ZEW Economic Studies

Publication Series of the Centre for European Economic Research (ZEW), Mannheim, Germany

AF810312

ZEW Economic Studies

Further volumes of this series can be found at our homepage: springeronline.com/series/4041

Vol. 11: K.L. Brockmann, M. Stronzik (Eds.)
Flexible Mechanisms for an Efficient Climate Policy
Cost Saving Policies and Business Opportunities
2000. VIII, 130 pp. ISBN 3-7908-1314-1

Vol. 12: W. Smolny
Endogenous Innovations and Knowledge Spillovers
A Theoretical and Empirical Analysis
2000. VIII, 277 pp. ISBN 3-7908-1320-6

Vol. 13: M. Lechner, F. Pfeiffer (Eds.)
Econometric Evaluation of Labour Market Policies
2001. X, 242 pp. ISBN 3-7908-1372-9

Vol. 14: M. Beise
Lead Markets
Country-Specific Success Factors of the Global Diffusion of Innovations
2001. XVI, 305 pp. ISBN 3-7908-1430-X

Vol. 15: O.H. Jacobs, C. Spengel
Effective Tax Burden in Europe
Current Situation, Past Developments and Simulations of Reforms
2002. X, 131 pp. ISBN 3-7908-1470-9

Vol. 16: U. Kaiser
Innovation, Employment, and Firm Performance in the German Service Sector
2002. X, 164 pp. ISBN 3-7908-1481-4

Vol. 17: J. Köke
Corporate Governance in Germany
An Empirical Investigation
2002. VIII, 184 pp. ISBN 3-7908-1511-X

Vol. 18: E. Wolf
What Hampers Part-Time Work?
An Empirical Analysis of Wages, Hours Restrictions and Employment from a Dutch-German Perspective
2003. X, 174 pp. ISBN 3-7908-0006-6

Vol. 19: P. Cecchini et al. (Eds.)
The Incomplete European Market for Financial Services
2003. XII, 255 pp. ISBN 3-7908-0013-9

Vol. 20: C. Böhringer, A. Löschel (Eds.)
Empirical Modeling of the Economy and the Environment
2003. VI, 326 pp. ISBN 3-7908-0078-3

Vol. 21: K. Rennings, T. Zwick (Eds.)
Employment Impacts of Cleaner Production
2003. VIII, 322 pp. ISBN 3-7908-0093-7

Vol. 22: O. Bürgel, A. Fier, G. Licht, G. Murray
The Internationalisation of Young High-Tech Firms
An Empirical Analysis in Germany and the United Kingdom
2003. XII, 291 pp. ISBN 3-7908-0120-8

Vol. 23: F. Hüfner
Foreign Exchange Intervention as a Monetary Policy Instrument
Evidence for Inflation Targeting Countries
2004. X, 175 pp. ISBN 3-7908-0128-3

Vol. 24: E. Lüders
Economic Foundation of Asset Price Processes
2004. XII, 121 pp. ISBN 3-7908-0149-6

Vol. 25: F. Reize
Leaving Unemployment for Self-Employment
An Empirical Study
2004. XII, 241 pp. ISBN 3-7908-0168-2

Vol. 26: Ch. Böhringer, A. Löschel (Eds.)
Climate Change Policy and Global Trade
2004. VIII, 381 pp. ISBN 3-7908-0171-2

Vol. 27: K. Jacob et al.
Lead Markets for Environmental Innovations
2005, XII, 273 pp.
ISBN 3-7908-0164-X

Vol. 28: L. Lammersen, R. Schwager
The Effective Tax Burden of Companies in European Regions
2005. XI, 251 pp. ISBN 3-7908-1562-4

Christina Elschner · Robert Schwager

The Effective Tax Burden on Highly Qualified Employees

An International Comparison

With 22 Figures
and 68 Tables

Physica-Verlag
A Springer Company

ZEW
Zentrum für Europäische
Wirtschaftsforschung GmbH
Centre for European
Economic Research

Series Editor
Prof. Dr. Dr. h.c. mult. Wolfgang Franz

Authors
Christina Elschner
Centre for European Economic Research (ZEW)
L 7,1
68161 Mannheim
Germany
elschner@zew.de

Professor Dr. Robert Schwager
Georg-August-University of Göttingen
Department of Economics
Platz der Göttinger Sieben 3
37073 Göttingen
Germany
rschwag@gwdg.de

Cataloging-in-Publication Data
Library of Congress Control Number: 2004117388

ISBN 3-7908-1568-3 Physica-Verlag Heidelberg New York

This work is subject to copyright. All rights are reserved, whether the whole or part of the material is concerned, specifically the rights of translation, reprinting, reuse of illustrations, recitation, broadcasting, reproduction on microfilm or in any other way, and storage in data banks. Duplication of this publication or parts thereof is permitted only under the provisions of the German Copyright Law of September 9, 1965, in its current version, and permission for use must always be obtained from Physica-Verlag. Violations are liable for prosecution under the German Copyright Law.

Physica-Verlag is a part of Springer Science+Business Media

springeronline.com

© Physica-Verlag Heidelberg 2005
Printed in Germany

The use of general descriptive names, registered names, trademarks, etc. in this publication does not imply, even in the absence of a specific statement, that such names are exempt from the relevant protective laws and regulations and therefore free for general use.

Cover design: Erich Dichiser, ZEW, Mannheim

SPIN 11365198 43/3130-5 4 3 2 1 0 – Printed on acid-free paper

Preface

This book is the result of a research project commissioned by the «IBC BAK International Benchmark Club»®, an initiative by BAK Basel Economics, and carried out by the Centre for European Economic Research (ZEW). It contributes to the IBC's effort to evaluate and compare economic performance and location factors across European regions. The book provides the background to the headline figures presented at the International Benchmark Forum on June 11th and 12th, 2003, in Basel, as well as many additional results.

This work has benefited from the help of many institutions and individuals. Above all, we are indebted to the sponsors for financing the project in times of limited fiscal resources. A panel of experts in human resources and taxation has advised us on characterising the compensation structure of typical highly qualified employees. We would like to thank the experts as well as the members of the Steering Committee of the IBC module on taxation for their enduring support. Special thanks go to Kurt Dütschler of the Swiss Federal Tax Administration who was always ready to provide information on detailed aspects of the Swiss tax system. We are grateful to Christoph Koellreuter and Martin Eichler from BAK Basel for organising and promoting research on taxation inside the IBC. Our colleague Lothar Lammersen (ZEW) provided many detailed comments which greatly improved our work. Our thanks go also to Otto H. Jacobs (University of Mannheim) and Christoph Spengel (University of Gießen and ZEW) for encouragement and advice. In addition, we are indebted to Gerd Gutekunst, Rico Hermann, and Thorsten Stetter (all ZEW) for helpful discussions. Finally, we owe thanks to Kristoph Baum and Irina Kremel (ZEW) and Monika Jackmann (University of Göttingen) who provided able help in preparing the final draft of this report. Of course, all remaining errors are our sole responsibility.

Mannheim and Göttingen, October 2004
Christina Elschner and Robert Schwager

Sponsors of the IBC Module Taxation

- Eidgenössische Steuerverwaltung, Bern, Switzerland
- Wirtschaftsministerium Baden-Württemberg, Stuttgart, Germany
- Tax and Finance Departments of the cantons of Basel-Landschaft, Basel-Stadt, Bern, Schwyz, St. Gallen, Ticino, Valais, and Zug, Switzerland

Panel of Experts

- Stefan Böhm, BASF AG, Ludwigshafen, Germany
- René G. Franzoni, UBS AG, Basel, Switzerland
- Günther Jordan, Ernst & Young AG, Stuttgart, Germany
- Markus Rappo, F. Hoffmann-La Roche AG, Basel, Switzerland
- Guido Richterich, Bottmingen, formerly Roche, Switzerland
- Karin Skiba, Ernst & Young AG, Frankfurt, Germany

Table of Contents

Executive Summary

This study presents estimates of the effective level of the tax burden on highly qualified employees in eight European countries and the United States. It is complementary to a companion project analysing the tax burden on capital.[1] Although both studies rely on different models for estimating effective tax burdens, they share the same spirit. The qualitative results of both can be compared, and common conclusions can be drawn. Hence, the results of both approaches provide a comprehensive picture of the level of taxation in the countries studied.

The study was prepared for the «IBC BAK International Benchmark Club»®, which evaluates and compares economic performance and location factors across European regions. The headline figures of this Executive Summary represent the *IBC Taxation Index* (see Table 0.1. on p. 5). This index will be updated regularly in the future so as to illustrate trends in the effective tax burdens of companies and on highly qualified employees.

The scope of the study is threefold: First, due to a great number of relevant tax rules, effective tax burdens may differ significantly from statutory tax burdens. Therefore, the analysis quantifies meaningful estimates of effective tax burdens. These estimates take into account the most important rules of all the relevant taxes. The study considers income taxes including surcharges, tax-like social security contributions as well as payroll taxes paid by the company. Second, taxation is deemed to be an important location factor. In order to compare the attractiveness of different locations from a tax perspective, the study compares effective tax burdens inter-regionally and internationally. Third, an effective tax rate is always the result of each particular case. To identify the general context, and to find out the most relevant tax provisions in different economic constellations, the so-called tax drivers, the study examines the effect of important tax provisions on effective tax burdens.

The measurement of the tax burden on highly skilled manpower is a new research field. Due to a lack of established methods a completely new approach has been developed which allows considering several components of the remuneration package, the family situation, and varying levels of compensation. This concept parallels established methodologies for the quantification of company tax burdens by calculating the effective average tax rate (EATR) as an indicator of the tax burden. The basic idea of our approach is that employers compete for highly qualified employees and therefore have to compensate these for taxes on labour income and tax-like social security contributions. As a consequence, the tax burden of differ-

---

1 See Lammersen and Schwager (2005).

ent regions is compared for a given *disposable income* after taxes which the employee can obtain at all locations.

The computer-based model determines the tax burden in an iterative procedure. At first the tax assessment of a typical qualified employee's income before taxes (the *total remuneration*) is conducted. If the resulting income after taxes falls short of (exceeds) the required disposable income, the assessment is repeated for a higher (lower) total remuneration. The model then iterates until the total remuneration necessary to obtain the predetermined disposable income is found. The effective average tax rate is calculated by dividing the difference between total remuneration and disposable income (the *tax wedge*) by the total remuneration. The EATR thus expresses how much the employer has to expend in addition to the predetermined disposable income. For example, if an employee with a disposable income of € 100,000 faces an EATR of 25 per cent this means that the tax wedge (€ 33,333) amounts to a quarter of the total remuneration (€ 133,333).

Taxes in this context are all income taxes including surcharges and state and municipality taxes, as well as payroll taxes paid by the company. Social security contributions are part of the tax burden inasmuch as the employee does not earn a specific, individual benefit by paying them. According to the basic idea of competition, there is little risk of unemployment for the kind of qualified employees considered here. Hence contributions to unemployment insurance, and by a similar reasoning also contributions to accident insurance, are defined as taxes. Health premiums, on the other hand, are not considered to be taxes since they are deemed to provide a genuine insurance.

Contributions to public pension schemes are considered to be partly taxes. The first pillar of old-age insurance is usually organised as a pay as you go system involving redistribution between generations and between high and low earning workers. Inasmuch as contribution payments do not result in actuarially fair pension entitlements, they constitute an implicit tax rather than an insurance premium. To account for this implicit tax, entitlements earned by the highly qualified employee are computed according to the legislation currently in force and offset against contributions.

Our model distinguishes between four kinds of compensation: (1) cash compensation, (2) contributions to old-age provision, (3) stock options and (4) perquisites. These components are taxable in different periods. Cash compensation and perquisites are taxable income in the year of payment whereas stock options are either taxable when the options are granted or when they are exercised. Contributions to old-age provisions may be excluded from taxable income and thus pension benefits are subject to taxation, or contributions may be paid out of taxed income implying that pensions are non-taxable income during retirement. Our model explicitly deals with the timing of tax and pension payments by using an intertemporal approach.

Geographically, the study covers twelve Swiss cantons, Austria, France, Germany, Ireland, Italy, the Netherlands, the United Kingdom, and the United States (Massachusetts). Currencies are converted with average nominal exchange rates of 2002. The effective average tax rates are calculated from the laws applying in 2002 and 2003.

The base case represents the *IBC Taxation Index* for highly skilled manpower. Here, we consider an employee's disposable income of € 100,000 that consists of 75 per cent cash compensation, 20 per cent old-age contributions, and 5 per cent perquisites. The employee is single and has no other income. The results show a threefold picture: The Swiss cantons Schwyz and Zug have the lowest tax burden with EATRs of 25.7 per cent and 25.9 per cent, followed by the other cantons analysed, the United States, and the United Kingdom with EATRs above 28 per cent and below 40 per cent. The highest tax burdens with effective tax rates between 40 per cent and 50 per cent occur in the other European countries considered, namely Ireland, Austria, the Netherlands, Germany, France, and Italy.

To illustrate these differences, it is instructive to translate back the EATRs into the total remuneration required in each location so as to provide the employee with a disposable income of € 100,000. To achieve this, a company has to spend € 134,589 in Schwyz, € 161,812 in Massachusetts, and € 199,203 in Italy. Thus, taxes interfere heavily in the international competition for talent.

Changing the disposable income to € 50,000 results in decreasing tax rates in almost all regions. With more than 10 percentage points, the reduction is particularly important in Switzerland and the Netherlands. This result illustrates the overall progressivity of the income tax and social security combined. The system becomes more progressive if tax rates rise steeply over the range of incomes considered, as in Switzerland, or if tax rates applying to low income brackets are very low, as in the Netherlands. On the other hand, ceilings on social security contributions reduce progressivity, as in Germany, Austria, and Italy.

Increasing the disposable income to € 200,000 results in relatively strong increases in the EATRs in Switzerland. This is due to the fact that, except in the case of unemployment insurance, there is no income ceiling in the Swiss social security system. Contributions still have to be paid on high income brackets. While Swiss cantons have the lowest effective tax burden among all countries analysed for low disposable incomes, Switzerland in part loses this top position once one moves to very high disposable incomes. In this respect, the United States, the United Kingdom, Ireland, and Austria compete successfully with Switzerland. In the United States, a highly qualified employee bears a lower effective average tax rate than in the cantons of Bern, Basel-Stadt, Basel-Landschaft, Genève, Ticino, Vaud. Austria ranks ahead of Genève, Ticino, and Vaud.

To analyse the taxation of *families* the effective average tax rates of an employee with a non-working spouse and two children have been calculated. All regions grant tax reliefs for families. On the one hand, families receive child benefits and/or tax credits. On the other hand, tax schedules differ depending on marital status and the number of children. Compared to other countries, families in Germany, Ireland, the USA, France, and Switzerland enjoy a particularly strong reduction of their tax burden relative to singles. In Italy, singles and families are taxed almost equally. A comparison of the effective tax rates for families at disposable incomes of € 50,000 and € 100,000 reveals that the tax advantage of families decreases with increasing income.

The *compensation structure* also influences the effective average tax rate. While increasing the share of old-age provision in the compensation package has only minor consequences for the EATR, in all countries except Germany and the Netherlands the effective tax burden decreases substantially if the employee is granted stock options.

Public pensions are responsible for a substantial part of the tax burden. To assess the quantitative importance of public pensions as a part of the overall tax burden, a simulation has been carried out assuming that contributions to the first pillar of old-age insurance yield a market rate of return. This results in a reduction in EATRs between 1.5 and 6.9 percentage points. The decrease is strongest in Italy, Ireland, and Germany.

The *IBC Taxation Index* presents the headline figures of both studies on the taxation of companies and on highly qualified employees (see Table 0.1.). A synthesis is provided in Fig. 0.1. For the twelve Swiss cantons considered and the median locations of the other countries, this figure displays the EATR at the corporate level together with the EATR of a single employee obtaining a disposable income of € 100,000 in 2003. Due to a number of conceptual differences, we cannot compare the IBC Taxation Index for companies with the IBC Taxation Index for highly qualified employees. Especially, both concepts of effective tax burdens do not permit straightforward conclusions on distributional issues. Nevertheless, we can compare the rankings and the relative differences in effective tax burdens between both studies.

For this purpose, we divide the effective tax burdens by the average of the included Swiss cantons. By definition, this average corresponds to an indexed effective tax burden of 100. We add a trend line which is based on the 20 observations included in order to illustrate the correlation between the tax burden on the production factor capital and on highly skilled employees.

It is striking that effective tax burdens appear to be closely correlated for most locations. This suggests that countries that impose large corporate tax burdens usually also impose large tax burdens on comparatively high personal incomes. A notable exception to these findings is the United States (Massachusetts). There, the tax burden on companies is among the highest of all regions considered, while qualified employees are taxed quite moderately. On the other hand, Ireland displays almost the lowest corporate tax burden of all regions together with a rather high tax burden on qualified employees. Despite these exceptions, however, from the point of view of a company, large corporate tax burdens usually are not compensated by small tax burdens on highly qualified employees, and vice versa. Therefore, those locations that already exhibit a competitive edge with respect to company taxation even improve their advantage when both types of taxes are considered.

Table 0.1. IBC Taxation Index for companies and highly qualified employees, 2003

			Companies			Highly qualified employees		
b)		Region	IBC Taxation Index, (EATR, %)	% of Swiss [a] average	Rank (out of 143)	IBC Taxation Index (EATR, %)	% of Swiss [a] average	Rank (out of 20)
CH	–	Zug	13.8	71.8	1	25.9	75.7	2
IR	–	Dublin	14.0	72.9	2	40.3	117.8	15
CH	–	Nidwalden	15.4	80.2	3	28.3	82.8	3
CH	–	Schwyz	16.5	85.9	4	25.7	75.1	1
CH	–	Ticino	18.5	96.0	5	38.2	111.6	11
CH	–	Bern	18.6	96.6	6	36.8	107.8	8
CH	–	Valais	19.7	102.5	7	35.4	103.6	5
CH	–	St. Gallen	20.3	105.5	8	36.8	107.5	7
CH	–	Vaud	20.5	106.7	9	39.3	114.9	14
CH	–	Zürich	21.0	109.6	10	32.6	95.2	4
CH	–	Genève	21.4	111.4	11	37.9	110.9	10
CH	–	Basel-Stadt	22.1	115.0	12	36.9	108.0	9
CH	–	Basel-Land.	22.8	118.9	13	36.6	106.9	6
GB	–	London	28.1	146.3	14	39.2	114.7	13
NL	Min	Amsterdam	30.2	–	15	42.9	–	–
NL	Med	Utrecht	30.2	157.4	16	42.9	125.5	17
NL	Max	Rotterdam	30.3	–	18	42.9	–	–
A		All State Capitals	30.4	158.2	19	41.7	122.0	16
I	Min	V. d'Aosta	31.6	–	28	49.8	–	–
I	Med	Cremona	31.8	165.5	44	49.8	145.6	20
I	Max	Venezia	31.8	–	54	49.8	–	–
F	Min	Paris	32.1	–	61	48.2	–	–
D	Min	Weilheim	32.9	–	62	47.6	–	–
F	Med	Doubs	34.5	179.5	99	48.2	140.9	19
D	Med	Bayreuth	34.6	180.1	103	47.6	139.3	18
F	Max	Isère	35.7	–	128	48.2	–	–
US	–	Boston	36.0	187.3	133	38.2	111.6	12
D	Max	Frankfurt	37.3	–	143	47.6	–	–

Remarks:

a) Average of the twelve cantons that have been included; the purpose of these columns is to provide the values used in Fig. 0.1.

b) Min/Med/Max: Region that displays the lowest/median/highest EATR for companies out of each country's assessed regions.

Fig. 0.1. Correlation of the tax burdens on companies and highly qualified employees, 2003

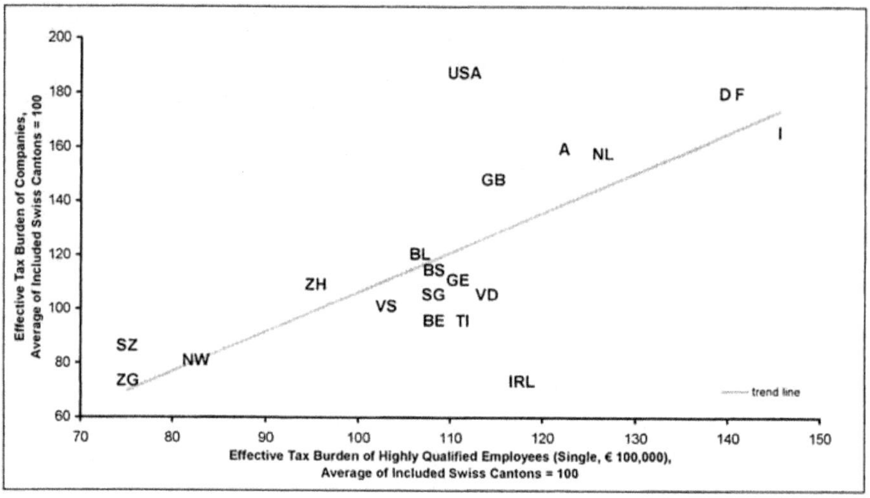

1 Aim of the Study

Taxes are an important determinant of the location of business activities. Consequently, numerous studies estimate the effective level of company tax burdens and compare these estimates across countries or regions. For example, the European Commission recently has presented a study of company taxation in the European Union,[2] and Gutekunst and Schwager (2002) and Lammersen and Schwager (2005) evaluate company taxation on a detailed regional basis. The aim of the present work is to complement these results with estimates of the tax burden on highly qualified employees, and to assess the relative attractiveness of locations with respect to the taxation of skilled manpower.

For this purpose, a new methodology is developed. The starting point of the analysis is the observation that highly skilled employees are very mobile internationally, which allows them to shift internationally differing tax burdens at least partially onto employers. In order to quantify the resulting burden for companies, we propose a comprehensive measure for the effective tax on highly skilled labour. The measure encompasses all taxes and all tax-like social security contributions which do not provide a specific benefit to the individual, whether they are paid by the employee or the employer. Moreover, we distinguish between cash compensation and other forms of remuneration such as perquisites, the grant of stock options and contributions to pension plans. The reason for this is that on the one hand, such diversified compensation packages are typical for highly qualified employees, and that on the other hand, different forms of compensation may be subject to different tax treatments. Finally, we vary the income level and the family status of the employee.

The method is applied to a number of locations in Europe and the United States and the resulting tax burdens are compared for the years 2002 and 2003. Moreover, the computation of tax burdens for different compensation packages and family conditions allows to identify the effects of specific tax or social security provisions.

Based on the inter-regional and international comparison of tax burdens presented in this study, tax administrations and economic development agencies can assess the competitive position of their own region relative to others. In addition, the detailed picture of the different taxes and contributions as well as their consequences presented here will allow regional decision makers to identify strengths and weaknesses of their own tax and social security systems. Beyond policy mak-

---

[2] Devereux, Lammersen, and Spengel (2000), (2001), European Commission (2002). For an early contribution in this line of research, see European Commission (1992).

ers setting tax rules, our study may also serve as a guide for firms comparing locations with respect to the tax part of labour costs. Last but not least, employees who share some of the characteristics of our model employees may find it interesting to learn to what extent tax burdens are different in other countries.

The present study is related to a companion study by Lammersen and Schwager (2005) on the taxation of companies. That report analyses the effective tax burden on investment, covering the same regions as the present work. Thus, a more complete picture of tax policy in the concerned regions emerges than would be possible by considering either the tax on labour or the tax on investment in isolation. In a wider sense, the present study contributes to a detailed and exhaustive assessment of location factors conducted by the «IBC BAK International Benchmark Club»® by BAK Basel Economics.[3] Thus, our focus on the taxation of manpower is not meant to imply that we deny the importance of other location factors such as infrastructure or environmental amenities. Rather, we concentrate on taxation so as to clearly isolate the impact of one specific location factor.

The book is structured as follows. In Chapter 2 we present the basic idea, the key assumptions and the structure of the concept used for assessing the tax burden on skilled labour. This is followed in Chapter 3 by a detailed description of the social security systems and tax regulations in the countries studied. The next three chapters contain the results, starting in Chapter 4 with a country by country presentation of effective tax rates. These results are combined in Chapter 5 in an international comparison. Chapter 6 provides some sensitivity analyses where the focus is on the impact of social security. The headline conclusions are summarised in Chapter 7. Some background information on taxes and social security and many detailed results are collected in the Appendix.

[3] See http://www.bakbasel.com.

2 The Methodology

In this chapter, we describe the concept used to measure the effective tax burden on highly skilled employees. The first section presents the basic idea motivating the concept. This is followed by a discussion of the main assumptions underlying the calculations. In the last two sections, we give a brief account of the regions and periods covered and compare our approach to existing measures of tax burden.

Since the present book is primarily focussed on the international comparison of the results we do not want to overburden the presentation with mathematical detail. Thus, throughout the chapter, we focus on the economic intuition and concentrate on explaining the basic structure and the principal working of the model. A comprehensive analytical presentation can be found in an accompanying working paper.[4]

2.1 Total Remuneration, Disposable Income, and the Effective Average Tax Rate

2.1.1 Mobility and Tax Shifting

We analyse the tax burden on qualified labour from the perspective of the company. We postulate that the tax to be paid on an employee's income is shifted at least partially onto the company and thus constitutes a competitive disadvantage for the employer, and by consequence also for the state or country where this tax is imposed. To see why this should be the case, observe that a qualified workforce is an important determinant for success, inducing companies to compete for these employees like for any scarce factor. This is most pronounced when the concerned employees are mobile across jurisdictional boundaries, as is typically the case for highly qualified specialists or managerial staff. Indeed, many studies[5] reveal an in-

---

4 See Elschner and Schwager (2004a).

5 According to Winkelmann et al. (2001: 33), 38.9 per cent of all companies in Germany employ university graduates originating from foreign countries. In Great Britain, the corresponding share is even 49.6 per cent. The industries most inclined to employ internationally mobile highly skilled staff are research and development, in-

creasing mobility of highly skilled employees in recent years. Such an individual will evaluate different employment opportunities on the basis of the income after taxes, that is, the amount of money he can spend for his own consumption or saving. This is the *disposable income* of the employee.

Our international comparison of tax burdens now is based on the assumption that the employee obtains a fixed disposable income which he can earn at all locations. Thus, the employee is perfectly mobile across regions and countries and refuses to accept any job which offers less than the disposable income which is generally paid for this kind of qualification. By imposing this assumption, we also implicitly abstract from all other factors which influence a job decision, such as job satisfaction, cost of living, local schools, or environmental amenities. While we do not question the relevance of any of these factors, we think it is fair to say that, nevertheless, a predominant aspect in deciding for or against a job offer is money.[6] Moreover, and more fundamentally, the present study aims at isolating the tax burden as one important factor for the attractiveness of locations. Adjusting disposable incomes according to other local characteristics would result in a combined measure which could not be related to taxes, nor to any other specific location factor.

To remain competitive, a firm seeking to attract or to keep an employee must provide him with the disposable income he obtains everywhere else. For a firm located in a region which taxes labour more heavily than others, this requires to increase the *gross income* before taxes and social security contributions payable by the employee so as to compensate for the high charges. Gross income is usually the quantity being negotiated and written down in the labour contract.[7] For this reason, gross income mostly serves as the base for calculating tax and social security liabilities.

While gross income is an important guide value for both, employer and employee, the firm's considerations will not stop here. In all countries, the employer also has to pay charges on the employee's gross income, e.g., employer's contributions to social insurance or special payroll taxes levied according to aggregated salaries and wages. Thus, total expenses connected with the compensation of a highly qualified employee consist of disposable income, employee's taxes as well as employer's taxes based on the employee's income. We define the total expenses which the company has to incur so as to be able to hire the employee as *total remuneration*. This is the quantity which defines the company's competitive position compared to companies located in other jurisdictions.

---

formation technology, and chemicals (Winkelmann et al. 2001: 34). See also Winkelmann (2002).

6 Especially concerning the competition between locations see Siebert (2000: 23 and 29). For a comprehensive inquiry into the motives and careers of internationally mobile university graduates in Europe, see Jahr et al. (2002).

7 There are some prominent exceptions to this rule. For example, in professional sports where employees are extremely mobile internationally, contracts often explicitly stipulate a net income, with the employer taking care of all taxes and social security contributions.

2.1.2 The Effective Average Tax Rate

The difference between total remuneration and disposable income is called the *tax wedge*. The tax wedge is the amount of money out of the total remuneration which does not benefit the employee. With a fixed disposable income, the expenses necessary to remunerate a highly skilled worker are the higher, the higher the tax wedge.

The tax wedge is a monetary quantity. In order to facilitate comparisons of tax burdens across income levels and family situations, a dimensionless measure is preferable which expresses taxes relative to labour costs. This measure is the *effective average tax rate* (EATR). It is defined as the tax wedge divided by the total remuneration. Denoting total remuneration by E^* and disposable income by E, this means

$$EATR = \frac{E^* - E}{E^*} \qquad (1)$$

As long as we consider a fixed disposable income, the EATR confers the same information as the tax wedge or the total remuneration. Thus, the higher the EATR, the less attractive is a country or region for companies employing highly qualified employees. Or, to express it from the perspective of the company, the higher the EATR, the more the employer has to spend in order to compensate an internationally mobile employee.

Symmetrically, a high EATR of one country does not mean that the highly skilled employee has a lower disposable income than in other countries with low EATRs. In order to make such a statement, one would have to compare the disposable incomes in the differing countries starting from the same, exogenously fixed total remuneration in each country. This would express the tax burden from an employee's point of view, assuming that he is not able to avoid these taxes by moving. Different levels of EATR resulting in different levels of disposable income would in this case supply information to the employee about the attractiveness of a region or country given a fixed willingness to pay of the employer. While the model would allow to compute such numbers, we prefer the comparison based on a fixed disposable income since it is the most useful way to measure the attractiveness of a location from a company's point of view.

2.1.3 Inter-Temporal Structure

Our aim is to quantify the tax burden on the income generated by working during one period, which we call the remuneration period for short. However, the compensation of highly qualified employees typically not only consists of income which is paid out in the remuneration period. The compensation components with this property considered in this study are long-term incentives and contributions to old-age provision. These forms of compensation also trigger tax liabilities in different periods. For this reason, a satisfactory assessment of the effective tax burden on employees earning mixed compensation packages has to account for the inter-temporal structure of income, tax and social security payments. Thus we extend the preceding discussion to account for disposable incomes generated in the remuneration period but accruing in different periods. In such an inter-temporal setting the EATR is defined as the difference between total remuneration and the sum of appropriately discounted disposable incomes generated by working in the remuneration period.

Formally, we denote by t_0 the remuneration period, by t_l the period in which the stock options are exercised after L years, and by t_r one out of P periods during which pensions are received, with retirement starting R periods after the remuneration period. Moreover, the disposable incomes in the three periods are denoted by E_0, E_l, and E_r. Evaluating total remuneration and disposable incomes in the period of remuneration, the EATR is then defined as

$$EATR = \frac{E^* - \left(E_0 + E_l \cdot \delta^L + E_r \cdot \delta^R \cdot \frac{1-\delta^P}{1-\delta} \right)}{E^*} \quad \text{with } \delta = \frac{1}{1+r} \tag{2}$$

In this expression, r is the market interest rate at which the individual can lend or borrow, independently of his location. This means that we assume a perfect and internationally integrated capital market. Moreover, we abstract from taxation of interest income. In general, taxation of interest income would reduce the interest rate relevant for the employee and thus give a greater weight to future disposable incomes. More fundamentally, a differential tax treatment of savings on the corporate and on the individual level will give rise to tax-reducing strategies using occupational pension schemes. We ignore these effects in order to keep the model simple, and in order to avoid the need to introduce assumptions concerning the employee's consumption and saving behaviour and concerning other kinds of income beside employment income.[8]

To sum up, the effective average tax rate *EATR* supplies information about current and future tax payments and charges that occur in context with the total remuneration earned in one period.

2.1.4 Computation

Our model is a computer-based simulation model. It can be structured into three elements (see Fig. 2.1.): data input, tax assessment, and calculation of the *EATR*. In the first element 'data input' the model reads the exogenous data concerning country-specific tax and social security regulations as well as the compensation structure and the level of the employee's compensation. In the second element, taxes and charges are calculated following the country-specific regulations. The

---

8 In Elschner and Schwager (2004a) we provide additional results for the case where the rate r relevant for the employee is given by the interest rate net of taxes while the firm still can accumulate at the gross market interest rate. See also Brassat and Kiesewetter (2003).

third element determines the total disposable income and the effective average tax rate according to equation (2).

As explained above, the compensation components are subject to tax and social insurance in different periods. We have identified three kinds of periods relevant in this respect: the period of remuneration, the period when the long-term incentives are exercised, and the pension periods. For the second element of the computation, this implies that the tax and social insurance contributions have to be assessed three times. Consequently, the model consists of three assessment blocks corresponding to the three periods (see Fig. 2.1.) in which tax and tax-like contributions are quantified.

Fig. 2.1. Structure of the model

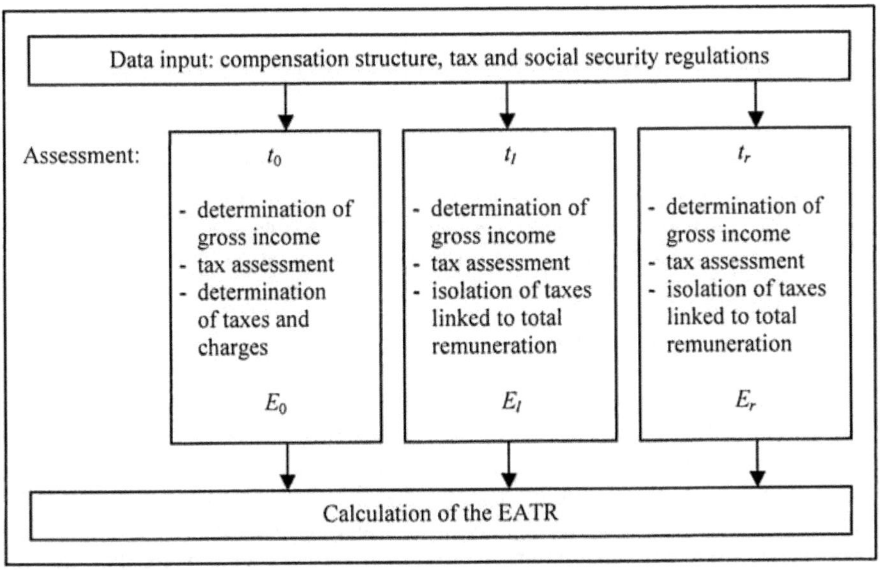

In each period, we first derive the gross income which is the base for social security contributions and taxes. This is done by determining analytically the value of gross income which, for a given total remuneration, is consistent both with the model assumptions, e.g., concerning the compensation structure, and the tax and social security regulations, e.g., about whether or not the employer's contributions themselves are part of gross income. Applying social security and tax schedules to gross income then gives the tax and social security payments. Finally, the disposable incomes E_0, E_l, and E_r are obtained by deducting these payments from the compensation component which yields income in the period considered.

In the three assessment blocks, the tax rules and social security regulations apply to the total income which is subject to tax and social security in each period. Because of progressive tax schedules, the assessment in the second and third blocks therefore requires some information about the income which is taxed in periods t_l and t_r but which is not generated by labour supplied in period t_0. We assume that in period t_l the employee earns the same gross income as in period

t_0.[9] For the retirement period t_r we postulate that the employee has been paying the same amount of old-age provisions as in t_0 throughout his career, and that he obtains the same retirement income in every year during retirement.[10]

The starting point of one round of tax assessment is total remuneration, the result is disposable income. Our measurement concept, however, treats the employee's disposable income as exogenous and seeks to derive the total remuneration necessary to achieve this disposable income. Therefore, we have to perform an iteration during which the simulation is repeated with changing amounts of total remuneration until the required disposable income is reached.

2.2 Model Specifications

In this section, we describe the assumptions and data used to implement the basic model structure outlined in the preceding section. After mentioning the macroeconomic data used, we define the characteristics of the analysed employee concerning his income level, composition of the compensation package, and family situation. We then define which taxes and which social security charges are part of the tax wedge. Finally, we give a brief account of the way the model integrates the tax and social security treatment of the various compensation components.

2.2.1 Macroeconomic Data

All present value calculations use an interest rate of 5 per cent. The income levels are all defined in Euro. We use the average nominal exchange rates for the year 2002 to convert the currencies of Switzerland, the United Kingdom, and the United States into Euros. We do not consider differences in purchasing power between or even within countries. This is motivated by our desire to clearly isolate tax effects from other determinants of an employee's choice of location, among which the cost of living is a prominent example.

2.2.2 The Employee's Characteristics: Income Level and Family Situation

The model employee whose effective average tax rate is to be determined in our analysis represents a typical highly qualified employee. He is defined by three main characteristics: the income level, the composition of compensation components, and as a personal characteristic the marital status including the number of children. In order to define the typical highly qualified employee we screened publications by personnel consultancies and research institutes.[11] The final selec-

9 See Section 2.2.4.3.

10 For details, see Section 2.2.4.4.

11 These included among others Towers Perrin (2002), Kienbaum (2001), Hören (1999), Brümmer (2001).

tion was prepared in co-operation with a panel composed of experts in human resource management as well as experts in the international taxation of employees.[12]

Altogether, we analyse eighteen different types of employees. We distinguish between a single person and the head of a family with a non-working spouse and two children between the ages of six and twelve.[13] These two types of personal characteristics do not cover completely the spread of interesting family types. In particular, we neglect the comparison of a working and a non-working spouse. Nevertheless, with our selection it is possible to show how much a country's tax system supports families.

We consider three different income levels of the highly qualified employee: One type with a *low*[14] income which consists of a disposable income of € 50,000, one with the *standard* disposable income of € 100,000, and one with *high* earnings of € 200,000 disposable income. It should be kept in mind that these income levels are defined on the basis of disposable income, and that the corresponding levels of gross income or even total remuneration will be noticeably higher.

Table 2.1. Compensation levels and structure of the compensation in per cent

Disposable income and components	Cash compensation	Perquisites	Long-term incentives	Old-age provision
Low: € 50,000				
Standard	75	-	-	25
Incentive-oriented	70	-	5	25
Pension-oriented	70	-	-	30
Standard: € 100,000				
Standard	75	5	-	20
Incentive-oriented	65	5	10	20
Pension-oriented	65	5	-	30
High: € 200,000				
Standard	75	5	-	20
Incentive-oriented	60	5	15	20
Pension-oriented	60	5	-	35

There are four different kinds of compensation components: cash compensation, perquisites, long-term incentives and old-age provisions. Concerning the structure of remuneration we identified three cases: the standard case with an average structure that implies a moderate proportion of old-age provision and perquisites, the incentive-oriented case with a high proportion of stock options and the pension-oriented case with a high proportion of old-age contributions. The weights of the single compensation components differ among the income levels

---

12 We are grateful to the panel members for their invaluable help at this stage of the project. Obviously, all remaining errors are the sole responsibility of the authors.

13 These ages have been chosen because of differing amounts of child tax allowances in some countries.

14 Of course, the label "low" is to be understood relative to the other two types analysed in our study. Compared to the wage distribution of the entire workforce, a yearly income of € 50,000 after taxes is high.

because the percentage of total compensation that is invested in compensation components other than cash, i.e. perquisites, long-term incentives, and contributions to the occupational pension scheme, typically increases with increasing total remuneration.

2.2.3 Taxes and Social Security Contributions

2.2.3.1 Taxes

When deriving disposable income from gross income, we deduct all direct taxes which are due because of the current employment relationship. Obviously, all personal income taxes including surcharges are part of the tax wedge. The same holds, where applicable, for state and local income taxes or surcharges. Contrary to that, church taxes are not part of the tax burden. Equally, property taxes are not counted as a labour related tax burden since the property does not directly refer to the remuneration of the employee in the current period.

We do not take into account any taxes which are levied on the spending side of the employee's budget. Thus no taxes on specific commodities such as tobacco or gasoline taxes enter the calculation. Most importantly, we do not consider the value added tax. The reason for excluding these taxes is that we want to assess the tax burden on income generation without having to make assumptions about the consumption and saving behaviour of the model employee.[15]

On the side of the company, we take into account payroll taxes which are levied on the aggregate wage costs. This applies to that part of France's *taxe professionnelle* which until 2002 was levied on the total payroll and to the Austrian *Kommunalsteuer* which is also based on aggregate wages and salaries. Until 2002, the Italian tax on productive activities IRAP had a similar effect as personnel expenses were not deductible. In our simulations, the additional amount of payroll tax triggered by paying the remuneration of the highly skilled employee is part of the tax wedge. A high payroll tax therefore increases the total remuneration required in order to achieve a given disposable income. This is a reasonable choice since our approach treats the tax burden on skilled employees as a management issue for the firm. In addition, the consistency with the companion study Lammersen and Schwager (2005) on the tax burden on investment requires to count payroll taxes exactly once. Since these taxes clearly are more closely related to labour input than to capital investment, it is natural to integrate them into the effective tax burden on highly skilled employees.

---

15 In a general equilibrium framework consumption and wage taxation are closely related since consumption taxes are likely to be shifted back onto workers (see e.g., Gaube and Schwager, 2003). The present research, however, aims at analysing the tax burden on the income of highly skilled employees in substantial detail. To keep the analysis manageable it is preferable to use a partial equilibrium approach and therefore to abstract from consumption taxes.

2.2.3.2 Social Security Contributions

Should the contributions to the various branches of social security be considered as taxes when computing the effective tax burden on highly skilled employees? The two possible extreme answers to this question are not entirely satisfactory. Ignoring social security contributions altogether would exclude a large, and in some countries the major component of non-wage labour costs from the consideration. On the other hand, counting all social security contributions into the tax wedge implies that differences between social security systems are not taken into consideration. Some countries like Germany have a nearly all-round social insurance including full health insurance, whereas other countries like, e.g., the United States only tender a basic social security implying that many risks have to be insured privately. If one counts contributions to public health insurance as taxes in this example, Germany would be less attractive than the United States because indispensable private insurance premiums in the United States are not part of the comparison, whereas social insurance premiums in Germany would decrease the employee's disposable income.

Assuming that the employee is willing to insure himself against all potential risks he will clearly consider not only charges but also benefits from social insurance and hence take out private insurance or not. Thus, in this example, contributions to social security appear almost as a substitute for a private expense which would have been undertaken anyway. Consequently, they should be part of the disposable income rather than the tax wedge.

This reasoning leads to the following guideline for integrating social security contributions into the tax wedge: We do not consider as tax-like those social security contributions which yield an individualised, specific benefit to the employee. In other words, we consider as taxes all those payments which do not yield an equivalent benefit to the taxpayer. Note that an individualised benefit is to be distinguished from the benefit which every citizen may derive from the spending of general tax revenues, say for schools or for infrastructure investment. Such benefits are not linked to the taxes or contributions paid by the individual, and indeed are also available to individuals who have not paid any tax at all.

Unfortunately, it is not possible to determine in any general way which branch of social security, or which part of the contribution to social security, qualifies as yielding an equivalent benefit, and which branch or part qualifies as a tax-like charge. In the following, we describe the assumptions which allow us to nevertheless quantify the tax-like part of social security contributions.

The most important insurance in this context is the first pillar of old-age insurance as everyone who reaches retirement age may benefit from this insurance. Thus, there clearly is a specific benefit linked to these contributions. However, the first pillar of old-age insurance being organised as a pay-as-you-go (PAYG) system, those contributions do not result in actuarially fair pensions. If the employee were to invest on the capital market instead of paying contributions to the first pillar of old-age insurance, in most countries he would obtain a higher retirement income than the public pension. Thus, in a public pension scheme, it is not the contribution in itself which has to be qualified as a tax but the loss in return compared to an investment on the capital market.

We take the low yield of public pension schemes explicitly into account when calculating the employee's income during the retirement period. In our model, the part of his old-age provisions that goes to the first pillar results in a public pension that is calculated with the actual pension formulae described in Section 3.1.1. Hence, inasmuch as contributions to the first pillar have to be seen as a tax-like charge, this charge appears in the form of a lower pension compared to a pension possible under market conditions. Contrary to that, we assume that the part of old-age provisions that goes into occupational pension schemes yields a pension under market conditions.

We calculate the pension entitlement from the regulations currently in force under the assumption that the employee has been earning the same income over his entire career. Thus, we do not use long-term projections about the likely future returns of the public pension systems in the different countries, nor do we consider possible future reforms. We are aware of the fact that this procedure eliminates a major source of concern about the long-term viability of public finances from our analysis. Moreover, since demographic trends differ between the countries studied, the international comparison would likely be affected if one were to integrate such projections. However, since the present study aims at quantifying the legal regulations both in the tax code and in social security, we consider it beyond the scope of our approach to integrate such long-term macroeconomic projections.

Victims of work incidents are mostly employees who work with dangerous equipment or substances whereas people working in the office typically are not exposed to such risks. This is why banks, for example, pay much lower premiums to accident insurance than companies in the chemical industry. For the same reason work incident insurance premiums paid for highly qualified employees have to be seen as taxes because those employees seldom work under dangerous conditions.

According to the basic idea of competition for a mobile highly skilled workforce, there is little risk of unemployment for the kind of qualified employees considered here. Hence contributions to unemployment insurance are considered as taxes.

In Switzerland, Italy, and France, the employer has to pay contributions for each employee to finance family allowances. These contributions have the character of charges as employees without children do not benefit from these contributions. On the other hand, employees with children receive family allowances which raise the disposable income.

There are some charges that are not levied within the bounds of social security but have to be paid from all employees for special purposes. Examples are in Austria the contributions to the *Arbeiterkammerumlage*, in France the *Contribution sociale généralisée CSG* and the *Contribution au remboursement de la dette sociale CRDS*, and in Switzerland contributions to the *Erwerbsersatzordnung EO* (see Section 3.1.4). All those charges qualify as tax-like contributions and are part of the effective average tax rate.

It is difficult to quantify a tax-like contribution in the health insurance systems of the analysed countries. The health insurance systems are organised and financed in widely varying ways (see Section 3.1.2). It is obvious that a system with contribution rates basing on the gross income cannot be an equivalent insurance: A low-earning worker gets the same health service as a high-earning employee but pays less contributions. Families may benefit from a public health insurance like in Germany as all non-working family members are co-insured in the working family member's health insurance without additional contributions. A high earning single person with a low risk of illness may prefer a private insurance because of lower contributions. To quantify the tax-like contribution one could assume a typical health insurance premium that would be paid to an equivalent private health insurance. The difference between state and private premium would then qualify as a charge or a profit. But risk groups and hence the amount of private health insurance premiums differ, for example according to the employee's age, weight, medical history, and country-specific regulations. For this reason it is not possible to determine a universally valid premium. Given this difficulty, for the purpose of this study, we refrain from quantifying the individual value of the benefit generated by contributions to public health insurance. Choosing between the extreme options of considering all such contributions as a tax or as an equivalent insurance premium, we prefer the latter. That is, we treat health insurance premiums always as a payment yielding an equivalent insurance benefit. Consequently, contributions to public health insurance are not considered in the effective average tax rate.[16] This choice is mainly made for the sake of simplicity. It should be kept in mind though that given the wide variation of public health care systems, this has an influence on the country rankings. In particular, countries where health care is financed out of general tax revenues like the United Kingdom would see their ranking improve once health insurance premiums in other countries were included in the tax burden.

2.2.4 Compensation Components

In this section, we discuss the valuation of compensation components for tax and social security purposes insofar as it is relevant in the context of our model. In addition, we describe the assumptions underlying the allocation of social security charges to the different compensation components. This is necessary in order to have a consistent definition of the compensation structure since the shares of the components according to Table 2.1. relate to total remuneration, which includes social security contributions. We adopt the following convention. Contributions to social security that refer to cash compensation and old-age contributions are distributed between them: Contributions to the first pillar of old-age insurance are part of old-age provisions, contributions to all other kinds of insurance belong to

[16] It is acknowledged that both choices are equally unsatisfactory. Thus, referring to health care, Heady (2003: 6) states that the "issue of comparability between countries with and without substantial private schemes is an issue that remains unresolved".

the cash compensation. The contributions that refer to the other two compensation components are part of the particular component.

2.2.4.1 Cash Compensation

Cash payments to the employee are part of gross income with their nominal value in the remuneration period. To this component belong the 'normal' compensation paid out in cash as well as bonus payments. In addition, according to the assumption specified above, social security contributions which are levied on cash income and on old-age provision, except those for the first pillar of old-age insurance, count towards the compensation component "cash".

2.2.4.2 Perquisites

As a concrete example for perquisites, we consider in our calculations a company car. Most countries offer the possibility to assess the company car at a standardised value instead of the true value which would be difficult to determine. Following our assumption on the allocation of social security charges, the share of total remuneration spent on perquisites is composed of the actual value of the company car plus the employer's contributions to social security weighing on the taxable standardised value of the company car.

In practice, companies usually lease their car pool and receive special prices from their leasing partner. Hence, the actual costs of the company car are equal to the total leasing rates plus prepayments and running costs less the revenue from selling the car at the end of the leasing period. This amount is not necessarily identical to the car price. According to a small internet research[17] screening leasing offers we assume that a standardised value of 1 per cent of the full price of the car per month is roughly equal to half of the actual monthly costs of the company car.

To substantiate our calculation consider the following example.[18] Daimler-Chrysler Bank offers to lease a Mercedes-Benz E 240 with a price of € 32,000 net of VAT for monthly rates of € 600 and a prepayment of 16 per cent of the net price. The leasing period is 36 months and at the end of the period the bank keeps the car. The employer then spends € 742 per month for the company car. In Germany, the standardised taxable value of company cars is fixed at 1 per cent of the gross price including VAT per month. In this example this amounts to € 371 taxable income per month, that is, half of the actual costs of € 742.

The ratio between actual costs and the standardised tax value depends on the type of car, possible company discounts, interest rates etc. The above example therefore can only be seen as an approximation. Generalising nevertheless, we express the tax treatment of perquisites by the ratio θ_p between actual costs and standardised value which is calculated by

---

17 We do not claim that this is representative.

18 Source: Internet research on the website www.daimlerchrysler-bank.com in June 2003, rounded values.

$$\theta_p = \frac{\text{full price} \cdot \text{standard percentage per month}}{\text{actual costs per month}} \tag{4}$$

The values for θ_p used for the different countries are summarised in Table A.3. on p. 90.

2.2.4.3 Long-Term Incentives

In our model, we assume that the employee receives stock options as long-term incentives. The options are granted in the period of remuneration, the vesting date, i.e. the earliest date to exercise the options, is after 5 years in this study. We assume that in the period of remuneration the employer anticipates the expected benefit of exercising the stock option.[19] Moreover, we assume that the vesting date and the date of exercise are identical, and we do not take into account capital gains from the sale of the shares.[20]

The tax treatment of stock options can be distinguished with respect to two aspects, the timing of taxation and the valuation of the benefit. The benefit may be subject to tax and social security at the date when the option is granted, i.e. in the remuneration period t_0, or at the vesting or exercise dates, i.e. in period t_l. The taxable value may be equal to, or different from, the actual benefit received by the employee.

Consider first the case of a taxation when the benefit is realised and without tax privileges for stock options. In this case, the true benefit of the option enters gross income at the date t_l. The costs of granting the stock options for the employer are the anticipated benefit plus, following our assumption about the attribution of social security charges, the employer's contributions to social security that are imposed on that benefit. Since the benefit accrues only in period t_l and the charges are also due only at that date, the compensation component "long-term incentives" in this case consists of the benefit plus the employer's contributions to social security discounted over the t_l-t_0 years elapsed between the remuneration period and the period of exercise.

If the option is taxed upon grant, as is the case in Switzerland, the taxable value enters gross income in the remuneration period. As long as the expected benefit of the option is correctly anticipated and fully taxed, however, this has no direct impact in our model.[21] This neutrality result arises because we do not distinguish between gross and net interest rates, so that the tax due in the remuneration period on the present value of the benefit is equal to the present value of the tax due on that same value in the period of exercise.

---

19 The benefit of stock options is of course unknown ex ante. However, throughout the analysis, we abstract from risk aversion considerations. Hence we can as well use the expected benefit from exercising the stock options.

20 See Elschner and Schwager (2004c) for effective average tax rates which take into account capital gains on the sale of shares.

21 A minor effect may arise from progressive tax schedules.

The actual benefit may, however, differ from the tax value on which the contributions to social security and the personal income tax are based. Several countries grant a special tax treatment to stock option plans which are considered as qualifying or approved option plans.[22] We generally assume that the stock options provided by the employer in our model satisfy all requirements necessary in order to benefit from such preferential treatment. To motivate our modelling of a reduced taxable value of options, consider the example of Switzerland where only a percentage of the expected benefit is taxable income. There, the estimated value of the option is reduced according to the time the options have to be held before they become exercisable. Options with a holding period of five years have a reduced tax value of around 75 per cent of the anticipated benefit. Hence, the anticipated benefit is obtained by dividing the tax value by the factor $\theta_l = 0.75$. Also in the other countries, we model a special tax treatment of stock options by the ratio θ_l of the taxable value over the true value of the option at the date of taxation. By consequence, when computing the compensation component "long-term incentives" for countries with a tax privilege for stock options, the actual benefit of exercising the option is set equal to the tax value divided by θ_l.

As explained in Section 2.1.4, we have to assume a basic income that flows to the employee in the period of exercising the stock options. Thus, beside the benefit from stock options the employee in our model receives the identical gross income as in the period of remuneration. The calculation of taxes and tax-like contributions imposed on the total income of the period of exercise follows the procedure in the period of remuneration. Taxes and tax-like contributions related to the long-term incentives then are isolated. They are equal to the amount by which the total tax liability exceeds the taxes and charges that would have been due if the options had not been exercised. Because the taxable income in the case of not exercising the options is equal to the taxable income of the period of remuneration, the tax liability related to the stock options is equal to the difference of tax and charge payments in the period of exercise less those in the period of remuneration.

2.2.4.4 Old-Age Contributions

Old-age contributions consist on the one hand of employer's and employee's compulsory contributions to the public pension scheme and on the other hand of employer's and employee's contributions to occupational pension plans. The percentage of total remuneration spent for old-age contributions is fixed by assumption according to Table 2.1. Also, the country-specific amount of contributions to the first pillar of the old-age insurance is fixed by law. As a consequence, the amount of contributions to the occupational pension scheme is the difference between the total amount of old-age contributions in the compensation package and the contributions to the first pillar. The contributions to occupational pension schemes therefore depend on the compensation structure and on the country-specific public pension scheme. To complete the description of the composition of

[22] See Section 3.3.3.

the remuneration component "old-age provision", recall from above that among the social security charges, only old-age contributions count towards this compensation component. Contributions to the other types of social security imposed on contributions to an occupational pension scheme are therefore counted in the compensation component "cash".

Assessing the tax liability on pensions procured by old-age provisions is one of the major challenges of the model. Contributions by employer and employee to company pension plans are invested in the period of remuneration into pension plans and yield interest. Together with contributions from other periods during working life they result in pension payments during retirement. In other words, at the end of his working life the employee has capital at his disposal which results from all previous old-age contributions. This capital has to be distributed over all following years of retirement to secure the living standard. In our model, the resulting annual pensions are calculated as annuities. The annuities together with the pensions received from the first pillar of social security are then equal to the annual income of the pensioner. However, the taxes imposed on those incomes are not directly linked to the contributions paid in the remuneration period but are the consequence of all invested contributions. Thus, the calculation of the tax burden on the old-age provisions of the remuneration period is split into two parts. First, the annual pension income is assessed. At this step, if special tax rules apply to proceeds from the first pillar of old-age insurance, they are taken into account. Dividing the resulting tax by the annual pension yields an average tax rate. The second part consists of computing an annual pension which would result from distributing only the contributions invested in the remuneration period over the whole retirement period. This annual mini-pension is then multiplied with the average tax rate calculated in the first part. The resulting amount is the tax on the old-age provisions linked to working in the remuneration period.

The average tax rate in the retirement period only consists of taxes paid, as social security contributions are not paid by pensioners. Contributions to health insurance have to be paid also by pensioners but are not characterised as tax-like contributions in our model. Finally, the implicit tax incorporated in the contributions to the first pillar of old-age insurance only are reflected in a lower income in the retirement period, not in directly measurable tax payments.

2.3 Geographical Coverage and Time Horizon

The study covers the tax and social security systems of Austria, France, Germany, Ireland, Italy, the Netherlands, Switzerland, the United Kingdom, and the United States. In all countries except Switzerland we provide only one national number per type of employee. This is justified by the fact that in these countries the taxation of labour income is entirely or almost entirely determined at the national level. Concerning personal income taxes, the only exception to this rule is a local and regional income tax in Italy which however varies very little.[23] In France, Italy, and Austria, there are payroll taxes levied at the local or regional level. In Switzerland personal income taxes vary substantially between cantons and municipalities. The study covers the cantons of Basel-Landschaft, Basel-Stadt, Bern, Genève, Nidwalden, St. Gallen, Schwyz, Ticino, Valais, Vaud, Zug, and Zürich. In each case, we compute local taxes using the tax multiple of the cantonal capital. In the United States as well, income taxes differ among the states. In this study, we consider solely the state of Massachusetts.

The time horizon of the study covers the tax years 2002 and 2003. We consider the situation at the beginning of each year. In the United Kingdom, the tax year starts in April of each calendar year. Thus, we consider in this case the tax years of 2001-2 and 2002-3. In Switzerland and France, the tax authorities change or fix tax schedules or allowances during or even at the end of a tax year. For those two countries, we have to consider the tax burden with a one-period time lag since more recent data are not available during the year. To justify this procedure one could argue that a potential investor will have the same problem und thus has to refer to the same (historic) tax data. In the analysis we will not explicitly mention this time lag and thus compare, for example, the tax burden in France based on tax data of 2002 with the tax burden of Germany based on data from 2003.

2.4 Comparison with Existing Approaches

2.4.1 Measures of Company Tax Burdens

Our concept of an EATR on the income of highly skilled employees follows acknowledged methods of measuring the tax burden of companies such as the effective marginal tax rate introduced by King and Fullerton, the effective average tax rate proposed by Devereux and Griffith, or the effective average tax rate computed with the *European Tax Analyzer* developed by the Centre for European Economic Research (ZEW) and the University of Mannheim.[24]

In all these concepts, a wedge between a pre-tax value and an after-tax value is divided by the pre-tax value so as to obtain an effective rate of taxation. The concepts by King and Fullerton and Devereux and Griffith only assess the tax burden on an additional unit of investment.[25] Contrary to that, we assess the tax on the to-

[23] Regions may impose an addition to the income tax rate between 0.9 and 1.4 per cent, and municipalities may add another 0.5 per cent. In the present study, the tax rate applicable to Roma is used.

[24] See King and Fullerton (1984), Devereux and Griffith (1999 and 2003), and Jacobs and Spengel (1996).

[25] These two concepts differ from each other in the assumption about the profitability of the investment considered. In the King/Fullerton approach, only the tax burden on such investments is measured which just yield a sufficient return to be undertaken, while the Devereux/Griffith model also evaluates the tax burden on highly profitable investments.

tal income of the individual rather than the tax on a marginal increase of his working time. In that respect our concept is closer to the *European Tax Analyzer* model which quantifies the tax burden of an entire company. In another respect, i.e. regarding the treatment of the employee's disposable income as exogenous, our approach has its counterpart in the measure of effective marginal tax rates by King and Fullerton. When calculating effective marginal tax burdens on investment, one can either fix the post-tax return to the investor (the so-called fixed-r-case) or the cost of capital which the investment earns (the so-called fixed-p-case). Since we fix the post-tax income, our approach corresponds to the fixed-r-case, whereas a computation of disposable incomes for exogenous total remuneration resembles rather the fixed-p-case.

2.4.2 Measures of Labour Tax Burdens

There are several alternative methods for calculating the tax burden on labour. In analogy to backward looking measures on the taxation of capital income, Mendoza et al. (1994) present effective average tax rates on labour income. These measures are computed by dividing aggregate taxes on labour income by a macroeconomic measure of such income. The advantage of these measures is that they are based on observed data, using actual tax payments. However, this also implies that they cannot provide any information about the effect of specific tax rules on the tax burden. Moreover, by their macroeconomic nature, one cannot determine the tax burden for different economic situations such as income levels or marital status. Backward looking measures are therefore not a suitable guide for the impact of taxation on economic decisions. Their main application lies in providing a quick reference figure for the way taxation interferes with the distribution of incomes among the factors of production on a macroeconomic level.

Contrary to the macroeconomic tax ratios presented by Mendoza et al. (1994) the EUROMOD model[26] takes a microeconomic approach. In this and in other tax and transfer simulation models, the tax and social security contributions as well as welfare entitlements are simulated for a representative sample of the population. This simulation is similar to the casuistic tax assessment performed in our model.[27] The results are then aggregated into society wide indicators, for example a Gini coefficient, so as to answer a variety of policy questions. Thus, the focus of microsimulation models is not to provide effective tax rates for specific categories of employees but on a microfoundation of aggregate policy analysis. Here, distributional issues are evidently at the centre of interest.

The approach most similar to ours is taken in the OECD publication series on "taxing wages".[28] Also there, the taxes and social security contributions of several

---

26 See the final report of the EUROMOD research consortium, Sutherland (2001).

27 There are however also backward looking elements in EUROMOD. In particular, pension entitlements are taken from the data and not simulated using the legal regulations. See Sutherland (2001: 5).

28 OECD (2002), for an introduction, see Heady (2003).

types of workers are assessed in a casuistic simulation. An effective average tax rate is then calculated by dividing the resulting tax wedge by total labour costs. As in our approach, income and payroll taxes are considered. However, there are two major differences between our model and the OECD approach. First, unlike the OECD we do not treat social security contributions as a whole as taxes. Instead, we take care to relate as precisely as possible individual benefits procured by social security contributions to the payment of these contributions. Thus, we quantify the pension resulting from the first pillar of old-age insurance, and unlike the OECD, we do not consider public health insurance premiums as taxes. Second, both approaches consider different types of employees. While the OECD concentrates on the average production worker and workers earning 67 or 167 per cent of this worker, our study is explicitly focussed on highly qualified employees. Beyond a mere change in the income level this has two structural consequences which make our model substantially richer than the OECD approach. Firstly, we take care to analyse the specific tax treatment of various compensation components. Secondly, since long-term incentives and in particular old-age provision are prominent in the compensation package of highly qualified employees this necessitates an inter-temporal approach.

2.4.3 Measures of the Tax Implicit in Public Pension Schemes

Several recent studies quantify the intensity of redistribution induced by public pension systems using a simulation approach that is related to ours. For example, Börsch-Supan and Reil-Held (2001) estimate the share of transfers, as opposed to insurance benefits, included in payments from the German pay-as-you-go pension system. Using data from the Socio-Economic Panel, a sample of German households, they simulate the pension entitlements of each household by applying the legal pension formula to an estimated earnings history. Fenge and Werding (2003) and Fenge et al. (2002) quantify the tax rates which are implicit in the pay-as-you-go pension systems of selected OECD countries. Hirte (2000) takes a similar approach for Germany but is focussed upon differences in the implicit tax rates faced by different age groups and cohorts.

Similarly to the method proposed in the present paper, this line of research is also based on an inter-temporal simulation model describing the earnings and pension entitlements of a representative individual. Since these studies exclusively focus on pensions they are able to include more details, in particular concerning life-expectancy and demographics. On the other hand, our approach is much broader in scope since we incorporate all taxes and social security contributions which are related to employing the highly qualified person. Also, these studies typically refer to an average person with more or less average income whereas the high-earning person who is in the centre of our model usually has to pay higher implicit taxes than an average earner.

To sum up, our model differs from all existing methods by addressing the issue of the tax burden on manpower from the point of view of the company, and by its careful modelling of the tax burden on highly skilled employees.

3 Description of Tax and Social Security Systems

The description of the tax and social security systems starts with a brief overview of the most important aspects concerning social security, the regulations referring to occupational pension plans, and specific charges which are neither social security contributions nor taxes. After that, we give a brief introduction into the tax systems of the countries studied, followed by a more detailed description of specific rules applying to the different compensation components.

3.1 Social Security, Occupational Pension Plans, and Various Charges

Concerning social security systems, we observe a comparable coverage of insured risks in all countries analysed.[29] Retirement, health, unemployment, and work injuries have to be covered by insurance.[30] Usually, compulsory insurance is financed as a pay-as-you-go system which secures at least a standard benefit. Especially in the case of health insurance, a private insurance applies in certain countries. In addition, there are other specific kinds of social insurance and other charges. In all countries, employers have the possibility to finance additional occupational pensions.

3.1.1 Old-Age, Disability, and Survivor Insurance and Occupational Pension Plans

The old-age insurance systems are organised as three pillar systems in all analysed countries. The first pillar represents the public pension scheme which is financed as a pay-as-you-go system involving redistribution between generations and in some countries also between high and low earning individuals. The second pillar also is associated with the employee's wage and salary. The employer and/or the employee pay into funded occupational pension plans. The form of occupational pension systems varies across and within the countries as there is often more than

---

29 See Table A.1. and Table A.2. on p. 89-90 for all contribution rates and income ceilings considered.

30 For an overview of social security regulations in Europe see MISSOC (2002 and 2003).

just one possibility of creating pension plans. The contributions to the second pillar are compulsory in some countries, in some countries they are not. Contributions to the third pillar of old-age provision are paid privately and are voluntary.

All in all one can summarise that the three pillar system intends to secure the culturally defined subsistence level with the first pillar whereas the additional second and third pillars guarantee the individual standard of living. The pension systems in the analysed countries differ from that guideline for political, social, and historical reasons.[31]

3.1.1.1 Austria

In Austria, the first pillar is dominant in the pension system. Employers and employees have to pay contributions into the first pillar depending on the employee's gross income. The contribution rates that have to be multiplied with the gross income are 10.25 per cent for employees and 12.55 per cent for employers. If the employee's gross income exceeds the income ceiling contributions have to be paid only to income up to the ceiling. In 2003, the income ceiling amounts to € 3,360 per month plus € 6,720 per year for bonus payments (€ 3,270 and € 6,540 in 2002). Examples for bonus payments are the Christmas bonus in December and the holiday bonus in summer. Assuming that those bonus payments amount to a full monthly salary the income ceiling adds up to € 47,040 per year. The employee earns a pension entitlement with all contributions paid. The resulting annual public pension out of all contributions to the first pillar paid during the whole working life is calculated by multiplying the reference income by the number of working years multiplied by 2 per cent. The maximum number of working years is 40 years. The reference income is determined by multiplying the average income of the 15 years with highest earnings by the factor 15/17.5. A reform of the first pillar has been adopted and will take effect in 2004. Cornerstones are the reform of early retirement, an increase in the number of years taken into account when calculating average earnings, and a decrease in the multiplying factor from 2 per cent to 1.78 per cent.

The second pillar is compulsory in one aspect. The so-called *Abfertigung Neu* regulates a minimum occupational pension scheme. For employees with contracts starting in 2003 or employees opting for the new system, the employer has to pay 1.53 per cent of gross income into a pension fund (the so-called *MV-Kasse*). At the end of his working life, the employee can decide whether he prefers a capital payment or a pension annuity. The three most important possibilities of financing the occupational pension scheme are direct guarantees, direct insurance, and pension funds. Direct guarantees are carried out by the companies themselves using pension reserves. The employee does not obtain a legal claim to a future pension payment. The occupational pension must not exceed 80 per cent of the actual income (§ 14 EStG). Direct insurance and pension funds are carried out by insurance companies. Thus, the employee obtains a legal claim to future pension payments.

---

[31] For an overview of old-age provision systems in Europe, see Fenge et al. (2003).

3.1.1.2 France

The French pension system is composed of several institutions. In the private sector, the system is separated into the pension scheme for workers and non-executive employees and the pension scheme for executives and highly qualified. Both groups have to pay contributions to the general social security system *Caisse nationale d'assurance vieillesse* (*CNAV*) at a rate of 6.55 per cent for the employee and 8.2 per cent for the employer up to a maximum of € 29,184 in 2003 (€ 28,224 in 2002). On income above this ceiling the contribution rates are 0.1 per cent for the employee and 1.6 per cent for the employer with no further income ceiling. The supplementary occupational schemes are compulsory and are financed as a pay-as-you-go system as well. Executives have to pay into two schemes (*AGIRC* and *ARCO*) with graduated contribution rates. There is a voluntary additional pension scheme which is fully funded and can be used as an occupational scheme or for private saving.

The public pension resulting from contributions to *CNAV* is calculated by multiplying the reference income by an individual pension factor and the number of insurance quarters. The reference income is equal to the average income of the 20 years with highest earnings, the individual pension factor depends on the pensioner's age. It amounts to 50 per cent for a pensioner who entered retirement at the age of 65. The number of insurance quarters must not exceed 160 which is equal to 40 years in which contributions were paid. The pensions of the supplementary schemes are calculated in the same way.

3.1.1.3 Germany

In Germany, the first pillar does not only provide a minimum income but also secures the living standard to a certain extent. Employee and employer each pay half of the compulsory contributions to the public pension scheme. The combined rate is 19.5 per cent of gross income in 2003 (19.1 per cent in 2002). It is applied up to an annual gross income of € 61,200 (€ 54,000 in 2002).[32] The public pension depends on pension points which are based on the amount of contributions paid and the number of years during which contributions were paid. The monthly pension is calculated by multiplying the pension points by the current pension value. Employees with incomes above the ceiling receive a pension point per year of about 1.8. The pension value in 2003 is € 26.13.

There are several alternatives of occupational old-age provision. Since it is the most common form, especially in big companies, we focus on old-age provision in the form of direct guarantees. In this case, the employer himself pays the pension to his former employee without any intermediary institution.

---

32 These ceilings apply to West Germany. In the East, the ceilings are € 51,000 for 2003 and € 45,000 for 2002.

3.1.1.4 Ireland

Unlike in most of the countries analysed, the Irish social security system is not split into several types of insurance. Overall contributions are paid into the entire system, not into separate insurance branches. It is not possible to determine objectively the proportion of contributions being used for public pensions. However, we know which sectors of social security are tax financed and which are contribution financed. Family allowances are tax financed, whereas the first pillar of old-age insurance, unemployment, and work injury insurance are financed out of the overall contribution. Health insurance is not included in the overall contribution. For the analysis, the approximate contribution to old-age insurance has been estimated. We assume that 20 per cent of the overall contributions correspond to unemployment and accident insurance, and the remaining 80 per cent to the first pillar of old-age insurance. The overall contribution rates are 4 per cent for employees up to incomes of € 40,420 in 2003 (€ 38,740 in 2002). Contributions are not levied on the first € 6,604 of income. Employers pay 8.5 per cent on the total gross income of employees with gross income less than € 356 per week. They pay 10.75 per cent for employees earning more than € 356 per week. Pensioners receive a base pension of currently € 147.30 per week if the employee has paid into the social security for 48 years. Dependent spouses receive an additional pension of € 116.70 per week.

Occupational pension plans are not compulsory and usually are organised as trustee-managed pension plans or pension schemes. The resulting pensions are not subject to any limitation.

3.1.1.5 Italy

The Italian system of old-age provision was reformed in 1992 and 1995. The first pillar was converted from a system with benefits depending on the earnings of the last five years to a system where benefits depend on life-time contributions and the life-expectancy of the pensioner's cohort at the age of retirement. However, the former pension system still influences the expectable pension, and the contributions are relatively high. Employers have to pay 23.81 per cent of gross income and the employees' contribution rate is 8.89 per cent. Contributions have to be paid up to an income ceiling of € 80,391. The annual public pension is calculated by multiplying the contributions by a conversion factor of 6.136 per cent for persons retiring at the age of 65 in 2003.

The second pillar of the Italian pension system is voluntary. There are two kinds of occupational pension schemes: direct guarantees with severance or pension payments as well as pension funds with severance payments. The pension plans with severance payments (*Trattamento de fine rapporto* TFR) were introduced in 1993 and are comparable to regular direct guarantees[33]. The employer has to contribute around 7.4 per cent of the employee's gross income into the TFR which can be transferred to a pension fund.

---

[33] See Fenge et al. (2003: 97-99) for more details.

3.1.1.6 The Netherlands

In the Netherlands, the first pillar of the pension system only offers a base pension in order to secure a minimum income. All tax payers with employment or rental income have to pay contributions to the public pension scheme at a rate of 17.9 per cent of the taxable income up to a ceiling of € 28,850 in 2003 (€ 27,850 in 2002). In addition, employees have to pay 1.25 per cent and employers have to pay 5.05 per cent of gross income for disability insurance, up to an income ceiling of € 30,260 in 2003. The base pension currently amounts to € 913 per month for singles and € 1,258 per month for married couples.

Because these base pensions are rather low, the second pillar is an important component of the pension system. Occupational pension plans usually are collectively agreed among employers' associations and unions. They often are financed through pension funds or direct insurance. The occupational pension plans are subject to certain limitations (Art. 18a Wet LB). The resulting pension of a defined contribution plan must not exceed 70 per cent of the annual earnings. This ceiling applies to an employee retiring at the age of 60. If he retires later, the ceiling of 70 per cent raises up to 100 per cent. The employee's contributions to a defined benefit plan are limited as well.

3.1.1.7 Switzerland

The Swiss pension system is explicitly organised as a three pillar system. Contributions to the first pillar have to be paid by all residents except pensioners. Work-related contributions to the first pillar (*Alters- und Hinterbliebenenversicherung* AHV) amount to 8.4 per cent of an employee's gross income without any ceiling paid half by employee and employer. Non-working spouses are exempt from such contributions if the working spouse contributes more than CHF 870 per month to the first pillar. The resulting base pension only secures a minimum income and depends little on contributions or life-time earnings. In 2003, the public pension for a single is between CHF 12,660 and CHF 25,320. With contributions based on annual earnings of CHF 75,960 the maximum pension is achieved. Contributions above this amount do not raise the resulting pension any more. Married couples receive a maximum pension of 1.5 times the maximum pension for singles, even if both couples paid contributions. The contributions to disability insurance (*Invalidenversicherung* IV) are levied at a rate of 0.7 per cent of gross income for both employee and employer without ceilings.

Employees with annual earnings above the maximum pension obtainable from the AHV are obliged to pay into an occupational pension plan. The pension plans are funded by the employers but have to meet special requirements. For example, the minimum rate of return currently has to be at least 3.25 per cent. The compulsory contribution rate rises with the employee's age.

3.1.1.8 United Kingdom

In the United Kingdom, the social security system is financed by overall contributions as well as by taxes. The first pillar of the old-age pension system and the contribution-based jobseeker's allowances are completely financed out of contributions. Health services are contribution-financed to a small extent. Work injuries and family allowances are tax financed. Hence, the overall contributions seem to be linked to the first pillar of old-age provision to a relatively high extent. As in the case of Ireland, we assume that 20 per cent of the contributions correspond to unemployment insurance and other charges. The employee's overall contribution rate amounts to 10 per cent up to a gross income of £ 30,420 in 2003 (£ 29,900 in 2002). The employer has to pay 11.8 per cent without ceiling. There are no contributions levied on the first £ 4,615. These contributions secure both a basic pension and an additional pension whose benefits are more closely linked to the contributions paid. If the employer provides a qualifying occupational pension scheme, the employee has the possibility to contract out of the additional public pension scheme. Thus, he is able to receive a higher pension with the same amount of contributions compared to the additional public pension. In this case, the contribution rate decreases to 8.4 per cent for the employer and to 8.3 per cent for the employee.. Pensioners receive a base pension of currently £ 72.50 per week provided that the employee has paid into social security for 44 years. Dependent spouses obtain an additional pension of £ 43.40 per week.

The second pillar of the pension system is not compulsory, but most big companies offer pension plans or pension schemes that are managed by trustees. The occupational pension plan is either a defined-benefit or a defined-contribution plan. The resulting benefits are limited to a maximum benefit of 1.5 times the final remuneration and an annual pension of two thirds of the final remuneration. In other words, the contributions are limited in so far as they must not result in pensions exceeding the above limits.

3.1.1.9 The United States

The old-age, survivor, and disability insurance *OASDI* builds the first pillar of the US pension system. The contribution rates amount to 6.2 per cent of gross income payable by both employee and employer up to a ceiling of $ 84,900 in 2002 and $ 87,000 in 2003. The resulting pension is calculated by multiplying the average incomes of the 35 years with highest earnings by a discount factor. The first $ 592 of average income are weighted by 90 per cent, income from $ 593 up to $ 3,567 is weighted by 32 per cent, and exceeding parts of average income are weighted by 15 per cent. Dependent spouses can claim one-half of their working spouse's benefit in addition.

The second pillar is usually financed through pension funds. Pension funds with tax privileges are either defined-benefit or defined-contribution plans. The contributions must not exceed 25 per cent of the employee's earnings or $ 35,000 per year.

3.1.2 Health Insurance

In our model, we do not consider contributions to health insurance as tax-like contributions (see Section 2.2.3.2). Thus, health insurance contributions qualify as disposable income. Nevertheless, we give an overview of the public health insurance systems in the countries analysed.

Austria has a compulsory health insurance system. The contribution rates amount to 3.4 per cent for employees and 3.5 per cent for employers. Contributions have to be paid for income not exceeding € 47,040 in 2003 (€ 45,780 in 2002).

Contributions to the health insurance in *France* mostly are paid by the employer. The contribution rate for the employer is 12.8 per cent whereas the employee's contribution rate is 0.75 per cent of gross income without any ceiling.

In *Germany,* in principle each employee has to pay into public health insurance. This system consists of several organisations among which the employee is free to choose. The contribution rates currently vary between 11.9 and 15.7 per cent of gross income half of which is paid by the employee and half by the employer. With this contribution, a non-working spouse and children are insured. Employees and employers have to pay an additional contribution to long-term care insurance of 1.7 per cent. Both types of insurance in West Germany are limited to gross incomes up to € 40,500 in 2002 and € 41,400 in 2003. These limits correspond to 75 per cent of the old-age insurance ceilings. Employees who earned more than € 40,500 in 2002 were able to opt out to a private health insurance with premiums according to individual health risk instead of gross income. Usually, this insurance is favourable for high earning singles. Families may be better off with public health insurance instead of paying insurance premiums for each family member. To finance the expanding costs of the existing health insurance system, the income ceiling for opting out of public health insurance was raised to € 45,900 in 2003.

In *Ireland,* employees pay 2 per cent of gross income into social health insurance.

The *Italian* health insurance system is financed by employers' contributions of 0.66 per cent of a white-collar employee's gross income. Manual workers are subject to other regulations. Since this insurance system only offers a fundamental medical service, most Italians take out an additional private health insurance.

The *Dutch* social health insurance is integrated in the income tax schedule and amounts to 10.25 per cent of taxable income up to earnings of € 28,850. Employees with a gross income of up to € 31,750 are subject to an additional health insurance with compulsory contribution rates of 1.7 per cent for the employee and 6.75 per cent for the employer.

In the *Swiss* health insurance system, mandatory health insurance premiums have to be paid by each resident. The premiums do not differ by age, sex or income. The maximum premiums are regulated by the cantons.

In the *United Kingdom,* social health insurance is part of the national insurance offering a basic medical service.

In the *United States*, the medicare tax is levied at contribution rates of 1.45 per cent for both employer and employee without any ceilings. The medicare system only supports old-aged persons. Personal health risks have to be insured privately.

3.1.3 Family Allowances

In all of the countries analysed, families receive family allowances, either in the form of tax privileges or as direct transfer payments (see Table 3.1. on p. 35). Most countries offer benefits as well as tax privileges. In several countries, the family allowances are financed out of contributions of the employers.

In 2002 and 2003, the family allowance in *Austria* amounts to at least € 112.70 per month and child and increases with the child's age and the number of children. The family allowance is tax financed.

France only grants a family allowance for families with two or more children. The child allowance amounts to at least € 111.26 per month with surcharges of € 30.77 for children above 11 years and € 54.70 for children above 16 years. Furthermore, there is a family benefit for families with low earnings. The family allowances are not subject to income tax.[34] The contribution rates for employers amount to 5.4 per cent of the aggregate salaries and wages.

Child allowances in *Germany* are tax financed. The child benefit is between € 154 and € 179 per month and child according to the number of children (§ 66 EStG). The family allowances are not subject to tax and social security. Tax payers with high incomes may receive a tax deduction instead of the child benefit if the former is more favourable.

In *Ireland,* child benefits are tax financed. The child allowance amounts to € 117.60 per month and child for the first two children, increasing with the number of children as well as for twins, triplets, and quadruplets. There are special family allowances for families with low incomes. The family benefits are not taxable nor subject to national insurance.

Italy grants a family allowance for employees if at least 70 per cent of the earnings derive from work. The child allowance depends on the number of children and the income. A family with two children for example receives € 250 if the income is below € 11,200. The allowance is reduced to zero for incomes above € 43,900. The benefits are not taxable nor subject to social security. The family allowances are financed by employers' contributions of 2.48 per cent of aggregate salaries and wages.

The *Netherlands* grant a child allowance which is graduated according to the child's age. For children born after 1994 the family allowance amounts to € 70.57 per month and child (Art. 12 AKW). The child benefits are not subject to tax and social security.

In *Switzerland,* the family allowances for employees are under cantonal sovereignty. The monthly cantonal family allowances range from CHF 150 to CHF 260

34 However, they are subject to the general social contribution CRDS at a rate of 0.5 per cent.

according to canton and number of children (see Table 3.1.). The child allowances are subject to personal income taxes. Employers have to pay contributions of up to 2 per cent of the aggregate salaries and wages to finance the cantonal family funds.

In the *United Kingdom*, family allowances are tax financed. The child allowance amounts to £ 68.25 per month for the oldest child and £ 45.85 for further children. The child benefit is not subject to tax and social insurance.

The *United States* does not grant child allowances. The family allowance is granted as an additional tax deduction.

Table 3.1. Family allowances: contribution rates and benefits, 2003

Country / canton	Employer's contribution rate	Child benefits per child and month
Austria	-*	€ 112.70 for children between 3 and 9 years
CH Basel-Landschaft	1.5	CHF 150**
CH Basel-Stadt	1.5	CHF 150**
CH Bern	1.8	CHF 160**
CH Genève	1.9	CHF 200**
CH Schwyz	1.7	CHF 160**
CH St. Gallen	2.0	CHF 170**
CH Ticino	1.5	CHF 183**
CH Valais	-*	CHF 260**
CH Vaud	2.0	CHF 150**
CH Zug	1.6	CHF 230**
CH Zürich	1.5	CHF 170**
France	5.4	€ 111.26 for children between 6 and 11 years
Germany		€ 154 - € 179 high incomes: tax allowance instead
Ireland	-*	at least € 117.60
Italy	2.48	graduated benefits for low incomes
The Netherlands	-*	€ 70.57 for children born after 1994
United Kingdom	-*	£ 68.25 for the first, £ 45.72 for further children
United States	-	-

* The child benefits are tax financed.
** The child benefits are taxable.
Source: MISSOC (2003), national ministries of social affairs.

3.1.4 Work Injury and Unemployment Insurance and Other Charges

In most of the countries studied, work injuries are covered by a compulsory insurance. The contributions are paid by the employer and differ according to industry. The average contributions are shown in Table 3.2.

Table 3.2. Average contribution rates to work injury insurance, 2003

Country	Average contribution rate in per cent	Income ceilings per employee
Austria	1.4	€ 47,040
France	2.26 [a)]	-
Germany	1.42	€ 61,356
Ireland	-	-
Italy	0.5 to 16; manufacturing: 3.0	-
The Netherlands	-	-
Switzerland	0.02 to 28.7	CHF 106,800
United Kingdom	-	-
USA	variable [b)]	-

[a)] According to the International Social Security Association ISSA (2002).
[b)] Current contribution rates are not available. According to ISSA, the average contribution rate was 2.05 per cent in 1995.
Source: MISSOC (2003) and national organisations charged with work injury insurance.

Contributions to unemployment insurance are limited by income ceilings in all analysed countries except Italy (see Table 3.3.). Switzerland has a federal insurance, in the United States, each state can levy premiums in addition to the federal unemployment insurance (FUTA). These premiums are deductible from federal insurance. One observes a great dispersion of contribution rates and ceilings. In particular, the rates in the United States are remarkably low.

Table 3.3. Contribution rates to unemployment insurance, 2003

Country	Contribution rate in per cent employee / employer	Income ceiling
Austria	3.0 / 3.7	€ 47,040
France	2.4 / 4.0	€ 116,736
Germany	3.25 / 3.25	€ 62,100
Ireland	included in the overall contribution	
Italy	0.3 / 4.41[a)]	-
The Netherlands	5.8 / 1.55	€ 30,260
Switzerland	1.5 / 1.5 up to:	CHF 106,800
	0.5 / 0.5 for exceeding income up to:	CHF 267,000
United Kingdom	included in the overall contribution	
USA	- / 6.2	$ 7,000
USA - Massachusetts	- / 2.125 (varying)	$ 10,800

[a)] For manufacturing companies with more than 50 employees.
Source: MISSOC (2003) and national organisations charged with unemployment insurance.

In Switzerland, Austria, and France, there are several charges which do not qualify neither as social insurance nor as income tax and which are levied to finance special purposes.

Austria levies two such fiscal charges. The *Arbeiterkammerumlage* – a contribution to a specific form of workers organisation – of 0.5 per cent for employees and a charge to boost the construction of homes with contributions of 0.5 per cent for both employees and employers. These charges are levied on incomes not exceeding € 40,320 in 2003 (€ 39,240 in 2002).

Tax payers in *France* have to pay a social tax. For employment income this is 8 per cent on 95 per cent of gross income. The contribution consists of a general social contribution (*Contribution sociale généralisée CSG)* and a tax for the purpose of reducing the public debt (*Contribution au remboursement de la dette sociale CRDS)*. Each employer has to pay an apprentice charge (*taxe d'apprentissage*) of 0.5 per cent of the employee's gross income. Companies with more than 10 employees are subject to a charge destined to promote the advancement of employees. The contribution rate amounts to 1.5 per cent of gross income. A housing charge which has to be paid by companies with more than 10 employees amounts to 0.45 per cent of the aggregate salaries and wages or 2 per cent for employers not participating in special housing programmes.

In *Switzerland*, a contribution has to be paid to finance the income compensation for military service (*Erwerbsersatzordnung EO*). This fund compensates for earnings lost during the military service of Swiss nationals. All residents with employment income including foreigners and women have to pay 0.15 per cent of gross income into the *EO*. The employer pays another 0.15 per cent. There is no income ceiling.

3.2 The Tax Systems in the Analysed Countries

For the tax burden on manpower personal income taxes including surcharges and state and municipality taxes as well as payroll taxes paid by the company are relevant. Contrary to that, the study does not deal with wealth taxes nor inheritance taxes since they are not linked directly to employment income. Church taxes as well are excluded from the study, assuming that all individuals have the possibility to leave church.

In the following, we describe the fiscal constitution, tax deductions, and tax schedules of the countries analysed.[35] For a brief overview of the tax schedules see Table 3.4. For tax allowances see Table A.4. - Table A.7. on p. 91-92.

[35] The description is based on IBFD (2003a and 2003b) and the national tax laws.

Table 3.4. Personal income tax: top rates

Country/Canton	Year	Highest income bracket	Top tax rate
Austria	'02-'03	€ 50,870	50.0 %
CH Basel-Landschaft	'02	CHF 1,119,067	42.6 %[a)]
	'03	CHF 1,122,724	42.6 %[a)]
CH Basel-Stadt	'02-'03	CHF 1,300,800	40.5 % [a)]
CH Bern	'02-'03	CHF 437,400	41.4 % [a)]
CH Genève		CHF 1,000,000	45.0 % [a)]
CH Nidwalden		CHF 300,000	26.7 % [a)]
CH Schwyz	'02	CHF 214,500	24.8 % [a)]
	'03	CHF 214,500	23.9 % [a)]
CH St. Gallen	'02-'03	CHF 248,000	35.9 % [a)]
CH Ticino	'02-'03	CHF 304,400	43.8 % [a)]
CH Valais	'02-'03	CHF 322,200	41.6 % [a)]
CH Vaud	'02-'03	CHF 189,800	45.4 % [a)]
CH Zug	'02-'03	CHF 130,500	23.3 % [a)]
CH Zürich	'02-'03	CHF 224,300	41.0 % [a)]
France	'02	€ 46,343	51.1 %
	'03	€ 47,131	49.6 %
Germany	'02-'03	€ 55,008	51.2 % [b)]
Ireland	'02-'03	€ 28,000	42.0 %
Italy	'02	€ 69,722	46.1 %*
	'03	€ 70,000	46.1 %*
Netherlands	'02	€ 47,746	52.0 %
	'03	€ 49,464	52.0 %
United Kingdom	'02	£ 29,400	40.0 %
	'03	£ 29,900	40.0 %
United States	'02	$ 307,050	43.9 % [a)]
	'03	$ 311,950	43.9 % [a)]

[a)] Combined tax rate with federal, state and municipal tax.
[b)] Including surcharge.

3.2.1 Austria

Fiscal constitution: The Republic of Austria comprises nine states. The fiscal constitution regulates the authority to levy taxes. The federation has the legislative competency for the income tax. Income tax revenues are shared among the federation, the states, and the municipalities. Employers pay a communal tax (*Kommunalsteuer*) on the aggregate salaries and wages. This tax is under legislative authority of the federation, but revenues accrue to the municipalities. The tax amounts to 3 per cent of the aggregate salaries and wages. The income tax on wages is withheld by the employer.

Tax base: The 13th and 14th monthly salaries are taxed at a rate of 6 per cent as long as they do not exceed one sixth of total income. All contributions to social security are tax deductible. For business-related expenses, there is a standard deduction of € 132 (§ 16 EStG) and, in addition, a tax credit of € 54. Further tax allowances are granted in the form of tax credits which are regulated in § 33 EStG. The personal tax credit is reduced as the income increases. It starts at € 887 and is equal to zero at a taxable income of € 35,421. There is an additional child tax credit of € 50.9 per child and month. The maximum pensioners' tax credit is € 400. It is reduced from taxable income of € 16,715 onwards and is equal to zero at an income of € 21,800.

Tax schedule: The income tax schedule is progressive. Married couples file separately. Incomes exceeding € 50,870 are subject to a statutory tax rate of 50 per cent.

3.2.2 France

Fiscal constitution: In the French Republic the most important types of taxes are levied by the central state. The central state is entitled to the entire revenue of the personal income tax. The French tax law is codified in the *Code Général des Impôts* (CGI) and its annexes. At the end of a year, the finance act (*Loi des Finances*) modifies the tax law for the current and the following years. The tax schedules are adjusted at the end of the tax year to account for inflation. The personal income tax is payable on the income of the preceding year. There is no withholding tax.

France levies several taxes or charges based on the employee's salary. The business tax (*taxe professionnelle*) was levied on 18 per cent of the aggregate salaries and wages until 2002. A reform in 1999 abolished this part of the business tax. Since in 2002, tax allowances for business tax based on wages and salaries amounted to € 914,694, many companies did not pay the tax any more. From 2003 on, it is completely abolished. In Paris, the rate of the business tax was 13.37 per cent in 2002 and 17.72 in 2001. The tax rate applies to 84 per cent of the tax base. Employers have to pay an additional payroll tax (*taxe sur les salaires*) if less than 10 per cent of the turnover are subject to value added tax. This applies for example to banks, insurance companies, or freelancers.[36] Companies who grant company cars to the employee's free disposal are subject to a special company tax. Since 1999, the tax due is € 282.03 per quarter for small cars and € 609.80 for larger cars. The company car tax is not deductible from the income tax base.

Tax base: In France, 10 per cent of gross income less social security contributions are deductible as business-related expenses. In 2002, the minimum and maximum deductions are € 370 and € 12,437.[37] From the resulting amount again twenty per cent are tax deductible up to a limit of € 22,780. The same deductions apply to pension income. Other tax allowances are integrated in the income tax schedule. The French income tax does not provide any special personal deductions. Old-aged persons with low incomes receive an additional degressive tax allowance. In 2002, the income ceiling for this allowance is € 16,090 for singles and

---

36 The *taxe sur les salaires* is not taken into account in the following analysis.

37 For the amounts of all tax allowances applying in 2002, see *Loi des finances pour 2003 du 30 décembre 2002.*

twice that amount for married couples. From 2001 to 2002, tax allowances increased by little.

Tax schedule: The income tax is progressive with a top tax rate of 49.58 per cent which applies to taxable incomes exceeding € 47,131. The top tax rate has been reduced since 2001 when it still amounted to 50.113 per cent. France uses family coefficients. To obtain the tax liability of a family, first the income of the family is divided by the coefficient applicable for the type of family considered, and then the tax due for this income is multiplied by the coefficient. The coefficient for a married couple is 2, for a couple with two children it is 3. However, the tax advantage for a family compared to a married couple must not exceed € 4,102. Otherwise the tax payment of a family with two children is obtained by using a family coefficient of 2 and then subtracting € 4,102 from the ensuing tax liability.

3.2.3 Germany

Fiscal constitution: The Federal Republic of Germany comprises 16 states. The federation has the authority to enact most tax laws. The revenues from the income tax accrue to the federation, the states, and the municipalities. The federation is entitled to the solidarity surcharge levied since 1995 to finance Germany's unification. The surcharge is 5.5 per cent of the income tax payment. The income tax on wage payments is withheld by the employer.

Tax base: In Germany, the employee's contributions to social insurance are deductible in limited amounts for purposes of personal income tax (§ 10c EStG). In principle, a deduction of 20 per cent of gross income is allowed for social security and contributions to other provision schemes for incomes up to € 12,228 for singles respectively € 24,456 for married couples.[38] The standard deduction is degressive and ends for gross incomes above € 19,175/€ 38,350 at an amount of € 2,001/€ 4,002. Furthermore, an additional deduction of € 36 is allowed for other special expenses, e.g., church tax or tax consultant if no exceeding costs are claimed.

Employees can claim a standard deduction of € 1,044 for business-related expenses (§ 9a No. 1 EStG). The deduction also is granted to pensioners who receive pensions related to a prior employment. German tax law grants a personal allowance of € 7,235 for singles respectively € 14,470 for married couples in 2002 and 2003 (§ 32a EStG). The personal allowance is integrated in the formulae of the tax schedule. A special old-age deduction is granted to old-aged persons who are still working (§ 24a EStG).

Tax payers with dependent children receive a child allowance deductible from the tax base or a non-taxable child benefit. The revenue office automatically takes account of the more favourable amount. That is, if the tax allowance reduces the tax liability by more than the non-taxable child benefit the allowance is used, otherwise the benefit. The child allowance (§ 32 EStG) amounts to € 1,824 plus

---

38 See Laux (2002) for detailed formulae to calculate the deduction for provision payments.

€ 1,080 for the costs of the children's education per child, per parent, and year. In 2002 and 2003, the allowance is more favourable than the benefit for taxable incomes above € 56,088 for married couples.

Tax schedule: The progressive tax rate of the personal income tax is expressed in formulae with continuously increasing marginal tax rates. From a taxable income of € 55,008 onwards, the top income tax rate of 48.5 per cent applies. Married couples can choose to file individually instead of jointly. If they file jointly the tax is computed by multiplying the joint taxable income by the average tax rate which applies to half the joint taxable income.

3.2.4 Ireland

Fiscal constitution: The Irish tax system is based on the British tax system. Like in the United Kingdom the tax law is regulated in the annually enacted Finance Act. Employment income is subject to withholding tax.

Tax base: Contributions to social security are not tax deductible. Instead of tax deductions tax credits are usual. A tax credit can be claimed by employees or pensioners with state or occupational pensions. It amounts to € 800 in 2003 and € 660 in 2002. Personal tax credits of € 1,520 for singles and € 3,040 for married couples apply. Married couples where one spouse stays at home caring for dependent persons receive an additional home carer's tax credit of € 770. Irish pensioners receive a tax credit of € 205 per person.

Tax schedule: Married couples file jointly. The top tax rate of 42.0 per cent is reached with taxable incomes of € 28,000.

3.2.5 Italy

Fiscal constitution: The Italian Republic is organised as a unitary state structured in 20 regions which are again subdivided into provinces and municipalities. Regions, provinces, and municipalities may only levy taxes that are permitted to them by the central state. The revenue of the personal income tax completely accrues to the central state. Regions levy a surcharge on the income tax. The surcharge ranges from 0.9 to 1.4 per cent of the personal income tax base. The tax rate is fixed by the regions. Municipalities may levy another surcharge up to a maximum of 0.5 per cent.[39] The income tax relating to employment income is withheld by the employer. There is a regional tax on productive activities (IRAP) payable by companies. Until the tax year of 2002 the IRAP effectively was levied on personnel expenses as they were not deductible from the tax base.

Tax base: Contributions to social security are fully tax deductible. With the tax reform of 2003, the deductions as well as the schedule have been changed.[40] From 2003 onwards, there is a basic deduction of € 3,000 which is increased to € 7,500

39 Rome has a municipal rate of 0.2 per cent and a regional rate of 0.9 per cent.

40 See *Agenzia delle Entrate, Circolare n. 2 del 15 gennaio 2003*, Roma.

for employment income and to € 7,000 for pensions. This deduction is degressive, equalling zero for incomes above € 26,000. Italy does not grant any personal tax credit. However, for non-working spouses a degressive tax credit is granted. In 2002 and 2003, this credit starts at € 546 for incomes up to € 15,494 and ends at € 422 for incomes above € 51,646. Families with low incomes may claim child allowance. Apart from this, individuals receive a tax credit of at least € 285 for each child. The working tax credit decreases because of the new basic deduction from up to € 1,146 in 2002 to at most € 235 in 2003. The tax credit for pensioners in 2003 is € 98 at the maximum for pensioners under 75, and up to € 222 for pensioners who are 75 years or older.

Tax schedule: The income tax schedule is progressive, married couples are assessed separately. From 2002 to 2003, tax rates and income brackets were adjusted to rounded amounts of Euro. The top tax rate stayed constant, lower tax rates and income brackets were raised. In 2003, the top tax rate of 45 per cent is reached with an income of € 70,000.

3.2.6 The Netherlands

Fiscal constitution: In the Netherlands, the state, the provinces, and the municipalities principally have the right to levy taxes. Nevertheless most taxes are levied by the central state. Tax revenues accrue to the state as well as to the provinces and municipalities. The Dutch personal income tax is structured as a box system with different tax schedules. Income from employment belongs to box 1. The tax rates of the two lowest income brackets of the tax schedule are combined with the social tax. The income tax on employment income is withheld by the employer.

Tax base: The contributions to workers' social security are partially deductible in the Netherlands. The contributions to the general public social security system are levied together with the personal income tax. These contributions are not tax-deductible. Contributions to social insurance which are paid out of gross income are deductible within limitations. Contributions to the workers' health insurance as well as other medical expenses are deductible in limited amounts. However, the contributions themselves stay below this limit. Contributions to unemployment insurance as well as contributions to occupational and personal pension plans are deductible for income tax purposes.

Tax rebates usually are accorded in the form of tax credits. In 2003, employees receive an employment tax credit of € 1,104 if they are under 57 years old. This credit decreases with increasing income and increases for older employees. Tax payers under 65 years obtain a personal tax credit of € 1,766. Non-working spouses obtain the personal tax credit as a transfer payment. For older persons the tax credit is reduced to € 806. Tax payers over 65 years may claim an old-age tax credit of € 346 if their income does not exceed € 29,592 (Art. 7 and 9 AOW and Art. 8.17-18 Wet LB). Taxpayers who receive a single-person's old-age pension get an additional tax credit of € 242. The child tax credit amounts to € 41 with an income limit of € 56,191. Families are entitled to a supplementary child credit of

€ 354 if their income does not exceed € 29,180 and to an additional credit of € 214 for each working spouse (Art. 8. 12-14 Wet LB).

Tax schedule: The income tax schedule of box 1 is combined with the social tax in the first two income brackets. In the lowest income brackets pensioners are therefore subject to other tax rates than employees. Married couples file separately. The top tax rate of 52 per cent is reached with a taxable income of € 49,464.

3.2.7 Switzerland

Fiscal constitution: In Switzerland, the confederation, the cantons, and the municipalities each levy their own taxes. Confederation and cantons have the sovereignty to levy taxes. Municipalities have a delegated sovereignty and may only levy taxes which they are empowered to by the canton. Regarding income taxes cantons and municipalities apply the same tax law. The confederation has a separate tax law. For reasons of flexibility and competition, cantons and municipalities fix annual multiples (*Steuerfuss*) by which the basic tax rates are multiplied yielding the rates of the canton or municipality tax.

In order to simplify the tax systems and to enhance the attractiveness for investors Switzerland has legislated the law on tax harmonisation in 1990.[41] Its objectives are to standardise the assessment periods for both individuals and legal entities and to harmonise the computation of taxable income. The schedules, tax rates, and tax-free allowances remain under the authority of each canton.

One big harmonisation concerning the tax assessment was the change from the *praenumerando* to the *postnumerando* taxation system which was completed in the tax year 2003. In the *praenumerando* taxation system the tax is assessed every two years for the income of the previous two years. In other words, the tax is paid for income that was earned during the two years before the assessment. The *postnumerando* taxation system is an annual assessment that is based on the income of the tax year. Taxes are paid during the whole tax period on an estimated base. At the beginning of the next year, the tax is finally assessed and tax payments may be corrected.

In the cantons Ticino, Vaud, and Valais, the 2-year-*praenumerando* system is still in force in the year 2002. The cantons will change to the annual *postnumerando* system in 2003. This implies that income from the years 2001 and 2002 will never be assessed as the taxes of 2002 and 2001 refer to income of 1999 and 2000 and the tax in 2003 refers to income of 2003. But incomes from 2001 and 2002 have nevertheless to be declared in order to account for extraordinary incomes or expenditures. In the following analysis, only Ticino, Vaud, and Valais are in this special situation.[42]

---

41 *Bundesgesetz über die Harmonisierung der direkten Steuern der Kantone und Gemeinden sowie über die direkte Bundessteuer.*

42 We use the tax regulations from 2000 in the calculations as the special regulations for 2002 income do not reflect the actual tax burden.

Most cantons changed on 01/01/2001 from the *prae*- to the *postnumerando* system. Schwyz still has a two-year tax period, but tax payers have the possibility to opt for the annual tax period. The other cantons analysed switched to a one-year assessment. Zürich already changed on 01/01/1999 and Basel-Stadt has always had the *postnumerando* system.

Tax base: The employee is subject to personal income tax with his gross income. In Switzerland, the employee's contributions to social insurance are completely tax-deductible. 3 per cent of the gross income less contributions to social security and occupational pension plans are deductible as business-related expenses. For the federal tax, the minimum deduction is CHF 1,900, the maximum deduction is CHF 3,800.[43] The cantons often follow this standard deduction where the limit varies. Some cantons have fixed standard deductions. For the detailed amounts of tax allowances in the cantons, see Table A.4. to Table A.7. on p. 91 ff.

Concerning the federal tax the personal deductions for the taxpayer or his spouse are integrated in the tax schedule. Income below CHF 15,770 or CHF 29,400, respectively is not taxable. Personal deductions in the cantons range from zero in Ticino up to CHF 6,500 for singles and CHF 13,000 for married couples in Zug. Tax allowances for taxpayers with children vary among the cantons reaching a maximum of CHF 8,000 per child in Zug and Ticino. The federal tax law grants a tax allowance of CHF 5,600 per child. In the cantons Vaud and Genève, the child allowances are part of the tax schedules. Some cantons grant deductions for pensioners of up to CHF 3,000 for singles and CHF 6,000 for married couples. These deductions often depend on the income and the net wealth of the pensioner.

Tax schedule: The income tax schedules of the confederation and the cantons are progressive. In contrast to other countries, the tax rate for the highest income is not always the highest statutory tax rate. The statutory tax rates increase up to the highest income bracket. From the highest income ceiling on, the income tax is calculated by multiplying the total taxable income with the tax rate instead of multiplying only the income in the bracket and adding the tax which is imposed on the lower income brackets. This form of progression is found in the confederation as well as in the cantons Zug, Basel-Stadt, Schwyz, and St. Gallen. For the tax rates as well as for the income brackets of the top rates see Table 3.4. on p. 38.

Married couples file jointly. In the cantons Zug and St. Gallen, married couples are taxed with the statutory average tax rate that would apply to half of their actual taxable income. The federal tax as well as the state income taxes of Basel-Landschaft, Basel-Stadt, Bern, Genève, Schwyz, Ticino, Zürich, and Nidwalden do not divide the income of married couples by two but by a smaller coefficient, or they have special tax schedules for married couples.

Vaud uses family coefficients within certain limits. Married taxpayers with or without children or singles with children divide their taxable income by the family coefficient which is 2.8 for a married couple with two children. The statutory tax rate which applies to the divided income is multiplied with the actual taxable in-

---

[43] For all deductions regarding the federal income tax, see *Kreisschreiben* No. 7 from 17/12/2001. For the state income taxes, see the canton-specific tax guides.

come. The tax advantage is cut off at high earnings of CHF 206,800 in 2003. For higher incomes the family coefficient is 1.8 for married couples and the tax base is reduced by an allowance of CHF 41,032.

In Genève, all personal tax allowances as well as the cantonal and municipal multiples are combined in the calculation of the tax payment. In a first step the tax is calculated taking deductions into account which results in the basic tax on net income. In addition, the basic tax on specific allowances according to marital status (CHF 15,000 for singles, CHF 27,500 for married couples), children (CHF 6,500 per child) and pensioners (decreasing in income for incomes up to CHF 74,160/CHF 111,240) is calculated as well. The difference between those two tax payments is the basic tax. In a second step the total tax payment is calculated. It consists of the basic tax plus the cantonal multiple of 47.5 per cent of the basic tax less a reduction of 12 per cent of the total plus an additional charge for the city of Genève (*Centime d'aide à domicile* at 1 per cent) and the municipal multiple.

The income tax of the canton Valais only has one schedule for both, singles and married couples, but married couples receive a reduction of 32 per cent of the tax payment. The reduction is at least CHF 600 and must not exceed CHF 3,500. Singles receive a decreasing tax credit for taxable incomes of up to CHF 28,900. From 2001 to 2002, only few changes in income taxes applied.

3.2.8 United Kingdom

Fiscal constitution: The tax system of the United Kingdom is organised centrally. The House of Commons enacts the Finance Act in which all taxes are regulated. The personal income tax is a non-permanent duty and has to be endorsed each year in the Finance Act. The tax year is from April to March of the following year. The personal income tax is structured as a scheduled system. Each schedule applies to different types of taxable income and stipulates different tax rates. Employment income is regulated in Schedule E.

Tax base: The contributions to social security are not tax-deductible. There is no standard deduction for business-related expenses. Tax payers receive a personal tax deduction of £ 4,615. Tax payers between 65 and 75 years instead obtain a tax allowance of £ 6,100, and tax payers beyond that age obtain £ 6,370. The married couple's allowance is £ 5,465 for persons born before 06/04/1935 and £ 5,535 for persons aged 75 or more. Above the income limit of £ 17,900 the old-age related allowances are reduced. Alternatively to the personal allowance for the old-aged the personal allowance may be claimed. The married couple's allowance has a minimum amount of £ 2,110. The United Kingdom reformed the child benefit system in 2002. Until 2002-2003, three types of child benefits applied: the general child benefit, working families tax credit for low-earning families and the child tax credit. In the tax year 2002-2003 the child tax credit is at most £ 529 for families with children, independent of the number of children.[44] The child tax credit decreases for tax payers whose income is in the higher tax rate band.[45]

Tax schedule: Married couples file separately in the United Kingdom. In Schedule E there are three tax rates, the lower, the basic, and the higher tax rate. The higher tax rate of 40 per cent applies to taxable income above £ 29,900.

3.2.9 United States

Fiscal constitution: In the United States, taxes are levied by the federation, the states, and the local governments. Personal income taxes usually are levied by the federation as well as by several states. Federal and state income taxes are not based on the same regulations. Some local governments also levy taxes on personal income. The state of Massachusetts analysed in our study levies a personal income tax, the city of Boston does not. Tax on employment income is withheld by the employer.

Tax base: For federal income tax purposes, the tax payer can choose between a standard deduction which is $ 4,750 for singles and $ 7,950 for married couples and itemised deductions (Code Sec. 63 (c), (d)). The itemised deductions include expenses for illness, health insurance premiums as well as taxes, interest payments or donations in limited amounts. The standard deduction is increased for persons over 65 by $ 1,150 for singles and by $ 900 per capita for married couples. Employees with low earnings receive an additional earned income tax credit (Sec. 32 IRC), pensioners with low earnings obtain a credit for the elderly (Code Sec. 22). There is an additional personal deduction of $ 3,050 for each member of the family (Code Sec. 152). Since 1997 there is a decreasing child tax credit of at most $ 600 (Sec. 24 IRC).

For state income tax purposes, social security contributions are tax deductible up to $ 2,000. There is a personal deduction of $ 3,300 ($ 6,600 for married couples), a child deduction of $ 1,000 per child as well as a deduction for pensioners of $ 700 ($ 1,400 for married couples).

Tax schedule: Married tax payers can choose between the possibilities to file jointly or separately. The top tax rate of the federal income tax is reached with an income of $ 311,950 whether filing separately or jointly. It amounts to 38.6 per cent. The state income tax of Massachusetts is proportional at a rate of 5.3 per cent.

---

44 ICTA 1988, s. 257AA, Sch. 138, FA 1999, s. 30, Sch. 3; FA 2000, s. 34.

45 From 2003/2004 onwards the credits are replaced by one child tax credit and a working tax credit for low-earning tax payers.

3.3 Compensation Components

3.3.1 Cash Compensation

For tax and social security purposes, employment income is defined as the compensation for the employee's work in all countries. Compensation can consist in cash or in kind.

In all countries cash compensation is subject to tax with its nominal value. Except for Austria, there are no special privileges concerning cash and bonus payments.[46] In Austria the 13th and 14th salaries are tax privileged. Up to a limit of one sixth of the regular salary the additional salary is taxed at a reduced tax rate of 6 per cent. Income exceeding this limit is subject to the regular tax schedule (§ 67 (1)-(2) EStG).

3.3.2 Perquisites: Company Car

Company cars which are put to the employee's free disposal are usually subject to tax as fringe benefits. The benefit of using the company car for private purposes can be evaluated referring to the intensity of private use or by a standardised value typically based on the price of the car. In Table A.3. on p. 90 we summarise for all countries the taxable fractions of the true monthly costs of a company car as expressed by the values θ_p. For the derivation of these values see Section 2.2.4.2.

In *Austria*, the standardised value is 1.5 per cent per month of the full price of the car up to a monthly maximum of € 510 in 2003. If the employee drives less than 500 kilometres per month the taxable value is reduced to 0.75 per cent up to a maximum of € 255 (§ 15 EStG and § 4 *Verordnung über die bundeseinheitliche Bewertung bestimmter Sachbezüge ab 2002*). Neglecting the case of an employee who drives little, we posit a θ_p of 0.75 for Austria.

In *France*, Art. 82 CGI stipulates that the valuation of company cars for tax purposes follows the regulations of social security. The valuation of company cars was reformed in 2003. The standard benefit of a leased car is now at 40 per cent of annual costs including the leasing fee, costs for fuel, insurance, and taxes. If the employee pays running costs on his own the standardised value is 30 per cent of the annual leasing fee.[47] Only the second version fits our approach because running expenses are unknown. The ratio θ_p between the standardised value and the actual costs is then 0.3. Before 2003 the benefit in kind was calculated based on the company's expenses in connection with the company car.[48] In addition to the

---

46 Tax privileges for bonus payments that refer to several years exist in some countries but are not analysed here.

47 See Direction de la Sécurité Sociale, *Circulaire DSS/SDFSS/5B/N°2003/07* from 07/01/2003, Part 2-2-3.

48 See Lefebvre, Fiscal 2002, Par. 1830.

personal income tax, the grant of the company car is subject to a special company car tax on the level of the firm.[49]

In *Germany* employees can choose between a valuation according to mileage or the standard value of 1 per cent of the full price of the car per month (§ 6 (1) No. 4 EStG and § 8 (2) EStG). Considering only the standardised valuation, θ_p results in 0.5.

In *Ireland* the taxable value of the company car is 30 per cent of the original market value per year. If the employee bears all running costs on his own the taxable benefit-in-kind of a car is reduced to 18.5 per cent of the original market value per year (TCA 1997, Part 5, Ch. 4). From 2004 on, this percentage will generally be set equal to 30 per cent. Employees with high mileage connected to their job obtain a reduced valuation. Fringe benefits are not subject to social security until 2003. Restricting attention to the case where the employee bears the running costs, we arrive at a value of $\theta_p = 0.77$ for Ireland.

The valuation of company cars for tax purposes in *Italy* does not fit the general approach outlined in Section 2.2.4.2. In that country, the fringe benefit provided by a company car is derived from tables on car values issued by the Italian automobile club ACI.[50] The costs of 15,000 kilometres for each type of car are multiplied by 30 per cent to obtain the annual fringe benefit. In order to standardise the calculation of the tax value of perquisites nevertheless, we assume a θ_p of 0.5 which corresponds roughly to the values in the ACI tables.

The annual benefit-in-kind of a company car in the *Netherlands* is valued at 25 per cent of the full price of the new car. The percentage is reduced under certain conditions (Art. 3. 145 Wet LB). Ignoring these, the Dutch value of θ_p is 1.04.

Swiss cantons have different regulations to evaluate the benefit of a company car. For example, Bern has a standardised measure of 1 per cent of the full price of the new car per month implying a θ_p of 0.5 which we use for all cantons. In other cantons, the fringe benefit is estimated individually or calculated with an approved regulation for such benefits.[51] With the new compensation certificate (*Lohnausweis*)[52] all cantons will adopt this standard valuation from 2004 onwards.

In the *United Kingdom,* the value of the benefit in kind depends on the CO_2 emissions figure for the company car from tax year 2002/2003 on. The maximum percentage of the price of the company car is 35 per cent per year, the minimum percentage is 15 per cent (Sch. 11 FA 2000). We assume that the lowest valuation applies, yielding a θ_p of 0.63. In earlier tax years, the taxable benefit of the car was 35 per cent of the list price. The price was limited to £ 80,000.[53]

In the *United States*, the fringe benefit is regularly measured according to the Lease Value Rule. Under the Lease Value Rule, the company car is valued with the annual lease value of the car which is indicated in the Lease Value Table. For automobiles with a list price above $ 600,000, the annual lease value is equal to 25

49 See Section 3.2.2.

50 See *Supplemento ordinario n. 231 alla Gazzetta Ufficiale del 17 dicembre 2002.*

51 See Bosshard and Funk (2000: 45).

52 The new certificate should be valid from 01/01/2004, but is now postponed.

53 See CCH (2001: par. 402).

per cent of the list price plus extra $ 500 (§ 1.61-21(d) Reg). This corresponds to a value of θ_p equal to 1.04.

3.3.3 Long-Term Incentives: Employer-Provided Stock Options

There are three possible dates when employer-provided stock options can become subject to tax: at the date of grant, at the date of the exercise of the option or at the date of vesting when the options can be exercised the first time. While for tradable stock options the date of taxation is often the date of grant, non-tradable options tend to be taxed at the date of exercise. In this study, we only consider non-tradable stock options.

The benefit of the stock options is usually equal to the market value of the underlying share at the time of exercise less the price actually paid. Some countries accord a preferential valuation of this benefit. Table A.3. on p. 90 presents the fractions θ_l of the true benefits which are subject to tax in the countries considered under the assumptions of our model.

Austria accords a preferential treatment to stock options as part of compensation if they satisfy several conditions (§ 3(1) EStG and § 67(10) EStG). Stock options are tax-privileged up to a fair value of the underlying shares of € 36,400 at the date of grant. A proportion of the benefit is tax-exempt which depends on the number of years elapsed since the date of grant. For each year ten per cent are granted, up to a maximum of 50 per cent. We assume a delay of 5 years, arriving at $\theta_l = 0.5$.

In *Germany*, stock options are not subject to a special tax treatment and hence are taxed at the date of exercise.[54] The benefit is equal to the difference between the market value at the date of exercise and the price actually paid. Stock options are subject to social security at the date of exercise as well.

In the *Netherlands*, employer-provided stock options are subject to tax on the vesting date with the full benefit. The employee can choose to be taxed at the date of exercise.[55] Since it is assumed that the options are exercised at the vesting date, this choice is not relevant in our model. Thus, in the Netherlands and in Germany θ_l is equal to one.

In *Switzerland*, stock options are taxed at the date of grant if the vesting date is up to five years after the grant of the options (*Reg. No. 5* from 30/04/1997). Otherwise the stock options are subject to tax in the period of exercise. The benefit then is the difference between market value and the price paid by the employee. We only consider the taxation of stock options upon grant. The taxable value of stock options in this case is estimated using the method of Black and Scholes. The value of employer-provided stock options has to be adjusted so as to reflect the restriction concerning the vesting date. The modification is fixed assuming a long-

54 BFH from 20. 06. 2001 VI R 105/99, BStBl. II 2001; following to BFH from 24. 01. 2001 I R 100/98, BFH/NV 2001 and I R 119/98, BFH/NV 2001.

55 Supreme Court decision BNB 1985/16, BNB 1992/231, BNB 1992/232 cited in European Commission (2003).

term capital market yield of 6 per cent. For options with a holding period of five years the modification amounts to 25.27 per cent. This results in a reduced value of the stock option of $\theta_l = 74.73$ per cent. Gains or losses resulting from the exercise of the qualified stock options which have been taxed upon grant do not affect the tax due.

Under certain conditions benefits from stock option plans are tax-exempt in *France*, *Ireland*, *Italy*, the *United Kingdom*, and the *United States*.[56] In *France*, gains resulting from the disposal of the stock are subject to tax if they exceed € 7,650 in 2002. In *Italy*, the full gain is subject to the capital gains tax of 12.5 per cent. In the tax year 2002/2003, gains are tax-exempt up to £ 7,700 in the *United Kingdom* and up to € 1,270 in *Ireland*. Exceeding gains are subject to capital gains tax in these two countries. In the United States, capital gains are taxed at rates according to the time the stock was held. In all these countries, θ_l is zero in our model because we do not consider the sale of the underlying stock.

3.3.4 Pension Schemes

In all of the analysed countries, the employer's contributions are deductible as personnel expenses from the company's tax base. Thus, we only refer to tax regulations concerning the employee's personal income tax. Since contributions to the first and the second pillars often are taxed differently, we start in Section 3.3.4.1 by considering the first pillar contributions and pensions. In Section 3.3.4.2 we then turn to the second pillar and where necessary to the third pillar of old-age insurance.

3.3.4.1 First Pillar of Old-Age Insurance

In *France*, *Italy*, and *Switzerland*, employees' contributions to the first pillar are fully deductible from the income tax base. As a consequence, public pensions are taxable income with their full amount.

In *Austria*, contributions are tax deductible as well. Furthermore, 25 per cent of public pensions deriving from the employee's contributions are subject to tax, the remaining 75 per cent are tax-exempt (§ 25(1) EStG and § 26 EStG).

In *Germany*, the employee's contributions are tax-deductible only within the standard deduction for personal expenses up to a maximum of € 2,001 for singles and € 4,002 for married couples. During the retirement period, public pensions therefore are subject to tax only with the income element of the pension annuity. For a person retiring at the age of 65, the income element amounts to 27 per cent of the whole public pension (§ 22 No. 1b EStG).

In the *Netherlands*, contributions to the first pillar are levied in combination with the personal income tax. As a consequence, they are not tax deductible (Art.

---

56 Ireland: S519D Taxes Consolidation Act 1997 and Schedule 12C; Italy: Article 9, Paragraph 4 Letter c) of the Italian Tax Code; UK: Section 135 and 185 ICTA 1988, Schedule 14 FA 2000; USA: Section 422 IRC.

11(1) Wet LB). However, public pensions are taxable income with their full amount (Art. 3.82 c, 3.100 in connection with Art. 1.7 (2) Wet LB, Art. 9 AOW).

Tax treatment in the *United Kingdom* and in *Ireland* is similar to the one found in the Netherlands: The employee's overall contributions are not tax deductible. Nevertheless, public pensions are subject to tax.

In the *United States*, employees' contributions are deductible in limited amounts within the standard deductions ($ 4,750) or within the itemised deductions. The tax treatment of the resulting public pensions depends on the taxable income. If the tax payer has an income below $ 34,000 for singles or below $ 44,000 for married couples filing jointly 50 per cent of the pension are tax-exempt. The tax-exempt proportion decreases according to income. With incomes above $ 43,000 and $ 56,000, respectively, 85 per cent of the public pension is taxable (Code Sec. 86).

3.3.4.2 Second Pillar of Old-Age Insurance

Contributions paid by the employee to the second pillar of old-age insurance usually are part of gross income and therefore are subject to social insurance. In contrast, typically no social insurance charges are levied on contributions to the second pillar paid by the employer.

The basic idea for taxing occupational pensions is either to exclude contributions from taxable income and thus subject pension benefits to taxation, or to require that contributions are paid out of after-tax income implying that pensions are tax-exempt during retirement. For contributions to the second pillar paid by the employer, generally the first alternative is chosen: They are not deemed taxable income of the employee before the period of retirement. Actually, there is a trend to treat the contributions paid by the employee in the same way, that is, to tax pensions from second pillar insurance when the resulting annuities are received and to exempt all contributions from personal income tax. The only country in our sample that does not allow deductibility of employees' contributions to the second pillar even in limited amounts is the United States. However, the tax treatment is diverse in the analysed countries which is shown in the following.

The taxation of contributions to the second pillar in *Austria* depends on the type of pension scheme. Employees can claim a tax credit of 5.5 per cent of the premium plus an additional percentage under certain conditions (§ 108a EStG). The tax credit is applicable up to a contribution of € 1,000. Alternatively, employees can deduct the contributions to pension funds within the limit of € 2,920 (§18(1) EStG). The employee's contributions to a direct insurance or to a direct guarantee are tax-exempt as long as the benefit is below 80 per cent of the employee's annual earnings (§ 14 EStG). Furthermore, contributions to other forms of old-age provision are tax-exempt up to an annual contribution of € 300 (§ 3 Z15a EStG). 25 per cent of occupational pensions resulting from the employee's contributions are not taxable, the remaining occupational pensions are taxable. The contributions to the *MV-Kasse* are not part of the employee's gross income and as a consequence they are not taxable nor subject to social security.[57] Contributions exceeding the compulsory amount of 1.53 per cent of gross income are subject to social insurance and personal income tax. The pension resulting from the *MV-Kasse* is tax-exempt (§ 29 Z 1 EStG).

In *France*, the employee's contributions are tax-deductible up to a limit of 19 per cent of 8 times the social security income ceiling (Art. 83.2 CGI) which is € 44,360 in 2003. The limit refers to all contributions of old-age provision including contributions to the first pillar and contributions by the employer. The sum of all contributions to the public and compulsory occupational pension schemes remains below this limit. Resulting pensions are subject to taxation. Contributions to the non-compulsory pension scheme exceeding the limit for deductibility are part of the taxable income of the employee (Art. 82 CGI). The resulting annuities are taxable with their income element which amounts to 40 per cent for tax payers who retired at an age between 60 and 69 (Art. 158 No. 6 CGI).

In *Germany*, the taxation of occupational pension plans varies. It depends on who pays the contributions (employer or employee), on the kind of pension scheme used (direct guarantee, direct insurance, pension funds), and on the amount paid. If the employee does not obtain a legal claim to a future pension the contributions are not seen as part of the compensation. For example, if the employer invests in a direct guarantee, the employee does not have taxable income before the pension is paid. Contrary to that, contributions to occupational pension plans where the employee receives a legal claim to future pensions are subject to personal income tax in the remuneration period. They may be tax-exempt in limited amounts (e.g. 4 per cent of the income ceiling of the first pillar for pension funds, § 3 No. 63 EstG). Exceeding contributions are subject to a tax rate of 20 per cent up to an amount of € 1,752 (§ 40b EstG). The taxation during the pension period depends on the tax treatment during the time when the contributions were paid. If the contributions were tax-exempt resulting pensions are subject to tax. If the contributions were paid out of taxed income the resulting pension is subject to tax only with its income element. They are thus treated in a way comparable to the public pension.

In *Ireland*, contributions to approved pension plans are deductible up to 15 per cent of the earnings. Since December 2002, there is an earnings cap of € 254,000. The annuities from occupational pension plans are subject to tax.

In *Italy*, the entire contributions paid by employer and employee into the second pillar of old-age provision are tax deductible up to 12 per cent of the total income subject to a maximum of € 5,165 per year. The resulting annuities during retirement are subject to income tax with their income element.[58] Unlike in the other countries, pension funds themselves have to pay a tax of 11 per cent on income.

The employee's contributions to a qualified occupational pension plan are tax deductible in the *Netherlands* as long as they do not exceed 2 per cent of income. Resulting pensions are subject to personal income tax. Contributions to a private

---

57 § 26 Z7 EStG and § 49 (3) Z18 ASVG; see as well Kristen et al. (2002).

58 See Fenge et al. (2003: 160), Towers Perrin (2001).

old-age provision are tax-deductible up to € 1,069. The resulting pensions are taxable with their income element.

Switzerland exempts all contributions to an occupational pension plan during the investment period. The resulting pensions are therefore subject to personal income tax.

In the *United Kingdom*, the employee can contribute to an occupational pension plan up to 15 per cent of the gross income with an annual maximum of £ 97,200 without having to pay tax on this contribution. Exceeding contributions are subject to tax.[59] However, for the contributions to be eligible for this exemption, the expected annual pension payment must not exceed two thirds of the final remuneration. The employee is not allowed to invest more into the occupational pension plan than the amount that results in this maximum pension. Additional investment has to be paid into funded unapproved retirement benefit schemes (*FURBS*) which are not tax privileged. The resulting pensions are taxable and double taxation occurs. A capital payment out of approved pension plans at the date of retirement of 1.5 per cent of the final remuneration is tax-exempt (ICTA 1988, s. 189).

In the *United States*, the employer's contributions to an occupational pension plan are tax-exempt and the resulting pensions are subject to personal income tax (Code Sec. 402-404). Contrary to that, the employee's contributions have to be paid out of taxed income and hence pensions resulting from the employee's contributions only are taxable with their income element during the retirement period. The tax-exempt element in pension payments starting after 1996 is calculated with the so-called simplified method (Code Sec. 72 (b) ff.). The employee's total contributions to the occupational pension plan are divided by the total number of expected monthly annuities. For lifetime annuities this number is estimated following average life expectancies. The estimated number thus depends on the age when the annuity starts. For a single retiring at the age of 65 it is 210, and for a married couple it is 310. The ratio of contributions divided by the number of annuities is the monthly tax-exempt amount of the occupational pension.

59 They can also be carried back or forward, ICTA 1988, s. 592 (7).

4 The Effective Tax Burden in the Analysed Countries

In the following, we present the effective average tax rates in the assessed countries. We proceed country by country. In each section, we describe the EATRs for each level of disposable income, type of compensation structure, and family situation (see Section 2.2.2). We then identify tax drivers which decrease or increase the tax burden. If there were important changes in taxation or social security systems from 2002 to 2003, we discuss the resulting changes in EATRs.

4.1 Austria

Fig. 4.1. illustrates the EATRs resulting for Austria for all types of employees at all income levels in the tax year 2003.[60] With increasing income, one can see a small increase in the EATR, by 4.6 percentage points, for singles and a moderate increase, by 10.6 percentage points, for families. This is due to the fact that the highest income bracket of the tax schedule already is reached with a taxable income of € 50,000.

The advantage in tax burden obtained by families is 8.0 percentage points for the low disposable income. Because married couples do not receive any privileges due to separate filing and because child allowances with roughly € 4,500 are not particularly high, the difference in the EATRs of singles and families is comparatively low and decreases rapidly with increasing income.

The variation of the compensation structure results in small changes of the EATRs of up to 2.2 percentage points for a long-term-incentive-oriented single. This stems from the fact that only 50 per cent of the option's benefit are taxed. Deferring income into the future as in the case of the pension-oriented (lti-oriented) employee results in a higher tax burden, as the deduction of old-age contributions is limited for employees.[61] Raising only the employer's contributions to the second pillar would result in a decrease of the tax burden, because they are not subject to social security and personal income tax during the period of remunera-

---

60 See Table A.8. and Table A.9. on p. 94.

61 When interpreting the results for the pension-oriented employee, it is important to remember that in our model, future income is discounted with the market interest rate before taxes. See Section 2.1.3 and the discussion in Section 5.2.

tion. However, for the international comparison we stick to the fixed split of the contributions to the second pillar between employee and employer.

The effective tax burden decreases from 2002 to 2003 by up to 0.8 percentage points, as illustrated by the bold lines in Fig. 4.1. There were small increases in tax credits but as well in social security contributions. The main reason for the decrease, however, is the introduction of the new compulsory occupational pension scheme (*MV-Kasse*) which allows the full deduction of contributions while exempting annuities from tax during retirement.

Fig. 4.1. Effective average tax rates for Austria in per cent, 2003 and 2002

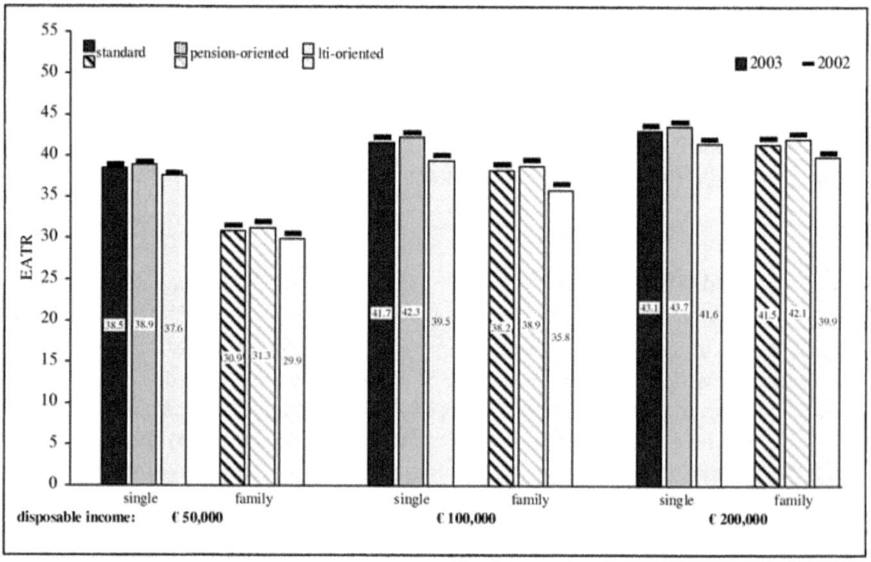

4.2 France

The effective average tax rates in France are illustrated in Fig. 4.2.[62] With increasing income, they vary over a span of 7.8 percentage points for singles and 15.9 percentage points for families. For the single the income starting from which the top tax rate applies is reached with our income levels. Families benefit from the French family quotient which can be seen in the comparably high increase in EATRs. The family quotient of 3 does not apply in our case as the maximum tax advantage compared to a married couple already is exhausted at the analysed income levels. Nevertheless, even the capped tax advantage leads to a substantial decrease in EATR.

The variation of the compensation structure reduces the EATR remarkably for the lti-oriented employee because the exercise of stock options is tax-exempt.

62 See Table A.34. and Table A.35. on p. 101.

Note that we ignore the tax liability on the capital gain procured by the sale of the shares. Taking this aspect into account would lead to a higher tax burden. For a pension-oriented employee, independently from his income level or family situation, the EATRs increase when increasing the contributions to old-age provision. This results from a rather unfavourable treatment of voluntary occupational pension plans. Although contributions to such pension plans are not deductible the resulting pensions are taxed with the standardised income element of 40 per cent.

From 2002 to 2003, the EATRs decrease for the low and the high income level. Several changes in the income tax (decreased tax schedule and increased tax allowances) and a decreased rate of the *taxe professionnelle* could not compensate the increase in income ceilings of social insurance totally.

Fig. 4.2. Effective average tax rates for France in per cent, 2003 and 2002

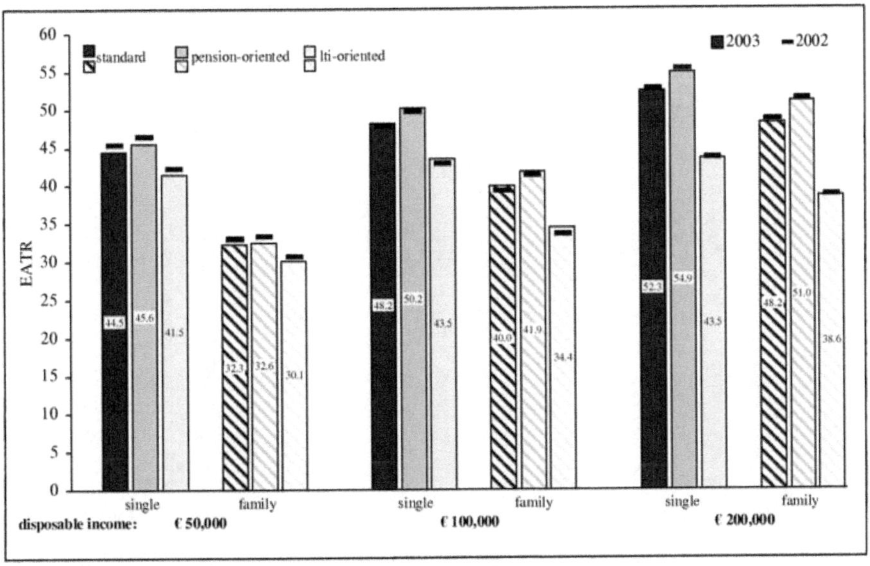

4.3 Germany

Fig. 4.3. represents the effective average tax rates of Germany for all analysed types and levels of income.[63] The tax schedule as well as the income ceiling of social security have a strong influence on the effective tax burden. A single with a disposable income of € 50,000 already is in the highest income bracket with a statutory tax rate of 48.5 per cent. His tax burden nearly stays constant over all income levels. In contrast to the other analysed countries, the German tax schedule is not based on income brackets with a constant rate applying to each bracket. Instead, marginal tax rates increase continuously starting from a rather high level

[63] See Table A.36. and Table A.37. on p. 96.

(19.9 per cent). Therefore even moderate incomes are subject to a rather high average tax rate. Put differently, the progressivity of the income tax schedule ends at comparatively low levels of taxable income. In addition, ceilings on social security contributions reduce progressivity as well.

The EATR for a family with the low level of disposable income is 18.6 percentage points below the EATR of a single. With increasing disposable income the family's tax advantage decreases to 5.4 percentage points at the income level of € 200,000. For married couples filing jointly, the top tax rate is achieved with a taxable income of around € 110,000. Families are therefore still in a progressive range of the tax schedule with the analysed income levels. As a consequence, with increasing income the EATR of a family increases faster than a single's EATR.

Fig. 4.3. Effective average tax rates for Germany in per cent, 2003 and 2002

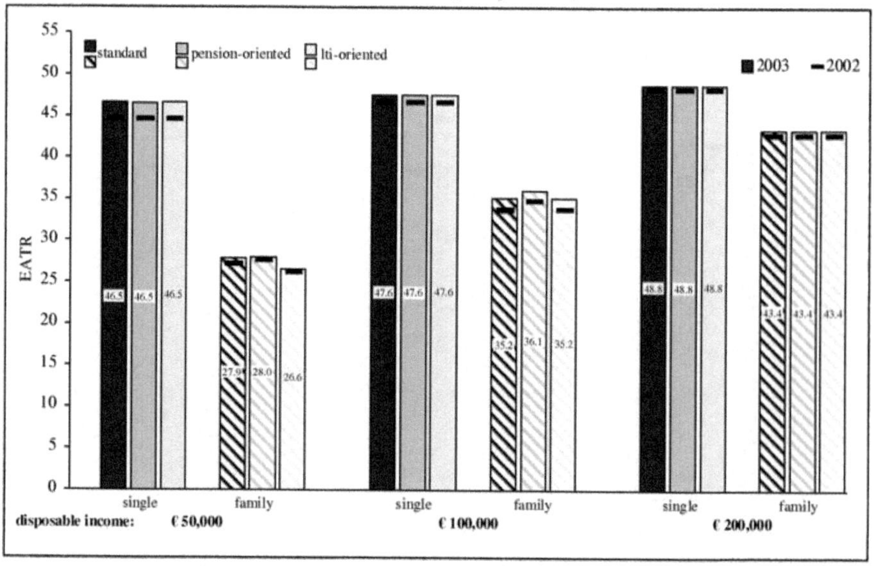

The structure of the employee's compensation does not have a noticeable influence on the tax burden. The EATRs of the standard and the incentive-oriented employee are equal for a single since there is no tax privilege for stock options. However, families at the low income level reduce their tax burden by 1.3 percentage points compared to the standard compensation structure if stock options are granted. This is due to the fact that this employee receives a gross income just below the income ceiling of social security at the low income level. In the exercise period gross income exceeds the ceiling due to the option benefit. By consequence there are no social security contributions on the option benefit.

A high proportion of old-age contributions does not affect the effective tax burden for singles. Families are hurt by deferring compensation. For the low and the standard level of disposable incomes, the EATR increases by 0.1 respectively 0.9 percentage points. The reason for this is that the family actually is subject to a higher statutory average tax rate in the retirement period because family allowances are no more available.

The increase in income ceilings and contribution rates of social security from 2002 to 2003 results in increased EATRs, as it is illustrated by the bold lines in Fig. 4.3. The single with low earnings and the family with the standard level of disposable income receive gross incomes that are just above the income ceilings of 2002. Thus, the increase is much higher for these types of employees than for the other income levels, reaching 1.9 percentage points for the single with a disposable income of € 50,000.

4.4 Ireland

The effective average tax rates for Ireland are depicted in Fig. 4.4.[64] If the income level is increased the effective tax burden increases by 8.0 percentage points for singles and 18.1 percentage points for families. Couples are filing jointly which results in a relatively high tax advantage for families especially at the low income level.

Fig. 4.4. Effective average tax rates for Ireland in per cent, 2003 and 2002

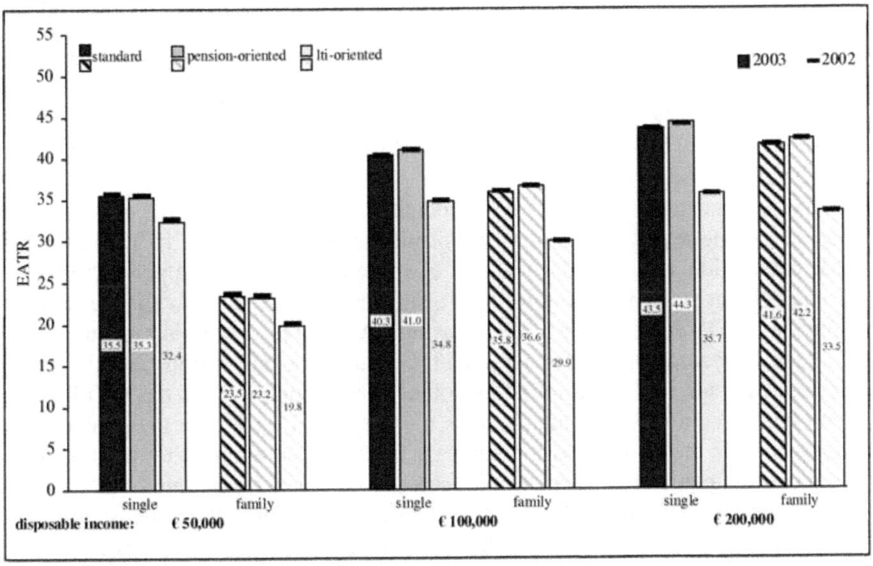

The EATR can be reduced remarkably with stock options, because they are tax-exempt at exercise. Note, however, that we do not consider the sale of the purchased stock. When capital gains tax occurs upon the sale of stock the effective tax burden rises.

Increasing the old-age contributions has different effects according to the income level. At low incomes, the employee's effective tax burden decreases. For

64 See Table A.38. and Table A.39. on p. 102.

the higher income levels, contributions to the second pillar exceed the tax-favoured limitation and the EATRs increase for both singles and families.

From 2002 to 2003 there are small changes of the tax schedule and the allowances. As a consequence the EATRs decrease somewhat. The introduction of the earnings cap for contributions to occupational pension plans in 2003 does not seem to have a noticeable influence on the attractiveness of occupational pension plans due to the earnings cap's level of € 254,000. Only for the single pension-oriented employee with high income the tax burden increases from 2002 to 2003 by 0.2 percentage points.

4.5 Italy

The effective average tax rates in Italy do not follow a clear trend as one can see in Fig. 4.5.[65] An employee with the standard compensation structure bears a tax burden that decreases by 0.8 percentage points as one passes from the low to the standard income level and increases again by 1.7 percentage points as one moves to the high level. For a pension-oriented employee the situation is reverse. There is a relatively large increase of 4.0 percentage points between the low and the standard level of disposable income and a small increase as one reaches the highest income level. With increasing income, an lti-oriented employee is faced with constantly decreasing EATRs. This diverse pattern is a consequence of our assumption of a compensation structure which varies with the income level even for the same type of employee.

If one calculates the EATRs with a compensation structure which remains fixed across income levels one obtains the results shown in brackets in Table A.41. In that calculation we keep the weights of the compensation components given in Table 2.1. on p. 15 for the low level of disposable income also for the other income levels. In this case we find increasing EATRs with increasing income.

Receiving stock options reduces the tax burden as stock options in Italy are tax-exempt and not subject to social insurance. The comparison of the EATRs using the variable compensation components illustrates that the higher the percentage of stock options the stronger is the decrease in EATR. In contrast to the lti-oriented employee, a pension-oriented employee does not necessarily enjoy a reduced effective tax burden compared to an employee with a standard compensation structure. An employee with a disposable income of € 50,000 experiences a small decrease in EATR whereas for employees with higher incomes the EATR increases. This is due to the limited deductibility of contributions to occupational pension plans. The low-earning employee is still within the limitation and thus benefits from that tax regulation.

65 See Table A.40. and Table A.41. on p. 102.

Fig. 4.5. Effective average tax rates for Italy in per cent, 2003 and 2002

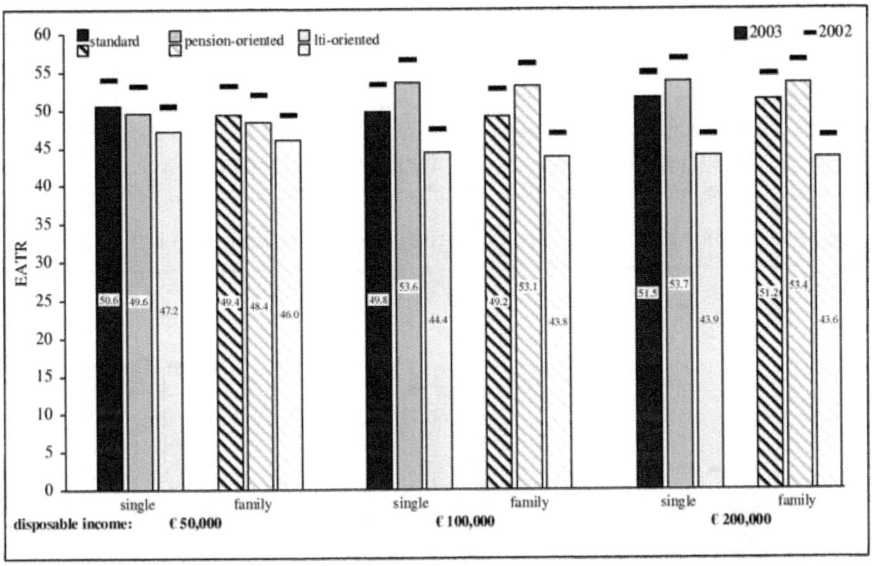

A striking result of our analysis concerns the taxation of families. In Italy, family allowances strongly depend on the family's income. The levels of disposable income which we analyse exceed the limitations on family allowances by far. Furthermore, married couples are taxed separately. The tax credit for a non-working spouse depends on the income as well. Hence, the differences between the EATRs of a single and of a family are very low. The advantage for a family is 1.2 percentage points at most.

Fig. 4.5. also includes the development of the EATRs from 2002 to 2003. The EATRs decrease by about 3.5 percentage points. The main reason for this is the reform of the regional tax on productive income IRAP that permits the deduction of personnel expenses from 2003 on. The introduction of the no tax area in the personal income tax in 2003 does not have any influence on the tax burden as our incomes are above the requested income ceilings.

4.6 The Netherlands

In the Netherlands, the combined tax schedule consisting of personal income tax and social security is reflected in the EATR shown in Fig. 4.6.[66] The highest tax bracket with a top rate of 52 per cent already is reached with the disposable income of € 50,000. But since a high proportion of the income is still in the first two income brackets with tax rates as low as 1.7 and 7.35 per cent the average tax rate

66 See Table A.42. and Table A.43. on p. 103.

is reduced.[67] This results in a strong increase in EATR as one passes from the low to the standard level of disposable income.

Like in Germany, where stock options are not privileged as well, the EATR stays constant if the proportion of stock options rises. With a higher proportion of old-age contributions, the EATR can be reduced to a small extent for all income levels. Only for families at the low income level the EATR increases because the increase in deductible old-age contributions cannot compensate for the increased tax rate due to the lack of family allowances during the retirement period.

Fig. 4.6. Effective average tax rates for the Netherlands in per cent, 2003 and 2002

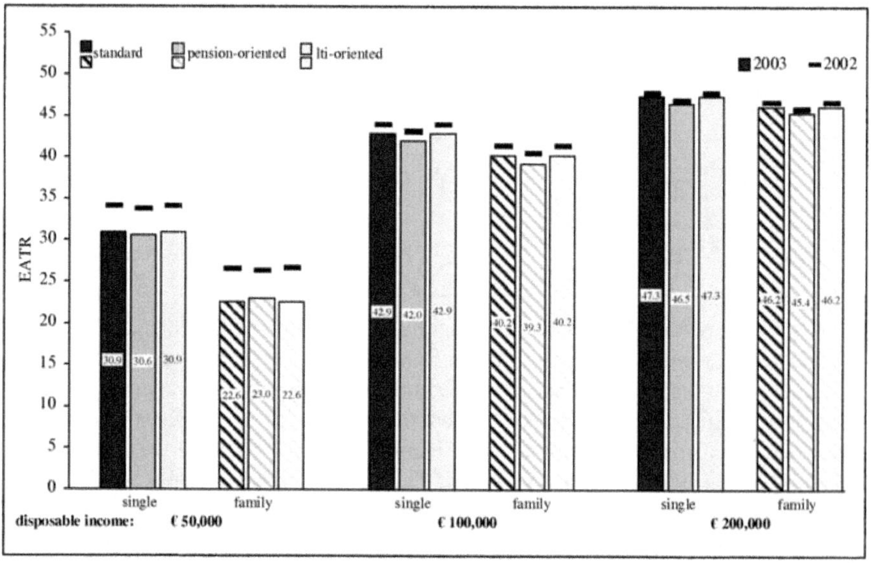

While families with the low income level bear an EATR which is 8.3 percentage points below the EATR of a single, the family advantage melts away to 2.7 percentage points at the standard and 1.1 percentage points at the high income level. This is due to the decreasing influence of the family allowances of € 1,900.

From 2002 to 2003, we observe a relatively strong decrease in the tax burden for the low income (up to 4.0 percentage points for families) and a smaller decrease for the higher levels of disposable income. This is due to changes in social security contributions and personal income tax. The contributions to public health insurance increased by around 2 percentage points. At the same time the personal income tax rates in the two lowest income brackets were decreased. Because we do not consider health insurance contributions as tax-like this has a reducing effect on the tax burden. Furthermore, the income brackets were raised and tax credits were increased.

67 Note that we define the contributions to the health insurance of 12.55 per cent on the first two income brackets as equivalent insurance contributions. They do not enter the effective tax burden.

4.7 Switzerland

Fig. 4.7. illustrates the effective average tax rates for the three income levels and the three variations of compensation structure for a single in the analysed twelve Swiss cantons.[68] In each graph, the cantons are sorted according to the EATR with the standard compensation structure. The displayed values above the bars refer to the respective EATRs of the standard compensation structure. There is a relatively high dispersion of the tax burden derived for different income levels.

Fig. 4.7. Effective average tax rates for a single in Switzerland in per cent, 2003

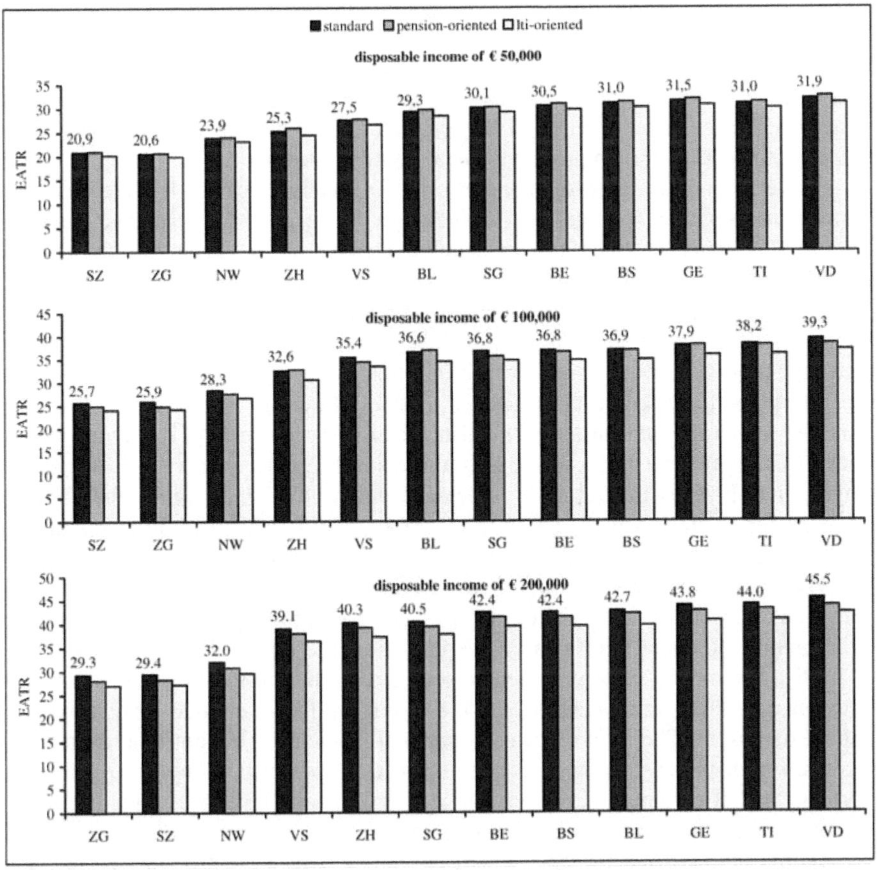

From a disposable income of € 50,000 to € 200,000, the span of EATR in the standard case amounts to 8.1 percentage points for the canton with lowest dispersion (Nidwalden) and to 15.0 percentage points for Zürich which shows the highest dispersion of effective tax rates. For the analysed income levels, the taxable income is still below the highest income bracket of the tax schedule in most

68 See Table A.10. to Table A.33. on p. 95 ff.

cantons[69]. Therefore, the EATR increases faster than it would do at income levels above the highest income bracket.

Another reason for the relatively steep increase in EATR is the Swiss social security system. Because there are no income ceilings (except for the unemployment insurance) and because the public pension hardly depends on the amount of contributions paid the proportion of tax-like contributions stays constant.

In all cantons, the tax burden decreases with the grant of stock options due to the uniformly favourable valuation of the options at the date of grant. For the high income level the reduction of the EATR is larger because we assume a higher percentage of stock options. However, one has to bear in mind that we do not consider any risk concerning the value of the options. If the actual stock price moves below the expected or even below the exercise price, the employee may tend not to exercise the stock option although he paid taxes on the expected benefit. In this case, the effective tax burden would increase compared to the standard compensation structure. On the other hand, if the stock turns out to be worth more than expected, the tax paid upon grant will seem relatively low ex post.

The effects of a high proportion of old-age contributions are less clear cut. For the high income level, the EATR decreases by up to 1.6 percentage points in Vaud. The same is true for the standard income level, except for the cantons Zürich, Basel-Landschaft, and Genève where the EATR rises with increasing old-age contributions. Regarding the low income level, the EATRs increase in all cantons. The highest increase occurs in the cantons Zürich and Vaud with 0.6 percentage points. However, the increases are fairly low.

The effective average tax rates for families shown in Fig. 4.8. give a similar picture as for the tax burden of singles. The dispersion of EATRs across income levels is larger than in the case of a single with differences between 11.6 percentage points in Schwyz and 20.8 percentage points in Ticino. Again, the effective tax burden decreases with the grant of stock options at all income levels and increases for pension-oriented employees with a low income level.

For the standard compensation structure and all income levels, Fig. 4.9. illustrates by how much families are favoured compared to singles. The bars represent the relative advantage for families expressed as the ratio between the EATRs of families and singles. The cantons are sorted according to the ratio derived for the low income level. In all cantons, the EATRs of families are remarkably lower than those of singles. The ratio reaches 67 per cent in Ticino. The family advantage decreases with increasing income level up to a 96 per cent ratio in Zug, Genève, Valais, and Nidwalden. However, for the high income level the ratios of all cantons are within a span of 5 percentage points.

From 2002 to 2003 there are changes scarcely worth mentioning due to minor changes in cantonal and municipal multiples of the state income taxes.

---

[69] For the income brackets and highest tax rates, see Table 3.4. on p. 38.

Fig. 4.8. Effective average tax rates for a family in Switzerland in per cent, 2003

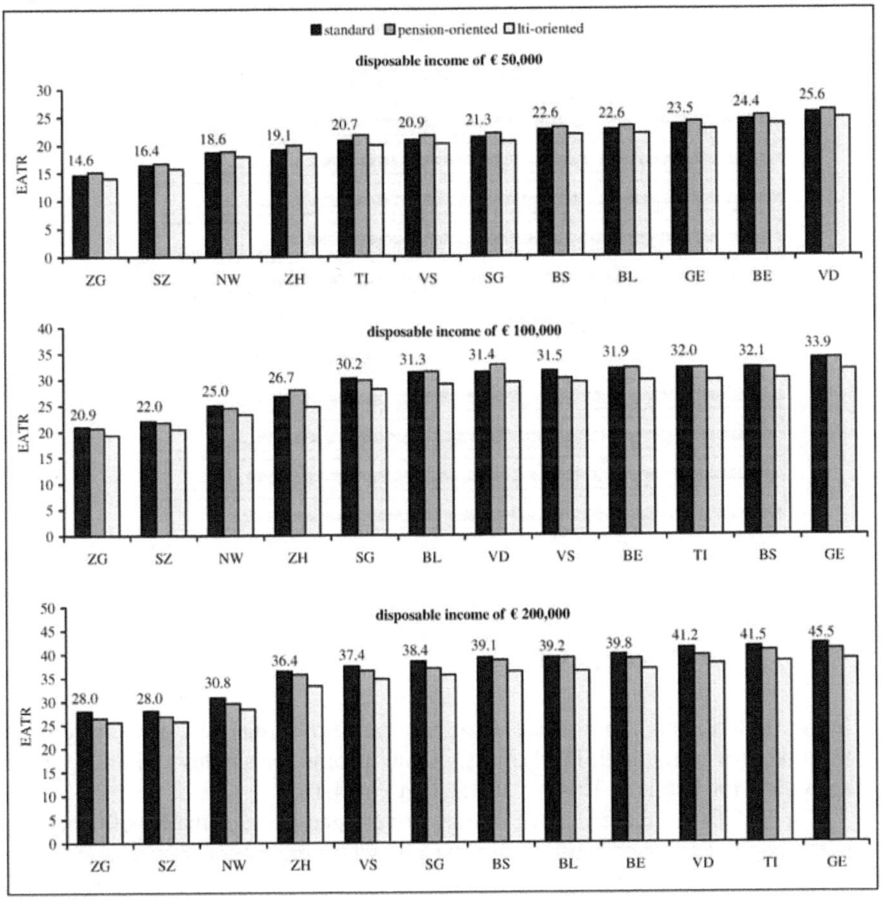

Fig. 4.9. Tax relief for families in Switzerland, 2003

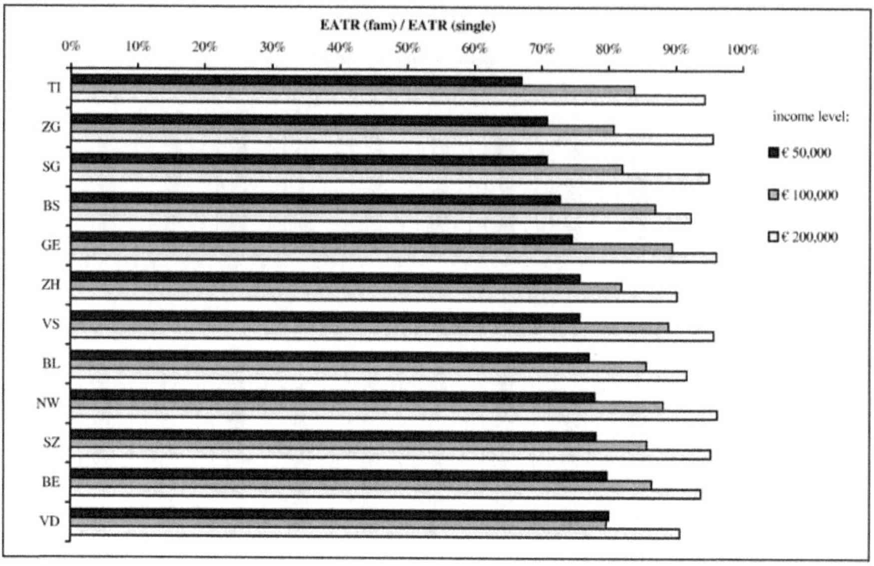

4.8 United Kingdom

In the United Kingdom, the EATRs span a range of around 9.1 percentage points from the low to the high level of disposable income for singles and 14.2 percentage points for families. This is illustrated in Fig. 4.10.[70]

The EATRs decrease if stock options are granted because the benefit conferred by the option is taxed neither at grant nor when the option is exercised.[71] The EATR rises with a higher proportion of old-age contributions over all income levels. This is because on the one hand, old-age contributions are tax deductible only in limited amounts and, on the other hand, the pensions resulting from an approved occupational pension plan are limited. Hence, the pension-oriented employee has to choose an unapproved pension plan which is taxed less favourably.

As married couples file separately and allowances for non-working spouses are only available for the elderly, the EATRs of families are not much lower than the EATRs of singles. At the high income level, the difference between single and family amounts to 0.8 percentage points.

From the 2002 to 2003, only a few changes apply to the tax and national insurance system. The EATRs decrease a little.

70 See Table A.44. and Table A.45. on p. 103.

71 Recall that we assume that the purchased stock is not sold, otherwise capital gains tax would occur.

Fig. 4.10. Effective average tax rates for the United Kingdom in per cent, 2003 and 2002

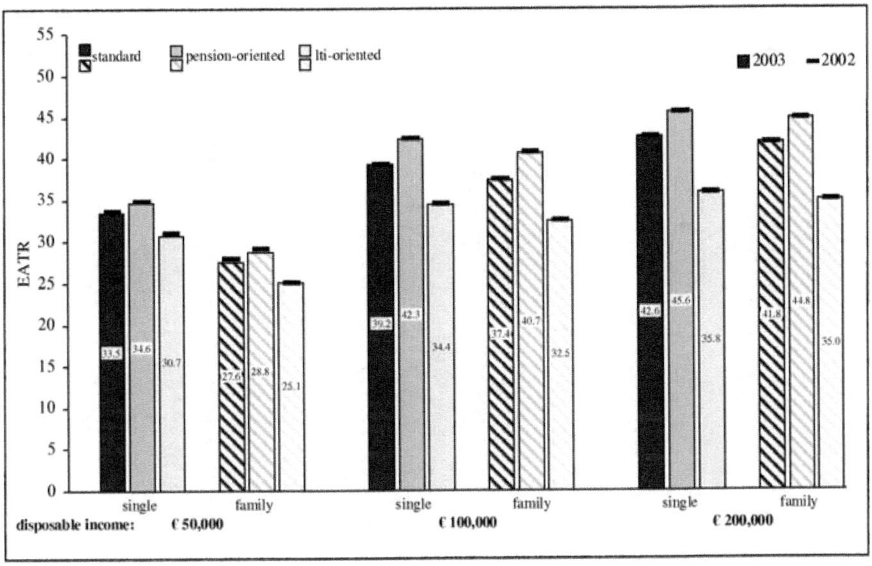

4.9 United States (Massachusetts)

The effective average tax rates of the state of Massachusetts are illustrated in Fig. 4.11.[72] The EATR obtained for a single employee rises by 7.8 percentage points as one increases the disposable income from € 50,000 to € 200,000. For families, the corresponding increase is by 16.8 percentage points. This result mainly stems from the high income necessary to reach the highest tax bracket.

The United States favours families to a relatively high extent. The EATR of families is up to 13.1 percentage points lower than the EATR of singles. Even for the high disposable income the family advantage remains on a relatively high level.

Lti-oriented employees have a lower effective tax burden than the standard employees. A rise in old-age contributions results in a higher EATR for all income levels. This is due to the fact that employees' contributions to an occupational pension plan are taxable at the time of investment. The regulations to determine the tax-exempt part of the resulting annuity cannot compensate for this disadvantage. In the calculations, we assume that 50 per cent of the contributions to the second pillar are paid by the employer. Increasing this proportion would lead to a lower EATR.

---

72 See Table A.46. and Table A.47. on p. 104.

Fig. 4.11. Effective average tax rates for the United States (Mass.) in per cent, 2003, 2002

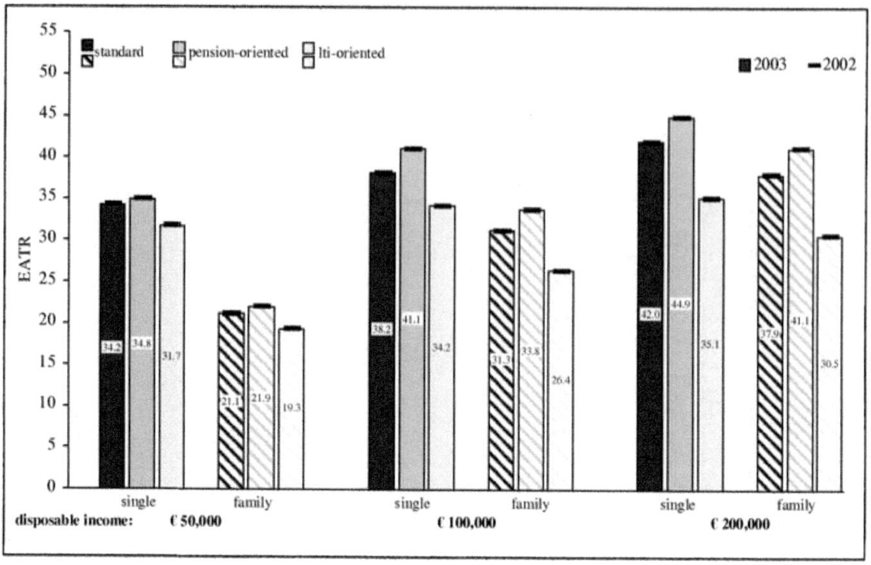

5 International and Inter-Regional Comparison

The results for the individual countries presented in the previous chapter are now combined so as to allow for an inter-regional and international comparison of the tax burden on highly qualified employees. We start by analysing the ranking of regions according to the tax burden on an employee living single and earning the standard compensation package. This is contrasted in Sections 5.2 and 5.3 to the tax burden resulting from other compensation structures. Section 5.4 presents results on the taxation of families. In the final section our results are related to the conclusions obtained in the companion study on company taxation.

5.1 The Standard Case

The basic international ranking is displayed in Fig. 5.1.[73] Here, the EATRs obtained in the standard case for the year 2003 are given for the three levels of disposable income considered. The regions are sorted according to the EATR obtained for the disposable income of € 100,000.

5.1.1 International Rankings

From this figure, it is evident that tax burdens on highly skilled employees vary widely across European countries. For the disposable income of € 100,000, the EATRs range from 25.7 per cent in Schwyz to 49.8 per cent in Italy. For the low disposable income of € 50,000 the span is even larger, from 20.6 per cent in Zug to 50.6 per cent in Italy. To illustrate these differences, it is instructive to translate the EATRs back into total remunerations.[74] In order to provide a highly qualified employee with a disposable income of € 100,000, a company has to spend € 134,574 in Schwyz, € 161,740 in Massachusetts, and € 199,084 in Italy. We conclude that taxes interfere heavily in the international competition for talent.

The Swiss cantons are ranked on top of the list in most comparisons. In particular, the three cantons of central Switzerland in our sample, Schwyz, Zug, and Nidwalden, share the three lowest EATRs for all income levels, only changing ranks among each other. On the other end of the scale, in the standard case, the

[73] This figure is based on Table A.54. to Table A.56. on p. 108 f.

[74] The total remuneration E^* is obtained by the formula $E^* = E / (1 - EATR)$, with the disposable income $E = 100{,}000$.

three countries with the highest EATRs always are Germany, France, and Italy. For a disposable income of € 100,000, the United States has a lower tax burden than all European Union countries, and for € 200,000 the United States places itself on 7th rank, leaving several Swiss cantons behind. On the other hand, the Netherlands move up to the 9th rank when one considers the income of € 50,000.

Fig. 5.1. International variation of EATRs for a single in the standard case in per cent, 2003

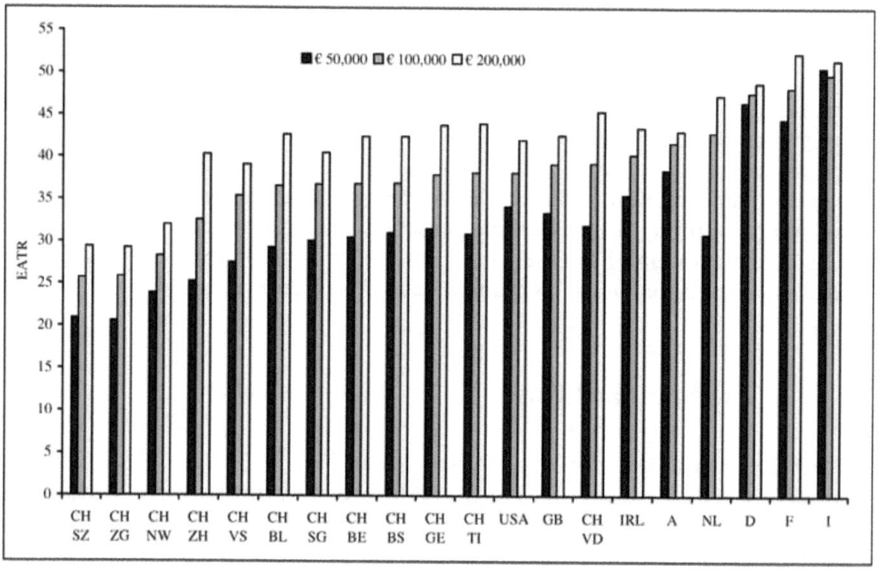

A main determinant of a country's position in the rankings is the income tax schedule. Obviously, large differences in the top rates[75] translate into differences in EATRs. This is exemplified by Zug and Schwyz with top rates below 25 per cent as opposed to Austria, France, and Germany with top rates close to or exceeding 50 per cent. However, since we compute an average tax rate, the rates applying to lower income brackets and the size of these brackets also have a major influence. For example, due to very low rates in the lower brackets and despite a very high statutory top income tax rate of 52 per cent, the Netherlands display an EATR similar to many Swiss cantons for the low disposable income.

The second main cause of a country's rank is the social security system, notably the first pillar of old-age insurance. As a rule, contributions to this part of social security yield a poor return and hence have to be considered as tax-like to a substantial degree. The higher the contribution rates of both employer and employee, the more this fact adds to the EATR. Italy sticks out with contribution rates of 23.81 per cent for the employer and 8.89 per cent for the employee, but also Austria, with 12.55 per cent for the employer and 10.25 per cent for the employee, and Germany, with 9.75 per cent for both employer and employee, have

75 See Table 3.4. on p. 38.

high rates.[76] To a substantial degree, the high EATRs of these countries stem from these social security contribution rates. Similarly, the United States owes its attractive position partly to the low contribution rates to old-age insurance which are 6.2 per cent for both employer and employee.

As we consider individuals with high earnings, ceilings on social security contributions are important. If there is a low ceiling, only a small fraction of the income is subject to social security, and the implicit tax burden is reduced. For example, the ceiling of € 28,850 substantially mitigates the effect of the high contribution rate of 17.9 per cent in the Netherlands. Conversely, since there is no ceiling on the contributions to the first pillar of the Swiss old-age insurance system, Switzerland loses some of the advantage procured by contribution rates which are about as low as in the United States.

In the United Kingdom, the Netherlands, and Ireland, the pension entitlements derived from contributions to the first pillar of old-age insurance are limited irrespective of the contributions paid. This implies that a high-earning employee pays much more into the system than he gets back in terms of pensions. Since we take the individual pension benefit into account, such base pensions or ceilings on entitlements raise the EATR.

Finally, other social security charges and payroll taxes add a noticeable amount to the tax wedge. This is particularly relevant for France with its variety of social charges and the *taxe professionnelle*.

5.1.2 The Progressivity of the Tax and Social Security System

As a second main feature Fig. 5.1. shows how the tax burden changes when the disposable income increases. As one expects, the EATR almost always rises as one passes from low to middle and high disposable income. However, the extent to which this happens differs substantially. In the Netherlands, the EATR on the high income exceeds the one on the low income by 16.4 percentage points. Also in most Swiss cantons the difference between the EATRs for the high and the low disposable incomes is large. For example, it is 15.0 percentage points in Zürich. On the other hand, in Austria, Germany, and Italy this difference is below 5 percentage points. Indeed, according to our definition of the standard employee, Italy even shows a decrease in the EATR as the income rises from € 50,000 to € 100,000.[77]

These comparisons give an impression of the overall progressivity of the tax and social security system. In France, Germany, and Austria the top income tax brackets start at taxable incomes of around € 50,000. Consequently, the average tax rate cannot increase by much anymore once a disposable income of € 50,000 or even € 100,000 is reached. Thus, in these countries the system does not appear to be progressive any more at the relatively high incomes considered in this study.

---

76 See Table A.2. on p. 90.

77 This effect however disappears if one adopts the same compensation structure across income levels (see Section 4.5).

Contrary to that, in the United States the highest tax rate starts at $ 311,950, and in both cantons of Basel as well as in Genève, one needs to earn CHF 1,000,000 or more in order to pay the top rate. As a consequence, the progressivity of the tax schedules is still visible at the incomes we analyse.

Ceilings on contributions to social security have a regressive effect since with increasing income, an increasing fraction of earnings exceeds the ceiling and is therefore exempt from charges. Together with high contribution rates, such ceilings counteract the progressivity of the income tax in France, Germany, Austria, and Italy.

Ceilings on pension entitlements or base pensions have the opposite effect. As the income rises the benefit conferred by a base pension becomes increasingly irrelevant relative to contributions. Thus, the tax implicit in social security increases as a share of income. This is a cause of the high differences in EATRs between high and low disposable incomes in the Netherlands, the United Kingdom, and most Swiss cantons. In Switzerland, this effect is reinforced by the lack of a ceiling on contributions.

5.1.3 The Changes from 2002 to 2003

To complete the analysis of the standard case, Fig. 5.2. shows the EATRs for the single employee with a disposable income of € 100,000 in the years 2002 and 2003.[78] In most regions, we observe a slight decrease in the EATR between these years. In the Swiss cantons, there have only been minor adjustments of the annual multiples. In Italy, the abolition of the payroll tax IRAP reduced the EATR by 3.6 percentage points. In the Netherlands, the decrease by 1.1 percentage points is mainly due to a shift of burden from the income tax to the public health insurance.[79]

Germany is the only country where the EATR rises for all income levels from 2002 to 2003. There, both the contribution rates to social security as well as the ceilings up to which contributions are levied have been increased in 2003. However, a reduction in income tax rates has already been legislated in Germany which will take effect in 2004 and 2005. This reform not only cuts the top rate from the current 48.5 per cent to 45 per cent in 2004 and to 42 per cent in 2005 but reduces tax rates across the board. Hence, a substantial decrease in German EATRs is the consequence.[80]

78 See Table A.48. to Table A.50. on p. 105 f.

79 Income tax rates have been reduced together with an increase in the contribution rates to public health insurance. As we do not count health insurance premiums as taxes, this reduces the EATR, see Section 4.6.

80 See Elschner and Schwager (2004b).

Fig. 5.2. Variation of EATRs in per cent in the standard case from 2002 to 2003

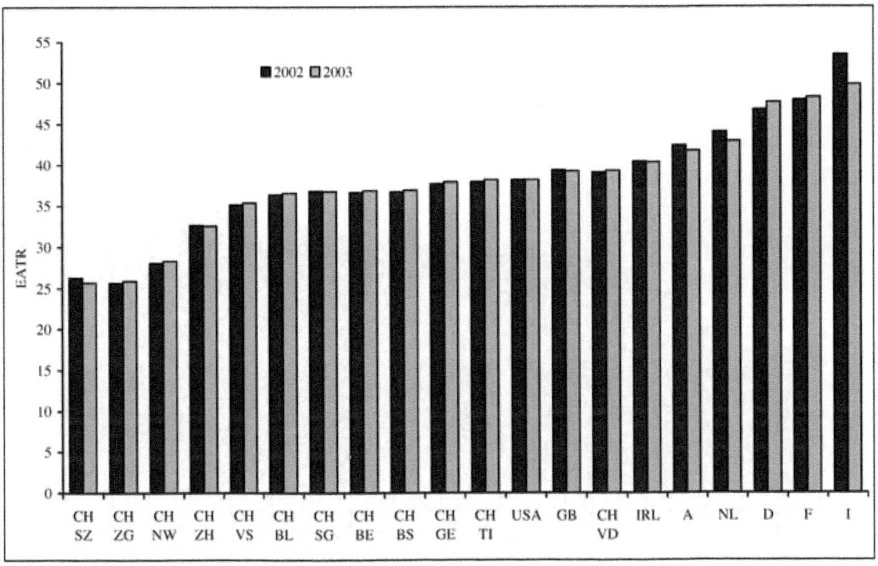

5.2 Pension-Oriented Employees

We now turn to the EATRs for pension-oriented employees.[81] For a disposable income of € 100,000, the resulting EATRs are compared with the EATRs of the standard compensation package in Fig. 5.3.[82] In the majority of cases, there is only a very small effect in the order of less than 1 percentage point. The only noticeable change in the ranking concerns the United Kingdom which falls back from 13th to 17th place.

In general, one would expect employees to benefit from deferred compensation payments by two effects. The first effect occurs because an increase in old-age provision shifts a fraction of income into periods with lower tax rates, as taxable income during retirement is usually lower than in active years. However, for the highly skilled employees considered here, this mechanism only has a very weak impact since the incomes are still very high even after retiring. The second effect arises from the possibility, conferred by occupational pension plans, to save with tax free interest earnings. This mechanism does not appear in our model since we calculate present values with the gross market interest rate before taxes,[83] implying that a hypothetical alternative form of saving is available the interest of which is tax free. Compared to this investment, contributions to the second pillar of old-age

81 For the shares of the compensation components, see Table 2.1. on p. 15.

82 See Table A.57. to Table A.59. on p. 108 f.

83 See Section 2.1.3.

provision are even disadvantageous unless either contributions are fully deductible or pensions are completely tax-exempt.[84]

Fig. 5.3. EATRs for a pension-oriented single with a disposable income of € 100,000, 2003

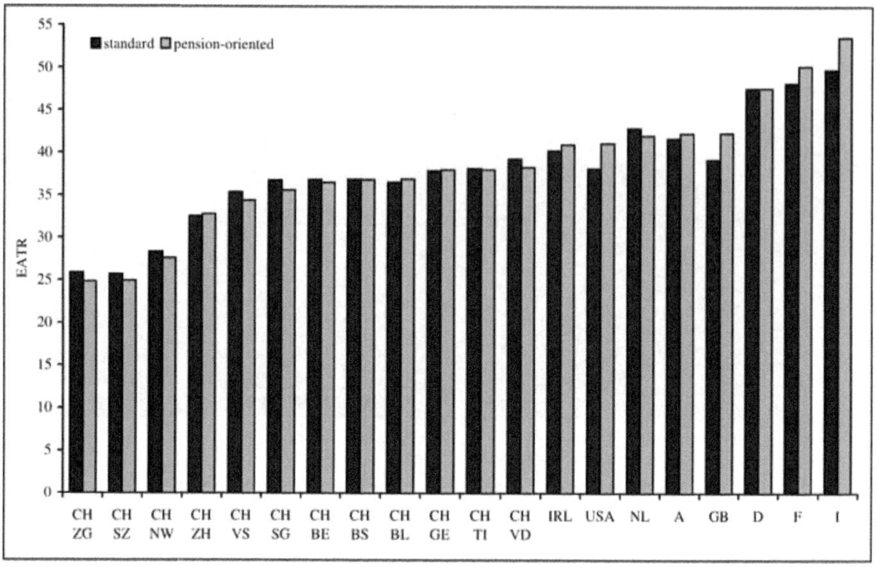

There are three countries where, for this reason, the EATR in our simulation is remarkably higher for a pension-oriented employee than with the standard compensation structure. In the United States, the United Kingdom, and Italy, the differences are 2.9, 3.1, and 3.8 percentage points respectively. In the United States, the employee's contributions to the second pillar of old-age insurance are fully taxed in the remuneration period. The pensions resulting from these contributions are then only partially tax-exempt according to the "simplified method". By consequence, these contributions are taxed more heavily than in other countries. For the United Kingdom, we assume that the employee invests in a defined-contribution scheme. Inasmuch as contributions to such schemes and the resulting pensions exceed certain limits, the contributions are taxable in the remuneration period while the resulting pensions in addition are taxable in the retirement period. In our analysis, these limits are surpassed by the employee earning a disposable income of € 100,000. Finally, in Italy a similar effect occurs since our pension-oriented employee has to invest some of his old-age provision into the third pillar of old-age insurance. Although these contributions are not deductible from the income tax base, 87.5 per cent of the resulting pensions are again subject to tax.

---

84 If interest income is taxed the discount rate relevant for the employee is the market rate of interest net of tax. In this case, occupational pension plans indeed provide a tax-efficient way of saving since contributions are deductible from the company's profit tax base. As shown in Elschner and Schwager (2004a: 15 ff.), the tax advantage conferred by occupational pension plans in such a scenario can be very large.

Thus, in these countries the income received in the form of old-age provision is taxed rather heavily. Compared to the standard employee, the pension-oriented employee invests a larger fraction of his income into this compensation component. By consequence, the average tax burden is larger for the pension-oriented employee.

These effects show the benefit of an explicitly inter-temporal model, as they are not captured by measures of the tax burden which are based on a one period consideration such as the OECD "taxing wages" approach or the EUROMOD simulations.[85] However, one has to bear in mind that our results also depend on the model's structure and the assumptions taken. In addition to the discount rate used, a crucial assumption concerns the allocation of the contributions to the second pillar of old-age insurance between employer and employee. We only consider a fixed ratio where both, employer and employee, pay the same amount into the second pillar. In reality, where the amount of employees' contributions eligible to preferential tax treatment is limited, the employer usually will pay a higher proportion into the second pillar and simultaneously will reduce the employee's gross income. In a model allowing for such tax reducing strategies, the EATRs of pension-oriented employees would be lower.

5.3 Long-Term-Incentive-Oriented Employees

As a second variation in the compensation structure, we consider an employee who obtains a fraction of his compensation in the form of stock options provided by the employer.[86] The EATRs which result from this compensation structure are depicted for the disposable income of € 100,000 in Fig. 5.4. and for the disposable income of € 200,000 in Fig. 5.5. In all countries with the exception of Germany and the Netherlands, the EATR is lower for a long-term-incentive-oriented employee than for an employee with the standard compensation structure. The decrease is substantial for the middle income employee, with the largest reductions in Ireland (5.5 percentage points), Italy (5.4 percentage points), France (4.7 percentage points), the United Kingdom (4.8 percentage points), and the United States (4.0 percentage points). For the high disposable income, we find that granting stock options reduces the EATRs by even more. Here, the differences compared to the EATRs for the standard compensation package are 8.8 percentage points in France, 7.8 percentage points in Ireland, 7.6 percentage points in Italy, 6.9 percentage points in the United States, and 6.8 percentage points in the United Kingdom.

---

85 See OECD (2002), Heady (2003), and Sutherland (2001).

86 For the shares of the compensation components, see Table 2.1. on p. 15.

Fig. 5.4. EATRs for an lti-oriented single with a disposable income of € 100,000, 2003

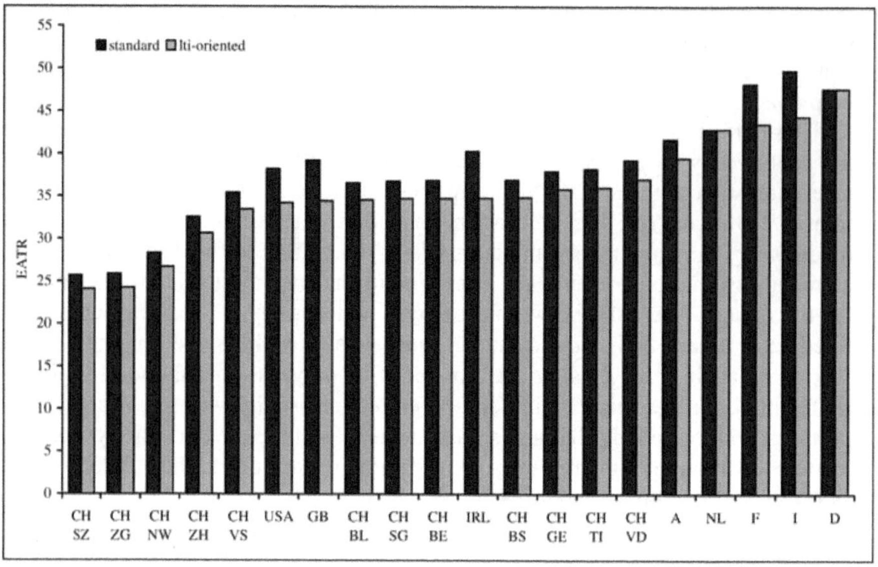

Fig. 5.5. EATRs for an lti-oriented single with a disposable income of € 200,000, 2003

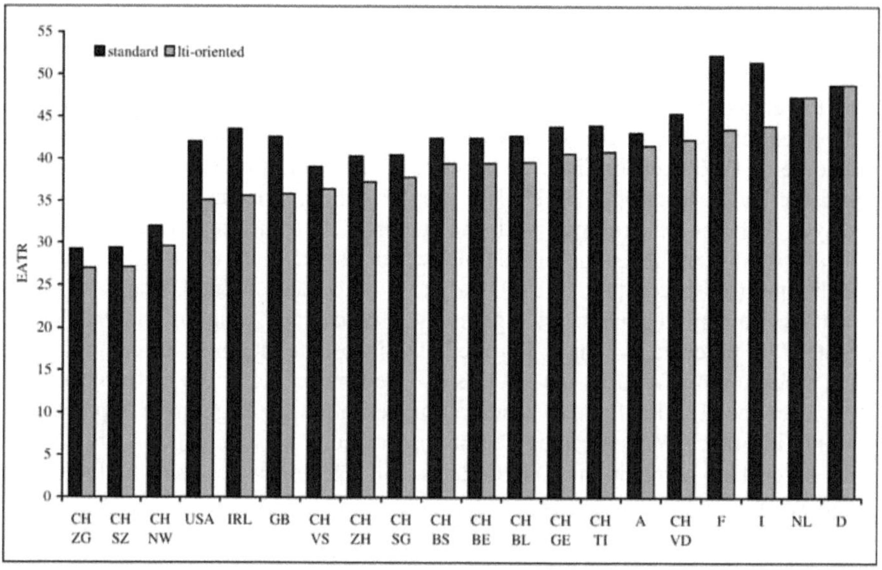

Given these huge reductions in their tax burdens, these countries gain many positions in the international rankings for the incentive-oriented employees compared to the standard case. Already for the disposable income of € 100,000, the United States, the United Kingdom, and Ireland have lower EATRs than many Swiss cantons. For the high income, the United States, Ireland, and the United

Kingdom move in front of all regions except the three low-tax cantons of central Switzerland. On the other hand, Germany is relegated to the last rank, and the Netherlands have the second-to-highest EATR for the high earning incentive-oriented employee.

These drastic changes in EATRs and international rankings reflect the strong discrepancies which exist between the taxation of stock option plans in the countries studied here. The Netherlands and Germany find themselves at the end of the list because they are the only two countries in our sample who tax stock options as regular income without granting any rebates or exemptions. In Switzerland and Austria, the taxable value of stock options falls short of the fair value. In the other countries, stock options are either completely or within limitations exempt from income tax if the stock option plan satisfies certain conditions.[87] Thus, firms in these countries can substantially reduce the tax burden on highly qualified employees by substituting stock option plans for cash compensation.

This strong conclusion has to be modified by two remarks. Firstly, it is important to recall that we exclude the effects of capital gains taxes from the model by assuming that the employee does not sell the shares. Since Italy, the United Kingdom, and the United States impose capital gains tax on the proceeds from selling shares obtained by exercising an option, our figures exaggerate the tax advantage procured by the preferential treatment.[88]

As a second caveat, it has to be noted that our model assumes a correct valuation of the stock options by the market and even by the tax authorities (unless there is an explicit rebate as in Switzerland). Moreover, we abstract from risk aversion considerations and assume that the employee and the firm just consider the expected value of the stock option plan and of the tax liability. These two simplifications imply that the date of taxation is irrelevant for the resulting tax burden. That is, if the options are taxed at the date of grant as in Switzerland, the tax paid is the same as the expected discounted tax which would have been paid if the options were taxable at the date of exercise, as is the case for example in Germany. However, a Swiss employee finding his options worthless at the end of the vesting period will have paid a tax on an income which was expected ex ante but which did not materialise ex post. Conversely, a German employee whose options turn out to be worth more than expected will have to pay the full tax on this gain.

5.4 Family Taxation

So far, the international comparison of effective tax rates has exclusively dealt with single persons. In this section, we extend the focus and consider the tax burden on highly qualified employees who are married and have two children. In

[87] In the calculations, we generally assume that these conditions are met. See Section 3.3.3.

[88] See Elschner and Schwager (2004c) for additional results taking capital gains into account.

these calculations, it is assumed that the spouse of the employee in question does not earn any taxable income from work or other sources.

Fig. 5.6. Comparison of EATRs for singles and families with an income of € 50,000, 2003

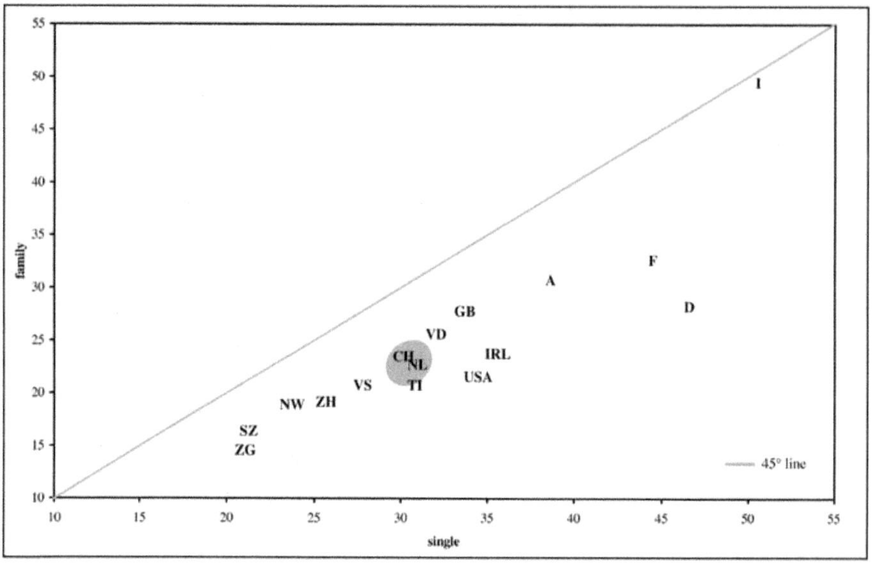

Fig. 5.7. Comparison of EATRs for singles and families with an income of € 100,000, 2003

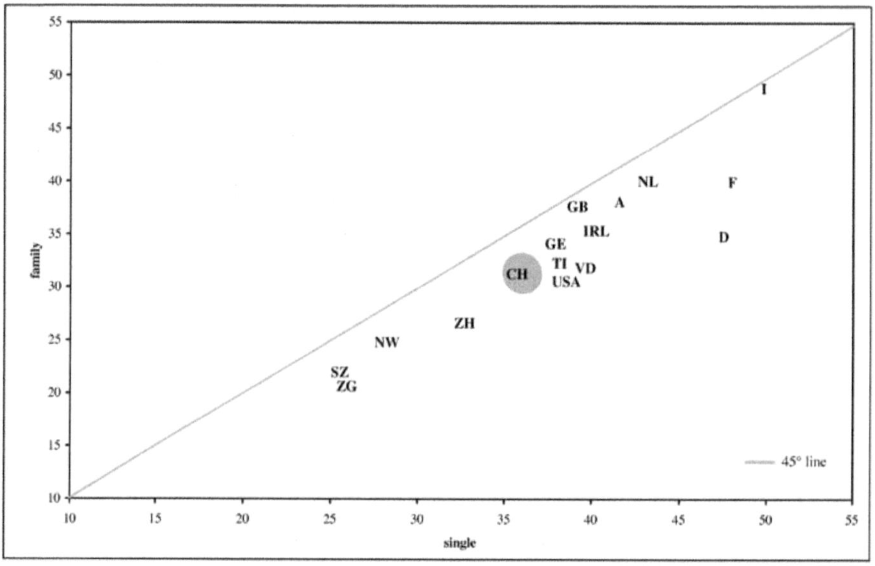

As can be seen by comparing Table A.57. to Table A.59. on p. 109 f. with Table A.54. to Table A.56. on p. 108 f., for a given disposable income, a family always pays less taxes than a single person. For the low and the middle disposable incomes, the effect of this tax relief for families is depicted in Fig. 5.6. and Fig. 5.7. In these figures, the EATR for a single person is measured on the horizontal axis and the EATR for a family on the vertical axis. Each point in the picture represents a region.[89] The 45-degree line in this diagram corresponds to situations where a family pays exactly the same amount of taxes as a single person. As mentioned, all countries exhibit some preferential treatment for families, so all points are placed below the diagonal in both pictures.

The extent of the family relief in a specific country is illustrated by the distance of the point representing this country from the 45-degree line. We notice a substantial family relief in many countries, but we also observe large differences between the locations in our sample. Considering first the standard disposable income of € 100,000, Germany sticks out with an EATR for families which is 12.4 percentage points below the EATR for singles. At some distance, France and Vaud follow with a corresponding reduction in EATRs for families compared to singles by 8.2 and 7.9 percentage points respectively. Also the United States, Sankt Gallen, and Ticino display a substantial family relief according to this measure. The countries which grant the lowest family relief are the Netherlands where the EATR for families is only 2.7 percentage points below the EATR for singles, the United Kingdom with a difference of 1.8 percentage points, and Italy with a reduction in EATR by only 0.6 percentage points. Ranking countries according to the EATR for families we find Germany on 14th place, ahead of Ireland, the United Kingdom, and the Netherlands.

For the low disposable income, the differences are even more striking. The German family relief expressed as the difference between the EATR for a family and for a single person in this case amounts to 18.6 percentage points. The United States (13.1 percentage points), Ireland (12.0 percentage points), and Ticino (10.2 percentage points) also display EATRs for families which are by more than 10 percentage points below the EATRs for singles. Contrary to that, in Italy the EATR for the family is only 1.1 percentage points below the EATR for the single person. This implies that for the family earning a disposable income of € 50,000, the EATR in Italy (49.4 per cent) exceeds the second highest EATR in the sample (France, 32.3 per cent) by nearly half.

For the high disposable income, the family relief does not vary so strongly among the countries. However, the greatest relief still occurs in Germany (5.3 percentage points) and the smallest is found in Italy (0.2 percentage points).

Three elements determine the extent to which the tax burden on families is reduced compared to singles. First, there are family or child allowances paid directly as transfers. Second, families may be allowed to deduct certain amounts from their income tax base. Third, the tax schedule applying to couples or families with children is important. As can be seen from Section 3.1.3, direct transfers to families are not negligible, but they do not differ as much among the countries studied as the resulting EATRs suggest. Deductions from the tax base are more important, and vary more among the countries. For example, Germany grants a deduction of

89 The cantons not labelled individually in Fig. 5.6. and Fig. 5.7. are placed in the shaded area marked "CH".

€ 5,808 for each child. However, by far the most important determinant of the difference between the effective tax burden on families and single persons is the tax schedule.

The large relief for families observed in some countries is brought about by a tax schedule which treats a family with a single earner essentially as if the income had been earned by two or more taxpayers. With a progressive tax schedule, this can reduce the average tax rate by a large amount. In Germany, couples file jointly and then pay a tax at an average rate which would apply to a single earner with half the taxable income. In France and Vaud, a similar result is achieved by applying a family divisor to the taxable income. On the other hand, in countries where married couples are assessed separately as in the Netherlands, the United Kingdom, and Italy there is only a very small family relief.

The importance of the tax schedule suggests that in the countries with a very favourable taxation of families, it is not so much the children who are favoured by the tax system but the non-working spouse. In Germany, the EATR of a family will move much closer to the EATR of a single person once one assumes that both spouses earn similar incomes. On the other hand, we do not count contributions to public health insurance as taxes. While this is generally justified because of the specific benefit provided by health insurance, it probably has an impact on the tax burden of families. We expect that integrating public health insurance into the tax wedge will reduce the tax burden in countries where non-working spouses and children are insured with the employee without having to pay additional premiums.

5.5 Comparison with the Effective Tax Burden of Companies

As mentioned in the introduction, the present study should be seen in connection with the companion study Lammersen and Schwager (2005) on the taxation of companies. That report covers the same countries as the present work, albeit in a much more regionally differentiated way. There, the effective tax burden on investment is measured using the approach by Devereux and Griffith (1999, 2003). In that model the tax burden on an indivisible, profitable investment is assessed. The model allows to evaluate the attractiveness of regions for the location of investment projects or companies. The tax burden is expressed as an effective average tax rate defined to be the difference between the pre-tax and the post-tax returns of an investment divided by the pre-tax return.

While Lammersen and Schwager (2004) produce effective average tax rates for a large variety of combinations of assets and sources of finance, for the comparison of Fig. 0.1. on p. 6, we only focus on the headline figures provided by that study. These figures represent the effective tax burden on an investment by a firm in the manufacturing sector. The investment earns a pre-tax real rate of return of 20 per cent. It is composed of intangibles, industrial buildings, machinery, financial assets, and inventories with equal weights, and it is financed by a mix of retained earnings, new equity and debt according to empirically observed weights.

The resulting effective average tax rates on the investment are compared to the EATR on a single employee with a standard compensation structure earning a disposable income of € 100,000. To make sure that we can compare[90] the results, we index effective tax burdens based on the average of the included Swiss cantons. By definition, this average corresponds to an indexed effective tax burden of 100. We add a trend line which is based on the 20 observations included in Fig. 0.1. in order to illustrate the correlation between the tax burden on the production factor capital and on highly skilled employees.

It is striking that effective tax burdens appear to be closely correlated for most locations. This suggests that – with the notable exceptions of Ireland and the United States – countries which impose large (small) tax burdens on highly skilled employees also impose large (small) corporate tax burdens. Thus, from the point of view of a company, in most cases small (large) corporate income tax burdens do not compensate for large (small) individual tax burdens. Therefore, those locations that already exhibit a competitive edge with respect to the taxation of qualified employees even improve their advantages when we consider both types of taxes.

90 Although both studies provide effective average tax rates, we cannot compare the numerical results of both studies due to a number of conceptual differences. Especially, note that both concepts of effective tax burdens do not permit straightforward conclusions on distributional issues.

6 The Importance of Social Security

The social security system influences the effective average tax rate in three ways. First, contributions to social insurance reduce the tax base and thus result in a lower tax payment. Second, the contributions themselves partly qualify as a kind of tax if there is no direct benefit procured by them. Third, the benefits from the public pension scheme increase the tax base in the retirement period and therefore the tax payment. Because of the complicated interaction of tax and social security regulations it is difficult to identify clearly the proportion of social security charges in the effective average tax rates.

Nevertheless, in this chapter we present some simulations which isolate the impact of social security on the effective average tax rate. It is structured into two parts. In the first part, we analyse the influence of the first pillar of old-age insurance by assuming that the contributions to the first pillar yield a market rate of return. In the second part, we analyse the influence of the entire social security system by assuming that this system provides an equivalent insurance and hence contributions are not to be considered as tax-like.

6.1 The First Pillar of Old-Age Insurance

The first pillar of old-age insurance is organised as a pay-as-you-go system in all of the analysed countries. The PAYG system usually redistributes not only between generations but also between high and low earning employees. The higher the contributions payable by an employee the higher is the tax implicit in the contribution. Countries which offer a basic pension that only depends on the number of years in which contributions were paid but not on the amount of contributions (e.g. the Netherlands, United Kingdom, or Ireland) or countries with a limited state pension but no ceiling on contributions (e.g. Switzerland) are expected to have higher implicit taxes within the public pension scheme than countries with income ceilings and with state pensions depending on the amount of contributions.

In this sensitivity analysis, we hypothetically assume that the contributions to the first pillar of old-age insurance payable by employer and employee are invested under market conditions and are paid out as an annuity during retirement. For tax purposes, contributions and resulting pensions are treated in the same way as in the standard case. This means that contributions are deductible to the same extent and that the "public" pensions benefit from the same privileges and tax regulations. The pension formulae are replaced by an investment yielding the market interest rate. We then compare the effective average tax rates in the standard case with those obtained in this simulation.

It would be wrong to interpret the difference between the two EATRs as the implicit tax stemming from the public pension scheme. The reason is that the impact of social security on the EATR is highly non-linear. To give just two examples, observe first that a higher pension resulting from the investment under market conditions also induces a higher tax payment during retirement. Second, a lower EATR also implies a lower gross income which in turn results in lower contributions to social security. Nevertheless, this difference provides a qualitative indicator for the impact of the first pillar of old-age insurance on the effective tax burden.

Fig. 6.1. Influence of the first pillar of old-age insurance on the EATR of a single, 2003

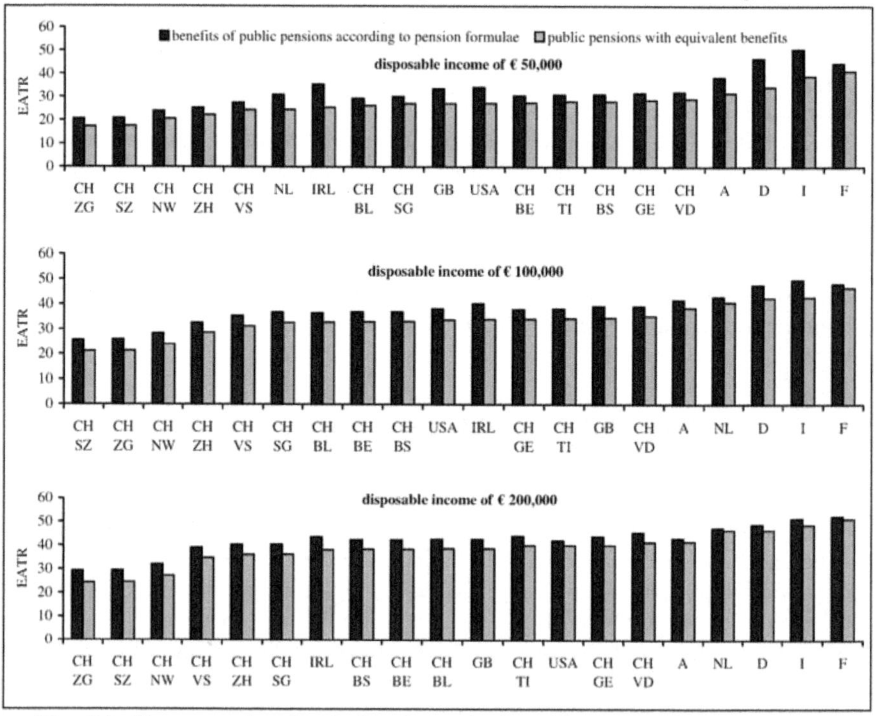

Fig. 6.1. illustrates the simulation for a single with the standard compensation structure at all income levels.[91] The EATRs decrease by varying amounts. In Switzerland, the charge implicit in the first pillar is larger for higher incomes because the state pension is limited while the contribution payments are not. Thus, the EATR without implicit taxes on the first pillar is lower than in the standard case by around 3 percentage points for the low and 4.2 percentage points for the high income level. In the other countries the difference between the two EATRs decreases with increasing income. This is due to income ceilings on the contribu-

91 See Table A.60. on p. 111.

tions to the public pension scheme which imply that the relative importance of the first pillar decreases with income. For example, in the Netherlands, the first pillar is very important for the low income level yielding a difference between the EATRs in the standard case and the simulation of 6.4 percentage points. After the ceiling on contributions is reached, at higher income levels the importance of the PAYG pension scheme decreases rapidly, leaving a difference between both EATRs of only 0.9 percentage points at a disposable income of € 200,000. The reduction in the EATRs for families (see Table A.61. on p. 112) is comparable to the one observed for singles.

6.2 All Social Insurances

For the analysis of the influence of the entire social security system, we assume that all contributions have the character of actuarially fair insurance premiums. The tax-like contributions then are equal to zero and, as already analysed above, contributions to the old-age insurance result in fair annuities. We then compare the EATR with the corresponding EATR in the standard case (see Fig. 6.2. and Table A.62. on p. 113).

At the low income level, the social insurance system has a very important influence on the EATR in France, Germany, and Italy with reductions in the tax burden by 18 percentage points or more. In Switzerland, the reduction is about 10 percentage points. This reduction remains constant over all income levels. For the low disposable income, the Netherlands still improve their position relative to Switzerland. For the two higher levels, on the contrary, the Netherlands have the highest tax rate. This is again due to comparably low income ceilings and a high top tax rate of 52 per cent.

As mentioned above, it is not possible to define the difference between the EATRs in the standard case and in the simulation carried out in the present section as the burden resulting from social security. This is evident especially for families (see Table A.63. on p. 114). In Germany, the EATR is below 5 per cent if one assumes that none of the contributions to social insurance qualifies as tax-like. To understand why the EATR is so low in this simulation in spite of Germany's high statutory income tax rate, note that we still assume that the employer's contributions to social security are not part of gross income. As they are not considered to be tax-like, these contributions are now part of the disposable income. Both assumptions together imply that employers' contributions now raise the disposable income one for one, that is, they are tax free income. Since these contributions amount to 20 per cent of gross income, the measured effective average tax rate must decrease substantially if they are considered to be tax free income. In addition, this effect also reduces the tax base which implies a lower statutory tax rate, driving down the EATR still further. Altogether, these considerations show that this simulation to some extent overstates the impact of social security.

Fig. 6.2. Influence of the social security on the EATR of a single, 2003

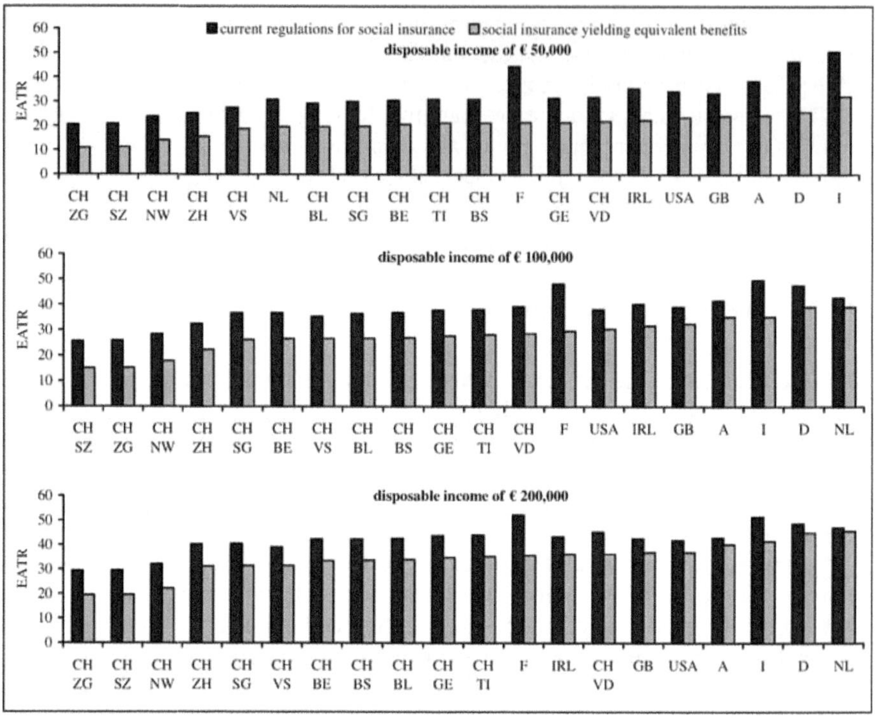

7 Summary and Conclusions

1. In this study, we calculate and compare the effective average tax rates on highly qualified employees in eight European countries and the United States for the years 2002 and 2003. Since there is no generally recognised approach for this research task we develop a new method. In our model the effective tax burden on highly qualified employees is quantified from a company's point of view.
2. The basic idea of our approach is that employers compete for highly qualified employees and therefore have to compensate these for taxes on labour income and tax-like social security contributions. As a consequence the tax burden of different regions is compared for a given disposable income after taxes which the employee can obtain at all locations. The tax burden is expressed by the effective average tax rate (EATR) which is defined as the ratio of taxes divided by total remuneration.
3. We derive EATRs for several income levels, structures of compensation and family situations which are typical for highly qualified employees. We consider income taxes including surcharges, tax-like social security contributions as well as payroll taxes paid by the company. The typical employee's income is assessed for tax and social security purposes in several periods during the life cycle.
4. The results show that there are considerable differences in tax burden across the countries studied. Swiss cantons generally have low or moderate EATRs. Throughout the analysis, Zug and Schwyz display the lowest tax burden. Germany, France, and Italy have the highest effective tax burdens in most cases. The United States, the United Kingdom, and Ireland mostly have moderate tax burdens.
5. Comparing our results with the effective tax burden on companies one finds that the rankings of countries with respect to both measures of tax burden are correlated. In general, countries which display a high tax burden on employees also tax companies quite heavily.
6. The EATR increases with increasing income in virtually all cases. However, the progressivity of the tax and social security system differs between countries.
7. Except for Germany and the Netherlands, the EATRs decrease substantially if employer-provided stock options are introduced into the compensation package since all the other countries grant tax privileges for such compensation.
8. In all countries, the EATRs for families are lower than the EATRs for singles with the same disposable income. The extent to which families are favoured

differs largely between the countries analysed. Germany by far accords the largest tax relief for families. Contrary to that, families in Italy almost bear the same effective tax burden as singles.

9. A sensitivity analysis shows that the first pillar of old-age insurance as well as the social security system as a whole contribute substantially to the overall effective tax burden.

A Appendix

A.1 Social Security Contributions and Charges

Table A.1. Contribution rates to social security and other charges, 2002

	old-age	health	unemployment	work injury	other charges	total	charge	income ceiling 1	income ceiling 2	income ceiling 3
A	10.25^2	3.40^2	3.00^2		1.00^1	17.65	4.00	39,240	45,780	
	12.55^2	3.50^2	3.70^2	1.40^2	0.50^1	22.10	5.60			
CH	4.20^0		1.50^1		0.15^0	6.55	1.65	106,800	267,000	
	4.20^0		1.50^1	1.00^1	0.15 - 2.15^0	7.55	2.65			
	0.70^0		0.50^2							
	0.70^0		0.50^2							
D	9.55^2	7.00^1	3.25^2			19.80	3.25	40,500	54,000	61,356
	9.55^2	7.00^1	3.25^2	1.42^3		21.22	4.67			
F	6.55^1	0.75^0	3.60^2		7.60^0	18.60	11.20	28,224	112,896	
	8.20^1	12.8^0	2.00^2	2.26	7.85^0	34.71	12.11			
	0.10^0									
	1.60^0									
I	8.89^1		0.30^0			9.19	0.30	80,391		
	23.81^1	0.66^0	4.41^0	0.50 - 16.00^0	2.48^0	31.86	7.39			
IRL	4.00^1	2.00^0	**	**		6.00	0.80	38,740		
	10.75^0					10.75	2.15			
NL	17.90^1	10.25^1	4.95^2			36.05	4.95	27,850	27,000	30,700
			3.60^2			16.20	3.60			
	1.25^2	1.70^3								
	5.85^2	6.25^3								
UK	8.40^1	**	**	**		8.40	1.68	29,900		
	8.30^0					8.30	1.66			
USA	6.20^2	1.45^0				7.65		7,000	84,900	
	6.20^2	1.45^0	6.20^1	2.05		13.85	6.20			

Note: Rates marked with a superscript ^{0} apply without ceiling. Rates marked with a superscript ^{1} (^{2},^{3}) apply to income in national currency up to ceiling 1 (2, 3) as given in the final three columns. The first row represents the employee's contribution rate, the second row the employer's contribution rate. Income ceilings are in national currency. **Overall contributions in column old-age.

Table A.2. Contribution rates to social security and other charges, 2003

	old-age	health	unemployment	work injury	other charges	total	charge	income ceiling 1	income ceiling 2	income ceiling 3
A	10.25[2]	3.40[2]	3.00[2]		1.00[1]	17.65	4.00	40,320	47,040	
	12.55[2]	3.50[2]	3.70[2]	1.40[2]	0.50[1]	22.10	5.60			
CH	4.20[0]		1.50[1]		0.15[0]	6.55	1.65	106,800	267,000	
	4.20[0]		1.50[1]	1.00[1]	0.15 - 2.15[0]	7.55	2.65			
	0.70[0]		0.50[2]							
	0.70[0]		0.50[2]							
D	9.75[2]	7.00[1]	3.25[2]			20.00	3.25	41,400	61,200	61,356
	9.75[2]	7.00[1]	3.25[2]	1.42[3]		21.42	4.67			
F	6.55[1]	0.75[0]	2.40[2]		7.60[0]	17.40	10.00	29,184	116,736	
	8.20[1]	12.80[0]	4.00[2]	2.26	7.85[0]	36.71	14.11			
	0.10[0]									
	1.60[0]									
I	8.89[1]		0.30[0]			9.19	0.30	80,391		
	23.81[1]	0.66[0]	4.41[0]	0.50 - 16.00[0]	2.48[0]	31.86	7.39			
IRL	4.00[1]	2.00[0]	**	**		6.00	0.80	40,420		
	10.75[0]					10.75	2.15			
NL	17.90[1]	10.25[1]	5.80[2]			36.90	5.80	28,850	30,260	31,750
			1.55[2]			13.35	1.55			
	1.25[1]	1.70[3]								
	5.05[2]	6.75[3]								
UK	8.40[1]	**	**	**		8.40	1.68	30,420		
	8.30[0]					8.30	1.66			
USA	6.20[2]	1.45[0]				7.65		7,000	87,000	
	6.20[2]	1.45[0]	6.20[1]	2.05		13.85	6.20			

For remarks see Table A.1.

Table A.3. Valuation of compensation components used in the simulation

Country	Value for company cars θ_p	Value for stock options θ_l
Austria	0.75	0.50
France	0.30	0.00
Germany	0.50	1.00
Ireland	0.77	0.00
Italy	0.50	0.00
Switzerland	0.50	0.75
The Netherlands	1.04	1.00
The United Kingdom	0.63	0.00
The United States (Mass.)	1.04	0.00

A.2 Tax Deductions and Tax Credits

Table A.4. Personal deductions and tax credits (in national currency)

Country	Year	Personal deductions / tax credits married couple	single	Deductions per child
Austria	'02-'03	3,640*	3,640*	
(tax credits)		887-0**	887-0**	613
CH Basel-Landschaft	'02-'03	14,372*	14,372*	5,000
CH Basel-Stadt	'02-'03	6,200	-	5,200
		14,600*	10,400*	
CH Bern	'02-'03	9,800	7,100	4,400
CH Confederation	'02	24,900	12,800	5,600
	'03	24,900*	15,770*	5,600
CH Genève [a)]	'02	8,000*	8,000*	-
	'03	12,100*	12,100*	-
CH Nidwalden	'02-'03	18,000*	10,000*	3,750
CH Schwyz	'02-'03	6,000	3,000	5,000
CH St. Gallen	'02-'03	4,400*	2,200*	6,000
CH Ticino	'02-'03	-	-	8,000
CH Valais	'02-'03	8,000*, [b)]	8,000*	5,000
CH Vaud [a)]	'02-'03	-	-	-
CH Zug	'02-'03	13,000	6,500	8,000
CH Zürich	'02-'03	11,000*	5,500*	5,400
France	'02	4,121*	4,121*	- [d)]
	'03	4,191*	4,191*	- [d)]
Germany	'02-'03	14,470*	7,235*	5,808
Ireland (tax credits)	'02-'03	3,040	1,520	-
Italy (tax credits)	'02-'03	546-422**	-	285
The Netherlands	'02	3,294	1,647	40
(tax credits)	'03	3,532	1,766	41
United Kingdom	'02	4,535	4,535	520-0**
(tax credits)	'03	4,615	4,615	529-0**
United States	'02	7,850 [c)]	4,700	
	'03	7,950 [c)]	4,750 [c)]	
	'02-'03	6,000	3,000	3,000
(tax credit)	'02-'03			600-0**
United States, Mass.	'02-'03	6,600	3,300	1,000

* Within the tax schedule. ** Degressive tax credit, which starts at a high level for low incomes and ends at zero for high incomes.

[a)] The personal allowances are combined with the tax schedule.

[b)] A tax credit of 32 per cent of the income tax for married couples, at the minimum 610 and at the maximum 3,560.

[c)] Standard deduction; alternatively itemised deductions may be claimed.

[d)] Within the family quotient.

Table A.5. Deductibility of employee's contributions to social security, 2002 and 2003

Country	Year	Deduction up to	Full deduction
Austria	'02-'03		x
France	'02-'03		x
Germany	'02-'03	€ 2,001 / € 4,002	
Ireland	'02-'03	-	
Italy	'02-'03		x
The Netherlands	'02-'03	within certain limits	
Switzerland	'02-'03		x
USA Federal income tax	'02-'03	-	
USA Massachusetts state income tax	'02-'03	$ 2,000	
United Kingdom	'02-'03	-	

Table A.6. Old-age deductions (in national currency)

Country	Year	Married couples	Singles
Austria (tax credits)	'02-'03	400-0*	400-0*
CH Basel-Stadt	'02-'03	500	500
		-	3,100 *, b)
CH Nidwalden	'02-'03	-	3,500-0 *, b)
CH Schwyz	'02-'03	6,000	3,000
CH St. Gallen	'02-'03	3,000-0*	2,000-0*
CH Ticino	'02-'03	8,000-0*	8,000-0*
CH Zug a)	'02-'03	3,000-0*	3,000-0*
Italy	'02-'03	7,000-0*	7,000-0*
(tax credits) c)		98-222*	98-222*
The Netherlands	'02	1,474	737
	'03	1,612	806
United Kingdom (tax credits)	'02-'03	6,100-4,615*	6,100-4,615*
		5,535-2,110 *, c)	
United States, Mass.	'02-'03	1,400	700

* Degressive tax credit/allowance, which starts at a high level for low incomes and ends at zero for high incomes.

a) The deduction depends not only on the income but on the property as well.

b) Only for single pensioners.

c) The allowance depends on the pensioner's age.

Table A.7. Standard deductions for business-related expenses (in national currency)

Country	Year	Deduction
Austria	'02-'03	132
(tax credit)		54
CH Basel-Landschaft	'02-'03	500
CH Basel-Stadt	'02-'03	700
CH Bern	'02-'03	3 % of income, between 1,900 and 3,800
CH confederation	'02-'03	3 %, between 1,900 and 3,800
CH Genève	'02-'03	3 %, between 500 and 1,500
CH Nidwalden	'02-'03	5 %, at the maximum 7,000
CH Schwyz	'02-'03	20 %, at the maximum 6,600
CH St. Gallen	'02-'03	10 %, between 700 and 2,400
CH Ticino	'02-'03	2,100
CH Valais	'02-'03	3 %, between 1,800 and 3,600
CH Vaud	'02-'03	3 %, between 1,800 and 3,600
CH Zug	'02-'03	3 %, between 1,900 and 3,800
CH Zürich	'02-'03	3 %, between 1,900 and 3,800
France	'02	10 %, between 364 and 12,229 *
	'03	10 %, between 370 and 12,437 *
Germany	'02-'03	1,044 *
Ireland (tax credit)	'02-'03	660 *
Italy	'02-'03	7,500-0
The Netherlands (tax credit)	'02	949
	'03	1,104
United Kingdom	'02-'03	-
United States	'02-'03	within the standard deduction
United States, Mass.	'02-'03	-

* For occupational pensions as well.

A.3 Detailed Results

Table A.8. EATR of singles and families in Austria 2002, in per cent

Disposable income (€)	50,000	100,000	200,000
Single			
Standard	38.9	42.4	43.8
Pension-oriented	39.3	42.9	44.3
Lti-oriented	38.0	40.1	42.2
Family			
Standard	31.7	39.1	42.2
Pension-oriented	32.1	39.7	42.8
Lti-oriented	30.6	36.6	40.5

Table A.9. EATR of singles and families in Austria 2003, in per cent

Disposable income (€)	50,000	100,000	200,000
Single			
Standard	38.5	41.7	43.1
Pension-oriented	38.9	42.3	43.7
Lti-oriented	37.6	39.5	41.6
Family			
Standard	30.9	38.2	41.5
Pension-oriented	31.3	38.9	42.1
Lti-oriented	29.9	35.8	39.9

Table A.10. EATR of singles and families in Basel-Landschaft 2002, in per cent

Disposable income (€)	50,000	100,000	200,000
Single			
Standard	34.4	38.2	42.1
Pension-oriented	35.0	41.1	45.0
Lti-oriented	31.9	34.2	35.2
Family			
Standard	21.2	31.3	38.0
Pension-oriented	22.0	33.8	41.2
Lti-oriented	19.4	26.4	30.7

Table A.11. EATR of singles and families in Basel-Landschaft 2003, in per cent

Disposable income (€)	50,000	100,000	200,000
Single			
Standard	29.3	36.6	42.7
Pension-oriented	29.7	36.9	42.1
Lti-oriented	28.4	34.5	39.6
Family			
Standard	22.6	31.3	39.2
Pension-oriented	23.3	31.4	39.1
Lti-oriented	21.9	29.1	36.3

Table A.12. EATR of singles and families in Basel-Stadt 2002, in per cent

Disposable income (€)	50,000	100,000	200,000
Single			
Standard	31.2	36.7	42.3
Pension-oriented	31.5	36.7	41.3
Lti-oriented	30.3	34.7	39.3
Family			
Standard	22.6	31.9	39.0
Pension-oriented	23.1	31.9	38.4
Lti-oriented	21.8	29.8	36.0

Table A.13. EATR of singles and families in Basel-Stadt 2003, in per cent

Disposable income (€)	50,000	100,000	200,000
Single			
Standard	31.0	36.9	42.4
Pension-oriented	31.3	36.8	41.4
Lti-oriented	30.1	34.8	39.4
Family			
Standard	22.6	32.1	39.1
Pension-oriented	23.0	32.1	38.6
Lti-oriented	21.8	30.0	36.2

Table A.14. EATR of singles and families in Bern 2002, in per cent

Disposable income (€)	50,000	100,000	200,000
Single			
Standard	30.6	36.6	42.4
Pension-oriented	31.0	36.4	41.4
Lti-oriented	29.7	34.6	39.4
Family			
Standard	24.8	31.9	39.8
Pension-oriented	25.6	32.1	39.0
Lti-oriented	24.1	29.8	36.7

Table A.15. EATR of singles and families in Bern 2003, in per cent

Disposable income (€)	50,000	100,000	200,000
Single			
Standard	30.5	36.8	42.4
Pension-oriented	30.9	36.5	41.4
Lti-oriented	29.7	34.7	39.5
Family			
Standard	24.4	31.9	39.8
Pension-oriented	25.1	32.1	38.9
Lti-oriented	23.7	29.7	36.8

Table A.16. EATR of singles and families in Genève 2002, in per cent

Disposable income (€)	50,000	100,000	200,000
Single			
Standard	31.5	37.7	43.7
Pension-oriented	31.9	37.8	42.5
Lti-oriented	30.7	35.6	40.5
Family			
Standard	24.0	33.9	42.0
Pension-oriented	24.6	34.0	40.8
Lti-oriented	23.2	31.7	38.8

Table A.17. EATR of singles and families in Genève 2003, in per cent

Disposable income (€)	50,000	100,000	200,000
Single			
Standard	31.5	37.9	43.8
Pension-oriented	31.9	38.0	42.7
Lti-oriented	30.7	35.8	40.6
Family			
Standard	23.5	33.9	42.1
Pension-oriented	24.1	34.0	40.9
Lti-oriented	22.7	31.7	38.8

Table A.18. EATR of singles and families in Nidwalden 2002, in per cent

Disposable income (€)	50,000	100,000	200,000
Single			
Standard	23.9	28.1	31.8
Pension-oriented	24.0	27.5	30.6
Lti-oriented	23.2	26.5	29.4
Family			
Standard	18.6	24.8	30.6
Pension-oriented	18.9	24.4	29.3
Lti-oriented	17.9	23.1	28.1

Table A.19. EATR of singles and families in Nidwalden 2003, in per cent

Disposable income (€)	50,000	100,000	200,000
Single			
Standard	23.9	28.3	32.0
Pension-oriented	24.0	27.6	30.8
Lti-oriented	23.2	26.7	29.6
Family			
Standard	18.6	25.0	30.8
Pension-oriented	18.9	24.5	29.6
Lti-oriented	17.9	23.3	28.4

Table A.20. EATR of singles and families in Schwyz 2002, in per cent

Disposable income (€)	50,000	100,000	200,000
Single			
Standard	21.6	26.3	30.0
Pension-oriented	21.8	25.6	28.9
Lti-oriented	20.9	24.7	27.7
Family			
Standard	17.1	22.6	28.6
Pension-oriented	17.4	22.4	27.4
Lti-oriented	16.4	21.0	26.2

Table A.21. EATR of singles and families in Schwyz 2003, in per cent

Disposable income (€)	50,000	100,000	200,000
Single			
Standard	20.9	25.7	29.4
Pension-oriented	21.0	24.9	28.3
Lti-oriented	20.2	24.1	27.2
Family			
Standard	16.4	22.0	28.0
Pension-oriented	16.7	21.8	26.8
Lti-oriented	15.7	20.5	25.7

Table A.22. EATR of singles and families in St. Gallen 2002, in per cent

Disposable income (€)	50,000	100,000	200,000
Single			
Standard	30.3	36.8	40.6
Pension-oriented	30.5	35.7	39.5
Lti-oriented	29.4	34.7	37.9
Family			
Standard	21.5	30.1	38.5
Pension-oriented	22.1	29.9	37.0
Lti-oriented	20.7	28.1	35.6

Table A.23. EATR of singles and families in St. Gallen 2003, in per cent

Disposable income (€)	50,000	100,000	200,000
Single			
Standard	30.1	36.8	40.5
Pension-oriented	30.2	35.6	39.4
Lti-oriented	29.2	34.7	37.8
Family			
Standard	21.3	30.2	38.4
Pension-oriented	22.0	29.8	37.0
Lti-oriented	20.6	28.1	35.5

Table A.24. EATR of singles and families in Ticino 2002, in per cent

Disposable income (€)	50,000	100,000	200,000
Single			
Standard	31.0	37.9	43.9
Pension-oriented	31.3	37.9	42.9
Lti-oriented	30.1	35.8	40.7
Family			
Standard	20.7	31.7	41.3
Pension-oriented	21.7	31.9	40.5
Lti-oriented	19.9	29.5	38.2

Table A.25. EATR of singles and families in Ticino 2003, in per cent

Disposable income (€)	50,000	100,000	200,000
Single			
Standard	31.0	38.2	44.0
Pension-oriented	31.3	38.0	43.0
Lti-oriented	30.1	36.0	40.9
Family			
Standard	20.7	32.0	41.5
Pension-oriented	21.7	32.0	40.7
Lti-oriented	19.9	29.7	38.3

Table A.26. EATR of singles and families in Valais 2002, in per cent

Disposable income (€)	50,000	100,000	200,000
Single			
Standard	27.5	35.2	38.9
Pension-oriented	27.7	34.2	37.9
Lti-oriented	26.6	33.2	36.3
Family			
Standard	20.9	31.3	37.2
Pension-oriented	21.7	30.0	36.2
Lti-oriented	20.2	29.2	34.5

Table A.27. EATR of singles and families in Valais 2003, in per cent

Disposable income (€)	50,000	100,000	200,000
Single			
Standard	27.5	35.4	39.1
Pension-oriented	27.7	34.4	38.1
Lti-oriented	26.6	33.4	36.4
Family			
Standard	20.9	31.5	37.4
Pension-oriented	21.7	30.1	36.4
Lti-oriented	20.2	29.4	34.7

Table A.28. EATR of singles and families in Vaud 2002, in per cent

Disposable income (€)	50,000	100,000	200,000
Single			
Standard	34.4	38.2	42.1
Pension-oriented	35.0	41.1	45.0
Lti-oriented	31.9	34.2	35.2
Family			
Standard	21.2	31.3	38.0
Pension-oriented	22.0	33.8	41.2
Lti-oriented	19.4	26.4	30.7

Table A.29. EATR of singles and families in Vaud 2003, in per cent

Disposable income (€)	50,000	100,000	200,000
Single			
Standard	31.9	39.3	45.4
Pension-oriented	32.5	38.3	43.8
Lti-oriented	31.1	37.0	42.3
Family			
Standard	25.6	31.4	41.2
Pension-oriented	26.1	32.7	39.6
Lti-oriented	24.7	29.4	37.8

Table A.30. EATR of singles and families in Zug 2002, in per cent

Disposable income (€)	50,000	100,000	200,000
Single			
Standard	20.6	25.7	29.0
Pension-oriented	20.7	24.7	27.9
Lti-oriented	19.9	24.0	26.7
Family			
Standard	14.6	20.7	27.7
Pension-oriented	15.1	20.6	26.2
Lti-oriented	14.0	19.2	25.3

Table A.31. EATR of singles and families in Zug 2003, in per cent

Disposable income (€)	50,000	100,000	200,000
Single			
Standard	20.6	25.9	29.3
Pension-oriented	20.7	24.8	28.1
Lti-oriented	19.9	24.2	27.0
Family			
Standard	14.6	20.9	28.0
Pension-oriented	15.1	20.7	26.4
Lti-oriented	14.0	19.3	25.5

Table A.32. EATR of singles and families in Zürich 2002, in per cent

Disposable income (€)	50,000	100,000	200,000
Single			
Standard	25.5	32.7	40.6
Pension-oriented	26.2	33.0	39.6
Lti-oriented	24.7	30.7	37.5
Family			
Standard	19.3	26.7	36.6
Pension-oriented	20.1	28.0	35.9
Lti-oriented	18.6	24.8	33.5

Table A.33. EATR of singles and families in Zürich 2003, in per cent

Disposable income (€)	50,000	100,000	200,000
Single			
Standard	25.3	32.6	40.3
Pension-oriented	25.9	32.8	39.3
Lti-oriented	24.4	30.6	37.3
Family			
Standard	19.1	26.7	36.4
Pension-oriented	19.9	27.9	35.7
Lti-oriented	18.4	24.8	33.3

Table A.34. EATR of singles and families in France 2002, in per cent

Disposable income (€)	50,000	100,000	200,000
Single			
Standard	45.5	47.9	52.8
Pension-oriented	46.6	49.8	55.4
Lti-oriented	42.4	43.0	43.6
Family			
Standard	33.1	39.4	48.7
Pension-oriented	33.4	41.4	51.5
Lti-oriented	30.8	33.6	38.8

Table A.35. EATR of singles and families in France 2003, in per cent

Disposable income (€)	50,000	100,000	200,000
Single			
Standard	44.5	48.2	52.3
Pension-oriented	45.6	50.2	54.9
Lti-oriented	41.5	43.5	43.5
Family			
Standard	32.3	40.0	48.2
Pension-oriented	32.6	41.9	51.0
Lti-oriented	30.1	34.4	38.6

Table A.36. EATR of singles and families in Germany 2002, in per cent

Disposable income (€)	50,000	100,000	200,000
Single			
Standard	44.6	46.7	48.4
Pension-oriented	44.6	46.7	48.4
Lti-oriented	44.6	46.7	48.4
Family			
Standard	27.2	33.9	42.9
Pension-oriented	27.7	34.9	42.9
Lti-oriented	26.3	33.9	42.9

Table A.37. EATR of singles and families in Germany 2003, in per cent

Disposable income (€)	50,000	100,000	200,000
Single			
Standard	46.5	47.6	48.8
Pension-oriented	46.5	47.6	48.8
Lti-oriented	46.5	47.6	48.8
Family			
Standard	27.9	35.2	43.4
Pension-oriented	28.0	36.1	43.4
Lti-oriented	26.6	35.2	43.4

Table A.38. EATR of singles and families in Ireland 2002, in per cent

Disposable income (€)	50,000	100,000	200,000
Single			
Standard	35.8	40.4	43.6
Pension-oriented	35.6	41.1	44.1
Lti-oriented	32.7	34.9	35.7
Family			
Standard	23.9	35.9	41.6
Pension-oriented	23.6	36.7	42.2
Lti-oriented	20.2	30.0	33.5

Table A.39. EATR of singles and families in Ireland 2003, in per cent

Disposable income (€)	50,000	100,000	200,000
Single			
Standard	35.5	40.3	43.5
Pension-oriented	35.3	41.0	44.3
Lti-oriented	32.4	34.8	35.7
Family			
Standard	23.5	35.8	41.6
Pension-oriented	23.2	36.6	42.2
Lti-oriented	19.8	29.9	33.5

Table A.40. EATR of singles and families in Italy 2002, in per cent

Disposable income (€)	50,000	100,000	200,000
Single			
Standard	54.1	53.4	54.9
Pension-oriented	53.2	56.6	56.8
Lti-oriented	50.6	47.5	46.8
Family			
Standard	53.2	52.8	54.7
Pension-oriented	52.1	56.2	56.6
Lti-oriented	49.4	47.0	46.5

Table A.41. EATR of singles and families in Italy 2003, in per cent

Disposable income (€)	50,000	100,000	200,000
Single			
Standard	50.6	49.8 (52.3*)	51.5 (53.4*)
Pension-oriented	49.6	53.6 (53.6*)	53.7 (54.1*)
Lti-oriented	47.2	44.4 (49.7*)	43.9 (50.9*)
Family			
Standard	49.4	49.2 (51.8*)	51.2 (53.2*)
Pension-oriented	48.4	53.1 (53.1*)	53.4 (53.9*)
Lti-oriented	46.0	43.8 (49.1*)	43.6 (50.7*)

* EATRs with identical weights of compensation components as for € 50,000.

Table A.42. EATR of singles and families in the Netherlands 2002, in per cent

Disposable income (€)	50,000	100,000	200,000
Single			
Standard	34.1	44.0	47.8
Pension-oriented	33.8	43.2	47.0
Lti-oriented	34.1	44.0	47.8
Family			
Standard	26.6	41.5	46.7
Pension-oriented	26.4	40.6	45.9
Lti-oriented	26.6	41.5	46.7

Table A.43. EATR of singles and families in the Netherlands 2003, in per cent

Disposable income (€)	50,000	100,000	200,000
Single			
Standard	30.9	42.9	47.3
Pension-oriented	30.6	42.0	46.5
Lti-oriented	30.9	42.9	47.3
Family			
Standard	22.6	40.2	46.2
Pension-oriented	23.0	39.3	45.4
Lti-oriented	22.6	40.2	46.2

Table A.44. EATR of singles and families in the United Kingdom 2002, in per cent

Disposable income (€)	50,000	100,000	200,000
Single			
Standard	33.7	39.3	42.7
Pension-oriented	34.9	42.5	45.6
Lti-oriented	31.0	34.5	35.9
Family			
Standard	28.0	37.6	41.9
Pension-oriented	29.2	40.8	44.9
Lti-oriented	25.2	32.6	35.0

Table A.45. EATR of singles and families in the United Kingdom 2003, in per cent

Disposable income (€)	50,000	100,000	200,000
Single			
Standard	33.5	39.2	42.6
Pension-oriented	34.6	41.1	45.6
Lti-oriented	30.7	34.4	35.8
Family			
Standard	27.6	37.4	41.8
Pension-oriented	28.8	40.7	44.8
Lti-oriented	25.1	32.5	35.0

Table A.46. EATR of singles and families in the United States (Mass.) 2002, in per cent

Disposable income (€)	50,000	100,000	200,000
Single			
Standard	34.4	38.2	42.1
Pension-oriented	35.0	41.1	45.0
Lti-oriented	31.9	34.2	35.2
Family			
Standard	21.2	31.3	38.0
Pension-oriented	22.0	33.8	41.2
Lti-oriented	19.4	26.4	30.7

Table A.47. EATR of singles and families in the United States (Mass.) 2003, in per cent

Disposable income (€)	50,000	100,000	200,000
Single			
Standard	34.2	38.2	42.0
Pension-oriented	34.8	41.1	44.9
Lti-oriented	31.7	34.2	35.1
Family			
Standard	21.1	31.3	37.9
Pension-oriented	21.9	33.8	41.1
Lti-oriented	19.3	26.4	30.5

Table A.48. EATR for a single with a disposable income of € 50,000 in 2002, in per cent

	Standard		Pension-oriented		Lti-oriented	
	EATR	Rk	EATR	Rk	EATR	Rk
Austria	38.9	17	39.3	17	38.0	17
CH Basel-Landschaft	29.4	6	29.8	6	28.5	6
CH Basel-Stadt	31.2	10	31.5	10	30.3	10
CH Bern	30.6	8	31.0	8	29.7	8
CH Genève	31.5	11	31.9	11	30.7	11
CH Nidwalden	23.9	3	24.0	3	23.2	3
CH Schwyz	21.6	2	21.8	2	20.9	2
CH St. Gallen	30.3	7	30.5	7	29.4	7
CH Ticino	31.0	9	31.3	9	30.1	9
CH Valais	27.5	5	27.7	5	26.6	5
CH Vaud	31.9	12	32.5	12	31.1	13
CH Zug	20.6	1	20.7	1	19.9	1
CH Zürich	25.5	4	26.2	4	24.7	4
France	45.5	19	46.6	19	42.4	18
Germany	44.6	18	44.6	18	44.6	19
Ireland	35.8	16	35.6	16	32.7	15
Italy	54.1	20	53.2	20	50.6	20
The Netherlands	34.1	14	33.8	13	34.1	16
United Kingdom	33.7	13	34.9	14	31.0	12
United States	34.4	15	35.0	15	31.9	14

Table A.49. EATR for a single with a disposable income of € 100,000 in 2002, in per cent

	Standard		Pension-oriented		Lti-oriented	
	EATR	Rk	EATR	Rk	EATR	Rk
Austria	42.4	16	42.9	16	40.1	16
CH Basel-Landschaft	36.4	6	36.8	9	34.4	7
CH Basel-Stadt	36.7	8	36.7	8	34.7	10
CH Bern	36.6	7	36.4	7	34.6	9
CH Genève	37.7	10	37.8	10	35.6	13
CH Nidwalden	28.1	3	27.5	3	26.5	3
CH Schwyz	26.3	2	25.6	2	24.7	2
CH St. Gallen	36.8	9	35.7	6	34.7	11
CH Ticino	37.9	11	37.9	11	35.8	14
CH Valais	35.2	5	34.2	5	33.2	5
CH Vaud	39.0	13	38.2	12	36.8	15
CH Zug	25.7	1	24.7	1	24.0	1
CH Zürich	32.7	4	33.0	4	30.7	4
France	47.9	19	49.8	19	43.0	17
Germany	46.7	18	46.7	18	46.7	19
Ireland	40.4	15	41.1	13	34.9	12
Italy	53.4	20	56.6	20	47.5	20
The Netherlands	44.0	17	43.2	17	44.0	18
United Kingdom	39.3	14	42.5	15	34.5	8
United States	38.2	12	41.1	14	34.2	6

Table A.50. EATR for a single with a disposable income of € 200,000 in 2002, in per cent

	Standard		Pension-oriented		Lti-oriented	
	EATR	Rk	EATR	Rk	EATR	Rk
Austria	43.8	14	44.3	14	42.2	15
CH Basel-Landschaft	42.6	10	42.0	9	39.5	12
CH Basel-Stadt	42.3	8	41.3	7	39.3	10
CH Bern	42.4	9	41.4	8	39.4	11
CH Genève	43.7	13	42.5	10	40.5	13
CH Nidwalden	31.8	3	30.6	3	29.4	3
CH Schwyz	30.0	2	28.9	2	27.7	2
CH St. Gallen	40.6	5	39.5	5	37.9	9
CH Ticino	43.9	15	42.9	11	40.7	14
CH Valais	38.9	4	37.9	4	36.3	7
CH Vaud	45.3	16	43.7	12	42.2	16
CH Zug	29.0	1	27.9	1	26.7	1
CH Zürich	40.6	6	39.6	6	37.5	8
France	52.8	19	55.4	19	43.6	17
Germany	48.4	18	48.4	18	48.4	20
Ireland	43.6	12	44.1	13	35.7	5
Italy	54.9	20	56.8	20	46.8	18
The Netherlands	47.8	17	47.0	17	47.8	19
United Kingdom	42.7	11	45.6	16	35.9	6
United States	42.1	7	45.0	15	35.2	4

Table A.51. EATR for a family with a disposable income of € 50,000 in 2002, in per cent

	Standard		Pension-oriented		Lti-oriented	
	EATR	Rk	EATR	Rk	EATR	Rk
Austria	31.7	18	32.1	18	30.6	18
CH Basel-Landschaft	22.7	10	23.3	10	21.9	11
CH Basel-Stadt	22.6	9	23.1	9	21.8	10
CH Bern	24.8	13	25.6	13	24.1	13
CH Genève	24.0	12	24.6	12	23.2	12
CH Nidwalden	18.6	3	18.9	3	17.9	3
CH Schwyz	17.1	2	17.4	2	16.4	2
CH St. Gallen	21.5	8	22.1	8	20.7	9
CH Ticino	20.7	5	21.7	6	19.9	6
CH Valais	20.9	6	21.7	5	20.2	7
CH Vaud	25.6	14	26.1	14	24.7	14
CH Zug	14.6	1	15.1	1	14.0	1
CH Zürich	19.3	4	20.1	4	18.6	4
France	33.1	19	33.4	19	30.8	19
Germany	27.2	16	27.7	16	26.3	16
Ireland	23.9	11	23.6	11	20.2	8
Italy	53.2	20	52.1	20	49.4	20
The Netherlands	26.6	15	26.4	15	26.6	17
United Kingdom	28.0	17	29.2	17	25.2	15
United States	21.2	7	22.0	7	19.4	5

Table A.52. EATR for a family with a disposable income of € 100,000 in 2002, in per cent

	Standard		Pension-oriented		Lti-oriented	
	EATR	Rk	EATR	Rk	EATR	Rk
Austria	39.1	17	39.7	16	36.6	18
CH Basel-Landschaft	31.1	7	31.3	7	28.9	7
CH Basel-Stadt	31.9	12	31.9	9	29.8	12
CH Bern	31.9	11	32.1	10	29.8	11
CH Genève	33.9	14	34.0	13	31.7	14
CH Nidwalden	24.8	3	24.4	3	23.1	3
CH Schwyz	22.6	2	22.4	2	21.0	2
CH St. Gallen	30.1	5	29.9	5	28.1	6
CH Ticino	31.7	10	31.9	8	29.5	10
CH Valais	31.3	8	30.0	6	29.2	9
CH Vaud	31.1	6	32.5	11	29.2	8
CH Zug	20.7	1	20.6	1	19.2	1
CH Zürich	26.7	4	28.0	4	24.8	4
France	39.4	18	41.4	19	33.6	16
Germany	33.9	13	34.9	14	33.9	17
Ireland	35.9	15	36.7	15	30.0	13
Italy	52.8	20	56.2	20	47.0	20
The Netherlands	41.5	19	40.6	17	41.5	19
United Kingdom	37.6	16	40.8	18	32.6	15
United States	31.3	9	33.8	12	26.4	5

Table A.53. EATR for a family with a disposable income of € 200,000 in 2002, in per cent

	Standard		Pension-oriented		Lti-oriented	
	EATR	Rk	EATR	Rk	EATR	Rk
Austria	42.2	16	42.8	15	40.5	17
CH Basel-Landschaft	39.1	9	39.0	9	36.2	11
CH Basel-Stadt	39.0	8	38.4	7	36.0	10
CH Bern	39.8	10	39.0	8	36.7	12
CH Genève	42.0	15	40.8	12	38.8	16
CH Nidwalden	30.6	3	29.3	3	28.1	3
CH Schwyz	28.6	2	27.4	2	26.2	2
CH St. Gallen	38.5	7	37.0	6	35.6	9
CH Ticino	41.3	12	40.5	11	38.2	14
CH Valais	37.2	5	36.2	5	34.5	7
CH Vaud	41.1	11	39.5	10	37.7	13
CH Zug	27.7	1	26.2	1	25.3	1
CH Zürich	36.6	4	35.9	4	33.5	5
France	48.7	19	51.5	19	38.8	15
Germany	42.9	17	42.9	16	42.9	18
Ireland	41.6	13	42.2	14	33.5	6
Italy	54.7	20	56.6	20	46.5	19
The Netherlands	46.7	18	45.9	18	46.7	20
United Kingdom	41.9	14	44.9	17	35.0	8
United States	38.0	6	41.2	13	30.7	4

Table A.54. EATR for a single with a disposable income of € 50,000 in 2003, in per cent

	Standard		Pension-oriented		Lti-oriented	
	EATR	Rk	EATR	Rk	EATR	Rk
Austria	38.5	17	38.9	17	37.6	17
CH Basel-Landschaft	29.3	6	29.7	6	28.4	6
CH Basel-Stadt	31.0	11	31.3	11	30.1	10
CH Bern	30.5	8	30.9	9	29.7	8
CH Genève	31.5	12	31.9	12	30.7	11
CH Nidwalden	23.9	3	24.0	3	23.2	3
CH Schwyz	20.9	2	21.0	2	20.2	2
CH St. Gallen	30.1	7	30.2	7	29.2	7
CH Ticino	31.0	10	31.3	10	30.1	9
CH Valais	27.5	5	27.7	5	26.6	5
CH Vaud	31.9	13	32.5	13	31.1	14
CH Zug	20.6	1	20.7	1	19.9	1
CH Zürich	25.3	4	25.9	4	24.4	4
France	44.5	18	45.6	18	41.5	18
Germany	46.5	19	46.5	19	46.5	19
Ireland	35.5	16	35.3	16	32.4	16
Italy	50.6	20	49.6	20	47.2	20
The Netherlands	30.9	9	30.6	8	30.9	13
United Kingdom	33.5	14	34.6	14	30.7	12
United States	34.2	15	34.8	15	31.7	15

Table A.55. EATR for a single with a disposable income of € 100,000 in 2003, in per cent

	Standard		Pension-oriented		Lti-oriented	
	EATR	Rk	EATR	Rk	EATR	Rk
Austria	41.7	16	42.3	16	39.5	16
CH Basel-Landschaft	36.6	6	36.9	9	34.5	8
CH Basel-Stadt	36.9	9	36.8	8	34.8	12
CH Bern	36.8	8	36.5	7	34.7	10
CH Genève	37.9	10	38.0	10	35.8	13
CH Nidwalden	28.3	3	27.6	3	26.7	3
CH Schwyz	25.7	1	24.9	2	24.1	1
CH St. Gallen	36.8	7	35.6	6	34.7	9
CH Ticino	38.2	11	38.0	11	36.0	14
CH Valais	35.4	5	34.4	5	33.4	5
CH Vaud	39.3	14	38.3	12	37.0	15
CH Zug	25.9	2	24.8	1	24.2	2
CH Zürich	32.6	4	32.8	4	30.6	4
France	48.2	19	50.2	19	43.5	18
Germany	47.6	18	47.6	18	47.6	20
Ireland	40.3	15	41.0	13	34.8	11
Italy	49.8	20	53.6	20	44.4	19
The Netherlands	42.9	17	42.0	15	42.9	17
United Kingdom	39.2	13	42.3	17	34.4	7
United States	38.2	12	41.1	14	34.2	6

Table A.56. EATR for a single with a disposable income of € 200,000 in 2003, in per cent

	Standard		Pension-oriented		Lti-oriented	
	EATR	Rk	EATR	Rk	EATR	Rk
Austria	43.1	12	43.7	12	41.6	15
CH Basel-Landschaft	42.7	11	42.1	9	39.6	12
CH Basel-Stadt	42.4	9	41.4	7	39.4	10
CH Bern	42.4	8	41.4	8	39.5	11
CH Genève	43.8	14	42.7	10	40.6	13
CH Nidwalden	32.0	3	30.8	3	29.6	3
CH Schwyz	29.4	2	28.3	2	27.2	2
CH St. Gallen	40.5	6	39.4	6	37.8	9
CH Ticino	44.0	15	43.0	11	40.9	14
CH Valais	39.1	4	38.1	4	36.4	7
CH Vaud	45.4	16	43.8	13	42.3	16
CH Zug	29.3	1	28.1	1	27.0	1
CH Zürich	40.3	5	39.3	5	37.3	8
France	52.3	20	54.9	20	43.5	17
Germany	48.8	18	48.8	18	48.8	20
Ireland	43.5	13	44.3	14	35.7	5
Italy	51.5	19	53.7	19	43.9	18
The Netherlands	47.3	17	46.5	17	47.3	19
United Kingdom	42.6	10	45.6	16	35.8	6
United States	42.0	7	44.9	15	35.1	4

Table A.57. EATR for a family with a disposable income of € 50,000 in 2003, in per cent

	Standard		Pension-oriented		Lti-oriented	
	EATR	Rk	EATR	Rk	EATR	Rk
Austria	30.9	18	31.3	18	29.9	18
CH Basel-Landschaft	22.6	11	23.3	12	21.9	11
CH Basel-Stadt	22.6	10	23.0	10	21.8	10
CH Bern	24.4	14	25.1	14	23.7	14
CH Genève	23.5	13	24.1	13	22.7	13
CH Nidwalden	18.6	3	18.9	3	17.9	3
CH Schwyz	16.4	2	16.7	2	15.7	2
CH St. Gallen	21.3	8	22.0	8	20.6	9
CH Ticino	20.7	5	21.7	6	19.9	7
CH Valais	20.9	6	21.7	5	20.2	8
CH Vaud	25.6	15	26.1	15	24.7	15
CH Zug	14.6	1	15.1	1	14.0	1
CH Zürich	19.1	4	19.9	4	18.4	4
France	32.3	19	32.6	19	30.1	19
Germany	27.9	17	28.0	16	26.6	17
Ireland	23.5	12	23.2	11	19.8	6
Italy	49.4	20	48.4	20	46.0	20
The Netherlands	22.6	9	23.0	9	22.6	12
United Kingdom	27.6	16	28.8	17	25.1	16
United States	21.1	7	21.9	7	19.3	5

Table A.58. EATR for a family with a disposable income of € 100,000 in 2003, in per cent

	Standard		Pension-oriented		Lti-oriented	
	EATR	Rk	EATR	Rk	EATR	Rk
Austria	38.2	17	38.9	16	35.8	18
CH Basel-Landschaft	31.3	7	31.4	7	29.1	7
CH Basel-Stadt	32.1	12	32.1	9	30.0	13
CH Bern	31.9	10	32.1	10	29.7	11
CH Genève	33.9	13	34.0	13	31.7	14
CH Nidwalden	25.0	3	24.5	3	23.3	3
CH Schwyz	22.0	2	21.8	2	20.5	2
CH St. Gallen	30.2	5	29.8	5	28.1	6
CH Ticino	32.0	11	32.0	8	29.7	10
CH Valais	31.5	9	30.1	6	29.4	9
CH Vaud	31.4	8	32.7	11	29.4	8
CH Zug	20.9	1	20.7	1	19.3	1
CH Zürich	26.7	4	27.9	4	24.8	4
France	40.0	18	41.9	19	34.4	16
Germany	35.2	14	36.1	14	35.2	17
Ireland	35.8	15	36.6	15	29.9	12
Italy	49.2	20	53.1	20	43.8	20
The Netherlands	40.2	19	39.3	17	40.2	19
United Kingdom	37.4	16	40.7	18	32.5	15
United States	31.3	6	33.8	12	26.4	5

Table A.59. EATR for a family with a disposable income of € 200,000 in 2003, in per cent

	Standard		Pension-oriented		Lti-oriented	
	EATR	Rk	EATR	Rk	EATR	Rk
Austria	41.5	12	42.1	14	39.9	17
CH Basel-Landschaft	39.2	9	39.1	9	36.3	11
CH Basel-Stadt	39.1	8	38.6	7	36.2	10
CH Bern	39.8	10	38.9	8	36.8	12
CH Genève	42.1	16	40.9	12	38.8	16
CH Nidwalden	30.8	3	29.6	3	28.4	3
CH Schwyz	28.0	2	26.8	2	25.7	2
CH St. Gallen	38.4	7	37.0	6	35.5	9
CH Ticino	41.5	13	40.7	11	38.3	14
CH Valais	37.4	5	36.4	5	34.7	7
CH Vaud	41.2	11	39.6	10	37.8	13
CH Zug	28.0	1	26.4	1	25.5	1
CH Zürich	36.4	4	35.7	4	33.3	5
France	48.2	19	51.0	19	38.6	15
Germany	43.4	17	43.4	16	43.4	18
Ireland	41.6	14	42.2	15	33.5	6
Italy	51.2	20	53.4	20	43.6	19
The Netherlands	46.2	18	45.4	18	46.2	20
United Kingdom	41.8	15	44.8	17	35.0	8
United States	37.9	6	41.1	13	30.5	4

Table A.60. Comparison of the EATR in the standard case and with a public pension scheme under market conditions, single in 2003, in per cent

Disposable income	€ 50,000		€ 100,000		€ 200,000	
	standard case	simula-tion	standard case	simula-tion	standard case	simula-tion
Austria	38.5	31.6	41.7	38.6	43.1	41.6
CH Basel-Landschaft	29.3	26.3	36.6	32.8	42.7	38.7
CH Basel-Stadt	31.0	28.0	36.9	33.0	42.4	38.3
CH Bern	30.5	27.5	36.8	32.9	42.4	38.4
CH Genève	31.5	28.6	37.9	34.1	43.8	40.1
CH Nidwalden	23.9	20.6	28.3	23.9	32.0	27.2
CH Schwyz	20.9	17.6	25.7	21.1	29.4	24.5
CH St. Gallen	30.1	27.0	36.8	32.6	40.5	36.3
CH Ticino	31.0	28.0	38.2	34.4	44.0	40.0
CH Valais	27.5	24.3	35.4	31.2	39.1	34.8
CH Vaud	31.9	29.1	39.3	35.4	45.4	41.4
CH Zug	20.6	17.2	25.9	21.3	29.3	24.3
CH Zürich	25.3	22.2	32.6	28.7	40.3	36.1
France	44.5	41.2	48.2	46.6	52.3	51.3
Germany	46.5	34.4	47.6	42.5	48.8	46.5
Ireland	35.5	25.4	40.3	34.0	43.5	38.2
Italy	50.6	39.0	49.8	42.9	51.5	48.7
The Netherlands	30.9	24.5	42.9	40.8	47.3	46.4
United Kingdom	33.5	27.1	39.2	34.6	42.6	38.7
United States	34.2	27.3	38.2	33.7	42.0	40.1

Table A.61. Comparison of the EATR in the standard case and a public pension scheme under market conditions, family in 2003, in per cent

Disposable income	€ 50,000		€ 100,000		€ 200,000	
	standard case	simula-tion	standard case	simula-tion	standard case	simula-tion
Austria	30.9	22.5	38.2	34.5	41.5	39.9
CH Basel-Landschaft	22.6	20.5	31.3	27.5	39.2	35.4
CH Basel-Stadt	22.6	20.4	32.1	28.4	39.1	35.2
CH Bern	24.4	22.3	31.9	28.2	39.8	35.8
CH Genève	23.5	21.3	33.9	30.3	42.1	38.0
CH Nidwalden	18.6	16.4	25.0	20.9	30.8	26.2
CH Schwyz	16.4	14.2	22.0	18.0	28.0	23.3
CH St. Gallen	21.3	19.2	30.2	26.4	38.4	34.2
CH Ticino	20.7	18.7	32.0	28.3	41.5	37.6
CH Valais	20.9	18.7	31.5	27.6	37.4	33.2
CH Vaud	25.6	23.4	31.4	28.0	41.2	37.1
CH Zug	14.6	12.5	20.9	16.8	28.0	23.2
CH Zürich	19.1	17.1	26.7	23.1	36.4	32.2
France	32.3	28.4	40.0	37.9	48.2	51.3
Germany	27.9	12.4	35.2	27.7	43.4	40.6
Ireland	23.5	9.1	35.8	28.6	41.6	35.9
Italy	49.4	37.6	49.2	42.1	51.2	48.4
The Netherlands	22.6	16.0	40.2	38.0	46.2	45.3
United Kingdom	27.6	21.2	37.4	32.8	41.8	37.9
United States	21.1	15.6	31.3	25.6	37.9	36.0

Table A.62. Comparison of the EATR in the standard case and with social security contributions yielding equivalent individual benefits, single in 2003, in per cent

Disposable income	€ 50,000		€ 100,000		€ 200,000	
	standard case	simulation	standard case	simulation	standard case	simulation
Austria	38.5	24.4	41.7	35.3	43.1	40.2
CH Basel-Landschaft	29.3	19.7	36.6	26.8	42.7	33.9
CH Basel-Stadt	31.0	21.3	36.9	27.1	42.4	33.6
CH Bern	30.5	20.7	36.8	26.6	42.4	33.4
CH Genève	31.5	21.5	37.9	27.7	43.8	34.8
CH Nidwalden	23.9	14.1	28.3	17.8	32.0	22.2
CH Schwyz	20.9	11.2	25.7	15.1	29.4	19.5
CH St. Gallen	30.1	19.9	36.8	26.2	40.5	31.3
CH Ticino	31.0	21.2	38.2	28.3	44.0	35.3
CH Valais	27.5	18.9	35.4	26.6	39.1	31.5
CH Vaud	31.9	22.0	39.3	28.7	45.4	36.3
CH Zug	20.6	10.9	25.9	15.2	29.3	19.5
CH Zürich	25.3	15.8	32.6	22.4	40.3	31.2
France	44.5	21.5	48.2	29.6	52.3	35.7
Germany	46.5	25.8	47.6	39.2	48.8	45.0
Ireland	35.5	22.4	40.3	31.8	43.5	36.2
Italy	50.6	32.1	49.8	35.3	51.5	41.5
The Netherlands	30.9	19.7	42.9	39.2	47.3	45.8
United Kingdom	33.5	24.1	39.2	32.6	42.6	37.0
United States	34.2	23.6	38.2	30.5	42.0	37.0

Table A.63. Comparison of the EATR in the standard case and with social security contributions yielding equivalent individual benefits, family in 2003, in per cent

Disposable income	€ 50,000		€ 100,000		€ 200,000	
	standard case	simulation	standard case	simulation	standard case	simulation
Austria	30.9	13.1	38.2	30.8	41.5	38.5
CH Basel-Landschaft	22.6	13.9	31.3	20.9	39.2	30.5
CH Basel-Stadt	22.6	13.6	32.1	21.9	39.1	30.3
CH Bern	24.4	15.5	31.9	21.5	39.8	30.5
CH Genève	23.5	13.8	33.9	23.4	42.1	33.0
CH Nidwalden	18.6	9.7	25.0	14.6	30.8	21.0
CH Schwyz	16.4	7.7	22.0	11.8	28.0	18.1
CH St. Gallen	21.3	12.1	30.2	19.4	38.4	28.9
CH Ticino	20.7	11.9	32.0	21.6	41.5	32.7
CH Valais	20.9	13.6	31.5	22.6	37.4	29.8
CH Vaud	25.6	15.8	31.4	21.2	41.2	31.5
CH Zug	14.6	6.1	20.9	10.7	28.0	18.0
CH Zürich	19.1	10.5	26.7	16.7	36.4	27.1
France	32.3	9.1	40.0	19.0	48.2	29.9
Germany	27.9	4.1	35.2	22.8	43.4	38.9
Ireland	23.5	5.4	35.8	26.2	41.6	33.9
Italy	49.4	30.3	49.2	34.6	51.2	41.2
The Netherlands	22.6	10.0	40.2	36.2	46.2	44.6
United Kingdom	27.6	18.6	37.4	30.7	41.8	36.2
United States	21.1	11.8	31.3	22.0	37.9	32.7

List of Tables

List of Figures

List of Abbreviations and Symbols

Abbreviations

A	Austria
ACI	Automobile Club d'Italia
AGIRC	Régime de retraite des cadres
AHV	Alters- und Hinterbliebenenversicherung
AKW	Algemene kinderbijslagwet
AOW	Algemene ouderdomswet
ARCO	Régime de retraite des non-cadres
ASVG	Allgemeines Sozialversicherungsgesetz
BE	Bern
BFH	Bundesfinanzhof
BL	Basel-Landschaft
BNB	Beslissingen in belastingzaken Nederlandse belastingrechtspraak (unofficial tax reporter)
BS	Basel-Stadt
BStBl	Bundessteuerblatt
CCH	Commerce Clearing House
CGI	Code général des impôts
CH	Switzerland
CNAV	Caisse nationale d'assurance vieillesse
CRDS	Contribution au remboursement de la dette sociale
CSG	Contribution sociale généralisée
D	Germany
EO	Erwerbsersatzordnung
ESRI	Economic and Social Research Institute (Tokyo)
EStG	Einkommensteuergesetz (Austria or Germany)
F	France
FA	Finance Act
FURBS	Funded unapproved retirement benefit scheme
FUTA	Federal unemployment tax act
GB	United Kingdom
GE	Genève
I	Italy
IBFD	International Bureau of Fiscal Documentation
ICTA	Income and Corporation Tax Act
IRAP	Imposta regionale sulle attività produttive
IRC	Irish Revenue Code
IRL	Ireland

ISSA	International Social Security Association
lti	long-term incentives
MISSOC	Mutual Information System on Social Protection in the EU Member States
MV	Mitarbeiter-Vorsorge
NL	Netherlands
NW	Nidwalden
OASDI	Old-age survivor and disability insurance
OECD	Organisation for Economic Co-Operation and Development
PAYG	pay-as-you-go
Rk	rank
SG	St. Gallen
SZ	Schwyz
TCA	Taxes Consolidation Act
TFR	Trattamento de fine rapporto
TI	Ticino
USA	United States
VD	Vaud
VS	Valais
Wet LB	Wet op de loonbelasting
ZG	Zug
ZH	Zürich

Symbols

δ	discount factor
E	disposable income
E_0	disposable income in the remuneration period
E_l	disposable income in the period when stock options are exercised
E_r	disposable income in a pension period
E^*	total remuneration
$EATR$	effective average tax rate
L	time between remuneration period and date of exercise, $L = t_l - t_0$
P	number of retirement periods
r	market interest rate
R	time between the beginning of retirement and the pension period
t_0	period of remuneration
t_l	period of exercising the stock options
t_r	any period during retirement
θ_l	share of the true value of the option which is subject to tax
θ_p	share of the lease value of the company car which is subject to tax

References

Börsch-Supan, A. and A. Reil-Held (2001), How Much Is Transfer and How Much Is Insurance in a Pay-As-You-Go System? The German Case, *Scandinavian Journal of Economics* 103, 505-524.

Bosshard, E. and P. Funk (2000), *Steueroptimierte Gehaltsleistungen* Bd. 1, Muri.

Brassat, M. and D. Kiesewetter (2003), Steuervorteile durch arbeitgeberfinanzierte Versorgungszusagen, *Zeitschrift für Betriebswirtschaft* 73, 1051-1076.

Brümmer, M.A. (2001), Vergütung in der IT-Branche, *Zeitschrift für Human Resource*, 304-309.

CCH (2001), *The CCH Tax Handbook 2001-02*, Bicester.

Devereux, M.P. and R. Griffith (1999), *The Taxation of Discrete Investment Choices*, IFS Working Paper 98/16 (Revision 2), London.

Devereux, M.P. and R. Griffith (2003), Evaluating Tax Policy for Location Decisions, *International Tax and Public Finance* 10, 107-126.

Devereux, M.P., L. Lammersen, and C. Spengel (2000), *The Effective Levels of Company Taxation in the Member States of the EU*, Report prepared for the Taxation and Customs Union Directorate General, Warwick.

Devereux, M.P., L. Lammersen, and C. Spengel (2001), *Changes in the Effective Levels of Company Taxation in the Member States of the EU: 1999 to 2001*, Supplementary report prepared for the Taxation and Customs Union Directorate General, Mannheim and Warwick.

Elschner, C. and R. Schwager (2004a), *A Method to Measure the Tax Burden on Highly Skilled Manpower*, ZEW Discussion Paper 04-59, Centre for European Economic Research, Mannheim.

Elschner, C. and R. Schwager (2004b), Das Haushaltsbegleitgesetz 2004 – ein Beitrag zur Wettbewerbsfähigkeit Deutschlands, *Betriebs-Berater* 6-58, Editorial.

Elschner, C. and R. Schwager (2004c), Do Employer-Provided Stock Options Reduce Compensation Costs?, Stock Option Watch, *ZEWnews English Edition* 3-2004, Mannheim, III-IV.

European Commission (1992), *Report of the Committee of Independent Experts on Company Taxation*, Brussels.

European Commission (2002), *Company Taxation in the Internal Market*, Commission Staff Working Paper, COM (2001) 582 final, Luxembourg.

European Commission (2003), *Employee Stock Options – the Legal and Adminstrative Environment for Employee Stock Options in the EU*, Final report of the expert group, Brussels.

Fenge, R., A. Gebauer, C. Holzner, V. Meier, and M. Werding (2003), *Alterssicherungssysteme im internationalen Vergleich: Finanzierung, Leistungen, Besteuerung*, ifo-Beiträge zur Wirtschaftsforschung 10, München.

Fenge, R., S. Übelmesser, and M. Werding (2002), *Old-Age Provision in Ageing Societies: Equity, Efficiency, and Sustainability*, Study commissioned by the ESRI, Tokyo.

Fenge, R. and M. Werding (2002), *Ageing and the Tax Implied in Public Pension Schemes: Simulations for Selected OECD Countries*, CESifo Working Paper 841, München.

Gaube, T. and R. Schwager (2003), Consumption vs. Wage Taxation and the Capital Levy, *Economics Letters* 79, 15-19.

Gutekunst G. and R. Schwager (2002), *Steuerbelastung von Unternehmen im Alpenraum*, ZEW Wirtschaftsanalysen 59, Baden-Baden.

Heady, C. (2003), *The 'Taxing Wages' Approach to Measuring the Tax Burden on Labour*, CES-ifo working paper 967, München.

Hirte, G. (2000), Struktur der impliziten Steuersätze der Gesetzlichen Rentenversicherung, *ifo-Studien* 46, 315-334.

Hören, M. v. (2000), Vergütung von Führungskräften: Aktueller Stand und Entwicklungstendenzen, *Personal: Zeitschrift für Human Resource Management*, 275-278.

IBFD (2003a), *European Tax Handbook*, Amsterdam.

IBFD (2003b), *Taxation of Individuals*, Amsterdam.

ISSA (2002), *Databases Social Security Worldwide*, International Social Security Association, www.issa.int/engl/homef.htm.

Jacobs, O.H. and C. Spengel (1996), *European Tax Analyzer*, ZEW Wirtschaftsanalysen 11, Baden-Baden.

Jahr, V., H. Schomburg, and U. Teichler (2002), *Internationale Mobilität von Absolventinnen und Absolventen Europäischer Hochschulen*, Werkstattberichte 61, Wissenschaftliches Zentrum für Berufs- und Hochschulforschung der Universität Kassel, Kassel.

Kienbaum (2001), Auszüge und Pressemitteilungen der *Vergütungsstudien 2001*, www.kienbaum.de.

King, M.A. and D. Fullerton (1984), *The Taxation of Income from Capital*, Chicago.

Kristen, S., W. Pinggera, and R. Schön (2002), Abfertigung Neu: Überblick über die Neuregelungen durch das Betriebliche Mitarbeitervorsorgegesetz, *Recht der Wirtschaft* 7, Article No. 389.

Lammersen, L. and R. Schwager (2005), *The Effective Tax Burden of Companies in European Regions: An International Comparison*, ZEW Economic Studies 28, Heidelberg.

Laux, H. (2002), Vorsorgeaufwendungen und Altersvorsorgebeiträge 2002, *Betriebs-Berater* 57, Beilage 4.

Lefebvre, F. (2002), *Mémento Pratique Francis Lefebvre Fiscal 2002*, Paris.

Mendoza, G., A. Razin, and L. Tesar (1994), Effective Tax Rates in Macroeconomics – Cross-Country Estimates of Tax Rates on Factor Incomes and Consumption, *Journal of Monetary Economics* 34, 297-323.

MISSOC (2002 and 2003), *Mutual Information System on Social Protection in the EU Member States and the EEA*, European Commission, http://europa.eu.int/comm/employment_social/missoc/index_en.html.

OECD (2002), *Taxing Wages 2001-2002*, Paris.

Siebert, H. (2000), *Zum Paradigma des Steuerwettbewerbs*, Beiträge zur Ordnungstheorie und Ordnungspolitik 165, Tübingen.

Sutherland, H. (2001), *Final Report Euromod: An Integrated European Benefit-Tax Model*, Euromod Working Paper No. EM9/01.

TowersPerrin (2001), Italy – New Tax Rules for Pensions and Termination Indemnities (TFR), *International Update* April 2001.

Towers Perrin (2002), *2001-2002 Worldwide Total Remuneration*, www.towers.com.

Winkelmann, R. (2002), Why Do Firms Recruit Internationally? – Results from the IZA International Employer Survey 2000, in: OECD, *International Mobility of the Highly Skilled*, Paris.

Winkelmann, R., A. Kunze, L. Locher et al. (2001), *Die Nachfrage nach internationalen hochqualifizierten Beschäftigten – Ergebnisse des IZA International Employer Surveys 2000*, IZA Research Report 4, Bonn.

Jens Borken
Andreas Patyk
Guido A. Reinhardt

Basisdaten für ökologische Bilanzierungen

AF810309

Aus dem Programm Umweltwissenschaften

Martin Kaltschmitt/Guido A. Reinhardt
Nachwachsende Energieträger
Grundlagen, Verfahren, ökologische Bilanzierung

Andreas Patyk/Guido A. Reinhardt
Düngemittel – Energie- und Stoffstrombilanzen

Mario Schmidt/Ulrich Höpfner
20 Jahre ifeu-Institut
Engagement für die Umwelt
zwischen Wissenschaft und Politik

Klaus Heinloth
Die Energiefrage
Bedarf und Potentiale, Nutzen, Risiken und Kosten

Andreas Heintz/Guido A. Reinhardt
Chemie und Umwelt

Egbert Boeker/Riek van Grondelle
Physik und Umwelt

Frithjof Staiß
Photovoltaik
Technik, Potentiale und Perspektiven der solaren Stromerzeugung

vieweg

Jens Borken
Andreas Patyk
Guido A. Reinhardt

Basisdaten für ökologische Bilanzierungen

Einsatz von Nutzfahrzeugen in Transport, Landwirtschaft und Bergbau

vieweg

Jens Borken, Dr. Andreas Patyk, Dr. Guido A. Reinhardt
ifeu-Institut für Energie- und Umweltforschung Heidelberg GmbH
Wilckensstraße 3
69120 Heidelberg
Tel.: 0 62 21-47 67-0
http://www.ifeu.de

Das vorliegende Werk wurde sorgfältig erarbeitet. Dennoch übernehmen Autoren und Verlag für die Richtigkeit von Angaben, Hinweisen und Ratschlägen sowie für eventuelle Druckfehler keine Haftung. Die Wiedergabe von Gebrauchsnamen, Handelsnamen, Warenbezeichnungen usw. in diesem Buch berechtigt auch ohne besondere Kennzeichnung nicht zu der Annahme, dass solche Namen im Sinne der Warenzeichen- und Warenschutzgesetzgebung als frei zu betrachten wären und daher von jedermann benutzt werden dürften.

Alle Rechte vorbehalten
© Springer Fachmedien Wiesbaden 1999
Ursprünglich erschienen bei Friedr. Vieweg &Sohn Verlagsgesellschaft 1999.

Das Werk einschließlich aller seiner Teile ist urheberrechtlich geschützt. Jede Verwertung außerhalb der engen Grenzen des Urheberrechtsgesetzes ist ohne Zustimmung des Verlags unzulässig und strafbar. Das gilt insbesondere für Vervielfältigungen, Übersetzungen, Mikroverfilmungen und die Einspeicherung und Verarbeitung in elektronischen Systemen.

http://www.vieweg.de

Konzeption und Layout des Umschlags: Ulrike Weigel, www.CorporateDesignGroup.de
Gedruckt auf Recyclingpapier

ISBN 978-3-322-91827-7 ISBN 978-3-322-91826-0 (eBook)
DOI 10.1007/978-3-322-91826-0

Vorwort

Keine Frage: Ökologisch relevante Daten zur Beschreibung von Prozessen recherchieren, validieren, abgleichen ist nicht nur ein wesentlicher Arbeitsschritt ökologischer Bewertungen, es macht als Teil der „Modellbildung" auch Spaß – zumindest kann es das. Dem unterschiedlich empfundenen Vergnügen an diesen Tätigkeiten stehen andere Aspekte gegenüber: begrenzte Zeit- und Kostenrahmen konkreter Projekte oder auch die Vergleichbarkeit verschiedener Studien untereinander. Unter diesen Aspekten ist es mehr als nur wünschenswert, geradezu notwendig, für Prozesse, die in sehr ähnlicher Form in zahlreichen Prozeßketten bzw. entlang von „Lebenswegen" von Produkten auftreten – und bei der ökologischen Bewertung oft ergebnisbestimmend sind (!) –, möglichst einheitlich definierte (Stichwort: Systemgrenze), dabei aber differenzierte und repräsentative Datensätze zu verwenden. Dazu kommt der Anspruch einer umfassenden Berücksichtigung relevanter Umweltkategorien (Stichwort: Schadstoffpalette) und die nachvollziehbare Dokumentation.

Mit diesem Buch versuchen wir einen Beitrag dazu zu leisten, diese Anforderungen zu erfüllen und für ökologische Bilanzierungen allgemein erfüllbar zu machen. Den Gegenstand bilden dabei Prozesse, mit denen wir uns seit einer Reihe von Jahren im Rahmen von Produkt-Ökobilanzen und anderen Studien zur ökologischen Bewertung beschäftigen: der Energieverbrauch und die Emissionen des Einsatzes von Nutzfahrzeugen in Gütertransport, Landwirtschaft und Bergbau. Insbesondere Gütertransporte liefern Beispiele für wichtige und in der Vergangenheit oft uneinheitlich und unzureichend behandelte Prozesse. Eine belastbare Modellierung des Einsatzes von Landmaschinen gewinnt mit der Diskussion um die ökologischen Vor- und Nachteile nachwachsender Rohstoffe und anderer landwirtschaftlicher Fragestellungen zusehends an Bedeutung. Bergbauprozesse schließlich spielen für die Lebenswege fast aller Produkte eine Rolle.

Ein Großteil des Zahlenmaterials wurde im Rahmen verschiedener Forschungs- und Fördervorhaben erarbeitet. Insbesondere sind hier Teile des unter anderem vom Umweltbundesamt geförderten Projekts „Energieverbrauch und Schadstoffemissionen aus dem motorisierten Verkehr in Deutschland 1980 bis 2020" und des von der Deutschen Bundesstiftung Umwelt geförderten Projekts „Ganzheitliche Bilanzierung nachwachsender Energieträger unter verschiedenen ökologischen Aspekten" zusammengefaßt. Darauf aufbauende zusätzliche Arbeiten wurden durch den ifeu-Verein für Energie- und Umweltfragen e. V. Heidelberg gefördert. Die hier publizierten Basisdaten sind inzwischen in eine Datenbank zur ökologischen Bilanzierung integriert und damit elektronisch verfügbar.

Bereits an dieser Stelle möchten wir auf einige weitere inhaltliche Punkte hinweisen:

- Erstmals wird in diesem Buch eine Methode zur detaillierten Bilanzierung von Feldarbeiten ausführlich vorgestellt und an ausgewählten Beispielen illustriert.
- Die Emissionsfaktoren werden nach Ortsklassen differenziert abgeleitet. Hierdurch wird unseres Erachtens eine spätere Bewertung der Bilanzierungsergebnisse wesentlich erleichtert.

- Neben dem Einsatz von Dieselkraftstoff wird auch der Einsatz der Bioenergieträger Rapsöl und Rapsmethylester in LKW bzw. Ackerschleppern behandelt.
- Außer den direkten Verbräuchen und Emissionen der Nutzfahrzeuge werden auch die „kumulierten“ Daten, d. h. einschließlich der Bereitstellung der jeweiligen Energieträger, ausgewiesen.

Unser Ziel war, die Ableitung der einzelnen Daten möglichst ausführlich zu beschreiben und die zugrundeliegenden Primärdaten weitestgehend vollständig zu dokumentieren. Dabei haben wir uns eng an die Ökobilanz-Methodik gehalten. Die betrachteten Prozesse sind mit dem gleichen räumlichen, zeitlichen und sachlichen Bezug abgeleitet. Sofern zukünftige Änderungen vorhersehbar sind, werden Fortschreibungen durchgeführt bzw. Anleitungen dazu gegeben.

Unsere Leserinnen und Leser bitten wir, uns Fehler und auch Unklarheiten in Ableitungen, Berechnungen oder Literaturzitaten erstens zu verzeihen und zweitens mitzuteilen; es droht ein Belegexemplar der zweiten Auflage.

Die Erstellung dieses Buches war – bei reiflicher Überlegung eigentlich nicht unerwartet – aufwendiger als optimistisch angenommen und wäre ohne direkte und indirekte Unterstützung unserer Umgebung kaum in dieser Form gelungen. Namentlich bedanken wir uns bei Wolfram Knörr für Berechnungen der Emissionsfaktoren für Straßentransporte mittels TREMOD und Mario Schmidt (beide IFEU) für seine Ausführungen zu speziellen Problemen bei der Bilanzierung von Gütertransporten und zur Integration der Daten in Umberto®. Auch Guido Zemanek sei herzlich gedankt für seine äußerst hilfreichen Anmerkungen bei der sorgfältigen Durchsicht des Manuskriptes. Und nicht zuletzt danken wir von ganzem Herzen auch unseren Freundinnen, Freunden und Familien. Leider konnten wir Zeitmangel und Defizite an Ausgeglichenheit nicht immer vermeiden.

Heidelberg, im März 1999

Jens Borken
Andreas Patyk
Guido A. Reinhardt

Inhaltsverzeichnis (Übersicht)

Inhaltsverzeichnis

Teil I Allgemeine Grundlagen

Teil II Ableitung der Basisdaten

Teil III Anhang

Teil I

Allgemeine Grundlagen

1 Einleitung

Welche ökologischen Vor- oder Nachteile haben Mehrweg- gegenüber Einwegflaschen? Welche Umweltwirkungen sind mit der Produktion von Brot verbunden? Wie ist die Bereitstellung von Kupfererz zur Produktion von Stromkabeln unter ökologischen Gesichtspunkten zu bewerten?

Diese und ähnliche Fragen werden seit einer Reihe von Jahren in „Ökobilanzen“ untersucht. Dabei hat sich gezeigt, daß der Einsatz von Nutzfahrzeugen – Transportmittel, Landmaschinen, Bergbaumaschinen – in vielen der untersuchten „Lebenswege“ eine wichtige, oft auch ergebnisbestimmende Rolle spielt. Diese nüchterne Feststellung bedeutet, unterstellt, daß Ökobilanzen Ziel und Zweck haben und ihre Ergebnisse Anwender finden (sollen): Die umweltbezogenen Schwachstellen – und damit auch Optimierungspotentiale – der Lebenswege zahlreicher Produkte liegen in Transportprozessen, im Bergbau, in der Landwirtschaft. Die folgenden Beispiele illustrieren die Bedeutung dieser Lebenswegabschnitte. Sie wurden aufgrund ihrer wirtschaftlichen und damit gesellschaftlichen Bedeutung ausgewählt oder weil an ihnen bestimmte Bilanzierungsprobleme besonders deutlich dargestellt werden können.

Beispiel Sojaschrot: Sojaschrot gehört zu den wichtigsten Futtermitteln in der heimischen Landwirtschaft. Die Bereitstellung von Sojaschrot läßt sich in drei Abschnitte unterteilen: Den landwirtschaftlichen Anbau der Sojabohnen in den Hauptanbauregionen Nord- und Südamerika und Asien, die industrielle Gewinnung des Schrotes, wobei Sojaöl als Kuppelprodukt gewonnen wird, und schließlich den Transport des Schrotes nach Deutschland. Die Energieaufwendungen in der Ölmühle sind der mit Abstand aufwendigste Teilschritt; mehr als ein Viertel des gesamten Energieeinsatzes entfällt auf den Transport, gefolgt von der maschinellen Feldarbeit; die Anteile der Lebenswegabschnitte sind in **Abb. 1-1** dargestellt. Die Gesamtaufwendungen der Sojaschrotbereitstellung – und damit auch sein Anbau und Transport – können sogar dann noch ihre Bedeutung behalten, wenn sie als Teil umfassender Lebenswege nur einen Aspekt der gesamten Fragestellung ausmachen, wie etwa bei der Bereitstellung von Rapsöl und RME. Dies wird ausführlich in Kapitel 8.2 dargestellt.

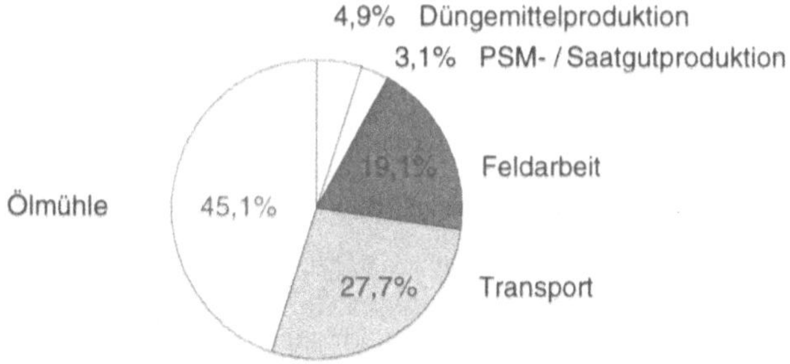

Abb. 1-1 Anteile der einzelnen Lebenswegabschnitte am gesamten Energieeinsatz der Bereitstellung von Sojaschrot in Deutschland (PSM: Pflanzenschutzmittel); eigene Berechnungen

Beispiel Kupferhalbzeuge: Die Bereitstellung von Primärkupfer-Halbzeugen in Deutschland umfaßt im wesentlichen den Abbau und die Anreicherung von Kupfererz z. B. in Chile, einem der Hauptförderländer, den Erztransport per Schiff, die Verhüttung in Deutschland und die Formgebung zu Blechen, Profilen oder Drähten. Die Anteile dieser Lebenswegabschnitte am gesamten Energieaufwand von knapp 70 GJ/t Rohr sind in **Abb. 1-2** zusammengefaßt. Der Anteil des Erzabbaus allein – ohne die grubennahe Aufarbeitung – liegt bei 20 %, der des Transports bei 4 %. Berücksichtigt man realistischerweise die hohe Recyclingquote bei Kupfer durch Abschreibung der Erzgewinnung, des Erztransports und der Verhüttung über mehrere Produktgenerationen, sinken diese Anteile natürlich, werden durch den relativ geringen Formgebungsaufwand aber nicht vernachlässigbar; der Anteil aller Transporte *einschließlich* der Schrottsammelfahrten ist im Falle der Sekundärkupferrohre mit einem Gesamtenergieaufwand von etwa 40 GJ/t Rohr sogar höher.

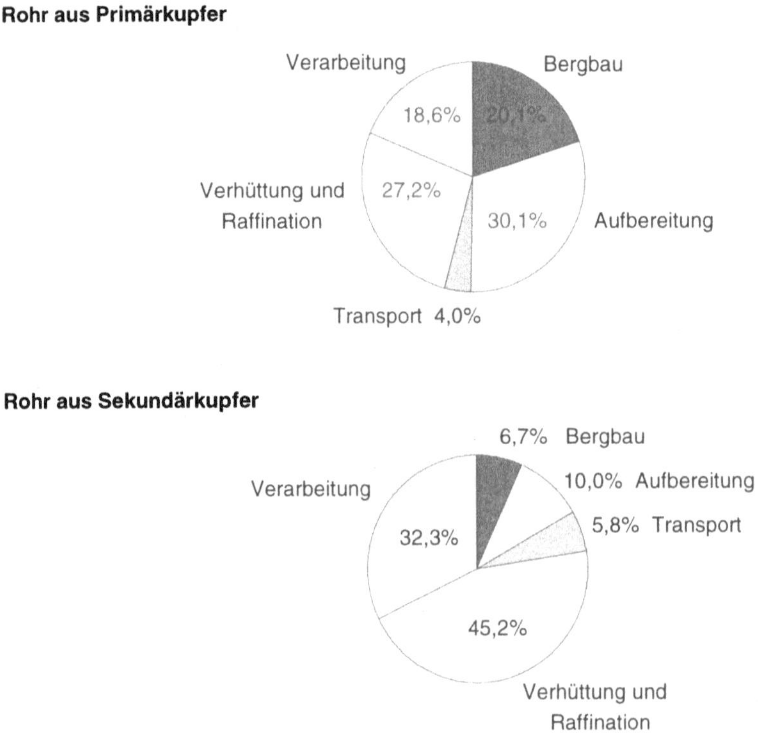

Abb. 1-2 Anteile der einzelnen Lebenswegabschnitte am gesamten Energieeinsatz für die Herstellung von Kupferrohren nach /BRUCH et al. 1995/ und eigenen Berechnungen

Beispiel Rapsöl: Die Bereitstellung dieses vieldiskutierten Bioenergieträgers wird in Kapitel 8.2 auf der Basis von /IFEU 1997a/ und eigenen Arbeiten detailliert behandelt. Für drei Parameter sind die Ergebnisse der Bilanzen über den *gesamten* Lebensweg, d. h. einschließlich der Nutzung in KFZ, in **Abb. 1-3** zusammengefaßt: Etwa 11 % des Einsatzes erschöpflicher Energie für die Bereitstellung von Rapsöl entfallen auf die maschinelle Feldarbeit, etwa 70 % auf die Produktion der eingesetzten Düngemittel. Die CO_2-Bilanz zeigt praktisch die gleiche Aufteilung wie die Energiebilanz, weil entlang des Lebensweges von Rapsöl fast ausschließlich fossile Energieträger eingesetzt werden. Für die Stickoxid-Bilanz stellen sich dagegen die Verhältnisse völlig anders dar: Fast 90 % der gesamten NO_X-Emissionen werden bei der Nutzung von Rapsöl freigesetzt, während auf die maschinelle Feldarbeit nur 3 % entfallen. Offenkundig ist der Energieverbrauch in diesem Fall kein aussagekräftiger Indikator für die Höhe anderer Umweltwirkungen. Wie weit Energieverbrauch und Emissionen korrelieren, hängt von den konkret betrachteten Lebenswegen und Schadstoffen ab. Den Verbrauch energetischer Ressourcen als Maßstab für Umweltverträglichkeit anzusetzen, empfiehlt sich damit nur für grobe Schätzungen. Die explizite Bilanzierung von Emissionen kann er nicht ersetzen. Letztere scheitert allerdings häufig an der Nichtverfügbarkeit von Basisdaten insbesondere für „nicht klassische" Luftschadstoffe.

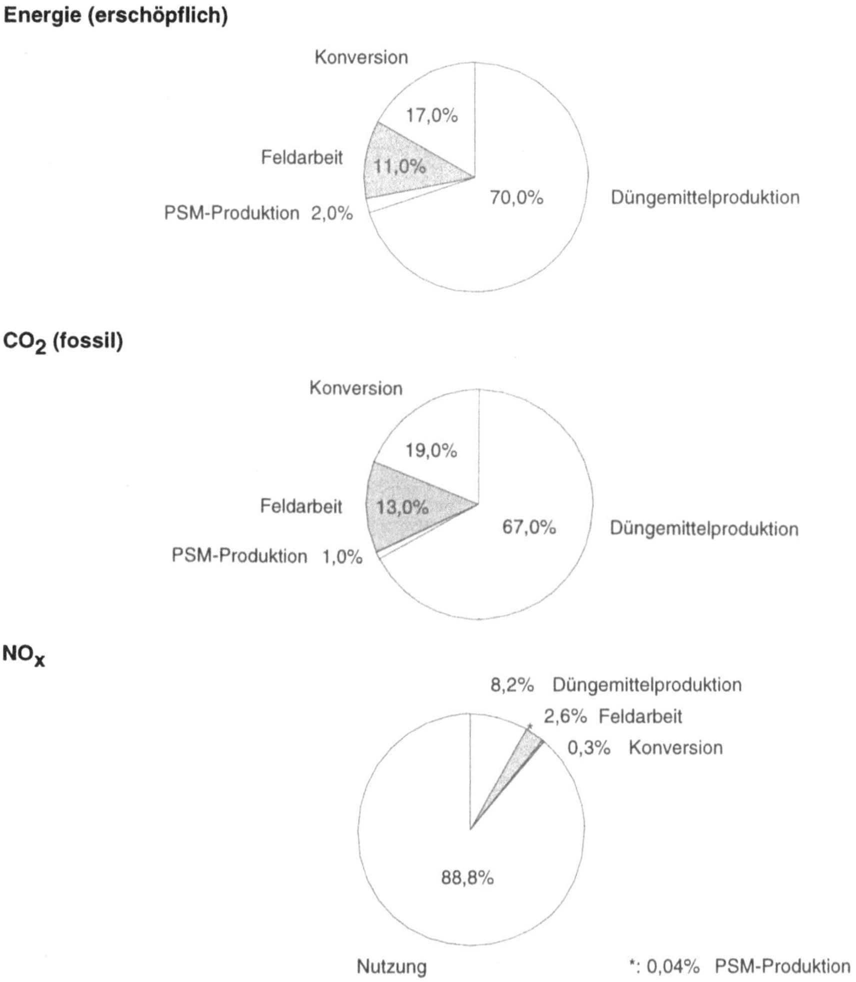

Abb. 1-3 Anteile der einzelnen Lebenswegabschnitte am Einsatz erschöpflicher Energie, den fossilen CO_2- und den NO_X-Emissionen des Lebensweges von Rapsöl nach /IFEU 1997a/ und eigenen Berechnungen (PSM: Pflanzenschutzmittel)

Beispiel Einweg kontra Mehrweg: In einer Studie des Umweltbundesamtes wurden die Umweltauswirkungen verschiedener üblicher Getränkeverpackungen – bei Milch: Schlauchbeutel, Pfandflasche, Blockpackung – untersucht /UBA 1995a/. Dabei zeigte sich, daß die Stickoxidemissionen *über den gesamten Lebensweg* kritisch von der Transportentfernung bei der Milchdistribution abhängen. Mit steigender Transportentfernung wandelt sich der Vorteil der Mehrwegflasche in einen Nachteil (**Abb. 1-4**). Dieses Beispiel zeigt eindrücklich nicht nur die Bedeutung von Transportprozessen, sondern auch die Notwendigkeit, Rahmenbedingungen und Annahmen in ökologischen Bilanzierungen sorgfältig und realistisch festzulegen bzw. zu treffen, gegebenenfalls durch Sensitivitätsanalysen zu variieren und mit den Ergebnissen zu dokumentieren.

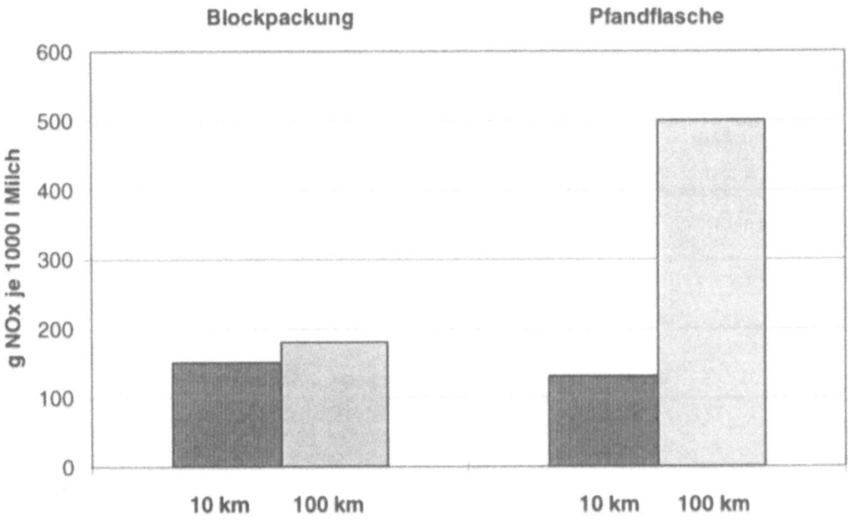

Abb. 1-4 NO_X-Emissionen entlang des Lebensweges von Einweg- und Mehrwegverpackungen für Milch in Abhängigkeit von der Transportentfernung /UBA 1995a/

Beispiel Dieselkraftstoff: Die Bereitstellung von Dieselkraftstoff umfaßt im wesentlichen die Erdölförderung und -aufbereitung, den Rohöltransport, die Produktion in der Raffinerie und die Kraftstoffdistribution. Die Anteile der Lebenswegabschnitte an den gesamten Partikelemissionen, die wegen ihrer humantoxischen bzw. kanzerogenen Wirkung relevant sind, sind in **Abb. 1-5** zusammengefaßt. Auch hier ist die Bedeutung des Lebenswegabschnitts Rohöltransport mit 35 % offensichtlich. Die Partikel werden jedoch zum überwiegenden Teil auf offener See ausgestoßen, hier mit Ortsklasse 3 bezeichnet, und sind damit – zumindest für den Menschen – praktisch unschädlich. Ungleich risikoreicher sind Dieselpartikel, die auf dem Kontinent und insbesondere in Ballungsräumen freigesetzt werden. Dazu tragen die Transporte aber nur wenig bei.

Das heißt, Emissionen mit räumlich begrenzter Wirkung sind differenziert nach Entstehungs- und Wirkungsorten zu bilanzieren. Dieser Gesichtspunkt wurde in ökologischen Bilanzierungen bisher häufig vernachlässigt. Die von uns vorgeschlagene und in diesem Buch angewandte Ortsklassen-Differenzierung wird in Kapitel 4.2.1 näher beschrieben.

Gesamt (bisher übliches Bilanzierungsverfahren)

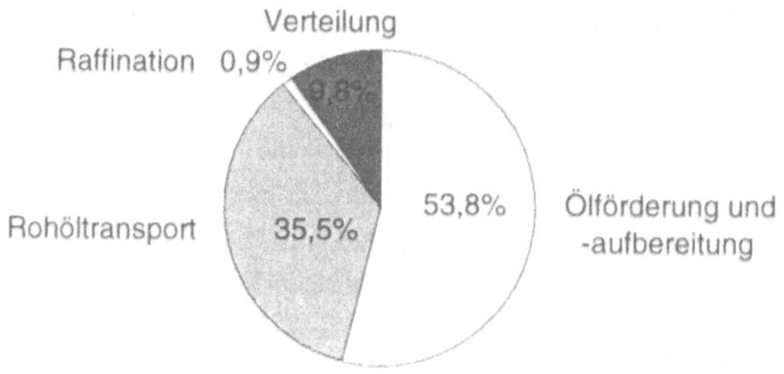

OK 2 (humantoxisch relevant)

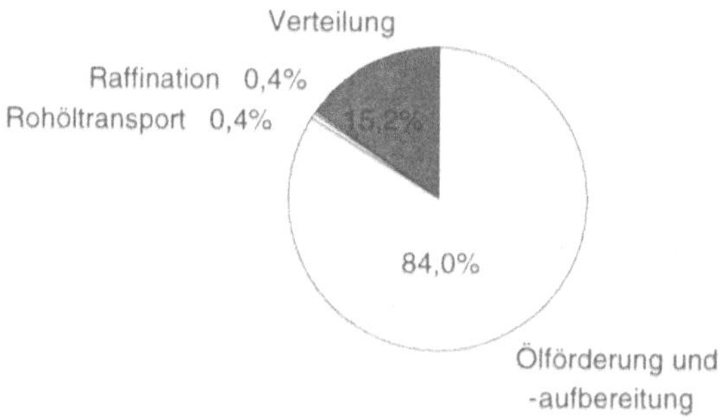

OK 3 (humantoxisch irrelevant)

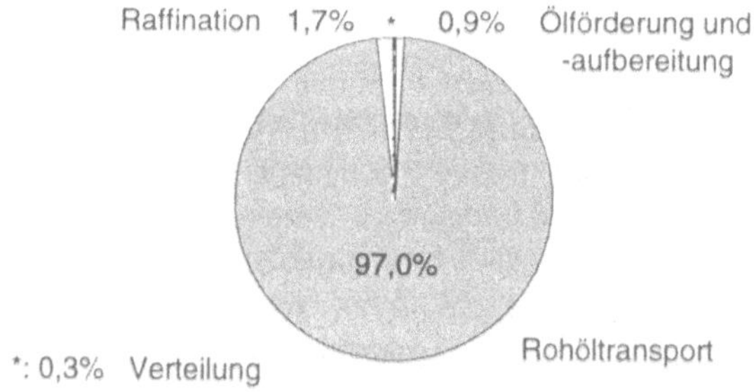

Abb. 1-5 Anteile der einzelnen Lebenswegabschnitte an den gesamten Partikelemissionen der Bereitstellung von Dieselkraftstoff frei Abnehmer differenziert nach Ortsklassen (OK); Anteile an Gesamt: OK 2: 63,7 %; OK 3: 36,3 %; eigene Berechnungen

Im Kontrast zur Umweltrelevanz des Einsatzes von Nutzfahrzeugen steht die vergleichsweise gering entwickelte Datenbasis. Einige wesentliche Probleme sind:

- Für heute als wichtig betrachtete Parameter, die über Energieverbrauch und „klassische" Schadstoffe hinausgehen, sind oft (noch) keine Daten verfügbar.
- Die Primär(Meß)datenbasis ist extrem schmal.
- Die räumlichen und/oder zeitlichen Bezüge verfügbarer Daten sind oft unklar oder für die zu untersuchenden Fragestellungen nicht oder nur bedingt geeignet.
- Die Differenzierungstiefe etwa nach Einsatzarten einer bestimmten Maschine ist in praktisch allen angesprochenen Bereichen unzureichend.

Diese Defizite zumindest ansatzweise zu beseitigen, ist das Ziel des vorliegenden Buches. Dazu werden spezifische Verbrauchs- und Emissionsdaten des Einsatzes von Nutzfahrzeugen abgeleitet, die

- konsistent mit einem einheitlichen funktionalen, sachlichen, räumlichen und zeitlichen Bezug,
- aktuell mit Bezug auf das Jahr 1996 und – wo dies sinnvoll und möglich ist – fortgeschrieben auf das Jahr 2000,
- repräsentativ für Deutschland,
- detailliert, insbesondere für LKW und Landmaschinen,
- umfassend, insbesondere für den Bereich der Luftschadstoffe hinsichtlich aller gängigen in Ökobilanzen betrachteten Umweltwirkungskategorien, und
- jeweils nach Ortsklassen differenziert

sind.

Neben dem Energieverbrauch und den Emissionen des Maschineneinsatzes selbst wird die Bereitstellung der verwendeten Energieträger – Kraftstoffe und Strom – erfaßt. Mit Rapsöl und RME werden auch regenerative Kraftstoffe berücksichtigt. Nicht betrachtet werden die Bereitstellung von Hilfs- und Betriebsstoffen wie Additiven und Schmierstoffen, der Maschinen selbst sowie die Aufwendungen für Bau, Unterhalt und Rückbau der Infrastruktur wie etwa Straßen und Gebäude.

Der Detaillierungsgrad und die Differenzierungstiefe der abgeleiteten Daten wächst mit dem Umfang und der Verläßlichkeit der verfügbaren Primärinformationen. Letztere hängen in der Regel von der ökonomischen und/oder der mutmaßlichen ökologischen Bedeutung der Maschinen ab. – Beispiele: Für den LKW-Transport, durch den fast zwei Drittel des gesamten Transportvolumens abgewickelt werden, können differenziertere und detailliertere Datensätze abgeleitet werden als für den Bahntransport. Für den Maschineneinsatz im Bergbau ist die Datenbasis deutlich schwächer als für den LKW-Transport, die Differenzierungstiefe auf der Ergebnisebene ist geringer.

Insgesamt gilt gleichwohl, daß für alle betrachteten Bereiche – Transport, Landwirtschaft, Bergbau – Daten abgeleitet werden, die detaillierter und belastbarer als das bisher vorliegende Material sind. Unter dem Aspekt „Detaillierung und Differenzierung" halten wir vor allem zwei methodische Ansätze bereits an dieser Stelle für erwähnenswert:

- Für die maschinelle Feldarbeit wird eine Methode zur differenzierten Erfassung einzelner Arbeitsgänge und – innerhalb dieser – einzelner Arbeitsschritte beschrieben. Zur Illustration des Verfahrens werden die Maschineneinsätze bei Anbau und Ernte wichtiger Feldfrüchte in Deutschland bilanziert; die Ergebnisse können direkt für weitergehende Bilanzierungen übernommen werden.

- Mit dem in /IFEU 1996b/ erstmals vorgestellten, hier detailliert beschriebenen und angewendeten Konzept der Ortsklassen ist es möglich, Emissionen in Ökobilanzen zumindest näherungsweise differenziert nach Wirkungsorten zu erfassen. Damit wird eine stärker an potentiellen ökologischen Wirkungen ausgerichtete und damit „realistischere" Bewertung möglich als im Falle der üblichen Summation aller Emissionen eines Schadstoffes über alle Orte.

Die Daten eignen sich sowohl für detaillierte Ökobilanzen komplexer Lebenswege als auch für andere ökologische Bilanzierungsinstrumente, insbesondere auch für Schwachstellenanalysen. Darüber hinaus können sie – wie bereits mit anderen Aggregationen und Bezugsgrößen für einige Basisdaten geschehen – in quasi makroskopischen Anwendungen in Energie- und Emissionsbilanzen, von Staaten etwa, eingesetzt werden.

2 Ökologische Bewertungsinstrumente

In diesem Kapitel wird der Rahmen dargestellt, in dem die vorgelegten Basisdaten angewendet werden können. Dazu werden verschiedene Bilanzierungsmethoden kurz besprochen und die Ökobilanzmethode ausführlich dargestellt.

2.1 Übersicht

In den sechziger Jahren wurden die ersten ökologischen Bewertungskonzepte entwickelt und ihre Anwendung zum Teil bereits seit den siebziger Jahren auch gesetzlich vorgeschrieben. Dazu gehören etwa das Environmental Impact Assessment (Umweltverträglichkeitsprüfung, UVP) auf gesetzlicher Basis in den USA oder die Schaffung einer Behörde zur Technikfolgenabschätzung beim amerikanischen Kongreß. In der Europäischen Union und in Deutschland wurden solche Maßnahmen erst in den späten achtziger Jahren begonnen. In der EU ist inzwischen eine UVP bei der Errichtung vieler Produktionsstätten und Anlagen Pflicht und es gilt eine Öko-Audit-Verordnung, nach der sich Betriebe – freiwillig – zertifizieren lassen können. Mit dem Technical Committee 207 der International Standardization Organisation (ISO) besteht eine private, weltweit tätige Organisation zur Standardisierung von Umweltbewertungs- und -managementinstrumenten. Die Ergebnisse der Arbeiten dieses Kommitees werden in Standards der sogenannten ISO 14.000-Familie zusammengefaßt. In der Bundesrepublik arbeitet der „Normenausschuß Grundlagen des Umweltschutzes" des Deutschen Instituts für Normierung (DIN-NAGUS) auf diesem Gebiet.

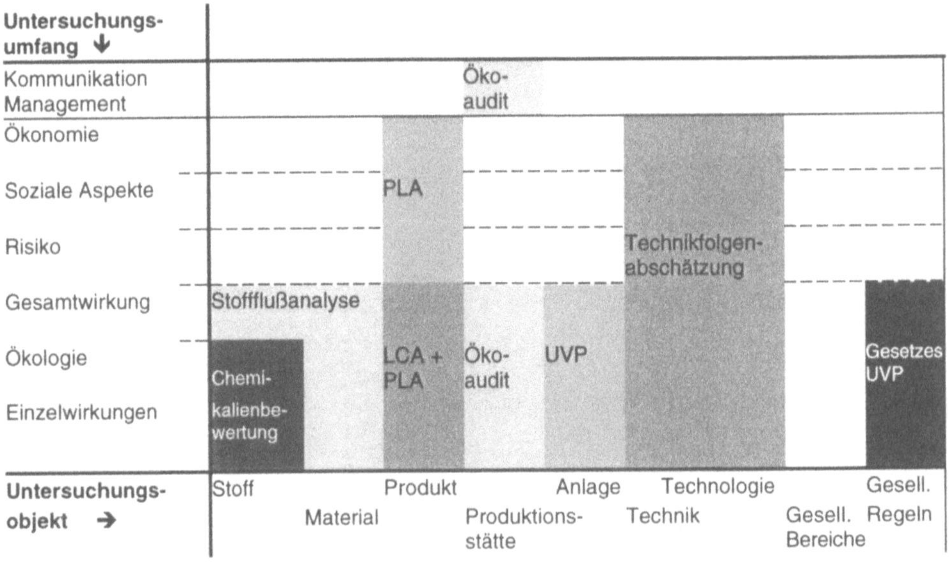

Abb. 2-1 Übersicht über verschiedene Umweltbewertungsinstrumente nach /IFEU 1994a/

Im Laufe der letzten Jahre wurde eine Vielzahl an Umweltbewertungsinstrumenten entwikkelt, die in der Regel für unterschiedliche Fragestellungen, unterschiedliche Untersuchungsobjekte bzw. einen unterschiedlichen Untersuchungsumfang konzipiert wurden. Inhaltliche Überschneidungen ließen sich dabei nicht vermeiden. Außerdem werden mit einigen Instrumenten nicht nur ökologische, sondern auch ökonomische und/oder soziale Aspekte aufgenommen. **Abb. 2-1** gibt eine Übersicht über den Untersuchungsumfang und die Untersuchungsobjekte einiger wichtiger ausgewählter ökologischer Bewertungsinstrumente.

Im folgenden wird nicht auf alle aufgeführten Umweltbewertungsinstrumente näher eingegangen, sondern nur auf solche, die in einem direkten Zusammenhang mit Ressourcen- und Emissionsbilanzen, die den Gegenstand dieses Buches bilden, stehen. Im einzelnen handelt es sich hierbei um die Technikfolgenabschätzung, die Produkt-Ökobilanz, die Produktlinienanalyse und das Öko-Audit. Eine ausführliche Darstellung auch der übrigen Verfahren findet sich in /IFEU 1994a/.

- **Technikfolgenabschätzung (TA):** Eine inzwischen knapp dreißigjährige Erfahrung mit Arbeiten zur TA besteht in den USA und teilweise auch in der Bundesrepublik. Die TA kann man als Bewertungsrahmen verstehen, da die Regelung allgemeiner Rahmenbedingungen zur Bewertung eines komplexen Sachverhaltes vorgenommen wird, ohne dabei Festlegungen im Detail zu treffen /IFEU 1994a/. Die TA bezieht in ihren Bewertungsumfang technische, ökologische, ökonomische, rechtliche und soziale Aspekte mit ein. Untersuchungsobjekte können bestimmte, eng begrenzte Techniken oder umfassend definierte Technologien sein. Da die TA deshalb auch im Vorfeld konkreter Umsetzungen, Anlagen, Maßnahmen oder Projekte angesiedelt ist, benötigt sie besondere Methoden der Prognose- und Szenarienbildung, um die abstrakten Fragestellungen handhabbar zu machen /RAKOS et al. 1988/, /JÖRISSEN et al. 1988/, /VDI 1992/.

  Eine Standardisierung TA-spezifischer Instrumente besteht nicht und wird auch nicht angestrebt, da sie aufgrund der Vielfalt der Fragestellungen nicht sinnvoll erscheint. Vielleicht aus diesem Grund hat sich statt dessen im TA-Bereich eine Art Institutionalisierung entwickelt, z. B. in Form von Beratungsbüros, die bei Regierungen und Parlamenten angesiedelt sind, wie etwa das ehemalige OTA in den USA, das TAB in der Bundesrepublik und NOTA in den Niederlanden (OTA: Office of Technology Assessment, TAB: Büro für Technikfolgenabschätzung beim Deutschen Bundestag, NOTA: Netherland Office of Technology Assessment).

- **Produkt-Ökobilanz:** Unter der Produkt-Ökobilanz wird die Bewertung eines Produktes hinsichtlich seiner Auswirkungen auf die Umwelt und die menschliche Gesundheit verstanden. Sie hat den Anspruch einer gesamtökologischen Bewertung; andere Aspekte werden nicht berücksichtigt. Dabei wird der gesamte Lebensweg des Produktes von der Rohstoffgewinnung über die Produktion und Nutzungsphase bis zur Entsorgung in die Untersuchung einbezogen und mit einem spezifischen Produktnutzen korreliert /PG LEBENSWEGBILANZEN 1992/, /SETAC 1993/. Deshalb heißt dieses Instrument im angelsächsischen Sprachraum auch Life Cycle Assessment (LCA). Untersuchungsobjekt sind Produkte, die einen Produktnutzen oder eine Dienstleistung repräsentieren.

  Zum jetzigen Zeitpunkt stellt die Produkt-Ökobilanz tendenziell eher noch einen Bewertungsrahmen dar. Jedoch sind sowohl national als auch international vielfältige Bemühungen zur Standardisierung dieses Instruments im Gange (ISO und DIN haben Normungsausschüsse gebildet). Mit zunehmender Anzahl verbindlicher Beschlüsse dieser Gremien bewegt sich die Ökobilanz von einem programmatischen Instrument auf ein konkretes Bewertungsverfahren zu. Dies führt zu einer weit höheren Verbindlichkeit der Bewertung und einer besseren Einschätzbarkeit der Ergebnisse. Details dazu finden sich in Kapitel 2.2.

- **Produktlinienanalyse:** Die Produktlinienanalyse wurde ebenfalls zur Bewertung von Produkten geschaffen. Der Begriff „Produkt" ist dabei sehr weit gefaßt und beinhaltet unter anderem auch Dienstleistungen oder eine Kombination aus Produkten und Dienstleistungen. Die Bewertungskriterien, die zwingend in einer Produktlinienanalyse zu betrachten sind, umfassen die ökologischen, ökonomischen und gesellschaftlichen Auswirkungen eines Produktes und seiner Produktion. Damit ist dieser Ansatz wesentlich breiter als andere Instrumente der Produktbewertung angelegt und ähnelt am ehesten der Technikfolgenabschätzung.

  Spezielle Forderungen an eine Produktlinienanalyse sind nach /RUBIK et al. 1987/:

  - Die Bedürfnisse und der Nutzen, die mit einem Produkt verbunden sind, sollen hinterfragt werden.
  - Alternativen zu dem Produkt sollen untersucht werden; dies können z. B. die Nullvariante, andere Verhaltensweisen, Dienstleistungen oder Produkte sein.
  - Der gesamte Produktlebensweg ist Untersuchungsgegenstand: Rohstoffgewinnung, Herstellung, Distribution, Gebrauch und Entsorgung. Auch Kuppelprodukte sind zu berücksichtigen.

  In der Produktlinienanalyse wird deutlich gemacht, daß dieses Instrument Prozeßcharakter hat. Während der Bearbeitung können das Planungsziel, die untersuchten Varianten, der Bilanzraum und andere Bestimmungsgrößen geändert werden.

- **Öko-Audit:** Das Öko-Audit in der EU ist ein Instrument des betrieblichen Umweltschutzes, das den Aufbau von Umweltmanagementsystemen und umweltbezogenen Controllingsystemen in Unternehmen umfaßt und damit auch eine Bewertung der betrieblichen Umweltwirkungen einschließt. Die Einführung des Öko-Audits ist freiwillig; bei erfolgreicher Teilnahme an einem Prüfungssystem wird ein wettbewerbswirksames Zertifikat ausgestellt. Die Anforderungen an die teilnehmenden Unternehmen sind in /EMAS 1993/ festgelegt; ein ähnliches Regelwerk wird zur Zeit durch die ISO erarbeitet.

  Das Umweltmanagementsystem soll die Einbeziehung von Umweltschutzanforderungen auf allen Entscheidungs- und Umsetzungsebenen sicherstellen, indem umweltrelevante Abläufe konkretisiert und Zuständigkeiten für umweltbezogene Aufgaben festgelegt werden. Da Umweltschutz im Betrieb nicht ohne die Mitwirkung der Mitarbeiterinnen und Mitarbeiter umgesetzt werden kann, ist durch Schulungen, Information usw. für die Motivation und Qualifikation der Beschäftigten zu sorgen. Gleichzeitig wird, ähnlich wie im betriebswirtschaftlichen Bereich, ein Controllingsystem eingeführt, das der Steuerung des betrieblichen Handelns unter Umweltgesichtspunkten dient: Die Unternehmen definieren Umweltleitlinien, Umweltziele und Maßnahmenprogramme und ermitteln in regelmäßigen Umweltbetriebsprüfungen, ob die selbst gesetzten Ziele erreicht werden konnten. Dafür sind geeignete Instrumente zur Erfassung und Bewertung der betrieblichen Umweltwirkungen notwendig. Welche Informations- und Analyseinstrumente zu diesem

Zweck eingesetzt werden, bleibt dem Unternehmen überlassen. In der Praxis variiert die Qualität der Datenerhebung und -bewertung stark: Während sich manche Unternehmen mit einer vereinfachten Input-Output-Analyse begnügen, nutzen andere Unternehmen umfassende Informationsinstrumente wie Ökobilanzen oder Stoffstromanalysen /FRINGS 1995/. Eine allgemeingültige Bewertungsprogrammatik gibt es bislang nicht, allerdings werden derzeit durch DIN-NAGUS und ISO geeignete Kennzahlen zum Vergleich der Umweltwirkungen zwischen verschiedenen Betrieben bzw. innerhalb eines Betriebes über eine Zeitreihe erarbeitet.

Neben den positiven Effekten auf die Umwelt hat das Öko-Audit im Zusammenhang mit Produkt-Ökobilanzen einen weiteren Vorteil: Die regelmäßige Erfassung und Bewertung von Umweltwirkungen – dabei spielen insbesondere auch Energie- und Emissionsbilanzen eine große Rolle – führt zu einer größeren Transparenz in den Betrieben und läßt auf eine verbesserte Datenverfügbarkeit für die Bilanzierung von Umweltwirkungen auch durch Produkt-Ökobilanzen hoffen. Außerdem ist die Zertifizierung auf eine ständige Weiterentwicklung und Verbesserung des Umweltschutzes hin angelegt.

Aus der Beschreibung dieser Umweltbewertungsinstrumente wird klar, daß für alle beschriebenen Verfahren Energie- und Emissionsbilanzen zu erstellen sind. Das heißt, Ressourcen- und Stoffstromanalysen können bzw. sollten sich an den für diese Bewertungsinstrumente aufgestellten Regeln oder Bilanzierungsvorschriften orientieren, damit sie in diesen Instrumenten Verwendung finden können. Von den genannten Umweltbewertungsinstrumenten ist die Ökobilanz bisher am weitesten entwickelt. Hier existieren die meisten Vereinbarungen, strukturelle und methodische Elemente sind zum Teil festgelegt oder es gibt Regeln, wie diese festzulegen sind. Darüber hinaus ist die Ökobilanz als Bewertungsinstrument schon weitgehend anerkannt; dies ist bei den anderen Bewertungsinstrumenten nur teilweise der Fall. Daher orientieren wir uns bei den hier beschriebenen Ableitungen von Basisdaten zur Ressourcen- und Emissionsbilanzierung an den Anforderungen der Ökobilanz-Methodik.

2.2 Spezialfall Ökobilanz

Wie erwähnt, bestehen bereits einige grundlegende, international abgestimmte Regeln zur Vorgehensweise bei der Erstellung von Produkt-Ökobilanzen; dies gilt beispielsweise für die Forderungen nach einer ausführlichen Beschreibung der Zieldefinition oder der Betrachtung der gesamten Lebenswege der Produkte von der Wiege bis zur Bahre („from cradle to grave"). Andere Elemente werden derzeit noch in der Bundesrepublik innerhalb des nationalen DIN-NAGUS-Ausschusses sowie international im Rahmen von länderübergreifenden ISO-Aktivitäten diskutiert. Dazu gehören z. B. die Fragen, wie Biodiversität zu bilanzieren ist und welche Bewertungsverfahren angewendet werden können oder sollten. Für derartige, gegenwärtig noch nicht geregelte Punkte ist nach heutigem Verständnis im Einzelfall zu beschreiben, warum welche Vorgehensweise gewählt wird. Damit sind Abweichungen von einer nicht vollständig bestimmten Standardmethode oder Ergänzungen durchaus möglich – bei einer entsprechenden Begründung. Insofern muß lediglich sichergestellt sein, daß ein sachgerechter Abgleich zwischen der Fragestellung des Themas und dem gewählten Bewertungskonzept stattfindet und die gesamte Methodik des gewählten Instruments durchgängig zum Einsatz kommt.

Im folgenden werden die Elemente einer Ökobilanz kurz skizziert. Insbesondere wird dargestellt, inwieweit das ökologische Bewertungsinstrument „Produkt-Ökobilanz" zur Beantwortung einer Fragestellung verwendet werden kann bzw. in welchen Punkten von dieser Vorgehensweise abgewichen wird und welche ökologischen Bilanzierungsinstrumente bzw. -ansätze statt dessen herangezogen werden.

Die Arbeitsschritte einer Produkt-Ökobilanz wurden erstmals von einem Workshop der SETAC definiert /SETAC 1991/. Seither wird von der ISO unter Einbindung einer Reihe von Vorschlägen verschiedener Expertengruppen /CML & TNO & B&G 1992/, /UBA 1992/, /SETAC 1993/, /DIN 1994/, /UBA 1995a/, /NORD 1995/ diese Standardmethodik weiterentwickelt. Sie ist inzwischen international verabschiedet und auch als europäische und deutsche Norm übernommen worden /DIN EN ISO 1997/.

Die in **Abb. 2-2** dargestellte Vorgehensweise zur Erstellung einer Ökobilanz ist durch die Unterteilung in vier Phasen gekennzeichnet. Zunächst werden das Bilanzierungsziel und die Rahmenannahmen festgelegt. Danach wird eine Sachbilanz erstellt, an die sich die Wirkungsabschätzung anschließt. Aufbauend auf der Wirkungsabschätzung erfolgt abschließend die Auswertung. Dabei ist zur Zeit noch umstritten, ob der bisher als Bewertung bezeichnete Teilschritt zur Wirkungsabschätzung oder zur Auswertung zu zählen ist. Hierbei handelt es sich allerdings nicht um eine streng konsekutiv anzuwendende Vorgehensweise; vielmehr werden die einzelnen Bilanzierungsschritte jeweils durch die anderen Schritte vor- bzw. mitbestimmt. Diese vier Einzelschritte werden im folgenden erläutert.

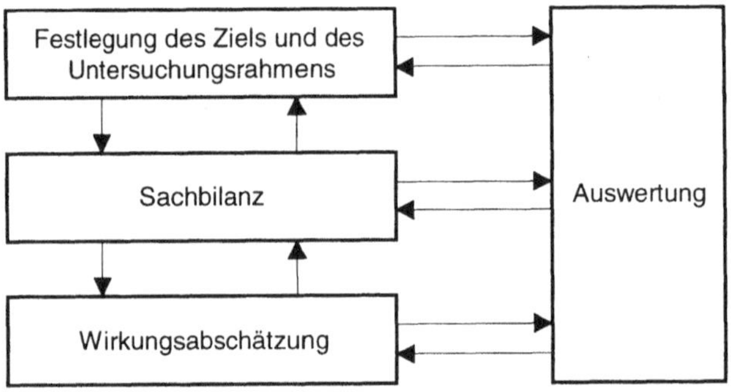

Abb. 2-2 Bestandteile einer Produkt-Ökobilanz nach /DIN EN ISO 1997/

2.2.1 Festlegung des Ziels und Untersuchungsrahmens

Dem ersten Schritt, der „Festlegung des Ziels und Untersuchungsrahmens", kommt eine Schlüsselstellung zu, da hier alle für die Bilanzierung wesentlichen und notwendigen Merkmale festgelegt werden. Dazu gehören z. B. die Festlegung der gesamten Lebenswege sowie Rahmenannahmen über geographische und zeitliche Systemgrenzen. Ebenso werden in diesem Schritt die umweltrelevanten Kenngrößen, ihre Aspekte und Rahmenbedingungen ausgewählt. Damit besteht die Ziel- und Rahmenfestlegung ihrerseits aus mehreren Teilschritten.

Die grundlegende Bedeutung einer möglichst präzisen Beschreibung der Ziel- und Rahmenfestlegung ist mittlerweile anerkannt. Die Zieldefinition soll gewährleisten, daß nicht an wichtigen Fragestellungen „vorbei" bilanziert wird und alle Beteiligten von der gleichen Sache sprechen. Die Rahmenfestlegung wiederum gibt Aufschluß über alle notwendigen Informationen zur Charakterisierung einer speziellen Ökobilanz.

Sowohl die grundlegende Struktur als auch die einzelnen Bestandteile der „Festlegung des Ziels und Untersuchungsrahmens" ist mittlerweile national wie international fast vollständig abgestimmt. Die entsprechende ISO-Norm 14041 /DIN EN ISO 1998/ ist 1998 in Kraft getreten. Auf der Basis dieser Norm sind in **Tabelle 2-1** die Bestandteile der Ziel- und Rahmenfestlegung aufgelistet. Sie sind hier in acht Teilschritte unterteilt, die sich in zahlreichen Anwendungsfällen bewährt haben und in großer Übereinstimmung mit den Anforderungsprofilen der einzelnen Normierungsgremien stehen /IFEU 1996a/.

Tabelle 2-1 Teilschritte bei der Festlegung des Ziels und Untersuchungsrahmens

1.	Hintergrund der Studie
2.	Ziel der Ökobilanz
3.	Anwender und Zielgruppen der Ökobilanz
4.	Allgemeine Informationen über die Ökobilanzstudie
5.	Allgemeine Beschreibung der Bilanzierungsobjekte/-optionen
6.	Allgemeine Systemannahmen
7.	Detaillierungsgrad
8.	Auswahl der Wirkungskategorien und der zur Wirkungsabschätzung und Auswertung verwendeten Methoden*

Quelle: /IFEU 1996a/; *: aktualisiert nach /DIN EN ISO 1998/

Entsprechend dem allgemeinen Anforderungsprofil für die „Festlegung des Ziels und Untersuchungsrahmens" sind deren einzelne Bestandteile jeweils gesondert und möglichst präzise darzustellen. Sinn und Inhalt lassen sich allgemein wie folgt beschreiben:

- **Hintergrund der Studie:** Hier werden Informationen zum Erkenntnisinteresse und zur möglichen Verwendung der Ergebnisse gegeben.
- **Ziel der Ökobilanz:** Mit dieser Festlegung soll eine einheitliche Verständigungsgrundlage geschaffen werden. Hier wird das eigentliche Erkenntnisinteresse einer Studie formuliert.
- **Anwender und Zielgruppen der Ökobilanz:** Die Wahl der Adressaten beeinflußt die Art und Weise, wie die Ökobilanz durchgeführt wird.
- **Allgemeine Informationen über die Ökobilanzstudie:** Hier erfolgen unter anderem die Dokumentation beteiligter Institutionen und Personen und Festlegungen, die in irgendeiner Weise Einfluß auf Form und Inhalt des Ökobilanz-Projektes haben. Beispiele: Projektleiter und -bearbeiter, Förderinstitution/Auftraggeber, Zeitplan, Vertraulichkeit, Einbindung eines wissenschaftlichen Begleitprozesses.
- **Allgemeine Beschreibung der Bilanzierungsobjekte/-optionen:** Diese Definitionen dienen dazu, zu vermeiden, daß verschiedene Personen sich auf das gleiche Produkt oder die gleiche Dienstleistung beziehen, aber eigentlich unterschiedliches meinen.

- **Allgemeine Systemannahmen:** Diese grundlegenden Annahmen bilden die Voraussetzung für die realistische und zielführende Abbildung der Grundstruktur des zu untersuchenden Produktlebensweges. Sie üben häufig einen entscheidenden Einfluß auf die Ergebnisse aus; deshalb sind die wichtigsten, potentiell ergebnisbestimmenden Annahmen bereits am Beginn eines Ökobilanz-Projektes zu treffen und mit den eventuell Betroffenen bzw. einem Expertengremium zu diskutieren und abzustimmen. Unter diese Annahmen fallen z. B. die zeitlichen und räumlichen Systemgrenzen oder auch die Abschneidekriterien, die bestimmen, ab wann was nicht mehr betrachtet wird.
- **Detaillierungsgrad:** Hier wird die Differenzierungstiefe der Analyse beschrieben. Aussagen dazu sind Hilfsmittel zur besseren Einschätzung der Erwartungen an die Ergebnisse der Ökobilanz.
- **Auswahl der Wirkungskategorien und der zur Wirkungsabschätzung und Auswertung verwendeten Methoden:** Festlegungen dazu sind von grundlegender Bedeutung für alle folgenden Phasen der Ökobilanz. Konkret beziehen sich die Festlegungen unter anderem darauf, wie die Größen quantifizierbarer Parameter des untersuchten Systems mit bestimmten Umweltauswirkungen in Zusammenhang gebracht werden können.

Die „Allgemeinen Systemannahmen" und die „Auswahl der Wirkungskategorien und der zur Wirkungsabschätzung und Auswertung verwendeten Methoden" werden wegen ihrer besonderen Bedeutung für die später abgeleiteten Basisdaten in Exkursen detailliert behandelt (Kapitel 2.3 und 2.4).

2.2.2 Sachbilanz

Die Sachbilanz folgt als zweiter Schritt auf die Zieldefinition und Rahmenfestlegung. Sie ist das technische Herzstück einer Ökobilanz. Die Sachbilanz unterteilt sich in mehrere Einzelschritte (**Tabelle 2-2**), die im Regelfall konsekutiv ausgeführt werden.

Tabelle 2-2 Teilschritte der Sachbilanz nach /DIN EN ISO 1998/

1	Vorbereitung der Datensammlung
2	Datensammlung
3	Berechnungsverfahren
3.1	Datenvalidierung
3.2	Bezug der Daten auf ein Modul
3.3	Bezug der Daten auf eine funktionale Einheit und Datenzusammenfassung
3.4	Verbesserung der Systemgrenzen
4	Auswertung der Ergebnisse der Sachbilanz

Im wesentlichen handelt es sich um das Sammeln und Aufbereiten der spezifischen Lebenswegdaten des Untersuchungsobjektes entsprechend den Vorgaben der Zieldefinition und Rahmenannahmen. Hierzu muß der gesamte Lebensweg des betrachteten Produktes bzw. Systems zuerst beschrieben und modelliert werden. Anschließend werden die benötigten Daten erhoben, um daraus die In- und Output-Ströme für das gesamte System oder – wenn gewünscht bzw. notwendig – bestimmter Untersysteme zu berechnen. Die hier diskutierten Ressourcen- und Emissionsdaten sind somit eine wesentliche Grundlage der Sachbilanz.

Ungeklärt ist zur Zeit noch, ob der letzte Unterpunkt „Interpretation und Präsentation" weiterhin ein Teilschritt der Sachbilanz bleibt oder in die vierte Phase der Produkt-Ökobilanz, die Auswertung, zu verlegen ist.

2.2.3 Wirkungsabschätzung

Im dritten Schritt der Produkt-Ökobilanz, der Wirkungsabschätzung, werden die betrachteten Sachbilanzparameter in Umweltwirkungen übertragen. Dies ist in allen Fällen notwendig, in denen die Grenze der Interpretation auf Sachbilanzebene erreicht ist, d. h., wenn ein Optionenvergleich ein uneinheitliches Bild bezüglich der betrachteten Input- und Outputparameter zeigt. Diese Situation findet man in den meisten Fällen, so daß der Schritt der Wirkungsabschätzung im Regelfall durchgeführt wird.

Nach der /DIN EN ISO 1999a/ wird die Wirkungsabschätzung in folgende, verbindlich zu berücksichtigende Teilschritte gegliedert:

- **Auswahl von Wirkungskategorien:** Sie erfolgt bereits in der ersten Phase der Produkt-Ökobilanz „Festlegung des Ziels und Untersuchungsrahmens"; Beispiel: Treibhauseffekt.
- **Klassifizierung:** Zuordnung von Sachbilanzergebnissen zu Wirkungskategorien; Beispiel: Festlegung der zu betrachtenden klimarelevanten Stoffe, deren Emissionen dann als Sachbilanzparameter zu erfassen sind.
- **Charakterisierung:** Zusammenführung der in der Klassifizerung festgelegten Größen z. B. über geeignete Äquivalenzfaktoren; Beispiel: CO_2-Äquivalente.

Die einzelnen Teilschritte gliedern sich wiederum in Unterpunkte, die Vorgehensweisen, Annahmen und Konventionen zum Gegenstand haben. Zusätzlich existieren optional zu behandelnde Bestandteile, die im Rahmen dieses Buches jedoch keine Rolle spielen.

In diesem Buch wird eine Wirkungsabschätzung, aufbauend auf den Sachbilanzergebnissen, zum Teil durchgeführt. Welche Wirkungskategorien im einzelnen betrachtet werden, wird in Kapitel 4 festgelegt.

2.2.4 Auswertung

Der letzte Schritt der Produkt-Ökobilanz ist entsprechend /DIN EN ISO 1999b/ die eigentliche Auswertung bzw. Interpretation. Hierbei werden die in der Sachbilanz und Wirkungsabschätzung erhaltenen Ergebnisse zu einem Gesamturteil zusammengeführt. Hierzu wurde in der Vergangenheit eine Reihe unterschiedlicher Bewertungskonzepte entwickelt. Bisher hat sich allerdings keines dieser Verfahren als alleine gültig erwiesen. Derzeit werden daher verschiedene Bewertungsverfahren – jeweils für verschiedene Randbedingungen – diskutiert und angewandt. Diese Diskussion spielt hier allerdings keine Rolle, da keine Bilanzen erstellt, sondern lediglich Basisdaten *für* ihre Erstellung abgeleitet werden.

2.3 Exkurs: „Allgemeine Systemannahmen“ in Ökobilanzen

Unter die allgemeinen Systemannahmen fallen verschiedene Bilanzierungskriterien und -para-meter sowie Rand- und Rahmenbedingungen, die einen entscheidenden Einfluß auf die Grundstruktur der Bilanz, die Art und Weise der Bilanzierung und damit letztlich auch auf die Gesamtergebnisse ausüben. Im folgenden werden dazu einige, im Hinblick auf die Bilanzierung von Gütertransporten, maschinellen Feldarbeiten und des Einsatzes von Bergbaumaschinen pragmatisch gewählte Systemannahmen im einzelnen dargestellt.

2.3.1 Funktionale Einheit/Bezugsgröße

Die funktionale Einheit beschreibt die Menge eines Produktes, auf die sich die Ökobilanz dieses Produktes bezieht. Wie der Begriff erkennen läßt, steht dabei die Funktion und damit der Nutzen im Vordergrund; dies ist vor allem in vergleichenden Bilanzen sehr wichtig. Zumindest wenn keine Vergleiche angestellt werden, bieten sich als funktionale Einheiten Massen- oder Energieeinheiten an. In diesen Fällen ist allerdings die Bezeichnung „Bezugsgröße“ anschaulicher.

2.3.2 Untersuchungsoptionen/Lebenswege

Prinzipiell sollen die gesamten Lebenswege der betrachteten Produkte von der Förderung der verwendeten Rohstoffe über die Produktion und Nutzung bis zur Entsorgung einschließlich aller Transportprozesse, der Energiebereitstellung, den dazwischen liegenden Einzelprozessen usw. erfaßt werden.

2.3.3 Systemgrenzen der Lebenswege

Für die Erstellung von Produkt-Ökobilanzen ist die Festschreibung von Lebensweggrenzen unumgänglich. Die Notwendigkeit der Grenzziehung hat hierbei verschiedene Ursachen.

Bilanzierungstiefe

Das Problem der Bilanzierungstiefe soll an einem Beispiel aus dem Lebensweg eines Agrarproduktes illustriert werden: Die Landmaschinen, deren Kraftstoffverbrauch und Emissionen bei die Erstellung des Produktes erfaßt werden, werden in Montagehallen mit Werkzeugmaschinen produziert. Die Hallen werden aus Stahl, Beton und Glas mit Maschineneinsatz gebaut, die Werkzeugmaschinen aus Metallen und Kunststoffen in anderen Hallen unter Einsatz anderer Maschinen. Für jede Montagehalle und jede Maschine müssen aus Rohstoffen erzeugte Werkstoffe bereitgestellt werden. Offensichtlich sind hier noch keineswegs sämtliche Ebenen erfaßt. Die konsequente Weiterführung würde quasi zu einem Weltmodell führen, in dem die Umweltauswirkungen jedes Lebenswegabschnittes auf einen bestimmten Arbeitsschritt anteilig abgeschrieben werden müßten. Dies ist – sowohl aus Gründen der Datenverfügbarkeit wie des enormen Rechenaufwandes – natürlich nicht realisierbar. Um das ganze Problem lösbar zu gestalten, muß daher irgendwo im Laufe der betrachteten Lebenswege „abgeschnitten“ werden.

Bislang bestehen keine festen Regeln zur Anwendung bestimmter Systemgrenzen bis auf die Grundregel, „von der Wiege bis zur Bahre“ des betrachteten Produktes zu bilanzieren. Danach ist der Lebensweg mindestens von der Entnahme der Rohstoffe aus der Umwelt, die in das Produkt selbst eingehen, bis zur Entsorgung des Produktes zu untersuchen. Somit bleiben viele weitere Abschneidekriterien zur Lebenswegabgrenzung offen. Diese sind aus Gründen der Nachvollziehbarkeit, Transparenz und einer einfacheren Handhabung im einzelnen zu benennen.

Eine weit verbreitete Abgrenzung ist der Ausschluß der Infrastruktur aus dem Bilanzraum – im obigen Beispiel der Montagehallen und Werkzeugmaschinen aller Produktionsebenen, aber auch der Landmaschinen selbst, in allgemeinerer Form: Gebäude, Maschinen, Industrieanlagen, Transportmittel und Verkehrswege.

Kuppelprodukte und Abfälle

Bei vielen Prozessen fallen neben den Hauptprodukten auch Nebenprodukte, sogenannte Kuppelprodukte, sowie Abfälle zur Verwertung bzw. zur Beseitigung an. So bleibt nach dem Abpressen von Rapsöl der proteinhaltige Rapskuchen übrig, der als Futtermittel importiertes Sojaschrot ersetzen kann. Und die Umesterung liefert nicht nur Rapsölmethylester, sondern auch Glyzerin, das in der chemischen Industrie Verwendung findet.

Für die bilanztechnische Behandlung von Kuppelprodukten und Abfällen in Produkt-Ökobilanzen gibt es unterschiedliche Verfahren. In einigen Fällen herrscht Konsens über die durchzuführende Vorgehensweise, in anderen Fällen, die aus methodischer Sicht nicht eindeutig lösbar sind, muß der Bilanzierer „seine“ Vorgehensweise beschreiben und begründen. Folgende Vorgehensweisen sind gebräuchlich /IFEU 1993a, b/, /VDI 1997/:

- **Abfälle zur Beseitigung:** Die Beseitigung von Abfällen verursacht Umweltauswirkungen. Diese werden den Kuppelprodukten des entsprechenden Prozesses zugerechnet, der diese Abfälle verursacht hat (siehe unten).
- **Abfälle zur Verwertung:** Hierfür gibt es eine Reihe unterschiedlicher Vorgehensweisen, die hier nicht näher erläutert werden, da sie für die hier betrachteten Prozesse keine Rolle spielen; eine detaillierte Beschreibung findet sich in /IFEU 1993a/. Wesentliche Zurechnungsverfahren werden im nächsten Punkt beschrieben.
- **Zurechnungsmethoden:** Die Umweltauswirkungen, die mit der Produktion aller Kuppelprodukte bzw. mit der Beseitigung oder Verwertung von Abfällen verbunden sind, sind den einzelnen Kuppelprodukten nach bestimmten Zuordnungsvorschriften zuzuordnen. Für die Aufteilung der Umweltauswirkungen auf die verschiedenen Kuppelprodukte haben sich zwei voneinander grundsätzlich verschiedene Verfahren etabliert:
    - **Allokationsverfahren:** Darunter werden Aufteilungsverfahren verstanden, bei denen nach einem bestimmten Verteilungsschlüssel die entstandenen Umweltauswirkungen den einzelnen Kuppelprodukten zugeordnet werden. Als Verteilungsschlüssel können z. B. Energieinhalte, Massen oder auch Marktpreise der Kuppelprodukte herangezogen werden.
    - **Gutschriftsverfahren:** In den Fällen, in denen die neben dem eigentlich betrachteten Produkt zusätzlich entstehenden Kuppelprodukte gleichartige Produkte aus anderen Produktionslinien substituieren (können), werden die mit diesen Produktionslinien ver-

bundenen Umweltauswirkungen vermieden. Diese Umweltauswirkungen werden im negativen wie im positiven Sinn dem betrachteten Produkt gutgeschrieben; man bezeichnet dieses Vorgehen als Äquivalenzprozeßbilanzierung. Als Basis für die Äquivalenzprozesse dient die Nutzengleichheit des betrachteten sowie des substituierbaren Produktes, z. B. Rapskuchen und Sojaschrot als Futtermittel.

Von diesen beiden Möglichkeiten soll vorrangig die Äquivalenzprozeßbilanzierung zur Anwendung kommen. Unter dem Aspekt einer möglichst realitätsnahen Abbildung soll die Äquivalenzprozeßbilanzierung nach dem „realen Substitutionsprinzip“ durchgeführt werden – sofern dies realisierbar ist (siehe dazu /REINHARDT 1993/). Das heißt, bei mehreren Möglichkeiten der Herstellung der anfallenden Kuppelprodukte soll derjenige Herstellungsprozeß als Äquivalenzprozeß betrachtet werden, der nach derzeitiger Kenntnis der wahrscheinlichste ist. Andere Prozesse können zur Abschätzung des Einflusses des gewählten Äquivalenzprozesses auf die Ergebnisse zusätzlich betrachtet werden.

Es gibt Fälle, in denen eine Äquivalenzprozeßbilanzierung nicht durchgeführt werden kann, da es keine entsprechenden Äquivalenzprozesse gibt. In solchen Fällen wird auf andere Bemessungsgrößen bzw. die Allokationsverfahren zugegriffen, die dem realen Substitutionsprinzip möglichst nahe kommen. Das können wirtschaftliche, energetische oder andere physikalische Größen sein. Die konkrete Wahl ist gesondert zu begründen.

Darüber hinaus kann aus pragmatischen Gründen von der Äquivalenzprozeßbilanzierung abgewichen werden, etwa wenn dadurch mögliche rechentechnische Vereinfachungen mit absehbar nur geringen Informationsverlusten verbunden sind.

Ob anfallende Stoffe als Kuppelprodukte bzw. als Abfälle betrachtet werden, hängt von den jeweiligen Gegebenheiten ab (Nutzung oder Entsorgung) und kann sich ändern. Die Verwendung, also Nutzung im Sinne eines Kuppelproduktes, von Stoffen, die bisher als zu entsorgende Abfälle betrachtet werden, wirft die Frage auf, ob diese überhaupt mit anteiligen Umweltauswirkungen belegt bzw. ob eine Gutschrift für die vermiedene Entsorgung vorgenommen werden muß. Spätestens zu dem Zeitpunkt, wo veränderte wirtschaftliche Strukturen dazu führen, daß sie von vornherein nicht mehr als Abfall, sondern als Wertstoff und damit als Kuppelprodukt angesehen werden, müssen sie wie alle anderen Kuppelprodukte behandelt werden und dementsprechend mit den Umweltauswirkungen der Produktion anteilig belastet werden.

2.3.4 Geographische und zeitliche Systemgrenzen

Die Festlegung räumlicher und zeitlicher Bezüge ist erforderlich, da die Mehrzahl technischer Prozesse in verschiedenen Ländern und Jahren unterschiedlich realisiert werden und damit mit unterschiedlichen Umweltauswirkungen verbunden sind. Dies gilt gleichermaßen für Prozesse die üblicherweise in Ökobilanzen über Mittelwerte erfaßt werden, wie etwa die Bereitstellung von Endenergieträgern, wie auch für Prozesse, die im Zentrum einer Ökobilanz stehen.

In der Praxis ist infolge von Mängeln der Datenbasis häufig die Verwendung von Daten mit anderen Bezugsräumen bzw. -zeiten als den für die Studie festgelegten unvermeidlich. Die Abweichungen sollten dokumentiert und begründet werden.

2.4 Exkurs: „Auswahl der Wirkungskategorien und der zur Wirkungsabschätzung und Auswertung verwendeten Methoden" in Ökobilanzen

Unter „Auswahl der Wirkungskategorien und der zur Wirkungsabschätzung und Auswertung verwendeten Methoden" versteht man unter anderem die Festlegung, welche Umweltauswirkungen überhaupt in Ökobilanzen zu betrachten sind, und die Zuordnung dieser Wirkungen zu bestimmten, mit dem Lebensweg des betrachteten Bilanzgegenstands verbundenen physikalischen Parametern.

Über die Ökobilanzphasen „Wirkungsabschätzung" und „Auswertung" sollen die Ergebnisse der Sachbilanz einer abschließenden ökologischen Bewertung zugeführt werden. Umgekehrt müssen natürlich zuvor in der Sachbilanz die für die Wirkungsabschätzung relevanten Parameter erfaßt worden sein. Daher muß bereits vor Beginn der Sachbilanzierung geklärt sein, welche Wirkungen berücksichtigt werden sollen. Für die Bewertung stehen eine Reihe von Methoden mit teilweise beträchtlichen Unterschieden in der Vorgehensweise zur Verfügung. Den methodischen Unterschieden entsprechend weichen auch die Ergebnisse zum Teil erheblich voneinander ab. Zu einer national bzw. international konsensfähigen Standardisierung ist es bislang noch nicht gekommen. Zumindest hinsichtlich der zu erfassenden Wirkungskategorien bestehen jedoch Ansätze zu einer Einigung.

Die folgende Darstellung von Kriterien zur Wirkungsabschätzung, den Wirkungskategorien, lehnt sich an den aktuellen Diskussionsstand des Unterausschusses „Wirkungsabschätzung und Bewertung" des DIN-NAGUS an /DIN 1995/. Dieser wiederum orientiert sich grob an der vorgeschlagenen Vorgehensweise nach /ISO 1995/ und /SETAC 1993/. Die in Teil II dieses Buches dokumentierten Basisdaten für Ressourcen- und Emissionsbilanzen aus Gütertransporten, maschineller Feldarbeit und dem Maschineneinsatz im Bergbau sind methodisch am aktuellen Stand der Bemühungen um Ökobilanznormierungen ausgerichtet, um einen möglichst großen Konsens über die erzielten Ergebnisse zu schaffen. **Tabelle 2-3** faßt die diskutierte Standardliste der Wirkungskategorien des DIN-NAGUS zusammen /DIN 1995/.

Tabelle 2-3 Standardliste der Umweltwirkungskategorien

1.	Ressourcenverbrauch
2.	Naturraumbeanspruchung
3.	Treibhauseffekt
4.	Abbau der Ozonschicht
5.	Versauerung
6.	Eutrophierung
7.	Ökotoxizität (Toxische Schädigung von Organismen)
8.	Humantoxizität (Toxische Schädigung von Menschen)
9.	Photosmog (Sommersmog)
10.	Lärmbelastung

Quelle: /DIN 1995/

Das Umweltbundesamt (UBA) erstellte eine Standardliste der Wirkungskategorien, die die Liste des DIN-NAGUS praktisch komplett einschließt und darüber hinaus folgende Kategorien enthält:

- allgemeine Risiken wie Transportunfälle und Störfallrisiken
- elektromagnetische Strahlungen verschiedener Frequenzbereiche und radioaktive Strahlung
- sonstige Belästigungen für Mensch, Pflanze und Tier wie Geruch, Lärm und Licht

Im folgenden werden die einzelnen Wirkungsindikatoren der Standardliste und die den Wirkungskategorien zugeordneten Sachbilanzparameter diskutiert. Auf diese Darstellung wird in Kapitel 4.2 im Zusammenhang mit den in diesem Buch erfaßten Parametern zurückgegriffen. Die Darstellung in diesem Kapitel soll eine möglichst allgemeine Grundlage liefern. Auf die später behandelten Prozesse wird daher im wesentlichen nur in einzelnen Beispielen Bezug genommen. Eine Abweichung von diesem Grundsatz besteht lediglich darin, daß auf die ausführliche Darstellung von Gewässerbelastungen durch die Einleitung von Abwasser im Kontext der Wirkungskategorien Eutrophierung und Human- und Ökotoxizität verzichtet wird. Dies ist darin begründet, daß mangels einer hinreichenden Datengrundlage die direkte Gewässerbelastung aus dem Einsatz von Nutzfahrzeugen nicht erfaßt werden konnte.

2.4.1 Ressourcenverbrauch

Den Hintergrund der Wirkungskategorie Ressourcenverbrauch bildet die grundsätzliche Begrenztheit von Rohstoffen. Unter Ressourcen werden dabei im Prinzip alle denkbaren Einsatzstoffe verstanden. Diese können z. B. Energieträger oder mineralische Rohstoffe, Wasser oder Naturraum sein. Eine Zuordnung zu einzelnen Ressourcenkategorien ist zwar hilfreich, aber nicht immer eindeutig. So wird etwa Erdgas sowohl als Energieträger (Heizgas), aber auch als Prozeßgas zur Mineraldüngemittelproduktion eingesetzt. Nach /UBA 1995a/ und /IFEU 1997b/ lassen sich in einer pragmatischen Einteilung folgende Ressourcenkategorien ableiten:

- **Ressource Energie:** Unter dieser Ressource werden fossile und regenerative Energieträger sowie das erschöpfliche Uranerz verstanden.
- **Mineralische Ressourcen:** Dazu zählen Rohstoffe wie Sand zur Glasproduktion, Phosphaterz und Schwefel zur Phosphatdüngerproduktion oder Eisenerz.
- **Ressource Naturraum:** Was unter dieser Ressource genau zu verstehen ist und wie sie ggf. bilanziert wird, wird derzeit in nationalen und internationalen Normierungsgremien diskutiert. Die Ideen reichen von einer Aufsummierung der einzelnen Flächengrößen bis hin zu unterschiedlichen Bewertungskategorien unterschiedlicher Flächen. Derzeit gibt es keine allgemein akzeptierte Vorgehensweise zur Bilanzierung des Naturraums.

Für die Ressource Naturraum verweisen wir auf die Ausführungen zur Wirkungskategorie Naturraumbeanspruchung. Die beiden anderen Ressourcenkategorien werden hier behandelt.

Energie

Energieträger bzw. ihre Energieinhalte werden – je nach Umwandlungsgrad – in unterschiedliche Kategorien eingeteilt, von denen jedoch nur die beiden im folgenden erstgenannten im eigentlichen Sinne Ressourcen-Charakter haben.

- **Naturenergie:** Energieinhalt der in der Natur, d. h. in Lagerstätten, vorliegenden Energieträger. Zur Überführung in Primärenergie müssen diese gefördert bzw. abgebaut werden.
- **Primärenergie:** Energieinhalt von Energieträgern, die noch keiner energetischen Umwandlung unterworfen, eventuell aber aufbereitet wurden. Hierzu zählt beispielsweise (aufbereitetes) Rohöl.
- **Sekundärenergie:** Energieinhalt von Energieträgern, die aus der Umwandlung von Primärenergieträgern (z. B. Ottokraftstoff oder Heizöl aus Rohöl, Uran aus Uranerz) oder aus anderen Sekundärenergieträgern (z. B. Strom aus Uran oder Heizöl) gewonnen werden.
- **Bezugsenergie:** Energieinhalt aller Energieträger, die der Verbraucher bezieht; dabei handelt es sich im wesentlichen um Sekundärenergie vermindert um Transportverluste (Netzverluste beim Stromtransport, Energieeinsatz zum Transport von Kraftstoffen von der Raffinerie zur Tankstelle usw.).
- **Endenergie:** Energieinhalt der vom Verbraucher verwendeten Energieträger; dies ist im wesentlichen die Bezugsenergie abzüglich des nicht energetischen Verbrauchs wie z. B. der Umfüllverluste bei Kraftstoffen.
- **Nutzenergie:** der Anteil der Energie, der nach der letzten energetischen Umwandlung dem Verbraucher zur Verfügung steht, z. B. als Licht, Wärme oder mechanische Arbeit.

Häufig erfaßte Energiekategorien sind der End- und der Primärenergieeinsatz. Die Bilanzierung der Primärenergieträger erfolgt dabei auf der Basis des ermittelten Endenergieträgereinsatzes. Für die fossilen Energieträger geschieht dies durch die Verknüpfung der Endenergieeinsätze mit den tatsächlichen Wirkungsgraden. Für die nicht fossilen Energieträger, also die regenerativen Energien und die Kernkraft, gibt es kein naturwissenschaftlich eindeutiges Verfahren der primärenergetischen Bewertung. Für die Ableitung der hier auftretenden Primärenergieäquivalente wurden mehrere Verfahren, die alle gewisse Vor- und Nachteile bzw. Inkonsistenzen aufweisen, entwickelt und in Bilanzen angewandt. Dazu zählen insbesondere folgende Ansätze.

- **Substitutionsmethode:** Hier wird der mittlere Wirkungsgrad der öffentlichen, mit fossilen Brennstoffen betriebenen Kraftwerke den regenerativen Energien angerechnet, da diese fossile Brennstoffe substituieren.
- **Äquivalenzmethode:** Hierbei finden derzeit zwei Zurechnungsvarianten Verwendung: Beim energieäquivalenten Ansatz beträgt der Wirkungsgrad 100 %. Beim zweiten wird der tatsächliche physikalische Wirkungsgrad der Energieumwandlungsanlagen (Wasserkraftwerk, Windkraftanlage, Solarmodul usw.) als Umrechnungsfaktor verwendet. Danach werden z. B. für Wasserkraft 85 %, für Windkraft 21 % und für Photovoltaik 8 % angesetzt (siehe dazu z. B. /MAUCH 1996/).

- **Ressourcenmethode:** Hier wird ausschließlich die Ausbeutung von Ressourcen als Bewertungskriterium herangezogen. Die regenerativen Energien werden demnach effektiv mit Null, die Kernenergie jedoch – entsprechend der Substitutionsmethode – mit einem Wirkungsgrad von 33 % bewertet (siehe dazu z. B. /AGE 1995/).

Aus diesen verschiedenen Möglichkeiten der Zurechnungsverfahren hat sich in der Bundesrepublik eine Konvention entwickelt, die inzwischen in vielen Produkt-Ökobilanzen und vor allem Energiebilanzen angewandt wird (siehe dazu /AGE 1995/, /MAUCH 1996/, /VDI 1997/). Danach gilt folgendes Verfahren:

- **Kernkraft:** Der primärenergetische Wirkungsgrad der Kernkraft wird entsprechend dem Substitutionsprinzip mit 33 % festgelegt.
- **Biomasse:** Die in der Biomasse letztlich enthaltene Sonnenenergie wird mit dem Energieinhalt der Biomasse bewertet. Zugrunde gelegt wird der Heizwert der tatsächlich „vom Feld" abtransportierten Biomasse.
- **Sonstige regenerative Energieträger:** Alle anderen regenerativen Energieträger werden mit einem primärenergetischen Wirkungsgrad von 100 % bewertet.

Offensichtlich unterscheiden sich diese Verfahren zum Teil beträchtlich voneinander, wirken sich in ihren Ergebnissen aber nur dann signifikant aus, wenn große Anteile nicht fossiler Energieträger in den Bilanzen auftreten.

Aggregation

Die Aggregation der Ressource Energie kann – auf der Basis von Primärenergie oder Primärenergieäquivalenten – unterschiedlich erfolgen. Die Unterschiede der einzelnen Konzepte bestehen im wesentlichen darin, ob – und wenn: wie – die Wertigkeit der einzelnen Primärenergieträger zueinander berücksichtigt wird. Unter dem Gesichtspunkt einer Erfassung aller Primärenergieträger bei der Aggregation stehen die beiden folgenden Konzepte im Vordergrund der Diskussion:

- Summe der Energieinhalte aller Primärenergieträger in Energieeinheiten; siehe dazu auch das Konzept des kumulierten Energieaufwandes (KEA) /VDI 1997/
- Summe der Energieinhalte als Arbeitsäquivalente aller Primärenergieträger in Energieeinheiten; siehe dazu /IFEU 1993b/

Während die erste Aggregationsmethode anschaulicher ist und so oder in Variationen in der Regel angewandt wird, ermöglicht der zweite Weg eine methodisch plausiblere Aggregation so unterschiedlicher Energieträger wie Wasserkraft und Kernenergie.

Sollen nur fossile Energieträger berücksichtigt werden, kann ein vom Umweltbundesamt entwickelter Berechnungsansatz auf der Basis von Erdöläquivalenzwerten Verwendung finden /UBA 1995a/. Als Berechnungsgrundlage dienen die statischen Reichweiten der betrachteten fossilen Energieträger, also Erdöl, Stein- bzw. Braunkohle und/oder Erdgas, unter Zugrundelegung der Weltreserven und des aktuellen Verbrauchs. Dieser Ansatz ist allerdings nicht unumstritten, da als Bewertungsgrundlage vornehmlich ökonomische Kenngrößen Berücksichtigung finden.

Nach einem anderen Ansatz wird in einer wachsenden Zahl von Ökobilanzen die Summe der Energieinhalte aller *erschöpflichen* Primärenergieträger in Energieeinheiten gewählt, also die Summe über die verschiedenen fossilen Energieträger und die primärenergetisch bewertete Kernenergie (siehe dazu z. B. /KALTSCHMITT & REINHARDT 1997/). Werden allerdings keine Lebenswegvergleiche, sondern lediglich Bilanzen für Einzelprodukte oder Dienstleistungen erstellt, so ist – neben der Auflistung aller einzelnen Energieträger – die Summe über alle Energieträger im Sinne des kumulierten Energieaufwandes (KEA) ebenso sinnvoll.

Die im Zusammenhang mit der Emission von Schadstoffen unter Umständen relevante Unterscheidung nach verschiedenen Orten und Zeiten spielt für den Verbrauch der Ressource Energie wie auch für den Verbrauch mineralischer Ressourcen keine Rolle.

Mineralische Ressourcen

Die zu bilanzierenden mineralischen Ressourcen ergeben sich aus den Grundstoffen zur Herstellung der betrachteten Produkte bzw. wichtiger Hilfsstoffe. Ähnlich den Energieträgern könnte eine Unterteilung in Rohstoffe in der Lagerstätte, geförderte Rohstoffe und aufbereitete Rohstoffe vorgenommen werden. Als festes Schema ist diese Unterteilung jedoch unüblich.

Die Bilanzierung der mineralischen Rohstoffe erfolgt auf der Basis des ermittelten Stoffeinsatzes der Produktionsprozesse. Dazu wird der Stoffeinsatz mit den Anteilen der tatsächlich stofflich genutzten Bestandteile der Rohstoffe, wie sie in der Lagerstätte vorliegen, verknüpft.

Aggregation

Anders als im Falle der Ressource Energie sind Aggregationen häufig nicht sinnvoll, da sie eine – zumindest ansatzweise – wechselseitige Ersetzbarkeit der einzelnen eingesetzten Ressourcen voraussetzen. Ein Beispiel für eine sinnvolle Aggregation ist die Zusammenfassung der verschiedenen schwefelhaltigen Ressourcen, die bei der Produktion von Schwefelsäure eingesetzt werden.

2.4.2 Naturraumbeanspruchung

Zu einer sinnvollen Bewertung der Ressource Fläche bedarf es der Einbeziehung einer Reihe unterschiedlicher Einzelfaktoren, die allerdings oftmals miteinander gekoppelt sind. Dazu sind beispielsweise Kenntnisse notwendig über den gegenwärtigen und zukünftigen Boden, sein ökologisches Potential, seinen biologischen Wert (einschließlich Biodiversität), seine physikalischen und/oder chemischen Eigenschaften (insbesondere bodenökologische Funktionen). Ferner ist unter Umständen die Einbeziehung angrenzender Flächen notwendig, von denen die Funktionsfähigkeit und damit auch der Wert einer betrachteten Fläche stark abhängen.

Im Rahmen der Ökobilanz-Methodik gibt es derzeit noch kein in sich schlüssiges Konzept zur Bewertung der Naturraumbeanspruchung. Einigkeit herrscht aber darüber, daß die Qualität des flächenbezogenen Naturraums und auch die Dauer, in der diese Qualität besteht, in die Wirkungsabschätzung mit einzubeziehen sind. In der Diskussion, wie dies geschehen könnte, hat insbesondere das Hemerobiekonzept nach /KLÖPFER & RENNER 1994/, das momentan als die aussichtsreichste methodische Basis für die Behandlung dieser Fragestellung gilt /IFEU 1996a/, große Bedeutung. Gerade unter dem Aspekt der landwirtschaftlichen Produktion von Pflanzen scheinen die Vielfalt der Pflanzen und Tiere, die genetische und Biotopvielfalt als Bewertungskriterien ebenso wichtig wie das vollständige Funktionieren von Biozönosen. In dieser Vielschichtigkeit wurde dies im Hemerobieansatz jedoch noch nicht präzisiert.

2.4.3 Treibhauseffekt

Unter der Wirkungskategorie Treibhauseffekt ist genauer der zusätzliche, vom Menschen verursachte (anthropogene) Treibhauseffekt zu verstehen. Die Notwendigkeit seiner Berücksichtigung in Produkt-Ökobilanzen ist unumstritten. Der anthropogene Treibhauseffekt wird durch die Emissionen klimawirksamer Spurengase bzw. deren Vorläufersubstanzen verursacht (direkt bzw. indirekt wirksame Emissionen). Zu den direkt klimawirksamen Spurengasen zählen im wesentlichen

- Kohlendioxid (CO_2),
- Methan (CH_4),
- Distickstoffoxid (N_2O, Trivialname: Lachgas),
- Wasserdampf,
- nahezu alle teil- und vollhalogenierten Fluorchlorkohlenwasserstoffe (FCKW; in der Natur nicht vorkommende, ausschließlich vom Menschen produzierte Verbindungen) sowie
- einige persistente Chlorkohlenwasserstoffe (CKW).

Die indirekt wirkenden Stoffe sind dagegen erst nach chemischen Umwandlungsprozessen innerhalb der Troposphäre klimawirksam. Zu diesen zählen kohlenstoffhaltige Verbindungen wie beispielsweise Kohlenmonoxid (CO) oder Kohlenwasserstoffe, die zu CO_2 als klimawirksamer Verbindung oxidiert werden. Andere indirekt wirksame Stoffe bilden unter bestimmten Voraussetzungen in komplizierten photochemischen Reaktionsmechanismen troposphärisches Ozon, das ebenfalls stark klimawirksam ist. Zu diesen sogenannten Vorläufersubstanzen zählen insbesondere Stickoxide (NO_X) und Kohlenwasserstoffe.

Aggregation

Für die Wirksamkeit der Emissionen von Schadstoffen können Ort und Zeit der Emissionen von Bedeutung sein. Für die wichtigsten klimarelevanten Schadstoffe gilt dies jedoch nur in geringem Maße. Durch die langen mittleren atmosphärischen Verweilzeiten der Gase findet eine globale Durchmischung statt; sie sind daher auch bei zeitlich leicht versetzten Emissionen in etwa gleich klimawirksam. Bei der Bilanzierung wird daher – unter dem Aspekt der Klimawirksamkeit – üblicherweise eine Aggregation über alle Emissionsorte und -zeiten vorgenommen.

Die Klimawirksamkeit einzelner Stoffe wird mit sogenannten GWP-Werten (Global Warming Potential) angegeben. Diese Faktoren bezeichnen die Menge CO_2, der eine äquivalente Klimawirksamkeit zugeschrieben wird (**Tabelle 4-7**). Die Produkte aus den GWP-Werten und der Schadstoffmenge ergeben die sogenannten CO_2-Äquivalente. Die Summe der CO_2-

Äquivalente beschreibt damit die gesamte Klimawirksamkeit der Emissionen des betrachteten Prozesses oder Systems.

Da der GWP-Wert ein Maß für die zeitlich integrierte Wirkung eines Stoffes relativ zu CO_2 darstellt, geht bei der Bestimmung der Umrechnungsfaktoren auf CO_2-Äquivalente die mittlere atmosphärische Verweildauer des Stoffes ein. Daher muß ein Zeithorizont gewählt werden, für den der Vergleich mit CO_2 gelten soll. Üblich sind GWP-Werte für Zeiträume von 20, 100 und 500 Jahren. Derzeit gängige Praxis in zahlreichen nationalen und internationalen Klimabilanzen ist die Berechnung der CO_2-Äquivalente für einen Integrationszeitraum von 100 Jahren. In **Tabelle 2-4** sind die Treibhauspotentiale ausgewählter Spurengase für verschiedene Zeithorizonte zusammengestellt. Die unterschiedliche Klimawirksamkeit eines Stoffes bei verschiedenen Integrationszeiträumen unter sonst gleichen Bedingungen ergibt sich aus den sehr verschiedenen atmosphärischen Lebensdauern der Gase. Besonders deutlich wird dies aus den Werten der halogenierten Kohlenwasserstoffe.

Tabelle 2-4 Treibhauspotential ausgewählter Spurengase für verschiedene Zeithorizonte

Substanz	Formel	Lebensdauer	Treibhauspotential bei Zeithorizont ...		
			20 Jahre	100 Jahre	500 Jahre
		Jahre	kg CO_2/kg	kg CO_2/kg	kg CO_2/kg
Kohlendioxid	CO_2	variabel	1	1	1
Distickstoffoxid	N_2O	120	280	310	170
Methan	CH_4	12,3	56	21	6,5
Schwefelhexafluorid	SF_6	3.200	16.300	23.900	34.900
FCKW 23	CHF_3	264	9.100	11.700	9.800
FCKW 32	CH_2F_2	5,6	2.100	650	200
FCKW 41	CH_3F	3,7	490	150	45

Quelle: /IPCC 1996/

2.4.4 Ozonabbau

Ähnlich dem Treibhauseffekt hat sich auch der stratosphärische Ozonabbau als wichtige und handhabbare Wirkungskategorie bei Produkt-Ökobilanzen etabliert. Zum Ozonabbau tragen Stoffe bei, die entweder direkt in der Stratosphäre freigesetzt werden oder aufgrund ihrer hohen Persistenz in der Troposphäre in die Stratosphäre diffundieren und dort ozonzerstörend wirken. In die erste Gruppe fallen neben den als gering einzuschätzenden Raketenemissionen vor allem die Emissionen der zivilen und militärischen Luftfahrt oberhalb der Tropopause. Bei den Stoffen, die in der Nähe des Erdbodens emittiert werden und in die Stratosphäre diffundieren, handelt es sich im wesentlichen um N_2O, SF_6 sowie voll- oder teilhalogenierte Kohlenwasserstoffe.

Aggregation

Alle Stoffe, die für die Ozonschicht schädlich sind, sind in den unteren Atmosphärenschichten chemisch nicht reaktiv. Aufgrund ihrer langen Lebensdauern werden sie global durchmischt; daher können ihre Emissionen über alle Orte und Zeiten aggregiert werden. Für die Klassierung von Flugzeugabgasen, die wegen der Höhe ihrer Freisetzung eventuell auch zum Ozonabbau beitragen können, ist bisher noch kein Standardverfahren abgeleitet worden.

Analog den CO_2-Äquivalenten als Kriterium zur Bewertung der klimarelevanten Gase haben sich für den Ozonabbau in der Stratosphäre als Bewertungsgröße die sogenannten Ozonabbaupotentiale (ODP-Potentiale) etabliert. Als Referenzsubstanz dient Trichlorfluormethan (FCKW 11). Aus den relativen ODP-Potentialen und den Massen der ozonzerstörenden Substanzen werden die FCKW-Äquivalente bestimmt. ODP-Werte wurden bisher allerdings lediglich für eine Vielzahl an voll- und teilhalogenierten Kohlenwasserstoffen und Halonen bestimmt, nicht jedoch für N_2O.

2.4.5 Versauerung

Die Versauerung von Böden und Gewässern wird durch die Immission säurebildender Gase verursacht, die entweder durch trockene oder nasse Deposition (Saurer Regen) in Boden oder Gewässer eingetragen werden. Wichtige säurebildende Gase sind

- Schwefeldioxid (SO_2),
- Stickoxide (NO, NO_2),
- Chlorwasserstoff (HCl) und
- Ammoniak (NH_3).

Daneben können bei manchen Prozessen noch weitere Stoffe wie andere Schwefelverbindungen und Fluorwasserstoff eine Rolle spielen. Es ist zu erwägen, ob basische Stäube wegen ihrer puffernden Wirkung den säurebildenden Stoffen gegenzurechnen sind. Allerdings liegen keine Informationen über die Zusammensetzung der hier erfaßten Stäube vor, so daß auf eine entsprechende Anrechnung verzichtet werden muß.

Aggregation

Für die Emission von säurebildenden Schadstoffen ist die Aggregation über alle Emissionsorte und -zeiten üblich. Analog der Verwendung von Treibhauspotentialen und CO_2-Äquivalenten werden die Emissionen der einzelnen säurebildenden Gase über sogenannte Säurebildungspotentiale mit SO_2 als Referenzsubstanz aggregiert (**Tabelle 4-8**).

2.4.6 Eutrophierung

Unter Eutrophierung versteht man den übermäßigen Nährstoffeintrag in Böden und Gewässer. Für Böden stellt der über die Atmosphäre eingetragene Stickstoff in Form von biogen wie anthropogen emittierten Stickstoffverbindungen den weitaus größten Anteil am Gesamteintrag, wenn die Flächen nicht landwirtschaftlich genutzt werden. Für Gewässer spielt die Einleitung nitrat- und phosphathaltiger Abwässer eine große Rolle. In /UBA 1995b/ wurde vorgeschlagen, die eutrophierenden Stoffe über Äquivalentwerte relativ zu Phosphat zu aggregieren (**Tabelle 2-5**). Die Werte gelten für eine „durchschnittliche" Zusammensetzung der Biomasse und lassen das lokale Nährstoffangebot unberücksichtigt.

Tabelle 2-5 Eutrophierungspotentiale in Phosphatäquivalenten

Substanz	Äquivalentwert kg PO_4^{3-}/kg
NO_X	0,13
NO	*0,20*
NO_2	*0,13*
NH_4^+	0,33
N-Inventar	0,42
PO_4^{3-}	1,00
P-Inventar	3,06

Quelle: /UBA 1995b/

2.4.7 Human- und Ökotoxizität

Eine Vielzahl von Verbindungen weist human- und/oder ökotoxische Wirkungen auf. Art und Ausmaß der Wirkung eines bestimmten Stoffes sind für verschiedene Arten von Lebewesen natürlich unterschiedlich; ausschließliche Human- *oder* Ökotoxizität sind allerdings selten. Umgekehrt können verschiedene Stoffe zu gleichen oder zumindest sehr ähnlichen Wirkungen führen. Beispiele für die gleichzeitige Human- *und* Ökotoxizität sowie ähnliche Wirkungen verschiedener Stoffe sind die Luftschadstoffe Schwefeldioxid und die Stickoxide, die beim Menschen zu Atemwegsproblemen führen und zur Bildung des pflanzenschädigenden Sauren Regens beitragen.

Um eine differenzierte Bewertung durchzuführen, ist die Unterscheidung verschiedener Formen der Toxizität sinnvoll wie z. B. akute und organbezogene Toxizität, Geno- und Neurotoxizität, Kanzerogenität oder Teratogenität /NORD 1995/. Eine entsprechende Einteilung toxischer Stoffe in dieser Differenzierungstiefe ist aber umstritten /IFEU 1996a/. Andere Einteilungen etwa nach Wirkungen mit und ohne Schwellenwerten und die damit verbundenen Bewertungsmöglichkeiten im Rahmen von Produkt-Ökobilanzen wurden in der Vergangenheit heftig diskutiert. Bisher wurde noch keine Einigung auf ein Bewertungsverfahren erreicht, mit der Folge, daß derzeit auch auf Sachbilanzebene nicht eindeutig klar ist, welche Substanzen unter welchen Randbedingungen zu erfassen bzw. zu bilanzieren sind – natürlich abgesehen davon, daß die Maximalforderung einer Bilanzierung aller Schadstoffe erhoben werden kann. In der Praxis werden meist die durch gesetzliche Regelungen (Abgasgrenzwerte, TA-Luft, GFAVO usw.) sogenannten limitierten Schadstoffe bilanziert sowie Stoffe, die nach jeweils aktuellem Kenntnisstand zu negativen Wirkungen führen können.

Aggregation

Die Verweildauer und damit die Reichweite human- und ökotoxischer Schadstoffe in der Atmosphäre ist begrenzt. Daher ist der Wirkungsort mehr oder weniger eng an den Emissionsort gebunden. So macht es hinsichtlich des Ausmaßes der Wirkung einen Unterschied, ob z. B. Dieselpartikel auf hoher See oder in Ballungszentren freigesetzt werden. Ein Weg, diese Unterschiede zu berücksichtigen, ist die Differenzierung der Emissionen nach drei Ortsklassen unterschiedlicher Bevölkerungsdichte, die bereits in mehreren Ökobilanzen durchgeführt wurde /IFEU 1996b/, /KALTSCHMITT & REINHARDT 1997/. Damit ist es zumindest tendenziell – wenn auch sicherlich unter Vorbehalten – möglich, Aussagen hinsichtlich der Schadwirkungen zu treffen. Dieses Konzept wird in Kapitel 4.2.1 erstmals ausführlich beschrieben.

Auch der Zeitpunkt der Emission hat Einfluß auf Art und Intensität der Immissionen. Zu unterscheiden ist z. B. zwischen kontinuierlich, pulsartig oder periodisch anfallenden Emissionen (tags/nachts, sommers/winters usw.). Eine weitere Kenngröße, die die Art und Intensität der Immissionen beeinflußt, ist die Höhe des Emissionsortes über dem Boden: Je höher der Freisetzungsort ist, um so niedriger sind die bodennahen Immissionen. In Produkt-Ökobilanzen sind diese Differenzierungen bislang nicht üblich.

Die Aggregation verschiedener Schadstoffe ist – über alle human- und ökotoxischen Schadstoffe betrachtet – eher die Ausnahme. Probleme bestehen zum einen hinsichtlich der zu betrachtenden Formen toxischer Wirkung (siehe oben) und zum anderen bei der Ableitung von Dosis/Wirkung-Korrelationen. Zu den Ausnahmen gehören die polychlorierten Dibenzodioxine und -furane, die Nichtmethan-Kohlenwasserstoffe (NMHC) und die Stickoxide. Diese Ausnahmen sind allerdings nur zum Teil auf identischen oder zumindest sehr ähnlichen Wirkungen begründet; sie sind im wesentlichen aus pragmatischen Gründen üblich geworden, wie etwa dem des meßtechnischen Aufwandes.

- Insgesamt existieren 75 unterschiedliche polychlorierte Dibenzodioxine und 135 unterschiedliche polychlorierte Dibenzofurane mit jeweils sehr unterschiedlicher Toxizität /HEINTZ & REINHARDT 1996/. Bei Messungen dieser Substanzen hat es sich inzwischen eingebürgert, eine bestimmte Auswahl dieser Substanzen, die die Gesamtheit der Dioxine/Furane repräsentieren sollen, zu messen. Für diese wurden sogenannte Toxizitätsäquivalente (TÄ) mit Bezug auf 2,3,7,8-TCDD (Tetrachlor-p-dibenzodioxin) ermittelt bzw. abgeschätzt. Damit lassen sich die einzelnen gemessenen Dioxine/Furane zu 2,3,7,8-TCDD-Toxizitätsäquivalenten zusammenfassen.
- In den NMHC wird die Gesamtheit aller Kohlenwasserstoffe *ohne* Methan erfaßt. Die Aussagekraft dieses Bilanzierungsparameters ist nur gering, da Hunderte von Stoffen mit extrem unterschiedlichen Schadwirkungen zusammengefaßt werden. Die gemeinsame Erfassung hat meßtechnische Gründe, beruht also nicht auf einer rechnerischen Aggregation. Eine Differenzierung nach Einzelstoffen ist sehr aufwendig und wird meist nur dann durchgeführt, wenn Anlaß zu der Vermutung besteht, daß nach aktuellem Kenntnisstand besonders toxische Stoffe in größerem Umfang emittiert werden. Ein Beispiel sind die Benzolemissionen von KFZ.
- Die Stickoxide (NO_X) werden meist als Stickstoffdioxid (NO_2) ausgewiesen. Diese Aggregation ist hinsichtlich der Wirkungscharakteristik der Stickoxide unproblematisch.

2.4.8 Photosmog

Unter Photosmog (auch als Sommersmog bezeichnet) versteht man die verstärkte Bildung von Photooxidantien wie Ozon und Peroxiacetylnitrat (PAN) in bodennahen Luftschichten. Da diese Substanzen sehr reaktiv sind, wirken sie in erhöhten Konzentrationen human- und ökotoxisch. Die Photooxidantien entstehen unter Sonneneinstrahlung im wesentlichen aus ungesättigten Kohlenwasserstoffen und Stickoxiden. Die modellhafte Abbildung der dabei stattfindenden unterschiedlichen, meist sehr komplexen Reaktionen ist äußerst schwierig. Die bisher ermittelten Ozonbildungspotentiale zur Aggregation der potentiell ozonbildenden Substanzen sind in Fachkreisen noch umstritten. Mit der Erfassung der NMHC- und Stickoxidemissionen werden jedoch zumindest auf der Sachbilanzebene Daten gewonnen, die zu einem späteren Zeitpunkt bei Vorliegen abgesicherter Modellierungsansätze unter Wirkungsaspekten ausgewertet werden können. Für die Aussagekraft des Parameters NMHC gelten dabei natürlich auch hier die gleichen Einschränkungen wie im Zusammenhang der Wirkungskategorien Human- und Ökotoxizität.

2.4.9 Lärmbelastung

Lärm ist eine Umweltbelastung, die ortsgebunden auftritt und dementsprechend ortsabhängig bewertet werden muß. Dies steht zum Teil im Widerspruch zum systemanalytischen, d. h. im wesentlichen ortsunabhängigen Ansatz der Produkt-Ökobilanz. Diskutiert werden hier pragmatische Ansätze, die zumindest Anhaltspunkte über mögliche Lärmbelästigungen entlang der Lebenswege geben sollen. Zu diesen gehört z. B. die Erfassung der Fahrleistung von Lastkraftwagen (in km pro funktionale Einheit) in Ballungszentren bzw. auf Außerortsstraßen. Insgesamt ist die Bilanzierungsweise noch umstritten.

3 Primärdaten: Messung und Repräsentativität

Repräsentative – oder als repräsentativ definierte (!) – Daten zur Beschreibung technischer Systeme basieren in aller Regel auf einer mehr oder weniger begrenzten Anzahl einzelner Meßwerte, die nach einem geeigneten Verfahren ausgewertet wurden. Der Grund ist offensichtlich: Es ist finanziell und zeitlich nicht möglich, z. B. Energieverbrauch und Emissionen des Gesamtbestandes an LKW eines Landes über sämtliche Einsätze etwa eines Jahres zu erfassen, um mittlere spezifische Verbräuche und Emissionsfaktoren zu erhalten. Andererseits müssen alle relevanten Einflußgrößen berücksichtigt werden. Darunter fallen fahrzeugtechnische Eigenschaften, Einsatzarten und die Häufigkeit, mit der diese auftreten. Das heißt, die begrenzte Anzahl an Fahrzeugen, die tatsächlich vermessen werden kann, und die Betriebszustände, in denen die Messungen erfolgen, müssen möglichst realistisch ausgewählt werden. Der Begriff „realistisch" meint dabei, daß die Fahrzeuge und Betriebszustände möglichst große Anteile am zu beschreibenden „Realbetrieb" ausmachen. Repräsentative Werte auf verschiedenen Aggregationsebenen werden durch die Gewichtung der Meßwerte mit ihren Anteilen am Realbetrieb erhalten.

Im folgenden werden einige allgemeine Aspekte der Bestimmung von spezifischen Energieverbräuchen und Emissionsfaktoren von Nutzfahrzeugen diskutiert. Die im Detail jeweils unterschiedlichen Ableitungen für die einzelnen Transportmittel, Feld- und Bergbaumaschinen finden sich in den entsprechenden Kapiteln in Teil II dieses Buches.

3.1 Technische Einflußfaktoren

Repräsentative Daten werden durch geeignete Gewichtung von Daten für einzelne Maschinen gewonnen. Der Energieverbrauch und die Emissionen *einer* dieselbetriebenen Maschine pro Zeiteinheit werden durch eine Reihe von Faktoren bestimmt, die im folgenden kurz diskutiert werden.

Nennleistung: Der Einfluß der Nennleistung ist im wesentlichen selbsterklärend: Unter sonst völlig gleichen Bedingungen emittiert ein großer Motor mehr Schadstoffe als ein kleiner. Ein weiterer Effekt besteht allerdings darin, daß diese Relation auch theoretisch nicht einfach proportional ist. Aus physikalischen Gründen wie etwa der günstigeren Volumen/Oberflächen-Relation bei großen Motoren sind ihre Verbräuche und Emissionen bezogen auf die Nennleistung niedriger als bei kleinen Motoren.

Motorauslastung: Die Auslastung ist durch das Produkt aus Drehzahl und Drehmoment jeweils bezogen auf die Nennwerte gegeben. Der Verbrauch steigt mit der Last. Der spezifische Verbrauch bezogen auf die mechanische Arbeit sinkt allerdings. Anschaulich: Bei Vollast ist die Umwandlung von Dieselkraftstoff in mechanische Arbeit effizienter als bei leichter Last. Die Emissionen verhalten sich je nach Schadstoff deutlich anders. Die zeitbezogenen CO- und HC-Emissionen hängen nur wenig vom Lastzustand ab. Bei Bezug auf den Verbrauch sind die Emissionen damit im Leerlauf besonders hoch. NO_X verhält sich *tendenziell* umgekehrt.

Ein zentrales Problem der Messung von Energieverbrauch und Emissionen der später diskutierten Maschinen besteht darin, die Messungen bei geeigneten Lastzuständen durchzuführen bzw. diese zu lokalisieren.

Motorkonzept: Bei den hier betrachteten Dieselmotoren unterscheidet man zwischen Vorkammermotoren und Direkteinspritzern. Beide können als Saugmotoren oder mit Aufladung ausgelegt sein, die Aufladung kann mit oder ohne Ladeluftkühlung erfolgen. Das bei Nutzfahrzeugen dominierende Konzept ist der Direkteinspritzer, der mit zunehmender Nennleistung zunehmend mit Turbolader und dieser in gleicher Tendenz mit Ladeluftkühlung ausgestattet ist. Vorkammermotoren sind im Verbrauch ungünstiger als Direkteinspritzer, zeigen jedoch für NO_X ein günstigeres Emissionsverhalten. Aufladung mindert CO-, HC- und Partikelemissionen, während Ladeluftkühlung die NO_X-Emissionen mindert.

Entwicklungsstand: Dieser Faktor ist ebenfalls im wesentlichen selbsterklärend: Innerhalb der Geschichte eines Motorkonzeptes finden Fortschritte statt.

Alter: Durch Verschleiß ändern sich Verbrauch und Emissionen. Bei der weiter unten besprochenen Ableitung repräsentativer Daten bzw. in Bilanzierungen ist dabei zu berücksichtigen, daß die jährliche Nutzungszeit in der Regel mit zunehmendem Alter abnimmt.

Wartungszustand: Gut gewartete Maschinen haben in der Regel niedrigere Verbräuche als schlecht gewartete. Für die Emissionen, inbesondere von HC und Partikeln, gilt ähnliches.

Kraftstoffqualität: Dieselkraftstoffe enthalten etwa 300 verschiedene Kohlenwasserstoffe. Die Zusammensetzung beeinflußt die Höhe verschiedener Emissionen. Für die Partikelemissionen ist vor allem der Schwefelgehalt des Kraftstoffes von Bedeutung sowie der Anteil von höher substituierten Aromaten, Diaromaten und kondensierten Aromaten. In der Regel wird bei Emissionsmessungen die Kraftstoffzusammensetzung nicht analysiert oder näher dokumentiert, da sie sich innerhalb des DIN-Normbereichs bewegt (vergleiche **Tabelle 8-10** in Kapitel 8.2). Ausnahmen bilden spezielle Emissionsuntersuchungen mit unterschiedlichen Kraftstoffqualitäten bzw. -zusammensetzungen. Die Verwertung der meisten Arbeiten erfordert damit die Annahme, daß sie mit „typischen" Kraftstoffen durchgeführt wurden.

Für einen bestimmten räumlichen und zeitlichen Bezug repräsentative spezifische Energieverbräuche und Emissionsfaktoren werden aus Meßwerten, die in ihrer Gesamtheit die genannten Einflußfaktoren berücksichtigen, durch Gewichtung mit ihren Anteilen an der Gesamtbetriebszeit im Bezugszeitraum bestimmt. Bilanzen werden entsprechend mit den absoluten Nutzungszeiten abgeleitet. Um repräsentative Daten zu bestimmen, sind daher zusätzlich zu Verbrauchs- und Emissionsmessungen die Analyse von Beständen und die Erhebung von Nutzungszeiten bzw. Fahrleistungen erforderlich. Beides ist fast nur gestützt auf Stichproben, Zusatzannahmen und Näherungen möglich.

Damit bestehen für repräsentative Verbräuche und Emissionen Quellen erheblicher Unsicherheiten auf zwei Ebenen:

- Definition von Fahrzeugklassen, die die dargestellten Einflußfaktoren in angemessener Differenzierungstiefe berücksichtigen, und korrekte Auswahl zu vermessender Fahrzeuge entsprechend der Klasseneinteilung
- Bestimmung der Gewichtungsfaktoren mit Bezug auf die Zeit, Fahr-, Transport- oder Arbeitsleistung

Die Unsicherheiten können in gut abgestimmten und meist sehr aufwendigen Projekten, die z. B. Emissionsmessungen, Fahrleistungs- und Fahrmustererhebungen enthalten, minimiert, aber – trivial – nie ausgeschlossen werden. Aus Literaturauswertungen resultieren zum Teil extreme Bandbreiten. Für Maschinen im Bergbau wird dies in Kapitel 7 ausführlich dargestellt, da ihre Verbrauchs- und Emissionsdaten in diesem Buch erstmals aus verschiedenen Quellen zusammengestellt werden.

3.2 Test- und Realbetrieb

Die Messung von Emissionen ist oftmals mit erheblichem Aufwand verbunden. Die gleichzeitige Messung einer größeren Anzahl von Schadstoffen im Betrieb von Fahrzeugen und anderen mobilen Maschinen kann allenfalls in Ausnahmen realisiert werden. Das übliche Vorgehen besteht darin, im realen Betrieb Drehzahl und Drehmoment aufzunehmen und die Drehzahl/Drehmoment-Kombinationen gewichtet mit ihrer zeitlichen Häufigkeit bzw. Dauer zu repräsentativen Fahrzyklen oder Lastkollektiven zu aggregieren; diese werden zur Verbrauchs- und Emissionsbestimmung auf Rollen- und Motorprüfständen „nachgefahren". Aus den Meßwerten, die diese Tests liefern, können EDV-gestützt somit auch für nicht erfaßte „Fahrmuster" Daten abgeschätzt werden.

Der wesentliche Unterschied zwischen Fahrzyklen und Lastkollektiven besteht darin, daß in Lastkollektiven der Gesamtbetrieb durch eine relativ kleine Anzahl von stationären Betriebspunkten (definiert durch Drehzahl und Drehmoment) dargestellt wird. Änderungen des Betriebszustandes, quasi die Übergänge zwischen zwei Punkten, werden dabei jedoch nicht erfaßt. Fahrzyklen umfassen demgegenüber Phasen positiver und negativer Beschleunigung und lassen sich z. B. durch mittlere Geschwindigkeiten und Streckenlängen charakterisieren. Für LKW, Off-Road-Fahrzeuge und andere mobile Maschinen werden bislang überwiegend Lastkollektive verwendet. Fahrzyklen sind mittlerweile vor allem für Messungen an PKW üblich. Die einzige Ausnahme bildet für LKW der US-HDTC (Heavy Duty Transient Cycle).

Bei geeigneter Aggregation in den Lastkollektiven können diese und die aufwendigeren „voll transienten" Fahrzyklen in Einzelfällen sehr ähnliche Ergebnisse liefern /SAE 1988/. Andererseits zeigen Vergleiche – nicht unerwartet – große Unterschiede zwischen den Ergebnissen verschiedener Tests untereinander und dem realen Betrieb /BUWAL 1994/. Grundsätzlich für alle Fahrzyklen und Lastkollektive (zusammenfassend: Zyklen) gilt, daß die auf ihrer Basis gewonnenen Daten starken Modellcharakter haben. In die Synthese eines Zyklus kann notwendigerweise nur eine begrenzte Anzahl von Einzelfahrten bzw. -einsätzen eingehen. Damit werden zwar die grundsätzlichen Eigenschaften z. B. des LKW-Einsatzes in Ballungsräumen im sogenannten 13-Punkte-Test im Vergleich zum Außerorts- und Autobahnverkehr gut erfaßt. Für eine bestimmte Strecke, den gesamten Verkehr eines Landes oder einer einzelnen Stadt kann jedoch die Gesamtheit der Fahrmuster eine deutlich andere Struktur aufweisen.

Die Mehrzahl der Zyklen wurde im Zusammenhang mit der Festlegung von Emissionsgrenzwerten zur einzelnen Typ-Zulassung der jeweiligen Nutzfahrzeuge entwickelt. Zur Definition der Testverfahren zur Typ-Zulassung gehören neben der Festlegung des Zyklus auch

Vorgaben zur Außentemperatur, zu Motor-Vorlaufzeiten vor Beginn der Emissionsmessungen, zur Unterteilung des Gesamtzyklus in mehrere verschieden zu gewichtende Abschnitte und zur analytischen Methode. Die Details werden hier nicht weiter diskutiert.

Einer der wichtigsten Zyklen ist der bereits erwähnte 13-Punkte-Test für LKW. Er beruht auf einem Lastkollektiv mit elf Betriebspunkten – der Leerlauf-Punkt wird dreimal angefahren –, das den LKW-Einsatz in Ballungsgebieten beschreiben soll. Der Zyklus wurde in den USA entwickelt und von der EU mit Änderungen bei der Gewichtung der einzelnen Punkte übernommen. Für Off-Road-Fahrzeuge bzw. mobile Dieselmaschinen im weitesten Sinne wurden von ISO Lastkollektive vorgeschlagen, die auch die Basis geplanter Vorschriften der EU werden sollen. Vier der Zyklen sollen bei Off-Road-Fahrzeugen im engeren Sinne, d. h. bei nicht schienengebundenen Rad- und Kettenfahrzeugen, Verwendung finden, eines bei Lokomotiven, zwei bei Schiffen und drei bei Gartengeräten. Keiner dieser Zyklen hat mehr als acht Lastpunkte; die Lage der Lastpunkte entspricht bei anderer Gewichtung meist der im 13-Punkte-Test (**Tabelle 3-1**). Die hohe Symmetrie der Lastpunktverteilung und -gewichtung wie auch die empfohlene Zuordnung von Tests und Maschinentypen ist dabei nicht unbedingt überzeugend.

Die eingeschränkte Realitätsnähe von etablierten Zyklen wie dem 13-Punkte-Test oder zukünftig maßgeblichen wie den ISO-Zyklen zeigt bereits ein *formaler* Vergleich mit nicht offiziellen, aber problemangepaßten Lastkollektiven. Der sogenannte 5-Punkte-Test für Ackerschlepper (siehe auch Kapitel 6.1.2), der KHD-Test für Gabelstabler und die beiden ISO-Zyklen C1 und C2 jeweils für Ackerschlepper *und* Gabelstabler weisen offensichtlich nur sehr geringe Ähnlichkeit auf (**Tabelle 3-1**). Dies gilt für die Lage der meisten Punkte im Motorkennfeld *und* – bei Punkten ähnlicher Lage – ihre Gewichtung. Zu einem Vergleich der Ergebnisse von 5- und 13-Punkte-Test am Beispiel eines Ackerschleppers siehe Kapitel 6.1.2.

Gerade die Gewichtung von Lastpunkten scheint eine wesentliche Fehlerquelle bei der Ableitung repräsentativer Zyklen zu sein. Auf eben die dadurch erhaltenen Testmittel nehmen jedoch die Grenzwerte zur Typ-Zulassung Bezug. Dies hat zwei negative Folgen:

- Die Typ-Zulassung orientiert sich an nur bedingt realistischen Betriebszuständen.
- In der Literatur sind im wesentlichen nur Mittelwerte aus Standard-Tests verfügbar.

Zumindest in ökologischen Bilanzierungen ist jedoch die Anwendung von differenzierten Daten aus angepaßten Tests angebracht. Für Maschinen im Bergbau können solche Daten gegenwärtig nicht abgeleitet werden; für Landmaschinen findet sich eine Ableitung aus Testergebnissen in Kapitel 6; für LKW erfolgt die Berechnung über mehrere Stufen mit einem komplexen Modell, bei dem diese Sachverhalte mit hoher Genauigkeit erfaßt werden (Kapitel 5.1).

Tabelle 3-1 Lastkollektive: relative Drehzahl, relatives Drehmoment und Gewichtung der Einzelpunkte im Testmittel

Standardzyklen: Lastpunkte												
Rel. DrehZ	Leerl.	60%	60%	60%	60%	60%	100%	100%	100%	100%	100%	
Rel. DrehM	0%	10%	25%	50%	75%	100%	100%	75%	50%	25%	10%	
MotorAL	0%	6%	15%	30%	45%	60%	100%	75%	50%	25%	10%	
Standardzyklen: Gewichtung												**ALG**
Zyklen nach ISO 8178												
C1	15%			10%	10%	10%	15%	15%	15%		10%	48%
C2	15%	10%	30%	32%	5%	2%				6%		20%
D1							30%	50%	20%			78%
D2							5%	25%	30%	30%	10%	47%
E1	40%		25%	15%	14%		6%					21%
E2							20%	50%	15%	15%		69%
F1	60%			15%			25%					30%
G1	5%	7%	30%	29%	20%	9%						28%
G2	5%						9%	20%	29%	30%	7%	47%
G3	10%						90%					90%
ARB J 2182	15%			10%	10%	10%	15%	15%	15%		10%	48%
ECE R49	25%	8%	8%	8%	8%	25%	10%	2%	2%	2%	2%	36%
US 13 Mode	20%	8%	8%	8%	8%	8%	8%	8%	8%	8%	8%	33%
Cal 8 Mode	15%			10%	10%	10%	15%	15%	15%		10%	48%
5-Punkte-Test			**A**	**B**	**C**	**D**	**E**					
Relative Drehzahl			95%	85%	53%	100%	40%					
Relatives Drehmoment			88%	48%	40%	15%	0%					
Motorauslastung			84%	41%	21%	15%	0%					40%
Gewichtung			31%	18%	19%	20%	12%					
KHD-Stapler-Test*			**A**	**B**	**C**	**D**	**E**	**F**	**G**	**H**		
Relative Drehzahl			28%	67%	75%	67%	62%	71%	83%	74%		
Relatives Drehmoment			0%	18%	10%	100%	15%	20%	12%	100%		
Motorauslastung			0%	12%	8%	67%	9%	14%	10%	74%		16%
Gewichtung			25%	8%	17%	7%	13%	17%	7%	7%		

Rel. DrehZ: Relative Drehzahl; Rel. DrehM: Relatives Drehmoment (Bezug jeweils Maximalwert); MotorAL: Motorauslastung; ALG: Motorauslastung im Testmittel

*: Im KHD-Stapler-Test wird die relative Drehzahl über das Intervall Leerlauf- bis Maximaldrehzahl definiert. Die hier dokumentierten Werte sind zur besseren Vergleichbarkeit auf das Intervall Stillstand bis Maximaldrehzahl umgerechnet. Sie gelten streng nur für Motoren mit Leerlauf- bzw. Maximaldrehzahlen von 650 und 2.300 U/min.

Quellen: /KHD 1998/, /VELLGUTH 1987/, /WELSCHOF 1981/

Teil II

Ableitung der Basisdaten

4 Basisinformationen und Rahmenannahmen

In Teil I dieses Buches wurde erläutert, daß und warum sich die Ableitung des hier diskutierten Ressourcenverbrauchs und der Emissionsdaten an der Methodik der Ökobilanz orientiert. Damit schließen wir auch formal an die Regeln für Ökobilanzen an. Im folgenden Unterkapitel wird zunächst der Teilschritt „Festlegung des Ziels und Untersuchungsrahmens" ausgeführt. Das heißt, die für die hier abgeleiteten Ressourcen- und Emissionsdaten notwendigen Basisinformationen und Rahmenbedingungen werden erläutert und dokumentiert. Die darüber hinausgehenden Konventionen für die beiden folgenden Teilschritte einer Ökobilanz, die Sachbilanz bzw. Wirkungsabschätzung, sind in Kapitel 4.2 näher beschrieben.

4.1 Festlegung des Ziels und Untersuchungsrahmens

Wie bereits in Kapitel 2.2.1 ausgeführt, umfaßt der Teilschritt der Festlegung des Ziels und des Untersuchungsrahmens einer Ökobilanz acht Einzelpunkte. Diese werden in Bezug auf die hier durchgeführten Ableitungen von Verbrauchs- und Emissionsdaten für den Einsatz von Nutzfahrzeugen in Gütertransport, Landwirtschaft und Bergbau sowie der dafür notwendigen Bereitstellung von Endenergieträgern im folgenden einzeln konkretisiert.

4.1.1 Hintergrund des Buches

In fast allen Ökobilanzen und zahlreichen anderen ökologischen Untersuchungen tritt als Teil der betrachteten Lebenswege bzw. Prozeßketten der Einsatz von Nutzfahrzeugen auf. Dabei haben Transportprozesse oft bedeutenden Einfluß auf die Ergebnisse. In Ökobilanzen zu landwirtschaftsbezogenen Fragestellungen spielt der Einsatz von Landmaschinen häufig eine wichtige Rolle. Schließlich werden für die Bereitstellung von Erzen und Kohlen Bergbaumaschinen eingesetzt, deren Umweltwirkungen ebenfalls erheblich sein können. Allerdings liegen für diese Prozesse nur in sehr begrenztem Maße aktuelle, repräsentative, belastbare und einfach handhabbare Daten vor. Hauptprobleme:

- fehlende Daten für heute als wichtig betrachtete Parameter, die über Energieverbrauch und „klassische" Schadstoffe hinausgehen
- unklare bzw. nicht oder nur bedingt geeignete räumliche und/oder zeitliche Bezüge der verfügbaren Daten
- unzureichende Differenzierungstiefe etwa nach Einsatzarten einer bestimmten Maschine in praktisch allen hier behandelten Bereichen

Aufbauend auf mehreren kürzlich beendeten und noch laufenden Projekten ist es inzwischen möglich, die Lücken zum Teil zu schließen. In einem vom Umweltbundesamt in Auftrag gegebenen Forschungsvorhaben /IFEU 1998a/ wird neben dem Personenverkehr der gesamte Güterverkehr in Deutschland differenziert nach Verkehrsart, Verkehrsmittel, Abgastechnologie, Fahrleistung, Straßenkategorie, Auslastungsgrad, zeitlichem Bezug usw. abgebildet.

Der Landmaschineneinsatz wurde in einem von der Deutschen Bundesstiftung Umwelt geförderten Forschungsvorhaben untersucht /KALTSCHMITT & REINHARDT 1997/. Darin wurden erstmals der Energieverbrauch und die Emissionen heute wesentlicher Luftschadstoffe durch den Maschineneinsatz in der Landwirtschaft für bundesdeutsche Verhältnisse erhoben und bilanziert. Verbrauchs- und Emissionsdaten für den Einsatz von Bergbaumaschinen werden auf der Grundlage einer umfangreichen schweizerischen Untersuchung abgeleitet /BUWAL 1994/. Die Bereitstellung der biogenen Kraftstoffe Rapsöl und Rapsölmethylester wurde in /IFEU 1997a/ bilanziert und zudem in weiteren themenübergreifenden eigenen Arbeiten modifiziert. Schließlich werden hier mehrere Arbeiten zur Bereitstellung konventioneller Endenergieträger zusammengefaßt; dabei stellt der entsprechende Teil in /PATYK & REINHARDT 1997/ die wichtigste Vorarbeit dar.

Im Zuge dieser Arbeiten und der Erstellung anderer Ökobilanzen entstand die Idee,

- Verbrauchs- und Emissionsdaten der wichtigsten Nutzfahrzeuge zusammenzustellen
- unter vollständiger Berücksichtigung des aktuellen Diskussionsstandes zur Normierung von Ökobilanzen,
- die erfaßten Parameter weiter zu differenzieren und für alle Parameter die gleiche Differenzierungstiefe zu erreichen,
- alle Parameter zu aktualisieren und aufeinander abzustimmen und schließlich
- die gesamten Ressourcen- und Emissionsdaten ausführlich zu dokumentieren.

4.1.2 Ziel des Buches

Das Ziel des Buches ist es, für ökologisch relevante Parameter repräsentative Basisdaten zum Einsatz verschiedener Nutzfahrzeuge in

- Gütertransport,
- Landwirtschaft und
- Bergbau

abzuleiten und zu dokumentieren. Als Basisdaten werden die Endenergieträgerverbräuche *und* die damit verbundenen Verbräuche fossiler und mineralischer Ressourcen sowie luftgetragene Emissionen erfaßt. Bei den Analysen sollen daher alle vorgelagerten Lebenswegabschnitte der Bereitstellung der Energieträger berücksichtigt werden. Die Daten sollen jeweils nach relevanten Einzelprozessen und Einsatzarten differenziert werden. Sie sollen für Datenbanken geeignet sein und für diese verfügbar gemacht werden.

Außerdem soll dieses Buch einen weiteren Schritt in Richtung auf die größtmögliche Transparenz von Ökobilanzen darstellen. Es soll als Beispiel dafür dienen, wie einer wichtigen Forderung an Ökobilanzen nachgekommen werden kann: der Nachvollziehbarkeit *aller* Primärdaten durch deren vollständige Offenlegung.

4.1.3 Zielgruppen

Zielgruppe sind alle, die Ökobilanzen oder andere ökologische Bilanzierungen erstellen, in deren Zusammenhang die besprochenen Prozesse auftreten. Darüber hinaus sollen auch

Praktiker angesprochen sein, die für die einzelnen Daten keine unmittelbare Verwendung haben, sich aber von der Ausführlichkeit der Darstellung anregen lassen wollen.

4.1.4 Allgemeine Informationen über das Buch

Die Ableitung und Zusammenstellung der Ressourcen- und Emissionsdaten der verschiedenen Nutzfahrzeuge wurde vom Verein für Energie- und Umweltfragen Heidelberg – ifeu e.V. gefördert. Die Arbeiten selbst wurden aufbauend auf mehreren Forschungsvorhaben im Herbst 1997 durchgeführt und im Sommer 1998 nochmals aktualisiert.

4.1.5 Allgemeine Beschreibung der Untersuchungsobjekte

Untersuchungsobjekt ist der Einsatz von Nutzfahrzeugen

- für Gütertransporte zu Land, zu Wasser und in der Luft (als einziges nicht-mobiles Gütertransportmittel werden zusätzlich auch Pipelines erfaßt),
- in der Land- bzw. Forstwirtschaft und
- im Bergbau.

Die Maschinen werden mit Kraftstoffen auf Erdölbasis, mit Strom oder auch mit Kraftstoffen aus nachwachsenden Rohstoffen angetrieben. Die Bereitstellung dieser Endenergieträger wird ebenfalls bilanziert. **Tabelle 4-1** gibt einen Überblick über die im einzelnen betrachteten Fahrzeuge, die Differenzierungstiefe und die eingesetzten Energieträger.

Tabelle 4-1 Differenzierung der betrachteten Nutzfahrzeuge

Einsatz	**Differenzierungstiefe** jeweils unterschieden nach Ortsklassen	**Energieträger** jeweils mit und ohne Vorkette
Gütertransport		
LKW	5 Typen, 3 Auslastungsgrade und	Dieselkraftstoff
	3 Straßenkategorien	Rapsölmethylester (RME)
Bahn	3 Zuggattungen	Dieselkraftstoff
		Strom
Binnenschiff	1 Typ	Dieselkraftstoff
Hochseeschiff	3 Typen	Schweröl
Flugzeug	Mittel- und Langstreckenflüge	Flugturbinentreibstoff (Kerosin)
Pipeline	2 Typen	Erdgas bzw. Strom
Feldarbeiten		
Traktor	3 Schlepperklassen, 5 Laststufen	Dieselkraftstoff
		Rapsöl und RME
Erntemaschine	2 Maschinenklassen, 2 Laststufen	Dieselkraftstoff
Bergbau		
Bagger	1 Typ	Dieselkraftstoff
Lader	1 Typ	Dieselkraftstoff
Dumper	1 Typ	Dieselkraftstoff

4.1.6 Allgemeine Systemannahmen

Die allgemeinen Systemannahmen setzen verschiedene Rand- und Rahmenbedingungen, die einen entscheidenden Einfluß auf die Ableitung der Daten und ihre Werte haben. Im folgenden werden die im Hinblick auf unsere Untersuchungsobjekte pragmatisch ausgewählten Systemannahmen im einzelnen dargestellt.

4.1.6.1 Funktionale Einheit

Als funktionale Einheit wird für die
- Güterverkehrsmittel die *Transportleistung in tkm*,
- Landmaschinen die *Einsatzzeit in min* und
- Bergbaumaschinen die *Einsatzzeit in h* sowie das *bewegte Volumen in* m^3 gewählt.

4.1.6.2 Untersuchungsoptionen/Lebenswege

Bilanziert wird sowohl der direkte Einsatz der Kraftstoffe in den Nutzfahrzeugen als auch die Bereitstellung der eingesetzten Energieträger inklusive Strom. Damit wird der Lebensweg der Kraftstoffe von der Entnahme der Rohstoffe in den entsprechenden Ländern (z. B. Rohöl zur Herstellung von Dieselkraftstoff oder Rohphosphat für die Düngemittel, die bei der Rapsproduktion eingesetzt werden und somit den regenerativen Kraftstoffen Rapsöl und RME zuzurechnen sind) über die Distribution der Energieträger (z. B. zu einer Tankstelle) bis hin zu ihrer Endnutzung in verschiedenen Nutzfahrzeugen bilanziert.

Da Verbrauchs- und Emissionsdaten von Landmaschinen hier erstmalig in dieser Ausführlichkeit abgeleitet werden, wird die Methodik zur Illustration und zur Diskussion einiger interessanter Zusammenhänge auf wichtige Feldfrüchte angewandt. Die Bilanzergebnisse können in weitergehenden Berechnungen direkt verwendet werden.

4.1.6.3 Systemgrenzen der Lebenswege

Bilanzierungstiefe

Die Lebenswege der eingesetzten Endenergieträger (Dieselkraftstoff bzw. andere Mineralölerzeugnisse, Strom, Rapsöl und RME) werden vollständig und mit allen Prozeßschritten von der Gewinnung und Aufbereitung der Rohstoffe bis zu ihrer Bereitstellung bilanziert. Für die untersuchten Nutzfahrzeuge werden ausschließlich die direkte Verwendung der Energieträger und die damit verbundenen gasförmigen Emissionen betrachtet.

Die ökologischen Wirkungen weiterer Materialien, die in der Nutzungsphase der Fahrzeuge verwendet werden, wie etwa Schmieröl, Reifen, Frostschutzmittel, Reinigungs- und Pflegemittel usw., sind hier nicht Bilanzierungsgegenstand. Ebensowenig werden die Bereitstellung und der Unterhalt der Infrastruktur – der Bau, die Wartung und Reparatur von Gebäuden, Maschinen, Industrieanlagen, Transportmitteln und Verkehrswegen – betrachtet.

Kuppelprodukte und Abfälle

Die Auswahl der Verfahren zur Behandlung von Kuppelprodukten und Abfällen – Äquivalenzprozeßbilanzierung oder Allokation – erfolgt nach dem Prinzip „Äquivalenzprozeßbilanzierung vor Allokation"; näheres hierzu findet sich in /KALTSCHMITT & REINHARDT 1997/. Dies wird hier für die Daten zur Bereitstellung von Rapsöl und Rapsölmethylester (RME) relevant.

4.1.6.4 Geographische Systemgrenzen

Der Bezugsraum für die Nutzfahrzeuge, die zum Gütertransport eingesetzt werden, ist Deutschland. Das heißt es werden nur die in Deutschland zugelassenen und üblichen Gütertransportmittel betrachtet. Für die Landwirtschaft wird ebenfalls nur der in Deutschland eingesetzte Maschinenpark berücksichtigt. Bergbaumaschinen werden in den meisten Fällen außerhalb Deutschlands eingesetzt; daher bilden die Hauptherkunftsländer der Erze und Abbauprodukte den Bezugsraum.

Für die Produktion der eingesetzten Energieträger wird ebenfalls Deutschland als Bezugsraum gewählt. Allerdings finden die Bereitstellung einzelner (Roh-)Stoffe wie z. B. Rohöl (für die Produktion von Dieselkraftstoff) oder verschiedene Produktionsprozesse wie etwa die Herstellung von Düngemitteln (die bei den rapsbasierten Kraftstoffen eingesetzt werden) nicht immer bzw. nicht ausschließlich in Deutschland statt. Bezugsraum dieser Stoffe ist dann das jeweilige Herkunftsland gewichtet mit dem durchschnittlichen Marktanteil des Produktes in Deutschland. Die jeweilige Wahl des Bezugsraums wird in den konkreten Fällen explizit begründet. Wenn Daten mit anderem Bezugsraum auf Deutschland übertragen werden, was infolge von Mängeln der Datenbasis notwendig sein kann, wird dies gleichfalls dokumentiert.

4.1.6.5 Zeitliche Systemgrenzen

Als Bezugsjahr wird das Jahr 1996 angesetzt, da für dieses Jahr bereits eine Reihe von „Realdaten" in Form amtlicher Statistiken vorliegt. Für Änderungen, die antizipiert werden können, werden außerdem Daten mit Bezug auf das Jahr 2000 ausgewiesen. Beispiele sind der LKW-Transport, für den neue Abgasgrenzwertstufen bereits festgelegt sind, oder die Elektrizitätsbereitstellung, für die eine vollständige Umsetzung der Großfeuerungsanlagenverordnung (GFAVO) in den ostdeutschen Bundesländern für das Jahr 2000 zu erwarten ist.

Stehen Kenngrößen oder Daten für das Jahr 1996 nicht zur Verfügung, werden entweder die Verhältnisse vergangener Jahre unverändert übernommen oder auf das Jahr 1996 fortgeschrieben. Entsprechendes gilt für Daten ohne konkreten zeitlichen Bezug. In allen Fällen werden die zugrunde gelegten Annahmen dargelegt und begründet.

4.1.7 Detaillierungsgrad

Die hier abgeleiteten Daten sollen über größenordnungsmäßige Abschätzungen deutlich hinausgehen. Es wird daher ein möglichst hoher Detaillierungsgrad unter Berücksichtigung der ausgewählten Systemgrenzen angestrebt. Konkret bedeutet dies

- für die Gütertransporte eine besonders detaillierte Behandlung der LKW-Transporte, die bei weitem den Hauptanteil an der Transportleistung stellen,
- für Landmaschinen eine Differenzierung bis hinunter zu einzelnen Feldarbeitsschritten,
- für den Bergbau eine Differenzierung nach den wichtigsten Maschinentypen und

- für die eingesetzten Energieträger eine weitgehende Differenzierung nach Produkten und Produktionsländern.

Die damit erforderlichen zusätzlichen Annahmen bei der Quantifizierung führen zu geringfügig erhöhten Unsicherheiten der einzelnen Ergebnisse. Diese Unsicherheiten werden jedoch unseres Erachtens durch den mit der Differenzierungstiefe verbundenen Informationsgewinn deutlich überwogen.

4.1.8 Auswahl der zur Wirkungsabschätzung verwendeten Kategorien

Die Kategorien, nach denen die Wirkungen auf die Umwelt aus dem Einsatz der verschiedenen Nutzfahrzeuge abgeschätzt werden, basieren auf der Standardliste der Wirkungskategorien nach /DIN 1995/ (**Tabelle 4-2**). Nicht betrachtet werden hier lediglich die Wirkungskategorien Naturraumbeanspruchung und Lärmbelastung, da für diese Kategorien bislang weder ein allgemein akzeptiertes Bilanzierungskonzept noch ein Bewertungskonzept vorliegt. Eine detaillierte Darstellung der verwendeten Bilanzierungsmethoden bzw. der den Wirkungskategorien zugeordneten Bilanzparameter findet sich im folgenden Kapitel.

Tabelle 4-2 Wirkungskategorien

1.	Ressourcenverbrauch
2.*	Naturraumbeanspruchung
3.	Treibhauseffekt
4.	Abbau der Ozonschicht
5.	Versauerung
6.	Eutrophierung
7.	Ökotoxizität (Toxische Schädigung von Organismen)
8.	Humantoxizität (Toxische Schädigung von Menschen)
9.	Photosmog (Sommersmog)
10.*	Lärmbelastung

*: Hier nicht erfaßte Wirkungskategorien
Quelle: /DIN 1995/

4.2 Festlegung der Bilanzierungsverfahren und -parameter

Im folgenden werden die Parameter zur Erfassung des Ressourcenbedarfs und der Emissionen beim Einsatz der betrachteten Nutzfahrzeuge ausgewählt. Ferner wird die Vorgehensweise bei der Bilanzierung dokumentiert und begründet. Die Ableitung der einzelnen Bilanzierungsparameter basiert auf den in Kapitel 4.1.8 angegebenen, in dieser Studie erfaßten Wirkungskategorien (**Tabelle 4-2**) und den Ausführungen in Kapitel 2.4.

4.2.1 Räumliche Differenzierung nach Ortsklassen

Üblicherweise werden in ökologischen Bilanzierungen die Emissionen luftgetragener Schadstoffe über alle Lebenswegabschnitte aufsummiert. Die so erhaltenen Bilanzsalden korrespondieren jedoch nicht notwendigerweise mit dem Ausmaß der tatsächlichen Wirkung. Abhängig von den Stoffeigenschaften und den jeweils betrachteten ökologischen Wirkungskategorien markieren sie zunächst nur das *maximale* Wirkungspotential.

Somit kann eine direkte Bewertung solcher Emissionsbilanzen zu verzerrten Ergebnissen führen, in manchen Fällen sogar das Ergebnis verfälschen. Beispielsweise ist es im Hinblick auf den Treibhauseffekt unproblematisch, alle CO_2-Emissionen unabhängig von ihren Emissionsorten aufzusummieren, da sich ihre Wirkungen räumlich nicht unterscheiden. Anders sind dagegen etwa die Emissionen von Dieselpartikeln hinsichtlich ihrer humantoxischen Wirkung zu behandeln, siehe **Abb. 1-5**. Ein weiteres Beispiel für ein verzerrtes Ergebnis einer Aggregation liefert die Bereitstellung von Rapsöl bzw. RME, die in Kapitel 8.2 detailliert dargestellt ist: Den größten Einzelbeitrag zur NO_X-Bilanz liefern die Emissionen von Frachtern auf offener See, die für den Transport des substituierten Futtermittels Sojaschrot eingesetzt werden. Soll die humantoxische Wirkung des NO_X beurteilt werden, dann darf nur der Teil der Emissionen angerechnet werden, der in bewohnten Gebieten, also über Land, niedergeht. In diesem Fall fällt die Bilanz zuungunsten von Rapsöl bzw. RME aus. Würden alle NO_X-Emissionen ohne Unterscheidung ihres Emissions- bzw. Wirkungsortes eingerechnet, fiele das Ergebnis zugunsten von Rapsöl bzw. RME aus (**Abb. 4-1**).

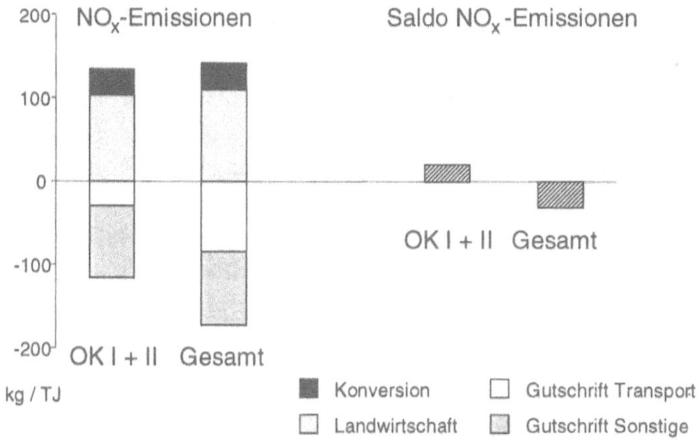

Abb. 4-1 NO_X-Emissionen der Bereitstellung von Rapsölmethylester differenziert nach Lebenswegabschnitten und Ortsklassen

Für die Emissionen des Flugverkehrs spielt auch die Höhe des Emissionsortes eine Rolle, da die Emissionen bestimmter Schadstoffe in den verschiedenen Schichten der Atmosphäre unterschiedliche Wirkungen haben.

Zwei Aspekte sind damit offensichtlich: Zum einen ist es in hohem Maße wünschenswert, in Sachbilanzen nicht ausschließlich Emissionssalden durch Addition über alle Lebenswegabschnitte zu erhalten. Zum anderen ist es praktisch undurchführbar, neben Emissionsdaten, die in aller Regel bereits Näherungen, Schätzungen usw. enthalten, belastbare Immissions-

und Populationsdaten der Orte, an denen die jeweiligen Einzelprozesse oder Lebenswegabschnitte stattfinden, zu erhalten.

Einen Ansatz, das dargestellte Dilemma zumindest zum Teil aufzulösen, stellt das im folgenden diskutierte Konzept der Ortsklassen dar. Es wurde erstmals in /IFEU 1996b/ und danach in weiteren Arbeiten zu Ökobilanzen wie /KALTSCHMITT & REINHARDT 1997/, /PATYK & REINHARDT 1997/ und /IFEU 1997a/ angewandt. Dabei wird versucht, näherungsweise zwischen dem Emissionsort und dem Immissionsort als dem wirkungsrelevanten Ort zu unterscheiden. Diese Unterscheidung hängt von den betrachteten Prozessen, die an jeweils unterschiedlichen Stellen stattfinden, und den untersuchten Stoffen mit ihren spezifischen atmosphärischen Lebensdauern ab. Daher werden im folgenden zunächst die Wirkungsorte grob klassifiziert, dann die Prozesse und schließlich die Stoffe charakterisiert. Gegenwärtig noch unberücksichtigt bleibt dabei die vertikale Auflösung (Stichwort Flugverkehr; siehe oben).

Ortsklassen

Die ökologischen Wirkungen fallen in bestimmten geographischen Räumen an, die sich grob nach dem Kriterium der Bevölkerungsdichte zu drei Ortsklassen zusammenfassen lassen. Die Ortsklassen 1 bis 3 sind wie folgt abgegrenzt:

OK 1: Gebiete hoher Bevölkerungsdichte: Innenstädte

OK 2: Gebiete mittlerer Bevölkerungsdichte: ländliche Gebiete, Industriegebiete

OK 3: Gebiete geringer Bevölkerungsdichte: Gebirgsregionen, Wüsten, offene See

Diese geographische Einteilung wird sowohl für Emissionen, die in diesen Gebieten freigesetzt werden, als auch für Immissionen, die in den entsprechenden Gebieten einwirken, angewendet. Bei der Anwendung des Ortsklassenkonzeptes (und ihrer Dokumentation) ist daher sorgfältig zu unterscheiden, ob gerade die Freisetzung eines Stoffes oder seine Einwirkung Gegenstand ist.

Zuordnung von Prozessen zu Emissionsortsklassen

Die in ökologischen Bilanzierungen relevanten Prozesse lassen sich in folgender Weise den Ortsklassen zuordnen:

OK 1: Distribution und Nutzung von Konsumgütern

OK 2: Distribution von Konsumgütern, Einsatz von Landmaschinen, Industrieproduktion, Energieumwandlung in Kraftwerken und Raffinerien, Rohstoffförderung

OK 3: Seetransport von Konsumgütern, Erzen und Energieträgern, Rohstoffförderung

Die bei den jeweiligen Prozessen anfallenden Emissionen werden getrennt nach diesen Ortsklassen erfaßt. Dabei ist offensichtlich, daß einige Prozesse in mehreren Ortsklassen auftreten können. In solchen Fällen ist je nach Fragestellung zu entscheiden.

Für die Zuordnung von Immissionen sind außerdem die Eigenschaften der Stoffe zu berücksichtigen, die im folgenden grob charakterisiert werden.

Verweildauer, Reichweite und Immissionsortsklassen

Die atmosphärische Verweildauer eines Stoffes hängt von der Geschwindigkeit seiner physikalischen Deposition und/oder seiner chemischen Umwandlung ab. Dabei kann die chemische Umwandlung sowohl deaktivierende als auch aktivierende Wirkung haben. Zum Beispiel wird das humantoxische CO zum bekanntermaßen nicht toxischen CO_2 oxidiert; umgekehrt entwickelt SO_2 seine versauernde Wirkung erst in Wasser gelöst, z. B. in Regentröpfchen, als schweflige Säure.

Je länger die Verweildauer, desto größer ist die Reichweite eines Stoffes. Je weiter er transportiert wird, desto schwächer wird der Zusammenhang zwischen Emissions- und Wirkungsort und um so schwieriger ist eine räumliche Abgrenzung. Natürlich hängt die Reichweite auch von den konkreten meteorologischen Verhältnissen ab. Für eine allgemeine Klassifikation müssen sie jedoch unberücksichtigt bleiben. Hier werden daher drei Reichweiten für die verschiedenen Stoffe betrachtet:

- **Globale Reichweite:** Stoffe mit atmosphärischen Verweildauern in der Größenordnung von Wochen oder größer werden in der gesamten Hemisphäre bzw. global verteilt. Damit wird ihr Immissionsort unabhängig vom Ort der Emission.
- **Regionale Reichweite:** Stoffe mit einer Verweildauer von einigen Tagen werden im Umkreis von etwa 1.000 km vom Emissionsort verteilt /EXTERNE 1995/. Ihre Immission ist daher in verschiedenen Ortsklassen zu berücksichtigen und wird im folgenden aufgeteilt.
- **Lokale Reichweite:** Stoffe mit sehr kurzer atmosphärischer Verweildauer sind nur in der unmittelbaren Umgebung des Emissionsortes wirksam. In diese Kategorie werden die Stoffe eingeordnet, die schnell deponieren bzw. an Partikel gebunden sind sowie Stoffe mit hoher chemischer Reaktivität und daher niedriger Verweildauer. Die Ortsklassen der Emission und der Immission sind für diese Stoffe somit gleich.

Die konkrete Einteilung der hier betrachteten Stoffe ist in **Tabelle 4-3** ausgewiesen.

Tabelle 4-3 Einteilung der Stoffe nach ihren Verweildauern bzw. Reichweiten

Verweildauer:	Lang	Mittel	Kurz
Reichweite:	**Global**	**Regional**	**Lokal**
	CO_2	SO_2	Partikel
	CH_4	CO	Staub
	N_2O	NO_X	Formaldehyd
		NMHC	Benzol
		HCl	Benzo(a)pyren*
		NH_3	TCDD*

*: im wesentlichen partikelgebunden

Zuordnung von Wirkungskategorien zu Ortsklassen

Bis hierher wurden Emissionsquellen nach ihrer Lage und Stoffe nach ihrem räumlichen Wirkungsbereich klassifiziert. Das gesamte Verfahren hängt jedoch zusätzlich von der untersuchten Wirkungskategorie ab. Für welche Wirkungen welche Ortsklassen zu berücksichtigen sind, wird im folgenden dargestellt.

- **Treibhauseffekt und stratosphärischer Ozonabbau:** Die Wirkungen sind unabhängig vom Emissionsort und die betreffenden Stoffe haben globale Reichweite. Daher können hier alle Emissionen aus allen Ortsklassen aufsummiert werden.
- **Photosmog, Versauerung und Eutrophierung:** Die Wirkungen sind regional begrenzt; sie lassen sich im wesentlichen OK 1 und OK 2 zuordnen (eine Ausnahme bildet z. B. die Eutrophierung der Nordsee). Auf der Seite der Emissionen sind alle drei Ortsklassen zu berücksichtigen, die Emissionen in OK 3 soweit, wie sie in OK 1 und OK 2 verfrachtet werden bzw. in bestimmten Fällen auch der über unbesiedeltem Gebiet verbleibende Teil (siehe oben: Nordsee-Eutrophierung).
  Für die hier diskutierten Anwendungen treten diese Zuordnungsfragen vor allem im Zusammenhang der Emissionen aus Hochseetransporten auf, die z. B. beim Rohölimport zur Produktion von Dieselkraftstoff, und damit bei allen hier betrachteten Maschineneinsätzen, anfallen. Dabei nehmen wir an, daß die Schiffe etwa die Hälfte der Fahrzeit in Küstennähe verbringen und daß dort jeweils zur Hälfte der Zeit Land- bzw. Seewind herrscht. Da hier nicht unterschieden wird, auf welchem Küstenstrich die Stoffe niedergehen (z. B. Afrika, Amerika oder Europa), werden damit 25 % der gesamten Emissionen von Stoffen mit regionaler Reichweite in kontinentale Gebiete und damit in OK 2 eingetragen. Für Stoffe kurzer atmosphärischer Verweildauer und entsprechend kurzer Reichweite wird kein Eintrag aus OK 3 in OK 2 angerechnet.
- **Human- und Ökotoxizität:** Für eine Wirkungsbewertung in diesen Kategorien ist eine Unterscheidung nach Ballungsraum (OK 1) und ländlichem Gebiet (OK 2) sinnvoll. In OK 1 werden nur die Mengen angerechnet, die auch in dieser Ortsklasse emittiert werden, da sie die Bilanz dominieren dürften. Aufgrund der großen Flächenunterschiede wird eine Verfrachtung von Emissionen aus OK 2 in der Regel vernachlässigbar sein. Dies ist jedoch gegebenenfalls zu prüfen und bei Bedarf zu berücksichtigen. Die Lebensdauer der Stoffe spielt für die Immission in OK 1 keine Rolle.
  Für die wirkungsseitige Aggregation in OK 1+2 werden wie oben alle Emissionen aus OK 1 und aus OK 2 zusammengenommen. Außerdem wird bei den Stoffen regionaler Reichweite ein 25 %iger Eintrag aus OK 3 berücksichtigt.

Die Emissionen der einzelnen Prozesse werden getrennt nach ihren Emissionsorten erfaßt und in Ortsklassen gemäß der obigen Aufteilungen ausgewiesen. Die **Tabelle 4-4** faßt die Aufteilung nach (Immissions)Ortsklassen für die verschiedenen Wirkungskategorien und Stoffe zusammen.

Mit diesem Vorgehen, dessen erster Ansatz zunächst grob erscheinen mag, werden unseres Erachtens die Daten einer Sachbilanz jedoch wesentlich besser für eine spätere Wirkungsabschätzung aufbereitet als ohne jede wirkungsspezifische Betrachtung. Nichtsdestotrotz handelt es sich – dies als Hinweis für den Benutzer – lediglich um Emissionsdaten, die räumlich differenziert erfaßt und ausgewiesen sind. Eine Analyse der Wirkungen ist damit nicht vorweggenommen.

Einen gewissen Mangel des Ortsklassen-Konzeptes bildet derzeit sicher die geringe Anzahl von Ortsklassen und die geringe Differenzierungstiefe nach Stoff-Lebenszeiten. Es stellt jedoch in jedem Fall einen erheblichen Fortschritt gegenüber der bisher üblichen undifferenzierten Addition der Emissionen über alle Orte dar.

Tabelle 4-4 Zuordnung der Emissionen zu Immissionsortsklassen differenziert nach Wirkungskategorien

Wirkungskategorie	Wirkungsbereich		
	Global	Ortsklasse 1	Ortsklasse 1+2
Treibhauseffekt	EOK 1 + EOK 2 + EOK 3		
Ozonabbau	EOK 1 + EOK 2 + EOK 3		
Versauerung		EOK 1	EOK 1 + EOK 2 + 25% EOK 3
Eutrophierung		EOK 1	EOK 1 + EOK 2 + 25% EOK 3
Photosmog		EOK 1	EOK 1 + EOK 2 + 25% EOK 3
Human- und Ökotox.			
SO_2		EOK 1	EOK 1 + EOK 2 + 25% EOK 3
CO		EOK 1	EOK 1 + EOK 2 + 25% EOK 3
NO_X		EOK 1	EOK 1 + EOK 2 + 25% EOK 3
NMHC		EOK 1	EOK 1 + EOK 2 + 25% EOK 3
Dieselpartikel		EOK 1	EOK 1 + EOK 2
Staub		EOK 1	EOK 1 + EOK 2
HCl		EOK 1	EOK 1 + EOK 2 + 25% EOK 3
NH_3		EOK 1	EOK 1 + EOK 2 + 25% EOK 3
Formaldehyd		EOK 1	EOK 1 + EOK 2 + 25% EOK 3
Benzol		EOK 1	EOK 1 + EOK 2 + 25% EOK 3
Benzo(a)pyren		EOK 1	EOK 1 + EOK 2
TCDD		EOK 1	EOK 1 + EOK 2

EOK: Emission in dieser Ortsklasse

4.2.2 Bilanzierte Parameter

Im folgenden werden die hier erfaßten Parameter und ihre Bilanzierungsmerkmale diskutiert.

4.2.2.1 Ressourcenverbrauch

Betrachtet werden energetische und mineralische Ressourcen.

Energetische Ressourcen

Bilanziert werden Primär- und Endenergieträger. Erfaßt werden die fossilen Primärenergieträger Erdöl, Erdgas, Stein- und Braunkohle sowie als weiterer erschöpflicher Primärenergieträger Uranerz. Als regenerative Energie wird standardmäßig Wasserkraft, für Rapsöl und Rapsölmethylester zusätzlich Biomasse erfaßt.

Aus der Kategorie der Endenergieträger werden alle diejenigen erfaßt, die in industriellen Produktionsprozessen oder in den bilanzierten Nutzfahrzeugen in relevanten Mengen eingesetzt werden bzw. sich aus den Bilanzierungsobjekten ergeben (**Tabelle 4-1**). Ottokraftstoff kann unberücksichtigt bleiben, da er in den genannten Einsatzbereichen praktisch keine Verwendung findet. Erdgas, Steinkohle und Braunkohle werden nicht nur als Primär-, sondern auch als Endenergieträger ausgewiesen. Im Falle der Ausweisung als Endenergieträger für einen Prozeß wird konsequenterweise lediglich die in diesem Prozeß zum Einsatz kommende Menge *ohne* den Aufwand zu ihrer Bereitstellung angegeben.

Bilanzierungsmerkmale

Folgende Merkmale liegen der Erstellung der Energie- bzw. Energieträgerbilanzen zugrunde:

- Alle in **Tabelle 4-5** ausgewiesenen Energieträger werden getrennt bilanziert.
- Die einzelnen Energieträger werden in energetischen Einheiten (Joule) ausgewiesen.
- Sowohl energetisch wie stofflich genutzte Energieträger werden als Energieträger bilanziert. Dies gilt z. B. für Erdgas, das bei der Stickstoffdüngemittelherstellung (zur Produktion von Raps) sowohl als Heizgas als auch als Prozeßgas, d. h. als materieller Input, eingesetzt wird.

Die Bilanzierung der Primärenergieträger erfolgt auf der Basis des ermittelten Endenergieträgereinsatzes. Für die fossilen Energieträger geschieht dies durch die Verknüpfung der Endenergieeinsätze mit den tatsächlichen Wirkungsgraden. Für die nicht fossilen Energien, also die regenerativen Energien und die Kernkraft, gibt es kein naturwissenschaftlich eindeutiges Verfahren der primärenergetischen Bewertung. Die zum Teil erheblich voneinander verschiedenen Verfahren wirken sich in ihren Ergebnissen aber nur dann signifikant aus, wenn große Anteile nicht fossiler Energien in den Bilanzen auftauchen. Aus der Gruppe der sonstigen regenerativen Energien spielt lediglich die Wasserkraft im Rahmen der Stromproduktion eine Rolle. Auch der Einsatz der Kernkraft ist auf die Stromerzeugung beschränkt. Für Kern- und Wasserkraft wenden wir daher der amtlichen Elektrizitätsstatistik folgend das Substitutionsprinzip an /BMWI 1995/. Für den Sonderfall der Rapsproduktion für die Biokraftstoffe Rapsöl und RME orientieren wir uns an /VDI 1997/ und nehmen die primärenergetische Bewertung der eingestrahlten Sonnenenergie über den Heizwert des Erntegutes jeweils nachrichtlich auf.

Tabelle 4-5 Bilanzierte Primär- und Endenergieträger

Primärenergieträger	Endenergieträger
Erschöpfliche	**Mineralölprodukte und Erdgas**
Erdöl	Leichtes Heizöl (Heizöl EL)
Erdgas	Schweres Heizöl (Heizöl S, Schweröl)
Steinkohle	Dieselkraftstoff
Braunkohle	Flugturbinenkraftstoff (Kerosin)
Uranerz	Erdgas
Regenerative	**Regenerative**
Wasserkraft	Rapsöl
Biomasse (nur für Rapsöl und RME)	Rapsölmethylester (RME)
	Sonstige konventionelle
	Strom (öffentliches Netz)
	Bahnstrom

Aggregation

Als aggregierte Größe wird der kumulierte Energieaufwand (KEA) ausgewiesen, darüber hinaus jedoch auch gesondert die Summe erschöpflicher Primärenergieträger.

Mineralische Ressourcen

Bei der Bilanzierung der rapsbasierten Kraftstoffe ist die Produktion der eingesetzten Düngemittel aus mineralischen Ressourcen zu berücksichtigten, ferner die Produktion von Betriebsstoffen für die Gewinnung von Rapsöl bzw. RME aus Rapssaat. Bilanziert werden die geförderten und – gegebenenfalls – die angereicherten Rohstoffe (**Tabelle 4-6**).

Tabelle 4-6 Betriebsmittel und erfaßte mineralische Ressourcen entlang der Lebenswege von Rapsöl bzw. RME

Betriebsmittel/Substanz	Mineralische Ressource
Stickstoffdünger	Kalkstein
Phosphatdünger	Phosphaterz
	Summe Schwefel
Kalidünger	Rohkali
Düngekalk	Kalkstein
Bleicherde	Tonmineralien
Glyzerin	Steinsalz

Für die Produktion von Phosphatdünger wird Schwefelsäure eingesetzt. Für den in der Schwefelsäure enthaltenen Schwefel wird hier ohne Differenzierung nach verschiedenen Ressourcen bzw. Ursprüngen – elementarer Schwefel aus natürlichen Vorkommen, sulfidischer Schwefel in Erzen, Kuppelprodukt der Entschwefelung von Mineralölprodukten – der Einsatz von Schwefel summarisch ausgewiesen. Eine detaillierte Ableitung findet sich in /PATYK & REINHARDT 1997/.

Nicht bilanziert werden hier natürliche Ressourcen wie Wasser, Luftsauerstoff und Luftstickstoff. Diese Ressourcen sind dort, wo sie eingesetzt werden, praktisch unbegrenzt vorhanden.

Bilanzierungsmerkmale

Folgende Merkmale liegen der Bilanzierung zugrunde:

- Alle in **Tabelle 4-6** ausgewiesenen Stoffe werden getrennt bilanziert.
- Die einzelnen Stoffe werden in Masseneinheiten ausgewiesen.

Die Bilanzierung der mineralischen Rohstoffe erfolgt auf der Basis des ermittelten Stoffeinsatzes der Produktionsprozesse. Dazu wird der Stoffeinsatz mit den Anteilen der tatsächlich stofflich genutzten Bestandteile der Rohstoffe, wie sie in der Lagerstätte vorliegen, verknüpft.

Aggregation

Eine Aggregation der bilanzierten mineralischen Rohstoffe wird nicht vorgenommen.

4.2.2.2 Naturraumbeanspruchung

Für die Naturraumbeanspruchung liegen zur Zeit noch keine allgemein akzeptierten Bilanzierungskriterien vor. Diese Wirkungskategorie wird daher hier nicht betrachtet.

4.2.2.3 Treibhauseffekt

Bilanziert werden die Emissionen von CO_2, CH_4 und N_2O. Andere klimarelevante Stoffe werden aus verschiedenen Gründen entweder gar nicht oder nicht unter dem Aspekt der Klimawirksamkeit erfaßt: So treten die teil- oder vollhalogenierten Kohlenwasserstoffe bei den hier betrachteten Prozessen praktisch nicht auf und werden daher nicht bilanziert. Wasserdampf als wichtigstes natürlich auftretendes klimarelevantes Gas wird nicht berücksichtigt, weil die vom Menschen verursachten Beiträge relativ zum natürlichen Wasserkreislauf vernachlässigbar klein sind; damit kann auch deren Wirksamkeit als verschwindend gering eingestuft werden. Eine Ausnahme hiervon bilden möglicherweise die Wasserdampfemissionen von Flugzeugen im Bereich der Tropopause. Wenn daraus Zirruswolken entstehen, können diese einen relevanten anthropogenen Beitrag zum Treibhauseffekt leisten. Da uns aber weder Bildungsraten von Zirruswolken infolge von Flugzeugemissionen noch deren Treibhauspotentiale bekannt sind, werden die Wasserdampfemissionen bei der Bestimmung von Gesamttreibhauspotentialen aller klimarelevanten Gase hier nicht berücksichtigt, sondern lediglich nachrichtlich dokumentiert. Bei besserer Kenntnis der entsprechenden Zusammenhänge und Wirkungen können sie in späteren Bilanzierungen berücksichtigt werden.

Die indirekte Wirkung von CO und der Kohlenwasserstoffe durch deren Oxidation zu CO_2 wird bei der CO_2-Bilanzierung berücksichtigt. Zur indirekten Klimawirksamkeit anderer Schadstoffe bzw. über andere Pfade, insbesondere von NO_X und Kohlenwasserstoffen über die Bildung von Ozon, liegen keine allgemein anerkannten Treibhauswirkungspotentiale vor. Unter dem Aspekt der Klimawirksamkeit werden diese Stoffe daher nicht berücksichtigt, wohl aber unter anderen Aspekten (Versauerung, Human- und Ökotoxizität, Photosmog).

Bilanzierungsmerkmale

Von den hier berücksichtigten klimarelevanten Gasen CO_2, N_2O und CH_4 erfordert lediglich die Bilanzierung von CO_2 weitere Konventionen:

- Die CO_2-Emissionen aus der Verbrennung fossiler Energieträger werden aus dem Kohlenstoffgehalt der Energieträger unter der Annahme einer vollständigen Oxidation berechnet.
- Die CO_2-Emissionen durch die Abspaltung von CO_2 aus Kalkstein bei der Branntkalkproduktion werden aus der Stöchiometrie der Reaktion berechnet. Dies wird bei den Daten für die rapsbasierten Kraftstoffe berücksichtigt.
- Die CO_2-Emissionen aus der direkten Verbrennung von Biokraftstoffen werden nicht dem Treibhauseffekt zugerechnet, da hierbei genau soviel CO_2 freigesetzt wird, wie zuvor der Atmosphäre beim Wachstum der Rapspflanze entzogen wurde. Die zeitweilige Bindung von CO_2 in der Pflanze bzw. dem Kraftstoff bis zur Verbrennung ist in der Regel auf maximal wenige Jahre beschränkt und erfordert daher keine Berücksichtigung.

Aggregation

Die Emissionen der klimarelevanten Gase werden über alle Emissionsorte und -zeiten aufsummiert und mit den GWP-Werten nach /IPCC 1996/ (Integrationszeitraum: 100 Jahre; **Tabelle 4-7**) gewichtet. Die Summe der drei Stoffe wird als gesamtes Treibhauspotential ausgewiesen.

Tabelle 4-7 Massenbezogene Treibhauspotentiale (GWP-Werte) der betrachteten klimawirksamen Gase über einen Zeithorizont von 100 Jahren relativ zu Kohlendioxid

Substanz	**Formel**	**Treibhauspotential** kg CO_2/kg
Kohlendioxid	CO_2	1
Distickstoffoxid	N_2O	310
Methan	CH_4	21
Quelle: /IPCC 1996/		

4.2.2.4 Ozonabbau

Als Bilanzierungsparameter für den stratosphärischen Ozonabbau werden ausschließlich N_2O-Emissionen erfaßt, da die hier betrachteten Lebenswege bzw. Prozesse nicht mit – nennenswerten – FCKW-Emissionen verbunden sind. Emissionen anderer Schadstoffe, insbesondere des Flugverkehrs, werden aufgrund der noch unklaren Wirkungszusammenhänge nicht berücksichtigt.

Bilanzierungsmerkmale

Die Bilanzierung von N_2O erfordert keine weiteren Konventionen.

4.2.2.5 Versauerung

Aus der von /CML & TNO & B&G 1992/ nach /UBA 1995b/ vorgeschlagenen Liste säurebildender Gase werden die Emissionen folgender Stoffe bilanziert:

- Schwefeldioxid (SO_2),
- Stickstoffmonoxid bzw. -dioxid (NO, NO_2),
- Chlorwasserstoff (HCl) und
- Ammoniak (NH_3).

Andere säurebildende Gase wie Fluorwasserstoff oder bestimmte andere Schwefelverbindungen treten im Verhältnis zu den genannten Verbindungen in so geringen Mengen auf, daß deren Anteile am Gesamteffekt – umgerechnet auf SO_2-Äquivalente – lediglich im Promillebereich liegen dürften. Darüber hinaus ist die Datenlage für diese Stoffe für eine verläßliche und repräsentative Erfassung aller Prozeßschritte unzureichend. Im folgenden werden sie daher nicht weiter berücksichtigt.

Bilanzierungsmerkmale

Folgende Merkmale liegen der Bilanzierung zugrunde:

- Die Stickoxide (NO_X) werden als Stickstoffdioxid (NO_2) erfaßt.
- Die SO_2-Emissionen aus dem Einsatz fossiler oder regenerativer Kraftstoffe werden aus deren Schwefelgehalten unter der Annahme einer vollständigen Oxidation berechnet.
- Die HCl-Emissionen werden analog den SO_2-Emissionen berechnet.

Aggregation

Die Emissionen der säurebildenden Gase werden differenziert nach Ortsklassen und aggregiert über alle Emissionszeiten aufsummiert und mit den Versauerungspotentialen nach /UBA 1995b/ (**Tabelle 4-8**) gewichtet. Die Summe der SO_2-Äquivalente der vier Stoffe wird als gesamtes Versauerungspotential ausgewiesen.

Tabelle 4-8 Massenbezogene Versauerungspotentiale der betrachteten säurebildenden Gase relativ zu SO_2

Substanz	**Formel**	**Versauerungspotential** kg SO_2/kg
Schwefeldioxid	SO_2	1
Stickoxide	NO_X	0,70
Stickstoffmonoxid	*NO*	*1,07*
Stickstoffdioxid	*NO_2*	*0,70*
Ammoniak	NH_3	1,88
Chlorwasserstoff	HCl	0,88
Quelle: /CML & TNO & B&G 1992/ nach /UBA 1995b/		

4.2.2.6 Eutrophierung

Der Nährstoffeintrag in Gewässer und Böden wird durch die Bilanzierung der luftgetragenen Stickstoffverbindungen (Kapitel 4.2.2.5) weitgehend erfaßt. Die Eutrophierung von Gewässern durch den Nitratablauf aus Kläranlagen – sie tritt z. B. bei der Produktion von Düngemitteln auf – wird hier nicht bilanziert, da uns kein hinreichend abgesichertes Datenmaterial für alle Abschnitte der betrachteten Lebenswege vorliegt.

Bilanzierungsmerkmale

Die Bilanzierung erfordert keine weiteren Konventionen.

Aggregation

Da bei unseren Bilanzen für die Eutrophierung nur die stickstoff- und keine phosphorhaltigen Schadstoffe (NO_X und NH_3) zu berücksichtigen sind, nehmen wir keine Aggregation nach Phosphatäquivalenten vor. Hierdurch werden zusätzliche Unsicherheiten vermieden. Die Werte werden aber so ausgewiesen, daß eine gewünschte Aggregation vom Leser leicht durchgeführt werden kann.

4.2.2.7 Human- und Ökotoxizität

Unter dem Aspekt der toxischen Gefährdung von Menschen und Organismen werden ausschließlich Luftschadstoffe betrachtet. Schadstoffhaltige Abwässer werden hier nicht bilanziert, da uns kein hinreichend abgesichertes Datenmaterial für alle Abschnitte der betrachteten Lebenswege vorliegt.

Die Auswahl der Luftschadstoffe orientiert sich im wesentlichen an der mehr oder weniger abschätzbaren Relevanz der Stoffe im Zusammenhang der untersuchten Prozesse wie auch der Datenverfügbarkeit. Die Emissionen der betrachteten Stoffe sind zum Teil durch gesetzliche Regelungen (Abgasgrenzwerte, TA-Luft, GFAVO usw.) limitiert. Dies kann zum einen als Hinweis auf ihre Umweltrelevanz gedeutet werden; zum anderen ist damit in der Regel eine relativ günstige Datenlage verbunden. Konkret werden folgende Luftschadstoffe bilanziert:

- Schwefeldioxid (SO_2)
- Kohlenmonoxid (CO)
- Stickoxide (NO_X)
- Flüchtige Kohlenwasserstoffe ausschließlich Methan (NMHC)
- Dieselpartikel (im folgenden kurz: Partikel)
- Staub (z. B. aus Kesselfeuerungen)
- Ammoniak (NH_3)

Die in Ökobilanzen noch nicht allgemein verbreitete Unterscheidung fester luftgetragener Emissionen in Partikel aus Motoren (einschließlich schwerölbetriebenen) und Staub aus Feuerungsanlagen ist sinnvoll, da sie sich chemisch – und damit auch in ihren Wirkungen – deutlich unterscheiden. Dieselpartikel bestehen im wesentlichen aus Kohlenstoff (Ruß) und enthalten organische Anhaftungen (etwa Benzo(a)pyren), während Staub z. B. aus Kohlefeuerungen große mineralische Anteile und mehr oder weniger große Schwermetallkonzentrationen aufweist. Allerdings ist auch klar, daß diese Unterscheidung wegen der komplexen Natur der emittierten Feststoffe nur sehr grob ist. Sie stellt jedoch gegenüber dem üblichen Vorgehen eine Verbesserung dar.

Die Aussagekraft des Bilanzierungsparameters NMHC ist nur gering, da in diesem Parameter Hunderte von Substanzen mit extrem unterschiedlichen Schadwirkungen zusammengefaßt werden. Die NMHC werden daher in dieser Studie ausschließlich aus dokumentarischen Gründen aufgeführt. Andererseits liegen für die meisten Prozesse der betrachteten Lebenswege nahezu keine abgesicherten bzw. öffentlich zugänglichen Emissionsmessungen oder Emissionsfaktoren für die einzelnen NMHC-Komponenten vor. Für folgende Einzelkomponenten werden wegen ihrer Toxizität und Kanzerogenität Abschätzungen vorgenommen; mögliche Inkonsistenzen sollen dabei helfen, Schwächen in der heutigen Datenlage aufzuspüren bzw. die Grenzen der Aussagefähigkeit der erhaltenen Ergebnisse zu verdeutlichen:

- Formaldehyd (FA)
- Benzol
- Benzo(a)pyren (BaP, als Leitkomponente für die PAH)
- polychlorierte Dioxine/Furane

Bilanzierungsmerkmale

Folgende Merkmale liegen der Bilanzierung zugrunde:

- Die Stickoxide (NO_X) werden als Stickstoffdioxid (NO_2) ausgewiesen.
- Die NMHC werden über die Gesamtmasse aller Kohlenwasserstoffe abzüglich Methan bilanziert.
- Die polychlorierten Dioxine/Furane werden als Toxizitätsäquivalente (TÄ) mit Bezug auf 2,3,7,8-TCDD (Tetrachlor-p-dibenzodioxin) bilanziert.

Aggregation

Außer den genannten Aggregationen für NO_X, NMHC und polychlorierte Dioxine/Furane werden keine weiteren Aggregationen durchgeführt. Zu diesen Aggregationen ist anzumerken, daß sie nicht unter dem Kriterium gemeinsamer und gleicher human- und/oder ökotoxischer Wirkungen erfolgen, sondern im wesentlichen aus Gründen technischer Praktikabilität üblich sind (siehe Kapitel 2.4.7).

4.2.2.8 Photosmog

Mit der Bilanzierung der Stickoxide und NMHC (siehe Kapitel 4.2.2.7) werden die wichtigsten Vorläufersubstanzen für die Bildung von Photooxidantien erfaßt. Ihr realer Beitrag zum Photosmog hängt jedoch von vielen verschiedenen, zum Teil lokalen Parametern ab, so daß er derzeit nicht pauschal bilanziert werden kann. Die Parameter sollten aber in entsprechend angepaßten Bilanzen Verwendung finden können.

Bilanzierungsmerkmale

Die Bilanzierung erfordert keine weiteren Konventionen.

Aggregation

Eine Aggregation erfolgt nicht. Die tatsächliche Photosmogbildung durch die bilanzierten Emissionen kann mangels verfügbarer Korrelationen nicht quantitativ ermittelt werden.

4.2.2.9 Lärmbelastung

Die Lärmbelastung ist (noch) keine in den Begriffen der Ökobilanzierung quantifizierbare Größe und wird daher hier nicht betrachtet.

4.2.3 Zusammenfassung der Bilanzierungsparameter

Die in den voranstehenden Abschnitten unter dem Aspekt der Wirkung festgelegten Bilanzierungsparameter lassen sich in den Kategorien Energieträger, mineralische Rohstoffe und luftgetragene Emissionen zusammenfassen (**Tabelle 4-9**). Für die Energieträger sind lediglich die Primärenergieträger aufgeführt, da nur diese – nicht aber die Endenergieträger – Ressourcen-Charakter haben. Mit aufgeführt sind neben den auf der Sachbilanzebene erfaßten Einzelgrößen die unter Wirkungsaspekten aggregierten Größen.

Tabelle 4-9 Erfaßte Bilanzierungsparameter und Wirkungskategorien

Mineralische Ressourcen	Energet. Ressourcen	Treibhaus-effekt	Ozon-abbau	Versaue-rung	Eutro-phierung	Toxizität	Photo-smog
Kalkstein	Erdöl	CO_2	N_2O	SO_2	NO_X	SO_2	NO_x
Phosphaterz	Erdgas	CH_4		NO_X	NH_3	CO	NMHC
Rohkali	Steinkohle	N_2O		HCl		NO_X	
Schwefel	Braunkohle	*CO_2-Äq.*		NH_3		HCl	
Tonmineralien	Uranerz			*SO_2-Äq.*		NH_3	
Steinsalz	*Σ Ersch. ET*					Partikel	
						Staub	
	Wasserkraft					FA	
	Biomasse*					Benzol	
						B(a)P	
	Σ Alle ET					TCDD-TÄ	

*: Nur für Rapsöl und Rapsölmethylester
Abkürzungen: Σ: Summe; ET: Energieträger; Äq.: Äquivalente; FA: Formaldehyd; B(a)P: Benzo(a)pyren; TCDD-TÄ: 2,3,7,8-TCDD-Toxizitätsäquivalente

4.3 Datenbasis und Datenqualität

Die Umsetzung der Zieldefinition auf der Sachbilanzebene, d. h. hier die Ableitung mittlerer spezifischer Ressourceneinsätze und Emissionen beim Einsatz verschiedener Transportmittel, Landmaschinen und im Bergbau eingesetzter Maschinen in Deutschland im Jahr 1996, ist in der Praxis mit erheblichen Problemen verbunden. Die Schwierigkeiten sind vor allem im Umfang und der Qualität der verfügbaren Basisdaten begründet.

Tatsächlich ist bereits die Zuordnung der Ergebnisse zu Deutschland 1996 weitgehend formaler Art. Um diese Zuordnung streng einzuhalten, wären statistische Durchschnittswerte notwendig, die für die meisten technischen Systeme nicht vorliegen. In die Ableitungen gehen daher notwendigerweise eine Reihe von Zusatzannahmen und Abschätzungen ein. Andererseits besteht der Anspruch, spezielle Einsätze durchschnittlicher Maschinen unter durchschnittlichen Bedingungen zu beschreiben. Das bedeutet, daß die hier abgeleiteten Daten nicht nur repräsentativ, sondern auch möglichst differenziert sein sollten. Anschaulich: Sie sollen z. B. wiedergeben, daß der mittlere Energieeinsatz für Anbau und Ernte von einem Hektar Raps mit „mittleren" Maschinen *un*gleich dem mittleren Energieeinsatz für Anbau und Ernte der „mittleren" Feldfrucht auf der gesamten Ackerfläche in Deutschland ist, oder daß der Transport einer Tonne über einen Kilometer mit dem gleichen LKW innerorts andere Emissionen verursacht als außerorts.

Natürlich stellt sich das Problem der Datenqualität nicht für alle Parameter in gleichem Maße. In der Regel sind Daten zum Energieeinsatz in größerer Zahl und besserer Belastbarkeit verfügbar als Emissionsdaten – nicht zuletzt eine Folge davon, daß Energie schon immer auch ein Kostenfaktor war. Andererseits relativiert der Anspruch an die Repräsentativität und zugleich Differenzierungstiefe der Daten zumindest zum Teil die günstigere Situation beim Parameter Energie.

Unterschiede bestehen ebenfalls hinsichtlich der Datenbasis zwischen den hier betrachteten Maschinen. Während LKW in umfassenden Großprojekten untersucht wurden, liegen für die in der Landwirtschaft und im Bergbau eingesetzten Maschinen allenfalls zusammenfassende Literaturstudien vor.

4.3.1 Vorgehensweise in diesem Buch

Grundsätzlich wird nur auf in der Literatur bzw. einem Computermodell (TREMOD) /IFEU 1998a/ vorhandene Daten zurückgegriffen. Diese Daten haben in der Regel andere Bezugsgrößen als die für ökologische Bilanzierungen geeigneten. Mit Hilfe von plausiblen Zusatzannahmen erfolgt die Ableitung der gewünschten Größen.

Die Datenbasis für die betrachteten Systeme ist hinsichtlich Umfang und Belastbarkeit sehr unterschiedlich. Außerdem erfordern unterschiedliche Datenstrukturen und Bezugsgrößen in unterschiedlichem Umfang Zusatzannahmen, die wiederum mehr oder weniger belastbar sein können. Letztlich gehen in die einzelnen Rechenschritte ausschließlich die von uns angesetzten Schätz- und berechneten Mittelwerte ein.

Auf Unsicherheiten, Bandbreiten usw. weisen wir hin, verzichten aber aus folgenden Gründen auf eingehende statistische Auswertungen: Für das System mit der besten Datengrundlage, den Transport mit LKW, wie auch für den Maschineneinsatz im Bergbau wurden die Rohdaten bereits in anderen Arbeiten aufbereitet. In anderen Fällen wie dem der Landmaschinen liegen für aussagekräftige statistische Auswertungen zu wenig Datensätze vor. So besitzt z. B. die Angabe einer Standardabweichung für einen Mittelwert aus einigen wenigen Einzelwerten, die jeweils in verschiedenen Labors mit verschiedenen Kraftstoffen und Maschinen gemessen wurden, keinen relevanten Informationsgehalt.

4.3.2 Belastbarkeit der Basisdaten

Eine qualitative Einschätzung der Belastbarkeit der Ergebnisdaten zum Energieverbrauch ist in **Tabelle 4-10** zusammengefaßt. Zum Verständnis der konkreten Bewertungen verweisen wir auf die entsprechenden Ausführungen in Kapitel 3 bzw. den jeweiligen Kapiteln zu Gütertransporten, Landwirtschaft, Bergbau und Energiebereitstellung (Kapitel 5 bis 8). Wir beschränken uns hier im wesentlichen auf einige eher formale Anmerkungen zu den Beurteilungskriterien:

- **Belastbarkeit der Mittelwerte:** Diese Rubrik erfaßt Umfang, Homogenität, Differenzierungsgrad und Aktualität der *gesamten* Datenbasis. Das heißt, daß zum Beispiel eine große Anzahl verschiedener Quellen hinsichtlich des Umfangs der Datenbasis positiv, unter dem Aspekt der Homogenität eher negativ gewertet wird.
- **Differenzierungstiefe:** In dieser Rubrik wird die erzielte Differenzierung hinsichtlich Maschinentyp und/oder Nennleistungsklasse *und* Einsatzarten bzw. Arbeiten oder Nutzungsmustern zusammengefaßt.
- **Belastbarkeit der differenzierten Daten:** Diese Rubrik erfaßt die Qualität der Mittelwerte *und* den Umfang zwar plausibler, in gewissem Maße aber willkürlicher Zusatzannahmen zur Durchführung der dargestellten Differenzierungen.

Das Bewertungsschema von A bis E (sehr gut / sehr hoch bis sehr schlecht / sehr niedrig) wird durch den Parameter Energie in **Tabelle 4-10** nicht ausgeschöpft. Für die Standardschadstoffe fällt die Bewertung der differenzierten Daten eine halbe bis ganze Stufe schlechter aus. Für andere Schadstoffe wie etwa Benzo(a)pyren ist bereits die Belastbarkeit der Mittelwerte deutlich geringer und eine Differenzierung kaum oder gar nicht möglich. Für die übrigen Transportmittel liegen die Datenqualitäten zwischen denen für LKW und für Bergbaumaschinen.

Unberührt davon kann jedoch für alle hier dokumentierten Daten davon ausgegangen werden, daß sie die belastbarsten gegenwärtig verfügbaren Daten zur Anwendung in ökologischen Bilanzierungen darstellen.

Tabelle 4-10 Qualitative Einschätzung der Belastbarkeit der Ergebnisdaten zum Energieverbrauch

	Belastbarkeit von Mittelwerten	**Differenzierungs-tiefe**	**Belastbarkeit der diff. Daten**
LKW	A	A	A
Landmaschinen	B	B	B
Bergbaumaschinen	B	C - D	C - D

A: sehr gut / sehr hoch; B: gut / hoch; C: mäßig; D: schlecht / niedrig; E: sehr schlecht / sehr niedrig

5 Gütertransport

Gegenstand dieses Kapitels sind Energieeinsatz und Emissionen der Gütertransportmittel

- LKW,
- Bahn,
- Binnenschiff,
- Seeschiff,
- Flugzeug und
- Pipeline.

Während Bahn und Binnenschiff und – als stationäre Anlagen – Pipelines für den kontinentalen Transport von Rohstoffen die Haupttransportmittel sind, wird die Distribution von Konsumprodukten durch den LKW-Transport dominiert. Seeschiffe werden auch zum Transport von Konsumgütern, überwiegend aber von Rohstoffen eingesetzt, Flugzeuge zum Transport teurer oder verderblicher Produkte.

Gemessen am Anteil an der gesamten Transportleistung haben die einzelnen Transportmittel *in* Deutschland eine sehr unterschiedliche Bedeutung: LKW: 66,2 %, Bahn: 15,9 %, Binnenschiff: 14,4 %, Pipeline: 3,4 %, Flugzeug 0,1 % (Bezug 1996) /VERKEHR 1997/. Einschließlich des Außenhandels, bei Bezug auf andere Länder bzw. im Welt-Mittel ergeben sich andere Relationen als für den Binnenverkehr in Deutschland. Für einzelne Produktgruppen ergeben sich andere Anteile als im Mittel aller transportierten Güter. Damit besteht zumindest die Möglichkeit, daß in einem bestimmten Produkt-Lebensweg nicht nur der in Deutschland dominierende LKW-Transport und der Seetransport von Rohstoffen eine entscheidende Rolle spielen. Grundsätzlich sind damit auch vergleichbar differenzierte und belastbare Datensätze für alle Transportmittel erstrebenswert. Diesem Ziel steht die sehr unterschiedliche Qualität der Primärdatenbasen entgegen. Damit werden für die Ableitung der spezifischen Daten der einzelnen Transportmittel zum Teil sehr unterschiedliche Vorgehensweisen erforderlich.

In den folgenden Kapiteln werden die Verfahren für die einzelnen Transportmittel detailliert beschrieben. Die spezifischen Energieverbräuche werden bezogen auf die Transportleistung in tkm ausgewiesen, die Emissionsfaktoren ebenfalls bezogen auf die Transportleistung und außerdem bezogen auf den Energieeinsatz. Der direkte Energieeinsatz und die damit verbundenen Emissionen werden in diesen Kapiteln dokumentiert. Im Anhang werden zusätzlich die kumulierten Energieaufwendungen und Emissionen, d. h. unter Einbeziehung der Energiebereitstellung, ausgewiesen.

Das Bezugsjahr der Ableitung ist 1996. Für LKW werden aufgrund der absehbaren Emissionsminderungen für die Schadstoffe NO_X, (NM)HC, CO und Partikel auch Faktoren mit Bezug auf das Jahr 2000 abgeleitet und im Anhang dokumentiert. Im Falle der übrigen Transportmittel, für die die Datenlage unsicherer ist, können im Bedarfsfall durch den Leser aus den dokumentierten Primärdaten entsprechende Fortschreibungen selbst vorgenommen werden. Die für 1996 abgeleiteten Daten können wegen der langen Zeiträume der Bestandsumschichtungen allerdings in akzeptabler Näherung für das Jahr 2000 angesetzt werden.

Schließlich können für alle Transportmittel die für den Bezugsraum Deutschland abgeleiteten Daten in akzeptabler Näherung auch für andere Bezugsräume angesetzt werden.

5.1 LKW

Im Falle des LKW-Transports ist aus zwei Gründen eine möglichst weitgehende Differenzierung bei der Erfassung von Energieeinsätzen und Emissionen wünschenswert: Der erste Grund ist der überragende Transportleistungsanteil in Deutschland (66 %) und den meisten industrialisierten Ländern. Da LKW in der Regel deutlich höhere spezifische Energieeinsätze und Emissionen als andere bodengebundene Transportmittel haben, resultiert für die ökologisch relevanten Größen eine noch größere Bedeutung des LKW-Transports als im Falle der ökonomischen Größe Transportleistung. Der zweite Grund für eine detaillierte Analyse des LKW-Transports liegt in den Emissionsorten: Ein großer Teil fällt in der Emissionsortsklasse 1, der Klasse mit der höchsten Bevölkerungsdichte, an. Die Emissionen der übrigen Transportmittel sind dagegen im wesentlichen auf die Ortsklassen 2 und 3 beschränkt.

Im folgenden werden nur LKW mit einem Zulässigen Gesamtgewicht von mindestens 7 t betrachtet. Da LKW bereits ab einem Gesamtgewicht von 3,5 t weit überwiegend von Dieselmotoren angetrieben werden, beziehen sich Verbrauchsangaben im folgenden stets auf Dieselkraftstoff. Die realistische Option, mit Rapsölmethylester einen Biokraftstoff im Nutzfahrzeugsektor zu verwenden, wird in einem eigenen Kapitel (5.1.5) behandelt.

Die Ergebnisse werden in der Differenzierung nach fünf repräsentativen LKW-Klassen, drei typischen Auslastungsgraden und den drei Straßenkategorien „Autobahn", „außerorts" (ohne Autobahn) und „innerorts" ausgewiesen. Den zeitlichen Bezug bildet das Jahr 1996; eine Fortschreibung mit Bezug auf das Jahr 2000 für die Schadstoffe NO_X, (NM)HC, CO und Partikel findet sich im Anhang (**Tabelle 9-2**). Für LKW-Transporte in anderen Regionen als Deutschland bzw. der EU, etwa Osteuropa, in denen auch längerfristig mit weniger strengen Grenzwerten bzw. einer langsameren Umsetzung als in der EU zu rechnen ist, liefern die hier abgeleiteten Daten zumindest Anhaltswerte.

Abschließend ist in Kapitel 5.1.6 die detaillierte Anwendung der Daten insbesondere bei variierenden Auslastungsgraden oder der Berücksichtigung von Rückfahrten beschrieben.

5.1.1 Grundlagen

Eine der Bedeutung des LKW-Transports angemessene Erfassung des Energieeinsatzes und der Emissionen muß eine Reihe technischer Parameter berücksichtigen:

Fahrzeugtechnik: LKW-Transporte – auch die *eines bestimmten* Produktes – werden mit einer Vielzahl verschiedener Fahrzeuge ausgeführt. Unterschiede bestehen typ- und baujahrabhängig in der Fahrzeugtechnik, im Wartungszustand und in der Größe der Fahrzeuge (Zulässiges Gesamtgewicht; siehe unten). Weiter ist zwischen verschiedenen Aufbauarten (Kasten, Tank, Mulde usw.) sowie zwischen Solo-LKW, LKW- und Sattelzügen zu unterscheiden. Besondere Bedeutung haben die für die einzelnen Baujahre gültigen Emissions-grenzwerte, die in Vorschriften der EU festgelegt sind. Die meisten Parameter können allerdings nur über pauschale Abschätzungen erfaßt werden.

Zulässiges Gesamtgewicht (ZGG): Das Zulässige Gesamtgewicht ist eine fahrzeugtechnische Größe. Im Unterschied zu den übrigen technischen Merkmalen kann das Zulässige Gesamtgewicht im Rahmen von ökologischen Bilanzierungen oft mit geringem Aufwand erhoben werden und in der Realität eines Produktlebensweges durch Entscheidungsträger z. B. im Bereich der Logistik beeinflußt werden. Die Abhängigkeit des spezifischen Energieverbrauchs und der Emissionen (Bezug: tkm) vom Zulässigen Gesamtgewicht ergibt sich daraus, daß der Anteil des LKW-Eigengewichts am Zulässigen Gesamtgewicht mit zunehmendem Zulässigen Gesamtgewicht sinkt. Anschaulich: Ein leerer LKW mit 15 t Zulässigem Gesamtgewicht wiegt weniger als zwei leere LKW mit 7,5 t Zulässigem Gesamtgewicht. Das Zusammentreffen von großer Sensitivität einerseits und relativ guter Beeinflußbarkeit andererseits machen eine differenzierte Betrachtung in Ökobilanzen sinnvoll und möglich.

Fahrmuster: Unter sonst gleichen Bedingungen sind der Energieeinsatz und die Emissionen eines Transports abhängig von der mittleren Geschwindigkeit, Anzahl und Art von Beschleunigungsvorgängen, der Steigung der Strecke und der Zuladung (Auslastungsgrad; siehe unten). Es ist offensichtlich, daß im Rahmen einer Ökobilanz Detailanalysen aller Transporte für die genannten Parameter unmöglich sind. Wie im Fall der Fahrzeugtechnik ist lediglich der Rückgriff auf Mittelwerte realistisch. Geeignete Aggregationsebenen stellen dabei die drei Straßenkategorien „Autobahn“, „außerorts“ und „innerorts“ dar.

Auslastungsgrad (ALG): Der Auslastungsgrad – das Verhältnis von tatsächlicher Zuladung zu Maximaler Nutzlast (MNL) – ist eine Größe, die das Fahrmuster mit definiert. Anders als die oben aufgeführten Parameter und ähnlich dem Zulässigen Gesamtgewicht kann der Auslastungsgrad im Rahmen von Ökobilanzen oft mit geringem Aufwand erhoben und in der betrieblichen Praxis relativ leicht beeinflußt werden. Die Abhängigkeit des spezifischen Energieverbrauchs und der Emissionen (Bezug: tkm) von der Auslastung besteht darin, daß das LKW-Eigengewicht mit zunehmender Auslastung über eine größere Masse an Transportgut „abgeschrieben“ wird. Wie für das Zulässige Gesamtgewicht ist eine differenzierte Betrachtung sinnvoll und möglich.

Bislang wurden die Einflußgrößen im wesentlichen unter dem Aspekt ihrer Berücksichtigung in Ökobilanzen betrachtet. Wie in Kapitel 3 diskutiert, ist jedoch bereits ihre Erfassung in Messungen problematisch: Auch in großen Meßprogrammen können

- Messungen nur für eine begrenzte Anzahl an Fahrmustern durchgeführt werden und
- nur wenige als besonders wichtig betrachtete LKW-Klassen berücksichtigt werden. Kriterien für die Auswahl sind die Anteile einzelner Klassen am Bestand nach /KBA/ bzw. an der Fahrleistung aller LKW.

Offensichtlich müssen bei der Ableitung von transportleistungsbezogenen Energieverbräuchen und Emissionen des LKW-Transports zahlreiche Näherungen und Vereinfachungen in Kauf genommen werden, die sich zum einen aus dem Aufwand der Erhebung von Meßdaten, zum anderen aus dem Anspruch einfacher Anwendbarkeit in Ökobilanzen ergeben. In den folgenden Unterkapiteln werden diese Näherungen und Zusatzannahmen detailliert erläutert. Hinsichtlich der Vorgehensweise der Ableitung ist zu unterscheiden zwischen dem spezifischen Energieeinsatz und den Emissionen limitierter, d. h. gesetzlich beschränkter Schadstoffe, die auf abgestimmten Meßprogrammen und Rechenmodellen basieren, und den Emissionen weiterer Schadstoffe, die durch Schätzwerte auf der Basis verschiedener Literaturangaben beschrieben werden.

5.1.2 Methodik

Die Basis der Ableitung bilden Rechenläufe eines im Auftrag des Umweltbundesamtes (UBA), Berlin, entwickelten Programms zur Berechnung des Energieeinsatzes und der Emissionen des motorisierten Verkehrs in Deutschland (TREMOD: Transport Emission Estimation Model; /IFEU 1998a/).

In TREMOD werden die Ergebnisse umfangreicher Projekte im Auftrag des Bundesministeriums für Verkehr und des Umweltbundesamtes zur Erhebung hoch differenzierter fahrleistungsbezogener Energieverbräuche und Emissionsfaktoren für limitierte Schadstoffe /TÜVRL 1995/, Fahrmuster und Fahrleistungsverteilungen /HEUSCH-BOESEFELDT 1996/ zusammengeführt. Diese Studien nehmen zwar Bezug auf verschiedene Jahre, enthalten aber zumindest zum Teil Änderungsfaktoren zur Fortschreibung. TREMOD selbst ist auf die Berechnung von Zeitreihen ausgelegt; die Entwicklungen von Größen wie der gesamten Fahrleistung und den Anteilen der einzelnen Fahrmuster daran werden in Szenarien nach /IFO 1995/, die auf der Bundesverkehrswegeplanung basieren, berechnet. Die zeitliche Änderung der Energieverbräuche und Emissionsfaktoren wird wie in /TÜVRL 1995/ dargestellt bzw. in Abstimmung verschiedener Institutionen – darunter IFEU, TÜVRL und UBA – modelliert. Im Fall der Emissionsfaktoren ist dabei vor allem die schrittweise Durchdringung des Bestandes mit LKW, die gerade rechtskräftig gewordenen oder zukünftig wirksamen Emissionsbegrenzungen unterliegen, von Bedeutung (EURO II ab 1996, EURO III ab 2000).

TREMOD liefert als Ergebnis den fahrleistungsbezogenen Kraftstoffverbrauch und die Emissionen differenziert nach Straßenkategorien und LKW-Klassen. Für die betrachteten Auslastungsgrade werden jeweils gesonderte Rechenläufe durchgeführt. In einem Rechenablauf wird die gesamte Fahrleistung auf dem Gebiet Deutschlands pro Jahr in den einzelnen Fahrmustern, die durch Straßenkategorie, Steigung und Geschwindigkeit definiert sind, mit den entsprechenden Kraftstoffverbräuchen und Emissionsfaktoren jeweils differenziert nach LKW-Klassen verknüpft. Die LKW-Klassen sind dabei lediglich über das Zulässige Gesamtgewicht definiert. Die in TREMOD enthaltene Unterscheidung verschiedener Aufbauarten (Kasten, Tank, Mulde usw.) führt einerseits nur zu geringen Differenzen für die einzelnen Parameter, ist andererseits aber mit relativ hohen Unsicherheiten behaftet, so daß eine Mittelung über alle Aufbauarten sinnvoll ist. Die Ergebnisse für die einzelnen Fahrmuster werden differenziert nach LKW-Klassen und Straßenkategorien zusammengefaßt. Die spezifischen Daten für eine Straßenkategorie, LKW-Klasse und einen Auslastungsgrad ergeben sich aus den Absolutwerten des Kraftstoffverbrauchs und der Emissionen dividiert durch die Fahrleistung.

Die Daten in TREMOD beziehen sich auf die Fahrleistung. Für die Beschreibung von Transportaufgaben in Ökobilanzen ist jedoch der Bezug auf die Transportleistung zweckmäßiger. Die Umrechnung fahrleistungsbezogener in transportleistungsbezogene Daten erfordert Annahmen zur Maximalen Nutzlast (MNL) der LKW-Klassen, nach denen in TREMOD differenziert wird. Für diese Umrechnung werden von den zehn LKW-Klassen nach TREMOD drei direkt übernommen sowie vier paarweise zusammengefaßt. Diese Reduktion gegenüber TREMOD ist aus verschiedenen Gründen sinnvoll:

- Die nach dem Kriterium „Anteil an der gesamten Fahrleistung" wichtigen LKW-Klassen werden in einer gut handhabbaren Anzahl von Datensätzen erfaßt.
- Den Daten des TREMOD-Inputs liegen teilweise nur sehr wenige Messungen zugrunde und die nach LKW-Klassen differenzierten Ergebnisse weisen einzelne, im wesentlichen geringfügige, Inkonsistenzen auf. Diese Inkonsistenzen betreffen die Relationen korrespondierender Daten verschiedener LKW-Klassen. Hier kann durch die Zusammenführung von LKW-Klassen, etwa von Sattel- und Lastzügen gleichen Zulässigen Gesamtgewichts, tendenziell von einer Verbesserung der Datenqualität ausgegangen werden.

Die hier angesetzten Werte für die Maximale Nutzlast sind Schätzwerte, die auf Auswertungen von LKW-Tests beruhen /LKW/. Die transportleistungsbezogenen Daten ergeben sich durch Division der fahrleistungsbezogenen Daten durch die tatsächliche Zuladung, dem Produkt aus Maximaler Nutzlast und Auslastungsgrad. **Tabelle 5-1** faßt die Spezifikation der hier betrachteten LKW-Klassen sowie ihre Anteile an der Fahrleistung in Deutschland im Jahr 1996 differenziert nach Straßenkategorien zusammen.

Tabelle 5-1 Kenngrößen der verwendeten LKW-Klassen und Anteile an der Gesamtfahrleistung differenziert nach Straßenkategorien in Deutschland 1996

Beschriebene LKW-Klassen						
Betriebsart	Solo	Solo	Solo	Zug	Zug	
ZGG in t	< 10	10 - 20	> 20	< 32	> 32	
Zur Klassenbeschreibung gewählte LKW						
ZGG, erfaßt, in t	7 – 7,5	14 – 20	20 – 28	30	40	
ZGG, gew. Mittel in t	7,5	16,5	23	30	40	
MNL in t	3,75	10,5	15,3	20,5	28	
Anteile an der Fahrleistung						**Summe**
Autobahn	7,5%	2,4%	3,1%	9,0%	28,7%	**50,7%**
Außerortsstraße	11,5%	3,3%	3,3%	3,8%	8,5%	**30,4%**
Innerortsstraße	9,8%	2,3%	1,8%	1,9%	3,1%	**18,9%**
Summe	**28,8%**	**8,0%**	**8,3%**	**14,7%**	**40,3%**	**100 %**

ZGG: Zulässiges Gesamtgewicht; MNL: Maximale Nutzlast
Quelle: /IFEU 1998a/, eigene Berechnungen

5.1.3 Kraftstoffverbrauch

Die nach dem oben dargestellten Verfahren erhaltenen spezifischen Kraftstoffverbräuche der fünf LKW-Klassen differenziert nach Straßenkategorien und Auslastungsgraden sind in **Tabelle 5-2** zusammengefaßt. Die Daten zeigen eindeutig die Notwendigkeit der Differenzierung nach LKW-Klassen und der Berücksichtigung verschiedener Auslastungsgrade. Der Kraftstoffverbrauch eines 7,5-t-LKW etwa ist bei einem Auslastungsgrad von 50 % um den Faktor 3 größer als der eines 40-t-Zuges (Mittel aller Straßenkategorien). Für einen 40-t-Zug ist der Verbrauch bei einem Auslastungsgrad von 50 % um den Faktor 1,6 größer als bei einem Auslastungsgrad von 100 %. Die Innerortsverbräuche sind um einen Faktor 1,1 bis 1,4

(7,5 bzw. 40 t) größer als die Verbräuche außerorts (Auslastungsgrad: 50 %); die Verbräuche auf Autobahnen liegen geringfügig über denen auf den übrigen Außerortsstraßen.

Die über alle LKW-Klassen gemittelten Verbräuche sind lediglich nachrichtlich aufgeführt; sie sollten allenfalls in Grobabschätzungen verwendet werden.

Tabelle 5-2 Energieeinsatz differenziert nach LKW-Klassen, Straßenkategorien und Auslastungsgraden

ZGG	7,5 t	16,5 t	23 t	30 t	40 t	gew. Mittel
Leerfahrt			— MJ / km —			
Autobahn	6,19	9,99	11,0	9,77	11,5	10,3
Außerorts	5,27	9,11	10,3	8,83	10,7	8,21
Innerorts	6,10	13,1	15,0	11,6	14,9	9,83
gew. Mittel	5,79	10,5	11,6	9,77	11,6	9,59
50 % ALG			— MJ / tkm —			
Autobahn	3,46	2,15	1,66	1,22	1,10	1,23
Außerorts	3,03	2,02	1,59	1,15	1,05	1,40
Innerorts	3,99	3,07	2,46	1,61	1,53	2,26
gew. Mittel	3,47	2,37	1,81	1,25	1,12	1,40
100 % ALG			— MJ / tkm —			
Autobahn	1,81	1,20	0,94	0,74	0,69	0,75
Außerorts	1,63	1,15	0,92	0,72	0,67	0,84
Innerorts	2,37	1,83	1,48	1,05	0,99	1,40
gew. Mittel	1,92	1,36	1,05	0,78	0,71	0,85

ZGG: Zulässiges Gesamtgewicht; ALG: Auslastungsgrad
Mittelwerte: Fahr- bzw. transportleistungsgewichtet (siehe Tabelle 5-1)
Quelle: /IFEU 1998a/, eigene Berechnungen

5.1.4 Emissionen

Für die Ableitung der Emissionsfaktoren sind drei Fälle zu unterscheiden:

- Schadstoffe, deren Emissionen sich unmittelbar aus Kraftstoffzusammensetzung und Kraftstoffverbrauch ergeben (inventargebundene Emissionen),
- Schadstoffe, deren Emissionen darüber hinaus bzw. ausschließlich vom Betriebszustand des Motors abhängen, zu denen entsprechende Informationen vorliegen und
- Schadstoffe, deren Emissionen wahrscheinlich ebenfalls vom Betriebszustand abhängen, für die jedoch keine differenzierten Primärdaten vorliegen.

Inventargebundene Emissionen

In diese Kategorie fallen CO_2, SO_2 und HCl. Die Berechnung aus Kraftstoffzusammensetzung und -verbrauch impliziert dabei eine vollständige Verbrennung des C-, S- und Cl-Inventars zu diesen Verbindungen. Im Falle des Schwefels entspricht dies praktisch der Realität. Für Kohlenstoff fallen mit CO, Methan, NMHC und den Partikeln relativ größere Mengen anderer Verbrennungsprodukte an; bezogen auf die CO_2-Emissionen liegt der C-Anteil, der mit diesen Verbindungen emittiert wird, jedoch im Promillebereich. Außerdem werden CO und NMHC schnell (im Vergleich zur atmosphärischen Verweildauer von CO_2) und fast ausschließlich zu CO_2 umgesetzt. Die Berechnung der CO_2- und SO_2-Emissionen aus Kraftstoffzusammensetzung und -verbrauch ist daher das anerkannte und übliche Verfahren zur Bestimmung der Emissionsfaktoren für diese Schadstoffe. Für HCl übernehmen wir diese Vorgehensweise.

Für den C-Gehalt von Dieselkraftstoff übernehmen wir den Wert aus /DGMK 1992/ von 86,6 M%. Für den S-Gehalt, der seit Anfang 1995 in der EU auf 0,05 M% begrenzt ist, nehmen wir als Rechenwert 0,045 M% an. Den Cl-Gehalt schätzen wir auf 0,0001 M% ab. Dieser Wert orientiert sich an einem Cl-Gehalt von 0,00012 M%, der in /CARBOTECH 1994/ als Obergrenze des in /ESSERS et al. 1992/ eingesetzten Dieselkraftstoffes angegeben wird. Die Emissionsfaktoren ergeben sich damit zu 73,9 g CO_2, 0,021 g SO_2 und 0,00023 g HCl je MJ Dieselkraftstoff.

Zur Umrechnung in energiebezogene Einheiten setzen wir den Energieinhalt von Dieselkraftstoff entsprechend /AGE 1998/ mit 42,96 MJ/kg an; die Faktoren sind in **Tabelle 5-3** dokumentiert. Die transportleistungsbezogenen Emissionsfaktoren ergeben sich daraus durch Multiplikation mit dem spezifischen Kraftstoffverbrauch.

Vom Betriebszustand abhängige Emissionen

Zu den hier betrachteten Schadstoffen, deren Emissionen vom Betriebszustand abhängig sind, gehören CO, NO_X, HC und Partikel. Für diese Schadstoffe können Faktoren – wie für den spezifischen Energieverbrauch beschrieben – auf der Basis von TREMOD-Abfragen bestimmt werden. Die Methan- und NMHC-Faktoren werden dabei aus den HC-Faktoren und einem Betriebszustand-unabhängigen Schätzwert für den Anteil von Methan an den HC-Emissionen von Diesel-KFZ nach /IFEU 1995b/ bestimmt. Analog werden die Faktoren für Benzol und Formaldehyd abgeleitet (diese Substanzen werden auch als Bestandteil der NMHC erfaßt). Folgende Anteile werden angesetzt: CH_4/HC: 2,4 M%; Benzol/HC: 1,9 M%; Formaldehyd/HC: 8,1 M%.

In **Tabelle 5-3** sind die verbrauchs- und transportleistungsbezogenen Emissionsfaktoren zusammengefaßt. Die verbrauchsbezogenen Faktoren für CO, NO_X, NMHC und Partikel sind Mittelwerte über *alle LKW-Klassen* und Straßenkategorien bei einem Auslastungsgrad von 50 %. Die transportleistungsbezogenen Faktoren dieser Schadstoffe basieren auf *nach den fünf LKW-Klassen differenzierten* verbrauchsbezogenen Faktoren im Mittel aller Straßenkategorien bei einem Auslastungsgrad von 50 %. Weiter differenzierte transportleistungsbezogene Daten finden sich im Anhang (**Tabelle 9-1**).

Emissionen weiterer Schadstoffe

Wahrscheinlich hängen die Emissionen von N_2O, NH_3 und von Dioxinen/Furanen zumindest teilweise ebenfalls vom Betriebszustand ab. Für diese Stoffe führen wir Grobabschätzungen (Bezug: Kraftstoffverbrauch) auf der Basis von Daten nach /BRADOW et al. 1980/ und /ESSERS et al. 1992/ (zusammengefaßt in /CARBOTECH 1994/) und einer Reihe von Zusatzannahmen durch. Für Benzo(a)pyren setzen wir die Mittelwerte der Daten nach /GRÄF et al. 1994/, /KRAHL 1993/, /WÖRGETTER et al. 1990/ und /WÖRGETTER et al. 1993/ für Ackerschlepper an (Bezug: Kraftstoffverbrauch). Die Faktoren sind ebenfalls in **Tabelle 5-3** dokumentiert.

Tabelle 5-3 Spezifischer Verbrauch und Emissionen von LKW bei einem Auslastungsgrad von 50 % im Mittel aller Straßenkategorien

ZGG		Alle*		7,5 t	16,5 t	23 t	30 t	40 t
Kraftstoffverbrauch								
Diesel			MJ/tkm	3,47	2,37	1,81	1,25	1,12
Emissionen								
		Global		**Global**	**Global**	**Global**	**Global**	**Global**
CO_2	g/MJ	73,9	g/tkm	256	175	134	92,5	82,9
CH_4	g/MJ	0,0026	g/tkm	0,018	0,0070	0,0049	0,0023	0,0018
N_2O	g/MJ	0,0077	g/tkm	0,027	0,018	0,014	0,0097	0,0087
		OK 1+2		**OK 1+2**	**OK 1+2**	**OK 1+2**	**OK 1+2**	**OK 1+2**
SO_2	g/MJ	0,021	g/tkm	0,073	0,050	0,038	0,026	0,024
CO	g/MJ	0,18	g/tkm	1,05	0,47	0,34	0,25	0,14
NO_X	g/MJ	0,74	g/tkm	1,95	1,72	1,39	0,92	0,89
NMHC	g/MJ	0,097	g/tkm	0,73	0,29	0,20	0,094	0,072
Partikel	g/MJ	0,038	g/tkm	0,18	0,10	0,064	0,054	0,036
Staub	g/MJ	0	g/tkm	0	0	0	0	0
HCl	g/MJ	0,000023	g/tkm	0,00008	0,00006	0,00004	0,00003	0,00003
NH_3	g/MJ	0,00047	g/tkm	0,0016	0,0011	0,00084	0,00058	0,00052
Formaldehyd	g/MJ	0,0088	g/tkm	0,060	0,024	0,016	0,0078	0,0060
Benzol	g/MJ	0,0021	g/tkm	0,014	0,0055	0,0039	0,0018	0,0014
Benzo(a)pyren	ng/MJ	180	ng/tkm	623	425	325	225	202
TCDD-TÄ	ng/MJ	0,0014	ng/tkm	0,0049	0,0033	0,0025	0,0018	0,0016

ZGG: Zulässiges Gesamtgewicht
*: Mittel über alle LKW und Straßenkategorien
Quellen: /CARBOTECH 1994/, /IFEU 1995b/, /IFEU 1998a/, eigene Berechnungen

Anwendung mittlerer Emissionsfaktoren

Wie unten gezeigt wird, ist die Differenzierung nach LKW-Klassen, Auslastungsgraden und Straßenkategorien für tiefergehende Analysen notwendig. Falls jedoch der Einsatz hier nicht dokumentierter LKW-Klassen erfaßt werden soll und/oder konkrete Verbrauchsdaten in MJ/tkm vorliegen, können mit der Verwendung mittlerer verbrauchsbezogener Emissionsfaktoren belastbare Ergebnisse erzielt werden. Für diese Faktoren ist eine Mittelung über LKW-Klassen, Auslastungsgrade und Straßenkategorien durchaus sinnvoll, da ihre Anwendung auf das ausschließliche Vorhandensein von Kraftstoffverbrauchsdaten, z. B. eines ganzen Fuhrparks, als Input abzielt. Die für die fünf hier betrachteten LKW-Klassen ausgewiesenen Daten können auch für detailliertere Untersuchungen unmittelbar verwendet werden, da sie sich auf realistische Werte für den Auslastungsgrad und die Anteile der einzelnen Straßenkategorien beziehen.

Weitere Differenzierungen

In **Tabelle 5-4** und **Tabelle 5-5** sind die spezifischen Kraftstoffverbräuche und Emissionsfaktoren für verschiedene Differenzierungen zusammengefaßt. Die Einflüsse des Zulässigen Gesamtgewichts, des Auslastungsgrades und der Straßenkategorie auf den Verbrauch wurden bereits diskutiert; wir beschränken uns daher hier auf einige Anmerkungen zu den Emissionen der Schadstoffe CO, NO_X, NMHC und Partikel. Die übrigen Schadstoffe sind, wie oben dargestellt, tatsächlich oder in der hier durchgeführten Ableitung unmittelbar an den Kraftstoffverbrauch gebunden.

Tabelle 5-4 faßt die Daten für die zwei LKW-Klassen mit der größten Fahrleistung und für drei Auslastungsgrade im Mittel aller Straßenkategorien zusammen. Vergleicht man die LKW miteinander, so zeigt sich, daß der 7,5-t-LKW fast immer mehr emittiert als der 40-t-Zug. Die größten Unterschiede bestehen bei den NMHC-Emissionen.

- Bei Leerfahrten (Bezug: Fahrleistung in km!) emittiert der 7,5-t-LKW durchschnittlich 17 bzw. 40 % mehr als der 40-t-Zug. Für NO_X und Partikel sind dagegen die Emissionen des 7,5-t-LKW um 70 bzw. 20 % kleiner als die des 40-t-Zuges.
- Bei halber Auslastung emittiert der 7,5-t-LKW immer mehr von den vier Schadstoffen als der 40-t-Zug. Dabei sind die NMHC-Emissionen um den Faktor 11 größer; für CO, Partikel und NO_X liegen die Relationen bei 9, 6 und 2.
- Für einen Auslastungsgrad von 100 % ergeben sich sehr ähnliche Relationen wie bei 50 % Auslastung.

Für einen 40-t-Zug sind die Emissionen bei halber Auslastung je nach Schadstoff um den Faktor 1,5 bis 2 größer als bei einem Auslastungsgrad von 100 %; für 7,5-t-LKW ist der Effekt etwas ausgeprägter.

Tabelle 5-4 Energieeinsatz und Emissionen von zwei LKW-Klassen differenziert nach Auslastungsgrad im Mittel aller Straßenkategorien

ZGG		**7,5 t**			**40 t**		
ALG		**0 %**	**50 %**	**100 %**	**0 %**	**50 %**	**100 %**
Dieselverb.	MJ/(t)km	5,79	3,47	1,92	11,6	1,12	0,71
CO	g/(t)km	1,75	1,05	0,58	1,68	0,14	0,080
NO_X	g/(t)km	3,19	1,95	1,10	9,17	0,89	0,56
NMHC	g/(t)km	1,22	0,73	0,40	0,92	0,072	0,039
Partikel	g/(t)km	0,29	0,18	0,10	0,43	0,036	0,021

ZGG: Zulässiges Gesamtgewicht; ALG: Auslastungsgrad; ALG 0 %: /km, ALG 50 und 100 %: /tkm
Quelle: /IFEU 1998a/, eigene Berechnungen

Tabelle 5-5 Energieeinsatz und Emissionen von zwei LKW-Klassen differenziert nach Straßenkategorien bei einem Auslastungsgrad von 50 %

ZGG		**7,5 t**			**40 t**		
Straßenkategorie		**AB**	**AO**	**IO**	**AB**	**AO**	**IO**
Dieselverb.	MJ/tkm	3,46	3,03	3,99	1,10	1,05	1,53
CO	g/tkm	0,89	0,84	1,40	0,13	0,13	0,23
NO_X	g/tkm	2,00	1,70	2,20	0,86	0,84	1,35
NMHC	g/tkm	0,43	0,46	1,27	0,066	0,065	0,15
Partikel	g/tkm	0,14	0,13	0,26	0,034	0,035	0,062

ZGG: Zulässiges Gesamtgewicht
AB: Autobahn; AO: Außerortsstraße ohne Autobahn; IO: Innerortsstraße
Quelle: /IFEU 1998a/, eigene Berechnungen

In **Tabelle 5-5** sind für zwei LKW-Klassen die Emissionsfaktoren für verschiedene Straßenkategorien bei einem Auslastungsgrad von 50 % zusammengefaßt. Die Emissionen auf Autobahnen und Außerortsstraßen sind für jede der LKW-Klassen recht ähnlich. Deutlich höher sind dagegen die Emissionen auf Innerortsstraßen. Sie liegen je nach Schadstoff um maximal den Faktor 3 (7,5-t-LKW, NMHC) über denen auf Außerortsstraßen.

In der Gesamtschau liegen die Einflüsse der drei Parameter

- Zulässiges Gesamtgewicht, genauer: die eingesetzten Motoren und ihre Einstellungen,
- Auslastungsgrad und
- Straßenkategorie

auf Kraftstoffverbrauch und Emissionen in ähnlichen Größenordnungen. Eine Differenzierung nach diesen drei Größen ist damit in tiefergehenden Analysen unbedingt sinnvoll. Für verschiedene Auslastungsgrade ist die Interpolation zwischen den hier ausgewiesenen Daten für 50 und 100 % möglich (Extrapolation für einen Auslastungsgrad < 50 %). Die Verwendung der über alle Straßenkategorien gemittelten Daten ist insofern gerechtfertigt, als die Mittelung gewichtet mit den für die einzelnen LKW-Klassen typischen Anteilen der Straßenkategorien erfolgt. Die über alle LKW-Klassen gemittelten Daten sollten dagegen nur in Grobabschätzungen eingesetzt werden.

5.1.5 Exkurs: Kraftstoffverbrauch und Emissionen im RME-Betrieb

In LKW werden fast nur Dieselmotoren eingesetzt, die grundsätzlich auch zur Verbrennung von RME (Rapsölmethylester) geeignet sind. Zu den speziellen Problemen der Ableitung von Emissionsfaktoren im RME-Betrieb verweisen wir auf die detaillierte Darstellung der RME- bzw. Rapsölnutzung in Landmaschinen (Kapitel 6.3). Wir beschränken uns hier auf einige Anmerkungen.

Einzelne Messungen weisen darauf hin, daß der energiebezogene Verbrauch (Einheit: MJ) im RME-Betrieb höher ist als im Dieselbetrieb; nach /SCHÄFER et al. 1998/ ist der Verbrauch im ECE-Zyklus unabhängig vom eingesetzten Kraftstoff. Allgemeingültige Aussagen lassen sich damit noch nicht ableiten. Wir gehen hier von gleichen Verbräuchen im RME- und Dieselbetrieb aus. Gravimetrisch ergibt sich wegen des geringeren Heizwertes von RME ein um etwa 15 % höherer Verbrauch des RME-Betriebs.

Die Emissionsfaktoren der inventargebundenen Schadstoffe CO_2, SO_2 und HCl werden unter der Annahme vollständiger Verbrennung aus dem massenbezogenen Verbrauch und dem C- und S-Gehalt von RME nach /KALTSCHMITT & REINHARDT 1997/ bzw. dem maximalen Cl-Gehalt nach /CONNEMANN 1998/ bestimmt (C-Gehalt: 77,3 M%, S-Gehalt: 0,005 M%, Cl-Gehalt: < 0,0001 M%).

Aufgrund der unterschiedlichen Zusammensetzungen von RME und Dieselkraftstoff und des damit nicht identischen – wenngleich natürlich sehr ähnlichen – Verbrennungsverhaltens sind grundsätzlich auch unterschiedliche Emissionen für Schadstoffe zu erwarten, deren Emissionen nicht direkt inventargebunden sind. Einzelmessungen bestätigen diese Erwartung. **Tabelle 5-6** faßt die Ergebnisse von Vergleichsmessungen an zwei Motoren-Baureihen zusammen (Mercedes-Benz BR 300 und BR 400). Bei diesen Baureihen handelt es sich um Direkteinspritzer, die im Dieselbetrieb die Abgasnorm EURO II erfüllen. Die Messungen erfolgten nach dem 13-Punkte-Test. Nach Angaben des Herstellers wird RME im Falle einer weiter verbreiteten Anwendung im wesentlichen in Motoren dieses Konzeptes eingesetzt werden. Die Ergebnisse sind als Relativwerte RME/Dieselkraftstoff ausgewiesen.

Tabelle 5-6 Emissionsdaten im 13-Punkte-Test: Mercedes-Benz-Nutzfahrzeugmotoren im RME-Betrieb

	E-Faktoren RME g/MJ RME	**RME / DK**
CO	0,14	80,5%
HC	0,31	54,0%
NO_X	0,12	113 %
Partikel	0,026	76,0%

Quelle: /SCHÄFER et al. 1998/

Nach /SCHÄFER 1997/ können die angegebenen Emissionsdaten für die derzeit mit RME betriebenen Mercedes-LKW angesetzt werden. Da die meisten zur Zeit mit RME betriebenen LKW Mercedes-Fahrzeuge sind, werden in **Tabelle 5-7** Faktoren auf der Basis von **Tabelle 5-6** zusammengestellt. Im Anhang (**Tabelle 9-4**) sind die kumulierten Energieaufwendungen und Emissionen einschließlich der RME-Bereitstellung ausgewiesen.

Tabelle 5-7 Spezifischer Verbrauch und Emissionen von LKW im RME-Betrieb bei einem Auslastungsgrad von 50 % im Mittel aller Straßenkategorien

ZGG		**Alle***		**7,5 t**	**16,5 t**	**23 t**	**30 t**	**40 t**
Kraftstoffverbrauch								
RME			MJ/tkm	3,47	2,37	1,81	1,25	1,12
Emissionen								
		Global		**Global**	**Global**	**Global**	**Global**	**Global**
CO_2**	g/MJ	76,2	g/tkm	264	180	138	95,3	85,5
CH_4	g/MJ	0,0023	g/tkm	0,015	0,0061	0,0042	0,0020	0,0015
N_2O	g/MJ	0,0067	g/tkm	0,023	0,016	0,012	0,0084	0,0075
		OK 1+2		**OK 1+2**	**OK 1+2**	**OK 1+2**	**OK 1+2**	**OK 1+2**
SO_2	g/MJ	0,0027	g/tkm	0,35	0,24	0,18	0,13	0,11
CO	g/MJ	0,12	g/tkm	0,73	0,32	0,24	0,18	0,10
NO_X	g/MJ	0,56	g/tkm	1,91	1,68	1,36	0,90	0,87
NMHC	g/MJ	0,050	g/tkm	0,34	0,13	0,093	0,044	0,034
Partikel	g/MJ	0,023	g/tkm	0,12	0,066	0,042	0,035	0,024
Staub	g/MJ	0	g/tkm	0	0	0	0	0
HCl	g/MJ	0,000028	g/tkm	0,000096	0,000065	0,000050	0,000035	0,00003
NH_3	g/MJ	0,00040	g/tkm	0,0014	0,0010	0,00073	0,00050	0,00045
Formaldehyd	g/MJ	0,0076	g/tkm	0,052	0,020	0,014	0,0067	0,0052
Benzol	g/MJ	0,0018	g/tkm	0,012	0,0048	0,0033	0,0016	0,0012
Benzo(a)pyren	ng/MJ	156	ng/tkm	540	368	282	195	175
TCDD-TÄ	ng/MJ	0,0012	ng/tkm	0,0042	0,0029	0,0022	0,0015	0,0014

ZGG: Zulässiges Gesamtgewicht
*: Mittel über alle LKW und Straßenkategorien; **: biogenes CO_2
Quelle: /IFEU 1997a/, eigene Berechnungen

Von anderen Herstellern als Mercedes-Benz liegen uns keine entsprechenden Daten vor. Vergleiche mit älteren Arbeiten zeigen uneinheitliche Ergebnisse; insbesondere sind keine systematischen Unterschiede zum Dieselbetrieb feststellbar, so daß die Verwendung gleicher Emissionsfaktoren wie für den Dieselbetrieb vertretbar ist.

Der geringe Schwefelgehalt von RME von 50 ppm gab verschiedentlich Anlaß zu dem Hinweis, RME sei besonders für den Einsatz in Fahrzeugen mit Oxidationskatalysator geeignet, durch den vor allem Partikelemissionen deutlich reduziert werden können. Gemäß den Beschlüssen der EU wird allerdings ab dem Jahr 2005 auch der Schwefelgehalt von Dieselkraftstoff maximal 50 ppm betragen und daher mögliche Unterschiede der Abgasbehandlung zwischen den beiden Kraftstoffen nicht mehr bestimmen.

5.1.6 Exkurs: Bilanzierung komplexer Gütertransporte*

Werden die oben abgeleiteten Basisdaten nicht auf einen „einfachen" Transport eines Gutes mit konstanter Auslastung angewendet, sondern auf komplexe Transportaufgaben im Rahmen der ökologischen Bilanzierung von Transport*gütern*, treten unter Umständen einige spezifische Problem auf, so z. B. bei variierenden Auslastungen, durch die Berücksichtigung von Rückfahrten oder bei unterschiedlichen Transportgütern. Die gesamten Aufwendungen müssen dann z. B. auf verschiedene Transportgüter aufgeteilt werden; dazu werden hier Allokationsverfahren vorgestellt. Diese Verfahren sind plausibel, stellen aber letztlich immer Konventionen dar, so daß der Anwender mit guten Gründen davon auch abweichen kann.

Die Allokationsmöglichkeiten werden im folgenden am Beispiel von Gütertransporten mit LKW erläutert, für die in diesem Buch auslastungsabhängige Verbräuche und Emissionsfaktoren abgeleitet wurden. Die Daten für die übrigen Transportmittel wurden jeweils für einen festen, durchschnittlichen Auslastungsgrad abgeleitet. Die Zusammenhänge und die formelmäßige Beschreibung sind jedoch bei Vorliegen entsprechender Daten identisch und können gegebenenfalls durch den Anwender selbst umgesetzt werden.

Die bisher behandelten spezifischen Daten beziehen sich auf die Transportleistung in tkm. Den Bezug der folgenden Ableitungen bildet die Fahrleistung in km. Die transportleistungsbezogenen Daten werden in fahrleistungsbezogene umgerechnet indem sie mit dem Auslastungsgrad und der Maximalen Nutzlast des betrachteten LKW multipliziert werden.

5.1.6.1 Unterschiedliche Auslastung

Eine besondere Bedeutung bei Gütertransporten hat der Auslastungsgrad. Der Auslastungsgrad gibt an, wie groß das Verhältnis zwischen der tatsächlichen Transportmenge und der Maximalen Nutzlast des Transportmittels ist. Bezug ist im Regelfall die Masse, also das Gewicht des Transportgutes, grundsätzlich kommen aber auch andere Bezugsgrößen in Frage wie z. B. das Volumen. Kraftstoffverbrauch und Emissionen hängen, wie in **Abb. 5-1** schematisch dargestellt, näherungsweise linear vom Auslastungsgrad ab.

* Unter Mitarbeit von Mario Schmidt

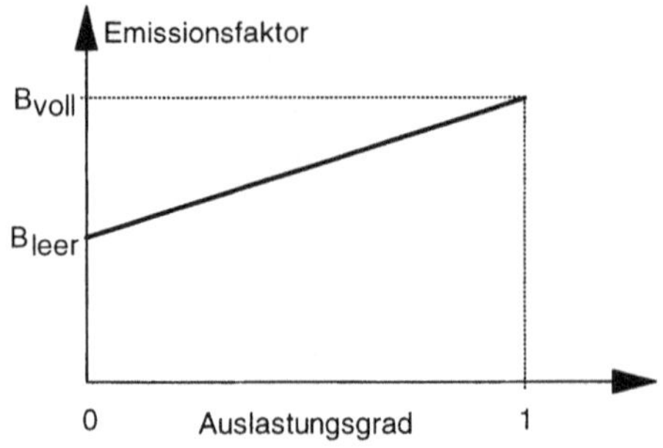

Abb. 5-1 Die Verbrauchs- und Emissionsfaktoren B eines LKW werden bezogen auf die Fahrstrecke als vom Auslastungsgrad linear abhängig angenommen.

Die Behandlung des Auslastungsgrades in ökologischen Bilanzierungen läßt sich an folgendem Beispiel gut demonstrieren: Beträgt die maximale Zuladung eines LKW 28 t und wird einer Bilanz ein Auslastungsgrad von 50 % zugrunde gelegt, dann werden pro LKW-Fahrt 14 t transportiert. Ergibt sich aus der Fragestellung, daß eine Menge von insgesamt 42 t transportiert werden soll, folgt, daß der LKW dreimal fahren muß; entsprechend werden Energieverbrauch und die Emissionen berechnet. Wenn von der gesamten Fracht nur 1 t interessiert (z. B. im Speditionsverkehr), dann ist es plausibel, diesem speziell betrachteten Transportgut nur 1/14 des Energieverbrauchs und der Emissionen dieser Fahrt anzurechnen. (Falls tatsächlich nur 1 t transportiert wird, muß der Auslastungsgrad entsprechend gewählt werden.)

In letzterem Fall wird also dem Transportgut (1 t) entsprechend dem Auslastungsgrad und der maximal zulässigen Zuladung nur ein Anteil des Energieverbrauchs und der Emissionen angelastet. Die anderen Transportgüter tauchen in der Rechnung nicht weiter auf. Im Grunde genommen handelt es sich um einen Kuppelprozeß, nämlich um den Transport mehrerer Güter mit einem Fahrzeug. Die Vernachlässigung der anderen Güter und die Zurechnung der Emissionen stellt dabei eine Allokation dar.

Wie erwähnt kann sich die Auslastung und die Zurechnung auch auf andere Größen beziehen, etwa auf das Volumen. Zum Beispiel könnte der LKW mit 1 t Schaumstoff oder ähnlichem bereits komplett ausgefüllt sein. Dann wären dem Transportgut Schaumstoff auch 100 % des Energieverbrauchs und der Emissionen anzulasten. Der massenbezogene Auslastungsgrad, für den hier die Daten abgeleitet wurden, ergibt sich dann aus der Dichte des Transportgutes, und müßte hier mit 1/28 = 3,6 % angegeben werden.

Der Anwender muß also sowohl den Bezug als auch die entsprechenden rechnerischen Zusammenhänge gemäß der zu bilanzierenden Fragestellung festlegen. Für Gütertransporte mit LKW sind in diesem Buch die Kraftstoffverbräuche und Emissionen für massenbezogene Auslastungsgrade von 0, 0,5 bzw. 1 angegeben; sie können somit für Leer-, halb und voll ausgelastete Fahrten direkt verwendet werden. Für andere Teilauslastungen als 50 % kann gemäß **Abb. 5-1** in guter Näherung linear interpoliert werden. Hierbei kann Bilanzierungssoftware, die speziell auf solche Fragestellungen ausgerichtet ist, wie etwa das im Anhang beschriebene Umberto, hilfreich sein.

5.1.6.2 Rückfahrten und Beifracht

In ökologischen Bilanzen stellt sich häufig die Frage, wie mögliche Rückfahrten von Transportmitteln zu behandeln sind /SCHMIDT et al. 1996/. Wird ein Transportgut angeliefert und das Transportmittel fährt anschließend wieder leer an seinen Ausgangsort zurück, so ist es naheliegend, die Aufwendungen für die Rückfahrt auch ganz dem Transportgut zuzuschlagen. Wenn das Transportmittel auf der Rückfahrt wieder voll beladen ist, kann es bei der alleinigen Zuordnung der Hinfahrt bleiben. Wenn allerdings auf der Rückfahrt andere Güter transportiert werden und das Transportmittel dabei nur teilausgelastet ist, sollte dem Transportgut der Hinfahrt ein Teil der Aufwendungen der Rückfahrt angerechnet werden. Auch hier sind also wieder Allokationen vorzunehmen, die im folgenden vorgeschlagen werden.

In allgemeiner Form gilt:

$$E_F = s * [(B_{voll}-B_{leer}) * \varepsilon + B_{leer}]$$

mit:

E_F	Kraftstoffverbrauch bzw. Emission der Fahrt in MJ bzw. g
s	Entfernung in km (gegebenenfalls nach Straßenkategorien unterschieden)
ε	Auslastungsgrad (bezogen auf das Gewicht) von 0 bis 1
B_{leer}	Verbrauchs- bzw. Emissionsfaktor der Leerfahrt (ε=0) in MJ bzw. g/Fz-km
B_{voll}	Verbrauchs- bzw. Emissionsfaktor der vollen Fahrt (ε=1) in MJ bzw. g/Fz-km

Im Leerzustand ist damit $E_F = s * B_{leer}$, im voll beladenen Zustand $E_F = s * B_{voll}$.

Dabei wird die lineare Abhängigkeit der spezifischen Daten vom Auslastungsgrad nach **Abb. 5-1** unterstellt und – trivial –, daß Gesamtverbrauch und -emissionen außerdem von der Fahrstrecke abhängen.

Leere oder volle Rückfahrt

Betrachtet man nun die Hin- und Rückfahrt eines Fahrzeugs getrennt, so lassen sich diese beiden Fahrten direkt aus obiger Formel wie folgt beschreiben, wobei gleiche Transportentfernung, aber eventuell verschiedene Auslastungen angesetzt werden.

$$E_{hin} = s * [(B_{voll}-B_{leer}) * \varepsilon_{hin} + B_{leer}] \qquad \text{(nur Hinfahrt)}$$

$$E_{rück} = s * [(B_{voll}-B_{leer}) * \varepsilon_{rück} + B_{leer}] \qquad \text{(nur Rückfahrt)}$$

Bei voll ausgelasteter Rückfahrt ist es plausibel, nur die Aufwendungen der einfachen Fahrt, also die Formel für E_{hin}, zu verwenden. Erfolgt die Rückfahrt leer, sollte sie der Hinfahrt zugerechnet werden, wenn man sich auf den Standpunkt stellt, daß sie durch die Hinfahrt verursacht wurde. Bei dieser Annahme wäre dann die folgende Formel zu verwenden:

$$E_{hin} = s * [(B_{voll}-B_{leer}) * \varepsilon_{hin} + 2 * B_{leer}] \qquad \text{(inkl. leere Rückfahrt)}$$

Damit sind die zwei eingangs erwähnten „einfachen" Sachverhalte beschrieben. Mit erfaßt sind auch die umgekehrten Fälle: Die Hinfahrt erfolgt leer und nur auf der Rückfahrt werden Güter transportiert. Das heißt die Hin- und Rückfahrt können vertauscht werden, ohne daß dies auf die Ergebnisse Auswirkungen hätte.

Teilbeladene Rückfahrt

Wie sollen die Aufwendungen verrechnet werden, wenn sowohl auf der Hin- als auch auf der Rückfahrt Güter transportiert werden, die Transportmittel aber nicht zu 100 % ausgelastet sind? Betrachtet man jede Fahrt als unabhängig von allen anderen, dann wären jeweils nur die Aufwendungen für die direkten Wege zu berücksichtigen. Hält man aber die Fahrten nicht für unabhängig voneinander, so ist eine Methode zur Anrechnung der einen Fahrt auf die andere zu finden.

Hier wird vorgeschlagen, die gesamten Aufwendungen im Verhältnis der transportierten Masse je Einzelfahrt zuzurechnen. Dazu werden zunächst die gesamten Aufwendungen E_{ges} für Hin- *und* Rückfahrt, berechnet:

$$E_{ges} = s * [(B_{voll}-B_{leer}) * (\varepsilon_{hin} + \varepsilon_{rück}) + 2 * B_{leer}]$$

Die jeweiligen Anteile von Hin- bzw. Rückfahrt werden dann durch das Verhältnis der transportierten Massen oder – gleichbedeutend – durch das Verhältnis der Auslastungsgrade bestimmt:

$$E_{hin} = E_{ges} * \varepsilon_{hin} / (\varepsilon_{hin} + \varepsilon_{rück})$$

$$E_{rück} = E_{ges} * \varepsilon_{rück} / (\varepsilon_{hin} + \varepsilon_{rück})$$

Durch Einsetzen der Formeln errechnet sich damit der Anteil der Hinfahrt an den gesamten Aufwendungen nach der folgenden Formel:

$$E_{hin} = s * [(B_{voll}-B_{leer}) * \varepsilon_{hin} + 2 * B_{leer} * \varepsilon_{hin} / (\varepsilon_{hin} + \varepsilon_{rück})] \qquad \text{(inkl. Rückfahrt)}$$

Die anteiligen Aufwendungen der Rückfahrt werden nach derselben Formel mit den entsprechenden Koeffizienten berechnet. In dieser Formel sind die beiden oben behandelten Grenzfälle eingeschlossen. Hin- und Rückfahrt können auch hier vertauscht werden; der Ansatz ist quasi symmetrisch.

Die dargestellte Allokationsvorschrift mit freier Wahl der Auslastungsgrade für einzelne Fahrten wird auch auf die Datensätze zu LKW-Transportprozessen in der Bilanzierungssoftware Umberto® angewendet, die im Anhang beschrieben ist. Steht ein solches Programm nicht zur Verfügung, kann der Bilanzierer folgendermaßen vorgehen: Gemäß Kapitel 5.1.6.1 werden aus den Tabellen in den Kapitel 5.1.3 und 5.1.4 die Daten für eine Fahrt mit einem bestimmten LKW und einem bestimmten Auslastungsgrad abgeleitet. Dabei dienen die Kraftstoffverbräuche und Emissionen bei den Auslastungsgraden 0 und 1 als Stützstellen. Die resultierenden Daten werden anschließend in die oben abgeleitete Formel eingesetzt.

Verschiedene Transportgüter / Zurechnung von Beifracht

Wie sollen die Transportaufwendungen zugerechnet werden, wenn das betrachtete Gut nur einen Teil der Ladung ausmacht? Analog zum oben dargestellten Vorgehen kann man die gesamten Aufwendungen nach dem Anteil der transportierten Masse an der Gesamtmasse aufteilen. Die Gesamtmasse ist $m_{max} * \varepsilon_{hin}$, so daß der Anteil dann $m_{Gut} / (m_{max} * \varepsilon_{hin})$ beträgt. Dabei bedeutet m_{max} die Maximale Nutzlast des LKW; m_{Gut} ist das Gewicht des betrachteten Transportgutes. Auf das Transportgut bezogen gilt also in Erweiterung der obigen Formel für die Hinfahrt, in der bereits der Anteil der Rückfahrt berücksichtigt ist:

$$E_{Gut} = s * m_{Gut} / (m_{max} * \varepsilon_{hin}) * [(B_{voll}-B_{leer}) * \varepsilon_{hin} + 2 * B_{leer} * \varepsilon_{hin} / (\varepsilon_{hin} + \varepsilon_{rück})]$$

mit:

E_{Gut}	Verbrauch bzw. Emissionen in MJ bzw. g, die dem Transportgut angerechnet werden
m_{Gut}	Gewicht des Transportgutes in t
m_{max}	Maximale Nutzlast des LKW in t

Wenn die Auslastung nicht massen-, sondern etwa volumenbezogen angegeben wird, dann sind analoge Formeln anzusetzen. Unterscheidet sich ferner die Transportentfernung für Hin- und Rückfahrt, dann muß der Parameter s entsprechend differenziert werden. Dazu werden die Gesamtaufwendungen aus den Einzelfahrten schrittweise zusammengesetzt. Auf der Grundlage dieser Formeln läßt sich die Berechnung außerdem auch auf längere Transportketten, also Mehrfachfahrten, erweitern.

Die Wahl von Allokationsvorschriften ist letztlich willkürlich. Sie sollten jedoch – natürlich – plausibel sein, entsprechend der ISO-Norm 14041 begründet und ausführlich dokumentiert werden. Schließlich muß aus Konsistenzgründen die Summe aller Beiträge wieder den Gesamtverbrauch bzw. die Gesamtemissionen des nicht allozierten Systems ergeben.

5.1.6.3 Alternative Zurechnung

Eine anderes plausibles Zurechnungsverfahren wurde im Rahmen der Ökobilanz für Getränkeverpackungen entwickelt /UBA 1995a/. Hier wird für den Transport (nur Hinfahrt) unterschieden nach den Transportgütern „Packmittel“ und „Packgut“. Beide werden zusammen transportiert. Aus der dort diskutierten Fragestellung heraus sollen nur der Verbrauch und die Emissionen, die dem Packmittel (E_{PackM}) angerechnet werden können, betrachtet werden. Folgende Gleichungen wurden angesetzt:

$$E_{PackG} = s * [m_{PackG} / (m_{PackM} + m_{PackG}) * (B_{voll} - B_{leer}) * \varepsilon + B_{leer} * m_{PackG} / m_{max}]$$

$$E_{PackM} = s * [m_{PackM} / (m_{PackM} + m_{PackG}) * (B_{voll} - B_{leer}) * \varepsilon + B_{leer} * (1 - m_{PackG} / m_{max})]$$

Der auslastungsabhängige Anteil $(B_{voll} - B_{leer}) * \varepsilon$ wird gemäß /UBA 1995a/ auf Packgut und Packmittel anteilig nach ihrem Gewicht verteilt. Der konstante Anteil B_{leer} wird entsprechend dem Verhältnis von Packgut-Gewicht zu Maximaler Nutzlast dem Packgut angerechnet. Den verbleibenden Rest trägt das Packmittel. Da der Auslastungsgrad $\varepsilon = (m_{PackM} + m_{PackG}) / m_{max}$ ist, vereinfachen sich die Formeln zu:

$$E_{PackG} = s * m_{PackG} / m_{max} * B_{voll}$$

$$E_{PackM} = s * [m_{PackM} / m_{max} * (B_{voll} - B_{leer}) + B_{leer} * (1 - m_{PackG} / m_{max})]$$

Im Idealfall, daß ein Packgut maximal zur Auslastung des LKW beiträgt, z. B. bei einem Transport mit einem Tankwagen, wird dem Packmittel der Term B_{leer} nicht angerechnet. Klaffen Packgut-Gewicht und Maximale Nutzlast auseinander, so wird dies dem Packmittel angelastet. Damit wird unterstellt, daß die schlechtere Auslastung eine Folge des Verpackungssystems ist.

Die beiden Beispiele zeigen, daß Teilfrachten und Rückfahrten je nach Fragestellung und Betrachtungsweise verschieden alloziert werden können.

Die in diesem Kapitel abgeleiteten Daten zu Kraftstoffverbrauch und Emissionen des Gütertransports mit LKW sind so dokumentiert, daß der Anwender die Möglichkeit hat, Bilanzen auf der Basis unterschiedlichster Fragestellungen zu erstellen. Für die anderen Transportmittel werden in diesem Buch, wie bereits erwähnt, mittlere Auslastungsgrade zugrunde gelegt; im Bedarfsfalle wäre die der Darstellung in diesem Kapitel zugundeliegende Differenzierung nach Auslastungsgraden durch den Anwender selbst abzuleiten. Eine Darstellung des Einsatzes einer Bilanzierungssoftware zur Bearbeitung der hier diskutierten Probleme findet sich im Anhang.

5.2 Bahn

Das wesentliche Differenzierungskriterium unter technischen und Umweltaspekten ist im Falle des Bahntransports die Traktionsart: „Elektro" oder „Diesel". Darüber hinaus sind eine Reihe weiterer Faktoren ähnlich denen beim LKW-Transport von Bedeutung für den Energieeinsatz und die damit verbundenen Emissionen wie etwa Lokomotivtyp, Waggontyp und -zusammenstellung (Zuggattung), Auslastung und Fahrweise.

Neben der Unterscheidung nach Traktionsarten ist für ökologische Untersuchungen vor allem die Differenzierung nach Zuggattungen sinnvoll, da die verschiedenen Zuggattungen sehr unterschiedliche Massenauslastungen und damit spezifische Verbräuche aufweisen. Die Zuggattung wird in der Regel durch die beförderten Güter bestimmt: Massengüter wie Erze oder Kohlen werden meist mit Ganzzügen befördert, Container im Kombinierten Ladungsverkehr (KLV) und Stückgut in Einzelwagenzügen. Nach /DIW & IFEU & IVU 1994/ betrug der mittlere Auslastungsgrad Ende der 80er Jahre für Ganzzüge 44 %, für den Kombinierten Ladungsverkehr 37 % und für Einzelwagenzüge 30 %.

Die Datenlage ist ungünstiger als beim LKW-Transport, gestattet aber bei begrenzter Differenzierung die Ableitung belastbarer Durchschnittswerte. Das gängige Verfahren ist die top-down-Berechnung aus der auf einem Bezugsgebiet bzw. von einem Unternehmen verbrauchten Energie und der damit erbrachten Transportleistung. Für den Bezug Deutschland 1996 ist dabei allerdings problematisch, daß die wichtigste Primärquelle, die sogenannte Gesamtkostenrechnung der Deutschen Bahn, 1993 eingestellt wurde. Differenzierungen nach Zuggattungen erfordern auch auf der Basis dieser relativ umfassenden und gut abgegrenzten Statistik Zusatzannahmen. Belastbare Emissionsfaktoren der Dieseltraktion lassen sich im wesentlichen nur mit Bezug auf den Energieverbrauch (Einheit: g Schadstoff/MJ bzw. g Dieselkraftstoff) – und damit ohne *unmittelbare* Berücksichtigung des Einflußes der Einsatzweise bzw. Motorauslastung – abschätzen.

Die hier dokumentierte Ableitung basiert im wesentlichen auf einer detaillierten Analyse in /DIW & IFEU & IVU 1994/ mit den Bezugsjahren 1988 (Basis) und 2010 (Szenario), die sich ihrerseits auf die Gesamtkostenrechnung /DB 1989a/ stützt. Im folgenden wird zunächst der Energieverbrauch differenziert nach den Traktionsarten „Elektro" und „Diesel" und den drei genannten Zuggattungen durchgeführt. Anschließend werden für die Dieseltraktion verbrauchsbezogene Emissionsfaktoren abgeschätzt und mit dem Verbrauch zu transportleistungsbezogenen Faktoren verknüpft.

5.2.1 Energieeinsatz

Bei den in /DIW & IFEU & IVU 1994/ ausgewerteten Informationen der Gesamtkostenrechnung /DB 1989a/ handelt es sich um mehr oder weniger stark aggregierte Daten zu Energieverbrauch und Transportleistungen einzelner Zuggattungen oder der – damaligen – Deutschen Bundesbahn insgesamt im Jahr 1988. Damit sind einige Zusatzannahmen erforderlich. Diese Zusatzannahmen betreffen im wesentlichen den technischen Bezug der abgeleiteten Daten, die Aufteilung der sogenannten Nebenfahrten bzw. -leistungen (Rangieren, Übergabezüge und Lok-Leerfahrten) auf die betrachteten Zuggattungen und die Anpassung an das Bezugsjahr 1996.

/DB 1989a/ enthält den Endenergieverbrauch und die Brutto-Transportleistung im Güterverkehr differenziert nach den Traktionsarten im Hauptlauf und den Zuggattungen. Die Brutto-Transportleistung bezeichnet dabei das Produkt aus der Brutto-Masse der Wagen und der tatsächlich zurückgelegten Strecke. Der spezifische Verbauch bezogen auf die Brutto-Transportleistung kann somit direkt berechnet werden. Für ökologische Bilanzierungen ist jedoch zum einen nur die tatsächlich transportierte Masse relevant und zum anderen nur die kürzeste Entfernung einfach angebbar. Die entsprechende, von der Bahn in sogenannten Tarif-Tonnenkilometern angegebene Transportleistung liegt allerdings nur undifferenziert als Gesamtbetriebsergebnis vor. Die Differenzierung erfolgt anhand der Betriebsstatistischen Kartei /DB 1989b/ und einigen Zusatzannahmen. In der genannten Statistik werden für zwei Stichtage neben der Brutto- auch die Netto-Transportleistung (das Produkt aus tatsächlich transportierter Masse und tatsächlich zurückgelegter Strecke) differenziert erfaßt. Unter der Annahme, daß die Brutto-/Netto-Relationen der verschiedenen Traktionsarten und Zuggattungen an diesen Tagen die Jahresmittel repräsentieren, können die Verbräuche auf die Netto-Transportleistung umgerechnet werden. Für die Umrechnung auf Tarif-tkm wird angenommen, daß das Verhältnis von Netto- zu Tarif-Transportleistung für alle Traktionsarten und Zuggattungen gleich ist.

Die Daten zu den Nebenleistungen sind nur wenig differenziert; insbesondere wird keine Unterscheidung zwischen Güter- und Personenverkehr durchgeführt. Die Nebenleistungen bzw. die mit ihnen verbundenen Energieverbräuche werden folgendermaßen aufgeteilt:

- Übergabezüge, die Waggons innerhalb eines Knotenpunktes verschieben, werden vollständig dem Güterverkehr zugerechnet. Die Aufteilung auf Traktionsarten und Zuggattungen erfolgt gemäß der Anzahl eingesetzter Waggons.
- Rangierfahrten werden zu 90 % dem Güterverkehr zugerechnet. Die Aufteilung auf Traktionsarten und Zuggattungen erfolgt gemäß der Anzahl eingesetzter Waggons mit der Zusatzannahme, daß der spezifische Aufwand für Ganzzüge und Züge des Kombinierten Ladungsverkehrs halb so hoch wie der für Einzelwagenzüge ist.
- Die Leerfahrten der Lokomotiven werden je zur Hälfte dem Güter- und dem Personenverkehr zugerechnet. Die Aufteilung auf Traktionsarten und Zuggattungen erfolgt gemäß der Anzahl der Züge.

Unabhängig von der Traktionsart im Hauptlauf werden Übergabe- und Rangierfahrten überwiegend mit Dieselloks, in geringerem Maße aber auch mit E-Loks durchgeführt. Beide Traktionsarten der Nebenleistungen werden auf beide Traktionsarten im Hauptlauf verteilt.

Damit ergibt sich auch für die Elektrotraktion ein Dieselverbrauch und umgekehrt für die Dieseltraktion ein – geringer – Stromeinsatz.

Die Ergebnisse für das Basis-Bezugsjahr 1988 werden mit Abschätzungen für das Szenario-Bezugsjahr 2010 durch Interpolation für 1996 fortgeschrieben. Dabei wird für Diesellokomotiven nach /DIW & IFEU & IVU 1994/ eine Verminderung des spezifischen Kraftstoffverbrauchs bis 2010 um 10 % gegenüber 1988 angenommen (bis 1996: -1,8 %), während der spezifische Strombedarf als konstant angesetzt wird. Damit wird unterstellt, daß sich Modernisierungseffekte vor allem bei Diesellokomotiven bemerkbar machen – wenngleich auch hier nur in sehr geringem Maße –, während bei der Elektrotraktion die Erhöhung der Transportgeschwindigkeit und damit des Verbrauchs kompensierend wirkt. Die Zulässigkeit, im wesentlichen unveränderte Daten mit Bezug auf 1988 für 1996 zu übernehmen, wird bestätigt durch Grobabschätzungen für die vergangenen Jahre auf der Basis höher aggregierter Daten nach /DB 1989c/ und folgende.

Die spezifischen Energieverbräuche differenziert nach Traktionsart im Hauptlauf, Zuggattungen und Hauptlauf und Nebenleistungen sind in **Tabelle 5-8** zusammengefaßt.

Tabelle 5-8 Spezifischer Endenergieeinsatz im Eisenbahngüterverkehr in Deutschland 1996

Hauptlauf	**Elektrotraktion**		**Dieseltraktion**	
Energieträger	**Strom** Wh/tkm	**Diesel** kJ/tkm	**Strom** Wh/tkm	**Diesel** kJ/tkm
Einzelwagenzüge				
Hauptlauf	64,0			661
Rangieren	0,11	44,3	0,26	111
Übergabezüge	0,63	48,1	1,57	119
Leerfahrten	1,17			17,7
Summe	**65,9**	**92,4**	**1,83**	**909**
Züge des KLV				
Hauptlauf	50,3			535
Rangieren	0,010	4,64	0,050	21,5
Übergabezüge	0,060	5,06	0,30	23,2
Leerfahrten	0,39			11,4
Summe	**50,8**	**9,70**	**0,35**	**591**
Ganzzüge				
Hauptlauf	31,0			337
Rangieren	0,010	5,48	0,050	21,9
Übergabezüge	0,080	5,91	0,31	23,6
Leerfahrten	0,30			8,01
Summe	**31,4**	**11,4**	**0,36**	**391**

KLV: Kombinierter Ladungsverkehr;
1 Wh = 3,6 kJ
Quellen: /DB 1989a, b/, /DIW & IFEU & IVU 1994/, eigene Berechnungen

5.2.2 Emissionen

Die Schadstoffemissionen der Elektrotraktion ergeben sich aus den Energieverbräuchen und den spezifischen Emissionen der Bahnstrombereitstellung (Bahnstrommix nach Kapitel 8.6).

Die Emissionen von Diesellokomotiven werden ebenfalls aus Verbrauch und verbrauchsbezogenen Emissionsfaktoren bestimmt. Für die inventargebundenen Schadstoffe CO_2, SO_2 und HCl nehmen wir – wie üblich – vollständige Oxidation des Dieselkraftstoffes und C-, S- und Cl-Gehalte von 86,6 M% bzw. 0,045 M% und 0,0001 M% an (Heizwert: 42,96 MJ/kg).

Zu den Schadstoffen, deren Emissionen von der Motorauslastung abhängen, liegen unseres Wissens keine repräsentativen Messungen vor. Für die limitierten Schadstoffe NO_X, HC, CO und Partikel setzen wir auf /DIW & IFEU & IVU 1994/ basierende Daten an (**Tabelle 5-9**). Dort werden aus verschiedenen Quellen Faktoren mit dem Bezugjahr 1988 abgeschätzt. Daraus werden über Minderungsraten Faktoren für das Jahr 2010 bestimmt. Die Minderungsraten haben dabei ausgesprochenen Abschätzungscharakter; sie sollen über den gesamten Zeitraum stattfindende Änderungen erfassen, die sowohl aus „allgemeinem motortechnischen Fortschritt", als auch der konkreten Umsetzung von Emissionsgrenzwerten und verbesserten Kraftstoffqualitäten rühren können. Die Minderung muß dabei nicht notwendigerweise kontinuierlich stattfinden. Gegenüber 1988 reduzierte Emissionen halten wir jedoch schon für 1996 für wahrscheinlich. Die Bestimmung der Faktoren führen wir daher hier durch – hilfsweise – lineare Interpolation zwischen den Bezugsjahren 1988 und 2010 durch.

Tabelle 5-9 Emissionsfaktoren von Diesellokomotiven: Literaturdaten und Rechenwerte

Quelle	**CO** g/MJ	**NO_X** g/MJ	**HC** g/MJ	**Partikel** g/MJ	**Bezug**
/HAHN 1989/	0,23	1,02	0,09	k. A.	Dieselloks 1983
/UBA 1989/	0,47	1,16	0,23	0,19	Dieselloks 1985
/IIASA 1991/	0,57	1,19	0,10	0,061	Dieselloks
/PROGNOS 1993/	0,42	1,28	0,15	0,033	Dieselloks im Güterverkehr 1988
daraus /DIW & IFEU & IVU 1994/					
	0,42	1,28	0,15	0,070	Dieselloks im Güterverkehr, ABL 1988
	0,34	1,28	0,12	0,04	Dieselloks im Güterverkehr, D 2010
	20%	0%	20%	40%	Reduktion 1988 => 2010
Diese Arbeit nach /DIW & IFEU & IVU 1994/					
	0,39	1,28	0,14	0,060	Dieselloks im Güterverkehr, D 1996
	7,27%	0%	7,27%	14,5%	Reduktion 1988 => 1996

ABL: Alte Bundesländer; D: Deutschland

Die Faktoren für Methan, NMHC, Benzol und Formaldehyd werden über Anteile am HC-Faktor wie für LKW beschrieben berechnet. Für die übrigen Schadstoffe übernehmen wir die verbrauchsbezogenen LKW-Emissionsfaktoren nach Kapitel 5.1.4.

In **Tabelle 5-10** sind die verbrauchsbezogenen Emissionsfaktoren für Diesellokomotiven und die transportleistungsbezogenen Faktoren für die drei Zuggattungen ausgewiesen; sie sind tendenziell unsicherer als die entsprechenden Faktoren für LKW.

Die Daten zum spezifischen kumulierten Energieaufwand und den damit verbundenen Emissionen des Betriebs einschließlich der Bereitstellung des Dieselkraftstoffes und Fahrstroms sind im Anhang (**Tabelle 9-5** bis **Tabelle 9-7**) differenziert nach Zuggattungen und Traktionsarten dokumentiert.

Tabelle 5-10 Spezifischer Verbrauch und Emissionen von dieselbetriebenen Güterzügen

		Diesel		Einzelwagen	KLV	Ganzzug
Kraftstoffverbrauch						
Diesel			MJ/tkm	0,91	0,59	0,39
Emissionen						
		Global		**Global**	**Global**	**Global**
CO_2	g/MJ	73,9	g/tkm	67,2	43,7	28,9
CH_4	g/MJ	0,0034	g/tkm	0,0031	0,0020	0,0013
N_2O	g/MJ	0,0077	g/tkm	0,0070	0,0046	0,0030
		OK 2		**OK 2**	**OK 2**	**OK 2**
SO_2	g/MJ	0,021	g/tkm	0,019	0,012	0,0082
CO	g/MJ	0,39	g/tkm	0,35	0,23	0,15
NO_X	g/MJ	1,28	g/tkm	1,16	0,76	0,50
NMHC	g/MJ	0,14	g/tkm	0,12	0,081	0,053
Partikel	g/MJ	0,060	g/tkm	0,054	0,035	0,023
Staub	g/MJ	0	g/tkm	0	0	0
HCl	g/MJ	0,00002	g/tkm	0,00002	0,00001	0,00001
NH_3	g/MJ	0,00047	g/tkm	0,00042	0,00028	0,00018
Formaldehyd	g/MJ	0,011	g/tkm	0,010	0,0067	0,0044
Benzol	g/MJ	0,0027	g/tkm	0,0024	0,0016	0,0010
Benzo(a)pyren	ng/MJ	180	ng/tkm	163	106	70,2
TCDD-TÄ	ng/MJ	0,0014	ng/tkm	0,0013	0,00083	0,00055

Nur Dieselanteil
KLV: Kombinierter Ladungsverkehr
Quellen: /DIW & IFEU & IVU 1994/, /IFEU & IVT & KuP 1994/, /IFEU 1995b/, eigene Berechnungen

5.3 Binnenschiffe

Wie bei anderen Transportmitteln hängen Energieverbrauch und Emissionen von Binnenschiffen von Parametern wie Größe (Tragfähigkeit), Nennleistung, Motortechnik und Motorauslastung ab, die wiederum mit dem Schiffsalter, der Frachtauslastung bzw. Fahrtrichtung – genauer: den Strömungsverhältnissen (Berg-, Tal- oder Kanalfahrt) – korrelieren. Für detaillierte Untersuchungen sollten Daten angesetzt werden, die zumindest Haupteinflußfaktoren wie Schiffsgröße, Auslastung und Strömungsverhältnisse berücksichtigen. Die Datenlage gestattet eine solche Differenzierung allerdings nur ansatzweise.

- Der spezifische Treibstoffverbrauch kann im wesentlichen nur top-down aus der auf einem Bezugsgebiet verbrauchten bzw. abgegebenen Kraftstoffmenge und der damit erbrachten gesamten Transportleistung ermittelt werden. Anders als im Falle der Eisenbahn (siehe Kapitel 5.2.1) ist dieses Vorgehen hier mit erheblichen Abgrenzungsproblemen verbunden: Aus Preisgründen wird der Treibstoff häufig außerhalb des „Verbrauchsgebietes“ gebunkert. Differenzierungen des Verbrauchs nach Schiffstypen und Fahrmustern müssen aus anderen Quellen und mit Zusatzannahmen abgeleitet werden.

- Eine Differenzierung des mittleren Verbrauchs nach Schiffstypen und Fahrmustern ist nur in grober Rasterung (Motorschiff/Schubverband bzw. Berg- und Talfahrt) möglich. Dazu wird der mittlere Verbrauch gemäß einiger Einzelmessungen aufgespalten, ohne daß allerdings eine Normierung auf den Gesamtverbrauch durchgeführt werden könnte.
- Wie im Falle der Bahn lassen sich belastbare Emissionsfaktoren nur mit Bezug auf den Treibstoffverbrauch angeben (Einheit: g Schadstoff/MJ bzw. g Dieselkraftstoff). Als die Emissionen *unmittelbar* beeinflußende Größe wird die Motorauslastung damit nicht erfaßt.

Im folgenden wird zunächst der Treibstoffverbrauch „top-down“ abgeschätzt. Zusätzlich wird ein Ansatz zur Ableitung von nach Schiffsklassen und Fahrmustern differenzierten Werten dokumentiert. Anschließend werden verbrauchsbezogene Emissionsfaktoren abgeschätzt und mit dem Verbrauch zu transportleistungsbezogenen Faktoren verknüpft.

5.3.1 Treibstoffverbrauch

Für eine Abschätzung des mittleren spezifischen Verbrauchs über alle Schiffsklassen und Fahrmuster orientieren wir uns an folgenden Angaben:

- /IIASA 1991/ erfaßt das Gesamtgebiet Bundesrepublik (alte Bundesländer), Frankreich und Niederlande, wodurch eine Bunkerung entlang der wichtigsten Binnenschiffahrtswege unabhängig von Grenzen berücksichtigt wird. Für das Jahr 1984 ergibt sich einschließlich Küstenschiffahrt ein spezifischer Verbrauch von 12,4 g/tkm.
- Die Erhebung des Ministeriums für Verkehrswesen der DDR /MVWDDR 1989/ differenziert nach Treibstoffverbrauch und Transportleistung der Binnenschiffflotte und gibt gemittelt über alle Wasserstraßen für 1988 einen spezifischen Verbrauch von 9,8 g/tkm an.
- In /ECOINVENT 1996/ wird für die Rheintanker eines schweizer Unternehmens ein durchschnittlicher Dieselverbrauch von 8,6 g/tkm angegeben.
- Aus der Treibstoffabgabe an und der Transportleistung durch Binnenschiffe in Deutschland 1994 resultiert ein spezifischer Verbrauch von 12,1 g/tkm /AGE 1998/, /STBA 1995a/. Einerseits ist in der Treibstoffabgabe die Küstenschiffahrt mit erfaßt, andererseits jedoch nicht der im benachbarten Ausland gebunkerte Treibstoff. Die Schwankungen der Werte für vergangene Jahre weisen auf erhebliche Unsicherheiten des Verfahrens hin: 1985: 14,5 g/tkm, 1989: 10,9 g/tkm, 1991: 11,7 g/tkm (alte Bundesländer).

Die einzelnen Werte können nur bedingt – für sich und in Relation zueinander – plausibel gemacht werden. Die sehr ähnlichen Daten mit den Bezugsjahren 1984 und 1994 sind beide in nicht aufschlüsselbarer Weise durch unterschiedliche Abgrenzungen von Energieverbrauch und Transportleistung mit bestimmt; der tatsächliche „Binnenschiffanteil“ dürfte allerdings bei beiden durch den Verkehr auf dem Rhein geprägt sein. Die Ursache des niedrigen Wertes nach /MVWDDR 1989/ könnte in einem mit einiger Wahrscheinlichkeit relativ hohen Auslastungsgrad liegen. Der Wert nach /ECOINVENT 1996/ kann – mit Vorbehalten aufgrund der geringen Hintergrundinformationen – als Anhalt für moderne, sehr gut ausgelastete Schiffe betrachtet werden.

Effekte etwa von Flottenumschichtungen hin zu größeren Einheiten, höheren motorischen Wirkungsgraden usw., oder Änderungen der Auslastungen lassen sich nicht ableiten. Wir halten daher die Abschätzung eines spezifischen Verbrauchs im Mittel über alle Schiffsklassen und Auslastungsgrade für das am besten geeignete Verfahren. Unseres Erachtens kann ein Wert von 10 g/tkm (0,43 MJ/tkm) für 1996 als realistisch gelten.

Nach Schiffsgröße, Fahrtrichtung und Auslastung differenzierte transportleistungsbezogene Verbrauchswerte lassen sich nach einem in /ENQUÊTE 1994/ angewendeten Verfahren ableiten. Im einzelnen gehen folgende Parameter in die Berechnung ein:

- **Verbrauch bezogen auf die mechanische Arbeit des Motors:** Dieser Parameter wird über alle Schiffstypen und Fahrmuster gemittelt angesetzt. In /ENQUÊTE 1994/ und /IWW et al. 1998/ werden 200 g (8,59 MJ) Dieselkraftstoff / kWh für 1992 und eine Reduktion bis 2010 um 10 % (Trendszenario) zugrunde gelegt; angesichts der oben dargestellten Unsicherheiten der top-down-Berechnung, die wir für übertragbar halten, verzichten wir auf eine Anpassung auf 1996 durch Interpolation.
- **Motornennleistung in kWh:** Betrachtet werden vier Schiffsklassen, die durch Motorleistung und Tragfähigkeit definiert sind (**Tabelle 5-11**).
- **Motorauslastung:** Sie variiert nur relativ wenig, da Schiffsdiesel im wesentlichen quasistationär betrieben werden /BIALONSKI et al. 1990/. Nach /ENQUÊTE 1993/ ändert sich die Auslastung vor allem mit der Strömungsgeschwindigkeit und -richtung, während die Frachtauslastung im wesentlichen die Fahrgeschwindigkeit beeinflußt. In **Tabelle 5-12** sind Daten differenziert nach freifließendem bzw. staureguliertem Fluß und Berg- bzw. Talfahrt zusammengestellt.
- **Fahrgeschwindigkeit in km/h:** Dieser Parameter wird wie die Motorauslastung und außerdem nach Frachtauslastung differenziert. Den Zahlenwerten liegen die Strömungsverhältnisse auf Rhein und Neckar zugrunde (**Tabelle 5-12**).
- **Tragfähigkeit in t:** Siehe Motorauslastung.
- **Auslastungsgrad:** Es werden 0 %, 50 % und 100 % angesetzt.

Aus diesen Größen wird der transportleistungsbezogene Verbrauch nach folgender Formel berechnet:

$$\text{Verbrauch g DK/tkm} = \frac{\text{Verbrauch g DK/kWh} * \text{Motornennleistung} * \text{Motorauslastung}}{\text{Fahrgeschwindigkeit} * \text{Tragfähigkeit} * \text{Auslastungsgrad}}$$

Die nach Schiffsklassen, Fahrtrichtung und Auslastung differenzierten Ergebnisse sind in **Tabelle 5-13** zusammengefaßt. Der spezifische Verbrauch der größten Schiffsklasse ist etwa ein Drittel niedriger als der der kleinsten; der Verbrauch der Bergfahrt auf freifließenden Wasserstraßen (Beispiel Rhein) liegt um den Faktor 2,5 über dem der Talfahrt, bei staugeregulierten um den Faktor 1,4; auf freifließenden Flüssen ist der Verbrauch der Bergfahrt um den Faktor 1,6 höher, der der Talfahrt um den Faktor 0,9 niedriger als auf staugeregulierten Wasserstraßen. Relevanter als die Schiffsgröße scheinen damit die Strömungsverhältnisse zu sein. Sie sind allerdings auch das problematischere Kriterium, da nicht immer belastbare Da-

Tabelle 5-11 Kenngrößen der betrachteten Binnenschiffsklassen

Beschriebene Schiffsklassen					
Tragfähigkeitsklassen	t	< 1.000	1.000-1.500	1.500-2.000	> 2.000
Zur Beschreibung gewählte Schiffe					
Tragfähigkeit	t	800	1.250	1.750	2.500
Motornennleistung	kW	400	550	710	820

Quelle: /BIALONSKI et al. 1990/

Tabelle 5-12 Kenngrößen des Transports mit Binnenschiffen

Wasserstraßentyp		**Freifließend**	**Stauреguliert**
Motorauslastung	Talfahrt	70%	60%
	Bergfahrt	90%	70%
Fahrgeschwindigkeit		km/h	km/h
Leerfahrt	Talfahrt	20,5	14
	Bergfahrt	10,25	12
ALG 50 %	Talfahrt	18	13
	Bergfahrt	9	11
ALG 100 %	Talfahrt	15,5	12
	Bergfahrt	7,75	10

ALG: Auslastungsgrad (Ladung)
Quellen: /ENQUÊTE 1994/, /IWW et al. 1998/, eigene Abschätzungen

Tabelle 5-13 Treibstoffverbrauch von Binnenschiffen differenziert nach Schiffstyp, Fahrtrichtung, Wasserstraßentyp und Auslastung

Wasserstraßentyp		**Freifließend**		**Staureguliert**	
Tragfähigkeit		Talfahrt	Bergfahrt	Talfahrt	Bergfahrt
Leerfahrt					
800 t	MJ/km	117	302	147	200
1.250 t	MJ/km	161	415	203	276
1.750 t	MJ/km	208	536	261	356
2.500 t	MJ/km	241	619	302	411
50 % ALG					
800 t	MJ/tkm	0,33	0,86	0,40	0,55
1.250 t	MJ/tkm	0,29	0,76	0,35	0,48
1.750 t	MJ/tkm	0,27	0,70	0,32	0,44
2.500 t	MJ/tkm	0,22	0,56	0,26	0,36
100 % ALG					
800 t	MJ/tkm	0,19	0,50	0,21	0,30
1.250 t	MJ/tkm	0,17	0,44	0,19	0,26
1.750 t	MJ/tkm	0,16	0,40	0,17	0,24
2.500 t	MJ/tkm	0,13	0,33	0,14	0,20

ALG: Auslastungsgrad (Ladung)
Quellen: /ENQUÊTE 1994/, /IWW et al. 1998/, eigene Berechnungen

ten für einen Wasserstraßenabschnitt zur Verfügung stehen und die Verwendung in Ökobilanzen in jedem Fall sehr aufwendig ist. Andererseits: Der Rhein, die mit 176 Mio. t Aufkommen größte deutsche und auch europäische Wasserstraße /VERKEHR 1997/, ist ein freifließendes Gewässer; die Auslastung der Bergfahrt ist im Mittel deutlich höher als die der Talfahrt /DIW & IFEU & IVU 1994/: 96 bzw. 60 %). Zwar reichen die Bestandsdaten und Informationen zu Transportleistungsanteilen nicht für eine gewichtete Mittelung aus. Zumindest eine halbquantitative Bestätigung für die oben durchgeführte Schätzung kann jedoch aus den differenzierten Werten gezogen werden. – Auf eine Empfehlung zur Verwendung der differenzierten Werte verzichten wir im Falle der Binnenschiffahrt.

5.3.2 Emissionen

Emissionsmessungen aus dem Betrieb oder praxisnahen Prüfstandtests liegen für Binnenschiffe unseres Wissens nicht vor. Die bisher verwendeten Faktoren beruhen auf Herstellerangaben für neue, korrekt eingestellte Motoren.

Die Faktoren der inventargebundenen Schadstoffe CO_2, SO_2 und HCl ergeben sich aus der Treibstoffzusammensetzung unter der Annahme vollständiger Oxidation (86,6 M% Kohlenstoff, 0,045 M% Schwefel, 0,0001 M% Chlor; Heizwert: 42,96 MJ/kg).

Für die limitierten Schadstoffe NO_X, HC, CO und Partikel setzen wir analog zum Vorgehen beim Bahntranport Daten nach /DIW & IFEU & IVU 1994/ an. Aus den Faktoren mit den Bezugsjahren 1988 und 2010 werden die Faktoren für 1996 durch Interpolation bestimmt (**Tabelle 5-14**).

Tabelle 5-14 Emissionsfaktoren von Binnenschiffen: Literaturdaten und Rechenwerte

Quelle	**CO** g/MJ	**NO_X** g/MJ	**HC** g/MJ	**Partikel** g/MJ	**Bezug**
/HAMBURG 1986/	0,33	0,93	0,13	0,056	Binnenschiffe 1982
/IIASA 1991/	0,32	1,09	0,14	k. A.	Binnenschiffe
/PROGNOS 1993/	0,15	1,26	0,079	0,023	Binnenschiffe 1987
daraus /DIW & IFEU & IVU 1994/					
	0,28	1,40	0,12	0,047	Binnenschiffe, ABL 1988
	0,22	1,40	0,093	0,028	Binnenschiffe, D 2010
	20%	0%	20%	40%	Reduktion 1988 => 2010
Diese Arbeit nach /DIW & IFEU & IVU 1994/					
	0,26	1,40	0,11	0,040	Binnenschiffe, D 1996
	7,27%	0%	7,27%	14,5%	Reduktion 1988 => 1996

ABL: Alte Bundesländer; D: Deutschland

Die verbrauchsbezogenen Faktoren für Methan, NMHC, Benzol und Formaldehyd werden aus dem HC-Faktor wie für LKW beschrieben berechnet, die für die übrigen Schadstoffe gleich denen von LKW gesetzt (siehe Kapitel 5.1.4).

In **Tabelle 5-15** sind die verbrauchs- und transportleistungsbezogenen Faktoren zusammengefaßt. Letztere beziehen sich auf den in Kapitel 5.3.1 abgeschätzten Durchschnittsverbrauch von 0,43 MJ/tkm; für spezielle Anwendungen können die verbrauchsbezogenen

Faktoren mit den nach Schiffsgrößen und Strömungsverhältnissen differenzierten Verbräuchen verknüpft werden. Die Emissionsfaktoren für Binnenschiffe sind, ähnlich denen für Diesellokomotiven, unsicherer als die für LKW.

Die Daten zum spezifischen kumulierten Energieaufwand und den damit verbundenen Emissionen des Betriebs von Binnenschiffen einschließlich der Bereitstellung des Dieselkraftstoffes sind im Anhang (**Tabelle 9-8**) dokumentiert.

Tabelle 5-15 Spezifischer Verbrauch und Emissionen von Binnenschiffen

Treibstoffverbrauch				
Diesel			MJ/tkm	0,43
Emissionen				
		Global		**Global**
CO_2	g/MJ	73,9	g/tkm	31,8
CH_4	g/MJ	0,0026	g/tkm	0,0011
N_2O	g/MJ	0,0077	g/tkm	0,0033
		OK 2		**OK 2**
SO_2	g/MJ	0,021	g/tkm	0,0090
CO	g/MJ	0,26	g/tkm	0,11
NO_X	g/MJ	1,40	g/tkm	0,60
NMHC	g/MJ	0,11	g/tkm	0,045
Partikel	g/MJ	0,040	g/tkm	0,017
Staub	g/MJ	0	g/tkm	0
HCl	g/MJ	0,000024	g/tkm	0,000010
NH_3	g/MJ	0,00047	g/tkm	0,00020
Formaldehyd	g/MJ	0,0087	g/tkm	0,0038
Benzol	g/MJ	0,0021	g/tkm	0,00088
Benzo(a)pyren	ng/MJ	180	ng/tkm	77,2
TCDD-TÄ	ng/MJ	0,0014	ng/tkm	0,00060

Quellen: /DIW & IFEU & IVU 1994/, /IFEU & IVT & KuP 1994/, /IFEU 1995b/, eigene Berechnungen

5.4 Seeschiffe

Seeschiffe lassen sich in drei Kategorien zusammenfassen, die sich hinsichtlich ihrer Größe und Auslastung und damit auch ihres spezifischen Verbrauchs und der damit verbundenen Emissionen unterscheiden:

- **Stückgutfrachter, Ro-Ro-Frachter und Containerschiffe:** Die Tragfähigkeit liegt zwischen 9.000 und 23.000 t /BIALONSKI et al. 1990/. Diese Schiffe sind auf allen Fahrten mehr oder weniger ausgelastet. Ro-Ro-Frachter werden im Fährverkehr auf kurzen Passagen eingesetzt.
- **Massengutschiffe:** Die Tragfähigkeit liegt im Mittel bei etwa 40.000 t. Diese Schiffe fahren häufig eine Richtung einer Route voll ausgelastet und die andere Richtung leer.

- **Tanker:** Diese meist zum Erdöltransport eingesetzten Schiffe haben mit 50.000 bis 200.000 t die größte Tragfähigkeit und werden mit Motoren ähnlich denen kleinerer Schiffe oder Turbinen angetrieben. Der Anteil turbinengetriebener Tanker lag 1990 weltweit bei 62 %; sie waren im Durchschnitt doppelt so groß wie die motorgetriebenen Tanker /KOLLE 1991/ nach /ECOINVENT 1996/. Tanker fahren meist voll ausgelastet bzw. leer.

Neben Faktoren wie Größe, Motorleistung, Geschwindigkeit und Auslastungsgrad bestimmen Wetterbedingungen und Strömung den Treibstoffverbrauch von Seeschiffen; diese nicht technischen Parameter sind kaum differenziert abbildbar, werden in Mittelwerten jedoch gut erfaßt.

Im folgenden wird zunächst der Energieverbrauch aus mittleren Flottenverbräuchen für die drei genannten Schiffskategorien abgeschätzt. Anschließend werden verbrauchsbezogene Emissionsfaktoren abgeschätzt und mit dem Verbrauch zu transportleistungsbezogenen Faktoren verknüpft.

5.4.1 Treibstoffverbrauch

Als Treibstoff wird hier Schweröl (Bunker C) angenommen; Dieselkraftstoff („marines Gasöl“ und „marines Dieselöl“; zu den Unterschieden siehe /DGMK 1992/) wird nur auf relativ kleinen – hier nicht betrachteten – Seeschiffen eingesetzt. Für den spezifischen Treibstoffverbrauch von Seeschiffen liegen verschiedene Angaben vor, die in **Tabelle 5-16** zusammengestellt sind. Aus diesen gut miteinander übereinstimmenden Angaben werden die spezifischen Treibstoffverbräuche für Seeschiffe mit Bezugsjahr 1996 abgeschätzt. Bei gleicher Größe haben turbinengetriebene Tanker etwas höhere Verbräuche als motorgetriebene. Da erstere jedoch im Mittel größer sind, kann in guter Näherung von gleichen spezifischen Verbräuchen ausgegangen werden.

Tabelle 5-16 Treibstoffverbrauch von Seeschiffen: Literaturdaten und Rechenwerte

Quelle	**Stückgut-frachter**	**Massengut-frachter**	**Tanker**	**Durch-schnitt**	**Bezug**
Verbrauch Schweröl	g/tkm	g/tkm	g/tkm	g/tkm	
/IEA 1992/	8,4 - 9,6	2,2 - 4	1,6 - 2,7	-	1988, weltweit
/UN 1995/				3,6	1985, weltweit
/BUWAL 1991/		4,9	2,6		
/MVWDDR 1989/, /STATDDR 1889/	6,7[a]				Flotte der DDR
/ECOINVENT 1996/	3,8	2,2	1,8[b]		c
/MASSERON 1982/			0,7 - 1,7 0,9 - 1,7		Motor: 250 - 50 kdwt Turbine: 300 - 50 kdwt
/KOLLE et al. 1991/			1,6 1,6		Motor: 140 kdwt Turbine: 280 kdwt
Rechenwert	**5**	**2,5**	**1,25**		

kdwt: kilo dead weight ton
a: Fast ausschließlich Trockenfrachter, zur Hälfte Stückgutfrachter;
b: Turbinen- und Motorantrieb;
c: Auslastungsgrade, Leer- und Ballastfahrten berücksichtigt

5.4.2 Emissionen

Wie bei dieselbetriebenen Transportmitteln werden die CO_2- und SO_2-Emissionen aus der Treibstoffzusammensetzung berechnet. Für Bunker C werden als internationale Mittelwerte ein C-Gehalt von 86,9 M%, ein S-Gehalt von 4,0 M% /DGMK 1992/ und ein Cl-Gehalt von 0,00088 M% /ECOINVENT 1996/ angenommen (Heizwert: 40,58 MJ/kg /AGE 1998/).

Für die Schadstoffe, deren Emissionen nicht durch die Treibstoffzusammensetzung bestimmt werden, ist zwischen den Antriebskonzepten zu unterscheiden: Verbrennungsmotor bei Frachtern und kleineren bis mittleren Tankern, Dampfturbine bei großen Tankern.

Verbrennungsmotoren

Für CO, NO_X, HC und Partikel liegen Emissionsmessungen aus dem Betrieb vor /LLOYDS 1990/, /LLOYDS 1991/, /LLOYDS 1995/, die zum Teil bereits in /IFEU & IVT & KuP 1994/ ausgewertet wurden. Diese verbrauchsbezogenen Daten übernehmen wir hier.

Die Faktoren der übrigen Schadstoffe werden wie für Diesellokomotiven und Binnenschiffe abgeschätzt, d. h. auf der Basis von LKW-Daten: Methan-, NMHC-, Benzol- und Formaldehydfaktoren werden aus dem HC-Faktor berechnet; für die übrigen Schadstoffe werden hilfsweise die verbrauchsbezogenen LKW-Emissionsfaktoren nach Kapitel 5.1.4 direkt übernommen. Es ist offensichtlich, daß dieses Verfahren für Seeschiffe weniger belastbar ist als für Diesellokomotiven und Binnenschiffe, da ein anderer Treibstoff eingesetzt wird. Die Faktoren stellen jedoch eine akzeptable Näherung dar; die Unsicherheiten können gegebenenfalls durch Sensitivitätsanalysen berücksichtigt werden.

Tabelle 5-17 Verbrauchsbezogene Emissionsfaktoren für Seeschiffe

Antrieb		Motor		Dampfturbine	
		Global		Global	
CO_2	g/MJ	78,5		78,5	
CH_4	g/MJ	0,0015		0,0018	
N_2O	g/MJ	0,0082		0,0020	
		OK 2+3	OK 2	OK 2+3	OK 2
SO_2	g/MJ	1,97	25%	1,97	25%
CO	g/MJ	0,22	25%	0,0074	25%
NO_X	g/MJ	2,07	25%	0,048	25%
NMHC	g/MJ	0,060	25%	0,0018	25%
Partikel	g/MJ	0,15	0%	0,028	0%
Staub	g/MJ	0	k. A.	0	k. A.
HCl	g/MJ	0,0022	25%	0,0022	25%
NH_3	g/MJ	0,00049	25%	0,00049	25%
Formaldehyd	g/MJ	0,0050	25%	0,00053	25%
Benzol	g/MJ	0,0012	25%	0,00004	25%
Benzo(a)pyren	ng/MJ	190	0%	60,0	0%
TCDD-TÄ	ng/MJ	0,029	0%	0,029	0%

OK: Ortsklasse

Quellen: /CARBOTECH 1994/, /ECOINVENT 1996/, /GEMIS 1997/, /IFEU & IVT & KuP 1994/, /IFEU 1995b/, /LLOYDS 1990/, /LLOYDS 1991/, /LLOYDS 1995/, /MHEP 1980/, eigene Berechnungen

Turbinen

Für CO, NO_X, HC und Partikel übernehmen wir Daten nach /MHEP 1980/ (Mittelwerte über Messungen bei 40, 70 und 100 % Motorauslastung). Für die übrigen Schadstoffe setzen wir die Werte stationärer Schwerölfeuerungen an (siehe Anhang, Kapitel 12.3).

In **Tabelle 5-17** sind die verbrauchsbezogenen Faktoren differenziert nach Antriebsarten, in **Tabelle 5-18** die transportleistungsbezogenen Faktoren differenziert nach Schiffstypen zusammengefaßt. Die transportleistungsbezogenen Faktoren für Tanker sind gewichtete Mittelwerte über die Daten für motor- und turbinengetriebene Schiffe (38 % Motor-, 62 % Turbinenantrieb; nach /KOLLE 1991/ zitiert in /ECOINVENT 1996/).

Tabelle 5-18 Spezifischer Verbrauch und Emissionen von Seeschiffen

		Stückgut-frachter	Massengut-frachter	Motor-tanker	Turbinen-tanker	Tanker (M+T-Mix)
Treibstoffverbrauch						
Bunker C	MJ/tkm	0,20	0,10	0,051	0,051	0,051
Emissionen						
		Global	**Global**	**Global**	**Global**	**Global**
CO_2	g/tkm	15,9	7,97	3,98	3,98	3,98
CH_4	g/tkm	0,00030	0,00015	0,00008	0,00009	0,00008
N_2O	g/tkm	0,0017	0,00083	0,00041	0,00010	0,00022
		OK 2+3	**OK 2+3**	**OK 2+3**	**OK 2+3**	**OK 2+3**
SO_2	g/tkm	0,40	0,20	0,10	0,10	0,10
CO	g/tkm	0,045	0,023	0,011	0,00038	0,0045
NO_X	g/tkm	0,42	0,21	0,11	0,0025	0,041
NMHC	g/tkm	0,012	0,0061	0,0031	0,00009	0,0012
Partikel	g/tkm	0,030	0,015	0,0075	0,0014	0,0037
Staub	g/tkm	0	0	0	0	0
HCl	g/tkm	0,00045	0,00023	0,00011	0,00011	0,00011
NH_3	g/tkm	0,00010	0,00005	0,00003	0,00003	0,00003
Formaldehyd	g/tkm	0,0010	0,00051	0,00025	0,00003	0,00011
Benzol	g/tkm	0,00024	0,00012	0,00006	0,00000	0,00002
Benzo(a)pyren	ng/tkm	38,6	19,3	9,65	3,04	5,55
TCDD-TÄ	ng/tkm	0,0058	0,0029	0,0015	0,0015	0,0015

Quellen: /CARBOTECH 1994/, /ECOINVENT 1996/, /GEMIS 1997/, /IFEU & IVT & KuP 1994/, /IFEU 1995b/, /LLOYDS 1990/, /LLOYDS 1991/, /LLOYDS 1995/, /MHEP 1980/, eigene Berechnungen

Wie in Kapitel 4.2.1 diskutiert, sollten die nicht global wirksamen Emissionen der Seeschiffe nach Ortsklassen differenziert werden; die verbrauchsbezogenen Faktoren sind entsprechend ausgewiesen. Den Partikelemissionen und den partikelgebundenen Schadstoffen, Benzo(a)pyren und Dioxine, wird Ortsklasse 3 zugeordnet, da sie schnell deponieren. Emissionen im Hafenbereich werden damit vernachlässigt und auch für die küstennahe Fahrt wird Partikeldeposition ausschließlich über dem Meer angenommen. Für die übrigen nicht partikelgebundenen Schadstoffe wird eine Verteilung auf die Ortsklassen 2 und 3 im Verhältnis 1 zu 3 angesetzt.

Die Daten zum spezifischen kumulierten Energieaufwand und den damit verbundenen Emissionen des Betriebs von Seeschiffen einschließlich der Schwerölbereitstellung sind im Anhang (**Tabelle 9-9**) dokumentiert.

5.5 Flugzeuge

Unter den Luftfrachtverkehr im weiteren Sinn fallen inländische Kurierflüge mit Propeller- und Turboprob-Maschinen, z. B. zum Transport einzelner Ersatzteile, wie auch interkontinentale Flüge mit Düsenmaschinen zum Transport von kompletten technischen Anlagen. Überwiegend werden verderbliche oder teure Güter und nahezu ausschließlich Stückgut befördert. Der Transport erfolgt in reinen Frachtmaschinen oder als Beifracht in Passagiermaschinen.

Spezifischer Verbrauch und Emissionen eines bestimmten Lufttransports hängen stark von der Fluglänge ab, da sich die spezifischen Werte der einzelnen Flugphasen deutlich unterscheiden und ihre Anteile am Gesamtflug mit der Strecke variieren. Steigflüge sind mit einem erheblich höheren Energieaufwand verbunden als Niveauflüge; der höchste spezifische Verbrauch fällt beim Start an, weil hier das höchste Gewicht gegen die größten Widerstände bewegt wird. Der mittlere spezifische Verbrauch eines Transports sinkt mit der Entfernung, weil der Anteil der Startphase sinkt. Bei Kurzstreckenflügen fallen außerdem Umwege stärker ins Gewicht. Schließlich werden auf kurzen Strecken tendenziell kleinere Maschinen als auf langen eingesetzt (zum Verhältnis „Fahrzeuggröße/Verbrauch" siehe Kapitel 5.1.3). Die Fluglängenabhängigkeit kann nicht ohne weiteres konsistent quantifiziert werden; eine halbquantitative Berücksichtigung ist jedoch geboten und möglich.

Im folgenden wird der mittlere spezifische Verbrauch von Düsenmaschinen im Kurz- bzw. Mittelstrecken- und im Langstreckenluftfrachtverkehr abgeleitet. Die Berechnung basiert auf Angaben zum in Deutschland abgegebenen Flugturbinenkraftstoff (Kerosin) und der damit erbrachten Transportleistung. Anschließend werden verbrauchsbezogene Emissionsfaktoren abgeschätzt und mit dem Verbrauch zu transportleistungsbezogenen Faktoren verknüpft.

5.5.1 Treibstoffverbrauch

In /IFEU 1996c/ wurde für das Jahr 1993 eine detaillierte Ableitung des spezifischen Verbrauchs aus Transportleistung und Kerosinabgabe durchgeführt, die hier aktualisiert wird.

Die Kerosinabgabe an die Luftfahrt *ohne* Unterscheidung zwischen Fracht- und Passagier- und Kurz- bzw. Mittelstrecken- und Langstreckenverkehr ist in /AGE 1998/ ausgewiesen. Die Aufteilung zwischen diesen Verkehrsarten erfolgt anhand *gewichteter* Transportleistungsanteile. Diese Gewichtungen werden im folgenden detailliert erläutert.

Die Verkehrs- bzw. Transportleistung wird im Luftverkehr nach verschiedenen Zurechnungsmethoden erfaßt. Sie unterscheiden sich im wesentlichen dadurch, ob die gesamte oder nur ein Teil der Transportentfernung in die Transportleistung eingeht. Die hier zugrunde gelegten Daten des Statistischen Bundesamtes /STBA 1995b/ werden nach dem sogenannten Standortprinzip erhoben; d. h. die Verkehrsleistung des aus Deutschland abgehenden Verkehrs bis zum ersten (Aussteige- bzw. Auslade-)Flughafen wird erfaßt. Diese Verkehrsleistung muß natürlich nicht notwendig mit der gemäß /AGE 1998/ getankten Kerosinmenge korrelieren; anschaulich: Der Treibstoff reicht weiter als bis zum ersten Flughafen (siehe dazu auch das im Prinzip identische Abgrenzungsproblem in der Binnenschiffahrt in Kapitel 5.3.1). Tatsächlich ergeben sich jedoch im Vergleich mit anders bestimmten Daten sehr gute Übereinstimmungen (siehe unten).

Die Daten zur Transportleistung in /STBA 1995b/ liegen differenziert nach Passagier- und Frachtverkehr, Linien- und Charterflügen sowie inländischem und grenzüberschreitendem Verkehr vor; die auf Passagierflügen transportierte Beifracht ist gewichtet in den Angaben in Personen-Kilometern enthalten. Für die Ableitung relevant ist neben der Passagier/Fracht-Differenzierung die Unterscheidung von inländischem und grenzüberschreitendem Verkehr.

Die der Transportleistung zugrunde gelegten sogenannten Großkreisentfernungen bezeichnen die kürzeste, nicht die real zurückgelegte Entfernung zwischen Start- und Zielflughafen. Umwegflüge, Warteschleifen usw. sind damit nicht berücksichtigt. Dies führt formal zu höheren spezifischen Kraftstoffverbräuchen gegenüber dem Bezug auf den reinen Streckenflug, da die gesamte verbrauchte Kraftstoffmenge auf die kürzest mögliche Entfernung umgelegt wird. Für ökologische Bilanzierungen ist der Bezug auf Großkreisentfernungen zweckmäßig, da nur diese mit akzeptablem Aufwand erhoben werden können; eine Korrektur auf reale Strecken erfolgt daher nicht.

Zur Aufteilung zwischen Fracht- und Passagierverkehr – differenziert nach inländischem und grenzüberschreitendem Verkehr – werden die Personenverkehrsleistungen in Personen-km formal in tkm umgerechnet. Dazu wird ein durchschnittliches Passagiergewicht inklusive Gepäck von 90 bzw. 96,5 kg (Inlands- bzw. Auslandsflüge) unterstellt. Die Kabinenausstattung wird durch einen Faktor berücksichtigt; die Lufthansa setzt zur Verteilung zwischen Passagieren und Beifracht einen Wert von 1,7 an, der in /IFEU 1996c/ für die Umrechnung der gesamten Leistung in Personen-km in tkm angesetzt wird.

Wie einleitend dargestellt, hängt der spezifische Verbrauch über unterschiedliche Anteile der verschiedenen Flugphasen von der Fluglänge ab. Aus /LUFTHANSA 1997/ ergibt sich, daß der Verbrauch auf Kurz- und Mittelstreckenflügen um durchschnittlich 50 % höher ist als auf Langstreckenflügen. Dies berücksichtigen wir wie folgt: Die inländische Transportleistung wird Kurz- bzw. Mittelstreckenflügen, die grenzüberschreitende Langstreckenflügen zugeordnet. Die Transportleistung auf Kurz- bzw. Mittelstreckenflügen wird mit dem Faktor 1,5 gegenüber der auf Langstreckenflügen gewichtet.

Aus den gewichteten Transportleistungen auf Kurz- bzw. Mittelstreckenflügen und Langstreckenflügen im Passagier- und Frachtverkehr in tkm werden die Anteile berechnet. Unter der Annahme gleicher Flotten und mittlerer Flugstrecken wird die Kerosinabgabe im gleichen Verhältnis aufgeteilt. Die mittleren spezifischen Verbräuche resultieren aus den tatsächlichen *ungewichteten* Verkehrsleistungen in Personen- bzw. tkm und den zugeordneten Kerosinmengen. Sie betragen im Frachtverkehr

- 16,4 MJ/tkm (381 g/tkm) auf Kurz- und Mittelstrecken und
- 10,9 MJ/tkm (253 g/tkm) auf Langstrecken.

Zum Vergleich: In einer aktuellen niederländischen Untersuchung werden für Kurz- und Mittelstrecken 19,5 MJ/tkm (453 g/tkm) und für Langstrecken 11,0 MJ/tkm (256 g/tkm) angegeben /CE 1997a/. Die Lufthansa gibt für ihre Frachtflotte einen durchschnittlichen Verbrauch von 10,5 MJ/tkm (245 g/tkm) /LUFTHANSA 1997/ an; dieser Wert wird von Langstreckenflügen mit sehr modernen Maschinen dominiert. Die Literaturwerte liegen damit zumindest in der gleichen Größenordnung (Kurz- und Mittelstrecken) oder stimmen mit den hier abgeleiteten überein (Langstrecken).

Trotz der guten Übereinstimmung mit anderen Quellen ist zu betonen, daß es sich bei den hier abgeleiteten Daten um Richtwerte handelt. Dies ergibt sich im wesentlichen aus den zahlreichen Annahmen, der Grobrasterung in nur zwei Entfernungsklassen und der Nichtberücksichtigung des Auslastungsgrades. – Der Transport von Schnittblumen aus Kolumbien kann mit volumen-, kaum aber massenausgelasteten Maschinen erfolgen. Der spezifische Verbrauch dürfte damit deutlich höher sein als etwa bei einem massenausgelasteten Transport von Maschinenteilen.

5.5.2 Emissionen

Wie bei dieselbetriebenen Transportmitteln werden die CO_2-, SO_2- und HCl-Emissionen aus der Treibstoffzusammensetzung berechnet. Für den in Deutschland gebräuchlichen Turbinenkraftstoff Jet A-1 wird der C-Gehalt mit 85 M% angegeben /DGMK 1992/. Der S-Gehalt kann zwischen 0,02 M% /DGMK 1992/ in Deutschland und dem internationalen Grenzwert von 0,3 M% liegen. Damit sollte zwischen Inlands- und Auslandsverkehr (Kurz- bzw. Mittel- und Langstrecke) unterschieden werden. Für den Inlandsverkehr setzen wir analog zu /IFEU 1996c/ 0,03 M% an. Dieser Wert wurde bei Messungen auf dem Frankfurter Flughafen im November 1994 bestimmt, wobei 40 % des dort abgegebenen Kerosins aus dem Ausland stammten. Für den Auslandsverkehr übernehmen wir ebenfalls den Wert nach /IFEU 1996c/. Dort wurde als internationaler Wert ein S-Gehalt von 0,05 M% abgeschätzt. Für den Cl-Gehalt übernehmen wir den Wert für Dieselkraftstoff von 0,0001 M%. Den Heizwert von Kerosin setzen wir einheitlich gleich 43 MJ/kg /AGE 1998/.

Für CO, NO_X und HC werden in /IFEU 1996c/ Emissionsfaktoren für das Bezugsjahr 1990 auf der Basis verschiedener Literaturangaben und darauf aufbauend – über Minderungsraten – für 2010 abgeschätzt. Nach bisherigem Kenntnisstand ist lediglich für CO eine Unterscheidung zwischen Kurz- bzw. Mittel- und Langstreckenverkehr erforderlich bzw. durchführbar. Die Emissionsfaktoren für das Bezugsjahr 1990 orientieren sich – unter Berücksichtigung der niedrigeren Faktoren neuerer Maschinen nach /LUFTHANSA 1995/ – an Arbeiten für die Enquête-Kommission „Schutz der Erdatmosphäre“ /IFEU & TÜVRL 1990/; das gleiche gilt für die Minderungsraten. Die Werte für 1996 werden hier aus denen für 1990 und 2010 durch lineare Interpolation bestimmt. Die Daten sind in **Tabelle 5-19** zusammengefaßt.

Die gegenläufigen Entwicklungen der NO_X- bzw. der CO- und HC-Emissionen werden aus vergangenen und zukünftigen Verbrauchsminderungen abgeleitet. Verbrauchsminderungen werden unter anderem durch höhere Verbrennungstemperaturen erreicht. Damit ist eine vollständigere Oxidation der Kohlenwasserstoffe zu CO_2 und H_2O verbunden; gleichzeitig wird bei höheren Temperaturen verstärkt NO_X gebildet.

Die Methan- und NMHC-Faktoren werden aus dem HC-Faktor und einem Methananteil von 5 % an den HC-Emissionen bestimmt /IFEU & TÜVRL 1990/. Die verbrauchsbezogenen Faktoren für Benzol und Formaldehyd werden in grober Näherung (!) aus dem HC-Faktor für Gasturbinen und den für Gasturbinen angesetzten Anteilen abgeschätzt, die für die übrigen Schadstoffe gleich denen von Gasturbinen gesetzt.

Tabelle 5-19 Emissionsfaktoren für Flugzeuge: Literaturdaten und Rechenwerte

Quelle	**CO** g/MJ	**NO_X** g/MJ	**HC** g/MJ	**Bezug**
/TÜVRL 1989/	0,23	0,28	0,058	Verkehr über Deutschland 1984
/BAZ 1987/	0,35	0,47	0,030	Schweiz 1987
/IFEU 1992/	0,23	0,26	0,070	Flugverkehr der DDR 1988
/DLR 1990/	0,042	0,23	0,014	ICAO 1988
/SWISSAIR 1991/	0,077	0,51	0,026	Swissair-Flotte 1989
/LUFTHANSA 1989/	0,088	0,35	0,035	Lufthansa-Flotte 1989
/IEA 1991/	0,047	0,42	0,023	
/BAZ 1993/	k. A.	0,35	0,070	1990
/BMV 1994/	0,42	0,37	0,17	Verkehr über Deutschland 1991
/DLR 1993/	0,014	0,42	0,035	1993
/LUFTHANSA 1995/	0,091	0,33	0,021	Lufthansa-Flotte 1994
daraus /IFEU 1996c/				
	0,14	0,35	0,035	Inland, Deutschland 1990
	0,093	0,35	0,035	Grenzüberschreitend 1990
	0,093	0,42	0,028	Inland, Deutschland 2010
	0,062	0,42	0,028	Grenzüberschreitend 2010
	33%	-20%	20%	Reduktion 1990 => 2010
Diese Arbeit nach /IFEU 1996c/				
	0,13	0,37	0,033	Inland, Deutschland 1996
	0,084	0,37	0,033	Grenzüberschreitend 1996
	10,0%	-6,0%	6,0%	Reduktion 1990 => 1996

ICAO: International Civil Aviation Organisation (Internationale Zivilluftfahrtorganisation der Vereinten Nationen)
Negatives Vorzeichen: Anstieg

Wie in Kapitel 4.2.1 erwähnt, hängt die qualitative und/oder quantitative Wirkung von Emissionen auch von der Höhe des Emissionsortes ab. Da die genauen Zusammenhänge noch relativ unklar sind, haben wir auf eine Erweiterung des Ortsklassenkonzeptes in die dritte Dimension verzichtet. Auch die Anwendung des Konzeptes in seiner gegenwärtigen Form ist jedoch zumindest im Zusammenhang lokaler Wirkung sinnvoll. Wir ordnen hier 10 bzw. 5 % (Kurz-/Mittel- bzw. Langstrecke) der gesamten Emissionen nicht global wirksamer Schadstoffe der Ortsklasse 2, die restlichen Emissionen der Ortsklasse 3 zu. Die Verteilung orientiert sich an den Emissionsanteilen unter- und oberhalb 3.000 ft (914 m) nach /CE 1997b/. Damit wird berücksichtigt, daß im wesentlichen die bodennahen Emissionen aus Warmlauf, Flugfeldbewegung sowie Starts und Landung unmittelbar humantoxische Wirkungen haben.

Die hier abgeleiteten Daten zum Energieaufwand und den damit verbundenen Emissionen des Luftfrachtverkehrs sind in **Tabelle 5-20** zusammengefaßt; die kumulierten Daten einschließlich der Kerosinbereitstellung sind im Anhang (**Tabelle 9-11**) dokumentiert.

In den oberen Schichten der Troposphäre können Wasserdampfemissionen die Wolkenbildung beeinflussen und damit mittelbar zum anthropogenen Treibhauseffekt beitragen. Wir geben daher hier nachrichtlich einen energieverbrauchsbezogenen Emissionsfaktor für Wasserdampf an. Aus dem Wasserstoffgehalt von Kerosin von 15 M% nach /DGMK 1992/ ergibt sich bei Annahme vollständiger Verbrennung ein Faktor von 31,4 g H_2O/MJ (1,35 kg H_2O/kg) Kerosin.

Tabelle 5-20 Spezifischer Verbrauch und Emissionen des Luftfrachtverkehrs

		Kurz-/Mittel-strecke	Langstrecke		Kurz-/Mittel-strecke	Langstrecke
Treibstoffverbrauch						
Kerosin				MJ/tkm	16,4	10,9
Emissionen						
		Global	**Global**		**Global**	**Global**
CO_2	g/MJ	74,1	74,1	g/tkm	1.215	810
CH_4	g/MJ	0,0016	0,0016	g/tkm	0,027	0,018
N_2O	g/MJ	0,0077	0,0077	g/tkm	0,13	0,084
		OK 2+3	**OK 2+3**		**OK 2+3**	**OK 2+3**
SO_2	g/MJ	0,014	0,023	g/tkm	0,23	0,25
CO	g/MJ	0,13	0,084	g/tkm	2,06	0,92
NO_X	g/MJ	0,37	0,37	g/tkm	6,06	4,04
NMHC	g/MJ	0,031	0,031	g/tkm	0,51	0,34
Partikel	g/MJ	0,012	0,012	g/tkm	0,19	0,13
Staub	g/MJ	0	0	g/tkm	0	0
HCl	g/MJ	0,00002	0,00002	g/tkm	0,00039	0,00026
NH_3	g/MJ	0,00047	0,00047	g/tkm	0,0076	0,0051
Formaldehyd	g/MJ	0,0023	0,0023	g/tkm	0,038	0,025
Benzol	g/MJ	0,0013	0,0013	g/tkm	0,022	0,014
Benzo(a)pyren	ng/MJ	180	180	ng/tkm	2.944	1.963
TCDD-TÄ	ng/MJ	0,0014	0,0014	ng/tkm	0,023	0,015
Anteil OK 2		10%	5%		10%	5%

Quellen: /CARBOTECH 1994/, /ECOINVENT 1996/, /IFEU 1995b/, /IFEU 1996c/, eigene Berechnungen

5.6 Pipelines

Der Transport per Rohr*fern*leitung spielt vor allem für Erdöl und Erdgas eine wesentliche Rolle. Daneben werden auch Mineralölprodukte und zunehmend Trinkwasser über größere Entfernungen mittels Pipelines transportiert. Der Energieaufwand des Pipelinetransports hängt unter anderem vom Leitungsdurchmesser, der Strömungsgeschwindigkeit bzw. den Druckunterschieden, der Höhendifferenz, dem Transportgut und der Auslastung ab. Wir unterscheiden hier im folgenden lediglich zwischen Gas- und Ölpipelines.

Gaspipelines

Die Verdichter von Gaspipelines werden mit Gasturbinen betrieben. Der Energieeinsatz liegt nach /GEMIS 1997/ bei 0,75 MJ/tkm bzw. 15,0 MJ/TJkm; diesen Wert übernehmen wir hier.

Die Emissionsfaktoren übernehmen wir ebenfalls im wesentlichen aus /GEMIS 1997/. Dabei wird zwischen Pipelines und Turbinen in der Bundesrepublik bzw. Westeuropa und in der GUS unterschieden. Die Formaldehyd- und Benzolfaktoren werden aus den NMHC-Emissionen und Anteilen daran nach /ECOINVENT 1996/ berechnet, die Benzo(a)pyren- und TCDD-Faktoren nach /IFEU 1998b/ bzw. /UBA 1995/ abgeschätzt. Neben den Verbrennungsemissionen werden die Methanverluste durch Leckagen berücksichtigt.

Die Daten sind in **Tabelle 5-21** zusammengefaßt. Für den Transport mit See-Pipelines empfiehlt sich die Aufteilung der nicht global wirksamen Schadstoffe in Ortsklassen wie für Seeschiffe dargestellt (siehe Kapitel 5.4.2).

Tabelle 5-21 Emissionsfaktoren für Gasturbinenverdichter an Gaspipelines in g/MJ Erdgas (verbrannt) und g/TJkm Erdgas (transportiert)

		D	GUS		D	GUS
Energieeinsatz						
Erdgas				MJ/TJkm	15,0	15,0
Emissionen						
		Global	**Global**		**Global**	**Global**
CO_2	g/MJ	55,2	55,4	g/TJkm	827	830
CH_4	g/MJ	0,0042	0,0084	g/TJkm	0,063	0,13
N_2O	g/MJ	0,0025	0,0025	g/TJkm	0,038	0,038
		OK 2	**OK 2**		**OK 2**	**OK 2**
SO_2	g/MJ	0,00043	0,00040	g/TJkm	0,0064	0,0060
CO	g/MJ	0,084	0,17	g/TJkm	1,26	2,51
NO_X	g/MJ	0,29	0,33	g/TJkm	4,41	5,01
NMHC	g/MJ	0,0084	0,021	g/TJkm	0,13	0,31
Partikel	g/MJ	0	0	g/TJkm	0	0
Staub	g/MJ	0,0042	0,0042	g/TJkm	0,063	0,063
HCl	g/MJ	0	0	g/TJkm	0	0
NH_3	g/MJ	0	0	g/TJkm	0	0
Formaldehyd	g/MJ	0,00084	0,0021	g/TJkm	0,013	0,031
Benzol	g/MJ	0,00084	0,0021	g/TJkm	0,013	0,031
Benzo(a)pyren	ng/MJ	1,00	1,00	ng/TJkm	15,0	15,0
TCDD-TÄ	ng/MJ	0,084	0,084	ng/TJkm	1,26	1,25

Für See-Pipelines: siehe Text
Quellen: /ECOINVENT 1996/, /GEMIS 1997/, /IFEU 1998b/, /UBA 1995/, eigene Berechnungen

Ölpipelines

Die Pumpen von Ölpipelines werden mit Elektromotoren angetrieben; der Energieeinsatz beträgt etwa 0,02 kWh/tkm (0,47 kWh/TJkm) /GEMIS 1997/. Die Emissionen des Rohöltransports ergeben sich aus den Emissionen der Stromerzeugung, die in den Kraftwerken der öffentlichen Versorgung (Kapitel 8.6) oder in betriebseigenen Kraftwerken stattfinden kann.

6 Landwirtschaft

Die Mehrzahl der Arbeiten in der Landwirtschaft wird heute maschinell oder maschinell unterstützt durchgeführt. Die wichtigsten – weil praktisch universell einsetzbaren – Maschinen sind Ackerschlepper; sie können mit entsprechenden Anbau- bzw. Anhängegeräten versehen zur Bodenbearbeitung wie Pflügen und Eggen, zum Transport, über die Zapfwelle zum Pumpen und zum Mähen eingesetzt werden. Das gesamte Einsatzspektrum von Schleppern reicht vom typischen Ackerbau über den Obst- und Gartenbau zur Forst- und Viehwirtschaft. Daneben werden zahlreiche motorisierte Spezialmaschinen für Ernte- und Pflanzzwecke eingesetzt.

Gegenstand der folgenden Darstellung ist die Ableitung von spezifischen Verbräuchen und Emissionen der maschinellen Feldarbeit *im engeren Sinne*, d. h. ohne expliziten Bezug auf Maschinen und Prozesse in Gartenbau, Forstwirtschaft und Viehzucht. Gegebenenfalls können für diese Sektoren Daten vergleichbarer Maschinen und Prozesse der maschinellen Feldarbeit übernommen werden.

In der landwirtschaftlichen Praxis werden Feldarbeiten mit sehr unterschiedlichem Energiebedarf mit Maschinen unterschiedlichster Motorleistung durchgeführt. Generell gilt, daß schwere Arbeiten wie z. B. Pflügen eher mit schweren Schleppern und Pflegearbeiten mit leichten Schleppern durchgeführt werden. Ferner werden große Schläge meist mit schweren und kleinere Schläge mit leichteren Schleppern bearbeitet. Schließlich fallen für verschiedene Kulturen, etwa Hackfrüchte und Getreide, nicht nur flächenbezogen unterschiedliche Gesamtzeitaufwendungen, sondern auch unterschiedliche Anteile schwerer und leichter Arbeiten an. Wegen der in Kapitel 3 dargestellten Abhängigkeit des absoluten Energieverbrauchs, des motorischen Wirkungsgrades und der Emissionen von Nennleistung und Motorauslastung sind für die hier betrachteten Parameter Differenzierungen nach Motorleistung und Lastzuständen unbedingt sinnvoll, sollen die Daten in detaillierten ökologischen Bilanzierungen eingesetzt werden.

Die Ableitung entsprechend differenzierter Daten wurde erstmals in /KALTSCHMITT & REINHARDT 1997/ und /PATYK & REINHARDT 1997/ kurz beschrieben. Im folgenden findet sich eine detaillierte Darstellung des Vorgehens, das die folgenden Schritte umfaßt:

- Einteilung der Maschinen in Nennleistungsklassen und Zuordnung der verschiedenen Feldarbeiten zu Laststufen
- Ableitung des Kraftstoffverbrauchs pro Zeiteinheit, differenziert nach Nennleistungsklassen und Laststufen
- Ableitung verbrauchsbezogener Emissionsfaktoren und Verknüpfung mit zeitbezogenen Verbräuchen, differenziert nach Nennleistungsklassen und Laststufen

Als Energieträger werden bei der Ableitung der spezifischen Verbräuche und Emissionen neben Dieselkraftstoff mit Rapsöl und seinem Umesterungsprodukt Rapsölmethylester (RME) auch regenerative Energieträger berücksichtigt.

In einem weiteren Kapitel werden die flächenbezogenen Zeitaufwendungen wichtiger landwirtschaftlicher Arbeitsgänge in den einzelnen Laststufen bestimmt. Diese Zeiten werden mit den zeitbezogenen Kraftstoffverbräuchen und Emissionen verknüpft, um Gesamtemissionen je Arbeitsschritt (z. B. Pflug aufsatteln oder Anfahrt oder Pflügen) bzw. in der Summe für ganze Arbeitsgänge (Pflügen inklusive Pflug aufsatteln, Anfahrt usw.) zu erhalten.

Die abgeleiteten Daten und die Methodik werden in einem letzten Kapitel auf die landwirtschaftliche Produktion von Rapssaat, Weizen, Zuckerrüben und Kartoffeln angewandt. Damit werden zugleich detaillierte Bilanzen der maschinellen Aufwendungen für einige der wichtigsten Feldfrüchte geliefert, die direkt in andere Anwendungen übernommen werden können.

Die Grundlage der Ableitungen bilden im wesentlichen fünf Datensätze. Aus dieser schmalen Datenbasis ergeben sich relativ große Unsicherheiten. Die Zuordnung zum Bezugsjahr 1996 hat im wesentlichen formalen Charakter. Den Schwerpunkt bildet die Darstellung zahlreicher, durch die Datenlage bedingter Näherungen.

6.1 Kraftstoffverbrauch

Die Ableitung des spezifischen Kraftstoffverbrauchs – und darauf aufbauend der Emissionsfaktoren – erfolgt differenziert nach Maschinenklassen und der Art der Arbeit. Den verschiedenen Arbeiten werden dabei unterschiedliche Lastpunkte eines speziell für Ackerschlepper entwickelten Testzykluses zugeordnet.

6.1.1 Differenzierung nach Maschinenklassen

Das gesamte Spektrum der selbstfahrenden Landmaschinen wird nach dem Kriterium der Nennleistung in drei Schlepperklassen und zwei Klassen für Erntemaschinen, die überwiegend deutlich stärker als Schlepper motorisiert sind, eingeteilt. Den Klassen wird jeweils eine Nennleistung als typischer Wert – im folgenden: Rechenwert – zugeordnet (**Tabelle 6-1**). Die Einsatzbereiche der Schlepperklassen bzw. die in den Erntemaschinenklassen erfaßten Maschinen lassen sich folgendermaßen abgrenzen:

- Leichte Schlepper: Pflegearbeiten auf kleinen Schlägen
- Mittlere Schlepper: Schwere Arbeiten auf kleinen Schlägen und Pflegearbeiten auf großen Schlägen
- Schwere Schlepper: Schwere Arbeiten auf großen Schlägen
- Erntemaschinen I: Schwere Mähdrescher und leichte Roder (Erntemaschinen für Hackfrüchte)
- Erntemaschinen II: Schwere Roder und Häcksler

Für selbstfahrende Erntemaschinen niedrigerer Leistung oder gezogene Erntemaschinen können die Daten einer geeigneten Schlepperklasse angesetzt werden.

Die Klasseneinteilung für Schlepper ist an der Bestandsstruktur in Deutschland 1996 nach /KBA 1997/ *und* dem Trend zu leistungsstarken Schleppern, wie ihn die Zulassungsstatistiken der vergangenen Jahre ausweisen, orientiert. Im Bestand stellen nach /KBA 1997/ die Schlepper mit Nennleistungen zwischen 37 und 59 kW mit 48 % die weitaus größte Gruppe

Tabelle 6-1 Klassifizierung von Landmaschinen nach Motorleistung und zugeordnete Rechenwerte

Maschinenklasse	Leistungsspektrum kW	Rechenwert kW
Leichte Schlepper	40 - 70	55,6*
Mittlere Schlepper	70 - 110	90
Schwere Schlepper	110 - 170	140
Erntemaschine I	170 - 280	225
Erntemaschine II	> 280	350

*: Mittelwert der hier untersuchten Schlepper

dar. Diese KBA-Klasse hat mit hoher Wahrscheinlichkeit in der gesamten landwirtschaftlichen Praxis über alle Schlaggrößen das weiteste Einsatzspektrum und bietet sich damit für die Definition des Mittleren Schleppers an. Angesichts des Trends zu schwereren Schleppern im Bestand und auch der wahrscheinlichen Anteile an der gesamten Arbeitsleistung halten wir die Zuordnung Leichter Schlepper zu dieser KBA-Klasse für zielführender. Der Rechenwert für Leichte Schlepper entspricht dem Mittelwert der Nennleistungen der Schlepper, deren Verbräuche und Emissionen die Basis der hier dargestellten Ableitung bilden; die übrigen Rechenwerte sind die Mittelwerte der repräsentierten Intervalle.

6.1.2 Differenzierung nach Art der Feldarbeit bzw. Lastpunkten

Die Differenzierung nach Betriebszuständen erfolgt auf der Basis eines speziell für Ackerschlepper entwickelten Lastkollektivs nach /VELLGUTH 1987/ und /WELSCHOF 1981/. Zur Ableitung dieses Zykluses wurden über ein Wirtschaftsjahr und sämtliche Arbeiten Drehzahl und Drehmoment eines Schleppers erfaßt, mit dem Ergebnis, daß sich die Mehrzahl der landwirtschaftlichen Arbeiten schon durch fünf Drehzahl/Drehmoment-Kombinationen ausreichend genau beschreiben läßt. Die Kenndaten des daraus abgeleiteten 5-Punkte-Tests – relative Drehzahl, Drehmoment und zeitliche Gewichtung in den Mittelwerten – sowie die den Punkten zugeordneten Arbeiten sind in **Tabelle 6-2** zusammengefaßt.

Tabelle 6-2 Typische Arbeiten, Kenndaten und mittlere Zeitanteile des 5-Punkte-Tests, gemessen für Schlepper mit Nennleistungen zwischen 50 und 74 kW

Typische Arbeit	Lastpunkt	rel. Drehzahl	rel. Drehmoment	Motorauslastung	mittlerer Zeitanteil
Schwere Zapfwellenarbeit, Pflügen	A	95 %	88 %	84 %	31 %
Normale Zapfwellenarbeit, Transport auf dem Feld und Feldwegen	B	85 %	48 %	41 %	18 %
Leichte Arbeit ohne Zapfwelle, langsame Arbeit, Kriechgang	C	53 %	40 %	21 %	19 %
Straßentransport, Rangieren	D	100 %	15 %	15 %	20 %
Leerlaufanteile aus allen Arbeiten	E	40 %	0 %	0 %	12 %
Zeitlich gewichtetes Mittel		**79 %**	**47 %**	**41 %**	**100 %**

Quellen: /WELSCHOF 1981/, /VELLGUTH 1987/

Im Zusammenhang mit der Differenzierung nach Lastpunkten sind zwei weitere Arbeiten interessant. In /LOGOS 1983/ wurden die fünf Kennfeldpunkte nach /WELSCHOF 1981/ hinsichtlich Lage und Zeitanteil nach Schlepper-Nennleistungsklassen differenziert. In /RINALDI & NÄF 1992/ wurde ein Lastkollektiv mit sechs Punkten vorgeschlagen; die Lage der den einzelnen Arbeiten zugeordneten Punkte im Motorkennfeld soll nur in geringem Maße von der Nennleistung abhängen. Für drei Punkte besteht eine gute Übereinstimmung der Lastkollektive nach /RINALDI & NÄF 1992/ und /VELLGUTH 1987/, ein Punkt des 5-Punkte-Tests liegt relativ genau zwischen zwei Punkten des 6-Punkte-Tests und je ein Punkt findet keine Entsprechung; dies sind ein zweiter Punkt für schwere Arbeiten im 6-Punkte-Test und der die Straßenfahrt abbildende Punkt im 5-Punkte-Test. Eine an sich wünschenswerte Verwendung der Arbeiten von /LOGOS 1983/ und /RINALDI & NÄF 1992/ kann nicht erfolgen, da keine bzw. nur ein Satz von Verbrauchs- und Emissionsdaten aus der Zyklenanwendung vorliegt.

Möglichkeiten der Erweiterung der Datenbasis für schwere Maschinen

Ziel der bislang erschienenen Arbeiten waren praktisch ausschließlich Erkenntnisse über Unterschiede im Emissionsverhalten bei Diesel- und Rapsöl- bzw. Rapsölmethylesterbetrieb. Zur Zeit liegen uns fünf nach Lastpunkten differenzierte Datensätze und einige weitere Sätze gewichteter Testmittelwerte für konventionelle Schlepper vor; letztere können nur zum Abgleich der Größenordnungen dienen; Daten für Elsbett-Schlepper im Dieselbetrieb werden hier nicht weiter behandelt. Die 5-Punkte-Tests wurden an Schleppern mit Nennleistungen zwischen 32 und 74 kW durchgeführt; schwere Schlepper und selbstfahrende Erntemaschinen sind somit in der Datenbasis nicht erfaßt. Eine Berücksichtigung von Daten aus 13-Punkte-Tests, die in größerer Zahl auch an schweren Schlepper- und LKW-Motoren durchgeführt wurden und werden, scheint daher zur Erweiterung der Datenbasis grundsätzlich unter zwei Aspekten wünschenswert:

- Für die nicht in 5-Punkte-Tests erfaßten schweren Schlepper können über Ähnlichkeitsbetrachtungen Daten aus 13-Punkte-Tests den Laststufen des 5-Punkte-Tests zugeordnet werden.
- Selbstfahrende Erntemaschinen, für die keine Emissionsdaten vorliegen, werden – anders als Schlepper – häufig nicht mit eigens für ihren Einsatzzweck, sondern mit vor allem für den Einbau in LKW konstruierten Motoren angetrieben.

Die Vermessung eines Schleppers sowohl im 5- als auch im 13-Punkte-Test erlaubt einen Vergleich der beiden Testverfahren /WÖRGETTER et al. 1993/. Die aggregierten Gesamtergebnisse der Tests weichen je nach Schadstoff unterschiedlich stark voneinander ab. Für den Lastpunkt A, Schwere Arbeit im 5-Punkte-Test, findet sich eine gute Näherung im 13-Punkte-Test (**Tabelle 6-3**). Durch die Zusammenfassung von zwei oder drei Punkten des 13-Punkte-Tests können andere Punkte des 5-Punkte-Tests ähnlich gut angenähert werden, meist jedoch nur für zwei der drei gemessenen Schadstoffe; die Gewichtung der Einzelpunkte erfolgt dabei in grober Näherung proportional zur Drehmoment-Differenz zwischen den Punkten des 5- und des 13-Punkte-Tests.

Mit solchen Zuordnungen und Gewichtungsfaktoren besteht somit prinzipiell die Möglichkeit, nur nach dem 13-Punkte-Test vorgenommene Messungen vergleichend zu betrachten. Es ist jedoch auch offensichtlich, daß nur eine größenordnungsmäßige Bestätigung, aber keine signifikante Verbesserung der in den folgenden Unterkapiteln abgeleiteten Rechenwerte möglich ist. Hinsichtlich der Verbrauchs- und Emissionsbestimmung für selbstfahrende Erntemaschinen halten wir die verschiedentlich vorgeschlagene direkte Verwendung von Daten des 13-Punkte-Tests aus drei Gründen für nicht stichhaltig:

- Der 13-Punkte-Test wurde nicht für LKW-*Motoren*, sondern zur Simulation des LKW-*Einsatzes* entwickelt; die Ähnlichkeit einzelner Punkte im 5- und im 13-Punkte-Test kann für oder auch gegen die Anwendung beider Tests interpretiert werden.
- Erntemaschinen werden korrekt nicht von LKW-Motoren, sondern von aus LKW-Motorbaureihen stammenden Aggregaten angetrieben. Einzelne Bauteile und vor allem die Motoreinstellung können erheblich von den für LKW-Motoren typischen abweichen.
- Unterschiede technischer Kenngrößen zwischen LKW- und Schleppermotoren stellen im wesentlichen eine Tendenz dar, die zahlreiche Ausnahmen – konkret: Überlappungen der Wertebereiche – zuläßt. So haben LKW insbesondere im unteren Leistungsbereich meist etwas höhere hubraumbezogene Leistungen und höhere Nenndrehzahlen als Schleppermotoren. Für die Leistungsklassen der in Erntemaschinen eingebauten Motoren gilt dies jedoch praktisch nicht mehr. Prinzipiell gleiches gilt auch für die in der früheren DDR bzw. in den neuen Bundesländern z. B. in Mähdrescher eingebauten luftgekühlten 3- und 4-Zylindermotoren, die auch stationär, nicht aber in LKW eingesetzt werden.

Tabelle 6-3 Vergleich von Schlepperemissionen bei zwei Arbeiten im 5- bzw. 13-Punkte-Test

Arbeit Test	Lastpunkt	CO g/h	HC g/h	NO_X g/h
Schwere Arbeit				
5-Punkte	A	58	46	436
13-Punkte	9	63	42	364
Leichte Arbeit				
5-Punkte	C	49	35	192
13-Punkte	1	54	20	29
13-Punkte	4	42	32	273
13-Punkte	5	56	34	362
13-Punkte	1 + 4 + 5	51	29	222
Gewichtetes Mittel				
5-Punkte	Alle	64	39	228
13-Punkte	Alle	89	35	259

Quelle: /WÖRGETTER et al. 1993/

Eine von uns durchgeführte Recherche und Auswertung von Daten aus 13-Punkte-Tests bestätigte die dargestellte kritische Einschätzung:

- Es sind überwiegend nur gewichtete Testmittelwerte zugänglich; Daten für die einzelnen Punkte sind als vertrauliche Firmendaten meist nur einseh-, nicht aber publizierbar. Anders als bei Untersuchungen nach dem 5-Punkte-Test ist somit die verfügbare Datenmenge sehr viel kleiner als die tatsächlich ermittelte.

- Bei den von uns einsehbaren Daten für einzelne Punkte handelt es sich um Meßwerte, die an neuen, modernen Motoren ermittelt wurden. Verbrauch und Emissionen waren daher insgesamt sehr niedrig und mit hoher Wahrscheinlichkeit bestandsuntypisch. Der Wartungszustand der Testschlepper aus den 5-Punkte-Tests, die sich überwiegend im Besitz von Forschungsanstalten befanden, dürfte dagegen zwar überdurchschnittlich gut gewesen sein, es handelte sich jedoch nicht um Neu- bzw. vor den Tests neu eingestellte Fahrzeuge.
- Die – nicht bestandstypischen (siehe oben) – Daten zeigen keine erkennbare Abhängigkeit des spezifischen Verbrauchs und der Emissionen von der Nennleistung bzw. dem Einsatzzweck der Motoren in Schleppern oder LKW.

Zusammenfassend ist daher festzustellen: Eine tatsächliche qualitative Verbesserung der Datenbasis für schwere Schlepper und Erntemaschinen würde nur durch Messungen an solchen Maschinen an den tatsächlich relevanten Lastpunkten erreicht. Daten aus 13-Punkte-Tests stellen somit keine quantifizierend verwertbare Erweiterung der Datenbasis dar und werden hier daher nicht berücksichtigt. Aufgrund dieser Datenlage sind unsere Werte nicht als statistische Durchschnittswerte anzusehen, sondern als Rechenwerte, die jedoch sicher in der richtigen Größenordnung liegen und untereinander korrekte größer/kleiner-Relationen aufweisen.

6.1.3 Kraftstoffverbrauch von Landmaschinen

Im folgenden werden die in Kapitel 6.1.1 und 6.1.2 formal eingeführten Differenzierungen nach Maschinenklassen und Feldarbeiten auf den Kraftstoffverbrauch von Landmaschinen angewendet. Dies geschieht zunächst für Schlepper und darauf aufbauend für Erntemaschinen. Für letztere wird dabei auch das für Schlepper abgeleitete Verfahren angewendet, ergänzt um Informationen aus dem Vergleich mit Praxisdaten.

6.1.3.1 Schlepper

Bisher sind praktisch nur leichte Schlepper nach dem 5-Punkte-Test vermessen worden. Die Ableitung der zeitbezogenen Kraftstoffverbräuche differenziert nach Lastpunkten erfolgt daher zunächst für die Klasse Leichte Schlepper nach Kapitel 6.1.1. Anschließend werden die einzelnen Verbrauchswerte gestützt auf plausible Zusatzannahmen für die anderen Klassen (Einteilung siehe **Tabelle 6-2**) modifiziert.

Die Bandbreiten der spezifischen Verbräuche (Bezug: Motorarbeit in kWh) bzw. Wirkungsgrade für die einzelnen Laststufen sind in den uns vorliegenden Datensätzen relativ gering; insbesondere ist innerhalb des erfaßten Leistungsintervalls von 32 bis 74 kW keine Nennleistungsabhängigkeit feststellbar. Wir setzen daher die Mittelwerte des Verbrauchs in MJ/h über die fünf Datensätze als Rechenwerte fest. Der Mittelwert der Nennleistungen der erfaßten Schlepper von 55,6 kW definiert, wie in Kapitel 6.1.1 dargestellt, den Rechenwert für Leichte Schlepper. In **Tabelle 6-4** sind die Verbrauchsdaten aus den hier berücksichtigten 5-Punkte-Tests zusammengestellt.

Tabelle 6-4 Kraftstoffverbrauch von Leichten Ackerschleppern, differenziert nach Lastpunkten des 5-Punkte-Tests: Literaturdaten und Rechenwerte (Bezüge: Motorarbeit in kWh und Zeit in h)

	MotorNL	**ZapfWL**	**Schwer**	**Normal**	**Leicht**	**Straße**	**Leerlauf**	**Gew. Mitt.**
Zeitanteil			31 %	18 %	19 %	20 %	12 %	
Quelle	kW	kW	MJ/kWh	MJ/kWh	MJ/kWh	MJ/kWh	MJ/kWh	MJ/kWh
a	32	26	12,0	14,8	15,6	33,4	-	-
b	52	45	9,87	11,5	11,2	24,9	-	-
c	60	49	9,96	11,2	11,7	22,9	-	-
d	60	52	9,96	11,2	11,7	22,9	-	-
a	74	60	12,4	14,5	12,0	39,5	-	-
Mittel	**55,6**	**46**	**10,8**	**12,7**	**12,5**	**28,7**	**-**	**-**
Quelle	kW	kW	MJ/h	MJ/h	MJ/h	MJ/h	MJ/h	MJ/h
a	32	26	265	157	86	130	30	156
b	52	45	371	211	107	168	29	211
c	60	49	411	225	123	168	41	230
d	60	52	433	238	129	179	37	242
a	74	60	633	404	279	344	49	397
Mittel	**55,6**	**46**	**423**	**247**	**145**	**198**	**37**	**247**

MotorNL bzw. ZapfWL: Motornenn- bzw. Zapfwellenleistung
Die Mittelwerte werden als Rechenwerte angesetzt.
Quellen:
a: /GRÄF et al. 1994/, b: /KRAHL 1993/, c: /WÖRGETTER et al. 1990/, d: /WÖRGETTER et al. 1993/

Obwohl die im 5-Punkte-Test erfaßten Daten keine Nennleistungsabhängigkeit erkennen lassen, halten wir eine Differenzierung nach Nennleistung aus physikalisch-technischen Gründen und unter dem Aspekt der Bestandsstruktur und ihrer Änderung für sinnvoll.

- Mit zunehmender Leistung steigt der Hubraum, wodurch das Verhältnis von Oberfläche zu Volumen der Brennräume günstiger wird und damit auch der Wirkungsgrad. Für Motorbaureihen mit modularem Aufbau der einzelnen Typen aus verschiedenen Anzahlen gleich großer Zylinder gilt dies allerdings nicht.
- Spezielle Techniken zur Leistungssteigerung, z. B. die Aufladung von Motoren, die auch mit Erhöhungen des Wirkungsgrades verbunden sind, werden mit zunehmender Nennleistung häufiger eingesetzt.
- Gemäß /KBA 1997/ ist das Durchschnittsalter von Schleppern um so höher, je geringer ihre Leistung ist. Dies läßt auf einen geringeren motortechnischen Standard und damit geringeren Wirkungsgrad in unteren Leistungsklassen schließen.
- Im Zusammenhang mit dem vorher Gesagten sinkt der Anteil leichter Schlepper am Gesamtbestand. Der Schwerpunkt motortechnischer Entwicklungsarbeit dürfte daher bereits seit mehreren Jahren eher bei schweren als bei leichten Schleppern gelegen haben, was möglicherweise zu Entwicklungsrückständen auch bei „modernen" leichteren Schleppern geführt hat.

Eine Berücksichtigung dieser Effekte ist allerdings nur in sehr pauschaler Form möglich und mit Unsicherheiten behaftet. Die im folgenden beschriebene Auswertung von Verbrauchsdaten zeigt aber auch die grundsätzliche Richtigkeit unserer Annahmen über die Nennleistungsabhängigkeit des Wirkungsgrades.

Die Differenzierung nach Schlepper-Nennleistung nehmen wir hier gestützt auf die Angaben in /DLG 1993/ vor. Dort sind etwa hundert nach OECD-Norm durchgeführte Tests an Schleppern mit Nennleistungen zwischen 33 und 182 kW zusammengefaßt. Für jeden Schlepper liegen Angaben zum spezifischen Verbrauch auf der sogenannten Abregelkurve, für den Zapfwellenbetrieb bei Nennleistung und den Zugbetrieb bei Nenndrehzahl oder Maximalleistung vor; für einen Teil der Schlepper werden Angaben zum Zapfwellenbetrieb bei Maximalleistung und beide Angaben zum Zugbetrieb gemacht; für die Abregelkurve und den Zapfwellenbetrieb werden Angaben zum Absolutverbrauch gemacht. Somit liegen acht unterschiedlich vollständige Datensätze vor. Nach der Normierung der Zapfwellen- und Zugbetriebsdaten auf Nennleistung wurden Regressionsanalysen für die Daten der Abregelkurve, die Daten zum Zapfwellenbetrieb bei Nenndrehzahl sowie die Gesamtheit der Zapfwellen- und Zugbetriebsdaten durchgeführt.

Für alle untersuchten Datensätze ergaben sich sinkende spezifische Verbräuche bei steigender Nennleistung. Über die gesamte Leistungsbreite der erfaßten Schlepper von 33 bis 182 kW betrug die Abnahme auf der Abregelkurve 5,6 % und für den Zapfwellen- und Zugbetrieb 11,5 bzw. 11,4 %. Zur Differenzierung des Verbrauchs nach Schlepper-Nennleistungen verwenden wir die Ausgleichsgerade des *absoluten* Verbrauchs in kg/h auf der Abregelkurve. Der relative Fehler der Konstante beträgt etwa 72 %, der Wert der Konstante (= fiktiver Verbrauch eines Schleppers mit 0 kW) beträgt jedoch lediglich 1,3 kg/h; für die Steigung von 0,135 kg/kWh beträgt der relative Fehler lediglich 2,1 %. Für den Zapfwellenbetrieb bei Nenndrehzahl ergaben sich folgende Werte: 2,4 kg/h ± 61 %, 0,18 kg/kWh ± 2,5 %; durch die kleinere Relation „Steigung / Konstante" ist der Gesamtfehler hier größer.

Tabelle 6-5 Spezifischer Kraftstoffverbrauch von Landmaschinen, differenziert nach Maschinenklassen und Lastpunkten des 5-Punkte-Tests

Maschinen-klasse	**MotorNL** kW	**Schwer** MJ/h	**Normal** MJ/h	**Leicht** MJ/h	**Straße** MJ/h	**Leerlauf** MJ/h	**Gew. Mittel** MJ/h
Leichte Schlepper	55,6	423	248	145	196	37	248
Mittlere Schlepper	90	641	376	222	299	56	376
Schwere Schlepper	140	965	564	333	448	85	564
Erntemaschine I	225	1.512	884	521	700	132	884
Erntemaschine II	350	2.315	1.358	794	1.076	205	1.354

MotorNL: Motornennleistung
Quellen:
/DLG 1993/, /GRÄF et al. 1994/, /KRAHL 1993/, /WÖRGETTER et al. 1990/, /WÖRGETTER et al. 1993/, eigene Berechnungen

Aus dieser Gleichung werden die Verbräuche auf der Abregelkurve für den 56-kW-Schlepper (Leichter Schlepper) und für Mittlere und Schwere Schlepper mit den Nennleistungen nach **Tabelle 6-1** berechnet. Die Verbräuche des Mittleren und Schweren Schleppers werden auf den des Leichten Schleppers bezogen. Diese Relativwerte werden mit den oben für den 55,6-kW-Schlepper festgelegten Rechenwerten der einzelnen Lastpunkte verknüpft. Für eine bestimmte Schlepperklasse erfolgt die Anpassung aller Lastpunkte somit durch einen Wert. Das bedeutet, daß für alle Lastpunkte die Wirkungsgrad-Relation zwischen zwei Schlepperklassen als gleich angenommen wird. Ferner sind in der Datenbasis lediglich moderne Schlepper erfaßt; zusätzliche Effekte der Altersstruktur des Bestandes müssen mangels belastbarer Informationen vernachlässigt werden. Die resultierenden Verbrauchswerte für die einzelnen Maschinenklassen und Lastpunkte sind in **Tabelle 6-5** zusammengestellt.

6.1.3.2 Erntemaschinen

Die Ableitung der Verbräuche selbstfahrender Erntemaschinen schließt sich methodisch an die Ableitung der Schlepperverbräuche an, d. h. die in Kapitel 6.1.3.1 aus den OECD-Tests bestimmte Ausgleichsgerade wird auf den Leistungsbereich der beiden Erntemaschinenklassen angewendet. Die damit für die Laststufen des 5-Punkte-Tests berechneten Werte sind ebenfalls in **Tabelle 6-5** aufgeführt.

In **Tabelle 6-6** sind zum Vergleich Bandbreiten und ungewichtete Mittelwerte des zeit- und flächenbezogenen Verbrauchs von Mähdreschern aus Praxistests zusammengefaßt; die Angaben sind aktuellen DLG-Prüfberichten entnommen. Die drei untersuchten Maschinen haben eine mittlere Nennleistung von 191 kW.

Tabelle 6-6 Zeit- und flächenbezogener Dieselkraftstoffverbrauch von Mähdreschern

Quelle	Hersteller	Leistung kW	Bandbreite MJ/h	Mittel MJ/h	Bandbreite MJ/ha	Mittel MJ/ha
/DLG 1995a/	Deutz	184	961 - 1.349	1.153	427 - 598	512
/DLG 1995b/	Fiat	191	952 - 1.422	1.209	363 - 517	440
/DLG 1995c/	MDW	199	922 - 1.597	1.260	363 - 632	500
	Mittel	**191**		**1.207**		**484**

Der ungewichtete mittlere Verbrauch von etwa 1.200 MJ/h kann für eine Nennleistung von 190 kW mit der hier dargestellten Methode durch die Punkte Schwere und Normale Arbeit im Verhältnis 4 : 1 reproduziert werden; mit diesen Gewichtungen ergibt sich die Motorauslastung zu etwa 75 %. Dieses Ergebnis stimmt gut mit älteren Testberichten für leichtere Maschinen überein, in denen auch spezifische Verbräuche bei verschiedenen Auslastungen angegeben sind. Gemäß Expertenbefragungen beträgt die Motorauslastung von Mähdreschern im praktischen Einsatz 50 bis 80 %. Dieses Intervall zeigt ebenfalls eine akzeptable Übereinstimmung mit der aus den Praxisdaten abgeleiteten Auslastung von 75 %. Der Mittelwert des Intervalls von 65 % Motorauslastung läßt sich durch die 1:1-Kombination der beiden Lastpunkte Schwere und Normale Arbeit sehr gut reproduzieren.

Zum Verbrauch selbstfahrender Roder liegt uns nur eine ältere Angabe vor, wonach der Verbauch einer Maschine mit 171 kW Nennleistung etwa 2.280 MJ/ha bzw. 1.160 MJ/h beträgt /DLG 1977/. Der Verbrauch in MJ/h kann nach unserer Methode durch den Punkt Schwere Arbeit mit einer Motorauslastungen von 84 % reproduziert werden. Expertenbefragungen, nach der Roder mit Motorauslastungen von 80 bis 90 % betrieben werden, stimmen damit sehr gut überein.

Die Bandbreite der Motorauslastung von Erntemaschinen *bei der Arbeit* ist somit in der Praxis – bedingt durch die Beschränkung auf jeweils einen Einsatzzweck – deutlich kleiner als bei Schleppern. Der Ernteeinsatz von Rodern läßt sich durch den Punkt Schwere Arbeit, der von Mähdreschern durch eine Kombination der beiden Lastpunkte Schwere und Normale Arbeit (Standard: 1:1) gut beschreiben. Die Lastpunkte Leichte, für Roder auch Normale Arbeit haben damit bei Erntemaschinen nur für die An- und Abfahrt auf Feldwegen usw. Bedeutung.

6.2 Emissionen

Im folgenden werden verbrauchsbezogene Emissionsfaktoren – für einige Schadstoffe differenziert nach Lastpunkten des 5-Punkte-Tests – abgeleitet. Durch die Verknüpfung mit nach Laststufen und Maschinenklassen differenzierten zeitbezogenen Kraftstoffverbräuchen können daraus zeitbezogene Faktoren berechnet werden.

Wie der Kraftstoffverbrauch hängen auch die Emissionen von Nennleistung und Laststufe ab. Zur Ableitung einer Nennleistungsabhängigkeit der Emissionsfaktoren ist die Datenbasis – im wesentlichen die vier zitierten Untersuchungen, die auch der Ableitung der Kraftstoffverbräuche zugrunde liegen – jedoch unzureichend. Ferner können nicht für alle in dieser Studie bilanzierten Schadstoffe nach Lastpunkten differenzierte Faktoren abgeleitet werden. Wie bereits in Kapitel 4.3 allgemein und in Kapitel 5.1.4 für LKW dargestellt, erfolgt die Ableitung der Faktoren für verschiedene Schadstoffe auf unterschiedliche Weise und ist mit unterschiedlichen Unsicherheiten verbunden.

Die Emissionsfaktoren für CO_2, SO_2 und HCl ergeben sich aus der Zusammensetzung von Dieselkraftstoff (86,6 M% Kohlenstoff, 0,045 M% Schwefel, 0,0001 M% Chlor; siehe Kapitel 5.1.4, LKW) und der Annahme vollständiger Verbrennung.

Für die Schadstoffe CO, NO_X, HC und Partikel, die vom Betriebszustand des Motors abhängen, sind die Meßwerte aus /WÖRGETTER et al. 1990/, /WÖRGETTER et al. 1993/, /KRAHL 1993/ und /GRÄF et al. 1994/ und die von uns daraus abgeschätzten mittleren verbrauchsbezogenen Emissionsfaktoren in **Tabelle 6-7** zusammengestellt (NMHC: siehe unten).

Für Schwere und Normale Arbeit, den Straßentransport und die durch die Schwere und Normale Arbeit dominierten gewichteten Testmittel liegen die relativen Bandbreiten (Maximal-/Minimalwert) der Einzeldaten zwischen 1,5 und 3. Für Leichte Arbeit und Leerlauf betragen die Bandbreiten 3 bis 17. Über alle Laststufen weisen die NO_X-Emissionen die geringsten Bandbreiten auf. Die relativen Bandbreiten im Leerlauf von 17 für HC und von 7 für CO ergeben sich durch jeweils einen extrem kleinen Wert. Werte von jeweils 6 für HC und CO bei Leichter Arbeit sind mit „gleichmäßigerer" Verteilung der Meßwerte verbunden. Für Partikelemissionen, für die allerdings nur drei Datensätze vorliegen, betragen die relativen Bandbreiten bei Leichter Arbeit und im Leerlauf bei „gleichmäßiger" Verteilung der Meßwerte 4 bzw. 8. Mit abnehmender Leistung – von Schwerer Arbeit zum Leerlauf – steigen die CO-, HC- und Partikelemissionen im Mittel aller Datensätze zum Teil drastisch an, während die NO_X-Emissionen bei Schwerer und Normaler Arbeit und im Leerlauf relativ ähnlich sind und bei Leichter Arbeit ein Maximum und bei Straßenfahrt ein Minimum aufweisen; einzelne Daten, insbesondere aus den Messungen von /GRÄF et al. 1994/, weichen von diesen Trends ab.

Sehr niedrige Emissionswerte wurden vor allem, aber nicht ausschließlich, an dem kleinsten Motor gemessen, bei dem es sich im Unterschied zu den anderen um einen Vorkammermotor handelt. Allgemein weist dieses Motorkonzept auch in anderen Anwendungsbereichen im Vergleich zu Direkteinspritzern geringere Emissionen auf. In Nutzfahrzeugen werden überwiegend Direkteinspritzer eingesetzt; Informationen zu den tatsächlichen Bestandsanteilen bei Ackerschleppern liegen jedoch nicht vor. Wir verzichten daher auf unterschiedliche Gewichtungen der einzelnen Datensätze bzw. Konzepte. Darüber hinaus erlaubt die geringe Anzahl von Datensätzen keine sichere Identifikation von „Ausreißern"; schließlich sind die einzelnen Studien als gleichermaßen solide zu betrachten. Die von uns verwendeten Rechenwerte stellen daher im wesentlichen Mittelwerte dar, in denen auch bei sehr großen Bandbreiten alle vorliegenden Daten berücksichtigt wurden. Zur Bestimmung der gewichteten Mittel wurden die verbrauchsbezogenen Emissionsdaten mit den zugehörigen zeitbezogenen Kraftstoffverbräuchen und den Zeitanteilen des 5-Punkte-Tests verknüpft.

Tabelle 6-7 Emissionsfaktoren leichter Ackerschlepper für CO, NO_X, HC und Partikel, differenziert nach Lastpunkten des 5-Punkte-Tests: Literaturdaten und Rechenwerte

Quelle	MotNL kW	ZapfWL kW	Schwer g/MJ	Normal g/MJ	Leicht g/MJ	Straße g/MJ	Leerlauf g/MJ	Gew. Mittel g/MJ
CO								
a	32	26	0,11	0,12	0,14	0,22	0,37	0,14
b	52	45	0,081	0,33	0,54	0,52	2,50	0,28
c	60	49	0,11	0,24	0,35	0,43	1,75	0,24
d	60	52	0,13	0,24	0,38	0,58	1,17	0,26
a	74	60	0,19	0,22	0,091	0,42	1,03	0,23
Rechenwert			**0,12**	**0,23**	**0,30**	**0,44**	**1,36**	**0,23**
NO_X								
a	32	26	0,47	0,65	0,73	0,52	0,65	0,54
b	52	45	1,08	1,09	1,59	0,59	1,37	1,06
c	60	49	0,90	0,78	1,32	0,46	0,70	0,86
d	60	52	1,01	0,81	1,49	0,49	0,87	0,94
a	74	60	0,64	0,53	0,54	0,51	0,85	0,58
Rechenwert			**0,82**	**0,77**	**1,13**	**0,51**	**0,89**	**0,80**
HC								
a	32	26	0,059	0,076	0,067	0,12	0,068	0,073
b	52	45	0,067	0,12	0,19	0,21	0,68	0,12
c	60	49	0,067	0,14	0,39	0,29	1,18	0,17
d	60	52	0,11	0,12	0,27	0,31	0,50	0,16
a	74	60	0,10	0,14	0,078	0,29	0,68	0,15
Rechenwert			**0,080**	**0,12**	**0,20**	**0,24**	**0,62**	**0,14**
Partikel								
a	32	26	0,065	0,071	0,058	0,10	0,056	0,072
b	52	45	0,033	0,077	0,093	0,12	0,46	0,069
c	60	49	k. A.	k. A.	k. A.	k. A.	k. A.	k. A.
d	60	52	k. A.	k. A.	k. A.	k. A.	k. A.	k. A.
a	74	60	0,058	0,054	0,023	0,12	0,20	0,066
Rechenwert			**0,052**	**0,068**	**0,058**	**0,12**	**0,24**	**0,069**

MotNL, ZapfWL: Motornenn- bzw. Zapfwellenleistung der Schlepper
Quellen:
a: /GRÄF et al. 1994/, b: /KRAHL 1993/, c: /WÖRGETTER et al. 1990/, d: /WÖRGETTER et al. 1993/

/GRÄF et al. 1994/, /KRAHL 1993/ und /WÖRGETTER et al. 1990/ haben Angaben zu Methan-, Benzol-, Formaldehyd- und Benzo(a)pyrenemissionen gemacht. Bei einer geringeren Zahl von Meßwerten als im Falle der limitierten Schadstoffe sind die relativen Bandbreiten allerdings deutlich größer. Wir setzen daher nur für Benzo(a)pyren die Mittelwerte der Literaturdaten als Rechenwerte an. Für Methan, Benzol und Formaldehyd gehen wir wie für LKW in Kapitel 5.1.4 beschrieben vor: Die Faktoren dieser Schadstoffe werden aus den nach Lastpunkten differenzierten HC-Emissionsfaktoren und den in /IFEU 1995c/ ermittelten Anteilen für Methan, Benzol und Formaldehyd an den gesamten HC-Emissionen von Diesel-KFZ (2,4, 1,9 bzw. 8,1 M%) berechnet.

Die Meßwerte und ihre Mittel sowie die angesetzten Rechenwerte sind in **Tabelle 6-8** zusammengestellt. Zur Bestimmung der gewichteten Mittel wurden die verbrauchsbezogenen Emissionsdaten mit den zugehörigen zeitbezogenen Kraftstoffverbräuchen und den Zeitanteilen des 5-Punkte-Tests verknüpft.

Tabelle 6-8 Emissionsfaktoren leichter Ackerschlepper für Methan, Formaldehyd, Benzol und Benzo(a)pyren, differenziert nach Lastpunkten des 5-Punkte-Tests: Literaturdaten und Rechenwerte

Quelle	MotNL	ZWL	Schwer	Normal	Leicht	Straße	Leerlauf	Gew. Mittel
	kW	kW	g/MJ	g/MJ	g/MJ	g/MJ	g/MJ	g/MJ
Methan								
c	60	49	0,00026	0,0010	0,0016	0,0021	0,0044	0,00089
Rechenwert			**0,0020**	**0,0028**	**0,0045**	**0,0056**	**0,0145**	**0,0032**
Formaldehyd								
a	32	26	0,017	0,015	0,015	0,013	0,019	0,016
b	52	45	0,0037	0,011	0,020	0,023	0,094	0,011
c	60	49	0,00075	0,0011	0,0017	0,0043	0,026	0,0020
a	74	60	0,0019	0,0041	0,0026	0,0029	0,0036	0,0026
Mittelwert			0,0059	0,0078	0,0098	0,011	0,036	0,0079
Rechenwert			**0,0066**	**0,0095**	**0,015**	**0,019**	**0,049**	**0,011**
Benzol								
a	32	26	0,0015	0,0011	0,0011	0,0011	0,00073	0,0013
c	60	49	0,00007	0,00016	0,00012	0,00560	0,00047	0,00092
a	74	60	0,0013	0,0018	0,0013	0,0019	0,00096	0,0015
Mittelwert			0,00094	0,00101	0,00084	0,00286	0,00072	0,0012
Rechenwert			**0,0016**	**0,0022**	**0,0036**	**0,0044**	**0,0011**	**0,0024**
Benzo(a)pyren			ng/MJ	ng/MJ	ng/MJ	ng/MJ	ng/MJ	ng/MJ
b	52	45	0,026	0,052	0,063	0,12	0,26	0,053
c	60	49	0,13	0,05	0,26	0,02	0,30	0,12
a	74	60	0,40	0,33	0,23	0,44	0,40	0,37
Rechenwert				**0,14**	**0,19**	**0,19**	**0,33**	**0,18**

MotNL, ZWL: Motor- bzw. Zapfwellenleistung der Schlepper
Rechenwerte für Methan, Benzol und Formaldehyd aus Anteilen an HC nach /IFEU 1995c/ und HC-Faktoren nach Tabelle 6-7; Rechenwerte für Benzo(a)pyren gleich Mittelwerte aus Quellen a bis c
Quellen: a: /GRÄF et al. 1994/, b: /KRAHL 1993/, c: /WÖRGETTER et al. 1990/

Für N_2O, NH_3 und Dioxine/Furane liegen keine an Schleppern gemessenen Daten vor. Wir übernehmen daher die für LKW abgeleiteten Werte, die nicht nach Lastpunkten differenziert werden können und daher für alle Punkte gleich angesetzt werden.

Alle Rechenwerte der verbrauchsbezogenen Emissionsfaktoren sind, differenziert nach Laststufen, in **Tabelle 6-9** zusammengefaßt. Die NMHC-Emissionsfaktoren ergeben sich aus der Differenz der oben abgeleiteten HC- und Methan-Faktoren; aufgrund der relativ geringen Methanemissionen liegen sie sehr nahe bei den HC-Faktoren. Die klimarelevanten Emissionen werden nicht nach Ortsklassen differenziert; die übrigen Schadstoffe ordnen wir der Ortsklasse 2 zu. Die Emissionen inklusive der Aufwendungen für die Bereitstellung von Dieselkraftstoff sind im Anhang (**Tabelle 10-1**) für den Mittelwert über alle Einsätze und Kulturen ausgewiesen.

Tabelle 6-9 Verbrauchsbezogene Emissionsfaktoren für Landmaschinen (Rechenwerte), differenziert nach Lastpunkten des 5-Punkte-Tests

	Schwer	Normal	Leicht	Straße	Leerlauf	Gew. Mittel
	g/MJ	g/MJ	g/MJ	g/MJ	g/MJ	g/MJ
	Global	**Global**	**Global**	**Global**	**Global**	**Global**
CO_2	73,9	73,9	73,9	73,9	73,9	73,9
CH_4	0,0019	0,0029	0,0047	0,0058	0,015	0,0032
N_2O	0,0077	0,0077	0,0077	0,0077	0,0077	0,0077
	OK 2	**OK 2**	**OK 2**	**OK 2**	**OK 2**	**OK 2**
SO_2	0,021	0,021	0,021	0,021	0,021	0,021
CO	0,12	0,23	0,30	0,43	1,35	0,23
NO_X	0,81	0,77	1,12	0,51	0,88	0,79
NMHC	0,08	0,12	0,19	0,23	0,60	0,13
Partikel	0,052	0,067	0,058	0,12	0,23	0,069
Staub	0	0	0	0	0	0
HCl	0,000023	0,000023	0,000023	0,000023	0,000023	0,000023
NH_3	0,00047	0,00047	0,00047	0,00047	0,00047	0,00047
Formaldehyd	0,0064	0,010	0,016	0,019	0,050	0,011
Benzol	0,0015	0,0023	0,0037	0,0046	0,012	0,0026
	ng/MJ	ng/MJ	ng/MJ	ng/MJ	ng/MJ	ng/MJ
Benzo(a)pyren	183	140	186	190	323	179
TCDD-TÄ	0,0014	0,0014	0,0014	0,0014	0,0014	0,0014

Quellen: /CARBOTECH 1994/, /ECOINVENT 1996/, /GRÄF et al. 1994/, /IFEU 1995c/, /KRAHL 1993/, /WÖRGETTER et al. 1990/, /WÖRGETTER et al. 1993/, eigene Berechnungen

6.3 Exkurs: Kraftstoffverbrauch und Emissionen im Rapsöl- und RME-Betrieb

Unter den gegenwärtigen Rahmenbedingungen – insbesondere aufgrund der Gasölbeihilfe – erscheint eine Verwendung von Rapsöl oder RME als Ersatz von Dieselkraftstoff in Landmaschinen aus ökonomischer Sicht unrealistisch. Bei veränderten Rahmenbedingungen könnte der Einsatz der beiden Biokraftstoffe in Landmaschinen jedoch praktische Bedeutung bekommen.

Technisch ist die Verwendung von RME in den Motoren von Landmaschinen ohne weiteres möglich, da seine Eigenschaften denen von Dieselkraftstoff sehr ähneln. Dagegen läßt sich Rapsöl mit seiner gegenüber Dieselkraftstoff zehnmal höheren Viskosität – nach heutigem Kenntnisstand – auf Dauer nur in speziellen Motoren, wie etwa Elsbett- oder elsbett-umgerüsteten Motoren, oder in großvolumigen Vorkammermotoren einsetzen /KRAHL 1998/. Großvolumige Vorkammermotoren werden jedoch nicht serienmäßig für den Nutzfahrzeugsektor gefertigt, da ihr spezifischer Kraftstoffverbrauch höher ist als bei vergleichbaren direkteinspritzenden Motoren oder Wirbelkammermotoren.

Für Rapsöl und RME weisen einzelne Messungen auf geringfügig kleinere motorische Wirkungsgrade als beim Einsatz von Dieselkraftstoff unter sonst gleichen Bedingungen hin. Diese ohnehin kleinen Unterschiede können jedoch nicht als gesichert betrachtet werden und werden daher hier vernachlässigt. Das heißt, daß hier für alle Lastzustände die gleichen zeitbezogenen spezifischen Verbräuche in MJ/h wie im Dieselbetrieb angenommen werden. Aufgrund unterschiedlicher spezifischer Energieinhalte und Dichten sind allerdings die massen- und volumenbezogenen Verbräuche unterschiedlich, was hier jedoch keine Rolle spielt, da diese Bezugsgrößen nicht verwendet werden.

Mit der Festlegung gleicher Energieverbräuche kann sich die Diskussion auf die verbrauchsbezogenen Emissionen beschränken. Eine weitere Einschränkung besteht darin, daß sie sich lediglich auf eine begrenzte Anzahl der hier betrachteten Schadstoffe bezieht, im wesentlichen NO_X, CO, NMHC und Partikel. Für CO_2, SO_2 und HCl werden die Emissionen der Biokraftstoffe wie bei Dieselkraftstoff aus ihren C-, S- und Cl-Inventaren berechnet; für eine Reihe anderer Schadstoffe, die nicht in den Basisarbeiten erfaßt wurden, wäre ohnehin die Übernahme von Faktoren aus Messungen an Dieselmotoren erforderlich.

Wie bereits erwähnt, stammen die Basisdaten der Emissionsfaktoren für Schlepper im Dieselbetrieb aus Arbeiten, die den Vergleich des Dieselbetriebs mit dem Rapsöl- und/oder RME-Betrieb zum Gegenstand hatten. Diese Arbeiten dienen auch hier als Basis. Sieben Messungen im Dieselbetrieb stehen fünf im Rapsöl- und zwei im RME-Betrieb gegenüber. Das heißt, für den Betrieb mit Rapsöl bzw. RME liegen jeweils noch weniger Messungen als für den mit Dieselkraftstoff vor. Für Rapsöl kommen zwei weitere Einschränkungen hinzu:

- Der Rapsöleinsatz in typischen Dieselmotoren ist technisch nicht praktikabel und der Dieseleinsatz in teureren rapsölgeeigneten Motoren ist ökonomisch nicht sinnvoll. Damit stellt sich die Frage eines geeigneten Vergleichsmotors. Zwei der vorliegenden Messungen wurden an Elsbett- bzw. elsbettisierten Motoren vorgenommen /KRAHL 1993/, drei Messungen wurden an Wirbelkammermotoren durchgeführt /KRAHL 1993/, /GRÄF et al. 1990/. Unabhängig von der Auswahl wird die Datenbasis noch schmäler.
- Für Rapsöl besteht gegenwärtig noch keine Norm, die Qualitätsstandards festlegt. Die Unterschiede der bei Messungen eingesetzten Kraftstoffe können damit deutlich größer als im Falle von Dieselkraftstoff oder RME gewesen sein.

Angesichts der problematischen Datenbasis ist es sinnvoll zu untersuchen, ob überhaupt die Notwendigkeit besteht Rapsöl- und RME-spezifische Emissionsfaktoren abzuleiten, oder ob eventuell die Faktoren des Dieselbetriebs in guter Näherung angesetzt werden können (wie oben dargestellt bezieht sich diese Frage ohnehin im wesentlichen nur auf die Schadstoffe NO_X, CO, NMHC und Partikel). Die Relation der Emissionen im Diesel- und Rapsöl- bzw.

RME-Betrieb unter sonst gleichen Bedingungen können dazu Informationen geben. Außerdem reduziert die Quotientenbildung den Einfluß systematischer Fehler. Beispielhaft sind hierzu für NO_X und CO die unseres Erachtens belastbarsten unter den publizierten Emissionsdaten für Wirbelkammermotoren, die aus drei Messungen im 5-Punkte-Test an zwei verschiedenen Motoren stammen, in **Tabelle 6-10** zusammengestellt. Die Daten zeigen folgendes:

- Für NO_X zeigen die Daten sowohl für die beiden Meßreihen am Deutz-Motor als auch im Vergleich zum KHD-Schlepper eine gute Übereinstimmung. Die Emissionen liegen im Rapsölbetrieb um etwa 20 % niedriger als im Dieselbetrieb – ausgenommen der wenig relevante Lastpunkt Leerlauf.
- Für CO dagegen weisen bereits die Daten der beiden Messungen am gleichen Motor (Deutz) große Abweichungen auf. Die dritte Meßreihe (KHD) wiederum weicht stark und in unterschiedlicher Richtung von den beiden anderen Datensätzen ab.

Ähnlich uneinheitliche Ergebnisse resultieren für den Vergleich RME/Dieselkraftstoff. Hinweise auf niedrigere NO_X- und Benzo(a)pyren- und höhere CO-, HC-, Formaldehyd- und Partikelemissionen beim Dieselbetrieb im Vergleich zum Betrieb mit Rapsöl- bzw. RME finden sich insgesamt nicht bestätigt.

Tabelle 6-10 Emissionsdaten im 5-Punkte-Test für Schlepper im Rapsölbetrieb relativ zum Dieselbetrieb, ausgewählt für NO_X und CO

	Nennleist. KW	**Schwer**	**Normal**	**Leicht**	**Straße**	**Leerlauf**
NO_X						
Deutz I	42	0,83	0,82	0,79	0,94	0,21
Deutz II	42	0,75	0,78	0,71	0,92	0,33
KHD	32	0,76	0,85	0,82	0,77	1,05
Mittel	**39**	**0,78**	**0,82**	**0,77**	**0,88**	**0,53**
CO						
Deutz I	42	0,72	1,00	2,34	1,19	8,58
Deutz II	42	1,23	1,73	2,58	1,66	5,64
KHD	32	1,78	1,31	1,82	1,46	2,95
Mittel	**39**	**1,25**	**1,35**	**2,24**	**1,44**	**5,72**

Quellen: Deutz I und II: /KRAHL 1994/ und /KRAHL 1997/; KHD: /GRÄF et al. 1994/

Aufgrund der schmalen Datenbasis und der großen Bandbreiten halten wir eine Ableitung von belastbaren Rapsöl- bzw. RME-spezifischen Emissionsfaktoren gegenwärtig für nicht durchführbar. Hilfsweise und zum Teil gerechtfertigt durch die uneinheitlichen Relationen der Emissionen im Betrieb mit Diesel- und Biokraftstoffen empfiehlt sich unseres Erachtens – außer für CO_2, SO_2 und HCl – die Verwendung der für den Dieselbetrieb abgeleiteten verbrauchsbezogenen Faktoren (siehe Kapitel 6.2). Die CO_2-, SO_2- und HCl-Faktoren ergeben sich direkt aus den C-, S- und Cl-Inventaren der Kraftstoffe bei Annahme vollständiger Oxidation (siehe Kapitel 5.1.5). Die Faktoren sind in **Tabelle 6-11** zusammengestellt. Die gesamten Aufwendungen und Emissionen unter Berücksichtigung der Bereitstellung der Kraftstoffe finden sich im Anhang (**Tabelle 10-2**).

Während die Gleichsetzung der Emissionsfaktoren für den Diesel- und Rapsöl- bzw. RME-Betrieb für den gegenwärtigen Bestand sicher nur eine Näherung darstellt, kann diese Annahme für moderne Maschinen bzw. zukünftige Bestände durchaus realistisch sein. Zukünftige Emissionsbegrenzungen werden motorseitige Maßnahmen oder eine Abgasnachbehandlung erfordern, die mit großer Wahrscheinlichkeit stark nivellierend auf Unterschiede zwischen dem Betrieb mit Diesel- und dem mit Biokraftstoffen wirken werden. Allerdings werden dann auch andere Emissionsfaktoren für den Dieselbetrieb als die hier abgeleiteten realistisch sein.

Tabelle 6-11 Verbrauchsbezogene Emissionsfaktoren für den Einsatz von Rapsöl und RME in Landmaschinen, differenziert nach Lastpunkten des 5-Punkte-Tests

	Schwer g/MJ	**Normal** g/MJ	**Leicht** g/MJ	**Straße** g/MJ	**Leerlauf** g/MJ	**Gew. Mittel** g/MJ
	Global	**Global**	**Global**	**Global**	**Global**	**Global**
CO_2*	76,4	76,4	76,4	76,4	76,4	76,4
CH_4	0,0017	0,0025	0,0041	0,0050	0,013	0,0028
N_2O	0,0067	0,0067	0,0067	0,0067	0,0067	0,0067
	OK 2	**OK 2**	**OK 2**	**OK 2**	**OK 2**	**OK 2**
SO_2	0,0054	0,0054	0,0054	0,0054	0,0054	0,0054
CO	0,11	0,20	0,26	0,37	1,17	0,20
NO_X	0,70	0,66	0,97	0,44	0,76	0,69
NMHC	0,067	0,10	0,17	0,20	0,52	0,11
Partikel	0,045	0,058	0,050	0,10	0,20	0,059
Staub	0	0	0	0	0	0
HCl	0,000020	0,000020	0,000020	0,000020	0,000020	0,000020
NH_3	0,00040	0,00040	0,00040	0,00040	0,00040	0,00040
Formaldehyd	0,0056	0,0084	0,014	0,017	0,043	0,0095
Benzol	0,0013	0,0020	0,0032	0,0040	0,010	0,0022
	ng/MJ	ng/MJ	ng/MJ	ng/MJ	ng/MJ	ng/MJ
Benzo(a)pyren	158	121	161	164	279	155
TCDD-TÄ	0,0012	0,0012	0,0012	0,0012	0,0012	0,0012

*: biogenes CO_2
Quellen: /CARBOTECH 1994/, /ECOINVENT 1996/, /GRÄF et al. 1994/, /IFEU 1995c/, /KRAHL 1993/, /WÖRGETTER et al. 1990/, /WÖRGETTER et al. 1993/, eigene Berechnungen

6.4 Arbeitszeiten

In Ökobilanzen von Agrarprodukten stellt die Anbaufläche zumindest für die Bilanzierung des Lebenswegabschnitts „Landwirtschaft" direkt oder mittelbar, über flächenbezogene Erträge als Inputdaten etwa, eine wichtige Bezugsgröße – nicht zu verwechseln mit der funktionalen Einheit der Gesamtbilanz (!) – dar. Um die nach Nennleistung und Laststufen differenzierten zeitbezogenen Verbräuche und Emissionsfaktoren ohne Informationsverlust einsetzen zu können, sind damit möglichst differenzierte Daten zum flächenbezogenen Zeitaufwand der unterschiedlichen Feldarbeiten erforderlich, die im folgenden abgeleitet werden.

Ausgangspunkt ist dabei, daß sich ein Arbeitsgang wie etwa das Pflügen, die Mahd oder die Aussaat in verschiedene Arbeitsschritte gliedert, die verschiedenen Betriebszuständen des Motors zugeordnet werden können. Diese verschiedenen Arbeitsschritte werden einzeln erfaßt und gemäß /DLG 1987/ und /JÄGER 1991/ einer Haupt- und verschiedenen Nebenzeiten zugeordnet. Diese Zeiten sind wie folgt charakterisiert:

- **Hauptzeit:** Damit wird die Zeit der tatsächlichen Arbeit der Maschine auf dem Feld, z. B. Pflügen, bezeichnet. Sie hängt flächenbezogen im wesentlichen von der Art der Arbeit, der Arbeitsbreite des Gerätes und der Arbeitsgeschwindigkeit ab; Arbeitsbreite und Arbeitsgeschwindigkeit wiederum werden durch die Schlaggröße bestimmt (große Geräte für große Schläge und umgekehrt; unter einem Schlag versteht man dabei eine zusammenhängende, mit der gleichen Kultur bepflanzte, einheitlich bewirtschaftete Fläche). Die Hauptzeit ist gleich der gesamten Zeit auf dem Feld abzüglich der Wende- und Verlustzeiten. Für Erntemaschinen bietet es sich in manchen Fällen auch an, die Hauptzeit als Quotient aus dem Ertrag und dem Durchsatz zu bestimmen und die übrigen Zeiten pauschal den Nebenzeiten zuzuordnen.
- **Rüstzeit:** Damit wird die Zeit zur Vorbereitung einer Maschine für die Arbeit, z. B. das Verbinden mit dem Schlepper, bezeichnet. Die Rüstzeit ist für zapfwellengetriebene Großgeräte länger als für einfache Anhängegeräte. Rüstzeiten fallen sowohl auf dem Hof als auch auf dem Feld an, z. B. beim Justieren von Spritzgerät oder Entfernen von Transportsicherungen.
- **Wegezeit:** Darunter fallen die Fahrzeiten von Schleppern mit Arbeitsgeräten bzw. Erntemaschinen zwischen Hof und Feld sowie Transportfahrten. Die Fahrten können auf der Straße und/oder auf Feldwegen erfolgen. Die Zeiten ergeben sich aus der Entfernung und der durchschnittlichen Geschwindigkeit.
- **Wendezeit:** Dies ist die Summe der Zeiten zum Wenden der Maschine am Feldrand zwischen zwei „Bahnen“. Die Dauer eines einzelnen Wendevorganges unterscheidet sich für verschiedene Arbeitsgänge nur wenig, während die gesamte Wendezeit von Schlaggröße und Arbeitsbreite abhängt.
- **Verlustzeit:** Als Verlustzeit werden die Zeiten des Maschinenstillstands auf dem Feld bezeichnet. Sie umfaßt gewollte Unterbrechungen der Arbeit, etwa für Umladevorgänge bei Erntemaschinen, ebenso wie ungewollte Stillstände, z. B. aufgrund von Pannen. Sie hängt vom Maschinentyp, der durchgeführten Feldarbeit, dem Wartungszustand der Maschine und den örtlichen Gegebenheiten ab und kann daher beträchtlich variieren. Sie wird hier für die einzelnen Maschinen pauschal als erfahrungsgestützter Anteil an der Hauptzeit angegeben.

Während die flächenbezogene Hauptzeit für eine bestimmte Arbeit nur mittelbar durch die Schlaggröße beinflußt wird (große Geräte für große Schläge und umgekehrt; siehe oben), ist für bestimmte Arbeitsschritte bzw. Nebenzeiten der Einfluß direkter: Sie sind für verschieden große Schläge mit dem gleichen absoluten Zeitaufwand verbunden, durch Abschreibung auf die Schlaggröße ergeben sich damit verschiedene flächenbezogene Zeiten. Ein Beispiel ist das Anbauen bzw. Anhängen von Geräten an Schlepper auf dem Hof. Schlepper-Nennleistung, Arbeitsbreite des Gerätes und Schlaggröße haben hier keinen Einfluß auf die Dauer des Arbeitsschrittes „Arbeitsgerät anhängen“.

Daten für die Haupt- und Nebenzeiten der einzelnen Arbeitsgänge finden sich in /DLG 1987/ und /JÄGER 1991/. Zur Verbindung der nach Laststufen differenzierten zeitbezogenenen Verbrauchs- und Emissionsdaten werden die Haupt- und verschiedenen Nebenzeiten bzw. die zugrundeliegenden Arbeitsschritte der verschiedenen Arbeitsgänge den Laststufen des 5-Punkte-Tests zugeordnet. **Abb. 6-1** zeigt dies schematisch.

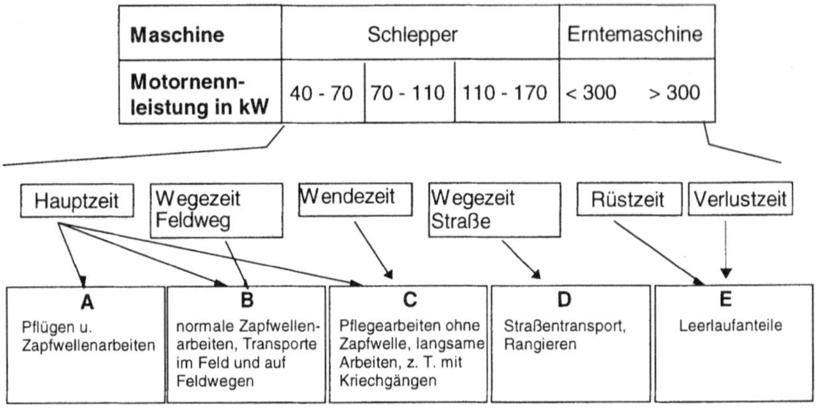

Abb. 6-1 Zuordnung der Haupt- und verschiedener Nebenzeiten zu den Laststufen des 5-Punkte-Tests nach /KALTSCHMITT & REINHARDT 1997/ (verändert)

Je nach Art der Arbeit läßt sich die *Hauptzeit* der Laststufe A, B oder C des 5-Punkte-Tests zuordnen:

- Laststufe A: schwere Arbeiten mit und ohne Zapfwelle wie Pflügen oder Erntegänge
- Laststufe B: normale Zapfwellenarbeiten wie die Ausbringung von Düngemitteln, Transporte im Feld
- Laststufe C: Pflegearbeiten ohne Zapfwelle, langsame Arbeiten wie die Aussaat von Getreide

Maschinenstillstände bei *Rüst-* und *Verlustzeiten* werden der Laststufe E (Leerlauf), *Wegezeit* auf Feldwegen Laststufe B (normale Arbeit), Straßentransporte Laststufe D und *Wendezeiten* Laststufe C (leichte Arbeit) zugeordnet.

Für ausgewählte Land- und Forstmaschinen, die typischerweise auf Schlägen zwischen 20 und 60 ha Größe eingesetzt werden, sind in **Tabelle 6-12** die technischen Kenndaten – Arbeitsbreite und Arbeitsgeschwindigkeit –, die Zuordnung der Arbeitsgeräte zu Schleppern sowie der Hauptzeiten zu Laststufen zusammengestellt. Auf kleineren Schlägen werden in der Regel Maschinen mit niedrigerer Arbeitsbreite eingesetzt, wodurch sich im wesentlichen die Hauptzeit verlängert. Die Angaben beruhen auf umfangreichen Datensammlungen nach /ISENSEE et al. 1992/, /KTBL 1993/, /FUNK 1995/ und zusätzlichen Schätzungen. **Tabelle 6-13** listet die spezifischen Daten für verschiedene Maschinen zur Ernte in Feld und Wald auf. Dabei hängt der Durchsatz einer bestimmten Erntemaschine wesentlich vom Erntegut, z. B. Rapssaat oder Weizenkörner, und dessen Erntefeuchte ab. Die angegebenen Werte sind daher als Orientierungsgrößen zu verstehen.

Tabelle 6-12 Kenndaten typischer schlepperbetriebener Land- und Forstmaschinen für Schlaggrößen von 20 bis 60 ha, zugeordnete Schlepperklassen und Laststufen der Hauptzeit

Maschine	**Motor-nennl.** kW	**Last-stufe**	**Geschw. Feld** km/h[a]	**Arbeits-breite** m	**Wende-zeit** min/W[b]	**Verlust-zeit** %[c]	**Rüstzeit Hof** min	**Rüstzeit Feld** min
Scheibenegge	110 - 170	C	8	7	0,25	4	16	4
Schwergrubber	110 - 170	A	8	6	0,25	4	11	3
Fräse	70 - 110	B	6	4	0,25	4	15	3
Achtschar-Aufsattelpflug	110 - 170	A	6	3	0,25	4	20	4
Saatbett-kombination	70 - 110	C	10	6	0,25	4	20	4
Kreiselegge	70 - 110	B	6	5	0,25	4	19	2
Drillmaschine	70 - 110	C	7	9	0,5	10	19	4
Bestellkombination	110 - 170	C	7	6	0,5	10	30	4
ZR-Einzelkorn-drillmaschine	70 - 110	C	5	12	0,5	10	18	3
Kartoffel-Legema-schine, 6-reihig	70 - 110	C	4	4,5	0,5	10	20	3
Netzegge	70 - 110	C	5	12	0,25	4	12	3
Hackstriegel	70 - 110	C	8	15	0,25	4	15	3
Häuflerstriegel, 6-reihig	70 - 110	C	8	4,5	0,25	4	12	3
Hackmaschine, 8-reihig	70 - 110	C	3	6	0,25	4	12	3
Krautschlegel, 6-reihig	70 - 110	B	3,5	4,5	0,25	4	12	3
Großraum-düngerstreuer	70 - 110	B	9	18	0,25	4	22	2
Anhängespritze	70 - 110	B	7	24	0,25	4	15	3
Front- und Heck-mähwerk	70 - 110	C	8	4,4	0,25	4	15	3
Doppelmesser-mähwerk	70 - 110	C	8	5,8	0,25	4	15	3
Kreiselzettwender	70 - 110	C	8	6,7	0,25	4	15	3
Kreiselschwader	70 - 110	C	8	5,6	0,25	4	15	3
Kreiselrechwender	70 - 110	C	8	6	0,25	4	15	3
Schlegelmulchgerät	110 - 170	B	5	7	0,25	4	15	3
Wiesenwalze	70 - 110	C	7	9	0,25	4	10	3
Chinaschilf-pflanzmaschine	70 - 110	C	2	3	0,5	40	30	3
Aufforstungs-maschine	70 - 110	B	2	2,25	0,5	10	30	3
Forst-Scheibenfräse (4 Scheiben)	70 - 110	B	8	2	0,25	4	30	3

MotornennL: Motornennleistung; ZR: Zuckerrübe
a: Geschwindigkeit im Feld, b: min/Wende, c: Anteil an der Hauptzeit
Quelle: /Kaltschmitt & Reinhardt 1997/, verändert

Tabelle 6-13 Kenndaten von Erntemaschinen in Land- und Forstwirtschaft

	Leistung kW	**Laststufe Hauptzeit**	**Durchsatz** Erntegut	t/h[a]	**Bemerkungen**
Mähdrescher	110 - 170	A	Rapskorn[b]	8	paralleles Überladen[d]
			Weizenkorn[c]	13,3	
Quaderballenpresse, gezogen	110 - 170	B	Stroh	16,8	126 kg/m^3, 472 kg[e]
			Knaulgras	19,2	185 kg/m^3, 693 kg[e]
Frontlader[f]	70 - 110	B	Stroh	9,2	Feldumschlag
			Knaulgras	13,4	
Köpfrodebunker, 6-reihig	170 - 300	A	Zuckerrüben	67,5[g]	paralleles Überladen[h]
Reinigungslader	110 - 170	B		120	-
Vollernter, gezogen, 2-reihig	110 - 170	A	Kartoffeln	19,2[i]	paralleles Überladen[j]
(Holz-)Feldhäcksler	170 - 300	B	Chinaschilf[k]	20,0	paralleles Überladen
			Holzschnitzel[l]	17,5	
Hackschnitzel-Vollernter	170 - 300	B	Hackschnitzel	7[m]	Fällen, Vorliefern, Hakken
Großhacker	70 - 110	B	Holz	11[m]	
Schlepper, 1 Anhänger, Übernahme	70 - 110	B	wie Mähdrescher		Parallelfahrt, Transportkapazität 8 t
Schlepper, 2 Anhänger	70 - 110	B	Abtransport Feld		Transportkapazität 16 t

a: Basis Trockenmasse
b: Wassergehalt Rapskorn 13 %
c: Wassergehalt Weizenkorn 17 %
d: Schüttgewicht Raps- und Weizenkorn: 650 kg TM/m^3
e: Stapeldichte bzw. Einzelgewicht auf Basis Trockenmasse
f: alle Umschlagprozesse mit Frontladern: 2 Ballen pro Lastspiel
g: Feuchtmasse Zuckerrüben, Wassergehalt 76,5 %
h: Schüttgewicht Zuckerrüben: 670 kg FM/m^3 bzw. 150 kg TM/m^3
i: Feuchtmasse Kartoffeln, Wassergehalt 75 %
j: Schüttgewicht Kartoffeln: 660 kg FM/m^3 mit zusätzlich 10 % Erdanhang beim Transport zum Lagerhaus
k: Dichte Häckselgut 91 kg TM/m^3
l: Dichte Hackschnitzel 232 kg TM/m^3 (Pappel, Weide, Buche) bzw. 166 kg TM/m^3 (Fichte)
m: Durchsatz in Festmeter fm/h

TM: Trockenmasse; FM: Feuchtmasse
Quelle: /KALTSCHMITT & REINHARDT 1997/

6.5 Anwendungshinweise, Beispiele und Diskussion

Die hier abgeleiteten Daten können auf sehr verschiedene Weisen in ökologischen Bilanzierungen genutzt werden. Die Unterschiede der einzelnen Anwendungsformen ergeben sich aus der Art des Erkenntnisinteresses und/oder der Verfügbarkeit weiterer Inputdaten. Zwei Anwendungsformen für sehr verschiedene Anforderungen und Datenlagen (Detail- bzw. Grobbilanz) werden im folgenden kurz beschrieben. Anschließend werden für Winterraps, Winterweizen, Zuckerrübe und Kartoffeln detaillierte flächenbezogene Energie- und Emissionsbilanzen der maschinellen Feldarbeit erstellt; für Raps erfolgt eine vollständige Dokumentation nach Arbeitsschritten, für die übrigen werden aggregierte Ergebnisse angegeben. Abschließend werden die Detailbilanzen der einzelnen Kulturen und für Winterraps eine zusätzlich erstellte Grobbilanz vergleichend diskutiert.

6.5.1 Anwendung

Die Art der Anwendung der hier abgeleiteten Daten hängt, wie erwähnt, von den Anforderungen an die Bilanzen ab. Zwei Vorgehensweisen, die die Bandbreite der Differenzierungsmöglichkeiten definieren, werden im folgenden beschrieben.

Grobbilanzierung

Aufgrund der in manchen Fällen absehbaren geringen Relevanz innerhalb eines bestimmten Lebensweges oder als Teil einer lediglich orientierenden Übersichtsbilanz bzw. einer Betriebsbilanz kann es ausreichen, die maschinelle Feldarbeit lediglich mit hoch aggregierten Basisdaten zu bilanzieren. In diesem Fall sollte der Dieselverbrauch pro Hektar der interessierenden Kultur bzw. des betrachteten Betriebes als Praxiswert bzw. Summe geeigneter Abschätzungen verfügbar sein. Der Verbrauch wird mit den verbrauchsbezogenen Emissionsfaktoren im Mittel des 5-Punkte-Tests verknüpft.

Detailbilanzierung

Aufgrund absehbar großer Relevanz innerhalb eines bestimmten Lebensweges oder als Teil einer sehr detaillierten Bilanz soll die maschinelle Feldarbeit hoch differenziert bilanziert werden. Die Bilanzierung umfaßt folgende Schritte:

- Die zu bilanzierenden Feldarbeiten und weitere landwirtschaftliche Rahmenbedingungen, insbesondere die Feldgröße, werden ermittelt bzw. festgelegt.
- Die eingesetzten Maschinen und Geräte werden bestimmt.
- Gemäß den Angaben zu flächenbezogenen Haupt- und Nebenzeiten, den Laststufen der Hauptzeiten und den realistisch anzunehmenden Nennleistungen der Schlepper bzw. Erntemaschinen nach **Tabelle 6-12** und **Tabelle 6-13** sowie zu den Laststufen der Nebenzeiten nach Kapitel 6.4 wird die „Arbeitszeitbilanz" über alle Arbeitsgänge differenziert nach Arbeitsschritten bzw. Laststufen und Nennleistung der eingesetzten Maschinen erstellt.
- Die nach Laststufen und Nennleistung differenzierte Arbeitszeitbilanz wird mit den entsprechend differenzierten zeitbezogenen Energieverbräuchen und Emissionsfaktoren verknüpft.
- Die Addition der Kraftstoffverbräuche und der direkten Emissionen aller Arbeitsschritte ergeben die entsprechenden Bilanzen der maschinellen Feldarbeit im Zusammenhang der zu bearbeitenden Fragestellung.

Grundsätzlich sind Kombinationen von Grob- und Detailbilanzierung möglich. Zum Beispiel kann der detailliert berechnete Kraftstoffverbrauch mit durchschnittlichen verbrauchsbezogenen Emissionsfaktoren verknüpft werden. Die Sinnhaftigkeit eines solchen Vorgehens hängt von der Fragestellung ab. Die Detailbilanzierung der maschinellen Feldarbeit wird im folgenden für vier Kulturen exemplarisch durchgeführt. Zum Vergleich wird für Raps zusätzlich eine Grobbilanz erstellt.

6.5.2 Beispiele: Anbau von Raps, Winterweizen, Zuckerrübe und Kartoffel

Im folgenden werden für die vier genannten Kulturen detaillierte Energie- und Emissionsbilanzen des Lebenswegabschnitts „Maschinelle Feldarbeit" gemäß dem beschriebenen Vorgehen erstellt; für die Rapsproduktion wird außerdem eine Grobbilanz erstellt (Kapitel 6.5.1). Der Rapsanbau wird detailliert beschrieben, während für Winterweizen, Zuckerrübe und Kartoffel lediglich die Bilanzergebnisse ausgewiesen werden. In Kapitel 6.5.3 werden die Ergebnisse diskutiert; den Schwerpunkt bildet dabei der Vergleich der Zeitanteile der einzelnen Laststufen, sowohl der Kulturen untereinander als auch – für Raps – mit denen des 5-Punkte-Tests.

Raps

Betrachtet wird der konventionelle Anbau von Winterraps, der wichtigsten hiesigen Ölsaat, nach guter fachlicher Praxis in Deutschland. Im konventionellen Landbau werden Mineraldünger und synthetische Pflanzenschutzmittel eingesetzt. Angenommen wird eine Schlaggröße zwischen 20 und 60 ha bei einem durchschnittlichen Ertrag von 3,1 t Rapskorn (bei 13 % Erntefeuchte) pro ha und Getreide als Vorfrucht.

Der Anbau von Winterraps beginnt mit der Einarbeitung der Stoppeln der Vorfrucht (Getreide) mit einer Scheibenegge in zwei Arbeitsgängen. Mit einem Aufsattelpflug wird das Feld umgebrochen. Die Aussaat erfolgt in einem Arbeitsgang mit einer Bestellkombination. Für diese Arbeitsgänge wird ein schwerer Schlepper der 140-kW-Klasse eingesetzt. Die Düngemittel werden in zwei Arbeitsgängen mit einem Großraumdüngerstreuer ausgebracht. Düngemittelausbringung und -transport erfolgen mit einem mittleren Schlepper. Pflanzenschutzmittel werden in drei Arbeitsgängen mit einer Anhängespritze und einem mittleren Schlepper ausgebracht. Das Rapskorn wird im Direktdrusch von einem mittleren Mähdrescher (110- bis 170-kW-Klasse) aus dem Stand geerntet. Parallel zum Mähdrescher fährt ein mittlerer Schlepper mit Anhänger. Ohne Umladen werden je zwei Anhänger von einem Schlepper gleichen Typs vom Feld zum Hof transportiert (Annahmen: 4 km Entfernung zwischen Feld und Hof, je zur Hälfte auf Straße und Feldweg; Geschwindigkeit: 15 km/h auf der Straße und 10 km/h auf Feldwegen). In zwei Arbeitsgängen mit einer Scheibenegge und einem schweren Schlepper werden die Stoppeln nach der Ernte eingearbeitet.

Für alle Arbeitsschritte werden die Daten nach **Tabelle 6-12** angesetzt. Die sich damit ergebende, nach Arbeitsgängen und -schritten differenzierte „Arbeitszeitbilanz" ist in **Tabelle 6-14** zusammengefaßt.

Für andere als den hier angesetzten Ertrag von 3,1 t Rapskorn je ha bei 13 % Feuchte muß die Arbeitszeit der Ernte aus Ertrag und Durchsatz der Erntemaschine neu berechnet werden. Die Hauptzeiten für Aussaat, Düngung und Spritzung hängen nur sehr wenig von den ausgebrachten Mengen ab. Das gleiche gilt für die Transportzeit dieser Stoffe zum Hof bzw. zum Feld. Im Rahmen plausibler Annahmen hierzu wird das Ergebnis kaum beeinflußt.

Tabelle 6-14 Arbeitszeitbilanz der maschinellen Feldarbeiten für den Anbau von Winterraps

	Maschinen-klasse kW	Laststufe Hauptzeit	Haupt-zeit	Wegezeit Feld	Wegezeit Straße	Wende-zeit	Verlust-zeit	Rüst-zeit
					— min / (ha*a) —			
Stoppelbe-arbeitung	140	A	44,2	2,4	1,6	1,6	1,8	2,0
Pflügen	140	A	33,8	1,9	1,3	1,0	1,4	1,8
Aussaat	140	C	17,3	1,1	0,7	1,1	1,8	1,4
Düngung	90	B	7,7	2,3	1,8	0,3	0,5	0,6
Spritzung	90	B	10,0	2,3	3,6	0,3	0,7	0,8
Ernte*	90/140	B/A	47,5	4,5	3,3	0,0	2,1	4,0

Laststufen der Nebenzeiten siehe Kapitel 6.4
*: Hauptzeit etwa je zur Hälfte auf Laststufe B mit 90-kW-Schlepper und auf Laststufe A mit 140-kW-Schlepper (Parallelernteverfahren)
Eigene Berechnungen

Die einzelnen flächenbezogenen Teilzeiten werden differenziert nach Feldarbeiten und Maschinen mit den entsprechenden zeitbezogenen Kraftstoffverbräuchen an den zugeordneten Laststufen des 5-Punkte-Tests nach **Tabelle 6-5** verknüpft. In **Tabelle 6-15** ist die resultierende, nach Arbeitsgängen und Laststufen differenzierte Energiebilanz zusammengefaßt.

Tabelle 6-15 Kraftstoffverbrauch beim Anbau von Winterraps differenziert nach Laststufen und Feldarbeitsschritten pro ha Anbaufläche und Wirtschaftsjahr

	Maschinen-klasse kW	Schwer	Normal	Leicht	Straße	Leerlauf	Summe
				— MJ / (ha*a) —			
Stoppelbearbeitung	140	710	23,4	9,4	12,4	5,4	760
Pflügen	140	543	17,8	5,3	9,4	4,5	580
Aussaat	140	0	10,2	101	5,4	4,6	121
Düngung	90	0	62,9	1,2	8,7	1,0	74
Spritzung	90	0	77,2	1,0	17,9	1,4	98
Ernte*	90/140	381	182	0,0	18,7	7,6	589
Summe		**1.634**	**373**	**118**	**72,4**	**24,5**	**2.222**

*: Hauptzeit etwa je zur Hälfte auf Laststufe B mit 90-kW-Schlepper und auf Laststufe A mit 140-kW-Schlepper (Parallelernteverfahren)
Eigene Berechnungen

Die nach Arbeitsgängen und -schritten differenzierten Emissionen können analog den Kraftstoffverbräuchen, d. h. aus den Arbeitszeiten und zeitbezogenen Emissionsfaktoren, oder aus den Verbräuchen und verbrauchsbezogenen Faktoren nach **Tabelle 6-9** berechnet werden. Die resultierenden Emissionen differenziert nach Laststufen sind in **Tabelle 6-16** gemeinsam mit den entsprechend aggregierten Verbräuchen zusammengefaßt. Differenziert nach Arbeitsgängen sind die Emissionen im Anhang (**Tabelle 10-3**) dokumentiert. Ferner sind dort (**Tabelle 10-4**) der kumulierte Energieaufwand und die entsprechenden Emissionen der maschinellen Feldarbeit beim Anbau von Winterraps, d. h. einschließlich der Bereitstellung des Kraftstoffes, ausgewiesen.

Tabelle 6-16 Anbau von Winterraps: Direkte Emissionen aus dem Einsatz von Dieselkraftstoff (Detail- und Grobbilanz)

	Detailbilanz						**Grobbilanz**
	Schwer	**Normal**	**Leicht**	**Straße**	**Leerlauf**	**Summe**	
	g/ha*a	g/ha*a	g/ha*a	g/ha*a	g/ha*a	g/ha*a	g/ha*a
	Global	**Global**	**Global**	**Global**	**Global**	**Global**	**Global**
CO_2	121.659	27.727	8.831	5.397	1.832	165.446	132.618
CH_4	3,14	1,07	0,56	0,42	0,37	5,56	5,81
N_2O	12,7	2,90	0,92	0,56	0,19	17,3	13,8
	OK 2	**OK 2**	**OK 2**	**OK 2**	**OK 2**	**OK 2**	**OK 2**
SO_2	34,5	7,86	2,50	1,53	0,52	46,9	37,6
CO	201	86,2	35,8	31,5	33,4	388	418
NO_X	1.336	287	134	37	22	1.817	1.421
NMHC	128	43,6	22,9	17,1	14,9	226	236
Partikel	85,1	25,1	6,89	8,43	5,79	131	123
Staub	0	0	0	0	0	0	0
HCl	0,038	0,0087	0,0028	0,0017	0,00058	0,052	0,042
NH_3	0,77	0,17	0,06	0,03	0,012	1,04	0,84
Formaldeh.	10,6	3,62	1,90	1,42	1,23	18,8	19,6
Benzol	2,48	0,85	0,45	0,33	0,29	4,40	4,60
	ng/ha*a	ng/ha*a	ng/ha*a	ng/ha*a	ng/ha*a	ng/ha*a	ng/ha*a
BaP	301	52,5	22,3	13,9	8,00	397	321
TCDD-TÄ	0,0023	0,000502	0,000107	0,00010	0,000035	0,0031	0,0025

BaP: Benzo(a)pyren; OK: Ortsklasse
Eigene Berechnungen

Die Grobbilanz wird hier erstellt, indem die gesamte Arbeitszeit lediglich differenziert nach Nennleistung der eingesetzten Maschinen mit dem Verbrauch und den Emissionen im Mittel des 5-Punkte-Tests verknüpft wird. Die Ergebnisse sind ebenfalls in **Tabelle 6-16** dokumentiert.

Die Bereitstellung der Betriebsstoffe Saatgut, Pflanzenschutzmittel und Mineraldünger ist hier nicht berücksichtigt, da lediglich das Bilanzierungsverfahren für den Maschineneinsatz beispielhaft dargestellt werden soll. Bei anderen Fragestellungen können diese Stoffe bzw. die mit ihrer Bereitstellung verbundenen Ressourcenverbräuche und Emissionen, insbesondere die der energieaufwendig produzierten Stickstoffdünger, die Bilanzen bestimmen. Detaillierte Bilanzen der Düngemittelbereitstellung finden sich in /PATYK & REINHARDT 1997/; die Bilanzierung der gesamten Bereitstellung von Rapssaat ist in Kapitel 8.2.1 dokumentiert.

Winterweizen, Zuckerrübe und Kartoffel

Mit der Bilanzierung der maschinellen Feldarbeit beim Anbau von Winterweizen, Zuckerrüben und Kartoffeln werden einige der in Deutschland wichtigsten Grundnahrungsmittel bzw. deren Vorprodukte betrachtet. Für diese Kulturen legen wir dieselben Anbaubedingungen wie für Raps zugrunde. Die Spezifikationen der eingesetzten Geräte finden sich in **Tabelle 6-12** und **Tabelle 6-13**. Das Vorgehen entspricht dem für Raps dargestellten. Für weitere Details sei auf /KALTSCHMITT & REINHARDT 1997/ verwiesen.

In **Tabelle 6-17** sind für Winterweizen, Zuckerrübe und Kartoffel sowie für Raps die flächenbezogenen Zeitaufwendungen differenziert nach Laststufen zusammengestellt. Mit ausgewiesen sind die daraus resultierenden Zeitanteile für die einzelnen Kulturen sowie die Zeitanteile der einzelnen Laststufen im 5-Punkte-Test. In **Tabelle 6-18** sind Energieeinsatz und Emissionen für alle Kulturen, für Raps gemäß der Grob- und der Detailbilanz, zusammengefaßt. Der kumulierte Energieaufwand und die entsprechenden Emissionen der maschinellen Feldarbeit, d. h. einschließlich der Bereitstellung des Kraftstoffes, sind im Anhang (**Tabelle 10-4**) ausgewiesen.

Tabelle 6-17 Zeitaufwand und -anteile der maschinellen Feldarbeit beim Anbau von Winterraps, Winterweizen, Zuckerrübe und Kartoffel differenziert nach Maschinenklassen und Laststufen (Bezug: 1 ha Anbaufläche und 1 Wirtschaftsjahr) und Zeitanteile nach dem 5-Punkte-Test

	Maschine kW	**Schwer** min/ha*a	**Normal** min/ha*a	**Leicht** min/ha*a	**Straße** min/ha*a	**Leerlauf** min/ha*a	**Summe** min/ha*a
Raps	90	0,0	49,3	0,6	7,7	4,9	62,5
	140	101,7	6,8	21,0	4,6	14,1	148,2
	Summe	**101,7**	**56,1**	**21,6**	**12,3**	**19,0**	**210,7**
	Rel. Anteil	*48 %*	*27 %*	*10 %*	*6 %*	*9 %*	*100 %*
Weizen	90	0,0	71,6	0,9	12,8	7,3	92,5
	140	87,6	6,1	20,1	4,0	13,5	131,3
	Summe	**87,6**	**77,6**	**21,0**	**16,8**	**20,8**	**223,8**
	Rel. Anteil	*39 %*	*35 %*	*9 %*	*8 %*	*9 %*	*100 %*
Zuckerrübe	90	0,0	92,7	96,9	12,8	16,4	218,8
	140	66,9	3,8	2,2	2,5	6,1	81,5
	225	56,0	2,1	0,0	7,9	7,5	73,4
	Summe	**122,9**	**98,5**	**99,2**	**23,2**	**29,9**	**373,8**
	Rel. Anteil	*33 %*	*26 %*	*27 %*	*6 %*	*8 %*	*100 %*
Kartoffel	90	0,0	323,5	92,4	65,3	41,0	522,2
	140	187,5	7,8	1,4	5,6	19,1	221,4
	Summe	**187,5**	**331,2**	**93,8**	**70,9**	**60,1**	**743,6**
	Rel. Anteil	*25 %*	*45 %*	*13 %*	*10 %*	*8 %*	*100 %*
5-Punkte-Test	Zeitanteile	31 %	18 %	19 %	20 %	12 %	100 %

Eigene Berechnungen auf der Basis von /KALTSCHMITT & REINHARDT 1997/

6.5.3 Diskussion

Die Ergebnisse der Energie- und Emissionsbilanzierung der maschinellen Feldarbeit beim Anbau von Winterraps, Winterweizen, Zuckerrübe und Kartoffel werden unter zwei Aspekten diskutiert: (I) Zeitaufwand und -anteile der Laststufen und Maschinenklassen und (II) Energieverbrauch und Emissionen, jeweils im Vergleich mit dem 5-Punkte-Test.

Tabelle 6-18 Kraftstoffverbrauch und direkte Emissionen beim Anbau von Winterraps, Winterweizen, Zuckerrübe und Kartoffel pro ha und Wirtschaftsjahr

		Raps - Grob	Raps	Weizen	Zuckerrübe	Kartoffel
Verbrauch	MJ/ha*a	1.794	2.238	2.161	3.742	5.933
Emissionen		**Global**	**Global**	**Global**	**Global**	**Global**
CO_2	g/ha*a	132.618	165.446	159.745	276.572	438.474
CH_4	g/ha*a	5,81	5,56	5,63	10,0	16,6
N_2O	g/ha*a	13,8	17,3	16,7	28,9	45,8
		OK 2	**OK 2**	**OK 2**	**OK 2**	**OK 2**
SO_2	g/ha*a	37,6	46,9	45,3	78,4	124
CO	g/ha*a	418	388	401	698	1.209
NO_X	g/ha*a	1.421	1.817	1.741	3.074	4.722
NMHC	g/ha*a	236	226	229	407	674
Partikel	g/ha*a	123	131	131	224	376
Staub	g/ha*a	0	0	0	0	0
HCl	g/ha*a	0,042	0,052	0,050	0,087	0,14
NH_3	g/ha*a	0,84	1,04	1,01	1,74	2,76
Formaldehyd	g/ha*a	19,6	18,8	19,0	33,8	55,9
Benzol	g/ha*a	4,60	4,40	4,46	7,92	13,1
Benzo(a)pyren	ng/ha*a	321	397	378	664	1.007
TCDD-TÄ	ng/ha*a	0,0025	0,0031	0,0030	0,0052	0,0083

OK: Ortsklasse
Eigene Berechnungen

Der Vergleich der vier Kulturen untereinander und mit dem 5-Punkte-Test hinsichtlich der Zeitanteile der einzelnen Laststufen zeigt folgendes:

- Die absoluten Einsatzzeiten pro Hektar Anbaufläche unterscheiden sich für Raps und Weizen auf der einen Seite und vor allem Kartoffeln auf der anderen Seite sehr deutlich. Der Gesamtzeitaufwand des Kartoffelanbaus ist fast fünfmal höher als der des Rapsanbaus. Eine wesentliche Ursache liegt im größeren Pflegeaufwand der Kartoffel.
- Gemeinsam ist den vier Kulturen der relativ niedrige Anteil der Straßenfahrten bzw. der Leerlaufzeiten von zusammen etwa 15 % der gesamten Maschinenzeit.
- Auf die übrigen drei – relevanteren – Laststufen Leichte bis Schwere Arbeit entfallen jeweils sehr unterschiedliche Anteile: So dominiert etwa beim Anbau von Raps und Weizen die höchste Laststufe, in der die Arbeitsgänge der Bodenbearbeitung der Ernte stattfinden. Demgegenüber fallen bei den Hackfrüchten vor allem die zeitaufwendige Pflanzung und Ernte stark ins Gewicht. Diese Arbeitsgänge entsprechen Normaler bzw. Leichter Arbeit.
- Schließlich werden die verschiedenen Maschinenklassen unterschiedlich stark beansprucht. Während für Raps und Weizen vor allem schwere Schlepper eingesetzt werden, überwiegen bei den Hackfrüchten die Maschinen mittlerer Leistung.
- Da bereits die vier betrachteten Kulturen deutliche Unterschiede untereinander zeigen, kann maximal eine Kultur ähnliche Zeitanteile der Laststufen aufweisen wie der 5-Punkte-Test. Tatsächlich ergibt sich lediglich für die Anteile der Schweren Arbeit beim Zuckerrübenanbau und im 5-Punkte-Test eine – allerdings sehr gute – Übereinstimmung. Für Raps und Weizen ergeben sich in der Detailberechnung sehr viel größere Anteile, für

Kartoffeln ein sehr viel kleinerer Anteil. Die Anteile Normaler Arbeit sind durchgängig deutlich höher als im 5-Punkte-Test. Die Anteile Leichter Arbeit weichen nach oben und unten stark von denen im 5-Punkte-Test ab. Straßenfahrt und Transport werden durch den 5-Punkte-Test sehr stark überschätzt.

Der Vergleich der Energie- und Emissionsbilanzen zeigt folgendes:

- Für eine Reihe von Parametern liefert Weizen niedrigere Werte als Raps, obwohl sein Anbau einen etwas höheren Zeitaufwand erfordert. Die gegenläufigen Zeit- und Verbrauchs- bzw. Emissionsdifferenzen sind in der Summe über die Laststufen allerdings relativ gering.
- Energieeinsatz und Emissionen aus dem Anbau von Kartoffeln sind nur etwa dreimal höher als die entsprechenden Werte für Raps, obwohl der Zeitaufwand fünfmal höher ist. Die längere Einsatzzeit leistungsschwächerer Maschinen beim Kartoffelanbau – begründet im hohen Pflegeaufwand (siehe oben) – wird durch ihren geringeren Kraftstoffverbrauch teilweise kompensiert.
- Der Vergleich der Grob- und Detailbilanz des Rapsanbaus spiegelt die Unterschätzung vor allem der Schweren und Normalen Arbeit im 5-Punkte-Test deutlich wider.

Zusammenfassend zeigt die Analyse der hier erstellten Bilanzen:

- Je nach Kultur entfallen völlig unterschiedliche Zeitanteile auf die einzelnen Laststufen. Insbesondere weichen die Zeitanteile deutlich von denen des 5-Punkte-Tests ab.
- Je nach Kultur werden unterschiedliche Schlepper mit sehr unterschiedlichen Zeitanteilen eingesetzt.
- Die Vernachlässigung dieser Aspekte spiegelt sich deutlich in den Bilanzergebnissen wider.

Unseres Erachtens sind diese Ergebnisse auch auf andere Kulturen übertragbar. In bestimmten Fällen mögen die Maschineneinsätze im Rahmen eines Gesamtlebensweges nicht ins Gewicht fallen, so daß auf eine detaillierte Behandlung verzichtet werden kann. Die vorliegenden Beispiele zeigen jedoch, daß für eine genaue Bilanzierung landwirtschaftlicher Arbeiten die vorgelegte Teilzeitmethode mit ihren Differenzierungen nach Laststufen und Maschinenklassen unbedingt vorzuziehen ist.

7 Bergbau

Im Bergbau – im weiteren Sinne der Förderung im Tief- und Tagebau *und* grubennahen Aufbereitung von Erzen und Kohlen – wird eine Vielzahl konzeptionell und hinsichtlich ihrer Nennleistung völlig unterschiedlicher mit Diesel- oder Elektromotoren betriebener Maschinen eingesetzt. Der Anteil, den der Einsatz dieser Maschinen an den Bilanzen einzelner Parameter bei bestimmten Produkten haben kann, wurde bereits in der Einleitung illustriert (**Abb. 1-2**). Belastbare spezifische Daten zu Energieeinsatz und Emissionen, die zur Anwendung in ökologischen Bilanzierungen geeignet sind, sind jedoch kaum vorhanden. Im folgenden werden solche Daten für eine Auswahl von im Bergbau relevanten dieselbetriebenen Maschinen abgeleitet:

- Bagger
- Schaufellader
- Off-Road-LKW, auch als Dumper bezeichnet

Nicht betrachtet werden damit Elektro-Bagger und die fast ausschließlich elektrisch betriebenen Förderbänder sowie Anreicherungs- und Aufbereitungsanlagen für Erze. Gegebenenfalls bekannte Stromverbräuche dieser Anlagen und die Verbräuche von Dieselgeneratoren in MJ/kWh können jedoch in akzeptabler Näherung mit den hier abgeleiteten verbrauchsbezogenen Emissionsdaten verknüpft werden.

Die Anforderungen an die Daten hier sind den für Gütertransport und Landwirtschaft dargestellten vergleichbar: Sie sollen repräsentativ für Bestände und Einsatzzwecke sein und zugleich eine differenzierte Beschreibung der betrachteten Prozesse ermöglichen. Damit bietet sich ein Vorgehen ähnlich dem für Landmaschinen an:

- Auswahl relevanter Maschinentypen und Nennleistungsklassen
- Definition relevanter Lastpunkte
- Ableitung von Kraftstoffverbräuchen mit geeignetem Bezug (Zeit, bewegte Masse), differenziert nach Nennleistungsklassen und Lastpunkten
- Ableitung verbrauchsbezogener Emissionsfaktoren, soweit möglich differenziert nach Nennleistungsklassen und Lastpunkten
- Verknüpfung von Kraftstoffverbrauch und Emissionsfaktoren

Den anschaulichsten Bezug bildet zweifellos für Bagger und Lader die bewegte Masse in t, für längere Off-Road-Transporte mit Dumpern in großen Gruben die Transportleistung in tkm. Um Angaben mit diesen Bezügen abzuleiten, sind neben den meist nur vorhandenen Daten mit Bezug auf die mechanische Motorarbeit in kWh Informationen über die Betriebsleistung in t/h bzw. tkm/h erforderlich. Letztere sind jedoch kaum belastbar verfügbar. Für Erze sind schließlich der Metallgehalt, für Erze und Kohlen die ebenfalls zu bewegenden Deckgesteine, Gangart usw. zu berücksichtigen, wenn, was der Regelfall sein dürfte, die Bilanzierung für gediegenes Metall (oder ein Metallprodukt) bzw. Kohle frei Abnehmer in t oder TJ durchgeführt wird. Diese komplexen Datenanforderungen sind der Grund dafür, daß Bergbauprozesse meist top-down bilanziert werden: Der Dieselverbrauch einer Grube wird durch die mit dem geförderten Erz ausgebrachte Metallmenge dividiert. Der spezifische Verbrauch wird mit verbrauchsbezogenen Emissionsfaktoren verknüpft.

Zusammenfassend läßt sich festhalten, daß sich Verbrauchs- und Emissionsdaten in der Differenzierungstiefe, die für Landmaschinen erreicht wurde, mit den vorliegenden Primärdaten nicht ableiten lassen. Die möglichst weitgehende Aufbereitung für Ökobilanz-Zwecke der wesentlichen Studie zum Thema wird im folgenden durchgeführt.

7.1 Datengrundlage

Die wichtigste Datengrundlage bildet die Studie „Schadstoffemissionen und Treibstoffverbrauch von Baumaschinen" in der Schweiz 1992 /BUWAL 1994/, die bereits als Basis für Emissionsbilanzen der Schweiz /BUWAL 1996/ und der EU /ANDRIAS et al. 1994/ diente. In /BUWAL 1994/ werden spezifische Daten abgeleitet und daraus exemplarisch die Energie- und Emissionsbilanzen von einzelnen Baustellen und des gesamten Baumaschineneinsatzes in der Schweiz erstellt. Das dabei gewählte Vorgehen läßt sich wie folgt zusammenfassen:

Über alle Maschinentypen werden Energieeinsatz und Emissionen bezogen auf die mechanische Arbeit der Motoren (pro kWh) gegen die Nennleistung aufgetragen. Dabei werden lediglich „aktuelle" Testverfahren, direkteinspritzende Dieselmotoren ohne Aufladung (DINA) und relativ neue Motoren berücksichtigt. Von insgesamt 300 verfügbaren Datensätzen genügen 130 diesen Anforderungen. Aus den Daten werden Ausgleichsfunktionen abgeleitet, mit denen typische *Basis*energieeinsätze und -emissionen pro kWh für repräsentative Nennleistungsklassen bestimmt werden. Während für Energieeinsatz und Emissionen im unteren Nennleistungsbereich noch eine starke Abhängigkeit festzustellen ist, gilt dies für Leistungen ab etwa 200 kW nicht mehr. **Tabelle 7-1** faßt die Daten zusammen.

Tabelle 7-1 Energieeinsätze und Basisemissionsfaktoren nach Nennleistungsklassen für direkteinspritzende Motoren ohne Aufladung

Nennleistung in kW		< 10	10 - 25	25 - 50	50 - 100	100 - 200	> 200
Dieselkraftstoff	g/kWh	> 280	270	267	262	256	254
Energie	MJ/kWh	> 12	11,5	11,4	11,2	10,9	10,8
CO	g/kWh	> 10	8,0	6,0	4,5	3,5	3,0
NO_X	g/kWh	14,3	14,3	14,3	14,3	14,3	14,3
HC	g/kWh	> 5	3,5	3,0	2,0	1,5	1,3
Partikel	g/kWh	> 2,5	2,0	1,7	1,3	1,2	1,1

Quelle: /BUWAL 1994/

Um andere Motorenkonzepte, den Entwicklungsstand der Motoren und die Gesamteinsatzzeit älterer Maschinen zu berücksichtigen, werden in /BUWAL 1994/ Korrekturfaktoren abgeschätzt:

- Für andere als DINA-Motoren werden unter der Annahme gleichen Entwicklungsstandes und Durchschnittsalters Korrekturfaktoren zwischen 0,7 (NO_X bei Vorkammermotoren mit Aufladung und Ladeluftkühlung) und 1,2 (Partikel bei unaufgeladenen Vorkammermotoren) abgeschätzt.

- Der Einfluß des Entwicklungsstandes (Baujahr) wird für alle Motorkonzepte zurückgehend vom Bezugsjahr der schweizer Untersuchung (1992) mit Verschlechterungen von 1 bis 3 % pro Jahr für den Energieeinsatz und die Emissionen angesetzt (Ausnahme: NO_X: 0 %).
- Der Alterungseffekt wird für alle Motorkonzepte mit Verschlechterungen von 2 % je Einsatzjahr für den Energieeinsatz und die Emissionen angesetzt (Ausnahme: NO_X: 0 %).

Tabelle 7-2 faßt die Faktoren zusammen.

Tabelle 7-2 Korrekturfaktoren für Motorenkonzept, Baujahr und Alterung relativ zu direkteinspritzenden Motoren ohne Aufladung des Baujahrs 1992

	Motorenkonzept						Baujahr	Alterung
	DINA	DIT	DITI	VKNA	VKT	VKTI		
Verbrauch DK	1	0,95	0,95	1,10	1,05	1,05	1,0 %	2 %
CO	1	0,80	0,80	1,00	0,95	0,90	1,5 %	2 %
NO_X	1	1,00	0,80	0,80	0,75	0,70	0,0 %	0 %
HC	1	0,80	0,80	1,00	0,95	0,90	1,5 %	2 %
Partikel	1	0,90	0,80	1,20	1,10	1,00	3,0 %	2 %

Motorenkonzepte: DI: Direkteinspritzer; VK: Vorkammermotor; NA: Nicht aufgeladen; T: Aufladung (Turbo-Aufladung); I: Intercooler (Ladeluftkühlung);
Baujahr: Verschlechterung für jedes Jahr früher als 1992
Alterung: Verschlechterung pro Jahr Einsatz
Quelle: /BUWAL 1994/

Durch Verknüpfung der *energie*bezogenen Daten mit Nennleistung und Auslastung werden *zeit*bezogene Daten erhalten. Die Nennleistung ist für die erfaßten Maschinen bekannt. Für den Auslastungsgrad kann der spezifische Wert eines Tests oder ein „Praxiswert" (Meßwert) angesetzt werden. In /BUWAL 1994/ wird an dieser Stelle eine sehr grobe Differenzierung nach Maschinentypen eingeführt: Es wird die Auslastung des Tests angesetzt, der gemäß ISO-Empfehlung für den Maschinentyp am besten geeignet ist (C1; siehe Kapitel 3.2); dabei wird nicht berücksichtigt, in welchem Maße dieser Test in der Datenbasis vertreten war.

Zur Berechnung der Emissionen von einer Baustelle werden die Betriebszeiten der einzelnen eingesetzten Maschinen mit den passenden zeitbezogenen Verbräuchen und Emissionen verknüpft, die Produkte werden aufsummiert. Die Bilanzierung für die Schweiz erfolgt im Prinzip genauso, allerdings unter Verwendung von einer Reihe von Zusatzannahmen zur Bestandsstruktur, dem Zusammenhang von Maschinenalter und jährlicher Nutzungsdauer usw.

Das Vorgehen in /BUWAL 1994/ ist unter verschiedenen Aspekten problematisch. Einige Punkte berühren die dort vorgelegten Ergebnisse, andere sind speziell für unsere Anwendungen relevant:

- Die Aggregation der Meßdaten erfolgt nur differenziert nach Nennleistung, nicht aber nach Maschinentyp. Das heißt, daß z. B. nicht zwischen einem Bagger und einem Kipper gleicher Leistung unterschieden wird. Die Differenzierung nach Maschinentypen wird erst im zweiten Schritt und nur in grober Näherung über Annahmen zur Motorauslastung eingeführt.

- Die gesamte Auswertung basiert auf Testmittelwerten. Das heißt, es erfolgt keine Differenzierung nach Lastzuständen. Auch wenn die Lastpunkte der Testverfahren realistisch gewählt sind, kann die Gewichtung für alle oder einige vermessene Maschinentypen unrealistisch sein. Dies beeinflußt Bilanzen wie in /BUWAL 1994/ und verhindert Differenzierungen wie in Kapitel 6 für die maschinelle Feldarbeit dargestellt.

- Es werden Daten aus verschiedenen Testverfahren angesetzt. Zur Überprüfung des Einflusses des Testverfahrens wurden acht Motoren verschiedener Konzepte mit Nennleistungen zwischen 12 und 608 kW vermessen. Im Mittel über alle Motoren und Testverfahren ergaben sich folgende *maximale* Abweichungen:

Kraftstoffverbrauch	4 %
CO	62 %
NO_X	17 %
HC	95 %
Partikel	16 %

  Diese Abweichungen bewegen sich für die Emissionen in der gleichen Größenordnung wie die Korrekturfaktoren für Motorkonzepte und Alterung. Eine gemeinsame Auswertung verschiedener Testverfahren ist damit nur bedingt zulässig.

- Der Gesamteffekt der verschiedenen Problempunkte wird in einer Vergleichsbetrachtung in /BUWAL 1994/ deutlich. Für den Kraftstoffverbrauch auf drei Baustellen ergibt sich im Mittel eine relative Differenz von +40 % zwischen den aus den Betriebszeiten der Maschinen berechneten und den gemessenen Werten (Bezug: Meßwerte). Nach Maschinen differenziert ergibt sich eine Bandbreite von -57 % bis +183 %. Eine von uns durchgeführte Analyse der Praxisdaten der einzelnen Baustellen nach /BUWAL 1994/ für Bagger, Lader und Dumper zeigt, daß sich bereits für gleiche Prozesse mit sehr ähnlichen Maschinen auf der gleichen oder verschiedenen Baustellen relative Bandbreiten des *volumenbezogenen* Energieverbrauchs von 500 bis 1.000 % (!) ergeben. Dabei ist keinerlei Abhängigkeit von der Nennleistung erkennbar. Andererseits lassen sich für zwei der von uns ausgewählten Maschinenklassen, Bagger und Lader, die Mittelwerte nach der BUWAL-Methode rechnerisch recht gut reproduzieren. Dabei ist zu beachten, daß die Berechnung der Mittelwerte nach verschiedenen Verfahren *und* mit deutlich verschiedenen Ergebnissen erfolgen kann (siehe dazu Kapitel 7.2). **Tabelle 7-3** faßt die Daten zusammen; die Basisdaten nach /BUWAL 1994/ sind im Anhang (**Tabelle 11-2**) dokumentiert.
  Die bisherige Diskussion hat die Unsicherheiten der Emissionsangaben ausgeklammert. Wir beschränken uns hier auf den Hinweis, daß die Bandbreiten von Emissionsdaten praktisch für alle technischen Systeme größer sind als die der korrespondierenden Energieeinsätze.

- Die Praxisdaten in /BUWAL 1994/ beziehen sich ausschließlich auf das bewegte Volumen; Angaben zur Dichte des Materials liegen nicht vor. Der andernfalls ableitbare *Massen*bezug ist für ökologische Bilanzierungen jedoch sehr viel zweckmäßiger als der *Volumen*bezug. Die dargestellten Bandbreiten der volumenbezogenen Daten erklären sich möglicherweise aus der unterschiedlichen Dichte der bearbeiteten Materialien, zu der keine Angaben gemacht werden.

- Zwar wird in /BUWAL 1994/ die Vielzahl der Baumaschinen erfaßt, doch gemäß den schweizer Verhältnissen mit dem Schwerpunkt auf relativ kleinen Maschinen (< 100 kW). Für die Bilanzierung von *Bergbau*prozessen ist das problematisch, da die dort eingesetzten Maschinen oft hinsichtlich ihrer Kapazität und Nennleistung (bis zu 1.000 kW) deutlich größer sind als übliche Baumaschinen.

Tabelle 7-3 Leistungsdaten und Kraftstoffverbrauch (gemessen und berechnet) von Baggern, Ladern und Dumpern

	Nenn-leistung	**Betriebs-leistung**	**Verbrauch DK Praxis**		**Theorie**		**Theorie / Praxis**	
	kW	m^3/h	MJ/h	MJ/m^3	MJ/h	MJ/m^3	MJ/h	MJ/m^3
Bagger								
Anzahl Daten	8	8	8	8	8	8		
Min	59	23,6	261	2,34	310	3,10	119%	133%
Max	155	183	680	23,4	796	33,7	117%	144%
Max / Min	263%	773%	261%	1.002%	257%	1.086%		
MW I	**112**	**93,6**	**493**	**8,53**	**575**	**10,9**	**117%**	**127%**
MW II				**5,26**		**6,15**		**117%**
MW I / MW II				162%		177%		
Lader								
Anzahl Daten	20	20	20	20	20	20		
Min	85	15,2	242	2,87	47$	4,88	195%	170%
Max	190	149	1149	34,8	1059	48,3	92%	139%
Max / Min	224%	982%	474%	1.210%	224%	990%		
MW I	**138**	**85,8**	**683**	**10,8**	**771**	**13,9**	**113%**	**128%**
MW II				**7,96**		**8,99**		**113%**
MW I / MW II				136%		155%		
Dumper								
Anzahl Daten	16	16	16	16	16	16		
Min	179	39,0	195	1,31	665	4,47	340%	340%
Max	192	149	346	7,40	714	18,3	206%	247%
Max / Min	107%	381%	177%	564%	107%	409%		
MW I	**185**	**91,4**	**269**	**3,52**	**686**	**9,00**	**255%**	**256%**
MW II				**2,94**		**7,51**		**255%**
MW I / MW II				120%		120%		
				MJ/m^3*km		MJ/m^3*km		MJ/m^3*km
Min				2,63		8,94		340%
Max				50,6		129		254%
Max / Min				1.926%		1.438%		
MW I				**15,8**		**42,4**		**268%**
MW IIa				**8,19**		**20,9**		**255%**
MW I / MW IIa				193%		203%		

DK: Dieselkraftstoff; NennL, BetriebsL: Nenn- bzw. Betriebsleistung
MW I: Mittel über alle Parameter = Summe (Einzelwerte) / Anzahl Werte
MW II: Mittel über EV in MJ/m^3 = Summe (EV in MJ/h) / Summe (BetriebsL in m^3/h)
MW IIa: Berechnet aus MW II mit der mittleren Weglänge gewichtet nach Transportleistung
Praxis: Meßdaten; Theorie: Berechnung über Ausgleichsfunktionen
Quellen: /BUWAL 1994/, eigene Berechnungen

Die Analysen in /BUWAL 1994/ erfolgten unseres Erachtens sehr sorgfältig, und die Datenbasis ist sehr umfangreich. Daher liegt die Ursache für sehr große Abweichungen im Einzelfall wahrscheinlich in grundsätzlich nur bedingt realistischen Lastkollektiven als Basis der Messungen. Zumindest die repräsentative zeitliche Gewichtung einzelner Punkte eines Lastkollektivs ist extrem schwierig, auch wenn die wesentlichen Lastpunkte gut lokalisierbar sind (siehe dazu Kapitel 3).

Trotz der soliden Qualität von /BUWAL 1994/ enthalten die einzelnen Daten offensichtlich große Unsicherheiten. Einige für ökologische Bilanzierungen zweckmäßige Datensätze können jedoch plausibel auf der Basis von /BUWAL 1994/ und einiger weiterer Arbeiten, insbesondere zu den Emissionen nicht limitierter Schadstoffe abgeleitet werden. Aufgrund der dargestellten Unsicherheiten verzichten wir dabei auf eine Anpassung an andere Bestandsstrukturen, etwa Deutschland – oder andere Länder – 1996. Dies läßt sich konkret rechtfertigen durch

- den ohnehin starken Näherungscharakter der gesamten Ableitung, vor allem aber dadurch, daß
- hinsichtlich der Anwendung der Daten Bezugsländer eine Rolle spielen, für die einerseits praktisch keine Daten vorliegen, andererseits aber von niedrigeren Standards als in Westeuropa ausgegangen werden kann.

Insbesondere unter dem letztgenannten Aspekt beschreiben vor allem die Emissionsdaten eher die untere Grenze der wahrscheinlichen Werte.

Betrachtet werden im folgenden die drei Maschinentypen Bagger, Schaufellader und Off-Road-LKW (Dumper), für die zunächst Kraftstoffverbräuche bezogen auf die Einsatzzeit und die Arbeitsleistung und anschließend verbrauchsbezogene Emissionsfaktoren abgeleitet werden. Abschließend werden die Verbräuche und die verbrauchsbezogene Emissionsfaktoren verknüpft.

7.2 Kraftstoffverbrauch

Für den Kraftstoffverbrauch von Baggern, Ladern und Dumpern setzen wir die Mittelwerte der Praxisdaten bezogen auf die Arbeitszeit und das bewegte Volumen an, die in **Tabelle 7-3** zusammengefaßt sind. Der für eine Ökobilanzierung häufig sinnvollere Bezug auf bewegte Masse – anstelle des bewegten Volumens – kann nicht ohne weiteres allgemeingültig hergestellt werden, da hierzu die Dichte des bewegten Materials bekannt sein muß.

Die hier erfaßten Maschinen sind kleiner als die im Bergbau üblicherweise eingesetzten. Da die Basisdaten keine Nennleistungsabhängigkeit zeigen, können die zeitbezogenen Daten für deutlich größere Maschinen linear extrapoliert werden.

Der mittlere Verbrauch bezogen auf das bewegte Volumen kann auf zwei Arten berechnet werden:

MW I: Mittelung über die einzelnen volumenbezogenen Verbräuche. Anschaulich: Alle Maschinen bewegen 1 m^3 Material; der Gesamtverbrauch wird durch die Anzahl der Maschinen dividiert.

MW II: Quotient aus dem gesamten zeitbezogenen Verbrauch und der gesamten Betriebsleistung. Anschaulich: Alle Maschinen arbeiten 1 h; der Gesamtverbrauch wird durch das Gesamtvolumen des bewegten Materials dividiert.

Tendenziell werden in MW I kleinere und in MW II größere Maschinen stärker bewertet. Daß hier vor allem Maschinen großer Nennleistung erfaßt werden sollen, würde für die Verwendung von MW II sprechen. Aufgrund der fehlenden Nennleistungsabhängigkeit unter den Einzelwerten orientieren wir uns hier am Mittel aus MW I und II. Aus dem gleichen Grund können die volumenbezogenen Daten für jede Nennleistungsklasse angesetzt werden.

Für Dumper ist der Bezug auf die Transportleistung sinnvoll. Die Weglängen auf den in /BUWAL 1994/ beschriebenen Baustellen betrugen zwischen 0,1 und 0,8 km. Eventuelle Effekte der Weglänge auf den spezifischen Verbrauch – z. B. mehr Lastwechsel und daher höherer Verbrauch auf 0,1 km gegenüber 0,8 km – werden durch andere Parameter überlagert. Eine entsprechende Differenzierung ist daher nicht möglich. Die oben beschriebene Unterscheidung von zwei Mittelwerten kann für den Bezug auf die Transportleistung fortgeführt werden (MW Ia und IIa). Die mittlere Weglänge in MW IIa ist mit der Transportleistung gewichtet. Wir setzen auch hier den Mittelwert von MW Ia und MW IIa an.

Ist die Dichte des bewegten Materials bekannt, können die Verbräuche und Emissionen von Volumenbezug auf Massenbezug umgerechnet werden. Die hier angesetzten Werte sind in **Tabelle 7-4** zusammengefaßt.

7.3 Emissionen

Für die inventargebundenen Schadstoffe CO_2, SO_2 und HCl nehmen wir – wie üblich – vollständige Oxidation des Dieselkraftstoffes und C-, S- und Cl-Gehalte von 86,6, 0,045 und 0,0001 M% an (Heizwert: 42,96 MJ/kg).

Die Emissionsfaktoren für NO_X, HC, CO und Partikel basieren auf Daten nach /BUWAL 1994/, die sich auf Bestandsstruktur und Betriebszeiten in der Schweiz 1992 beziehen. Diese Daten werden in /BUWAL 1994/ in g/h ausgewiesen. Daraus und aus den ebenfalls dokumentierten Kraftstoffverbräuchen pro Stunde werden die Faktoren in g/MJ berechnet (**Tabelle 7-4**). Wir setzen hier die gemeinsamen Mittelwerte für Bagger, Lader und Dumper an, da die Daten zwischen den Maschinentypen nur eine relativ geringe Bandbreite aufweisen (vergleiche die Maximal-/Minimalwerte), andererseits aber, wie dargestellt, der Kraftstoffverbrauch schon für einen Maschinentyp eine erhebliche Bandbreite zeigt.

Die Differenzierung von HC in Methan und NMHC sowie die Ableitung der Faktoren für die übrigen betrachteten Schadstoffe erfolgt wie für LKW und Landmaschinen in Kapitel 5.1.4 und 6.2 dargestellt.

Tabelle 7-4 Spezifikationen, Energieverbrauch und Emissionen von Baggern, Ladern und Dumpern in der Schweiz 1992

Maschine	**Anm.**	**Gewicht**	**NLKlasse**	**Mittlere NL**	**Lastfaktor**
		t	kW	kW	
Hydraulikbagger	Raupe	23 - 47	100 - 200	150	0,47
Ladeschaufler	Rad	12 - 24	100 - 200	150	0,51
	Rad	> 24	> 200	250	0,51
Großdumper	Rad	< 24	100 - 200	150	0,34
	Rad	> 24	> 200	250	0,34
Maschine	**DK**	**CO**	**NO_X**	**HC**	**Partikel**
	g/h	g/h	g/h	g/h	g/h
Hydraulikbagger	22.055	246	1.004	108	110
Ladeschaufler	24.110	268	1.090	118	121
	41.026	447	1.799	196	209
Großdumper	18.016	198	726	87	100
	29.228	318	1.196	140	157
	MJ/h	g/MJ	g/MJ	g/MJ	g/MJ
Hydraulikbagger	942	0,26	1,07	0,11	0,12
Ladeschaufler	1.029	0,26	1,06	0,11	0,12
	1.752	0,26	1,03	0,11	0,12
Großdumper	769	0,26	0,94	0,11	0,13
	1.248	0,25	0,96	0,11	0,13
Mittelwert		**0,26**	**1,01**	**0,11**	**0,12**
Max / Min		103%	113%	102%	111%

DK: Dieselkraftstoff; NL: Nennleistung
Quelle: /BUWAL 1994/, eigene Berechnungen

7.4 Zusammenführung

Die hier abgeleiteten spezifischen Energieverbräuche und Emissionsfaktoren mit verschiedenen Bezügen sind in **Tabelle 7-5** zusammengefaßt. Die Daten zum spezifischen kumulierten Energieaufwand und den damit verbundenen Emissionen einschließlich der Bereitstellung von Dieselkraftstoff sind im Anhang (**Tabelle 11-1**) dokumentiert.

Das dargestellte Vorgehen – insbesondere die Kombination von Daten verschiedener Herkunft, der Verzicht auf die Anpassung von Bezugsraum und -zeit sowie weitere Differenzierungen – ist angesichts der oben diskutierten Bandbreiten und Unsicherheiten gerechtfertigt. Die hier abgeleiteten Daten erlauben, zumindest wesentliche Grubenprozesse zu unterscheiden, falls die komplementären Input-Daten wie Zeit oder Gesamtenergieverbräuche vorliegen. Andernfalls bilden die kraftstoffbezogenen Emissionsfaktoren immer noch eine gut belastbare Basis für „top-down"-Bilanzierungen.

Tabelle 7-5 Spezifischer Energieeinsatz und Emissionen von Baggern, Ladern und Dumpern

Maschinen			**Bagger**	**Lader**	**Dumper**	**Bagger**	**Lader**	**Dumper**
Bezug		**MJ**	**h**	**h**	**h**	**m^3**	**m^3**	**m^3*km**
Kraftstoffverbrauch								
Diesel	MJ	1	493	683	269	6,90	9,40	12,0
Emissionen		**Global**	**Global**	**Global**	**Global**	**Global**	**Global**	**Global**
CO_2	g	74,4	36.634	50.803	19.993	513	699	893
CH_4	g	0,0027	1,34	1,86	0,73	0,019	0,026	0,033
N_2O	g	0,0034	1,66	2,30	0,90	0,023	0,032	0,040
		OK 2	**OK 2**	**OK 2**	**OK 2**	**OK 2**	**OK 2**	**OK 2**
SO_2	g	0,021	10,4	14,4	5,67	0,15	0,20	0,25
CO	g	0,26	127	176	69,3	1,78	2,42	3,10
NO_X	g	1,01	498	691	272	6,97	9,50	12,1
NMHC	g	0,11	54,5	75,5	29,7	0,76	1,04	1,33
Partikel	g	0,12	60,1	83,3	32,8	0,84	1,15	1,46
Staub	g	0	0	0	0	0	0	0
HCl	g	0,00044	0,22	0,30	0,12	0,0030	0,0041	0,0053
NH_3	g	0,0027	1,34	1,86	0,73	0,019	0,026	0,033
Formaldehyd	g	0,0092	4,52	6,27	2,47	0,063	0,086	0,11
Benzol	g	0,0022	1,06	1,47	0,58	0,015	0,020	0,026
Benzo(a)Pyren	ng	181	89.059	123.504	48.603	1.247	1.699	2.171
TCDD-TÄ	ng	0,0014	0,69	0,96	0,38	0,010	0,013	0,017

OK: Ortsklasse
Quelle: /BUWAL 1994/, eigene Berechnungen

8 Energiebereitstellung

Die wesentlichen Endenergieträger im Gütertransport, in der Landwirtschaft und im Bergbau sind Mineralölprodukte und Strom. Sie werden in komplexen Prozeßketten, die den Einsatz unterschiedlichster bergbaulicher Verfahren und Fördertechniken, chemischer oder physikalischer Trenn- und Anreicherungsverfahren, Transport- und Umwandlungsprozesse umfassen, bereitgestellt. Während dabei Mineralölprodukte im wesentlichen auf dem Primärenergieträger Erdöl basieren, werden zur Stromerzeugung alle fossilen Energieträger sowie Kern- und Wasserkraft und, in geringerem Maße, weitere regenerative Energien genutzt.

Im folgenden wird die Bereitstellung frei Abnehmer von Mineralölprodukten, Rapsöl und Rapsölmethylester (RME) als Diesel-Substituten, von Stein- und Braunkohle, Erdgas und Uran zur Verstromung sowie die Strombereitstellung selbst behandelt. Den Schwerpunkt bildet die Bereitstellung der Energieträger in Deutschland im Jahr 1996. Für Mineralölprodukte, Strom und die beiden Biokraftstoffe werden darüber hinaus im Anhang Bilanzen mit Bezug auf das Jahr 2000 ausgewiesen, da durch Änderungen der Rohölqualitäten und Produktpaletten in Raffinerien bzw. durch Fortschritte bei der Emissionsminderung in der ostdeutschen Elektrizitätswirtschaft Änderungen der gesamten Bereitstellungsaufwendungen und -emissionen zu erwarten sind.

Generell werden für die Bilanzierung der Energiebereitstellung die aktuellsten verfügbaren Daten angesetzt; die Bezugsjahre der Basisdaten liegen zwischen 1994 /AGE 1998/ und 1996 /BMWI 1998/. Damit sind bereits für das Bezugsjahr 1996 Fortschreibungen erforderlich, die anhand weniger differenzierter, jedoch aktueller Statistiken erfolgen (Beispiel: Fortschreibung von /AGE 1998/ mit /MWV 1997/ für 1996). Die eigentliche Raffinerie- und Stromproduktion im Jahr 2000 wird im wesentlichen basierend auf /PROGNOS 1996/ bilanziert. Für die Herkunftsstruktur und den Förderaufwand der fossilen Energieträger sind Entwicklungen weniger zuverlässig vorhersagbar; die vorliegenden Daten werden daher ohne Modifikationen für das Jahr 2000 übernommen.

8.1 Energieträger auf Erdölbasis

Die in Deutschland abgesetzten Mineralölprodukte (1996: 132 Mio. t) werden überwiegend im Land aus importiertem Rohöl (103 Mio. t) erzeugt, das zu 40 % aus Westeuropa stammt. Die Förderung in Deutschland lag bei 2,9 Mio. t, der Export bei 1,8 Mio. t. Auch der Außenhandel von Zwischen- und Endprodukten der Mineralölverarbeitung hat einen erheblichen Umfang, wobei der Import mit 46,2 Mio. t gegenüber 14,1 Mio. t den Export deutlich überwiegt. Der Austausch findet im wesentlichen in Westeuropa statt, wobei der größte Anteil auf die Niederlande entfällt. Daneben liefern lediglich die Länder Osteuropas, insbesondere die GUS, noch in relevantem Umfang. Die Relationen zwischen importierten und in Deutschland produzierten Mengen sind für verschiedene Produkte sehr unterschiedlich; vor allem leichtes Heizöl wird in großem Umfang importiert (in 1996: 15,4 Mio. t, bei einer Produktion von 24,4 Mio. t) /MWV 1997/.

Da die importierten Mineralölprodukte überwiegend aus westeuropäischen Ländern stammen, können für alle in Deutschland abgesetzten Mineralölprodukte in guter Näherung gleiche Produktionsbedingungen, und zwar die für Deutschland typischen, angenommen werden.

8.1.1 Rohölbereitstellung

Die Rohölbereitstellung umfaßt drei Prozeßschritte: die Förderung von Rohöl, seine Aufbereitung und den Transport zur Raffinerie.

Herkunft: Das in Deutschland verarbeitete Rohöl stammt im wesentlichen aus Großbritannien, Norwegen, der GUS und einigen OPEC-Staaten; der Anteil der inländischen Förderung ist nur gering (**Tabelle 8-1**).

Tabelle 8-1 Rohölbereitstellung in Deutschland 1996: Herkunftsregionen, Fördertechniken und Transportentfernungen

	Herkunft		Fördertechniken		Transport-entfernung
		Primär	Sekundär	Tertiär	
	Anteil	Anteil	Anteil	Anteil	km
Westeuropa	40,2%	50%	50%	0%	500
OPEC	30,8%	80%	20%	0%	8.800
GUS	26,2%	100%	0%	0%	2.500
Deutschland	2,9%	14%	70%	16%	200

Die Anteile der Herkunft sind auf 100 % normiert.
Quellen: /GEMIS 1997/, /MWV 1997/, eigene Berechnungen

Förderung: Rohöl wird auf dem Festland und küstennah auf dem Meer gefördert (off shore). Während in Europa der Anteil der off-shore-Förderung bei etwa 95 % liegt /ECOINVENT 1996/, ist er in Osteuropa und Nahost sehr gering; weltweit beträgt er etwa ein Drittel /SHELL 1994/. Die Fördertechniken lassen sich in drei Kategorien unterscheiden:

- **Primär:** Förderung durch elektrisch, mit Dieselmotoren oder Gasturbinen betriebene Pumpen
- **Sekundär:** Förderung durch Einpressen von Wasser in nicht durch Pumpen ausbeutbare Vorkommen
- **Tertiär:** Förderung durch Einpressen von Dampf oder Kohlendioxid

Der Energieaufwand der Förderung hängt stark von der eingesetzten Technik ab. Die Anteile der einzelnen Techniken weisen erhebliche Unterschiede zwischen den Förderregionen auf; die hier angesetzten Daten sind in **Tabelle 8-1** zusammengefaßt.

Aufbereitung: Im Anschluß an die Förderung werden Gas und Wasser aus dem Rohöl entfernt. Das Öl wird dazu entweder erhitzt, chemisch behandelt oder der Schwerkraft bzw. elektrischen Feldern ausgesetzt. Als Energieträger wird dazu in OPEC-Ländern und der GUS Schweröl eingesetzt, auf den Ölfeldern in der Nordsee Erdölgas. Wir unterstellen hier den Einsatz thermischer Verfahren; die Aufbereitungsanlagen werden näherungsweise durch Kesselfeuerungen beschrieben.

Transport: Der Transport aus den OPEC-Staaten erfolgt mit Großtankern. Nordseeöl und Öl aus der GUS werden überwiegend über Pipelines importiert; innerhalb Deutschlands erfolgt der Transport des hier geförderten und des importierten Rohöls praktisch ausschließlich über Pipelines. Die Pumpen der Pipelines werden in der Regel elektrisch betrieben. Die hier angesetzten Transportweiten sind in **Tabelle 8-1** zusammengefaßt.

Der Endenergieeinsatz der Bereitstellung ist für die verschiedenen Förderregionen und Prozeßschritte in **Tabelle 8-2** zusammengestellt.

Tabelle 8-2 Spezifischer Endenergieeinsatz der Rohölbereitstellung in Deutschland 1996, differenziert nach Förderregionen und Prozeßschritten

Herkunft	Förderung Primär	Sekundär	Tertiär	Tertiär	Aufbereit.	Transport
Anlage / Energieträger						
Westeuropa	Gasturbine	Gasturbine			HS-Kessel	Pipeline (Gas)
OPEC	Diesel-Pumpe	Diesel-Pumpe			HS-Kessel	Tanker
GUS	Diesel-Pumpe				HS-Kessel	Pipeline (Gas)
Deutschland	E-Pumpe	E-Pumpe	E-Pumpe	HS-Kessel	HS-Kessel	Pipeline (E)
Endenergieeinsatz in GJ/GJ Rohöl						
Westeuropa	0,0033	0,010	k. A.	k. A.	0,0027	0,0030
OPEC	0,0029	0,0077	k. A.	k. A.	0,0029	0,021
GUS	0,0066	k. A.	k. A.	k. A.	0,059	0,015
Deutschland	0,0011	0,0033	0,0033	0,30	0,0027	0,0004

HS: Schweröl; E: EVU-Strom; Gas: Gasturbinen-Kraftwerk
Quellen: /GEMIS 1997/, eigene Berechnungen

Tabelle 8-3 faßt die resultierenden Primärenergieaufwendungen differenziert nach Förderregionen und Prozeßschritten zusammen. Für den Primärenergieaufwand zur Bereitstellung (Förderung, Aufbereitung, Transport bis zur Raffinerie in Deutschland) des durchschnittlichen in Deutschland verarbeiteten Rohöls ergeben sich die ebenfalls in **Tabelle 8-3** dokumentierten Anteile nach Herkunftsländern und Prozeßschritten. Die größten Einzelposten des herkunftsgewichteten mittlere Primärenergieaufwandes von 0,040 GJ/GJ Rohöl sind mit 44 % die Aufbereitung in der GUS und mit 18 % der Transport aus OPEC-Ländern.

Die spezifischen Emissionen der Bereitstellung von Rohöl ergeben sich durch Verknüpfung der Energieeinsätze in den einzelnen Prozessen der Bereitstellung mit energieeinsatzbezogenen Emissionsfaktoren.

- Für die bei der Ölförderung eingesetzten dieselbetriebenen Pumpen werden die in Kapitel 7.3 für Generatoren und Pumpen abgeleiteten Emissionsfaktoren angesetzt. Eine Anpassung an die Verhältnisse in OPEC-Ländern oder der GUS erfolgt nicht.
- Für Gasturbinen und Kessel, die bei der Förderung, der Aufbereitung und dem Transport eingesetzt werden, verwenden wir Daten nach /GEMIS 1997/ und /ECOINVENT 1996/ sowie eigene Abschätzungen. Die Faktoren der Standard-Schadstoffe sind nach Westeuropa/Deutschland und OPEC/GUS differenziert.
- Für den Tankertransport setzen wir die Faktoren nach Kapitel 5.4.2 an.

Neben den Emissionen aus der Nutzung von Energieträgern werden die bei der Förderung aus dem Erdöl freigesetzten CO_2-, Methan- und NMHC-Emissionen nach /GEMIS 1997/ berücksichtigt; die Benzolemissionen schätzen wir orientiert am Anteil der Benzol- an den NMHC-Emissionen in Raffinerien nach /GOETHEL 1993/ ab (0,39 %). Die Faktoren und ihre Ableitung sind im Anhang (**Tabelle 12-3**) dokumentiert.

Tabelle 8-3 Spezifischer Primärenergieeinsatz der Rohölbereitstellung in Deutschland 1996, differenziert nach Förderregionen und Prozeßschritten

Herkunft	Anteil	Förderung	Aufbereitung	Transport	Summe
		GJ/GJ Rohöl			
Westeuropa	40,2%	0,0067	0,0030	0,0030	0,013
OPEC	30,8%	0,0043	0,0032	0,023	0,031
GUS	26,2%	0,0075	0,066	0,015	0,089
Deutschland	2,9%	0,061	0,0030	0,0011	0,065
Gew. Mittelwert	**100 %**	**0,0077**	**0,020**	**0,012**	**0,040**
		Anteil am Bereitstellungsaufwand (Gew. Mittel)			
Westeuropa	40,2%	6,8%	3,0%	3,0%	12,8%
OPEC	30,8%	3,4%	2,5%	18,1%	24,0%
GUS	26,2%	4,9%	43,8%	9,8%	58,5%
Deutschland	2,9%	4,5%	0,2%	0,1%	4,8%
Gew. Mittelwert	**100 %**	**19,5%**	**49,5%**	**31,0%**	**100,0%**

Die Anteile der Herkunft sind auf 100 % normiert.
Quellen: /GEMIS 1997/, /MWV 1997/, eigene Berechnungen

Die Daten zu Energieeinsatz und Emissionen der Bereitstellung von Erdöl in Deutschland sind in **Tabelle 8-4** zusammengefaßt. Die Emissionen nicht global wirksamer Schadstoffe sind als Summe über die Ortsklassen ausgewiesen.

Die Anteile der Ortsklasse 2 sind in **Tabelle 8-5** als Prozentwerte ausgewiesen. Die Anteile der Ortsklasse 3 ergeben sich als Differenz zu 100 %, da in der Ortsklasse 1 (hohe Bevölkerungsdichte, Innenstadt) keine Emissionen anfallen.

8.1.2 Raffinerieprozeß

Grundlagen

Der größte Teil des Energieaufwandes zur Bereitstellung von Erdölprodukten fällt in den Raffinerien an. Neben Rohöl, das den Hauptteil des sogenannten Produkten- oder Umwandlungseinsatzes in Raffinerien stellt, werden dabei eine Reihe in Raffinerien selbst erzeugter, grundsätzlich absatzfähiger Endprodukte zu anderen Produkten umgesetzt oder gemischt. Der Energieeigenverbrauch wird im wesentlichen durch Raffinerieprodukte wie Schweröl und Raffineriegas sowie in Raffineriekraftwerken und öffentlichen Kraftwerken erzeugten Strom gedeckt.

Rohöl selbst und die meisten Erdölprodukte sind Mischungen einer Vielzahl von Kohlenwasserstoffen. Im einfachsten Fall besteht die Produktion aus einer Trennung des Rohöls in verschiedene Fraktionen durch Destillation. Dabei können die einzelnen Fraktionen nicht unabhängig voneinander erhalten werden (Kuppelproduktion): Um eine „mittlere" Fraktion zu erhalten muß eine „leichte" entfernt und eine zurückbleibende „schwere" (Sumpf) mit erhitzt werden. In einfachen Raffinerien bestimmt die Zusammensetzung des Rohöls weitgehend die Anteile der Fraktionen an der Gesamtproduktion. Die Nachfrage nach den einzelnen Fraktionen ist allerdings unterschiedlich groß und entspricht meist nicht den Vorgaben durch die Rohölzusammensetzung. In komplexen Raffinerien werden daher weniger nachgefragte Fraktionen entsprechend umgewandelt (Cracken, Reforming, Isomerisierung usw.). Die meisten dieser Reaktionen sind relativ energieaufwendig; die Höhe des Energieeinsatzes in einer Raffinerie hängt daher stark von der Produktpalette ab. Während einfache Raffinerien einen Energiebedarf von 2 bis 4 % des Inputs aufweisen, steigt der Energiebedarf bei komplexen Raffinerien bis auf 6 bis 10 % /WEC 1988/, /SHELL 1991/, /DGMK 1992/.

Tabelle 8-4 Spezifischer Primärenergieeinsatz und Emissionsfaktoren der Bereitstellung von Erdöl frei Raffinerie in Deutschland 1996

Herkunft		**Nordsee**	**OPEC**	**GUS**	**Deutschland**	**Mittel**
Primärenergieeinsatz						
Erdöl	GJ/GJ	1,003	1,019	1,072	1,054	1,027
Erdgas	GJ/GJ	0,010	0,00018	0,016	0,0011	0,0081
Steinkohle	GJ/GJ	0,00001	0,00005	0,00020	0,0028	0,00015
Braunkohle	GJ/GJ	0,00001	0,00007	0,00024	0,0033	0,00018
Uran	GJ/GJ	0,00001	0,00002	0,00009	0,0039	0,00015
Summe Erschöpfl. ET	*GJ/GJ*	*1,013*	*1,019*	*1,088*	*1,065*	*1,036*
Wasser	GJ/GJ	0,00000	0,00000	0,00001	0,00015	0,00001
Summe	**GJ/GJ**	**1,013**	**1,019**	**1,088**	**1,066**	**1,036**
Emissionen						
		Global	**Global**	**Global**	**Global**	**Global**
CO_2	g/GJ	1.026	2.214	8.921	5.187	3.576
CH_4	g/GJ	2,29	5,48	28,8	4,65	10,3
N_2O	g/GJ	0,030	0,086	0,23	0,14	0,10
CO_2-Äquivalente	*g/GJ*	*1.083*	*2.356*	*9.596*	*5.327*	*3.823*
		OK 2+3	**OK 2+3**	**OK 2+3**	**OK 2+3**	**OK 2+3**
SO_2	g/GJ	1,44	24,6	57,3	29,2	24,0
CO	g/GJ	0,94	2,20	8,73	2,54	3,41
NO_X	g/GJ	3,19	13,2	21,5	7,26	11,2
NMHC	g/GJ	1,33	4,11	19,9	2,88	7,07
Partikel	g/GJ	0,0020	1,25	0,83	0,042	0,60
Staub	g/GJ	0,075	0,17	2,81	0,68	0,84
HCl	g/GJ	0,0041	0,029	0,093	0,11	0,038
NH_3	g/GJ	0,00001	0,0070	0,0033	0,00023	0,0030
Formaldehyd	g/GJ	0,0095	0,061	0,12	0,028	0,056
Benzol	g/GJ	0,013	0,027	0,12	0,014	0,046
Benzo(a)pyren	ng/GJ	182	2.097	5.038	3.217	2.128
TCDD-TÄ	ng/GJ	0,89	0,45	2,99	1,64	1,32
SO_2-Äquivalente	*g/GJ*	*3,67*	*33,9*	*72,4*	*34,3*	*31,8*

OK: Ortsklasse; in OK 1 fallen keine Emissionen an.
Quellen: /AGE 1998/, /ECOINVENT 1996/, /GEMIS 1997/, /GOETHEL 1993/, /IFEU 1998b/, /JESS & HEDDEN 1994/, /MWV 1997/, /UBA 1995c/, /UBA 1998/, eigene Berechnungen

Tabelle 8-5 Anteile der Emissionen in der Ortsklasse 2 an den Gesamtemissionen der Bereitstellung von Erdöl frei Raffinerie in Deutschland 1996

Herkunft	Nordsee	OPEC	GUS	Deutschland	Mittel
SO_2	29,3%	36,6%	99,9%	98,9%	78,2%
CO	25,9%	67,9%	100,0%	98,8%	85,4%
NO_X	25,8%	51,0%	99,9%	97,3%	73,6%
NMHC	27,2%	95,3%	100,0%	99,2%	93,6%
Partikel	63,9%	37,8%	99,7%	60,6%	60,2%
Staub	4,0%	99,8%	100,0%	99,8%	96,5%
HCl	29,1%	40,4%	99,9%	99,7%	82,7%
NH_3	68,2%	44,5%	99,6%	67,3%	60,2%
Formaldehyd	26,6%	71,2%	99,9%	98,1%	85,2%
Benzol	26,2%	86,2%	100,0%	98,0%	89,0%
Benzo(a)pyren	4,8%	44,8%	99,9%	99,2%	79,9%
TCDD-TÄ	0,7%	30,8%	99,9%	98,6%	65,8%
SO_2-Äquivalente	*27,2%*	*40,5%*	*99,9%*	*98,7%*	*77,0%*

Die Anteile der Ortsklasse 3 ergeben sich als Differenz zu 100 %. In der Ortsklasse 1 (hohe Bevölkerungsdichte, Innenstadt) fallen keine Emissionen an.
Quellen: /AGE 1998/, /ECOINVENT 1996/, /GEMIS 1997/, /GOETHEL 1993/, /IFEU 1998b/, /JESS & HEDDEN 1994/, /MWV 1997/, /UBA 1995c/, /UBA 1998/, eigene Berechnungen

Im Mittel lag nach /GEMIS 1997/ der Eigenbedarf in Westeuropa in den frühen 90er Jahren bei 5,5 % Prozeßwärme und 0,5 % Strom bezogen auf den Energieinhalt der Produkte.

Diese Zusammenhänge lassen sich besonders deutlich am Beispiel von Kraftstoffen illustrieren: Die Deckung der Nachfrage nach Ottokraftstoff macht in großem Umfang die Umwandlung anderer Fraktionen notwendig. Dieselkraftstoff läßt sich dagegen zu größeren Teilen allein durch Destillation gewinnen. Dabei erfordert die Produktion von Dieselkraftstoff (Mitteldestillat) aber die Abtrennung der leichteren, vor allem in Ottokraftstoff enthaltenen Fraktionen des Rohöls. In der Realität ist tatsächlich vor allem die Nachfrage nach Ottokraftstoff und nach Rohbenzin (Naphtha) für die chemische Industrie Ursache der hohen Komplexität moderner Raffinerien. Daneben spielt aber auch der generelle Trend zu leichteren Produkten eine Rolle. Bei abnehmender Nachfrage nach Schweröl und steigender nach leichtem Heizöl werden auch Mitteldestillate (Dieselkraftstoff, Kerosin, leichtes Heizöl) verstärkt durch Cracken hergestellt.

Der mittlere Energieaufwand zur Produktion von Erdölprodukten läßt sich durch Division des Saldos der Energiebilanz einer Raffinerie oder der Raffinerien eines Landes durch den Produkt-Ausstoß bestimmen. Aufgrund der relativ umfassenden Statistikführung im Bereich der Energiewirtschaft kann diese Rechnung für die Bundesrepublik in jährlicher Folge durchgeführt werden. Der mittlere Energieaufwand ist jedoch nur dann, wenn die Produktion in einfachen Raffinerien erfolgt, eine plausible Kenngröße. Im Falle komplexer Raffinerien führt diese Größe zu einer unangemessenen Belastung auch „einfach" in ausreichender Menge erhältlicher Produkte (siehe oben). Wie fast stets im Zusammenhang mit Kuppelproduktionen besteht damit auch hier ein Zuordnungsproblem bezüglich des Energieaufwandes und der damit verbundenen Emissionen. Allerdings kann hier, anders als z. B. bei der NaCl-Elektrolyse oder Buntmetallverhüttung mit Schwefelsäuregewinnung, der Gesamtprozeß durch entsprechenden Energieaufwand auf eine ökonomisch optimale Produktverteilung eingestellt werden.

Eine Lösung dieses Zuordnungsproblems findet sich in /JESS & HEDDEN 1994/. Für die „Modell-Raffinerie Deutschland" im Bezugsjahr 1992 wird dort die Ableitung spezifischer Energieaufwendungen für verschiedene Erdölprodukte aus Umwandlungs- und spezifischem Prozeßenergieeinsatz in den einzelnen Raffinerieanlagen dargestellt. Die Modell-Raffinerie ist dabei durch die gesamte bundesdeutsche Raffinerieproduktion definiert. Die Ergebnisdaten finden sich im wesentlichen in /FFE & IFE 1995/ (siehe auch /HEDDEN & JESS 1992/).

Bilanzierung

Der spezifische Energieaufwand und die Emissionen der Produktion von Mineralölprodukten in einem bestimmten Bezugsjahr werden in vier Schritten berechnet:

- Aus dem Eigenverbrauch der Raffinerien differenziert nach verschiedenen Energieträgern auf Erdölbasis, anderen fossilen Energieträgern, Fernwärme und Strom gemäß der amtlichen Energiestatistik oder einer strukturgleichen Fortschreibung und den entsprechenden Emissionsfaktoren wird die Eigenverbrauchs-Energie- und Emissionsbilanz der Raffinerien erstellt. Diese Bilanz wird zunächst auf der Endenergieebene erstellt und anschließend mit den Bereitstellungsaufwendungen der eingesetzten Energieträger zu einer Bilanz der Primärenergieträger erweitert.
- Aus dem Umwandlungsausstoß, Umwandlungs(wieder)einsatz und dem Eigenverbrauch von Sekundärenergieträgern auf Erdölbasis wird der Netto-Umwandlungsausstoß berechnet. Um den unterschiedlichen spezifischen Energieaufwand für die Produktion der verschiedenen Produkte zu berücksichtigen, wird mit Faktoren, die aus /JESS1994/ abgeleitet werden, ein „gewichteter" Netto-Ausstoß bestimmt.
- Die spezifischen Energieaufwendungen und Emissionen der Produktion von Mineralölprodukten werden aus der Energie- und Emissionsbilanz berechnet durch Verteilung der Bilanzwerte gemäß den Anteilen der einzelnen Produkte am gewichteten Netto-Ausstoß und Division durch die Absolutwerte der *un*gewichteten Netto-Ausstöße der einzelnen Produkte.
- Die spezifischen ausstoßbezogenen Energieaufwendungen und Emissionen der Bereitstellung von Rohöl werden aus der Energie- und Emissionsbilanz der Rohölbereitstellung durch Division durch den gesamten *un*gewichteten Netto-Ausstoß aller Produkte berechnet. Die so erhaltenen Werte werden zu den entsprechenden Daten der Rohölverarbeitung (vorhergehender Spiegelstrich) addiert.

Die offizielle Energiebilanz für 1996 liegt noch nicht vor; wir setzen hier die Bilanz an, die sich aus der Fortschreibung der aktuellsten Bilanz /AGE 1998/ (Bezug: 1994) mit Daten für 1994 und 1996 nach /MWV 1997/ ergibt. Struktur und Umfang der Angaben nach /MWV 1997/ erfordern einige Zusatzannahmen, die wichtigste: Die Anteile der einzelnen Energieträger – raffinerieeigene Brennstoffe, importierte Brennstoffe und Strom – am gesamten Eigenverbrauch bleiben zwischen 1994 und 1996 konstant. Gemäß /HEDDEN & JESS 1992/ wird für den Stromverbrauch ein Bezug von 62 % aus dem öffentlichen Netz und 38 % Eigenerzeugung unterstellt (weitere Annahmen: Stromerzeugung mit Gegendruckturbinen und Dampfbereitstellung, 30 % elektrischer Wirkungsgrad; Brennstoffe: Schweröl, Petrolkoks, Kokereigas, Erdgas). Für die Bereitstellung von Fernwärme setzen wir den Wirkungsgrad gleich 80 % mit Erdgas als Brennstoff.

Tabelle 8-6 Umwandlungseinsatz und -ausstoß und Brennstoffeinsatz deutscher Raffinerien 1996 (berechnet)

	Umwandlungs- Einsatz	**Umwandlungs- Ausstoß**	**Brennst.einsatz Prozeß-wärme**	**Brennst.einsatz Raffin-KW**	**Netto-Ausstoß**		**Gew. Faktor**	**Gew. Netto-Ausstoß**
	TJ	TJ	TJ	TJ	TJ	Anteil	GJ/GJ	Anteil
Rohöl	4.448.020	0	0	0	0	k. A.	k. A.	k. A.
Mineralölprodukte								
Motorenbenzin	151.567	1.136.734	0	0	985.167	23,6%	0,105	36,3%
Rohbenzin	45.909	412.104	86	0	366.109	8,8%	0,032	4,1%
Flugbenzin	0	0	0	0	0	0,0%	0,105	0,0%
Kerosin	922	144.180	0	0	143.259	3,4%	0,060	3,0%
Diesel	669	930.699	42	0	929.987	22,3%	0,060	19,4%
Heizöl leicht	48.251	1.095.580	752	0	1.046.577	25,1%	0,060	21,9%
Heizöl schwer	160.246	547.570	49.067	14.856	323.401	7,7%	0,047	5,3%
Petrolkoks	0	56.991	22.587	900	33.503	0,8%	0,089	1,0%
Andere	62.239	293.256	13.269	0	217.749	5,2%	0,070	5,3%
Flüssiggas	10.541	138.307	7.115	0	120.651	2,9%	0,081	3,4%
Raffineriegas	10.866	173.140	142.588	8.553	11.133	0,3%	0,074	0,3%
Summe	*491.210*	*4.928.561*	*235.506*	*24.310*	*4.177.536*	*100,0%*	*0,068*	*100,0%*
Andere								
Sonstige	0	k. A.	67	0	k. A.	k. A.	k. A.	k. A.
Kokereigas	0	k. A.	2.926	1.801	k. A.	k. A.	k. A.	k. A.
Erdgas	0	k. A.	8.692	2.701	k. A.	k. A.	k. A.	k. A.
Summe	**4.939.230**	**4.928.561**	**247.191**	**28.811**	**4.177.536**	**100,0%**	**0,068**	**100,0%**

Erläuterungen: siehe Text
Quellen: /AGE 1998/, /JESS & HEDDEN 1994/, /MWV 1997/, eigene Berechnungen

Tabelle 8-6 faßt den aus /AGE 1998/ und /MWV 1997/ abgeleiteten Umwandlungseinsatz und -ausstoß und Brennstoffeinsatz in deutschen Raffinerien 1996 (ohne Strom und Fernwärme) zusammen. Neben den Kategorien nach /AGE 1998/ ist der Netto-Ausstoß ausgewiesen und – als besonders wichtige Größe – der mit den Faktoren zum Eigenverbrauch nach /JESS & HEDDEN 1994/ gewichtete Netto-Ausstoß. **Tabelle 8-7** faßt den Eigenverbrauch der Raffinerien von End- und Primärenergie zusammen.

Emissionsfaktoren

Emissionsfaktoren für Raffinerien bezogen auf den eingesetzten Brennstoff werden aus verschiedenen Quellen übernommen bzw. abgeleitet, da kein konsistenter, alle hier erfaßten Schadstoffe umfassender Faktorensatz vorliegt. Eine detaillierte Dokumentation der Faktoren und ihrer Ableitung findet sich Anhang (**Tabelle 12-4**). Die Quellen der Faktoren lassen sich in zwei Gruppen unterscheiden:

- Für die CO_2-, Methan-, N_2O-, SO_2-, NO_X-, CO-, NMHC- und Staubemissionen aus Kesselfeuerungen werden die Faktoren nach /UBA 1998/ mit dem Bezug Westdeutschland 1994 angesetzt.

- Für HCl, Benzol, Formaldehyd, Benzo(a)pyren und TCDD-Toxizitätsäquivalente werden Emissionsfaktoren nach /GEMIS 1997/, /UBA 1995c/, /ECOINVENT 1996/ und /IFEU 1998b/ angesetzt.

Neben den Emissionen aus Feuerungsanlagen werden zwei prozeßspezifische Emissionen erfaßt, die nicht aus der Energieumwandlung stammen: Zum einen die Verdunstungsemissionen aus diffusen Quellen der Raffinerien und zum anderen die SO_2-Emissionen aus Entschwefelungsanlagen. Diese Emissionen werden über den ungewichteten Netto-Ausstoß den einzelnen Produkten zugeordnet. Die Faktoren werden aus Daten nach /UBA 1998/ abgeleitet (1,8 g SO_2/GJ Produkt, 0,75 g Methan/GJ Produkt, 6,74 g NMHC/GJ Produkt); die Benzolverdunstung schätzen wir orientiert am Anteil der Benzol- an den NMHC-Emissionen nach /GOETHEL 1993/ auf 0,39 % ab. Die SO_2-Emissionen werden ohne Belastung der Schwefel-Folgeprodukte vollständig den Mineralölprodukten als den eigentlich gewünschten Produkten der Entschwefelung zugeschlagen.

Tabelle 8-7 Eigenverbrauch von End- und Primärenergie deutscher Raffinerien 1996 (berechnet)

	Endenergie			**Primärenergie**		
	Raffinerie-produkte	**Import**	**Summe**	**Raffinerie-produkte**	**Import**	**Summe**
	TJ	TJ	TJ	TJ	TJ	TJ
Prozeßwärme						
Raffinerieprodukte	235.506	0	235.506	263.055	0	263.055
Sonstige	0	67	67	0	70	70
Kokereigas	0	2.926	2.926	0	3.088	3.088
Erdgas	0	8.692	8.692		9.260	9.260
Summe	*235.506*	*11.685*	*247.191*	*263.055*	*3.158*	*266.213*
Fernwärme	0	3.424	3.424	0	4.559	4.559
Strom						
RaffinerieKW	8.593	0	8.593	27.153	4.778	31.932
EVU-Strom	0	14.021	14.021	0	43.753	43.753
Summe	*8.593*	*14.021*	*22.614*	*27.153*	*48.531*	*75.685*
Summe	**244.099**	**29.129**	**273.228**	**290.208**	**56.249**	**346.457**

Erläuterungen: siehe Text
Quellen: /AGE 1998/, /JESS & HEDDEN 1994/, /MWV 1997/, eigene Berechnungen

8.1.3 Distribution

Die Distribution von Mineralölprodukten hat nur einen geringen Einfluß auf die Gesamtbilanz. Daher wird vereinfachend unterstellt, daß sie für alle Produkte gleich jeweils über 50 km per Bahn, LKW und Binnenschiff erfolgt. Energieeinsatz und Emissionen werden mit den spezifischen Daten nach Kapitel 5 berechnet.

8.1.4 Zusammenführung

Tabelle 8-8 faßt den Primärenergieeinsatz und die Emissionen der Bereitstellung von Dieselkraftstoff in Deutschland im Jahr 1996 differenziert nach Prozeßschritten bzw. Sektoren zusammen. Der primärenergetische Aufwand der Rohölbereitstellung liegt in einer ähnlichen Größenordnung wie der Energieeinsatz in der Raffinerie. Im Vergleich zum Einsatz fossiler Brennstoffe ist der Anteil von EVU-Strom an den gesamten Bereitstellungsaufwendungen relativ gering. Noch niedriger sind die Anteile für die Bereitstellung von Kohle und Erdgas sowie die Aufwendungen für die Verteilung der Produkte.

Tabelle 8-8 Primärenergieeinsatz und Emissionen der Bereitstellung von Dieselkraftstoff in Deutschland im Jahr 1996 differenziert nach Prozeßschritten bzw. Sektoren

	Summe		**davon**				
			Bereitstellung Rohöl	**Bereitstellung Kohle/Gas**	**Raffinerie ohne EVU**	**EVU inkl. Vorkette**	**Distribution**
Primärenergieeinsatz							
Erdöl	1,088	GJ/GJ	94,8%	0,0%	5,0%	0,0%	0,2%
Erdgas	0,013	GJ/GJ	67,9%	1,7%	26,0%	3,9%	0,5%
Steinkohle	0,0038	GJ/GJ	4,2%	1,1%	26,0%	62,5%	6,2%
Braunkohle	0,0030	GJ/GJ	6,4%	0,0%	0,0%	91,1%	2,5%
Uran	0,0036	GJ/GJ	4,3%	0,0%	0,0%	90,5%	5,2%
Σ Erschöpfl. ET	*1,111*	*GJ/GJ*	*93,7%*	*0,0%*	*5,3%*	*0,8%*	*0,2%*
Wasser	0,00013	GJ/GJ	6,2%	0,1%	0,0%	77,5%	16,3%
Summe	**1,111**	**GJ/GJ**	**93,7%**	**0,0%**	**5,3%**	**0,8%**	**0,2%**
Emissionen							
	Global		**Global**	**Global**	**Global**	**Global**	**Global**
CO_2	8.510	g/GJ	44,4%	0,2%	46,7%	6,5%	2,2%
CH_4	13,9	g/GJ	77,9%	6,3%	6,2%	8,6%	1,0%
N_2O	0,28	g/GJ	38,9%	0,3%	47,6%	7,3%	5,9%
CO_2-Äquivalente	*8.888*	*g/GJ*	*45,4%*	*0,4%*	*45,4%*	*6,5%*	*2,2%*
	OK 2+3		**OK 2+3**	**OK 2+3**	**OK 2+3**	**OK 2+3**	**OK 2+3**
SO_2	38,7	g/GJ	65,5%	0,1%	30,5%	3,5%	0,4%
CO	4,66	g/GJ	77,4%	0,7%	11,5%	2,8%	7,6%
NO_X	18,0	g/GJ	65,6%	0,5%	20,2%	3,0%	10,8%
NMHC	14,5	g/GJ	51,4%	0,0%	47,2%	0,1%	1,2%
Partikel	0,71	g/GJ	89,3%	0,2%	0,0%	0,7%	9,8%
Staub	1,14	g/GJ	77,5%	0,1%	19,3%	2,8%	0,3%
HCl	0,105	g/GJ	38,5%	0,3%	28,8%	30,5%	1,9%
NH_3	0,004	g/GJ	77,6%	0,1%	0,0%	0,5%	21,8%
Formaldehyd	0,087	g/GJ	67,8%	0,5%	16,3%	0,6%	14,7%
Benzol	0,084	g/GJ	57,7%	0,4%	37,8%	0,4%	3,7%
Benzo(a)pyren	3.917	ng/GJ	57,4%	0,1%	33,2%	0,3%	9,0%
TCDD-TÄ	3,13	ng/GJ	44,7%	0,5%	52,9%	1,5%	0,4%
SO_2-Äquivalente	*51,4*	*g/GJ*	*65,5%*	*0,2%*	*28,0%*	*3,4%*	*3,0%*

OK: Ortsklasse; in OK 1 fallen keine Emissionen an.
Quellen: /AGE 1998/, /ECOINVENT 1996/, /GEMIS 1997/, /GOETHEL 1993/, /IFEU 1998b/, /JESS & HEDDEN 1994/, /MWV 1997/, /UBA 1995c/, /UBA 1998/, eigene Berechnungen

Tabelle 8-9 faßt den Primärenergieeinsatz und die Emissionen der Bereitstellung von Dieselkraftstoff, Kerosin und Schweröl in Deutschland im Jahr 1996 zusammen. Im Anhang (**Tabelle 12-1**) finden sich die entsprechenden Daten mit Bezug auf das Jahr 2000.

Tabelle 8-9 Primärenergieeinsatz und Emissionen der Bereitstellung von Dieselkraftstoff, Kerosin und Schweröl in Deutschland im Jahr 1996

		Diesel/Kerosin		**Schweröl**	
Primärenergieeinsatz					
Erdöl	GJ/GJ	1,088		1,076	
Erdgas	GJ/GJ	0,013		0,012	
Steinkohle	GJ/GJ	0,0038		0,0031	
Braunkohle	GJ/GJ	0,0030		0,0024	
Uran	GJ/GJ	0,0036		0,0029	
Summe Erschöpfl. ET	*GJ/GJ*	*1,111*		*1,096*	
Wasser	GJ/GJ	0,00013		0,00011	
Summe	**GJ/GJ**	**1,111**		**1,096**	
Emissionen					
		Global		**Global**	
CO_2	g/GJ	8.510		7.486	
CH_4	g/GJ	13,9		13,3	
N_2O	g/GJ	0,28		0,24	
CO_2-Äquivalente	*g/GJ*	*8.888*		*7.841*	
		OK 2+3	**OK 2**	**OK 2+3**	**OK 2**
SO_2	g/GJ	38,7	85,5%	35,9	84,6%
CO	g/GJ	4,66	88,5%	4,49	88,2%
NO_X	g/GJ	18,0	82,3%	17,1	81,6%
NMHC	g/GJ	14,5	96,7%	14,4	96,7%
Partikel	g/GJ	0,71	63,7%	0,71	64,0%
Staub	g/GJ	1,14	97,3%	1,08	97,2%
HCl	g/GJ	0,10	93,3%	0,091	92,3%
NH_3	g/GJ	0,0041	68,7%	0,0041	69,2%
Formaldehyd	g/GJ	0,087	89,8%	0,084	89,5%
Benzol	g/GJ	0,084	93,6%	0,082	93,5%
Benzo(a)pyren	ng/GJ	3.917	88,3%	3.625	87,5%
TCDD-TÄ	ng/GJ	3,13	84,6%	2,74	82,6%
SO_2-Äquivalente	*g/GJ*	*51,4*	*84,8%*	*48,0*	*83,9%*

OK: Ortsklasse; in OK 1 fallen keine Emissionen an.
Quellen: /AGE 1998/, /ECOINVENT 1996/, /GEMIS 1997/, /GOETHEL 1993/, /IFEU 1998b/, /JESS & HEDDEN 1994/, /MWV 1997/, /UBA 1995c/, /UBA 1998/, eigene Berechnungen

8.2 Energieträger auf pflanzlicher Basis: Rapsöl und RME

Pflanzenöle bzw. ihre Umesterungsprodukte können unter bestimmten Voraussetzungen in Dieselmotoren von Nutzfahrzeugen, z. B. von LKW oder Landmaschinen, eingesetzt werden. Für deutsche und teilweise auch europäische Verhältnisse ist dabei Raps – zumindest hinsichtlich seines Potentials – die wichtigste Ölsaat, während in den USA etwa Soja oder in Malaysia Palmöl größere Bedeutung haben. Aus Rapssaat lassen sich Rapsöl und durch Umesterung Rapsölmethylester (RME) gewinnen. Beide Kraftstoffe können entweder rein oder mit Dieselkraftstoff gemischt verwendet werden. Die Eigenschaften von RME ähneln denen von Dieselkraftstoff so sehr (**Tabelle 8-10**), daß fast alle konventionellen Dieselmotoren ohne besondere Umrüstung für die Verbrennung von RME geeignet sind; lediglich Komponenten des kraftstofführenden Systems müssen gegebenenfalls durch spezielle RME-beständige Teile ersetzt werden. Rapsöl mit einer gegenüber Dieselkraftstoff zehnmal höheren Viskosität läßt sich – nach heutigem Kenntnisstand – auf Dauer nur in großvolumigen Kammermotoren oder in speziell umgerüsteten Motoren einsetzen /KRAHL 1998/. Da der Einsatz dieser Motoren in LKW gegenwärtig nicht üblich und auch zukünftig nicht zu erwarten ist, beschränkt sich das Einsatzfeld von Rapsöl auf Landmaschinen. (Wegen dieser technischen Einschränkungen werden hier spezifische Verbräuche und Emissionsfaktoren für den RME-Einsatz in LKW *und* Landmaschinen und den Rapsöleinsatz in Landmaschinen diskutiert; Kapitel 5.1.5 und 6.3.)

Die Lebenswege der Bereitstellung von Rapsöl bzw. RME sind in **Abb. 8-1** schematisch dargestellt. Neben den Prozessen der „Rapslinien“ sind die der Bereitstellung jener Produkte, die durch Kuppelprodukte der Rapslinien substituiert werden, abgebildet (Sojaschrot, synthetisches Glyzerin) sowie das landwirtschaftliche Referenzsystem. Letzteres stellt die Nutzung einer landwirtschaftlichen Fläche in dem Fall dar, daß kein Raps angebaut wird.

Für die Bereitstellung von Rapsöl und RME wird neben dem Einsatz energetischer Ressourcen und den damit verbundenen Emissionen luftgetragener Schadstoffe auch der Verbrauch mineralischer Ressourcen bilanziert. Dies ist sinnvoll, da – anders als bei fossilen Energieträgern – entlang der Lebenswege dieser Kraftstoffe relativ große Mengen verschiedener mineralischer Ressourcen verbraucht werden. Ebenfalls im Unterschied zu den hier betrachteten fossilen Energieträgern fallen bei der Rapsöl- und RME-Bereitstellung Kuppelprodukte an, deren Nutzung zu Gutschriften führt (siehe oben), die in den Bilanzen zu berücksichtigen sind.

Im folgenden wird zunächst die landwirtschaftliche Produktion der Rapssaat beschrieben. Die weitere Bilanzierung erfolgt für Rapsöl und RME getrennt, da sich die Weiterverarbeitung der Rapskörner für die beiden Kraftstoffe deutlich unterscheidet:

- **Rapsöl:** Vor dem Hintergrund, daß der Rapsöleinsatz lediglich für Landmaschinen eine realistische Option ist (siehe oben), unterstellen wir eine dezentrale, kleintechnische Ölgewinnung. Die Anlagen können auf Höfen oder bei Genossenschaften stehen, so daß eine Distribution des Treibstoffes entfällt. Als Kuppelprodukt fällt Rapskuchen an, der Sojaschrot als Futtermittel substituieren kann.

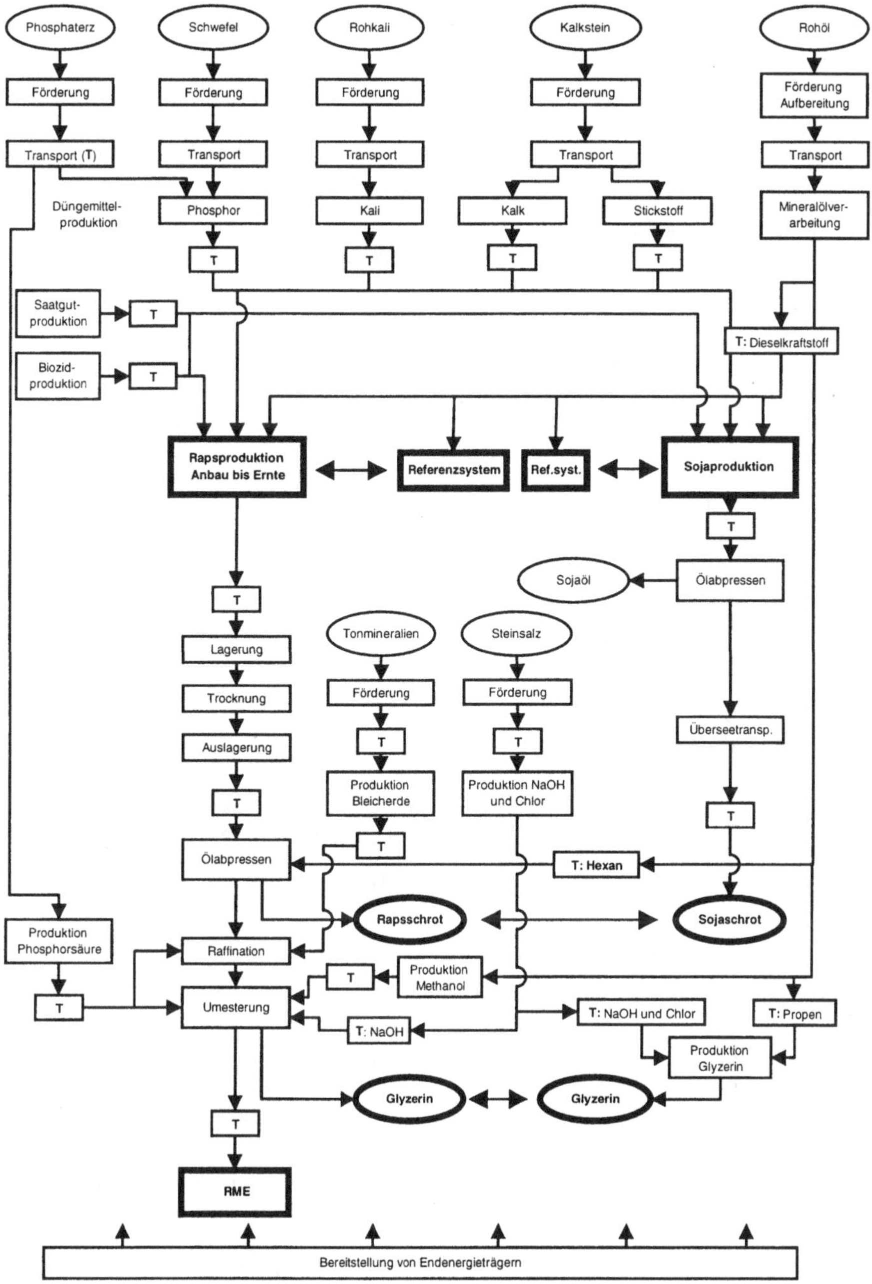

Abb. 8-1 Bereitstellung von RME, Rapsöl („Ölabpressen") und von Produkten, die durch Kuppelprodukte der RME-Produktion substituiert werden (T: Transport) /IFEU 1997a/

- **RME:** Für die komplexere RME-Produktion nehmen wir die zentrale Verarbeitung des Rapskorns in Ölmühlen an, in denen die Extraktion, Raffination und Umesterung im großtechnischen Maßstab durchgeführt wird. Die Anlagen haben im Vergleich zu kleineren eine höhere Ölausbeute. Neben dem Rapsextraktionsschrot, das wie Rapskuchen als Futtermittel verwendet werden kann, fällt als weiteres Kuppelprodukt Glyzerin aus der Umesterung an. Ferner sind bei der RME-Bereitstellung längere Transporte zur und von der Ölmühle zu berücksichtigen.

Die durch den Rapsanbau vermiedene Referenznutzung der Anbaufläche (hier: aktiv begrünte Brache) wird im Zusammenhang mit der landwirtschaftlichen Rapssaatproduktion bilanziert. Die Bereitstellung des durch Rapskuchen und -extraktionsschrot (Rapsöl bzw. RME) in ähnlichem – aber nicht gleichem Umfang – substituierbaren Sojaschrots wird im Zusammenhang mit der Rapsölproduktion behandelt.

Tabelle 8-10 Ausgewählte Normanforderungen an Dieselkraftstoff und Kennwerte von RME und Rapsöl

Kennwert	Einheit	Diesel[a]	RME[e]	Rapsöl[d]
Dichte (15 °C)	g/ml	0,815 - 0,855	0,875 - 0,900	0,914 - 0,922
kin. Viskosität (20 °C)	mm^2/s	2 - 8	3,5 - 5,0[f]	78,7
Flammpunkt	°C	> 55	> 110	324
Filtriergrenze	°C	0[b] / -12[c]	0[b] / -20[c]	+5
Cetanzahl	-	> 45	> 49	37-38
Koksrückstand	M%	< 0,1	< 0,05	0,20 - 0,30
Schwefelgehalt	M%	< 0,05	< 0,01	0,009
Heizwert[d]	MJ/kg	42,96	37,2	37,2
angenäherte Summenformel[d]	-	$C_{15}H_{32}$	$C_{19}H_{35}O_2$	$C_{57}H_{102}O_6$

a: nach /DIN 1986/; b: Sommer; c: Winter; d: Durchschnittswerte (keine Norm); e: nach /DIN 1997/; f: bei 40 °C
Quellen: /DIN 1997/, /HARTMANN 1995/, /TÜVBAYERN 1996/

8.2.1 Produktion von Rapssaat

Die Rapskornproduktion erfolgt für Rapsöl und RME in gleicher Weise und wird daher hier für beide Kraftstoffe gemeinsam behandelt. Allerdings resultiert nur aus dem in diesem Kapitel gewählten Bezug auf die Anbaufläche *ein* Datensatz für beide Kraftstoffe. Bei Bezug auf den Energiegehalt der Endenergieträger ist zu berücksichtigen, daß die Ölausbeuten für Rapsöl (dezentrale Gewinnung) und RME (zentrale Gewinnung) unterschiedlich angesetzt werden.

Die durch den Rapsanbau vermiedenen Aufwendungen der Referenznutzung der Anbaufläche „aktiv begrünte Brache" bzw. die Rahmenannahmen der damit verbundenen Gutschriften werden in Kapitel 8.2.1.2 dokumentiert.

8.2.1.1 Landwirtschaftliche Produktion von Rapssaat

Betrachtet wird der konventionelle Anbau von Winterraps nach guter fachlicher Praxis in Deutschland. Im konventionellen Landbau werden Mineraldünger und synthetische Pflanzenschutzmittel eingesetzt. Angenommen wird eine Schlaggröße zwischen 20 und 60 ha bei einem durchschnittlichen Ertrag von 3,1 t Rapskorn (bei 13 % Erntefeuchte) pro ha und Getreide als Vorfrucht.

Die maschinelle Feldarbeit beim Rapsanbau wurde bereits in Kapitel 6.5.2 detailliert behandelt; wir beschränken und daher hier auf die stichwortartige Auflistung der zu erfassenden Arbeitsgänge:

- Einarbeitung der Stoppeln der Vorfrucht in zwei Arbeitsgängen mit einer Scheibenegge
- Umbrechen mit einem Aufsattelpflug
- Aussaat in einem Arbeitsgang mit einer Bestellkombination
- Düngemittelausbringung in zwei Arbeitsgängen mit einem Großraumdüngerstreuer
- Pflanzenschutzmittelausbringung in drei Arbeitsgängen mit einer Anhängespritze
- Mahd im Direktdrusch
- Einarbeitung der Rapsstoppeln in zwei Arbeitsgängen mit einer Scheibenegge

Die hier angesetzten flächenbezogenen Daten zum Einsatz der Betriebsmittel Saatgut, Dünge- und Pflanzenschutzmittel sind in **Tabelle 8-11** zusammengefaßt /IFEU 1997a/. Die Daten für den konventionellen Anbau von Soja, die für die Gutschriften relevant sind (Kapitel 8.2.2.2), sind bereits hier zum Vergleich mit aufgeführt. Im Anhang (**Tabelle 12-7**) sind die Aufwendungen und Emissionen für die Bereitstellung dieser Betriebsmittel dokumentiert.

Tabelle 8-11 Betriebsmittel beim Anbau von Winterraps und Sojabohnen

Betriebsmittel	**Raps** kg/(ha*a)	**Soja** kg/(ha*a)
Saatgut	3	60
Düngemittel		
N-Dünger	145,6	5
P_2O_5-Dünger	54	10
K_2O-Dünger	30	20
CaO	19	-
Pflanzenschutzmittel (aktive Substanz)	1,23	1,25
Quelle: /IFEU 1997a/		

Neben den Emissionen aus der Bereitstellung und Ausbringung der Düngemittel fallen N_2O- und NH_3-Emissionen aus Nitrifikations- und Denitrifikationsprozessen an, deren Höhe an die Höhe der Stickstoffdüngung gekoppelt ist. Allerdings ist dieser Zusammenhang bisher nur ungenau quantifizierbar. Neben den direkten Emissionen aus dem Boden entsteht N_2O auch indirekt: aus der Umwandlung von NO_X oder NH_3 in der Atmosphäre sowie durch Nitrifikations- und Denitrifikationsprozesse nach Auswaschung der Düngemittel in Gewässer. Für den Rapsanbau setzen wir die Werte der **Tabelle 8-12** an.

Tabelle 8-12 Emissionsfaktoren für anthropogen induzierte N_2O- und NH_3-Emissionen mikrobieller Herkunft

		Bandbreite	mittlerer Emissionsfaktor
direktes N_2O aus Boden (Düngemittel)	g N_2O-N / kg Dünger-N	2,5 - 22,5	12,5
indirektes N_2O aus NO_X bzw. NH_3	g N_2O-N / kg NH_3-N bzw. NO_X-N	2 - 20	10
indirektes N_2O aus Wasser ausgewaschen	g N_2O-N / kg N-ausgewaschen	0,6 - 40	7,5
direktes NH_3 aus Boden (Düngemittel)	g NH_3 / kg Dünger-N	7,2 - 72	40

Quellen: /IPCC 1995/, /IFEU 1997a/

8.2.1.2 Gutschrift: Referenznutzung der Anbaufläche

Als Referenznutzung wird eine aktiv begrünte Brache angenommen. Damit sind die Arbeitsgänge Bodenbearbeitung, Aussaat und Mahd verbunden (für Details siehe /KALTSCHMITT & REINHARDT 1997/). Ressourceneinsatz und Emissionen der Bereitstellung des Saatgutes (Welsches Weidelgras) wurden detailliert für die vorliegende Publikation berechnet (Anhang, **Tabelle 12-7**). Die Zeitanteile in den einzelnen Laststufen sind in **Tabelle 8-13** zusammengestellt. Im Anhang (**Tabelle 12-8**) sind die resultierenden Aufwendungen des Referenzlandbaus detailliert dokumentiert.

Tabelle 8-13 Zeitanteile und Kraftstoffeinsatz beim Maschineneinsatz der Referenznutzung

	Leistung kW	Schwer min/ha	Normal min/ha	Leicht min/ha	Straße min/ha	Leerlauf min/ha	Kraftstoff MJ DK/ha
Schlepper	90	0	0,015	0	0,011	0,0021	0,15
	140	22,1	21,0	19,6	2,20	6,61	691
Summe		22,1	21,0	19,6	2,21	6,61	691

Eigene Berechnungen

8.2.2 Rapsöl

Die Bereitstellung von Rapsöl wird hier unter der Annahme einer kleintechnischen, erzeugernahen Ölgewinnung behandelt. Gutschriften ergeben sich aus der Substitution von Sojaschrot als Futtermittel durch den stark proteinhaltigen Rapskuchen.

8.2.2.1 Dezentrale Ölgewinnung

Die Rapssaat mit einem Wassergehalt von 13 % wird nach der Einlagerung zunächst gereinigt, auf einen Wassergehalt von 8,3 % getrocknet und kühl gelagert. Anschließend wird aus der Saat mit einem durchschnittlichen Ölgehalt von 41 % im Kaltpreßverfahren Rapsöl gewonnen. Dabei wird ein mittlerer Entölungsgrad von 81 % erreicht. Als Kuppelprodukt fällt Rapskuchen an, der nicht weiter aufgearbeitet wird. Das Rapsöl wird durch Sedimentation und Filtration gereinigt und direkt „an der Ölpresse" an den Endverbraucher abgegeben. Die Daten zur Rapsölgewinnung sind in **Tabelle 8-14** zusammengefaßt.

Tabelle 8-14 Strom- und Heizöleinsatz zur Rapsölgewinnung aus Rapssaat

	Bezug	Heizöl kg	Strom kWh	Bemerkungen
Ein- und Auslagerung	t Korn (Erntegut)		3,7	13 % Erntefeuchte
Trocknung	kg Wasserentzug	0,10	0,10	8,3 % Lagerfeuchte
Kühlung	t Korn (Lagergut)		8,8	
Pressung	t Korn (Lagergut)		42,0	Ertrag: 332 kg Rohöl

Quelle: /KALTSCHMITT & REINHARDT 1997/

8.2.2.2 Gutschriften

In der Bilanz von Rapsöl sind zwei Gutschriften zu berücksichtigen: für die unterbliebene Referenznutzung, die bereits diskutiert wurde, und für die Substitution von Sojaschrot als Futtermittel durch das Kuppelprodukt Rapskuchen.

Die Bereitstellung von Sojaschrot umfaßt den landwirtschaftlichen Anbau der Bohnen, die Schrotproduktion mit Sojaöl als Kuppelprodukt und den transatlantischen Transport des Schrots. Als Herkunftsland unterstellen wir die USA. In **Tabelle 8-11** und **Tabelle 8-15** sind die Basisdaten zusammengestellt. Der Überseetransport des Sojaschrots (10.000 km) erfolgt per Massengutfrachter, der kontinentale Transport per Binnenschiff (500 km).

Die Allokation zwischen Sojaschrot und -öl erfolgt für die Aufwendungen der Lebenswegabschnitte Landwirtschaft und Ölgewinnung massenbezogen im Verhältnis 81,2 zu 18,8. Andere Allokationen wie über „Masse * Heizwert" oder „Masse * Marktpreis" führen nicht zu signifikant anderen Ergebnissen. Die Gutschrift für Rapskuchen wird auf der Basis durchschnittlicher Proteingehalte nach /REINHARDT 1993/ von 37,5 % für Rapskuchen und 42 % für Sojaschrot berechnet.

Tabelle 8-15 Energetische und stoffliche Einsätze der Produktion von Sojaschrot aus Sojabohnen

	Input	Bezug	Menge kg	Strom kWh	Dampf MJ	Bemerkungen
Ein- u. Auslagerung	Energie	t Bohnen		3,7		
Trocknung	Heizöl	kg Wasserentzug	0,10	0,10		
Kühlung	Energie	t Bohnen		8,8		
Pressung	Energie	t Bohnen		60	1.000	
Extraktion	Hexan	t Bohnen	0,7			Ertrag: 812 kg SES

SES: Sojaextraktionsschrot
Quelle: Eigene Abschätzungen nach /AHMED et al. 1994/

8.2.2.3 Zusammenführung

Tabelle 8-18 faßt den Einsatz mineralischer Ressourcen, den Primärenergieeinsatz und die Emissionen der Bereitstellung von Rapsöl frei Endverbraucher in Deutschland im Jahr 1996 zusammen; die Fortschreibung auf das Jahr 2000 findet sich im Anhang (**Tabelle 12-9**). Die Bilanzen sind die Summen der Teilbilanzen der landwirtschaftlichen Produktion der Rapssaat und der Rapsölproduktion aus Rapssaat. Der Verbrauch mineralischer Ressourcen resultiert aus dem Düngemitteleinsatz.

8.2.3 RME

Die Bereitstellung von RME wird hier unter der Annahme einer großtechnischen Produktion behandelt. Gutschriften ergeben sich aus der Substitution von Sojaschrot als Futtermittel durch Rapsextraktionsschrot und von synthetischem Glyzerin durch Glyzerin aus der Umesterung von Rapsöl zu RME.

8.2.3.1 Zentrale Ölgewinnung

RME wird aus gereinigtem Rapsöl durch Umesterung gewonnen. Um die Ölausbeute zu erhöhen, werden die Ölanteile, die beim Pressen im Rapskuchen zurückgeblieben sind, mit Hexan extrahiert. Dadurch kann eine Ölausbeute von 99 % erreicht werden. Das Hexan verbleibt zum Teil (hier 25 %) im Öl bzw. im Preßrückstand. Das in der Ölmühle freigesetzte Hexan kann teilweise nachverbrannt oder in Biofiltern abgebaut werden; der Rest (hier 50 %) entweicht in die Atmosphäre. Als Emissionsfaktor setzen wir 0,375 kg NMHC je t Saat an /KALTSCHMITT & REINHARDT 1997/; mit diesem Wert werden strengere Maßnahmen zur Emissionsminderung in Ölmühlen vorweggenommen.

Im Unterschied zur dezentralen Rapsölproduktion ist die zentrale RME-Produktion mit Ferntransporten zur Anlieferung der Rapssaat verbunden. Annahmen: mittlerer Gesamtweg 240 km, 70 % per Binnenschiff, je 15 % per Bahn und LKW (40-t-Zug).

8.2.3.2 Raffination und Umesterung

Vor der Umesterung ist eine (Teil-)Raffination des Rapsöls notwendig, um Schleim-, Farb- und sonstige Begleitstoffe sowie freie Fettsäuren zu entfernen, die die Haltbarkeit des Öls, seine Verarbeitungseigenschaften und/oder seinen Geruch beeinflussen. Die Raffination kann chemisch oder physikalisch erfolgen.

Bei der chemischen Raffination wird das rohe Rapsöl durch Säurezusatz entschleimt, filtriert, mit Laugen neutralisiert, mit Bleicherde entfärbt, nochmals filtriert und durch Wasserdampfdestillation desodoriert. Bei der physikalischen Raffination werden dem rohen Rapsöl Wasser, Phosphorsäure und Bleicherde zur Entschleimung und Entfärbung in einem Prozeßschritt zugesetzt. Nach dem Abtrennen der Feststoffe erfolgt die Entsäuerung und Desodorierung des Rapsöls ebenfalls in einem Schritt durch Wasserdampfdestillation. Details zu den Verfahren finden sich in /KALTSCHMITT & REINHARDT 1997/.

Die physikalische Raffination löst zunehmend die chemische ab. Wir gehen daher hier von einem physikalischen Verfahren aus. **Abb. 8-2** skizziert die Verfahrensschritte. Die mit der Raffination verbundenen Verluste schätzen wir auf 4 % der nutzbaren Masse.

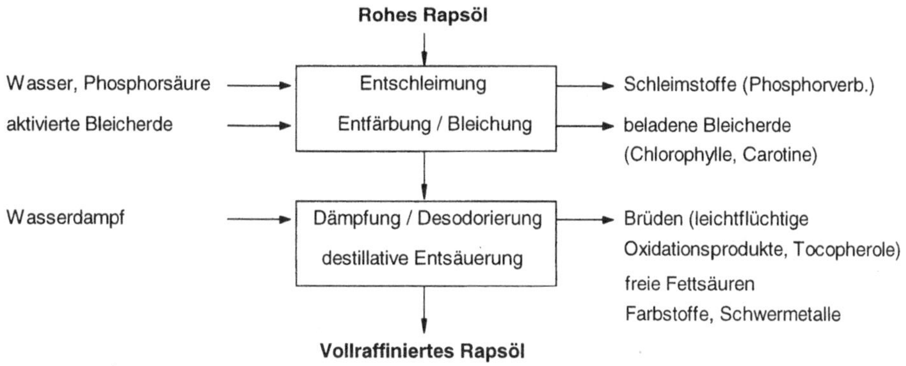

Abb. 8-2 Physikalische Raffination nach /KALTSCHMITT & REINHARDT 1997/

Die Umesterung erfolgt durch Zusatz von Methanol und eines alkalischen Katalysators (hier: Natronlauge). Diese wird nach der Umsetzung mit einer Säure neutralisiert (hier: Phosphorsäure). Die Ausbeute erreicht bei optimierter Prozeßführung (Eduktrückführung) bis zu 98 %.

Als Kuppelprodukt entsteht in wässriger Lösung Glyzerin mit einem vorsichtig geschätzten Gehalt von 80 %. Nach Anreicherung durch Destillation auf einen Glyzeringehalt von etwa 99 % kann damit synthetisch erzeugtes Glyzerin substituiert werden. Da erst durch die Aufarbeitung des Glyzerins aus der Umesterung ein Produkt entsteht, das synthetisches Glyzerin substituieren kann, sind die notwendigen Aufwendungen RME „schlechtzuschreiben". Die Basisdaten sind in **Tabelle 8-16** zusammengefaßt.

Für die Distribution von RME an Tankstellen nehmen wir an, daß der Transport über 150 km mit 40-t-LKW-Zügen erfolgt.

8.2.3.3 Gutschriften

In der Bilanz von RME sind drei Gutschriften zu berücksichtigen: für die unterbliebene Referenznutzung, für die Substitution von Sojaschrot als Futtermittel durch das Kuppelprodukt Rapskuchen und für die Substitution von synthetischem Glyzerin durch das Kuppelprodukt Glyzerin aus der Umesterung. Die ersten beiden Gutschriften fallen in gleicher bzw. ähnlicher Weise für Rapsöl an und wurden bereits behandelt. Im Falle des Rapsextraktionsschrots ist allerdings der gegenüber Rapskuchen etwas geringere Proteinanteil von 35 % zu berücksichtigen /REINHARDT 1993/.

Die Gutschrift für das Kuppelprodukt Glyzerin umfaßt den Ressourceneinsatz und die damit verbundenen Emissionen der großtechnischen, synthetischen Glyzerindarstellung. Die Basisdaten sind in **Tabelle 8-17** zusammengefaßt. Eine detaillierte Darstellung der Ressourcen- und Emissionsbilanzen findet sich im Anhang (**Tabelle 12-8**).

Tabelle 8-16 Energetische und stoffliche Einsätze der Produktion von RME

	Input	Bezug	Menge kg	Strom kWh	Dampf MJ	Bemerkungen
Ein- und Auslagerung	Energie	t Korn		3,7		13 % Erntefeuchte
Trocknung	Heizöl	kg Wasserentzug	0,10	0,10		8,3 % Lagerfeuchte
Kühlung	Energie	t Korn		8,8		8,3 % Lagerfeuchte
Pressung	Energie	t Korn		34,0	580	
Extraktion	Hexan	t Korn	1			Ausbeute: 405 kg Rohöl
Raffination	Energie	t Rohöl		6	296[a]	Ausbeute: 960 kg
	Bleicherde	t Rohöl	6			raffiniertes Öl
	Phosphorsäure[b]	t Rohöl	1			
Umesterung	Energie	t raff. Öl		45,5	1.346	Ausbeute: 990 kg
	Methanol	t raff. Öl	108			RME, 116 kg Glyze-
	Natronlauge (98%ig)	t raff. Öl	6			rin (80%ig)
Aufbereitung Glyzerin	Energie	t Glyzerin (80%ig)			1.299	obere Abschätzung

a: inkl. 3 kg Heizöl; mittlere Dampfenthalpie 2,1 MJ/kg, b: inkl. Neutralisation bei Umesterung
Quelle: /KALTSCHMITT & REINHARDT 1997/, eigene Abschätzungen

Tabelle 8-17 Energetische und stoffliche Einsätze für die Produktion von Glyzerin (Bezug: 1 kg Glyzerin)

	Menge kg	Strom kWh	Dampf MJ
Energie		0,9	63
Chlor	2,0		
Natronlauge	1,4		
Propylen	0,8		

Quelle: /IFEU 1997a/

8.2.3.4 Zusammenführung

Tabelle 8-18 faßt den Einsatz mineralischer Ressourcen, den Primärenergieeinsatz und die Emissionen der Bereitstellung von RME frei Tankstelle in Deutschland im Jahr 1996 zusammen; die Fortschreibung auf das Jahr 2000 findet sich im Anhang (**Tabelle 12-9**). Die Bilanzen sind die Summen der Teilbilanzen der landwirtschaftlichen Produktion der Rapssaat und der RME-Produktion aus Rapssaat. Der Verbrauch mineralischer Ressourcen resultiert aus dem Düngemitteleinsatz.

Differenziert nach den hier diskutierten Prozeßschritten sind die Daten im Anhang (**Tabelle 12-8**) dokumentiert.

Tabelle 8-18 Spezifischer Einsatz mineralischer und energetischer Ressourcen und Emissionen der Bereitstellung von Rapsöl und RME frei Abnehmer in Deutschland im Jahr 1996

		Rapsöl		**RME**	
Mineralische Ressourcen					
Kalkstein	g/GJ	3.055		2.668	
Phosphaterz	g/GJ	5.227		4.716	
Schwefel	g/GJ	348		323	
Rohkali	g/GJ	4.999		4.862	
Kochsalz	g/GJ	0		-7.343	
Tonmineralien	g/GJ	0		204	
Primärenergieträger					
Erdöl	GJ/GJ	-0,020		-0,16	
Erdgas	GJ/GJ	0,11		0,14	
Steinkohle	GJ/GJ	0,024		-0,031	
Braunkohle	GJ/GJ	0,013		-0,050	
Uran	GJ/GJ	0,015		-0,048	
Σ Erschöpfl. ET	*GJ/GJ*	*0,14*		*-0,15*	
Wasser	GJ/GJ	0,0024		-0,0056	
Summe*	**GJ/GJ**	**0,145**		**-0,159**	
Emissionen					
		Global		**Global**	
CO_2 **	g/GJ	7.803		-6.963	
CH_4	g/GJ	31,0		5,20	
N_2O	g/GJ	133		116	
CO_2-Äquivalente	*g/GJ*	*49.682*		*29.030*	
		OK 2	**OK 3**	**OK 2**	**OK 3**
SO_2	g/GJ	7,29	-67,4	-102	-49,0
CO	g/GJ	6,09	-7,57	2,58	-5,47
NO_X	g/GJ	23,8	-70,6	19,8	-50,8
NMHC	g/GJ	-10,2	-2,06	18,5	-1,54
Partikel	g/GJ	0,33	-6,72	0,93	-4,84
Staub	g/GJ	11,1	-0,00088	7,27	-0,0044
HCl	g/GJ	0,39	-0,081	-0,32	-0,060
NH_3	g/GJ	180	-0,010	157	-0,0062
Formaldehyd	g/GJ	-0,073	-0,17	0,11	-0,12
Benzol	g/GJ	-0,022	-0,040	0,045	-0,029
Benzo(a)pyren	ng/GJ	2.057	-8.656	-60,3	-6.249
TCDD-TÄ	ng/GJ	5,05	-1,43	2,29	-1,09
SO_2-Äquivalente	*g/GJ*	*363*	*-117*	*207*	*-84,6*

*Nachrichtlich: Energieinhalt von Rapskorn: 2,028 bzw. 1,749 GJ je bereitgestelltem GJ Rapsöl bzw. RME.

** Nur fossiles CO_2.

Bei negativen Zahlen überwiegen die Gutschriften aus Kuppelprodukten die Aufwendungen der Produktion.

Zur Umrechnung der Ergebnisdaten von Energie- auf Massen- bzw. Volumenbezug (von GJ auf kg bzw. l) siehe die Heizwerte und Dichten von Rapsöl bzw. RME nach Tabelle 8-10.

Eigene Berechnungen

8.3 Stein- und Braunkohle

Die wesentlichen Unterschiede zwischen Stein- und Braunkohle bestehen im Kohlenstoffgehalt und – damit verbunden – Heizwert. Steinkohle weist für beide Größen deutlich höhere Werte auf. Steinkohle wird in Deutschland nur untertage, in anderen Ländern auch im Tagebau gefördert; Braunkohle wird nur im Tagebau gefördert. Als Energieträger zur Stein- und Braunkohleförderung wird sowohl im Tagebau als auch im Untertagebau praktisch ausschließlich Strom eingesetzt, der in grubennahen Kohlekraftwerken erzeugt wird.

Der Energieaufwand der Stein- und Braunkohleförderung in Deutschland wird aus den Angaben in /KOHLE 1997/ abgeleitet. Für den Abbau in den Hauptherkunftsländern der Importsteinkohle (1996: 25,5 % vom Absatz) werden die Daten aus /GEMIS 1997/ übernommen. Der sehr geringe Anteil importierter Braunkohle wird hier nicht betrachtet.

Der Überseetransport von Steinkohle aus den USA, Australien und Südafrika in die Bundesrepublik erfolgt mit Massengutschiffen, der Transport aus Polen per Bahn. Für inländische Transporte werden zu gleichen Teilen Binnenschiffe und die Bahn angesetzt. Braunkohle wird in Deutschland weit überwiegend nahe dem Förderort verstromt; Transporte werden daher hier vernachlässigt.

In **Tabelle 8-19** sind die Primärenergieaufwendungen zur Bereitstellung von Steinkohle differenziert nach Förderregionen und Prozeßschritten zusammengefaßt.

Tabelle 8-19 Primärenergieeinsatz zur Bereitstellung von Steinkohle differenziert nach Förderland bzw. -region (Bezug: Energieinhalt der geförderten Kohle)

Herkunft	Anteil	Förderung	Transport				Summe
			Bahn	Schiff	Bahn	Schiff	
		GJ/GJ	km	km	GJ/GJ	GJ/GJ	GJ/GJ
Deutschland	74,5%	0,048	200	100	0,00075	0,0014	0,050
Polen	6,7%	0,019	500	0	0,0065	0	0,026
USA/Kanada	4,3%	0,011	500	8.000	0,0065	0,027	0,045
Südafrika	12,0%	0,019	500	15.000	0,0065	0,051	0,077
Australien	2,3%	0,011	500	25.000	0,0065	0,085	0,10
Gew. Mittelwert	**100 %**	**0,040**	**276**	**2.811**	**0,0022**	**0,010**	**0,053**

Quellen: /GEMIS 1997/, /KOHLE 1997/, eigene Berechnungen

Die Emissionen der Stein- und Braunkohlebereitstellung ergeben sich aus den Emissionen der Kraftwerke (siehe Kapitel 8.6), die den Strom zur Förderung erzeugen, und der Transportprozesse. Daneben fallen prozeßspezifische Emissionen an, im wesentlichen Staub- und Kohlenwasserstoff-Freisetzungen aus den Lagerstätten selbst, die nach den Angaben in /GEMIS 1997/ berücksichtigt werden.

Die Daten zu Energieeinsatz und Emissionen der Bereitstellung von Steinkohle in Deutschland sind in **Tabelle 8-20** zusammengefaßt. Die Emissionen nicht global wirksamer Schadstoffe sind als Summe über die Ortsklassen ausgewiesen. Die Anteile der Ortsklasse 2 sind in **Tabelle 8-22** als Prozentwerte ausgewiesen. Die Anteile der Ortsklasse 3 ergeben sich als Differenz zu 100 %, da in der Ortsklasse 1 (hohe Bevölkerungsdichte, Innenstadt) keine

Emissionen anfallen. Die Daten für in Deutschland abgebaute Braunkohle finden sich in **Tabelle 8-21**.

Tabelle 8-20 Spezifischer Primärenergieeinsatz und Emissionsfaktoren der Bereitstellung von Steinkohle frei Abnehmer (Kraftwerke und Industrie) in Deutschland 1996

Herkunft		**D**	**Polen**	**USA/Kanada**	**Südafrika**	**Australien**	**Gew. Mittel**
Primärenergieeinsatz							
Erdöl	GJ/GJ	0,0016	0,0073	0,037	0,063	0,10	0,013
Erdgas	GJ/GJ	0,00022	0,00008	0,00036	0,00061	0,0010	0,00028
Steinkohle	GJ/GJ	1,049	1,019	1,011	1,019	1,011	1,041
Braunkohle	GJ/GJ	0,00022	0,00003	0,00013	0,00022	0,00034	0,00021
Uran	GJ/GJ	0,00072	0,00001	0,00005	0,00008	0,00012	0,00055
Σ Erschöpfl. ET	*GJ/GJ*	*1,052*	*1,027*	*1,049*	*1,084*	*1,113*	*1,055*
Wasser	GJ/GJ	0,00011	0,00000	0,00001	0,00001	0,00001	0,00008
Summe	**GJ/GJ**	**1,052**	**1,027**	**1,049**	**1,084**	**1,113**	**1,056**
Emissionen							
		Global	**Global**	**Global**	**Global**	**Global**	**Global**
CO_2	g/GJ	4.690	2.320	3.943	6.783	9.001	4.850
CH_4	g/GJ	518	609	106	505	106	495
N_2O	g/GJ	0,21	0,13	0,33	0,56	0,82	0,27
CO_2-Äquival.	*g/GJ*	*15.625*	*15.153*	*6.262*	*17.562*	*11.491*	*15.324*
		OK 2	**OK 2**	**OK 2+3**	**OK 2+3**	**OK 2+3**	**OK 2+3**
SO_2	g/GJ	3,77	17,0	66,0	122	185	25,8
CO	g/GJ	1,38	3,11	9,17	14,7	22,3	3,93
NO_X	g/GJ	5,43	17,1	70,6	124	192	27,7
NMHC	g/GJ	0,26	1,17	3,49	5,54	8,44	1,29
Partikel	g/GJ	0,070	0,46	4,53	8,08	13,2	1,56
Staub	g/GJ	0,18	1,38	0,87	1,52	1,03	0,47
HCl	g/GJ	0,35	0,14	0,14	0,26	0,28	0,31
NH_3	g/GJ	0,00069	0,0031	0,017	0,029	0,046	0,0060
Formaldehyd	g/GJ	0,015	0,082	0,22	0,34	0,52	0,080
Benzol	g/GJ	0,0049	0,020	0,056	0,087	0,13	0,021
Benzo(a)pyren	ng/GJ	280	1.218	6.534	11.189	17.835	2.337
TCDD-TÄ	ng/GJ	0,38	0,18	0,99	1,81	2,84	0,63
SO_2-Äquival.	*g/GJ*	*7,87*	*29,1*	*116*	*209*	*320*	*45,5*

OK: Ortsklasse; in OK 1 fallen keine Emissionen an.
Quellen: /ECOINVENT 1996/, /GEMIS 1997/, /IFEU 1998b/, /KOHLE 1997/, /UBA 1995c/, /UBA 1998/, eigene Berechnungen

Tabelle 8-21 Spezifischer Primärenergieeinsatz und Emissionsfaktoren der Bereitstellung von Braunkohle frei Kraftwerk in Deutschland 1996

Primärenergieeinsatz		
Erdöl	GJ/GJ	0
Erdgas	GJ/GJ	0
Steinkohle	GJ/GJ	0
Braunkohle	GJ/GJ	1,040
Uran	GJ/GJ	0
Summe Erschöpfl. ET	*GJ/GJ*	*1,040*
Wasser	GJ/GJ	0
Summe	**GJ/GJ**	**1,040**
Emissionen		
		Global
CO_2	g/GJ	4.422
CH_4	g/GJ	1,66
N_2O	g/GJ	0,14
CO_2-Äquivalente	*g/GJ*	*4.500*
		OK 2
SO_2	g/GJ	29,0
CO	g/GJ	0,73
NO_X	g/GJ	4,00
NMHC	g/GJ	0,062
Partikel	g/GJ	0
Staub	g/GJ	0,38
HCl	g/GJ	0,23
NH_3	g/GJ	0
Formaldehyd	g/GJ	0,0012
Benzol	g/GJ	0,0012
Benzo(a)pyren	ng/GJ	8,04
TCDD-TÄ	ng/GJ	0,35
SO_2-Äquivalente	*g/GJ*	*32,0*

Quellen: /ECOINVENT 1996/, /GEMIS 1997/, /IFEU 1998b/, /KOHLE 1997/, /UBA 1995c/, /UBA 1998/, eigene Berechnungen

Tabelle 8-22 Anteile der Emissionen in der Ortsklasse 2 an den Gesamtemissionen der Bereitstellung von Steinkohle frei Abnehmer (Kraftwerke und Industrie) in Deutschland 1996

Herkunft	D	Polen	USA/Kanada	Südafrika	Australien	Gew. Mittel
SO_2	99,4%	99,7%	38,4%	37,5%	31,3%	46,1%
CO	99,8%	99,9%	50,2%	41,9%	36,1%	60,2%
NO_X	99,7%	99,7%	39,8%	35,9%	30,9%	47,5%
NMHC	99,6%	99,8%	64,3%	57,9%	54,0%	67,0%
Partikel	97,6%	99,5%	10,5%	6,0%	3,8%	11,1%
Staub	100,0%	100,0%	99,9%	99,9%	99,8%	99,9%
HCl	100,0%	100,0%	67,7%	66,4%	48,4%	94,9%
NH_3	99,2%	99,6%	39,1%	33,4%	30,4%	41,6%
Formaldehyd	99,7%	99,9%	53,5%	43,9%	37,9%	56,0%
Benzol	99,7%	99,9%	56,6%	47,9%	42,4%	60,5%
Benzo(a)pyren	99,2%	99,7%	20,1%	12,6%	8,6%	23,6%
TCDD-TÄ	99,7%	98,5%	18,8%	17,2%	12,0%	56,1%
SO_2-Äquivalente	*99,6%*	*99,8%*	*39,0%*	*36,8%*	*31,1%*	*47,6%*

Die Anteile der Ortsklasse 3 ergeben sich als Differenz zu 100 %. In der Ortsklasse 1 (hohe Bevölkerungsdichte, Innenstadt) fallen keine Emissionen an.
Quellen: /ECOINVENT 1996/, /GEMIS 1997/, /IFEU 1998b/, /KOHLE 1997/, /UBA 1995c/, /UBA 1998/, eigene Berechnungen

8.4 Erdgas

Erdgas besteht im wesentlichen aus Methan, daneben weiteren Kohlenwasserstoffen (vor allem Ethan), Schwefelwasserstoff (H_2S) sowie Stickstoff und CO_2. Abhängig vom H_2S-Gehalt, der bis zu 24 % betragen kann /ECOINVENT 1996/, unterscheidet man Süß- und Sauergas.

Das in Deutschland verbrauchte Erdgas wird zum überwiegenden Teil importiert. Norwegisches Erdgas wird off-shore gefördert. In den beiden anderen wichtigen Lieferländern, den Niederlanden und der GUS, sowie in Deutschland findet die Förderung auf dem Land statt. Zur Förderung wird praktisch ausschließlich Strom eingesetzt, der durch Gasturbinenkraftwerke am Förderort erzeugt wird.

Zur Aufbereitung des Erdgases am Förderort, im wesentlichen Trocknung und – im Falle von Sauergas – Entschwefelung, wird Prozeßwärme aus gasgefeuerten Anlagen eingesetzt. Das in Deutschland geförderte Erdgas besteht etwa zur Hälfte aus Sauergas, während in den hier betrachteten übrigen Förderländern vor allem schwefelärmeres Gas gefördert wird. Die Aufbereitung umfaßt daher hier nur für deutsches Erdgas eine Entschwefelung.

Der Transport zu Großabnehmern (Industrie oder Kraftwerke) erfolgt vorwiegend per Pipeline. Der Antrieb der Verdichter erfolgt durch Gasturbinen, die mit dem transportierten Gas betrieben werden.

In **Tabelle 8-23** sind die Primärenergieaufwendungen zur Bereitstellung von Erdgas differenziert nach Förderregionen und Prozeßschritten zusammengefaßt.

Tabelle 8-23 Primärenergieeinsatz zur Bereitstellung von Erdgas differenziert nach Förderland bzw. -region und Prozeßschritten nach /GEMIS 1997/ (Bezug: Energieinhalt des geförderten Erdgases)

Herkunft	Anteil	Förderung	Aufbereit.	Verluste[a]	Transport		Verl.[b]	Summe
		GJ/GJ	GJ/GJ	GJ/GJ	km	GJ/GJ	GJ/GJ	GJ/GJ
Deutschland	21%	0,0033	0,022	0,0010	250	0,0040	0,00002	0,030
Niederlande	27%	0,0033	0,0043	0,0015	600	0,010	0,00004	0,019
Norwegen	19%	0,0033	0,0043	0,0024	1.500	0,024	0,00009	0,034
GUS	33%	0,0042	0,015	0,011	7.000	0,11	0,0040	0,15
Gew. Mittel	**100%**	**0,0036**	**0,011**	**0,0047**	**2.810**	**0,045**	**0,0013**	**0,065**

a: Verluste bei Förderung und Aufbereitung; b: Verluste beim Transport
Quellen: /GEMIS 1997/, /WEG 1997/, eigene Berechnungen

Die Emissionen der Erdgasbereitstellung ergeben sich aus den Emissionen der Gasturbinenkraftwerke, die den Strom zur Förderung erzeugen, der Kesselfeuerungen der Trocknungs- und Entschwefelungsanlagen und der Verdichter an den Pipelines. Die Emissionsfaktoren sind im Anhang (**Tabelle 12-3**) und in Kapitel 5.6 zusammengefaßt.

Neben den Emissionen aus der Nutzung von Erdgas werden die bei Förderung, Aufbereitung und Transport durch Leckagen auftretenden Verluste berücksichtigt /GEMIS 1997/. Die Entschwefelung von Sauergas ist mit prozeßspezifischen SO_2-Emissionen verbunden. Den Emissionsfaktor für die Entschwefelung in Deutschland leiten wir aus Angaben nach /UBA 1994/ für die Entschwefelung in deutschen Raffinerien, der geförderten Erdgasmenge und der produzierten Schwefelmenge nach /WEG 1994/ ab. Die SO_2-Emissionen werden ohne Belastung der Schwefel-Folgeprodukte vollständig dem Erdgas als dem eigentlich gewünschten Produkt der Entschwefelung zugeschlagen.

Die Daten zu Energieeinsatz und Emissionen der Bereitstellung von Erdgas in Deutschland sind in **Tabelle 8-24** und **Tabelle 8-25** zusammengefaßt; die Emissionen nicht global wirksamer Schadstoffe sind als Summe über die Ortsklassen ausgewiesen. Die Anteile der Ortsklasse 2 sind in **Tabelle 8-26** als Prozentwerte ausgewiesen. Die Anteile der Ortsklasse 3 ergeben sich als Differenz zu 100 %, da in der Ortsklasse 1 keine Emissionen anfallen.

Tabelle 8-24 Spezifischer Primärenergieeinsatz der Bereitstellung von Erdgas frei Abnehmer (Kraftwerke und Industrie) in Deutschland 1996: Primärenergieeinsatz

Herkunft		D	NL	NOR	GUS	Mittel
Primärenergieeinsatz						
Erdöl	GJ/GJ	0	0	0	0	0
Erdgas	GJ/GJ	1,030	1,018	1,033	1,145	1,065
Steinkohle	GJ/GJ	0	0	0	0	0
Braunkohle	GJ/GJ	0	0	0	0	0
Uran	GJ/GJ	0	0	0	0	0
Summe Erschöpfl. ET	*GJ/GJ*	*1,030*	*1,018*	*1,033*	*1,145*	*1,065*
Wasser	GJ/GJ	0	0	0	0	0
Summe	**GJ/GJ**	**1,030**	**1,018**	**1,033**	**1,145**	**1,065**

Quellen: /ECOINVENT 1996/, /GEMIS 1997/, /IFEU 1998b/, /UBA 1995c/, /UBA 1998/, eigene Berechnungen

Tabelle 8-25 Emissionen der Bereitstellung von Erdgas frei Abnehmer (Kraftwerke und Industrie) in Deutschland 1996

Herkunft		**D**	**NL**	**NOR**	**GUS**	**Mittel**
Emissionen						
		Global	**Global**	**Global**	**Global**	**Global**
CO_2	g/GJ	1.586	919	1.663	7.441	3.353
CH_4	g/GJ	20,4	30,8	49,9	301	121
N_2O	g/GJ	0,065	0,040	0,074	0,33	0,15
CO_2-Äquivalente	*g/GJ*	*2.034*	*1.578*	*2.735*	*13.864*	*5.948*
		OK 2	**OK 2**	**OK 2+3**	**OK 2**	**OK 2+3**
SO_2	g/GJ	0,057	0,0071	0,013	0,054	0,034
CO	g/GJ	2,06	1,33	2,46	21,8	8,46
NO_X	g/GJ	7,12	4,63	8,60	43,5	18,7
NMHC	g/GJ	0,21	0,13	0,25	2,69	1,01
Partikel	g/GJ	0	0	0	0	0
Staub	g/GJ	0,10	0,066	0,12	0,54	0,24
HCl	g/GJ	0	0	0	0	0
NH_3	g/GJ	0	0	0	0	0
Formaldehyd	g/GJ	0,021	0,013	0,025	0,27	0,10
Benzol	g/GJ	0,021	0,013	0,025	0,27	0,10
Benzo(a)pyren	ng/GJ	28,7	16,7	30,2	134	61
TCDD-TÄ	ng/GJ	2,13	1,34	2,48	10,9	4,87
SO_2-Äquivalente	*g/GJ*	*5,04*	*3,25*	*6,03*	*30,5*	*13,1*

OK: Ortsklasse; in OK 1 fallen keine Emissionen an.
Quellen: /ECOINVENT 1996/, /GEMIS 1997/, /IFEU 1998b/, /UBA 1995c/, /UBA 1998/, eigene Berechnungen

Tabelle 8-26 Anteile der Emissionen in der Ortsklasse 2 an den Gesamtemissionen der Bereitstellung von Erdgas frei Abnehmer (Kraftwerke und Industrie) in Deutschland 1996

Herkunft	**D**	**NL**	**NOR**	**GUS**	**Mittel**
SO_2	100%	100%	25,0%	100%	94,6%
CO	100%	100%	25,0%	100%	95,9%
NO_X	100%	100%	25,0%	100%	93,5%
NMHC	100%	100%	25,0%	100%	96,5%
Partikel	100%	100%	0%	100%	0%
Staub	100%	100%	0%	100%	90,4%
HCl	100%	100%	0%	100%	0%
NH_3	100%	100%	0%	100%	0%
Formaldehyd	100%	100%	25,0%	100%	96,5%
Benzol	100%	100%	25,0%	100%	96,5%
Benzo(a)pyren	100%	100%	0,8%	100%	90,6%
TCDD-TÄ	100%	100%	0,3%	100%	90,4%
SO_2-Äquivalente	*100%*	*100%*	*25,0%*	*100%*	*93,5%*

Die Anteile der Ortsklasse 3 ergeben sich als Differenz zu 100 %. In der Ortsklasse 1 (hohe Bevölkerungsdichte, Innenstadt) fallen keine Emissionen an.
Quellen: /ECOINVENT 1996/, /GEMIS 1997/, /IFEU 1998b/, /UBA 1995c/, eigene Berechnungen

8.5 Uran

Zu Uranerzabbau, Erz- und Isotopenanreicherung sowie Brennstabproduktion liegen nur sehr wenige technische und wirtschaftliche Informationen vor. Viele Daten unterliegen einer weitaus größeren Vertraulichkeit als bei herkömmlichen Kraftwerken und Brennstoffen. Daher werden hier die Energiedaten weitgehend aus /GEMIS 1997/ übernommen; für die Erz- und Isotopenanreicherung sowie die Brennstabproduktion wird der mittlere Strom in Deutschland angesetzt. Der Transportaufwand wird in /GEMIS 1997/ als sehr gering eingeschätzt und daher hier vernachlässigt. **Tabelle 8-27** faßt die Energie- und Emissionsdaten zusammen.

Tabelle 8-27 Spezifischer Primärenergieeeinsatz und Emissionsfaktoren der Bereitstellung von Uran frei Kernkraftwerk

Primärenergieeinsatz			
Erdöl	GJ/GJ	0,0043	
Erdgas	GJ/GJ	0,0028	
Steinkohle	GJ/GJ	0,010	
Braunkohle	GJ/GJ	0,014	
Uran	GJ/GJ	1,013	
Summe Erschöpfl. ET	*GJ/GJ*	*1,044*	
Wasser	GJ/GJ	0,0006	
Summe	**GJ/GJ**	**1,044**	
Emissionen			
		Global	
CO_2	g/GJ	2.885	
CH_4	g/GJ	5,20	
N_2O	g/GJ	0,12	
CO_2-Äquivalente	*g/GJ*	*3.031*	
		OK 2+3	**OK 2**
SO_2	g/GJ	16,1	99,2%
CO	g/GJ	1,37	98,9%
NO_X	g/GJ	7,43	98,3%
NMHC	g/GJ	0,52	99,1%
Partikel	g/GJ	0,40	97,1%
Staub	g/GJ	0,94	100,0%
HCl	g/GJ	0,15	99,9%
NH_3	g/GJ	0,0016	97,9%
Formaldehyd	g/GJ	0,032	99,0%
Benzol	g/GJ	0,0088	99,0%
Benzo(a)pyren	ng/GJ	664	97,6%
TCDD-TÄ	ng/GJ	0,25	98,1%
SO_2-Äquivalente	*g/GJ*	*21,5*	*99,0%*

Die Anteile der Ortsklasse 3 ergeben sich als Differenz zu 100 %. In der Ortsklasse 1 (hohe Bevölkerungsdichte, Innenstadt) fallen keine Emissionen an.
Quellen: /ECOINVENT 1996/, /GEMIS 1997/, /IFEU 1998b/, /UBA 1995c/, /UBA 1998/, eigene Berechnungen

8.6 Strom

Elektrische Energie wird fast ausschließlich durch die Umwandlung fossiler Energieträger bzw. in Kernkraftwerken erzeugt. Daneben hat nur die Wasserkraft noch eine gewisse Bedeutung. Sonnen- und Windenergie wie auch die Nutzung von Bioenergieträgern spielen bislang in Deutschland eine sehr geringe Rolle.

Der durchschnittliche Energieeinsatz und die Emissionen hängen stark von der Zusammensetzung des Kraftwerkparks im jeweiligen Bezugsgebiet ab. 1996 wurden in Deutschland 8,3 % des in das öffentliche Netz eingespeisten Stroms exportiert, 7,2 % des eingespeisten Stroms wurden importiert, vor allem aus Westeuropa /BMWI 1998/. Wegen dieser ausgeglichenen Bilanz und der relativ geringen Import- und Exportanteile wird im folgenden nur der Bezugsraum Deutschland betrachtet.

Die inländische Stromerzeugung kann in die der Unternehmen der öffentlichen Versorgung (im folgenden EVU: Elektrizitätsversorgungsunternehmen), der Bahn- und der Industriekraftwerke unterteilt werden. Neben der Produktion aus eigenen Kraftwerken deckt die Bahn ihren Strombedarf zu etwa einem Viertel aus dem EVU-Netz. In der Industrie wird branchenabhängig in unterschiedlichem Maße öffentlicher und selbst erzeugter Strom eingesetzt. Zum Teil speisen Industriekraftwerke überschüssigen Strom auch in das öffentliche Netz ein; 1996 betrug der Anteil des Industriestromes am öffentlichen Strom etwa 5 % /BMWI 1998/. Da im Zusammenhang dieses Buches Strom vor allem für den Betrieb von Eisenbahnen genutzt wird, wird die Industriestromproduktion hier nicht behandelt. In dem Maße, in dem Industriestrom in die Bereitstellung anderer Energieträger eingeht, wird er dort behandelt.

Im folgenden wird die Stromerzeugung und -bereitstellung der EVU und der Deutschen Bahn in Braun- und Steinkohle-, Erdgas-, Schweröl-, Kern- und Wasserkraftwerken in Deutschland im Jahr 1996 bilanziert.

8.6.1 Energieeinsatz

Die Ableitung des mittleren spezifischen Energieeinsatzes der Stromproduktion in Kraftwerken der EVU basiert im wesentlichen auf /BMWI 1998/ (Bezug: 1996). Dort finden sich nach Energieträgern differenzierte Angaben zum Energieeinsatz sowie zur Brutto- und Netto-Stromproduktion des gesamten Kraftwerkparks, aus denen „top-down“ die spezifischen Energieaufwendungen berechnet werden. Die Ableitung zur Bahnstromproduktion wird mit Zusatzannahmen zu den Netto-Wirkungsgraden, die nicht unmittelbar aus /BMWI 1998/ abgeleitet werden können, auf die gleiche Weise durchgeführt. Der von der Bahn verbrauchte Strom (Bahn-Mix) stammte 1996 zu etwa 75 % aus eigener Produktion. Abweichend von /BMWI 1998/ ordnen wir dabei den Anteil der Stromerzeugung des Großkraftwerks Neckarwestheim II, der in das Bahnnetz eingespeist wird, der Bahnstromerzeugung zu; der Strom wird wie bei anderen EVU-Kraftwerken über Umformer, jedoch ohne „Umweg“ über das öffentliche Netz in das Bahnnetz eingespeist. Die spezifischen Aufwendungen für den Bahn-Mix ergeben sich aus den Anteilen der beiden Kraftwerkparks.

Die Umspann- und Leitungsverluste werden für den in der Industrie genutzten Strom der EVU-Kraftwerke Deutschlands mit einem Wirkungsgrad von 95,7 %, für den an die Bahn abgegebenen Strom mit einem Wirkungsgrad von 95,0 % berücksichtigt. Für den in Bahnkraftwerken erzeugten Strom wird angenommen, daß diese Verluste nicht auftreten („der Verbraucher liegt direkt am Kraftwerk").

8.6.2 Emissionen

Die spezifischen Emissionen der Stromerzeugung ergeben sich durch Verknüpfung der Energieeinsätze, differenziert nach Energieträgern, mit energieeinsatzbezogenen Emissionsfaktoren für Kraftwerke. Die Emissionsfaktoren werden aus verschiedenen Quellen übernommen bzw. abgeleitet, da kein konsistenter, alle hier erfaßten Schadstoffe umfassender Faktorensatz vorliegt. Im wesentlichen lassen sich folgende Vorgehensweisen unterscheiden:

- Übernahme von Faktoren nach /UBA 1998/: CO_2, Methan, N_2O, CO und NMHC
- Anpassung von Faktoren nach /UBA 1998/: SO_2, NO_X und Staub
- Übernahme oder Ableitung aus anderen Quellen: HCl, Benzol, Formaldehyd, Benzo(a)pyren und TCDD-Toxizitätsäquivalente

Eine detaillierte Dokumentation der Faktoren und ihrer Ableitung findet sich im Anhang (**Tabelle 12-5** und **Tabelle 12-6**).

8.6.3 Zusammenführung

Energieeinsatz und Emissionen der gesamten Strombereitstellung ergeben sich aus Energieeinsatz und Emissionen der eigentlichen Stromproduktion einschließlich Verteilungsverlusten und denen der Bereitstellung fossiler Energieträger und von Uran in Kraftwerken. **Tabelle 8-28** faßt die Daten zum spezifischen Energieeinsatz und den Emissionen der Bereitstellung von EVU-Strom frei industrieller Abnehmer und Strom der Bahnkraftwerke und Bahn-Mix frei Oberleitungsnetz einschließlich Brennstoffbereitstellung in Deutschland im Jahr 1996 zusammen. Die Emissionen nicht global wirksamer Schadstoffe sind als Summe über die Ortsklassen 2 und 3 ausgewiesen, die Anteile der Emissionen in der Ortsklasse 2 davon als Prozentwerte. Die Anteile der Ortsklasse 3 ergeben sich als Differenz zu 100 %, da in der Ortsklasse 1 (hohe Bevölkerungsdichte, Innenstadt) keine Emissionen anfallen. Die Fortschreibung auf das Jahr 2000 findet sich im Anhang in **Tabelle 12-2**.

Tabelle 8-28 Spezifischer Energieeinsatz und Emissionen der Strombereitstellung: EVU Strom frei industrieller Abnehmer, Strom der Bahnkraftwerke und Bahn-Mix frei Oberle tungsnetz einschließlich Brennstoffbereitstellung in Deutschland im Jahr 1996

		EVU frei Industrie		**BahnKW frei Oberleitung**		**Bahn-Mix frei Oberleitung**	
Primärenergieeinsatz							
Erdöl	MJ/kWh	0,15		0,18		0,17	
Erdgas	MJ/kWh	0,60		0,91		0,84	
Steinkohle	MJ/kWh	2,92		4,90		4,42	
Braunkohle	MJ/kWh	3,39		0,49		1,32	
Uran	MJ/kWh	4,05		3,27		3,55	
Σ Erschöpfl. ET	*MJ/kWh*	*11,11*		*9,76*		*10,30*	
Wasser	MJ/kWh	0,13		0,52		0,42	
Summe	**MJ/kWh**	**11,23**		**10,28**		**10,72**	
Emissionen							
		Global		**Global**		**Global**	
CO_2	g/kWh	678		533		583	
CH_4	g/kWh	1,47		2,44		2,21	
N_2O	g/kWh	0,025		0,021		0,023	
CO_2-Äquivalente	*g/kWh*	*717*		*590*		*636*	
		OK 2+3	**OK 2**	**OK 2+3**	**OK 2**	**OK 2+3**	**OK 2**
SO_2	g/kWh	1,68	97,6%	0,47	85,9%	0,82	92,7%
CO	g/kWh	0,16	97,1%	0,19	95,9%	0,18	96,2%
NO_X	g/kWh	0,66	93,7%	0,55	87,3%	0,59	89,3%
NMHC	g/kWh	0,017	92,8%	0,017	87,8%	0,017	89,2%
Partikel	g/kWh	0,0060	34,8%	0,0087	24,5%	0,0080	26,7%
Staub	g/kWh	0,039	100,0%	0,020	99,9%	0,026	99,9%
HCl	g/kWh	0,040	99,9%	0,030	99,8%	0,033	99,8%
NH_3	g/kWh	0,00002	57,2%	0,00003	50,4%	0,00003	51,8%
Formaldehyd	g/kWh	0,00066	84,7%	0,00080	78,9%	0,00077	80,3%
Benzol	g/kWh	0,00037	93,0%	0,00040	89,5%	0,00040	90,4%
Benzo(a)pyren	ng/kWh	15,9	68,3%	20,1	58,0%	19,2	60,4%
TCDD-TÄ	ng/kWh	0,059	98,2%	0,051	96,6%	0,054	97,1%
SO_2-Äquivalente	*g/kWh*	*2,17*	*96,8%*	*0,88*	*86,9%*	*1,26*	*91,8%*

OK: Ortsklasse; in OK 1 fallen keine Emissionen an.

Quellen: /BMWI 1998/, /ECOINVENT 1996/, /GEMIS 1997/, /IFEU 1998b/, /UBA 1995c/, /UBA 1998/, /VDEW 1998/, eigene Berechnungen

Teil III

Anhang

9 Gütertransport

Über den *direkten* Energieverbrauch und die Emissionen des Transports allein werden die Umweltauswirkungen eines Transports nicht vollständig erfaßt. Mit zu berücksichtigen ist die Bereitstellung des verbrauchten Kraftstoffes bzw. Energieträgers (hier: Dieselkraftstoff, Rapsölmethylester (RME), Bunker C, Kerosin, Erdgas, Strom). Die Daten dazu werden in Kapitel 8 abgeleitet. Der gesamte Energieeinsatz (kumulierter Energieverbrauch) ergibt sich durch Multiplikation des Verbrauchs in MJ (Strom: kWh) mit dem Energieeinsatz zur Bereitstellung des Energieträgers in MJ/MJ (Strom: MJ/kWh), die gesamten Emissionen durch Multiplikation der Emissionen der Bereitstellung mit dem Verbrauch und Addition zu den direkten Emissionen. Im folgenden werden diese Daten für die betrachteten Transportmittel dokumentiert.

Neben den Daten mit dem „Standard"-Bezugsjahr 1996 werden für LKW wegen der Einführung neuer Emissionsrichtlinien auch Daten mit dem Bezugsjahr 2000 ausgewiesen. Dies ist sinnvoll, da die Bestandsumschichtung bei LKW relativ schnell erfolgt. Neufahrzeuge bzw. deren Spezifikationen bekommen damit schnell Einfluß auf bestandstypische Mittelwerte.

Für die übrigen Transportmittel können die Daten mit Bezug auf 1996 in guter Näherung auch für das Jahr 2000 angesetzt werden. Im Bedarfsfalle können für die direkten spezifischen Verbräuche und Emissionsfaktoren Fortschreibungen aus den dokumentierten Primärdaten durch den Leser selbst vorgenommen werden. Diese „direkten" Daten können mit den im Anhang (**Tabelle 12-1** und **Tabelle 12-2**) dokumentierten Daten zur Energiebereitstellung im Jahr 2000 verknüpft werden.

Für LKW werden außer den kumulierten Daten differenzierte Emissionsfaktoren für die Schadstoffe NO_X, NMHC, CO und Partikel dokumentiert, ebenfalls für die Jahre 1996 und 2000.

Hilfsweise können alle Daten für andere Bezugsräume als Deutschland angesetzt werden.

Die hier dokumentierten Daten werden in den folgenden Abschnitten kurz mit ihren konkreten Bezügen auf die einzelnen Transportmittel beschrieben und gegebenenfalls kommentiert.

9.1 LKW: Kumulierte Daten (Diesel und RME) und Emissionsfaktoren 2000

In **Tabelle 9-1** sind die transportleistungsbezogenen kumulierten Daten des Gütertransports mit LKW für zwei Beispiele zusammengefaßt: 7,5-t-LKW und 40-t-Zug jeweils im Mittel aller Straßenkategorien bei einem Auslastungsgrad von 50 % (Dieselbetrieb).

Nach Kapitel 8.1 liegt der Energieaufwand zur Bereitstellung von Dieselkraftstoff bei etwa 10 % des Energieinhaltes des erzeugten Energieträgers. Für die Schadstoffemissionen liegt der Anteil der Bereitstellung an der Summe aus Bereitstellung und Nutzung pro tkm zwischen 1 und 90 %. Für die einzelnen Luftschadstoffe sind die Verhältnisse damit extrem unterschiedlich. Im Falle der Methanemissionen etwa ist der Anteil der Bereitstellung mit über 90 % (40-t-Zug) sehr viel größer als im Falle der Partikelemissionen mit etwa 6 %. Die Unterschiede zwischen den direkten Emissionen der LKW-Klassen bleiben auch in den kumulierten Emissionen erkennbar. Mit der Ausnahme NO_X sind die Anteile der direkten Schadstoffemissionen für den 40-t-Zug immer niedriger als für den 7,5-t-LKW. Der Anteil der direkten Methanemissionen etwa ist für den 40-t-Zug nur ein Drittel so groß wie für den 7,5-t-LKW.

Die transportleistungsbezogenen Emissionsfaktoren für CO, NO_X, NMHC und Partikel, die nach dem in Kapitel 5.1.4 dargestellten Verfahren abgeleitet wurden, sind in **Tabelle 9-2** und **Tabelle 9-3** differenziert nach den fünf LKW-Klassen, drei Straßenkategorien und drei Auslastungsgraden für die Bezugsjahre 1996 und 2000 zusammengefaßt. Die Fortschreibung auf das Jahr 2000 ist sinnvoll, da im Bereich des LKW-Transports durch die Einführung der Emissionsrichtlinien EURO II und III bereits mittelfristig mit deutlichen Emissionsminderungen zu rechnen ist.

In **Tabelle 9-4** sind die transportleistungsbezogenen kumulierten Daten des Gütertransports mit **LKW im RME-Betrieb** für zwei Beispiele zusammengefaßt: 7,5-t-LKW und 40-t-Zug jeweils im Mittel aller Straßenkategorien bei einem Auslastungsgrad von 50 %.

Zur Produktion von RME werden bei konventioneller Wirtschaftsweise unter anderem mineralische Düngemittel eingesetzt. Diese Stoffe basieren zum Teil auf mineralischen Ressourcen, die in den Bereitstellungsaufwendungen mit zu berücksichtigen sind. Wie in Kapitel 8.2 dargestellt fällt bei der Bilanzierung der RME-Produktion eine Reihe von Gutschriften an, da „Nebenprodukte“ wie Glyzerin konventionell erzeugte Produkte substituieren können. Bei negativen Werten überwiegen die angerechneten Gutschriften den Energieeinsatz bzw. die Emissionen der RME-Bereitstellung und -Nutzung.

Tabelle 9-1 Spezifischer kumulierter Energieaufwand und Emissionen des Gütertransports mit LKW am Beispiel zweier LKW-Klassen im Mittel aller Straßenkategorien bei einem Auslastungsgrad von 50 % (Dieselbetrieb)

ZGG		**7,5 t**		**40 t**	
Primärenergieeinsatz					
Erdöl	MJ/tkm	3,77		1,22	
Erdgas	MJ/tkm	0,043		0,014	
Steinkohle	MJ/tkm	0,013		0,0043	
Braunkohle	MJ/tkm	0,010		0,0034	
Uran	MJ/tkm	0,013		0,0034	
Summe Erschöpfl. ET	*MJ/tkm*	*3,85*		*1,25*	
Wasser	MJ/tkm	0,00047		0,00051	
Summe	**MJ/tkm**	**3,85**		**1,25**	
Emissionen					
		Global		**Global**	
CO_2	g/tkm	286		92,5	
CH_4	g/tkm	0,066		0,017	
N_2O	g/tkm	0,028		0,0090	
CO_2-Äquivalente	*g/tkm*	*296*		*95,6*	
		OK 2+3	**OK 2**	**OK 2+3**	**OK 2**
SO_2	g/tkm	0,21	90,6%	0,067	90,6%
CO	g/tkm	1,06	99,8%	0,14	99,6%
NO_X	g/tkm	2,01	99,5%	0,91	99,6%
NMHC	g/tkm	0,78	99,8%	0,089	99,4%
Partikel	g/tkm	0,18	99,5%	0,037	99,2%
Staub	g/tkm	0,0040	97,3%	0,0013	97,3%
HCl	g/tkm	0,00045	94,5%	0,00014	94,5%
NH_3	g/tkm	0,0016	99,7%	0,00053	99,7%
Formaldehyd	g/tkm	0,061	99,9%	0,0061	99,8%
Benzol	g/tkm	0,014	99,9%	0,0015	99,6%
Benzo(a)pyren	ng/tkm	637	99,8%	206	99,8%
TCDD-TÄ	ng/tkm	0,016	89,3%	0,0051	89,3%
SO_2-Äquivalente	*g/tkm*	*1,62*	*98,3%*	*0,71*	*98,8%*

OK: Ortsklasse
Eigene Berechnungen

Tabelle 9-2 Transportleistungbezogene Emissionsfaktoren für LKW differenziert nach LKW-Klasse, Straßenkategorie und Auslastungsgrad; Bezug: Deutschland 1996: CO und NO_X

ZGG	7,5 t	16,5 t	23 t	30 t	40 t	Gew. Mittel
			— CO —			
Leerfahrt			— g/km —			
Autobahn	1,61	1,79	2,09	1,99	1,61	**1,72**
Außerorts	1,50	1,83	2,05	1,86	1,59	**1,67**
Innerorts	2,15	3,35	3,74	2,71	2,51	**2,57**
Gew. Mittel	**1,75**	**2,26**	**2,45**	**2,05**	**1,68**	**1,86**
50 % ALG			— g/tkm —			
Autobahn	0,89	0,35	0,28	0,24	0,13	**0,18**
Außerorts	0,84	0,35	0,27	0,23	0,13	**0,25**
Innerorts	1,40	0,75	0,58	0,36	0,23	**0,56**
Gew. Mittel	**1,05**	**0,47**	**0,34**	**0,25**	**0,14**	**0,25**
100 % ALG			— g/tkm —			
Autobahn	0,46	0,18	0,14	0,14	0,075	**0,10**
Außerorts	0,44	0,18	0,14	0,14	0,075	**0,14**
Innerorts	0,83	0,43	0,34	0,23	0,14	**0,33**
Gew. Mittel	**0,58**	**0,25**	**0,18**	**0,15**	**0,080**	**0,14**
			— NO_X —			
Leerfahrt			— g/km —			
Autobahn	3,50	6,62	7,78	7,02	8,90	**7,59**
Außerorts	2,87	6,27	7,44	6,34	8,55	**5,76**
Innerorts	3,33	10,5	12,3	9,11	13,4	**7,31**
Gew. Mittel	**3,19**	**7,60**	**8,66**	**7,11**	**9,17**	**6,98**
50 % ALG			— g/tkm —			
Autobahn	2,00	1,43	1,21	0,89	0,86	**0,92**
Außerorts	1,70	1,39	1,19	0,84	0,84	**1,01**
Innerorts	2,20	2,46	2,04	1,26	1,35	**1,69**
Gew. Mittel	**1,95**	**1,72**	**1,39**	**0,92**	**0,89**	**1,04**
100 % ALG			— g/tkm —			
Autobahn	1,07	0,80	0,70	0,55	0,54	**0,57**
Außerorts	0,94	0,80	0,71	0,53	0,54	**0,61**
Innerorts	1,31	1,46	1,23	0,82	0,87	**1,05**
Gew. Mittel	**1,10**	**0,99**	**0,82**	**0,58**	**0,56**	**0,64**

ZGG: Zulässiges Gesamtgewicht; ALG: Auslastungsgrad
Die Mittelwerte sind mit den Anteilen an der Fahr- bzw. Transportleistung gewichtet.
Quelle: /IFEU 1998a/, eigene Berechnungen

Tabelle 9-2 (Fortsetzung) Transportleistungbezogene Emissionsfaktoren für LKW differenziert nach LKW-Klasse, Straßenkategorie und Auslastungsgrad; Bezug: Deutschland 1996: NMHC und Partikel

ZGG	7,5 t	16,5 t	23 t	30 t	40 t	Gew. Mittel
			— NMHC —			
Leerfahrt			— g/km —			
Autobahn	0,79	0,97	1,12	0,80	0,86	**0,86**
Außerorts	0,83	1,02	1,15	0,75	0,85	**0,88**
Innerorts	2,02	2,15	2,31	1,52	1,70	**1,96**
Gew. Mittel	**1,22**	**1,33**	**1,40**	**0,88**	**0,92**	**1,08**
50 % ALG			— g/tkm —			
Autobahn	0,43	0,19	0,15	0,083	0,066	**0,085**
Außerorts	0,46	0,20	0,15	0,077	0,065	**0,13**
Innerorts	1,27	0,49	0,37	0,18	0,15	**0,42**
Gew. Mittel	**0,73**	**0,29**	**0,20**	**0,094**	**0,072**	**0,14**
100 % ALG			— g/tkm —			
Autobahn	0,22	0,10	0,075	0,043	0,035	**0,045**
Außerorts	0,24	0,11	0,076	0,041	0,035	**0,066**
Innerorts	0,74	0,29	0,21	0,11	0,090	**0,24**
Gew. Mittel	**0,40**	**0,16**	**0,11**	**0,051**	**0,039**	**0,074**
			— Partikel —			
Leerfahrt			— g/km —			
Autobahn	0,25	0,38	0,37	0,43	0,40	**0,38**
Außerorts	0,23	0,39	0,36	0,39	0,41	**0,33**
Innerorts	0,40	0,68	0,61	0,54	0,68	**0,52**
Gew. Mittel	**0,29**	**0,47**	**0,42**	**0,44**	**0,43**	**0,39**
50 % ALG			— g/tkm —			
Autobahn	0,14	0,077	0,054	0,051	0,034	**0,041**
Außerorts	0,13	0,079	0,054	0,050	0,035	**0,053**
Innerorts	0,26	0,16	0,098	0,074	0,062	**0,11**
Gew. Mittel	**0,18**	**0,10**	**0,064**	**0,054**	**0,036**	**0,053**
100 % ALG			— g/tkm —			
Autobahn	0,076	0,041	0,030	0,030	0,019	**0,024**
Außerorts	0,073	0,042	0,030	0,031	0,020	**0,030**
Innerorts	0,15	0,091	0,058	0,047	0,038	**0,068**
Gew. Mittel	**0,10**	**0,056**	**0,036**	**0,033**	**0,021**	**0,031**

ZGG: Zulässiges Gesamtgewicht; ALG: Auslastungsgrad
Die Mittelwerte sind mit den Anteilen an der Fahr- bzw. Transportleistung gewichtet.
Quelle: /IFEU 1998a/, eigene Berechnungen

Tabelle 9-3 Transportleistungbezogene Emissionsfaktoren für LKW differenziert nach LKW-Klasse, Straßenkategorie und Auslastungsgrad; Bezug: Deutschland 2000: CO und NO_X

ZGG	7,5 t	16,5 t	23 t	30 t	40 t	Gew. Mittel
			— CO —			
Leerfahrt			— g/km —			
Autobahn	1,10	1,11	1,32	1,26	0,98	**1,06**
Außerorts	1,02	1,13	1,29	1,19	0,97	**1,06**
Innerorts	1,46	2,07	2,36	1,72	1,52	**1,65**
Gew. Mittel	**1,19**	**1,39**	**1,54**	**1,31**	**1,02**	**1,17**
50 % ALG			— g/tkm —			
Autobahn	0,61	0,21	0,18	0,15	0,080	**0,11**
Außerorts	0,57	0,22	0,17	0,15	0,081	**0,16**
Innerorts	0,95	0,46	0,37	0,23	0,14	**0,35**
Gew. Mittel	**0,71**	**0,29**	**0,22**	**0,16**	**0,085**	**0,15**
100 % ALG			— g/tkm —			
Autobahn	0,31	0,11	0,090	0,091	0,046	**0,062**
Außerorts	0,30	0,11	0,087	0,090	0,046	**0,085**
Innerorts	0,56	0,27	0,21	0,15	0,084	**0,21**
Gew. Mittel	**0,39**	**0,15**	**0,12**	**0,10**	**0,048**	**0,085**
			— NO_X —			
Leerfahrt			— g/km —			
Autobahn	2,94	5,37	6,40	5,78	7,24	**6,27**
Außerorts	2,41	5,08	6,11	5,23	6,95	**4,79**
Innerorts	2,80	8,51	10,1	7,48	10,9	**6,05**
Gew. Mittel	**2,68**	**6,14**	**7,10**	**5,86**	**7,45**	**5,79**
50 % ALG			— g/tkm —			
Autobahn	1,68	1,16	0,99	0,73	0,70	**0,75**
Außerorts	1,43	1,13	0,98	0,69	0,69	**0,82**
Innerorts	1,85	1,99	1,67	1,04	1,10	**1,38**
Gew. Mittel	**1,64**	**1,39**	**1,14**	**0,76**	**0,72**	**0,84**
100 % ALG			— g/tkm —			
Autobahn	0,90	0,65	0,58	0,45	0,44	**0,46**
Außerorts	0,79	0,65	0,58	0,44	0,44	**0,50**
Innerorts	1,10	1,18	1,01	0,67	0,71	**0,86**
Gew. Mittel	**0,92**	**0,80**	**0,67**	**0,47**	**0,46**	**0,52**

ZGG: Zulässiges Gesamtgewicht; ALG: Auslastungsgrad
Die Mittelwerte sind mit den Anteilen an der Fahr- bzw. Transportleistung gewichtet.
Quelle: /IFEU 1998a/, eigene Berechnungen

Tabelle 9-3 (Fortsetzung) Transportleistungbezogene Emissionsfaktoren für LKW differenziert nach LKW-Klasse, Straßenkategorie und Auslastungsgrad; Bezug: Deutschland 2000: NMHC und Partikel

ZGG	7,5 t	16,5 t	23 t	30 t	40 t	Gew. Mittel
			— NMHC —			
Leerfahrt			— g/km —			
Autobahn	0,63	0,74	0,87	0,62	0,66	**0,66**
Außerorts	0,67	0,78	0,89	0,59	0,65	**0,69**
Innerorts	1,62	1,64	1,79	1,17	1,29	**1,54**
Gew. Mittel	**0,98**	**1,01**	**1,08**	**0,68**	**0,70**	**0,83**
50 % ALG			— g/tkm —			
Autobahn	0,34	0,15	0,11	0,064	0,050	**0,064**
Außerorts	0,37	0,16	0,12	0,060	0,050	**0,096**
Innerorts	1,02	0,38	0,28	0,14	0,11	**0,32**
Gew. Mittel	**0,58**	**0,22**	**0,15**	**0,073**	**0,055**	**0,10**
100 % ALG			— g/tkm —			
Autobahn	0,18	0,078	0,058	0,034	0,027	**0,034**
Außerorts	0,19	0,082	0,059	0,031	0,026	**0,050**
Innerorts	0,59	0,22	0,17	0,082	0,068	**0,19**
Gew. Mittel	**0,32**	**0,12**	**0,082**	**0,039**	**0,030**	**0,056**
			— Partikel —			
Leerfahrt			— g/km —			
Autobahn	0,17	0,24	0,24	0,28	0,25	**0,24**
Außerorts	0,16	0,24	0,23	0,26	0,26	**0,22**
Innerorts	0,28	0,43	0,39	0,35	0,43	**0,34**
Gew. Mittel	**0,20**	**0,30**	**0,27**	**0,28**	**0,26**	**0,25**
50 % ALG			— g/tkm —			
Autobahn	0,10	0,049	0,035	0,033	0,021	**0,026**
Außerorts	0,093	0,050	0,035	0,033	0,022	**0,033**
Innerorts	0,18	0,10	0,063	0,048	0,039	**0,073**
Gew. Mittel	**0,12**	**0,064**	**0,041**	**0,035**	**0,022**	**0,033**
100 % ALG			— g/tkm —			
Autobahn	0,052	0,026	0,019	0,020	0,012	**0,015**
Außerorts	0,050	0,027	0,020	0,020	0,012	**0,019**
Innerorts	0,10	0,058	0,038	0,031	0,024	**0,044**
Gew. Mittel	**0,069**	**0,035**	**0,023**	**0,021**	**0,013**	**0,019**

ZGG: Zulässiges Gesamtgewicht; ALG: Auslastungsgrad
Die Mittelwerte sind mit den Anteilen an der Fahr- bzw. Transportleistung gewichtet.
Quelle: /IFEU 1998a/, eigene Berechnungen

Tabelle 9-4 Spezifischer Einsatz mineralischer und energetischer Ressourcen und kumulierte Emissionen des Gütertransports mit LKW im *RME-Betrieb* am Beispiel zweier LKW-Klassen im Mittel aller Straßenkategorien bei einem Auslastungsgrad von 50 %

ZGG		**7,5 t**		**40 t**	
Mineralische Ressourcen					
Kalkstein	g/tkm	9,25		2,99	
Phosphaterz	g/tkm	16,4		5,29	
Schwefel	g/tkm	1,12		0,36	
Rohkali	g/tkm	16,9		5,45	
Kochsalz	g/tkm	-25,5		-8,24	
Tonmineralien	g/tkm	0,71		0,23	
Primärenergieträger					
Erdöl	MJ/tkm	-0,56		-0,18	
Erdgas	MJ/tkm	0,48		0,15	
Steinkohle	MJ/tkm	-0,11		-0,034	
Braunkohle	MJ/tkm	-0,17		-0,056	
Uran	MJ/tkm	-0,17		-0,054	
Summe Erschöpfl. ET	*MJ/tkm*	-0,53		-0,17	
Wasser	MJ/tkm	-0,019		-0,0063	
Summe*	**MJ/tkm**	**-1,079**		**-0,351**	
Emissionen					
		Global		**Global**	
CO_2	g/tkm	-24,2**	264***	-7,81**	85,5***
CH_4	g/tkm	0,034		0,0074	
N_2O	g/tkm	0,42		0,14	
CO_2-Äquivalente	*g/tkm*	*108*		*34,9*	
		OK 2	**OK 3**	**OK 2**	**OK 3**
SO_2	g/tkm	-0,0085	-0,17	-0,018	-0,055
CO	g/tkm	0,74	-0,019	0,88	-0,0061
NO_X	g/tkm	1,98	-0,18	0,056	-0,057
NMHC	g/tkm	0,40	-0,0053	0,044	-0,0017
Partikel	g/tkm	0,12	-0,017	0,0010	-0,0054
Staub	g/tkm	0,025	-0,000015	0,0082	-0,0000049
HCl	g/tkm	-0,0010	-0,00021	0,000094	-0,000067
NH_3	g/tkm	0,55	-0,000021	0,18	-0,0000069
Formaldehyd	g/tkm	0,053	-0,00043	0,0013	-0,00014
Benzol	g/tkm	0,012	-0,00010	175	-0,000033
Benzo(a)pyren	ng/tkm	539	-21,7	-0,066	-7,01
TCDD-TÄ	ng/tkm	0,012	-0,0038	0,0026	-0,0012
SO_2-Äquivalente	*g/tkm*	*2,40*	*-0,29*	*0,36*	*-0,095*

OK: Ortsklasse
*: Nachrichtlich: Energieinhalt von Rapskorn: 6,07 MJ/tkm bzw. 1,96 MJ/tkm für LKW 7,5 t bzw. LKW 40 t
**: Fossiles CO_2: ausschließlich für CO_2-Äquivalente angerechnet.
***: Nachrichtlich: Biogenes CO_2 aus der Nutzung von RME.
Bei negativen Zahlen überwiegen die Gutschriften aus Kuppelprodukten die Aufwendungen der Produktion.
Eigene Berechnungen

9.2 Bahn: Kumulierte Daten

In **Tabelle 9-5** bis **Tabelle 9-7** sind die transportleistungsbezogenen kumulierten Daten des Gütertransports mit der Bahn differenziert nach Zuggattungen (Einzelwagenzug, Züge des Kombinierten Ladungsverkehrs (KLV) und Ganzzug) und Traktionsart im Hauptlauf (Elektro, Diesel) dokumentiert. Der relativ hohe Erdölanteil am Primärenergieverbrauch von Einzelwagenzügen auch mit Elektrotraktion im Hauptlauf resultiert aus dem verhältnismäßig hohen Rangieraufwand für Einzelwagenzüge, der fast ausschließlich mit Diesellokomotiven erbracht wird.

Tabelle 9-5 Spezifischer kumulierter Energieaufwand und Emissionen des Gütertransports mit *Einzelwagenzügen*

Hauptlauftraktion		**Elektro**		**Diesel**		**Mix**	
Primärenergieeinsatz							
Erdöl	MJ/tkm	0,11		0,99		0,20	
Erdgas	MJ/tkm	0,056		0,013		0,052	
Steinkohle	MJ/tkm	0,29		0,012		0,26	
Braunkohle	MJ/tkm	0,087		0,0052		0,079	
Uran	MJ/tkm	0,23		0,0098		0,21	
Σ Erschöpfl. ET	*MJ/tkm*	*0,78*		*1,03*		*0,81*	
Wasser	MJ/tkm	0,028		0,00089		0,025	
Summe	**MJ/tkm**	**0,81**		**1,03**		**0,83**	
Emissionen							
		Global		**Global**		**Global**	
CO_2	g/tkm	46,0		76,0		49,0	
CH_4	g/tkm	0,15		0,020		0,13	
N_2O	g/tkm	0,0022		0,0073		0,0027	
CO_2-Äquivalente	*g/tkm*	*49,8*		*78,7*		*52,7*	
		OK 2+3	**OK 2**	**OK 2+3**	**OK 2**	**OK 2+3**	**OK 2**
SO_2	g/tkm	0,059	92,5%	0,056	90,7%	0,059	92,4%
CO	g/tkm	0,048	99,0%	0,36	99,9%	0,079	99,4%
NO_X	g/tkm	0,16	97,2%	1,18	99,7%	0,26	98,4%
NMHC	g/tkm	0,015	98,9%	0,14	99,7%	0,027	99,3%
Partikel	g/tkm	0,0061	93,2%	0,055	99,6%	0,011	96,4%
Staub	g/tkm	0,0018	99,8%	0,0011	97,4%	0,0017	99,6%
HCl	g/tkm	0,0022	99,8%	0,00018	96,3%	0,0020	99,7%
NH_3	g/tkm	0,00005	97,6%	0,00043	99,7%	0,00008	98,7%
Formaldehyd	g/tkm	0,0011	99,0%	0,010	99,9%	0,0020	99,5%
Benzol	g/tkm	0,00028	98,9%	0,0025	99,8%	0,00050	99,4%
Benzo(a)pyren	ng/tkm	18,2	97,0%	167	99,7%	33,1	98,4%
TCDD-TÄ	ng/tkm	0,0040	96,3%	0,0042	89,5%	0,0040	95,5%
SO_2-Äquivalente	*g/tkm*	*0,17*	*95,6%*	*0,88*	*99,2%*	*0,24*	*96,9%*

Mix: 90 % Elektrotraktion und 10 % Dieseltraktion
Eigene Berechnungen

Tabelle 9-6 Spezifischer kumulierter Energieaufwand und Emissionen des Gütertransports mit *Zügen des Kombinierten Ladungsverkehrs*

Hauptlauftraktion		**Elektro**		**Diesel**		**Mix**	
Primärenergieeinsatz							
Erdöl	MJ/tkm	0,019		0,64		0,082	
Erdgas	MJ/tkm	0,043		0,0077		0,039	
Steinkohle	MJ/tkm	0,22		0,0038		0,20	
Braunkohle	MJ/tkm	0,067		0,0022		0,061	
Uran	MJ/tkm	0,18		0,0034		0,16	
Σ Erschöpfl. ET	*MJ/tkm*	*0,53*		*0,66*		*0,55*	
Wasser	MJ/tkm	0,021		0,00023		0,019	
Summe	**MJ/tkm**	**0,55**		**0,66**		**0,57**	
Emissionen							
		Global		**Global**		**Global**	
CO_2	g/tkm	30,4		48,9		32,2	
CH_4	g/tkm	0,11		0,011		0,10	
N_2O	g/tkm	0,0012		0,0047		0,0016	
CO_2-Äquivalente	*g/tkm*	*33,1*		*50,6*		*34,9*	
		OK 2+3	**OK 2**	**OK 2+3**	**OK 2**	**OK 2+3**	**OK 2**
SO_2	g/tkm	0,042	92,7%	0,036	90,6%	0,041	92,5%
CO	g/tkm	0,013	97,3%	0,23	99,9%	0,035	99,0%
NO_X	g/tkm	0,043	92,4%	0,77	99,8%	0,12	97,3%
NMHC	g/tkm	0,0024	95,7%	0,090	99,7%	0,011	98,9%
Partikel	g/tkm	0,0010	69,6%	0,036	99,6%	0,0045	93,6%
Staub	g/tkm	0,0013	99,9%	0,00068	97,3%	0,0012	99,8%
HCl	g/tkm	0,0017	99,8%	0,00009	95,2%	0,0015	99,8%
NH_3	g/tkm	0,00001	87,5%	0,00028	99,7%	0,00003	97,7%
Formaldehyd	g/tkm	0,00015	94,8%	0,0068	99,9%	0,00081	99,1%
Benzol	g/tkm	0,00005	95,7%	0,0016	99,8%	0,00020	99,0%
Benzo(a)pyren	ng/tkm	2,76	85,8%	109	99,7%	13,3	97,2%
TCDD-TÄ	ng/tkm	0,0028	96,9%	0,0027	89,4%	0,0028	96,2%
SO_2-Äquivalente	*g/tkm*	*0,073*	*92,7%*	*0,57*	*99,2%*	*0,12*	*95,7%*

Mix: 90 % Elektrotraktion und 10 % Dieseltraktion
Eigene Berechnungen

Tabelle 9-7 Spezifischer kumulierter Energieaufwand und Emissionen des Gütertransports mit *Ganzzügen*

Hauptlauftraktion		**Elektro**		**Diesel**		**Mix**	
Primärenergieeinsatz							
Erdöl	MJ/tkm	0,018		0,42		0,059	
Erdgas	MJ/tkm	0,027		0,0052		0,024	
Steinkohle	MJ/tkm	0,14		0,0031		0,13	
Braunkohle	MJ/tkm	0,042		0,0017		0,038	
Uran	MJ/tkm	0,11		0,0027		0,10	
Σ Erschöpfl. ET	*MJ/tkm*	*0,34*		*0,44*		*0,35*	
Wasser	MJ/tkm	0,013		0,00020		0,012	
Summe	**MJ/tkm**	**0,35**		**0,44**		**0,36**	
Emissionen							
		Global		**Global**		**Global**	
CO_2	g/tkm	19,2		32,4		20,6	
CH_4	g/tkm	0,070		0,0075		0,063	
N_2O	g/tkm	0,00080		0,0031		0,0010	
CO_2-Äquivalente	*g/tkm*	*21,0*		*33,5*		*22,2*	
		OK 2+3	**OK 2**	**OK 2+3**	**OK 2**	**OK 2+3**	**OK 2**
SO_2	g/tkm	0,026	92,7%	0,024	90,6%	0,026	92,5%
CO	g/tkm	0,010	97,8%	0,15	99,9%	0,025	99,1%
NO_X	g/tkm	0,033	94,0%	0,51	99,8%	0,081	97,6%
NMHC	g/tkm	0,0023	97,2%	0,059	99,7%	0,0080	99,0%
Partikel	g/tkm	0,00094	80,0%	0,024	99,6%	0,0032	94,4%
Staub	g/tkm	0,00082	99,9%	0,00045	97,4%	0,00078	99,7%
HCl	g/tkm	0,0010	99,8%	0,00006	95,5%	0,00095	99,8%
NH_3	g/tkm	0,00001	92,4%	0,00018	99,7%	0,00002	98,0%
Formaldehyd	g/tkm	0,00015	96,8%	0,0045	99,9%	0,00059	99,2%
Benzol	g/tkm	0,00004	97,1%	0,0011	99,8%	0,00015	99,1%
Benzo(a)pyren	ng/tkm	2,69	90,9%	71,7	99,7%	9,59	97,5%
TCDD-TÄ	ng/tkm	0,0017	96,8%	0,0018	89,4%	0,0017	96,1%
SO_2-Äquivalente	*g/tkm*	*0,051*	*93,4%*	*0,38*	*99,2%*	*0,084*	*96,0%*

Mix: 90 % Elektrotraktion und 10 % Dieseltraktion
Eigene Berechnungen

9.3 Binnenschiffe: Kumulierte Daten

In **Tabelle 9-8** sind die verbrauchs- und transportleistungsbezogenen kumulierten Daten des Gütertransports mit Binnenschiffen dokumentiert. Ihnen liegt der hier abgeschätzte mittlere spezifische Verbrauch von 0,43 MJ/tkm zugrunde. Liegen detaillierte Daten über den betrachteten Schiffahrtsweg (Strömungsverhältnisse), Transportrichtung, Auslastungsgrad und Schiffsgröße vor, können die differenzierten Verbräuche nach Kapitel 5.3.1 angesetzt oder mit der dort angegebenen Formel berechnet werden.

Tabelle 9-8 Spezifischer kumulierter Energieaufwand und Emissionen des Gütertransports mit Binnenschiffen

Bezug	**Energie**		**Transportleistung**		
Primärenergieeinsatz					
Erdöl	MJ/MJ	1,09	MJ/tkm	0,47	
Erdgas	MJ/MJ	0,013	MJ/tkm	0,0054	
Steinkohle	MJ/MJ	0,0038	MJ/tkm	0,0016	
Braunkohle	MJ/MJ	0,0030	MJ/tkm	0,0013	
Uran	MJ/MJ	0,0036	MJ/tkm	0,0016	
Summe Erschöpfl. ET	*MJ/MJ*	*1,11*	*MJ/tkm*	*0,48*	
Wasser	MJ/MJ	0,00013	MJ/tkm	0,00006	
Summe	**MJ/MJ**	**1,11**	**MJ/tkm**	**0,48**	
Emissionen					
		Global		**Global**	
CO_2	g/MJ	82,4	g/tkm	35,4	
CH_4	g/MJ	0,017	g/tkm	0,0071	
N_2O	g/MJ	0,0080	g/tkm	0,0034	
CO_2-Äquivalente	*g/MJ*	*85,2*	*g/tkm*	*36,6*	
		OK 2+3		**OK 2+3**	**OK 2**
SO_2	g/MJ	0,060	g/tkm	0,026	90,6%
CO	g/MJ	0,26	g/tkm	0,11	99,8%
NO_X	g/MJ	1,41	g/tkm	0,61	99,8%
NMHC	g/MJ	0,12	g/tkm	0,051	99,6%
Partikel	g/MJ	0,040	g/tkm	0,017	99,4%
Staub	g/MJ	0,0011	g/tkm	0,00049	97,3%
HCl	g/MJ	0,00013	g/tkm	0,00006	94,5%
NH_3	g/MJ	0,00047	g/tkm	0,00020	99,7%
Formaldehyd	g/MJ	0,0088	g/tkm	0,0038	99,9%
Benzol	g/MJ	0,0021	g/tkm	0,00092	99,7%
Benzo(a)pyren	ng/MJ	184	ng/tkm	78,8	99,8%
TCDD-TÄ	ng/MJ	0,0045	ng/tkm	0,0019	89,3%
SO_2-Äquivalente	*g/MJ*	*1,05*	*g/tkm*	*0,45*	*99,3%*

OK: Ortsklasse
Eigene Berechnungen

9.4 Seeschiffe: Kumulierte Daten

In **Tabelle 9-9** sind die transportleistungsbezogenen kumulierten Daten des Gütertransports mit Seeschiffen differenziert nach Stückgutfrachtern, Massengutfrachtern, Motortankern, Turbinentankern und im gewichteten Mittel von Motor- und Turbinentankern (M+T-Mix) dokumentiert. Dem M+T-Mix liegen Transportleistungsanteile (38 bzw. 62 %) nach /KOLLE 1991/ zugrunde. **Tabelle 9-10** gibt hierzu die jeweiligen Anteile an der Ortsklasse 2 an.

Tabelle 9-9 Spezifischer kumulierter Energieaufwand und Emissionen des Gütertransports mit Seeschiffen

		Stückgut-frachter	Massengut-frachter	Motor-tanker	Turbinen-tanker	Tanker (M+T-Mix)
Primärenergieeinsatz						
Erdöl	MJ/tkm	0,22	0,11	0,055	0,055	0,055
Erdgas	MJ/tkm	0,0023	0,0012	0,00059	0,00059	0,00059
Steinkohle	MJ/tkm	0,00062	0,00031	0,00016	0,00016	0,00016
Braunkohle	MJ/tkm	0,00049	0,00025	0,00012	0,00012	0,00012
Uran	MJ/tkm	0,00059	0,00030	0,00015	0,00015	0,00015
Summe Erschöpfl. ET	*MJ/tkm*	*0,22*	*0,11*	*0,056*	*0,056*	*0,056*
Wasser	MJ/tkm	0,00002	0,00001	0,00001	0,00001	0,00001
Summe	**MJ/tkm**	**0,22**	**0,11**	**0,056**	**0,056**	**0,056**
Emissionen						
		Global	**Global**	**Global**	**Global**	**Global**
CO_2	g/tkm	17,5	8,73	4,36	4,36	4,36
CH_4	g/tkm	0,0030	0,0015	0,00075	0,00077	0,00076
N_2O	g/tkm	0,0017	0,00085	0,00043	0,00011	0,00023
CO_2-Äquivalente	*g/tkm*	*18,0*	*9,02*	*4,51*	*4,41*	*4,45*
		OK 2+3	**OK 2+3**	**OK 2+3**	**OK 2+3**	**OK 2+3**
SO_2	g/tkm	0,41	0,20	0,10	0,10	0,10
CO	g/tkm	0,046	0,023	0,011	0,00060	0,0047
NO_X	g/tkm	0,42	0,21	0,11	0,0033	0,042
NMHC	g/tkm	0,015	0,0076	0,0038	0,00082	0,0019
Partikel	g/tkm	0,030	0,015	0,0075	0,0015	0,0038
Staub	g/tkm	0,00022	0,00011	0,00005	0,00005	0,00005
HCl	g/tkm	0,00047	0,00023	0,00012	0,00012	0,00012
NH_3	g/tkm	0,00010	0,00005	0,00003	0,00003	0,00003
Formaldehyd	g/tkm	0,0010	0,00051	0,00026	0,00003	0,00012
Benzol	g/tkm	0,00025	0,00013	0,00006	0,00001	0,00003
Benzo(a)pyren	ng/tkm	39,3	19,7	9,83	3,23	5,73
TCDD-TÄ	ng/tkm	0,0064	0,0032	0,0016	0,0016	0,0016
SO_2-Äquivalente	*g/tkm*	*0,70*	*0,35*	*0,18*	*0,10*	*0,13*

M+T-Mix: Transportleistungsgewichtung; 38 % Motor- und 62 % Turbinentanker
OK: Ortsklasse
Eigene Berechnungen

Tabelle 9-10 Anteile der Emissionen nicht global wirksamer Schadstoffe in der Ortsklasse 2 an den gesamten Emissionen des Frachttransports mit Seeschiffen

	Stückgut-frachter	**Massengut-frachter**	**Motor-tanker**	**Turbinen-tanker**	**Tanker (M+T-Mix)**
SO_2	26,1%	26,1%	26,1%	26,1%	26,1%
CO	26,2%	26,2%	26,2%	48,7%	28,0%
NO_X	25,5%	25,5%	25,5%	39,6%	26,1%
NMHC	38,9%	38,9%	38,9%	88,9%	51,9%
Partikel	0,3%	0,3%	0,3%	1,6%	0,6%
Staub	97,2%	97,2%	97,2%	97,2%	97,2%
HCl	27,7%	27,7%	27,7%	27,7%	27,7%
NH_3	25,3%	25,3%	25,3%	25,3%	25,3%
Formaldehyd	26,0%	26,0%	26,0%	33,7%	27,3%
Benzol	29,5%	29,5%	29,5%	72,8%	35,2%
Benzo(a)pyren	1,6%	1,6%	1,6%	4,9%	2,8%
TCDD-TÄ	7,2%	7,2%	7,2%	7,2%	7,2%
SO_2-Äquivalente	*25,8%*	*25,8%*	*25,8%*	*26,4%*	*26,1%*

M+T-Mix: Transportleistungsgewichtung; 38 % Motor- und 62 % Turbinentanker
Eigene Berechnungen

9.5 Flugzeuge: Kumulierte Daten

In **Tabelle 9-11** sind die transportleistungsbezogenen kumulierten Daten des Frachttransports mit Düsenflugzeugen differenziert nach Kurz- bzw. Mittelstrecken- und Langstreckenflug dokumentiert.

Tabelle 9-11 Spezifischer kumulierter Energieaufwand und Emissionen des Frachttransports mit Flugzeugen differenziert nach Kurz- bzw. Mittel- und Langstreckenflug

		Kurz-/Mittelstrecke		Langstrecke	
Primärenergieeinsatz					
Erdöl	MJ/tkm	17,8		11,9	
Erdgas	MJ/tkm	0,21		0,14	
Steinkohle	MJ/tkm	0,062		0,041	
Braunkohle	MJ/tkm	0,049		0,033	
Uran	MJ/tkm	0,060		0,040	
Summe Erschöpfl. ET	*MJ/tkm*	*18,2*		*12,1*	
Wasser	MJ/tkm	0,0022		0,0015	
Summe	**MJ/tkm**	**18,2**		**12,1**	
Emissionen					
		Global		**Global**	
CO_2	g/tkm	1.355		903	
CH_4	g/tkm	0,26		0,17	
N_2O	g/tkm	0,13		0,087	
CO_2-Äquivalente	*g/tkm*	*1.401*		*934*	
		OK 2+3	**OK 2**	**OK 2+3**	**OK 2**
SO_2	g/tkm	0,86	65,5%	0,68	55,3%
CO	g/tkm	2,14	12,8%	0,97	9,4%
NO_X	g/tkm	6,36	13,3%	4,24	8,5%
NMHC	g/tkm	0,75	37,6%	0,50	34,1%
Partikel	g/tkm	0,20	13,0%	0,13	8,3%
Staub	g/tkm	0,019	97,3%	0,012	97,3%
HCl	g/tkm	0,0021	77,8%	0,0014	76,9%
NH_3	g/tkm	0,0077	10,5%	0,0051	5,5%
Formaldehyd	g/tkm	0,039	12,9%	0,026	8,0%
Benzol	g/tkm	0,023	15,0%	0,015	10,3%
Benzo(a)pyren	ng/tkm	3.008	11,6%	2.005	6,8%
TCDD-TÄ	ng/tkm	0,074	61,6%	0,050	60,0%
SO_2-Äquivalente	*g/tkm*	*5,33*	*21,8%*	*3,65*	*17,2%*

OK: Ortsklasse
Eigene Berechnungen

9.6 Pipelines: Kumulierte Daten

In **Tabelle 9-12** sind die transportleistungsbezogenen kumulierten Daten des Erdgastransports mit Pipelines mit Gasturbinenverdichtern dokumentiert. Für die elektrisch betriebenen Ölpipelines ergeben sich die kumulierten Daten durch Verknüpfung des Stromverbrauchs mit den entsprechenden Daten der unterstellten Strombereitstellung.

Tabelle 9-12 Spezifischer kumulierter Energieaufwand und Emissionen des Erdgastransports mit Pipelines

		D		GUS	
Primärenergieeinsatz					
Erdöl	MJ/TJkm	0		0	
Erdgas	MJ/TJkm	16,0		16,0	
Steinkohle	MJ/TJkm	0		0	
Braunkohle	MJ/TJkm	0		0	
Uran	MJ/TJkm	0		0	
Summe Erschöpfl. ET	*MJ/TJkm*	*16,0*		*16,0*	
Wasser	MJ/TJkm	0		0	
Summe	**MJ/TJkm**	**16,0**		**16,0**	
Emissionen					
		Global		**Global**	
CO_2	g/TJkm	878		881	
CH_4	g/TJkm	1,88		1,95	
N_2O	g/TJkm	0,040		0,040	
CO_2-Äquivalente	*g/TJkm*	*930*		*934*	
		OK 2+3	**OK 2**	**OK 2**	**OK 2**
SO_2	g/TJkm	0,0069	99,6%	0,0065	100,0%
CO	g/TJkm	1,39	99,6%	2,63	100,0%
NO_X	g/TJkm	4,69	99,6%	5,27	100,0%
NMHC	g/TJkm	0,14	99,6%	0,33	100,0%
Partikel	g/TJkm	0	k. A.	0	k. A.
Staub	g/TJkm	0,067	99,5%	0,066	100,0%
HCl	g/TJkm	0	k. A.	0	k. A.
NH_3	g/TJkm	0	k. A.	0	k. A.
Formaldehyd	g/TJkm	0,014	99,6%	0,033	100,0%
Benzol	g/TJkm	0,014	99,6%	0,033	100,0%
Benzo(a)pyren	ng/TJkm	15,9	99,5%	15,8	100,0%
TCDD-TÄ	ng/TJkm	1,33	99,5%	1,32	100,0%
SO_2-Äquivalente	*g/TJkm*	*3,29*	*99,6%*	*3,70*	*100,0%*

Eigene Berechnungen

10 Landwirtschaft

In den folgenden Tabellen werden Daten zum spezifischen kumulierten Energieaufwand und den damit verbundenen Emissionen der maschinellen Feldarbeit, die entsprechenden Daten für Anbaubeispiele und – für Raps – nach einzelnen Arbeitsgängen und Laststufen differenzierte Daten zu den direkten Emissionen dokumentiert.

10.1 Kumulierte Daten im Diesel-, Rapsöl- und RME-Betrieb

Tabelle 10-1 und **Tabelle 10-2** enthalten den spezifischen Primärenergieeinsatz und die kumulierten Emissionen von Landmaschinen im Mittel des 5-Punkte-Tests (Dieselbetrieb,

Tabelle 10-1 Spezifischer kumulierter Energieaufwand und Emissionen des Einsatzes von Landmaschinen (Dieselbetrieb) im Mittel des 5-Punkte-Tests

Primärenergieträger				
Erdöl	MJ/MJ	1,09		
Erdgas	MJ/MJ	0,013		
Steinkohle	MJ/MJ	0,0038		
Braunkohle	MJ/MJ	0,0030		
Uran	MJ/MJ	0,0031		
Summe Erschöpfl. ET	*MJ/MJ*	*1,11*		
Wasser	MJ/MJ	0,00045		
Summe	**MJ/MJ**	**1,11**		
Emissionen				
		Global		
CO_2	g/MJ	82,3		
CH_4	g/MJ	0,17		
N_2O	g/MJ	0,0080		
CO_2-Äquivalente	*g/MJ*	*85,1*		
		OK 2	**OK 3**	**OK 2+3**
SO_2	g/MJ	0,053	0,0056	0,058
CO	g/MJ	0,24	0,00054	0,24
NO_X	g/MJ	0,81	0,0032	0,81
NMHC	g/MJ	0,15	0,00048	0,15
Partikel	g/MJ	0,069	0,00026	0,069
Staub	g/MJ	0,0013	0,000031	0,0014
HCl	g/MJ	0,00012	0,0000071	0,00013
NH_3	g/MJ	0,00047	0,0000013	0,00047
Formaldehyd	g/MJ	0,011	0,0000089	0,011
Benzol	g/MJ	0,0026	0,0000054	0,0026
Benzo(a)pyren	ng/MJ	182	0,46	183
TCDD-TÄ	ng/MJ	0,0040	0,00048	0,0045
SO_2-Äquivalente	*g/MJ*	*0,62*	*0,0078*	*0,63*
Eigene Berechnungen				

Rapsöl- bzw. RME-Betrieb). Für die biogenen Kraftstoffe sind zusätzlich die Verbräuche mineralischer Ressourcen durch den Düngemitteleinsatz bzw. aus der Umesterung ausgewiesen.

Tabelle 10-2 Spezifischer Ressourceneinsatz und kumulierte Emissionen des Einsatzes von Landmaschinen im Rapsöl- und RME-Betrieb im Mittel des 5-Punkte-Tests

		Rapsöl		**RME**	
Mineralische Ressourcen					
Kalkstein	g/MJ	3,05		2,67	
Phosphaterz	g/MJ	5,23		4,72	
Schwefel	g/MJ	0,35		0,32	
Rohkali	g/MJ	5,00		4,86	
Kochsalz	g/MJ	0		-7,34	
Tonmineralien	g/MJ	0		0,20	
Primärenergieträger					
Erdöl	MJ/MJ	-0,020		-0,16	
Erdgas	MJ/MJ	0,11		0,14	
Steinkohle	MJ/MJ	0,024		-0,031	
Braunkohle	MJ/MJ	0,013		-0,050	
Uran	MJ/MJ	0,015		-0,048	
Summe Erschöpfl. ET	*MJ/MJ*	*0,14*		*-0,15*	
Wasser	MJ/MJ	0,0024		-0,0056	
Summe*	**MJ/MJ**	**0,14**		**-0,16**	
Emissionen					
		Global		**Global**	
CO_2	g/MJ	7,80**	76,4***	-6,96**	76,4
CH_4	g/MJ	0,031		0,0085	
N_2O	g/MJ	0,13		0,12	
CO_2-Äquivalente	*g/MJ*	*49,8*		*31,5*	
		OK 2	**OK 3**	**OK 2**	**OK 3**
SO_2	g/MJ	0,010	-0,067	-0,10	-0,049
CO	g/MJ	0,013	-0,0076	0,24	-0,0055
NO_X	g/MJ	0,048	-0,071	0,82	-0,051
NMHC	g/MJ	-0,0061	-0,0021	0,15	-0,0015
Partikel	g/MJ	0,0024	-0,0067	0,070	-0,0048
Staub	g/MJ	0,011	-0,00000088	0,0073	-0,0000044
HCl	g/MJ	0,00042	-0,000081	-0,00029	-0,000060
NH_3	g/MJ	0,18	-0,000010	0,16	-0,0000062
Formaldehyd	g/MJ	0,00026	-0,00017	0,011	-0,00012
Benzol	g/MJ	0,000057	-0,000040	0,0026	-0,000029
Benzo(a)pyren	ng/MJ	7,58	-8,66	180	-6,25
TCDD-TÄ	ng/MJ	0,0051	-0,0014	0,0024	-0,0011
SO_2-Äquivalente	*g/MJ*	*0,38*	*-0,12*	*0,77*	*-0,085*

*: Nachrichtlich: Energieinhalt von Rapskorn: 2,028 bzw. 1,749 MJ je bereitgestelltem MJ Rapsöl bzw. RME.
**: Fossiles CO_2; ausschließlich für CO_2-Äquivalente angerechnet.
***: Nachrichtlich: Biogenes CO_2 aus der Nutzung von Rapsöl bzw. RME.
Bei negativen Zahlen überwiegen die Gutschriften aus Kuppelprodukten die Aufwendungen der Produktion.
Eigene Berechnungen

Den Bezug der Daten in **Tabelle 10-1** und **Tabelle 10-2** bildet der Energieverbrauch. Nach Laststufen differenzierte verbrauchsbezogene Emissionen können vom Anwender aus den entsprechenden direkten Emissionen und den Daten zur Dieselbereitstellung durch einfache Addition selbst berechnet werden. Zur Bilanzierung der maschinellen Feldarbeit beim Anbau einer bestimmten Kultur werden die so erhaltenen Daten mit dem Kraftstoffverbrauch in den einzelnen Laststufen multipliziert. Der Verbrauch wiederum wird aus Einsatzzeit und zeitbezogenem Verbrauch der einzelnen Maschinenklassen bestimmt.

10.2 Anbaubeispiele: Differenzierungen und kumulierte Daten

Tabelle 10-3 faßt die direkten Emissionen der maschinellen Feldarbeit beim Anbau von Winterraps differenziert nach Arbeitsschritten zusammen (Dieselbetrieb; Bezug: Anbaufläche). **Tabelle 10-4** dokumentiert den spezifischen Primärenergieeinsatz und die damit verbundenen Emissionen der maschinellen Feldarbeit beim Anbau von Winterraps, Winterweizen, Kartoffeln und Zuckerrüben (Dieselbetrieb; Bezug: Anbaufläche und Wirtschaftsjahr).

Tabelle 10-3 Anbau von Winterraps: Direkte Emissionen der maschinellen Feldarbeit (Dieselbetrieb), differenziert nach Arbeitsschritten (Bezug: 1 ha Anbaufläche und 1 Wirtschaftsjahr)

		Stoppelbearbeitung	Pflügen	Ausbringung*	Ernte und Transport	Summe
		Global	**Global**	**Global**	**Global**	**Global**
CO_2	g/ha*a	56.627	43.164	21.816	43.839	165.446
CH_4	g/ha*a	1,63	1,24	1,22	1,48	5,56
N_2O	g/ha*a	5,91	4,51	2,28	4,58	17,28
		OK 2	**OK 2**	**OK 2**	**OK 2**	**OK 2**
SO_2	g/ha*a	16,0	12,2	6,18	12,4	46,9
CO	g/ha*a	108	82,8	89,6	107	388
NO_X	g/ha*a	620	472	256	468	1.817
NMHC	g/ha*a	66,2	50,5	49,4	60,0	226
Partikel	g/ha*a	41,8	31,9	21,5	36,0	131
Staub	g/ha*a	0	0	0	0	0
HCl	g/ha*a	0,018	0,014	0,0069	0,014	0,052
NH_3	g/ha*a	0,36	0,27	0,14	0,28	1,04
Formaldehyd	g/ha*a	5,50	4,19	4,10	4,98	18,8
Benzol	g/ha*a	1,29	0,98	0,96	1,17	4,40
Benzo(a)pyren	ng/ha*a	139.916	106.700	49.083	101.792	397.491
TCDD-TÄ	ng/ha*a	1,07	0,82	0,41	0,83	3,13

*: Aussaat und Ausbringung von Dünge- und Pflanzenschutzmitteln
OK: Ortsklasse
Eigene Berechnungen

Tabelle 10-4 Spezifischer kumulierter Energieaufwand und Emissionen der maschinellen Feldarbeit des Anbaus von Winterraps, Winterweizen, Zuckerrüben und Kartoffeln

		Raps	Weizen	Zuckerrüben	Kartoffeln	
Primärenergieträger						
Erdöl	MJ/ha*a	2.439	2.355	4.078	6.464	
Erdgas	MJ/ha*a	28,1	27,1	46,9	74,4	
Steinkohle	MJ/ha*a	8,53	8,24	14,3	22,6	
Braunkohle	MJ/ha*a	6,71	6,48	11,2	17,8	
Uran	MJ/ha*a	6,84	6,60	11,4	18,1	
Σ Erschöpfl. ET	*MJ/ha*a*	*2.489*	*2.404*	*4.161*	*6.597*	
Wasser	MJ/ha*a	1,01	0,98	1,69	2,68	
Summe	**MJ/ha*a**	**2.490**	**2.405**	**4.163**	**6.600**	
Emissionen						
		Global	**Global**	**Global**	**Global**	
CO_2	g/ha*a	184.114	177.771	307.780	487.950	
CH_4	g/ha*a	36,8	35,8	62,2	99,3	
N_2O	g/ha*a	17,9	17,3	29,9	47,4	
CO_2-Äquiv.	*g/ha*a*	190.430	183.875	318.353	504.728	
		OK 2+3	**OK 2+3**	**OK 2+3**	**OK 2+3**	**OK 2***
SO_2	g/ha*a	131	126	218	346	90,4%
CO	g/ha*a	399	411	716	1.237	99,7%
NO_X	g/ha*a	1.858	1.780	3.142	4.831	99,6%
NMHC	g/ha*a	259	260	461	760	99,6%
Partikel	g/ha*a	133	132	227	381	99,6%
Staub	g/ha*a	3,02	2,92	5,05	8,01	97,7%
HCl	g/ha*a	0,28	0,27	0,47	0,75	94,4%
NH_3	g/ha*a	1,05	1,01	1,76	2,79	99,7%
Formaldehyd	g/ha*a	19,0	19,2	34,1	56,4	99,9%
Benzol	g/ha*a	4,59	4,64	8,23	13,6	99,8%
Benzo(a)pyren	ng/ha*a	405.969	386.202	678.541	1.029.420	99,7%
TCDD-TÄ	ng/ha*a	10,0	9,66	16,7	26,5	89,2%
SO_2-Äquiv.	*g/ha*a*	*1.433*	*1.374*	*2.422*	*3.734*	*98,8%*

OK: Ortsklasse;
*: Anteil nährungsweise für alle Kulturen
Eigene Berechnungen

11 Bergbau

In **Tabelle 11-1** sind die Daten zum spezifischen kumulierten Energieaufwand und den damit verbundenen Emissionen des Einsatzes von Maschinen im Bergbau dokumentiert.

In **Tabelle 11-2** und **Tabelle 11-3** sind die hier ausgewerteten technischen Daten und Kraftstoffverbräuche von Baumaschinen nach /BUWAL 1994/ zusammengefaßt. Die „Praxiswerte" stammen aus Messungen der Verbräuche, die „Theoriedaten" wurden aus den Basiswerten in **Tabelle 7-1** berechnet, die ihrerseits auf einer Analyse der Meßwerte beruhen.

Tabelle 11-1 Spezifischer kumulierter Energieaufwand und Emissionen von Baggern, Ladern und Dumpern

Maschinen		**Bagger**	**Lader**	**Dumper**	**Bagger**	**Lader**	**Dumper**	
Bezug		**h**	**h**	**h**	**m^3**	**m^3**	**m^3*km**	
Primärenergieeinsatz								
Erdöl	MJ	539	748	294	7,55	10,3	13,1	
Erdgas	MJ	6,21	8,62	3,39	0,087	0,12	0,15	
Steinkohle	MJ	1,88	2,60	1,02	0,026	0,036	0,046	
Braunkohle	MJ	1,49	2,07	0,82	0,021	0,029	0,036	
Uran	MJ	1,80	2,50	0,98	0,025	0,034	0,044	
Σ Erschöpfl. ET	*MJ*	*551*	*764*	*300*	*7,71*	*10,5*	*13,4*	
Wasser	MJ	0,067	0,092	0,036	0,00093	0,0013	0,0016	
Summe	**MJ**	551	764	301	7,71	10,5	13,4	
Emissionen								
		Global	**Global**	**Global**	**Global**	**Global**	**Global**	
CO_2	g	40.856	56.658	22.297	572	779	996	
CH_4	g	8,24	11,4	4,50	0,12	0,16	0,20	
N_2O	g	3,96	5,50	2,16	0,055	0,076	0,097	
CO_2-Äquivalente	*g*	*42.258*	*58.602*	*23.062*	*592*	*806*	*1.030*	
		OK 2+3	**OK 2+3**	**OK 2+3**	**OK 2+3**	**OK 2+3**	**OK 2+3**	**OK 2**
SO_2	g	29,6	41,0	16,1	0,41	0,56	0,72	90,6%
CO	g	129	179	70,6	1,81	2,47	3,15	99,8%
NO_X	g	507	703	277	7,09	9,67	12,4	99,7%
NMHC	g	61,7	85,5	33,7	0,86	1,18	1,50	99,6%
Partikel	g	60,4	83,8	33,0	0,85	1,15	1,47	99,8%
Staub	g	0,57	0,78	0,31	0,0079	0,011	0,014	97,3%
HCl	g	0,064	0,089	0,035	0,00089	0,0012	0,0016	94,5%
NH_3	g	0,23	0,32	0,13	0,0033	0,0044	0,0057	99,7%
Formaldehyd	g	4,56	6,33	2,49	0,064	0,087	0,11	99,9%
Benzol	g	1,10	1,53	0,60	0,015	0,021	0,027	99,8%
Benzo(a)pyren	ng	92.520	128.305	50.492	1.295	1.765	2.256	99,8%
TCDD-TÄ	ng	2,24	3,11	1,23	0,031	0,043	0,055	89,3%
SO_2-Äquivalente	*g*	*385*	*534*	*210*	*5,39*	*7,34*	*9,38*	*99,0%*

OK: Ortsklasse
Eigene Berechnungen

Tabelle 11-2 Technische Daten und Kraftstoffverbrauch von Baggern und Ladern

Maschinentyp	**NennL**	**BetriebsL**	**Verbrauch**				**/BUWAL 1994/**	
Arbeit			**Praxis**		**Theorie**		**Kapitel**	**Seite**
	kW	m3/h	MJ/h	MJ/m3	MJ/h	MJ/m3		
Bagger								
Humusabtrag	110	80,6	639	7,94	565	7,01	A 5-1	1
Ausbruch	113	25,0	409	16,3	581	23,2	A 5-4	17
Ausbruch	113	175	408	2,34	581	3,32	A 5-6	20
Tunnelbau	59	100	329	3,29	310	3,10	A 5-10	27
Tunnelbau	59	50,0	261	5,22	310	6,20	A 5-10	28
Tunnelbau	155	183	661	3,62	796	4,36	A 5-7	22
Tunnelbau	155	23,6	554	23,4	796	33,7	A 5-9	23
Aushub	129	112	680	6,08	663	5,93	A 5-2	4
MW I	**112**	**93,6**	**493**	**8,53**	**575**	**10,9**		
MW II				**5,26**		**6,15**		
Lader								
Aufladen	85	25,0	678	27,1	474	19,0	A 5-9	23
Aufladen	95	75,2	637	8,48	530	7,04	A 5-7	22
Aufladen	95	94,6	523	5,53	530	5,60	A 5-8	22
Aufladen	116	92,1	265	2,87	647	7,02	A 5-7	22
Aufladen	116	15,2	242	16,0	647	42,7	A 5-9	23
Aufladen	157	30,0	583	19,4	875	29,2	A 5-4	17
Aufladen	157	48,4	583	12,0	875	18,1	A 5-5	19
Aufladen	157	149	583	3,92	875	5,88	A 5-6	20
Aufladen	175	65,7	762	11,6	976	14,8	A 5-10	24
Aufladen	175	100	623	6,23	976	9,76	A 5-10	24
Aufladen	190	21,9	763	34,8	1.059	48,3	A 5-8	22
Aufladen	190	53,3	515	9,67	1.059	19,9	A 5-7	22
Aufstockung	112	116	723	6,22	624	5,37	A 5-2	3
Schüttung	120	115	497	4,32	669	5,81	A 5-1	2
Fundationsschicht	120	111	551	4,94	669	6,01	A 5-1	3
Abtrag	112	120	774	6,45	624	5,20	A 5-2	4
Abtrag	157	114	996	8,74	875	7,68	A 5-2	4
Humusabtrag	120	137	1.149	8,37	669	4,88	A 5-1	1
Humusabtrag	157	91,4	1.074	11,7	875	9,58	A 5-2	3
Aushub	160	141	1.146	8,15	892	6,34	A 5-1	1
MW I	**138**	**85,8**	**683**	**10,8**	**771**	**13,9**		
MW II				**7,96**		**8,99**		

NennL bzw. BetriebsL: Nenn- bzw. Betriebsleistung; KV: Kraftstoffverbrauch
MW I: Mittel über alle Parameter = Summe (Einzelwerte) / Anzahl Werte
MW II: Mittel über KV in MJ/m^3 = Summe (KV in MJ/h) / Summe (BetriebsL in m^3/h)
Praxis: Meßdaten; Theorie: Berechnung über Ausgleichsfunktionen
Quelle: /BUWAL 1994/, eigene Berechnungen

Tabelle 11-3 Technische Daten und Kraftstoffverbrauch von Dumpern

Maschinentyp	NennL	BetriebsL	Verbrauch				/BUWAL 1994/	
Arbeit			Praxis		Theorie		Kapitel	Seite
	kW	m^3/h	MJ/h	MJ/m^3	MJ/h	MJ/m^3		
Dumper								
Transport	179	51,7	196	3,79	665	12,9	A 5-4	18
Transport	179	62,5	316	5,06	665	10,6	A 5-4	18
Transport	179	78,9	195	2,48	665	8,43	A 5-5	19
Transport	179	82,3	316	3,84	665	8,08	A 5-5	19
Transport	179	115	235	2,04	665	5,77	A 5-4	18
Transport	179	129	234	1,82	665	5,16	A 5-5	19
Transport	179	149	195	1,31	665	4,47	A 5-6	20
Transport	179	149	316	2,13	665	4,47	A 5-6	21
Transport	179	149	235	1,58	665	4,47	A 5-6	21
Transport	192	39,0	242	6,21	714	18,3	A 5-9	23
Transport	192	46,6	345	7,40	714	15,3	A 5-8	22
Transport	192	59,1	308	5,20	714	12,1	A 5-8	22
Transport	192	60,0	229	3,81	714	11,9	A 5-9	23
Transport	192	90,7	315	3,47	714	7,87	A 5-7	22
Transport	192	97,6	278	2,84	714	7,31	A 5-9	23
Transport	192	103	346	3,35	714	6,91	A 5-7	22
MW I	**185**	**91,4**	**269**	**3,52**	**686**	**9,00**		
MW II				**2,94**		**7,51**		

NennL bzw. BetriebsL: Nenn- bzw. Betriebsleistung; KV: Kraftstoffverbrauch
MW I: Mittel über alle Parameter = Summe (Einzelwerte) / Anzahl Werte
MW II: Mittel über KV in MJ/m^3 = Summe (KV in MJ/h) / Summe (BetriebsL in m^3/h)
Praxis: Meßdaten; Theorie: Berechnung über Ausgleichsfunktionen
Quelle: /BUWAL 1994/, eigene Berechnungen

12 Energiebereitstellung

In den folgenden Tabellen werden der spezifische kumulierte Energieeinsatz und die damit verbundenen Emissonen der Bereitstellung von Kraftstoffen auf Mineralölbasis, von Rapsöl und RME sowie von Strom in Deutschland im Jahr 2000 dokumentiert. Für die RME-Bereitstellung werden nach Lebenswegabschnitten differenzierte Daten ausgewiesen. Ferner werden Ableitung bzw. Herkunft der verbrauchsbezogenen Emissionsfaktoren für mit unterschiedlichen Brennstoffen betriebene Kesselfeuerungen, die bei der Rohölaufbereitung und in Raffinerien eingesetzt werden, und Kraftwerksfeuerungen beschrieben und dokumentiert.

Die Fortschreibung der Energiebereitstellung auf das Jahr 2000 ist aus verschiedenen Gründen sinnvoll. Im Falle der Mineralölprodukte ist mittel- bis längerfristig mit Änderungen der Rohölqualitäten und Produktpaletten in Raffinerien zu rechnen. Erwartet werden ein verstärkter Einsatz „schwererer" Rohöle und eine weiter steigende Nachfrage nach leichten Produkten. Beide Trends würden zu einem erhöhten Energieeinsatz in Raffinerien führen. Bei der Strombereitstellung sind durch die Angleichung der ostdeutschen Elektrizitätswirtschaft an westdeutsche Verhältnisse insbesondere im Bereich der Emissionsminderung – vollständige Umsetzung der GFAVO –, aber auch hinsichtlich der Wirkungsgrade Reduktionen der gesamten Bereitstellungsaufwendungen und -emissionen im bundesdeutschen Mittel zu erwarten. Für RME schließlich ist die Fortschreibung sinnvoll, da dieser biogene Kraftstoff gegenwärtig nur relativ geringe Bedeutung hat, sich dies aber *zukünftig* ändern kann. Für seine ökologische Bewertung sind damit auch zukünftige Rahmenbedingungen, soweit sie erkennbar sind, maßgeblich.

12.1 Energieträger auf Erdölbasis – Bezugsjahr 2000

In **Tabelle 12-1** sind die Daten der Bereitstellung von Mineralölprodukten im Jahr 2000 zusammen. Die Raffinerieenergiebilanz für das Jahr 2000 wird durch lineare Interpolation aus der Bilanz für 1996 (Kapitel 8.1.2) und der für das Jahr 2010 nach /PROGNOS 1996/ abgeleitet. Gegenüber dem Bezugsjahr 1996 hat sich die Produktpalette zu leichteren Produkten verschoben, woraus ein insgesamt niedrigerer Wirkungsgrad resultiert. Geringer und teilweise gegenläufig sind Änderungen bei der Bereitstellung des von Raffinerien importierten EVU-Stroms: der Energieträgersplit der EVU, Kraftwerkswirkungsgrade und -emissionen (vollständige Umsetzung der GFAVO in den neuen Bundesländern bis 2000). Die Rohölbereitstellung im Jahr 2000 wird gleich der im Jahr 1996 angesetzt.

Tabelle 12-1 Primärenergieeinsatz und Emissionen der Bereitstellung von Dieselkraftstoff, Kerosin und Schweröl in Deutschland im Jahr 2000

		Diesel/Kerosin		Schweröl	
Primärenergieeinsatz					
Erdöl	GJ/GJ	1,089		1,078	
Erdgas	GJ/GJ	0,012		0,011	
Steinkohle	GJ/GJ	0,0037		0,0030	
Braunkohle	GJ/GJ	0,0029		0,0023	
Uran	GJ/GJ	0,0034		0,0028	
Summe Erschöpfl. ET	*GJ/GJ*	*1,112*		*1,097*	
Wasser	GJ/GJ	0,00014		0,00012	
Summe	**GJ/GJ**	**1,112**		**1,097**	
Emissionen					
		Global		**Global**	
CO_2	g/GJ	8.286		7.311	
CH_4	g/GJ	13,9		13,3	
N_2O	g/GJ	0,27		0,24	
CO_2-Äquivalente	*g/GJ*	*8.660*		*7.663*	
		OK 2+3	**OK 2**	**OK 2+3**	**OK 2**
SO_2	g/GJ	37,1	84,9%	34,7	84,1%
CO	g/GJ	4,56	88,2%	4,39	87,9%
NO_X	g/GJ	17,5	81,8%	16,6	81,1%
NMHC	g/GJ	14,5	96,7%	14,4	96,7%
Partikel	g/GJ	0,70	62,8%	0,69	63,0%
Staub	g/GJ	1,12	97,2%	1,06	97,1%
HCl	g/GJ	0,10	93,1%	0,088	92,1%
NH_3	g/GJ	0,0041	68,4%	0,0041	68,9%
Formaldehyd	g/GJ	0,086	89,6%	0,083	89,4%
Benzol	g/GJ	0,083	93,5%	0,082	93,5%
Benzo(a)pyren	ng/GJ	3.830	88,0%	3.554	87,2%
TCDD-TÄ	ng/GJ	3,05	84,1%	2,68	82,2%
SO_2-Äquivalente	*g/GJ*	*49,4*	*84,1%*	*46,4*	*83,3%*

OK: Ortsklasse; in OK 1 fallen keine Emissionen an.
Quellen: /AGE 1998/, /ECOINVENT 1996/, /GEMIS 1997/, /GOETHEL 1993/, /IFEU 1998b/, /JESS & HEDDEN 1994/, /MWV 1997/, /PROGNOS 1996/, /UBA 1995c/, /UBA 1998/, eigene Berechnungen

12.2 Strom – Bezugsjahr 2000

In **Tabelle 12-2** sind der spezifische Energieeinsatz und die Emissionen der Bereitstellung von Strom im Jahr 2000 zusammengestellt. Der Brennstoffsplit für das Jahr 2000 wird durch lineare Interpolation aus dem von 1996 (Kapitel 8.6.1) und dem für das Jahr 2010 nach /PROGNOS 1996/ abgeleitet. Gegenüber dem Bezugsjahr 1996 wird eine Angleichung der Kraftwerkswirkungsgrade und Netzverluste in Ostdeutschland an westdeutsche Verhältnisse und die vollständige Umsetzung der Vorgaben der GFAVO in Ostdeutschland angenommen. Die Brennstoffbereitstellung wird gleich der im Jahr 1996 angesetzt.

Tabelle 12-2 Spezifischer Energieeinsatz und Emissionen der Strombereitstellung: EVU-Strom frei industrieller Abnehmer, Strom der Bahnkraftwerke und Bahn-Mix frei Oberleitungsnetz einschließlich Brennstoffbereitstellung in Deutschland im Jahr 2000

		EVU frei Industrie		BahnKW frei Oberleitung		Bahn-Mix frei Oberleitung	
Primärenergieeinsatz							
Erdöl	MJ/kWh	0,14		0,19		0,18	
Erdgas	MJ/kWh	0,64		1,13		1,00	
Steinkohle	MJ/kWh	2,89		4,91		4,39	
Braunkohle	MJ/kWh	3,31		0,35		1,24	
Uran	MJ/kWh	3,92		3,03		3,35	
Σ Erschöpfl. ET	*MJ/kWh*	*10,90*		*9,61*		*10,16*	
Wasser	MJ/kWh	0,14		0,55		0,44	
Summe	**MJ/kWh**	**11,05**		**10,16**		**10,60**	
Emissionen							
		Global		**Global**		**Global**	
CO_2	g/kWh	668		531		581	
CH_4	g/kWh	1,46		2,47		2,21	
N_2O	g/kWh	0,025		0,021		0,022	
CO_2-Äquivalente	*g/kWh*	*706*		*590*		*634*	
		OK 2+3	**OK 2**	**OK 2+3**	**OK 2**	**OK 2+3**	**OK 2**
SO_2	g/kWh	0,47	91,6%	0,43	84,6%	0,45	86,8%
CO	g/kWh	0,17	97,2%	0,19	96,0%	0,19	96,3%
NO_X	g/kWh	0,58	92,8%	0,55	87,2%	0,57	88,9%
NMHC	g/kWh	0,017	92,5%	0,017	87,5%	0,017	89,0%
Partikel	g/kWh	0,0058	33,6%	0,0085	22,5%	0,0078	25,0%
Staub	g/kWh	0,028	99,9%	0,019	99,8%	0,022	99,9%
HCl	g/kWh	0,039	99,9%	0,029	99,7%	0,033	99,8%
NH_3	g/kWh	0,00002	55,8%	0,00003	48,2%	0,00003	49,9%
Formaldehyd	g/kWh	0,00064	84,3%	0,00080	78,7%	0,00076	80,1%
Benzol	g/kWh	0,00036	92,9%	0,00042	89,7%	0,00041	90,5%
Benzo(a)pyren	ng/kWh	15,4	67,5%	20,1	57,7%	19,0	60,1%
TCDD-TÄ	ng/kWh	0,058	98,1%	0,052	96,4%	0,055	97,0%
SO_2-Äquivalente	*g/kWh*	*0,91*	*92,5%*	*0,84*	*86,3%*	*0,88*	*88,2%*

OK: Ortsklasse; in OK 1 fallen keine Emissionen an.
Quellen: /BMWI 1998/, /ECOINVENT 1996/, /GEMIS 1997/, /IFEU 1998b/, /PROGNOS 1996/, /UBA 1995c/, /UBA 1998/, /VDEW 1998/, eigene Berechnungen

12.3 Emissionsfaktoren für Kesselfeuerungen

Die brennstoffeinsatzbezogenen Emissionsfaktoren für Standard-Schadstoffe aus Feuerungen in Anlagen zur Rohölaufbereitung übernehmen wir aus /GEMIS 1997/. Faktoren der Schadstoffe, die nicht in /GEMIS 1997/ enthalten sind, leiten wir in gleicher Weise wie die für Raffineriefeuerungen aus verschiedenen anderen Quellen ab (siehe unten). Die Faktoren sind in **Tabelle 12-3** zusammengefaßt.

Tabelle 12-3 Brennstoffeinsatzbezogene Emissionsfaktoren für Kesselfeuerungen in Anlagen zur Rohölaufbereitung

		Kessel (Schweres Heizöl)		Erdgaskessel	
		Westeuropa	**GUS/OPEC**	**Westeuropa**	**GUS**
		Global	**Global**	**Global**	**Global**
CO_2	g/GJ	78.773	78.323	55.151	55.376
CH_4	g/GJ	3,01	3,02	2,52	2,51
N_2O	g/GJ	2,01	2,02	1,01	1,11
		OK 2 (+ 3*)	**OK 2**	**OK 2 (+ 3*)**	**OK 2**
SO_2	g/GJ	491	884	0,43	0,40
CO	g/GJ	43,0	72,0	14,0	69,6
NO_X	g/GJ	115	144	28,0	111
NMHC	g/GJ	3,01	3,02	2,52	2,51
Partikel	g/GJ	0	0	0	0
Staub	g/GJ	11,5	43,2	0,14	1,39
HCl	g/GJ	1,44	1,44	0	0
NH_3	g/GJ	0	0	0	0
Formaldehyd	g/GJ	0,45	0,45	0,25	0,25
Benzol	g/GJ	0,030	0,030	0,25	0,25
Benzo(a)pyren	ng/GJ	60.000	60.000	1.000	1.000
TCDD-TÄ	ng/GJ	28,7	28,8	28,0	27,8

Westeuropa: Deutschland, Niederlande, Nordsee
*: Anteil der off shore Förderung in OK 3
Quellen: /ECOINVENT 1996/, /GEMIS 1997/, /IFEU 1998b/, /UBA 1995c/, /UBA 1998/, eigene Berechnungen

Die brennstoffeinsatzbezogenen Emissionsfaktoren für Kesselfeuerungen zur Prozeßwärme- und Strombereitstellung in Raffinerien werden aus verschiedenen Quellen übernommen bzw. abgeleitet. Eine wichtige Grundlage bilden die Faktoren nach /UBA 1998/, die differenziert nach Ost- und Westdeutschland in einer Zeitreihe für die Jahre 1980 bis 1994 vorliegen. Sie enthalten allerdings nicht alle hier betrachteten Schadstoffe. Ferner sind die Minderungen der Emissionen ostdeutscher Raffinerien, die nach unserer Einschätzung in den letzten Jahren stattgefunden haben, nicht erfaßt. Die damit erforderlichen Zusatzannahmen und Verfahren werden im folgenden beschrieben:

- Für Westdeutschland kann von im wesentlichen konstanten spezifischen Emissionen ausgegangen werden /GOETHEL 1993/. In ostdeutschen Raffinerien entsprechen die Emissionsstandards inzwischen westdeutschen Verhältnissen. Für die CO_2-, Methan-, N_2O-, SO_2-, NO_X-, CO-, NMHC- und Staubemissionen von Feuerungen in Raffinerien werden daher die Faktoren nach /UBA 1998/ für Westdeutschland 1994 angesetzt.
- Die HCl-Emissionsfaktoren werden aus /GEMIS 1997/ übernommen.
- Formaldehyd- und Benzolemissionsfaktoren werden aus Angaben zu den Anteilen dieser Verbindungen an den NMHC-Emissionen nach /ECOINVENT 1996/ berechnet.
- Für Benzo(a)pyren setzen wir die Faktoren an, die in /IFEU 1998b/ abgeleitet wurden.
- Emissionsfaktoren für TCDD-Toxizitätsäquivalente werden aus /UBA 1995c/ abgeleitet. Dort werden Näherungswerte – Obergrenzen bzw. Bandbreiten – für die Emissionskonzentrationen in der Abluft in ng TÄ/m^3 ausgewiesen. Für kohle-, öl- und gasbetriebene

Feuerungsanlagen werden jeweils Konzentrationen < 0,1 ng TÄ/m³ angegeben. Die Verknüpfung mit den energiebezogenen Abluftmengen von Feuerungsanlagen nach /GEMIS 1997/ ergibt energiebezogene Emissionsfaktoren. Gemäß /UBA 1995c/ liegen die so erhaltenen Emissionsfaktoren im oberen Bereich der für Kesselfeuerungen zu erwartenden Emissionen.

Die Faktoren sind in **Tabelle 12-4** zusammengestellt.

Tabelle 12-4 Brennstoffeinsatzbezogene Emissionsfaktoren für Kesselfeuerungen in Raffinerien

		Heizöl EL	Heizöl S	Petrol-koks	And.Min. ölprod.	Flüssig-gas	Raffin.-gas	Kokerei-gas	Erdgas
		Global	**Global**	**Global**	**Global**	**Global**	**Global**	**Global**	**Global**
CO_2	g/GJ	74.000	78.000	101.000	80.000	65.000	60.000	44.000	56.000
CH_4	g/GJ	3,10	3,70	0,50	3,70	1,30	1,30	1,30	1,30
N_2O	g/GJ	1,50	3,50	4,00	3,50	1,50	1,50	1,50	1,50
		OK 2	**OK 2**	**OK 2**	**OK 2**	**OK 2**	**OK 2**	**OK 2**	**OK 2**
SO_2	g/GJ	85,0	442	531	442	1,70	9,00	12,0	0,50
CO	g/GJ	10,0	20,6	41,9	20,6	10,0	10,0	10,0	10,0
NO_X	g/GJ	70,0	93,3	101	93,2	44,1	44,1	44,1	44,1
NMHC	g/GJ	3,10	3,70	0,50	3,70	1,30	1,30	1,30	1,30
Partikel	g/GJ	0	0	0	0	0	0	0	0
Staub	g/GJ	1,50	9,00	14,6	9,00	0,10	0,10	0,10	0,10
HCl	g/GJ	0,094	1,44	1,44	1,44	0	0	0	0
NH_3	g/GJ	0	0	0	0	0	0	0	0
Formaldehyd	g/GJ	0,46	0,55	0,075	0,55	0,13	0,13	0,13	0,13
Benzol	g/GJ	0,031	0,037	0,0050	0,037	0,13	0,13	0,13	0,13
BaP	ng/GJ	30.000	60.000	60.000	60.000	1.000	1.000	1.000	1.000
TCDD-TÄ	ng/GJ	29,0	29,0	29,0	29,0	28,0	28,0	28,0	28,0

Quellen: /ECOINVENT 1996/, /GEMIS 1997/, /GOETHEL 1993/, /IFEU 1998b/, /UBA 1995c/, /UBA 1998/, eigene Berechnungen

12.4 Emissionsfaktoren für Kraftwerke

Die brennstoffeinsatzbezogenen Emissionsfaktoren für Kraftwerke werden aus verschiedenen Quellen übernommen bzw. abgeleitet. Die Grundlage für die Standard-Schadstoffe bilden die Faktoren nach /UBA 1998/, die in einer Zeitreihe für die Jahre 1980 bis 1994 differenziert nach Ost- und Westdeutschland vorliegen. Sie enthalten allerdings nicht alle hier betrachteten Schadstoffe.

Aus dem erfaßten Zeitraum ergibt sich ferner, daß Emissionsminderungen in Ostdeutschland nicht vollständig beschrieben sind. Schließlich ergeben sich aus unterschiedlichen Abgrenzungen bei der Ableitung der Emissionsfaktoren Abweichungen zwischen den von uns berechneten „rohen" Emissionsbilanzen für SO_2, NO_X und Staub nach /UBA 1998/ und /BMWI 1998/ und den Emissionsbilanzen der EVU-Stromproduktion nach /VDEW 1998/. Die damit erforderlichen Zusatzannahmen und Verfahren werden im folgenden beschrieben:

- Die CO_2-, Methan-, N_2O-, CO- und NMHC-Faktoren für Ost- bzw. Westdeutschland 1994 nach /UBA 1998/ werden unverändert für 1996 übernommen. Soweit sich die Daten für Ost- und Westdeutschland unterscheiden werden sie gewichtet mit den auf Ost- bzw. Westdeutschland entfallenden Anteilen am Gesamteinsatz in Deutschland gemittelt.
- Die SO_2-, NO_X- und Staub-Faktoren für Ost- und Westdeutschland 1994 nach /UBA 1998/ werden mit den Emissionsbilanzen der EVU nach /VDEW 1998/ für Ost- und Westdeutschland 1996 abgeglichen und wie oben beschrieben gemittelt.
- Die HCl-Emissionsfaktoren werden aus /GEMIS 1997/ übernommen.
- Emissionsfaktoren für Formaldehyd und Benzol werden aus Angaben zu den Anteilen dieser Verbindungen an den NMHC-Emissionen nach /ECOINVENT 1996/ berechnet.
- Für Benzo(a)pyren setzen wir die Faktoren an, die in /IFEU 1998b/ abgeleitet wurden.
- Für TCDD-Toxizitätsäquivalente werden die Emissionsfaktoren, die oben für allgemeine Kesselfeuerungen abgeleitet wurden, angesetzt.

Die Emissionsfaktoren sind in **Tabelle 12-5** zusammengefaßt.

Tabelle 12-5 Brennstoffeinsatzbezogene Emissionsfaktoren für Kraftwerke in Deutschland 1996

		Steinkohle	Braunkohle	Erdgas	Schweröl	Übrige
		Global	Global	Global	Global	Global
CO_2	g/GJ	92.000	110.229	56.000	78.000	15.000
CH_4	g/GJ	1,50	1,53	0,30	3,50	5,03
N_2O	g/GJ	4,00	3,50	1,50	3,50	3,00
		OK 2	OK 2	OK 2	OK 2	OK 2
SO_2	g/GJ	69,7	395	0,52	180	78,0
CO	g/GJ	19,2	18,5	37,5	27,3	34,5
NO_X	g/GJ	67,1	93,3	64,1	59,6	125
NMHC	g/GJ	1,50	1,53	0,30	3,50	5,03
Partikel	g/GJ	0	0	0	0	0
Staub	g/GJ	3,35	7,06	0,094	5,81	9,73
HCl	g/GJ	7,00	5,80	0	0,50	2,00
NH_3	g/GJ	0	0	0	0	0
Formaldehyd	g/GJ	0,030	0,031	0,030	0,53	0,10
Benzol	g/GJ	0,030	0,031	0,030	0,035	0,10
Benzo(a)pyren	ng/GJ	200	200	0	60.000	200
TCDD-TÄ	ng/GJ	7,57	8,71	5,60	5,80	8,71

Quellen: /ECOINVENT 1996/, /GEMIS 1997/, /IFEU 1998b/, /UBA 1995c/, /UBA 1998/, /VDEW 1998/, eigene Berechnungen

Für das Bezugsjahr 2000 werden die SO_2-, NO_X- und Staub-Faktoren für Westdeutschland 1994 nach /UBA 1998/ mit der Emissionsbilanz der EVU nach /VDEW 1998/ für Westdeutschland 1996 abgeglichen. Damit wird berücksichtigt, daß bis zum Jahr 2000 auch in Ostdeutschland die GFAVO vollständig umgesetzt sein wird. Die Emissionsfaktoren sind in **Tabelle 12-6** zusammengefaßt.

Tabelle 12-6 Brennstoffeinsatzbezogene Emissionsfaktoren für Kraftwerke in Deutschland 2000

		Steinkohle	Braunkohle	Erdgas	Schweröl	Übrige
		Global	Global	Global	Global	Global
CO_2	g/GJ	92.000	109.841	56.000	78.000	15.000
CH_4	g/GJ	1,51	1,58	0,30	3,50	70,0
N_2O	g/GJ	4,00	3,50	1,50	3,50	3,00
		OK 2	OK 2	OK 2	OK 2	OK 2
SO_2	g/GJ	48,0	60,0	0,25	256	123
CO	g/GJ	19,0	21,0	49,0	29,0	175
NO_X	g/GJ	85,9	54,7	58,5	57,2	108
NMHC	g/GJ	1,50	1,50	0,30	3,50	70,0
Partikel	g/GJ	0	0	0	0	0
Staub	g/GJ	4,70	2,35	0,047	6,11	18,8
HCl	g/GJ	7,00	5,80	0	0,50	2,00
NH_3	g/GJ	0	0	0	0	0
Formaldehyd	g/GJ	0,030	0,030	0,030	0,53	1,40
Benzol	g/GJ	0,030	0,030	0,030	0,035	1,40
Benzo(a)pyren	ng/GJ	200	200	0	60.000	200
TCDD-TÄ	ng/GJ	7,57	8,71	5,60	5,80	8,71

Quellen: /ECOINVENT 1996/, /GEMIS 1997/, /IFEU 1998b/, /UBA 1995c/, /UBA 1998/, /VDEW 1998/, eigene Berechnungen

12.5 Rapsöl und RME: Detailbilanz und Bereitstellung 2000

In den folgenden Tabellen werden differenzierte Darstellungen des spezifischen Einsatzes mineralischer und energetischer Ressourcen sowie der Emissionen der Bereitstellung von Rapsöl und RME gegeben.

Tabelle 12-7 faßt die Bereitstellungsaufwendungen der beim Rapsanbau eingesetzten Betriebsmittel – Saatgut, Düngemittel und Pflanzenschutzmittel – zusammen. Dabei fallen nur für Phosphatdünger nennenswerte Emissionen in der Ortsklasse 3 an; bei allen anderen Betriebsmitteln liegt der Anteil an den gesamten Emissionen bei weniger als 3 %.

In **Tabelle 12-8** sind die Aufwendungen für die RME-Bereitstellung differenziert nach einzelnen Lebenswegabschnitten einschließlich der verschiedenen Gutschriften dokumentiert. Um Redundanzen zu vermeiden, werden die Aufwendungen für die Bereitstellung von Rapsöl nicht gesondert ausgewiesen: Der Lebenswegabschnitt Landwirtschaft ist mit Bezug auf die Anbaufläche für beide Kraftstoffe identisch. Das Ölpressen aus der Rapssaat erfolgt in zentralen Ölmühlen (RME) mit 20 % höherer Ausbeute als in dezentralen Anlagen (Rapsöl). Die folgenden Schritte der Extraktion und Raffination entfallen bei der Bereitstellung von Rapsöl. Außerdem ist die Rapsölbereitstellung mit geringerem Transportaufwand verbunden. Als Gutschriften sind für Rapsöl nur der Referenzlandbau sowie der Anbau und Transport von Soja(schrot) anzurechnen; Glyzerin fällt nur bei der Produktion von RME als Kuppelprodukt an.

In **Tabelle 12-9** sind der spezifische Ressourcenverbrauch und die Emissionen der Bereitstellung von Rapsöl und RME im Jahr 2000 zusammengestellt. Die Unterschiede resultieren aus Änderungen bei der Bereitstellung der eingesetzten Endenergieträger.

Tabelle 12-7 Spezifischer Ressourceneinsatz und Emissionen der Bereitstellung von Betriebsmitteln zum Anbau von Winterraps (Fortsetzung nächste Seite): Saatgut (Raps und Referenzkultur) und Pflanzenschutzmittel (PSM)

		Saatgut		**PSM**
Bezug		**Rapskorn**	**Gras**	**Akt. Sub.**
		1 kg	1 kg	1 kg
Mineralische Ressourcen				
Kalkstein	kg	0,038		
Phosphaterz	kg	0,073		
Schwefel	kg	0,0049		
Rohkali	kg	0,11		
Primärenergie				
Erdöl	MJ	1,43	1,06	100
Erdgas	MJ	1,98	2,03	81,6
Steinkohle	MJ	0,22	0,24	30,7
Braunkohle	MJ	0,048	0,053	27,2
Uran	MJ	0,072	0,082	27,5
Σ Erschöpfl. ET	*MJ*	*3,75*	*3,46*	*267*
Wasser	MJ	0,017	0,019	3,57
Summe	**MJ**	**3,76**	**3,48**	**270**
Emissionen				
		Global	**Global**	**Global**
CO_2	g	231	210	11.231
CH_4	g	0,44	0,44	25,2
N_2O	g	1,69	0,89	1,74
CO_2-Äquivalente	*g*	*765*	*496*	*12.301*
		OK 2	**OK 2**	**OK 2**
SO_2	g	0,45	0,49	35,7
CO	g	0,31	0,24	5,1
NO_X	g	1,48	1,16	15,3
NMHC	g	0,12	0,087	1,85
Partikel	g	0,051	0,031	0,16
Staub	g	0,15	0,17	1,39
HCl	g	0,0048	0,0065	0,54
NH_3	g	2,27	0,29	0,16
Formaldehyd	g	0,0078	0,0052	0,034
Benzol	g	0,0020	0,0014	0,024
Benzo(a)pyren	ng	180	118	638
TCDD-TÄ	ng	0,073	0,073	3,12
SO_2-Äquivalente	*g*	*5,76*	*1,84*	*47,2*

Eigene Berechnungen

Tabelle 12-7 (Fortsetzung) Spezifischer Ressourceneinsatz und Emissionen der Bereitstellung von Betriebsmitteln zum Anbau von Winterraps und der Referenzkultur: Düngemittel

Bezug		**Kalk** **CaO** 1 kg	**Stickstoff** **N** 1 kg	**Phosphor** **P_2O_5** 1 kg	**P_2O_5** 1 kg	**Kalium** **K_2O** 1 kg
Mineralische Ressourcen						
Kalkstein	kg	1,84	0,55			
Phosphaterz	kg			4,06		
Schwefel	kg			0,27		
Rohkali	kg					10,5
Primärenergie						
Erdöl	MJ	0,38	9,16	6,64		1,17
Erdgas	MJ	0,38	35,7	7,27		7,00
Steinkohle	MJ	0,49	3,13	1,82		1,19
Braunkohle	MJ	0,65	0,31	0,60		0,50
Uran	MJ	0,43	0,63	1,10		0,52
Σ Erschöpfl. ET	*MJ*	*2,32*	*48,9*	*17,4*		*10,4*
Wasser	MJ	0,069	0,18	0,28		0,079
Summe	**MJ**	**2,39**	**49,1**	**17,7**		**10,5**
Emissionen						
		Global	**Global**	**Global**		**Global**
CO_2	g	284	2.820	1.117		617
CH_4	g	0,29	7,45	2,07		1,38
N_2O	g	0,019	15,1	0,038		0,049
CO_2-Äquivalente	*g*	*296*	*7.643*	*1.172*		*661*
		OK 2	**OK 2**	**OK 2**	**OK 3**	**OK 2**
SO_2	g	0,090	5,07	7,92	4,06	0,23
CO	g	3,00	2,79	0,96	0,46	0,42
NO_X	g	0,50	15,7	4,32	4,26	1,11
NMHC	g	0,050	0,57	0,41	0,13	0,13
Partikel	g	0,018	0,087	0,10	0,41	0,043
Staub	g	0,95	2,31	1,11	0,00020	0,85
HCl	g	0,013	0,068	0,020	0,00095	0,074
NH_3	g	0,00089	6,69	0,0066	0,0059	0,0019
Formaldehyd	g	0,0034	0,021	0,022	0,010	0,0080
Benzol	g	0,00087	0,0074	0,0059	0,0024	0,0022
Benzo(a)pyren	ng	83,9	696	443	522	196
TCDD-TÄ	ng	0,031	1,28	0,23	0,0068	0,25
SO_2-Äquivalente	*g*	*0,45*	*28,7*	*11,0*	*7,05*	*1,07*

Quelle: /PATYK & REINHARDT 1997/

Tabelle 12-8 Bereitstellung von RME differenziert nach Lebenswegabschnitten: Mineralische Ressourcen (Bezug: 1 GJ RME)

Lebenswegabschnitt	**Kalkstein** g/GJ	**Phosphaterz** g/GJ	**Schwefel** g/GJ	**Rohkali** g/GJ	**Steinsalz** g/GJ	**Tonmineralien** g/GJ
Landwirtschaft						
Saatgut	2,71	5,16	0	7,41	0	0
N-Dünger	1.883	0	0	0	0	0
P-Dünger	0	5.155	343	0	0	0
K-Dünger	0	0	0	7.406	0	0
Düngekalk	822	0	0	0	0	0
Zwischensumme	*2.708*	*5.160*	*343*	*7.414*	*0*	*0*
Konversion						
Bleicherde	0	0	0	0	0	204
Phosphorsäure	0	64,1	13,4	0	0	0
Natronlauge	0	0	0	0	92,7	0
Zwischensumme	*0*	*64,1*	*13,4*	*0*	*92,7*	*204*
Gutschriften RME						
Referenzlandbau (Saatgut)	-8,28	-43,7	-2,90	-147	0	0
Saatgut (Soja)	-0,76	-11,2	-0,74	-57,7	0	0
N-Dünger (Soja)	-30,7	0	0	0	0	0
P-Dünger (Soja)	0	-454	-30,2	0	0	0
K-Dünger (Soja)	0	0	0	-2.347	0	0
Chlor (Glyzerin)	0	0	0	0	-5.302	0
Natronlauge (Glyzerin)	0	0	0	0	-2.134	0
Zwischensumme	*-39,8*	*-509*	*-33,8*	*-2.552*	*-7.436*	*0*
Summe gesamt	**2.668**	**4.716**	**323**	**4.862**	**-7.343**	**204**

Bei negativen Zahlen überwiegen die Gutschriften aus Kuppelprodukten die Aufwendungen der Produktion.
Eigene Berechnungen

Tabelle 12-8 (Fortsetzung) Bereitstellung von RME differenziert nach Lebenswegabschnitten: Erschöpfliche Energie und klimarelevante Gase (Bezug: 1 GJ RME)

Lebenswegabschnitt	Ersch. Energie GJ/GJ	CO_2-Äq. g/GJ	CO_2 (fossil) g/GJ	CH_4 g/GJ	N_2O g/GJ
Landwirtschaft					
Eggen	0,020	1.532	1.482	0,29	0,14
Pflügen	0,015	1.168	1.129	0,22	0,11
Ausbringung	0,0077	591	571	0,13	0,055
Ernte	0,016	1.186	1.147	0,23	0,11
Saatgut	0,00026	54,0	16,3	0,031	0,12
N-Dünger	0,17	26.166	9.655	25,5	51,5
P-Dünger	0,022	1.488	1.418	2,63	0,049
K-Dünger	0,0073	466	435	0,97	0,035
Düngekalk	0,0010	132	127	0,13	0,0087
Pflanzenschutzmittel	0,0077	355	325	0,73	0,050
Emissionen Feld	0	20.846	0	0	67,2
Zwischensumme	*0,26*	*53.985*	*16.305*	*30,8*	*119*
Konversion					
Zwischenlagerung	0,032	2.292	2.230	2,17	0,053
Anlieferung	0,010	734	707	0,30	0,066
Ölmühle	0,071	4.220	4.036	6,91	0,13
Hexan	0,0036	38,5	37,1	0,050	0,0012
Raffination	0,012	727	697	1,14	0,020
Bleicherde	0,00043	33,8	33,3	0,0070	0,0011
Phosphorsäure	0,00034	22,8	22,0	0,029	0,00069
Umesterung*	0,062	3.660	3.509	5,78	0,099
Methanol	0,11	8.189	8.091	4,00	0,048
Natronlauge	0,0027	186	176	0,37	0,0076
Auslieferung	0,0050	385	372	0,070	0,036
Zwischensumme	*0,31*	*20.488*	*19.909*	*20,8*	*0,46*
Gutschriften RME					
Referenzlandbau	-0,019	-1.558	-1.412	-0,43	-0,44
Sojaschrot Anbau	-0,10	-7.398	-6.512	-7,47	-2,35
Sojaschrot Transport	-0,047	-3.782	-3.658	-0,65	-0,36
Glyzerin-Synthese	-0,24	-17.634	-17.264	-10,9	-0,46
Chlor	-0,093	-6.412	-6.064	-12,7	-0,26
Natronlauge	-0,062	-4.284	-4.051	-8,50	-0,17
Propylen	-0,16	-4.373	-4.217	-5,79	-0,11
Zwischensumme	*-0,73*	*-45.442*	*-43.176*	*-46,5*	*-4,16*
Summe gesamt	**-0,15**	**29.030**	**-6.963**	**5,20**	**116**

*: inkl. Glyzerinaufbereitung
Bei negativen Zahlen überwiegen die Gutschriften aus Kuppelprodukten die Aufwendungen der Produktion.
Eigene Berechnungen

Tabelle 12-8 (Fortsetzung) Bereitstellung von RME differenziert nach Lebenswegabschnitten: SO_2 und NO_X, differenziert nach Ortsklassen (Bezug: 1 GJ RME)

Lebenswegabschnitt	SO_2-Äquiv. OK 2 g/GJ	SO_2 OK 2 g/GJ	SO_2 ges. g/GJ	NO_X OK 2 g/GJ	NO_X ges. g/GJ
Landwirtschaft					
Eggen	11,4	0,95	1,05	14,9	14,9
Pflügen	8,66	0,72	0,80	11,3	11,4
Ausbringung	4,66	0,37	0,41	6,13	6,15
Ernte	8,60	0,74	0,81	11,2	11,3
Saatgut	0,41	0,031	0,037	0,10	0,11
N-Dünger	98,1	17,4	17,7	53,6	54,0
P-Dünger	13,9	10,1	15,2	5,48	10,9
K-Dünger	0,76	0,16	0,19	0,78	0,81
Düngekalk	0,20	0,040	0,047	0,22	0,23
Pflanzenschutzmittel	1,36	1,03	1,03	0,44	0,44
Emissionen Feld	258	0	0	0	0
Zwischensumme	*406*	*31,5*	*37,2*	*104*	*110*
Konversion					
Zwischenlagerung	4,34	3,22	3,36	1,53	1,64
Anlieferung	7,29	0,49	0,54	9,70	9,74
Ölmühle	9,55	5,23	5,33	6,07	6,20
Hexan	0,17	0,13	0,14	0,059	0,070
Raffination	1,49	0,79	0,80	1,00	1,02
Bleicherde	0,26	0,13	0,13	0,18	0,18
Phosphorsäure	0,31	0,27	0,36	0,061	0,16
Umesterung*	7,67	4,19	4,27	4,91	5,01
Methanol	8,07	5,85	6,29	3,17	3,45
Natronlauge	0,62	0,47	0,48	0,20	0,21
Auslieferung	2,81	0,24	0,26	3,67	3,68
Zwischensumme	*42,6*	*21,0*	*22,0*	*30,5*	*31,3*
Gutschriften RME					
Referenzlandbau	-11,3	-1,03	-1,17	-14,3	-14,4
Sojaschrot Anbau	-34,6	-8,14	-8,90	-30,4	-31,1
Sojaschrot Transport	-39,5	-18,9	-71,5	-29,4	-84,5
Glyzerin-Synthese	-103	-86,3	-87,2	-23,6	-24,3
Chlor	-21,4	-16,3	-16,6	-6,82	-7,18
Natronlauge	-14,3	-10,9	-11,1	-4,59	-4,84
Propylen	-17,5	-13,4	-14,1	-5,75	-6,18
Zwischensumme	*-241*	*-155*	*-211*	*-115*	*-173*
Summe gesamt	**207**	**-102**	**-151**	**19,8**	**-31,1**

*: inkl. Glyzerinaufbereitung
Bei negativen Zahlen überwiegen die Gutschriften aus Kuppelprodukten die Aufwendungen der Produktion.
Eigene Berechnungen

Tabelle 12-8 (Fortsetzung) Bereitstellung von RME differenziert nach Lebenswegabschnitten: Weitere Emissionen I (Bezug: 1 GJ RME)

Lebenswegabschnitt	**NH_3 OK 2** g/GJ	**HCl OK 2** g/GJ	**Partikel OK 2** g/GJ	**Partikel ges.** g/GJ	**Staub OK 2** g/GJ
Landwirtschaft					
Eggen	0,0084	0,0021	0,99	1,00	0,024
Pflügen	0,0064	0,0016	0,76	0,76	0,018
Ausbringung	0,0032	0,00082	0,51	0,51	0,0092
Ernte	0,0065	0,0017	0,85	0,86	0,018
Saatgut	0,16	0,00034	0,0036	0,0041	0,010
N-Dünger	22,9	0,23	0,30	0,33	7,91
P-Dünger	0,0084	0,026	0,13	0,64	1,40
K-Dünger	0,0013	0,052	0,030	0,033	0,60
Düngekalk	0,00040	0,0059	0,0082	0,0089	0,43
Pflanzenschutzmittel	0,0047	0,015	0,0047	0,0047	0,040
Emissionen Feld	137	0	0	0	0
Zwischensumme	*160*	*0,34*	*3,58*	*4,14*	*10,5*
Konversion					
Zwischenlagerung	0,000061	0,051	0,0098	0,019	0,075
Anlieferung	0,0038	0,0034	0,31	0,31	0,013
Ölmühle	0,000042	0,080	0,0066	0,014	0,21
Hexan	0,0000087	0,00045	0,0014	0,0023	0,0053
Raffination	0,0000066	0,010	0,0011	0,0020	0,036
Bleicherde	0,00042	0,00012	0,0080	0,0081	0,0032
Phosphorsäure	0,000084	0,00028	0,0010	0,010	0,023
Umesterung*	0,035	57,3	5,59	10,6	184
Methanol	0,0012	0,0083	0,076	0,097	0,17
Natronlauge	0,00012	0,010	0,0027	0,0037	0,011
Auslieferung	0,0021	0,00054	0,15	0,15	0,0060
Zwischensumme	*0,042*	*57,5*	*6,14*	*11,2*	*184*
Gutschriften RME					
Referenzlandbau	-0,11	-0,0042	-1,01	-1,02	-0,080
Sojaschrot Anbau	-2,69	-0,11	-1,58	-1,64	-0,68
Sojaschrot Transport	-0,0080	-0,023	-0,32	-5,56	-0,053
Glyzerin-Synthese	-0,00046	-0,11	-0,075	-0,12	-2,12
Chlor	-0,0039	-0,36	-0,089	-0,12	-0,36
Natronlauge	-0,0027	-0,24	-0,062	-0,084	-0,24
Propylen	-0,0018	-0,043	-0,083	-0,12	-0,38
Zwischensumme	*-2,82*	*-0,88*	*-3,22*	*-8,67*	*-3,93*
Summe gesamt	**158**	**57,0**	**6,51**	**6,72**	**191**

*: inkl. Glyzerinaufbereitung
Bei negativen Zahlen überwiegen die Gutschriften aus Kuppelprodukten die Aufwendungen der Produktion.
Eigene Berechnungen

Tabelle 12-8 (Fortsetzung) Bereitstellung von RME differenziert nach Lebenswegabschnitten: Weitere Emissionen II (Bezug: 1 GJ RME)

Lebenswegabschnitt	NMHC OK 2 g/GJ	Formaldehyd OK 2 g/GJ	Benzol OK 2 g/GJ	BaP OK 2 ng/GJ	TCDD-TÄ OK 2 ng/GJ
Landwirtschaft					
Eggen	1,81	0,13	0,032	3.350	0,072
Pflügen	1,38	0,10	0,024	2.554	0,055
Ausbringung	1,26	0,097	0,023	1.177	0,028
Ernte	1,61	0,12	0,029	2.440	0,056
Saatgut	0,0087	0,00055	0,00014	12,7	0,0052
N-Dünger	1,94	0,070	0,025	2.382	4,38
P-Dünger	0,52	0,027	0,0074	563	0,29
K-Dünger	0,090	0,0056	0,0016	138	0,18
Düngekalk	0,023	0,0015	0,00039	37,5	0,014
Pflanzenschutzmittel	0,054	0,0010	0,00070	18,4	0,090
Emissionen Feld	0	0	0	0	0
Zwischensumme	*8,69*	*0,55*	*0,14*	*12.672*	*5,17*
Konversion					
Zwischenlagerung	0,34	0,003	0,0018	568	0,14
Anlieferung	0,85	0,062	0,015	1.477	0,036
Ölmühle	0,66	0,045	0,025	420	0,50
Hexan	26,3	0,00027	0,0012	13,6	0,012
Raffination	0,12	0,0086	0,0052	83,9	0,090
Bleicherde	0,024	0,0015	0,00037	28,8	0,0012
Phosphorsäure	0,0051	0,00027	0,000089	4,52	0,0061
Umesterung*	0,61	0,042	0,025	409	0,45
Methanol	1,21	0,021	0,0090	516	0,30
Natronlauge	0,011	0,00058	0,00021	12,5	0,018
Auslieferung	0,36	0,025	0,0060	828	0,018
Zwischensumme	*30,5*	*0,21*	*0,089*	*4.362*	*1,57*
Gutschriften RME					
Referenzlandbau	-2,17	-0,16	-0,039	-2.912	-0,091
Sojaschrot Anbau	-11,1	-0,27	-0,076	-5.596	-0,71
Sojaschrot Transport	-1,92	-0,11	-0,029	-1.480	-0,108
Glyzerin Synthese	-2,96	-0,055	-0,017	-5.344	-0,95
Chlor	-0,38	-0,019	-0,0072	-420	-0,61
Natronlauge	-0,26	-0,013	-0,0049	-288	-0,41
Propylen	-1,86	-0,020	-0,015	-1.054	-1,58
Zwischensumme	*-20,7*	*-0,65*	*-0,19*	*-17.094*	*-4,45*
Summe gesamt	**18,5**	**0,11**	**0,045**	**-60,3**	**2,29**

*: inkl. Glyzerinaufbereitung
Bei negativen Zahlen überwiegen die Gutschriften aus Kuppelprodukten die Aufwendungen der Produktion.
Eigene Berechnungen

Tabelle 12-9 Spezifischer Einsatz mineralischer und energetischer Ressourcen und Emissionen der Bereitstellung von Rapsöl und RME frei Abnehmer in Deutschland im Jahr 2000

		Rapsöl		RME	
Mineralische Ressourcen					
Kalkstein	g/GJ	3.055		2.668	
Phosphaterz	g/GJ	5.227		4.716	
Schwefel	g/GJ	348		323	
Rohkali	g/GJ	4.999		4.862	
Kochsalz	g/GJ	0		-7.343	
Tonmineralien	g/GJ	0		204	
Primärenergieträger					
Erdöl	GJ/GJ	-0,020		-0,16	
Erdgas	GJ/GJ	0,11		0,14	
Steinkohle	GJ/GJ	0,024		-0,031	
Braunkohle	GJ/GJ	0,012		-0,046	
Uran	GJ/GJ	0,014		-0,047	
Σ Erschöpfl. ET	*GJ/GJ*	0,14		-0,15	
Wasser	GJ/GJ	0,0023		-0,0051	
Summe*	**GJ/GJ**	**0,14**		**-0,16**	
Emissionen					
		Global		**Global**	
CO_2	g/GJ	7.776**		-6.739**	
CH_4	g/GJ	31,1		4,76	
N_2O	g/GJ	133		116	
CO_2-Äquivalente	*g/GJ*	*49.657*		*29.248*	
		OK 2	**OK 3**	**OK 2**	**OK 3**
SO_2	g/GJ	3,11	-67,4	-81,0	-49,0
CO	g/GJ	6,13	-7,57	2,43	-5,47
NO_X	g/GJ	23,6	-70,6	21,3	-50,9
NMHC	g/GJ	-10,2	-2,06	18,5	-1,54
Partikel	g/GJ	0,33	-6,72	0,93	-4,84
Staub	g/GJ	11,1	-0,00088	7,48	-0,0044
HCl	g/GJ	0,39	-0,081	-0,30	-0,060
NH_3	g/GJ	180	-0,010	157	-0,0062
Formaldehyd	g/GJ	-0,073	-0,17	0,11	-0,12
Benzol	g/GJ	-0,022	-0,040	0,044	-0,029
Benzo(a)pyren	ng/GJ	2.067	-8.656	-51,0	-6.250
TCDD-TÄ	ng/GJ	5,05	-1,43	2,31	-1,09
SO_2-Äquivalente	*g/GJ*	*359*	*-117*	*230*	*-84,6*

*: Nachrichtlich: Energieinhalt von Rapskorn: 2,028 bzw. 1,749 MJ je bereitgestelltem MJ Rapsöl bzw. RME.

**: Fossiles CO_2.

Bei negativen Zahlen überwiegen die Gutschriften aus Kuppelprodukten die Aufwendungen der Produktion.

Zur Umrechnung der Ergebnisdaten von Energie- auf Massen- bzw. Volumenbezug (von GJ auf kg bzw. l) siehe die Heizwerte und Dichten von Rapsöl bzw. RME nach Tabelle 8-10.

Eigene Berechnungen

12.6 Heizwerte und Dichten von Energieträgern

Zur Umrechnung zwischen Energie-, Massen- und Volumeneinheiten werden, wenn nicht anders vermerkt, die Daten nach **Tabelle 12-10** angesetzt.

Tabelle 12-10 Heizwerte und Dichten von Energieträgern

Energieträger	**Heizwert**	**Dichte**	
	MJ/kg	kg/l	kg/m3
Erdöl (roh)	42,611		
Dieselkraftstoff	42,960	0,832	
Kerosin	43,000	0,795	
Schweröl	40,582	0,970	
Steinkohle	29,704		
Braunkohle	8,797		
Erdgas	44,010		0,792

Quellen: /AGE 1998/, /DGMK 1992/, eigene Abschätzungen

13 Bereitstellung der Daten in einer Datenbank

Von Mario Schmidt

13.1 Anforderungen an Bilanzierungssoftware

Gerade in Ökobilanzen von Produkten, aber auch in anderen Stoffstromanalysen sind Einsätze von Nutzfahrzeugen von entscheidender Bedeutung. Da die meisten Stoffstromanalysen computergestützt erstellt werden, müssen die Daten für diese Prozesse EDV-gerecht bereitgestellt werden. Dabei sind insbesondere folgende Anforderungen zu stellen, die hier am Beispiel von Transportprozessen erläutert werden:

- **Generischer Prozeß mit standardisiertem Datensatz:** Ein Transportvorgang wird aufgrund der unzureichenden Datenlage nicht individuell betrachtet, sondern einer bestimmten Kategorie von Transporten zugeordnet, für die standardisierte Daten vorliegen. Je nachdem, wie differenziert diese Daten sind, können für die Zuordnung zahlreiche Aspekte berücksichtigt und damit der individuelle Transportvorgang möglichst genau beschrieben werden.
- **Modularer Aufbau:** In einer Prozeßkette wird ein Transportprozeß als ein Modul neben vielen anderen aus Produktion, Konsumtion, Entsorgung oder anderen Transporten verstanden. Die Daten sind gekapselt und der Prozeß tritt mit dem restlichen System nur über die Stoffströme in Verbindung. Dieser modulare Aufbau erlaubt die mehrfache Verwendung des gleichen Datensatzes in unterschiedlichen Systemen bzw. Fragestellungen.
- **Verknüpfungsmöglichkeit mit anderen Prozessen:** Der Transportprozeß muß so gestaltet sein, daß er mit ganz unterschiedlichen Prozessen verknüpft werden kann, um z. B. den Transport unterschiedlicher Güter beschreiben zu können.
- **Variationsmöglichkeit von Parametern:** Der Transportvorgang wird mit verschiedenen prozeßbeschreibenden Parametern gekennzeichnet. Dazu gehören z. B. die Transportentfernung, das zulässige Gesamtgewicht oder die Größe eines LKW, die Auslastung, die verschiedenen Fahrmodi usw.
- **Auswertung der Gesamtbilanz nach Einzelprozessen, z. B. Transporten:** Wird die Input-/Outputbilanz eines größeren Stoffstromsystems erstellt, so sollte der Anwender in der Lage sein, den Beitrag der Transporte, z. B. an den Emissionen oder am Energieverbrauch, einfach zu ersehen.

Diese Anforderungen werden von verschiedenen auf dem Markt erhältlichen Programmen erfüllt. Hier wird im folgenden die Ökobilanz-Software Umberto® vorgestellt, die vom IFEU–Institut für Energie- und Umweltforschung Heidelberg zusammen mit dem ifu-Institut für Umweltinformatik Hamburg entwickelt wurde. Die im Hauptteil dieses Buches abgeleiteten Daten sind in die Prozeßbibliothek von Umberto® integriert; ihre Anwendung wird am Beispiel von Transportprozessen illustriert.

13.2 Die Bilanzierungssoftware Umberto®

Umberto® ist ein Programm für Stoffstromanalysen, das auf einzelnen PCs und in Client-Server-Netzen unter Microsoft Windows 95/98 oder NT läuft. Es ermöglicht die Erstellung von Produkt-Ökobilanzen, standortbezogenen oder betrieblichen Ökobilanzen und komplexen Stoffstromanalysen. Umberto® basiert auf der Methode der Stoffstromnetze, bei der ein Lebensweg oder ein Produktionssystem als ein Netz von Umwandlungsprozessen dargestellt wird /SCHMIDT & HÄUSLEIN 1997/. Der Begriff *Stoff*strom umfaßt dabei neben massebehafteten Strömen in gleicher Weise auch Energieströme. Das Programm eignet sich gleichermaßen zur Aufstellung umfangreicher Sachbilanzen als auch zur Wirkungsanalyse und Bewertung dieser Sachbilanzergebnisse.

In **Abb. 13-1** ist die Benutzeroberfläche unter Microsoft Windows abgebildet. Der Anwender kann mittels eines komfortablen Netzwerkeditors sein Stoffstromnetz, z. B. den Produktlebensweg oder die Prozeßkette, graphisch aufbauen. Die quadratischen Symbole stehen dabei für die Umwandlungsprozesse. Die Kreise definieren Bestände oder Verteilerknoten und können z. B. zur flexiblen Beschreibung von Bilanzgrenzen oder Umweltmedien im System oder zur Modellierung von Recyclingsystemen verwendet werden. Die einzelnen graphischen Objekte werden durch Mausklick „geöffnet". Dahinter verbergen sich die Definitionen, z. B. von Prozessen, oder die Information, wieviel und welche Materialien zwischen den Netzobjekten fließen.

Die Stoffstromnetze können dabei hierarchisch aufgebaut werden: Hinter einem Prozeß (in **Abb. 13-1** in T3 ganz rechts) kann sich wieder ein ganzes Netz aus Einzelprozessen – also ein Subnetz – verbergen. Damit lassen sich sehr komplexe Systeme aufbauen und analysieren.

Ziel der Modellierung ist es, bekannte Stoffströme und Prozeßinformationen mit bekannten Funktionalitäten dazu zu verwenden, um unbekannte Ströme und Bestände im System zu berechnen. Im Fall einer Produkt-Ökobilanz sind üblicherweise alle Prozeßinformationen bekannt und es werden aus einem speziellen Stoffstrom, nämlich aus der funktionellen Einheit des Produktes (1 Stück, 1 kg usw.), alle Ressourcenverbräuche, Emissionen, Abfälle usw. berechnet. Es können allerdings auch andere Systeme vorliegen, in denen einzelne Prozeßabläufe nicht weiter bestimmt sind oder in denen mehrere Stoffströme bereits bekannt sind. Das Programm ermittelt dann jene Größen, die aus den bekannten Informationen und Abhängigkeiten berechenbar sind. Der Anwender geht zur Erstellung eines Stoffstromnetzes folgendermaßen vor:

- Festlegung der relevanten Materialien, d. h. Stoffe und Energien, die in dem System fließen. Der Anwender ist bei der Definition einzelner Materialien völlig frei.
- Aufbau des Stoffstromnetzes, also des Lebensweges eines Produktes oder der Prozeßkette, mittels des graphischen Netzwerkeditors.
- Definition der einzelnen Umwandlungsprozesse zur Beschreibung der Produktion, Energieerzeugung, Transporte usw. Hierbei werden zahlenmäßige Zusammenhänge zwischen den Inputströmen und den Outputströmen angegeben. Die Zusammenhänge können für fortgeschrittene Anwender auch nichtlinear und zeitperiodenabhängig modelliert werden.

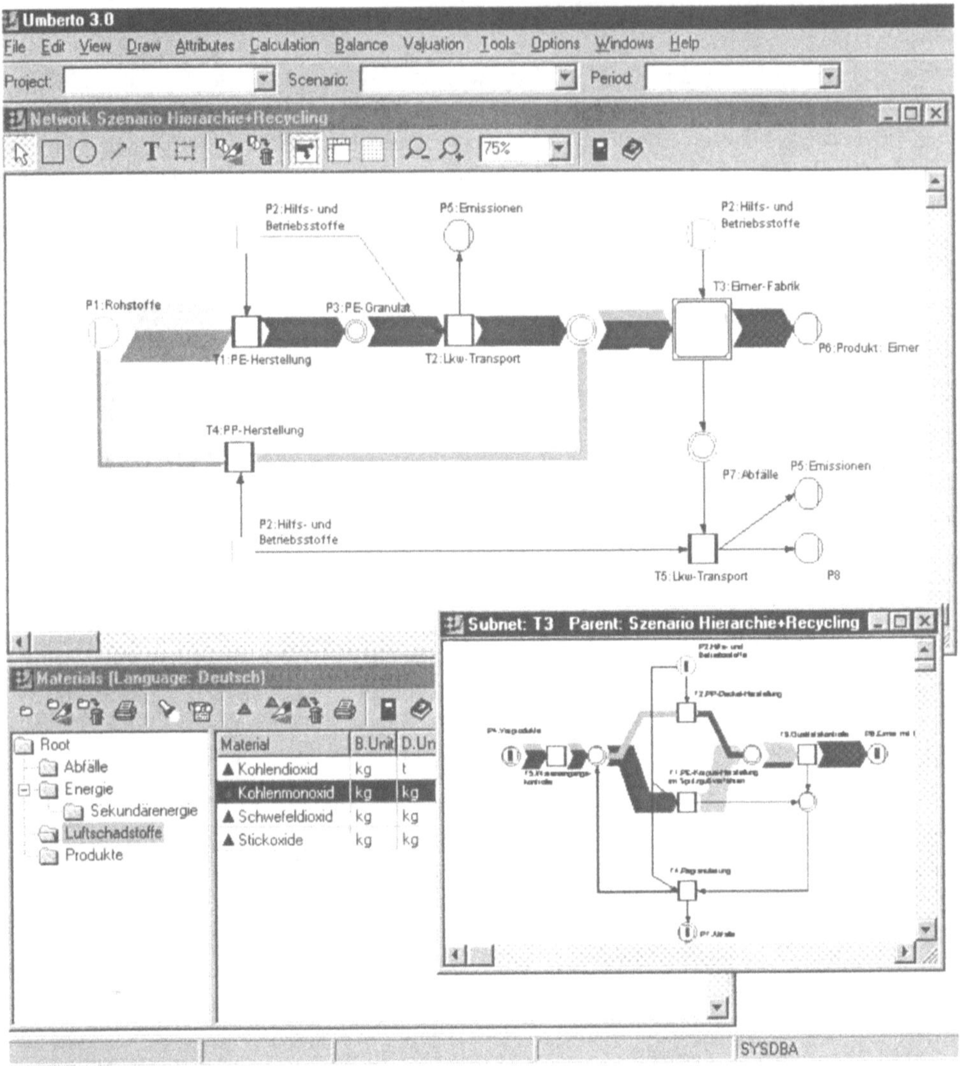

Abb. 13-1 Die Benutzeroberfläche von Umberto® 3.0. In einem Netzwerkeditor werden die Stoffstromnetze erstellt. Dabei sind hierarchische Systeme möglich. Der Prozeß T3 kann wieder als ein eigenes Stoffstromnetz (Fenster unten rechts) aufgefaßt werden. Links unten – teilweise verdeckt – ist das Fenster mit der Verwaltung der Materialstammdaten zu sehen.

- Eingabe von bekannten Strom- oder Bestandsdaten, z. B. der funktionellen Einheit, zur Berechnung des Systems.

Nach der Berechnung sind an jeder Stelle im Netz die Ströme und Bestände von Stoffen und Energien bekannt und können ausgewertet werden. Zur Anzeige der Werte reicht ein Doppelklick mit der Maus auf das betreffende Netzelement. Aus der Aggregation dieser Detaildaten über das gesamte System oder über spezielle Netzausschnitte, die man manuell wählen kann, folgt schließlich eine Bilanz in Form einer Input/Outputliste der relevanten Stoff- und Energieströme (siehe Beispiel in **Abb. 13-2**). Diese Bilanz kann – entsprechend der Aufgabestellung der Untersuchung – nach verschiedenen Prozessen oder Umweltmedien ausgewertet werden. Ferner lassen sich Kennzahlen bilden oder Wirkungsanalysen und Bewertungen auf die Bilanz anwenden.

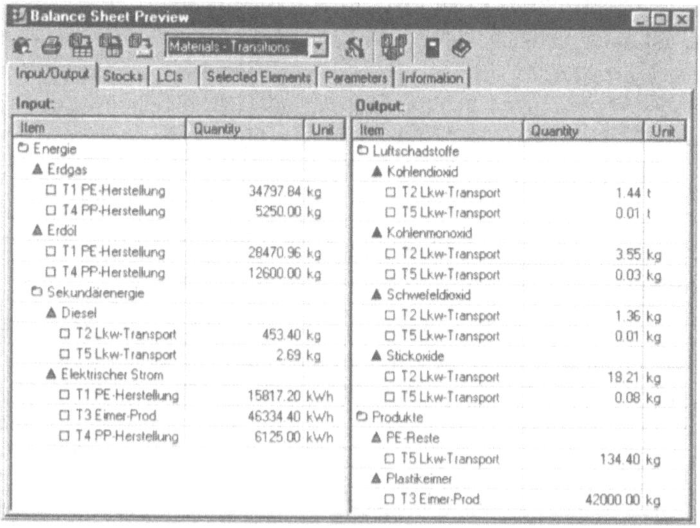

Abb. 13-2 Input- und Outputliste eines einfachen Beispiels. In diesem Fall werden die Input- und Outputströme des Gesamtsystems zusätzlich nach den Beiträgen der einzelnen Prozesse dargestellt.

Folgende Eigenschaften der Software Umberto® sind besonders hervorzuheben:

- Der spezielle Ansatz der Stoffstromnetze ermöglicht sowohl eine Periodenrechnung als auch eine Stückrechnung. Damit ist das Programm universell für Produkt- *und* Betriebsbilanzen einsetzbar. Für Betriebsbilanzen werden nicht nur Ströme, sondern auch Bestände im System berücksichtigt.
- Der Anwender hat nahezu alle Freiheiten in der Definition der Umwandlungsprozesse. Sie können entweder sehr einfach mit Verhältniszahlen der Input- zu Outputströmen zueinander aufgebaut werden oder mittels mathematischer Funktionen auch nichtlineare Abhängigkeiten berücksichtigen. Außerdem steht unter Umberto® eine Bibliothek mit bereits vordefinierten Datensätzen aus den Bereichen der Energieerzeugung, Abfallentsorgung, Transporte und wichtiger Produktionsprozesse zur Verfügung.
- Das Programm überprüft die innere Konsistenz des Systems. So können z. B. Energie oder Stoffe nicht „verschwinden", wenn der Anwender die Prozesse richtig definiert hat.

- Durch den Ansatz der Stoffstromnetze kann der Anwender bei einem bestehenden bzw. berechneten System die Bilanzgrenzen nahezu beliebig verändern und somit das System flexibel auswerten.
- Allokationsvorschriften einzelner Prozesse oder ganzer Systeme können vielseitig modelliert werden.
- Mit den Stoffstromnetzen können auch komplizierte Materialrückflüsse, wie sie z. B. beim Recycling auftreten, modelliert werden /SCHMIDT & SCHORB 1995/.
- Aufbauend auf der Sachbilanz können Wirkungsanalysen und Bewertungen durchgeführt werden. Umberto® ist dabei nicht auf eine bestimmte Bewertungsmethode festgelegt. Mit dem Programm wird eine Methodendatenbank mit den gängigen Bewertungsverfahren ausgeliefert. Der fortgeschrittene Anwender kann unter Umberto® auch eigene Bewertungsmethoden definieren und in der Datenbank abspeichern.
- Es bestehen komfortable Schnittstellen zum Datenaustausch (Import und Export) mit anderen Programmen. Mit einer SQL-Schnittstelle kann auf Datenbestände der gängigen Datenbanksysteme zurückgegriffen werden.
- Umberto® ermöglicht neben der reinen Stoffstromrechnung auch eine Kostenrechnung. Dabei können die Stoff- und Energieströme im System mit Preisen bewertet werden. Zusätzlich ist die Definition weiterer Kostenarten (Personalkosten, Abschreibungen usw.) möglich, die bei der Kostenrechnung berücksichtigt werden. Das Programm führt eine interne Leistungsverrechnung und eine Kostenträgerrechnung durch /SCHMIDT & MÖLLER 1998/.
- Das Programm Umberto® verfügt über ein umfangreiches Dokumentationssystem. Alle Objekte, z. B. Materialien, Prozesse, Projekte usw., können mit Texten genauer beschrieben werden. Zu den bereitgestellten Prozeßmodulen liegen online-Beschreibungen der Datenherkunft oder Prozeßannahmen vor. Schließlich existiert ein online-Hilfesystem, das das Benutzerhandbuch ergänzt.

Umberto® ist damit nicht nur eine Software zur Erstellung von Produkt-Ökobilanzen. Es ist vielmehr ein Datenbank-basiertes Modellierprogramm für den Aufbau von betrieblichen Umweltinformationssystemen. (Weitere Auskünfte: ifu-Institut für Umweltinformatik, Hamburg.)

13.3 Transportprozesse in Umberto®

Auch Transportvorgänge werden in Stoffstromanalysen als Umwandlungsprozesse aufgefaßt. Zwar bleibt im Idealfall das Transportgut invariant, d. h. es verändert sich durch den Transportprozeß nicht in seinen materiellen Eigenschaften, jedoch wird Energie benötigt und verschiedene Schadstoffemissionen werden freigesetzt. Im folgenden wird beispielhaft beschrieben, wie Transportprozesse in Umberto® modelliert werden und wie die in Kapitel 5 abgeleiteten Daten in der Datenbank verfügbar sind.

Ein Anwender modelliert einen Transportvorgang, indem er zuerst graphisch einen Prozeß in das Netz einfügt und dann die Prozesse durch Pfeile miteinander verbindet. Danach wählt er in einer Prozeßbibliothek die entsprechende Klasse von Transportprozessen aus, also z. B. LKW, Bahn, Flugzeug usw. In **Abb. 13-3** ist das Fenster der Bibliothek mit den verschiedenen Prozeßgruppen und – im Falle der LKW-Transporte – mit den einzelnen Modulen zu erkennen. Diese Module enthalten bereits die Prozeßdefinitionen, die auf den Daten aus diesem Buch basieren. Das Modul wird in ein Prozeßnetz eingefügt. Innerhalb des Prozesses muß der Anwender dann festlegen, welche Transportgüter von dem Prozeß transportiert werden sollen, woher der Kraftstoff oder die Energie kommt, wohin die Emissionen gehen, und gegebenenfalls prozeßbestimmende Parameter angeben.

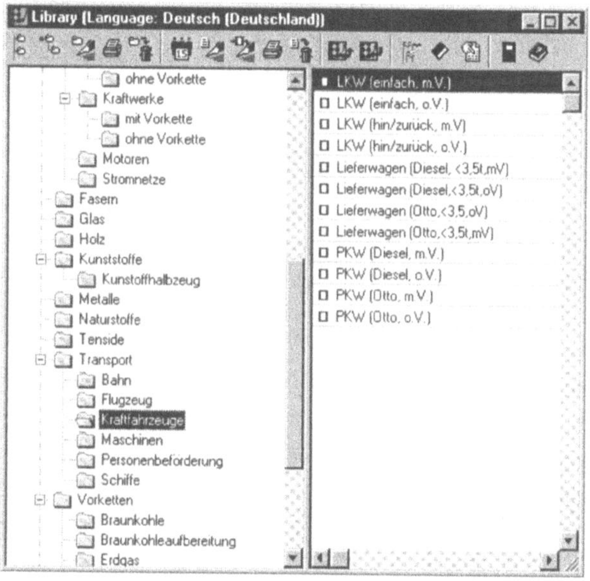

Abb. 13-3 Die Bibliothek mit vorgefertigten Prozeßmodulen, die ausgewählt und in ein Stoffstromnetz einbezogen werden können.

Das Prinzip ist in **Abb. 13-4** dargestellt: In den Prozeß fließen auf der Inputseite die Transportgüter. Dieser Fluß wird durch die Masse in kg oder t bestimmt und erscheint wieder unverändert auf der Outputseite. Das Transportgut soll eine bestimmte Entfernung mit einer gewissen Fahrzeugauslastung transportiert werden. Aus der Menge und den prozeßbestimmenden Parametern errechnet das Modul den Bedarf an Energie (z. B. Dieselkraftstoff) und fordert diese auf der Inputseite an. Auf der Outputseite fallen die Emissionen an.

In den Modulen können die Bilanzgrenzen des Transportvorgangs unterschiedlich weit gezogen werden: Zum einen kann tatsächlich nur der Transport als Elementarprozeß betrachtet werden. Dann stehen bei einem LKW auf der Inputseite Dieselkraftstoff und auf der Outputseite die unmittelbaren Auspuffemissionen. Bei einem Bahntransport mit Elektrotraktion wird lediglich auf der Inputseite elektrischer Strom bilanziert.

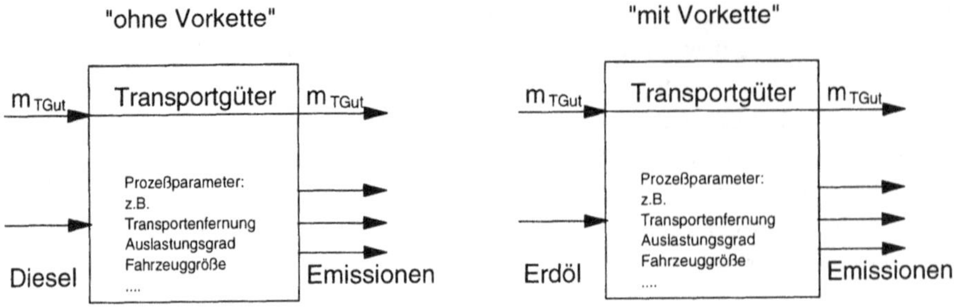

Abb. 13-4 Prinzip der Transportprozesse. Die Transportgüter bestimmen mit ihrer Masse und zusammen mit einstellbaren Prozeßparametern das Aktivitätsniveau des Prozesses. Die Transportgutmenge (m_{TGut}) bleibt auf Input- und Outputseite gleich. Das Modul berechnet den Energiebedarf und die Emissionen.

Zum anderen kann man die Bereitstellung dieser Sekundärenergien (die Vorkette) bereits berücksichtigen und in die Moduldefinition einbeziehen. Der LKW-Transport würde dann auf der Inputseite „Erdöl" anfordern, obwohl der LKW nicht direkt mit Erdöl betrieben wird; er wäre vielmehr als ein System aus Vorkette und dem eigentlichen Transportvorgang zu verstehen. Analog beim Bahntransport: Hier entstünden nun Emissionen und auf der Inputseite würden z. B. Kohle, Erdöl und Uran für die Strombereitstellung auftreten.

Eine besondere Bedeutung haben die prozeßbestimmenden Parameter. Bei einem LKW-Transport müssen z. B. folgende Parameter vorgegeben werden:

- Transportentfernung in km
- Auslastungsgrad in %
- LKW-Größenklasse (1 bis 6)
- Fahrleistungsanteil Autobahn in %
- Fahrleistungsanteil Außerortsstraße in %
- Fahrleistungsanteil Innerortsstraße in %

Für die LKW-Größe kann zwischen sechs Klassen nach Zulässigem Gesamtgewicht (< 7,5 t, 14 - 20 t, > 20 t, Züge < 32 t, Züge >32 t, Durchschnitt) gewählt werden. Zusammen mit den Fahrleistungsanteilen für die verschiedenen Straßenkategorien werden dann die entsprechenden Emissions- und Verbrauchsfaktoren für die Berechnung ausgewählt.

Die Unterscheidung der Emissionen nach Ortsklassen, wie in diesem Buch durchgeführt, wird in den Datensätzen unter Umberto® nicht berücksichtigt. Die Prozeßbeschreibungen lassen sich allerdings nachträglich leicht ändern und um diese zusätzliche Unterscheidung ergänzen. Für die Auswertung ist dabei das sogenannte Stellenkonzept in Stoffstromnetzen hilfreich, bei dem eine weitere Untergliederungsmöglichkeit der Input- und Outputströme, wie z. B. nach Umweltmedien oder Ortsklassen, möglich ist.

14 Abkürzungen und Einheiten

ALG	Auslastungsgrad
Äq., Äquiv., Äquival.	Äquivalente
BaP	Benzo(a)pyren
CaO	Calciumoxid, Bezugsgröße für Düngekalk
CH_4	Methan
CO	Kohlenmonoxid
CO_2	Kohlendioxid
DIN-NAGUS	Deutsches Institut für Normung, Normenausschuß Grundlagen des Umweltschutzes
Erschöpfl. ET	Erschöpfliche Energieträger
EU	Europäische Union
EVU	Elektrizitätsversorgungsunternehmen
GFAVO	Großfeuerungsanlagenverordnung
GUS	Gemeinschaft Unabhängiger Staaten
HC	Hydrocarbons (Kohlenwasserstoffe)
H_2S	Schwefelwasserstoff
H_2SO_4	Schwefelsäure
H_3PO_4	Phosphorsäure
HCl	Chlorwasserstoff
HNO_3	Salpetersäure
ISO	International Standardization Organization
K-Dünger	Kaliumdünger
K_2O	Kaliumoxid, Bezugsgröße für Kaliumdünger
M%	Massenprozent
MNL	Maximale Nutzlast
N	Stickstoff, Bezugsgröße für Stickstoffdünger
N-Dünger	Stickstoffdünger
N_2O	Distickstoffoxid (Lachgas)
NH_3	Ammoniak
NL	Niederlande
NOR	Norwegen
NMHC	Non Methane Hydrocarbons (Nicht-Methan Kohlenwasserstoffe)
NO	Stickstoffmonoxid
NO_2	Stickstoffdioxid
NO_X	Stickoxide
OECD	Organization of Economic Cooperation and Development
OK	Ortsklasse
OPEC	Organization of Petroleum Exporting Countries
P-Dünger	Phosphatdünger
P_2O_5	Phosphorpentoxid, Bezugsgröße für Phosphatdünger
PCDD	Polychlorierte Dibenzodioxine
PCDF	Polychlorierte Dibenzofurane
RME	Rapsölmethylester
SETAC	Society of Environmental Toxicology and Chemistry
Σ	Summe
SO_2	Schwefeldioxid
TÄ	Toxizitätsäquivalente
TCDD	Tetrachlordibenzodioxin
tkm	Tonnenkilometer
ZGG	Zulässiges Gesamtgewicht

15 Literatur

/AGE 1995/ Arbeitsgemeinschaft Energiebilanzen (Hrsg.): Beschlußlage und Empfehlungen zur Reform der Energiebilanzen. Positionspapier, Essen 1995

/AGE 1998/ Arbeitsgemeinschaft Energiebilanzen (Hrsg.): Energiebilanzen der Bundesrepublik Deutschland 1994. Essen 1998

/AHMED et al. 1994/ Ahmed, I., Decker, J., Morris, D.: How much energy does it take to make a gallon of soydiesel? Bericht für das National Soy Diesel Development Board, Jefferson City, Missouri. Institute for Local Self-Reliance Environmentally Sound Economic Development, Minneapolis/Washington/Philadelphia 1994

/ANDRIAS et al. 1994/ Andrias, A., Samaras, Z., Zierock, K. H.: The estimation of the emissions of other mobile sources and maschinery - Subpart „Off-road vehicles and machines". EU Study Contract number B4-3040/93/000803/B3, Brüssel 1994

/BAZ 1987/ Bundesamt für Zivilluftfahrt (Hrsg.): Schadstoffemissionen und Treibstoffverbrauch des Zivilluftverkehrs in der Schweiz pro 1987. Bern 1987

/BAZ 1993/ Bundesamt für Zivilluftfahrt, Bundesamt für Militärflugplätze (Hrsg.): Die Auswirkungen der Luftfahrt auf die Umwelt, Technischer Bericht B: Teilbereich Luft/Energieverbrauch. Bearbeitet durch Elektrowatt Ingenieurunternehmungen. Bern 1993

/BIALONSKI et al. 1990/ Bialonski, W. et al.: Spezifischer Energieeinsatz im Verkehr – Ermittlung und Vergleich der spezifischen Energieverbräuche. Verkehrswissenschaftliches Institut an der RWTH Aachen, Aachen 1990

/BMV 1994/ Hotes, A., Hüttig, G. (TU Berlin); Koschel, W. (RWTH Aachen): Abschätzung der Schadstoffemissionen ziviler Flugzeuge mit Strahlantrieben – Bewertung für den Flughafennahbereich und das Gebiet der Bundesrepublik Deutschland. Forschungsbericht im Auftrag des Bundesministers für Verkehr (BMV), FE-Nr. 500 96/91. 1994 (unveröffentlicht)

/BMWI 1998/ Bundesministerium für Wirtschaft (Hrsg.): Die Elektrizitätswirtschaft in der Bundesrepublik Deutschland im Jahre 1996. Elektrizitätsstatistik, 48. Bericht, Frankfurt a. M. 1998

/BRADOW et al. 1980/ Bradow, R., Dietzmann, H., Parness, M.: Emissions from trucks by chassis version of 1983 transient procedures. SAE Paper 801371, 1980

/BRUCH et al. 1995/ Bruch, K. H., Gohlke, D., Kögler, C., Krüger, J., Reuter, M., v. Röpenack, I., Rombach, E., Rombach, G., Winkler, P.: Sachbilanz einer Ökobilanz der Kupfererzeugung und Verarbeitung. (Sonderdruck) Metall 49 (1995)

/BUWAL 1991/ Bundesamt für Umwelt, Wald und Landschaft (Hrsg.): Ökobilanz von Packstoffen, Stand 1990. Schriftenreihe Umwelt Nr. 132, Bern 1991

/BUWAL 1994/ Bundesamt für Umwelt, Wald und Landschaft (Hrsg.): Schadstoffemissionen und Treibstoffverbrauch von Baumaschinen. Umwelt-Materialien Nr. 23, Bern 1994

/BUWAL 1996/ Bundesamt für Umwelt, Wald und Landschaft (Hrsg.): Schadstoffemissionen und Treibstoffverbrauch im Offroad-Sektor. Umwelt-Materialien Nr. 49, Bern 1996

/CARBOTECH 1994/ Schläpfer, K. et al. (Carbotech): Emissionsfaktoren nichtlimitierter Schadstoffe des Straßenverkehrs. Im Auftrag des Bundesamtes für Umwelt, Wald und Landschaft, Bern 1994

/CE 1997a/ Dijkstra, W., Dings, J. (CE - Centre for Energy Conservation and Environmental Technology): Specific energy consumption and emissions of freight transport – A comparison between road, water, rail and air. Delft/NL 1997

/CE 1997b/ Roos, J., Bleijenberg, A., Dijkstra, W. (CE - Centre for Energy Conservation and Environmental Technology): Energy and emission profiles of aircraft and other modes of passenger transport over European distances. Im Auftrag des Niederländischen Ministeriums für Wohnen, Raumplanung und Umwelt, Abschlußbericht, Delft/NL 1997

/CML & TNO & B&G 1992/ Heijungs, R., Guinée, J. B., Huppes, G., Lamkreijer, R. M., Udo de Haes, H. A., Wegener Sleeswijk, A., Ansems, A. M. M., Eggels, P. G., van Duin, R., de Goede, H. P.: Environmental Life Cycle Assessment of Products. Guide (Part 1) and Backgrounds (Part 2), prepared by CML, TNO and B&G, Leiden 1992 (Englisch: 1993)

/CONNEMANN 1998/ Connemann, J., Leer: Persönliche Mitteilung, Nov. 1998

/DB 1989a/ Deutsche Bundesbahn (DB), Zentrales Rechnungswesen (Hrsg.): Auszüge aus der Gesamtkostenrechnung 1988 – Betriebsartenrechnung. Frankfurt a. M. 1989

/DB 1989b/ Deutsche Bundesbahn (DB), Zentrales Rechnungswesen (Hrsg.): Betriebstatistische Kartei 1988 – Betriebsartenrechnung. Frankfurt a. M. 1989

/DB 1989c/ Deutsche Bundesbahn (DB, Hrsg.): Die Bahn in Zahlen 89. Frankfurt a. M. 1989

/DGMK 1992/ Deutsche Wissenschaftliche Gesellschaft für Erdöl, Erdgas und Kohle (DGMK, Hrsg.): Ansatzpunkte der Potentiale zur Minderung des Treibhauseffektes aus der Sicht der fossilen Energieträger. DGMK-Forschungsbericht 448-2, Hamburg 1992

/DIN 1986/ Deutsches Institut für Normung (DIN, Hrsg.): DIN 51601. Flüssige Kraftstoffe - Dieselkraftstoff - Mindestanforderungen. Beuth Verlag, Berlin 1986

/DIN 1994/ Normenausschuß Grundlagen des Umweltschutzes des Deutschen Instituts für Normung (DIN-NAGUS, Hrsg.): Grundsätze produktbezogener Ökobilanzen. Übereinkunft des Arbeitsausschusses 3 des DIN-NAGUS, DIN-Mitt. 73, Nr. 3 (1994) 208-212

/DIN 1995/ Normenausschuß Grundlagen des Umweltschutzes des Deutschen Instituts für Normung (DIN-NAGUS, Hrsg.): Wirkungsabschätzung und Bewertung. Nationales Positionspapier zu DIN ISO 14042. Arbeitspapier (1. Entwurf) des Arbeitsausschusses 3/Unterausschuß 2 des DIN-NAGUS (AA3/UA2) 4-53

/DIN 1997/ Deutsches Institut für Normung (DIN, Hrsg.): DIN 51606. Dieselkraftstoff aus Fettsäuremethylestern - Mindestanforderungen. Beuth Verlag, Berlin 1997

/DIN EN ISO 1997/ Deutsches Institut für Normung (DIN, Hrsg.): DIN EN ISO 14040. Umweltmanagement - Ökobilanz - Prinzipien und allgemeine Anforderungen. Beuth Verlag, Berlin 1997

/DIN EN ISO 1998/ Deutsches Institut für Normung (DIN, Hrsg.): DIN EN ISO 14041. Umweltmanagement – Ökobilanz – Festlegung des Ziels und des Untersuchungsrahmens sowie Sachbilanz. Beuth Verlag, Berlin 1998

/DIN EN ISO 1999a/ Deutsches Institut für Normung (DIN, Hrsg.): DIN EN ISO 14042. Umweltmanagement – Ökobilanz – Wirkungsabschätzung (Entwurf, Februar 1999). Beuth Verlag, Berlin 1999

/DIN EN ISO 1999b/ Deutsches Institut für Normung (DIN, Hrsg.): DIN EN ISO 14043. Umweltmanagement – Ökobilanz – Auswertung (Entwurf, Januar 1999). Beuth Verlag, Berlin 1999

/DIW & IFEU & IVU 1994/ Höpfner, U., Knisch, H. (IFEU): Arbeitspaket Wirkungsanalyse und -prognose. In: Verminderung der Luft- und Lärmbelastung des Güterfernverkehrs 2000/2010. DIW, IFEU und IVU im Auftrag des Umweltbundesamt, UFOPLAN-Nr. 104 05 962, Berlin 1994

/DLG 1977/ Deutsche Landwirtschafts-Gesellschaft (Hrsg.): Prüfbericht 2577, Frankfurt a. M. 1977

/DLG 1987/ Deutsche Landwirtschafts-Gesellschaft (Hrsg.): Pflichtenheft für die Datenverarbeitung in der Pflanzenproduktion. DLG-Verlag, Frankfurt a. M. 1987

/DLG 1993/ Deutsche Landwirtschafts-Gesellschaft (Hrsg.): Ackerschlepper in der Prüfung. DLG-Verlag, Frankfurt a. M. 1993

/DLG 1995a/ Deutsche Landwirtschafts-Gesellschaft (Hrsg.): Prüfbericht 4382, Frankfurt a. M. 1995

/DLG 1995b/ Deutsche Landwirtschafts-Gesellschaft (Hrsg.): Prüfbericht 4386, Frankfurt a. M. 1995

/DLG 1995c/ Deutsche Landwirtschafts-Gesellschaft (Hrsg.): Prüfbericht 4383, Frankfurt a. M. 1995

/DLR 1990/ Nüsser, H.-G., Schmitt, A. (DLR): The global distribution of air traffic at high altitudes, related fuel consumption and trends. In: Schumann, U. (Hrsg.): Air traffic and the Environment – Background, Tendencies and Potential Global Atmospheric Effects. Springer Verlag, Heidelberg 1990

/DLR 1993/ Schumann, U. (DLR): On the effect of emissions from aircraft engines on the state of the atmosphere. Deutsche Forschungsanstalt für Luft- und Raumfahrt e.V. (DLR), Institut für Physik der Atmosphäre; Report No. 1. Oberpfaffenhofen 1993

/ECOINVENT 1996/ Baumann, T., Frischknecht, R., Gränicher, H.-P., Hofstetter, P., Knoepfel, I., Ménard, M., Sprecher, F.: Ecoinvent – Ökoinventare für Energiesysteme: Grundlagen für den ökologischen Vergleich von Energiesystemen und den Einbezug von Energiesystemen in Ökobilanzen für die Schweiz. Im Auftrag des Bundesamtes für Energiewirtschaft und des Nationalen Energie-Forschungs-Fonds, 3.Aufl., Bern 1996

/EMAS 1993/ Verordnung (EWG) Nr. 1836/93 des Rates vom 29. Juli 1993 über die freiwillige Beteiligung gewerblicher Unternehmen an einem Gemeinschaftssystem für das Umweltmanagement und die Umweltbetriebsprüfung. Abl. Nr. L. 168 vom 10. Juli 1993

/ENQUÊTE 1994/ Enquête-Kommission „Schutz der Erdatmosphäre" (Hrsg.): Systemvergleich für unterschiedliche verkehrliche Prozeßabläufe und Transportketten hinsichtlich des Energieeinsatzes und klimarelevanter Emissionen im Güterverkehr. Bd. 4/II Verkehr, Economia Verlag, Bonn 1994

/ESSERS et al. 1992/ Essers, U., Hagenmaier, H., Hutzinger, O.: Untersuchungen zur Emission halogenierter Dibenzodioxine und Dibenzofurane aus Verbrennungsmotoren beim Betrieb mit handelsüblichen Betriebsstoffen. GSF-Forschungszentrum für Umwelt und Gesundheit, Forschungsbericht 4/92, München 1992

/EXTERNE 1995/ Kommission der Europäischen Gemeinschaften (Hrsg.): ExternE – Externalties of Energy. Volume 1 (Summary), Luxemburg 1995

/FFE & IFE 1995/ Bauer, H., Hoffmann, C., Ilmberger, F. (FfE) und Brunner, T., Ebersperger, R., Fleißner, T., Kawollek, R. (IfE): Kumulierter Energieaufwand und energieoptimierte Nutzungsdauer von Personenkraftwagen. Bayerisches Zentrum für Angewandte Energieforschung e. V. (Hrsg.) im Auftrag des Bayerischen Staatsministeriums für Wirtschaft und Verkehr, München 1995

/FRINGS 1995/ Frings, E.: Ergebnisse und Empfehlungen der Enquête-Kommission „Schutz des Menschen und der Umwelt" zum Stoffstrommanagement. In: Schmidt, M., Schorb, A. (Hrsg.): Stoffstromanalysen in Ökobilanzen und Ökoaudits. Springer-Verlag, Berlin/Heidelberg 1995

/FUNK 1995/ Funk, M. (KTBL): Schriftliche Mitteilung vom 07.04.95, Kuratorium für Technik und Bauwesen in der Landwirtschaft, Darmstadt

/GEMIS 1997/ Fritsche, U. R., Leuchtner, J., Matthes, F. C., Rausch, L., Simon, K. H.: Gesamt-Emissions-Modell Integrierter Systeme (GEMIS) Version 3.0. Im Auftrag des Hessischen Ministeriums für Umwelt, Energie und Bundesangelegenheiten, Wiesbaden 1997

/GOETHEL 1993/ Goethel, G. F., Altmann, B.-R.: Emissionsminderung in deutschen Raffinerien. Erdöl, Erdgas, Kohle 109/5 (1993) 224-227

/GRÄF et al. 1994/ Gräf, D., Barnefsky, K., König, W., Maurer, K., Reiser, W.: Projekt Naturdiesel. Zwischenergebnisse eines laufenden Projekts zu den Abgasemissionen von Ackerschleppern, Uffenheim 1994

/HAHN 1989/ Hahn, J. (Deutsche Bundesbahn): Schadstoffmindernde Maßnahmen an den Dieselmotoren von Schienenfahrzeugen. Eisenbahntechnische Rundschau 38/6 (1989) 377

/HAMBURG 1986/ Umweltbehörde Hamburg (Hrsg.): Luftreinhalteplan Hamburg. Hamburg 1986

/HARTMANN & STREHLER 1995/ Hartmann H., Strehler A.: Die Stellung der Biomasse im Vergleich zu anderen erneuerbaren Energieträgern aus ökologischer, ökonomischer und technischer Sicht. Schriftenreihe „Nachwachsende Rohstoffe" Band 3, Landwirtschaftsverlag Münster-Hiltrup, 1995

/HEDDEN & JESS 1992/ Hedden, K., Jess, A.: Instrumente für Klimagas-Reduktions-Strategien (IKARUS) – Daten: Umwandlungssektor, Unterbereich: Raffinerien und Ölveredlung, (Teilprojekt 4). Im Auftrag des Bundesministeriums für Forschung und Technologie, Entwurf des Endberichts, Bonn 1992

/HEUSCH-BOESEFELDT 1996/ Palm, I., Regniet, G., Schmidt, G. (Heusch-Boesefeldt): Ermittlung der Pkw- und Nfz-Jahresfahrleistungen 1993 auf allen Straßen in der Bundesrepublik Deutschland. Im Auftrag des Bundesministeriums für Verkehr, Aachen 1996

/IEA 1991/ International Energy Agency (Hrsg.): Energy and the environment. Paris 1991

/IEA 1992/ International Energy Agency (Hrsg.): Energy and environment: Transport system responses in the OECD – Greenhouse gas emissions and road transport technology. Draft, Paris 1992

/IFEU & IVT & KuP 1994/ Höpfner, U, Knörr, W., Lambrecht, U., Patyk, A., Reichmuth, M. (IFEU); Hamacher, R., Hautzinger, H., Heidemann, D. (IVT); Kessel, P., Selz, T. (Kessel und Partner): Motorisierter Verkehr in Niedersachsen 1990 und 2010. Im Auftrag des Niedersächsischen Umweltministeriums, Hannover 1994

/IFEU & TÜVRL 1990/ Höpfner, U. et al. (IFEU); Waldeyer, H. et al. (TÜV Rheinland): Emissionsminderung durch rationelle Energienutzung und emissionsmindernde Maßnahmen im Verkehrssektor. Studienschwerpunkt A.1.4 in: Enquête-Kommission „Vorsorge zum Schutz der Erdatmosphäre" des Deutschen Bundestages (Hrsg.): Energie und Klima: Band 2. Economica Verlag, Bonn 1990

/IFEU 1992/ Höpfner, U., Knörr, W. (IFEU): Motorisierter Verkehr in Deutschland – Energieverbrauch und Luftschadstoffemissionen des motorisierten Verkehrs in der DDR, Berlin (Ost) und der Bundesrepublik Deutschland im Jahr 1988 und in Deutschland im Jahr 2005. Im Auftrag des Umweltbundesamtes und der Senatsverwaltung für Stadtentwicklung und Umweltschutz von Berlin (West), Erich Schmidt Verlag, Berlin 1992

/IFEU 1993a/ Giegrich, J., Mampel, U. (IFEU): Ökologische Bilanzen in der Abfallwirtschaft. Vorstudie: Schadstoffaspekte der Verwertung und Behandlung/Ablagerung von Abfällen (Toxizitätsparameter). Im Auftrag des Umweltbundesamtes, Berlin 1993

/IFEU 1993b/ Franke, B. (IFEU): Ecological balances as an instrument for the evaluation of waste management alternatives. Im Auftrag der EG-Kommission, DG 11, Brüssel 1993

/IFEU 1994a/ Giegrich, J., Reinhardt, G. A. (IFEU): Aufgabenstellung und Konzepte bei der ökologischen Bewertung von nachwachsenden Rohstoffen als Energieträger. In: Fortbildungszentrum Gesundheits- und Umweltschutz Berlin (Hrsg.): Tagungsband zum Seminar „Nachwachsende Rohstoffe als Energieträger – Neueste Bewertungskonzepte" am 08. September in Berlin, S. 41-59, Berlin 1994

/IFEU 1995a/ Giegrich, J., Mampel, U., Duscha, M. (IFEU): Bilanzbewertung in produktbezogenen Ökobilanzen. In: Umweltbundesamt (Hrsg.): Methodik der produktbezogenen Ökobilanzen – Wirkungsbilanz und Bewertung. UBA-Texte 23/95, Berlin 1995

/IFEU 1995b/ Höpfner, U., Patyk, A. (IFEU): Komponenten-Differenzierung der Kohlenwasserstoffemissionen von KFZ. Im Auftrag des Umweltbundesamtes Berlin, F+E Nr. 105 06 069, Heidelberg 1995

/IFEU 1995c/ Höpfner, U., Patyk, A. (IFEU): Komponenten-Differenzierung der Kohlenwasserstoffemissionen von KFZ. Im Auftrag des Umweltbundesamtes Berlin, F+E Nr. 105 06 069, Heidelberg 1995

/IFEU 1996a/ Giegrich, J., Detzel, A. (IFEU): Ökologischer Vergleich graphischer Papiere – ein methodischer Leitfaden (Zwischenbericht). Im Auftrag des Umweltbundesamtes, Heidelberg 1996

/IFEU 1996b/ Eden, T. U., Höpfner, U., Patyk, A., Reinhardt, G. A., Zenger, A. (IFEU): Ökologische Bilanzierung von Elektrofahrzeugen. In BMBF (Hrsg.): Erprobung von Elektrofahrzeugen der neuesten Generation auf der Insel Rügen. Bonn 1997

/IFEU 1996c/ Knisch, H., Reichmuth, M. (IFEU): Verkehrsleistung und Luftschadstoffemissionen des Personenflugverkehrs in Deutschland von 1980 bis 2010 unter besonderer Berücksichtigung des tourismusbedingten Flugverkehrs (Zwischenbericht). In: Umweltbundesamt (Hrsg.): Maßnahmen zur verursacherbezogenen Schadstoffreduzierung des zivilen Flugverkehrs. UBA-Texte 16/96, Berlin 1996

/IFEU 1997a/ Reinhardt, G. A., Borken, J., Patyk, A., Vogt, R., Zemanek, G. (IFEU): Ressourcen- und Emissionsbilanzen: Rapsöl und RME im Vergleich zu Dieselkraftstoff. Im Auftrag des Umweltbundesamtes, FKZ 36 301 002, Heidelberg 1997 und Aktualisierung: Heidelberg 1999

/IFEU 1997b/ Fehrenbach, H., Giegrich, J. (IFEU): Ökologische Bilanzen in der Abfallwirtschaft. Im Auftrag des Umweltbundesamtes, Berlin 1997

/IFEU 1998a/ Knörr, W., Höpfner, U., Lambrecht, U., Nagel, H.-J., Patyk, A. (IFEU): Daten- und Rechenmodell: Energieverbrauch und Schadstoffemissionen aus dem motorisierten Verkehr in Deutschland 1980 bis 2020 – Beschreibung der Software TREMOD: Bedienungsanleitung, Rechenabläufe und Datendokumentation. Im Auftrag des Umweltbundesamtes. Abschluß bevorstehend

/IFEU 1998b/ Detzel, A., Fehrenbach, H., Franke, B., Giegrich, J., Lell, M., Patyk, A., Vogt, R. (IFEU): Ermittlung von Emissionen und Minderungsmaßnahmen für persistente organische Schadstoffe in der Bundesrepublik Deutschland. Im Auftrag des Umweltbundesamtes, Forschungsvorhaben Nr. 104 02 365, Heidelberg 1998

/IFO 1995/ Hild, R., Ratzenberger, R., Langmantel, E. (ifo): Vorausschätzung der Verkehrsentwicklung in Deutschland bis zum Jahr 2010. Im Auftrag des Bundesministers für Verkehr, München 1995

/IIASA 1991/ Lübkert, B. et al. (IIASA): Life-Cycle Analysis-Idea – An International Data Base for Ecoprofile Analysis: A Tool for Decision Makers. Laxenburg 1991

/IPCC 1995/ Intergovernmental Panel of Climate Change (Hrsg.): Climate change 1994 – Radiative forcing of climate change and an evaluation of the IPCC IS92 emission scenarios. University Press, Cambridge 1995

/IPCC 1996/ Intergovernmental Panel of Climate Change (Hrsg.): Climate change 1995 – The science of climate change. University Press, Cambridge 1996

/ISENSEE et al. 1992/ Isensee, E., Ohls, J., Quest, D.: Pflanztechnik für Miscanthus. Landtechnik 47, 11, 1992, 550-554

/IWW et al. 1998/ IWW, IFEU, KuP, PÖU, PTV: Entwicklung eines Verfahrens zur Erstellung umweltorientierter Fernverkehrskonzepte als Beitrag zur Bundesverkehrswegeplanung. Im Auftrag des Umweltbundesamtes, F+E-Vorhaben Nr. 10506001, Karlsruhe/Berlin 1998

/JÄGER 1991/ Jäger, P.: Zeitbedarf von Feldarbeiten, Teil 1 – 3. Landtechnik 46, Sonderdruck, 1991

/JESS & HEDDEN 1994/ Jess, A., Hedden, K.: Die „Modellraffinerie Deutschland". Ein Instrument für Prognosen des zukünftigen Energieverbreauchs der deutschen Mineralölverarbeitung. Erdöl, Erdgas, Kohle 110, Heft 11/12 (1994) 454-458

/JÖRISSEN et al. 1988/ Jörissen, J. et al.: Die Umweltverträglichkeitsprüfung in den USA. Analyse US-amerikanischer Erfahrungen und deren Relevanz für die Implementation der UVP-Richtlinie der EG in der Bundesrepublik Deutschland, Erich-Schmidt-Verlag, Berlin 1988

/KALTSCHMITT & REINHARDT 1997/ Kaltschmitt, M., Reinhardt, G. A. (Hrsg.): Nachwachsende Energieträger: Grundlagen, Verfahren, ökologische Bilanzierung. Verlag Vieweg, Braunschweig/Wiesbaden 1997

/KBA/ Kraftfahrt-Bundesamt (Hrsg.): Bestand an Kraftfahrzeugen und Kraftfahrzeuganhängern am 1. Juli. Bonn-Bad Godesberg, verschiedene Jahrgänge

/KHD 1998/ Knuth, H.W., KHD: Persönliche Mitteilung. Köln 1998

/KLÖPFFER & RENNER 1994/ Klöpffer, W., Renner, I.: Methodik der Wirkungsbilanz im Rahmen von Produkt-Ökobilanzen unter Berücksichtigung nicht oder nur schwer quantifizierbarer Umwelt-Kategorien. In: Umweltbundesamt (Hrsg.): Methodik der produktbezogenen Ökobilanzen – Wirkungsbilanz und Bewertung. UBA-Texte 23/95, Berlin 1995

/KOHLE 1997/ Zahlen der Kohlenwirtschaft. In: Statistik der Kohlenwirtschaft e. V., Glückauf, Essen 1997

/KOLLE et al. 1991/ Kolle, L. et al.: Emissions from inland and coastal shipping and potential for improvement. In: Kroon, M. et al. (Hrsg.): Freight transport and the environment. Studies in Environmental Sciences 45, Elsevier Science Publications, Amsterdam 1991

/KRAHL 1993/ Krahl, J.: Bestimmung der Schadstoffemissionen von landwirtschaftlichen Schleppern beim Betrieb mit Rapsölmethylester im Vergleich zu Dieselkraftstoff. Fortschritt-Berichte VDI, Reihe 15, Nr. 100. VDI-Verlag, Düsseldorf 1993

/KRAHL 1998/ Krahl, J., FH Coburg: Persönliche Mitteilung, 11.02.1998

/KTBL 1993/ Kuratorium für Technik und Bauwesen in der Landwirtschaft (KTBL, Hrsg.): Datensammlung für die Betriebsplanung in der Landwirtschaft. 13. Auflage, Darmstadt 1993

/LKW/ lastauto-omnibus-Katalog. Vereinigte Motor-Verlage, Stuttgart, verschiedene Jahrgänge

/LLOYDS 1990/ Lloyd's Register of Shipping (Hrsg.): Marine exhaust emission research programme – Steady state operation. London 1990

/LLOYDS 1991/ Lloyd's Register of Shipping (Hrsg.): Marine exhaust emission research programme – Steady State operation – Slow speed addendum. London 1991

/LLOYDS 1995/ Lloyd's Register of Shipping (Hrsg.): Marine exhaust emissions research programme. Croydon/UK 1995

/LOGOS 1983/ Logos, J. N.: Ackerschleppermotoren, Stand der Technik, Entwicklungstendenzen. Landtechnik 38 (1983) 474-480

/LUFTHANSA 1989/ Deutsche Lufthansa AG: Schriftliche Mitteilung. Frankfurt a.M. 7.9.1989

/LUFTHANSA 1995/ Deutsche Lufthansa AG (Hrsg.): Umweltbericht 1994. Frankfurt a.M. 1995

/LUFTHANSA 1997/ Deutsche Lufthansa AG (Hrsg.): Umweltbericht 1996/97. Frankfurt a.M. 1997

/MASSERON 1982/ Masseron, J.: L'economie des hydrocarbures. Publications Institut Francais du Petrole, Paris 1982

/MAUCH 1996/ Mauch, W.: Bereitstellungsnutzungsgrade für Brennstoffe und für elektrische Energie in der Bundesrepublik Deutschland. Studie der Forschungsstelle für Energiewirtschaft (FfE), München 1996

/MHEP 1980/ Ministry of Health and Environmental Protection (Hrsg.): Handbook of Emission Factors, Part 1: Non Industrial Sources. Den Haag/NL, 1980

/MVWDDR 1989/ Ministerium für Verkehrswesen der DDR (Hrsg.): Energiewirtschaftliche Jahresanalyse des Verkehrswesens 1988. Berlin 1989

/MWV 1997/ Mineralölwirtschaftsverband (Hrsg.): Die Mineralöl-Zahlen 1997, Hamburg 1997

/NORD 1995/ Arbeitsgruppe der skandinavischen Umweltminister (Hrsg.): Nordic Guidelines on LCA. Stockholm 1995

/PATYK & REINHARDT 1997/ Patyk, A., Reinhardt, G. A.: Düngemittel – Energie- und Stoffstrombilanzen. Verlag Vieweg, Braunschweig/Wiesbaden 1997

/PG LEBENSWEGBILANZEN 1992/ Projektgemeinschaft Lebenswegbilanzen (GVM Wiesbaden, IFEU Heidelberg, ILV München, Hrsg.): Methode für Lebenswegbilanzen von Verpackungssystemen. Wiesbaden/Heidelberg/München 1992

/PROGNOS & IFEU 1993/ Becker, U. et al. (Prognos), Höpfner, U. et. al. (IFEU): Entwicklung der Emissionen von Luftschadstoffen und CO_2 durch den Verkehr in Ost- und Westdeutschland bis 2010. Im Auftrag des Bundesministers für Verkehr, FE-Nr. 90344/91, Basel 1993

/PROGNOS 1996/ Prognos AG (Hrsg.): Die Energiemärkte Deutschlands im zusammenwachsenden Europa – Perspektiven bis zum Jahr 2020. Im Auftrag des Bundesministeriums für Wirtschaft, Bonn 1996

/RAKOS et al. 1988/ Rakos, C. et al.: Technikbewertung und Umweltverträglichkeitsprüfung. Ein internationaler Vergleich. Österreichische Akademie der Wissenschaften, Wien 1988

/REINHARDT 1993/ Reinhardt, G. A.: Energie- und CO_2-Bilanzierung nachwachsender Rohstoffe – Theoretische Grundlagen und Fallstudie Raps. 2. Aufl., Verlag Vieweg, Braunschweig/Wiesbaden 1993

/RINALDI & NÄF 1992/ Rinaldi, M., Näf, E.: Motorauslastung von Landwirtschaftstraktoren. Berichte der Eidgenössischen Forschungsanstalt für Betriebswirtschaft und Landtechnik (FAT) 426, Tänikon/CH 1992

/RUBIK et al. 1987/ Rubik, F. et al.: Produktlinienanalyse – Bedürfnisse, Produkte und ihre Folgen. Volksblatt Verlag, Köln 1987

/SCHÄFER 1997/ Schäfer, A., Daimler-Benz, Persönliche Mitteilungen, Stuttgart 1997

/SCHÄFER et al. 1998/ Schäfer, A., Naber, D., Gairing, M.: Biodiesel als alternativer Kraftstoff für Mercedes-Benz-Dieselmotoren. Mineralöltechnik 3, Hamburg 1998

/SCHMIDT & HÄUSLEIN 1997/ Schmidt, M., Häuslein, A.: Ökobilanzierung mit Computerunterstützung. Springer-Verlag, Berlin/Heidelberg/New York 1997

/SCHMIDT & MÖLLER 1998/ Schmidt, M., Möller, A.: Öko-Controlling und Kostenrechnung. Springer-Verlag, Berlin/Heidelberg/New York 1998

/SCHMIDT & SCHORB 1995/ Schmidt, M., Schorb, A.: Stoffstromanalysen in Ökobilanzen und Ökoaudits. Springer-Verlag, Berlin/Heidelberg/New York 1995

/SCHMIDT et al. 1996/ Schmidt, M. et al.: Prozeßmodellierung und Datenstruktur in Stoffstromnetzen. In: Scheer, A.-W. et al. (Hrsg.): Computergestützte Stoffstrommanagement-Systeme. Marburg 1996

/SETAC 1991/ Society of Environmental Toxicology and Chemistry (SETAC, Hrsg.): A Technical Framework for Life Cycle Assessment. Workshop Report, Smugglers Notch (USA)

/SETAC 1993/ Society of Environmental Toxicology and Chemistry (SETAC, Hrsg.): Guidelines for Life Cycle Assessment: A Code of Practice. Übereinkunft einer Arbeitsgruppe der SETAC, Brüssel 1993

/SHELL 1991/ Fabri, J., Krumm, H., Reglitzky, A. A. (Shell): Minderung der Kohlendioxidemissionen – Eine Herausforderung an zukünftige Kraftstoffe. Shell Technischer Dienst, Hamburg 1991

/SHELL 1994/ Shell (Hrsg.): Erdöl- und Erdgasförderung im Offshore-Bereich. Shell Briefing Service, 1/1994, Hamburg 1994

/STBA 1995a/ Statistisches Bundesamt (Hrsg.): Statistisches Jahrbuch. Metzler Poeschel Verlag, Stuttgart/Wiesbaden 1995

/STBA 1995b/ Statistisches Bundesamt (Hrsg.): Luftverkehr – 1994. Verkehr, Fachserie 8, 6, Wiesbaden 1995

/SWISSAIR 1991/ Swissair (Hrsg.): Ökobilanz Swissair: Eine Querschnittsanalyse über sämtliche umweltrelevanten Aktivitäten am Standort Zürich-Kloten und über alle Luftemissionen der Swissair-Flotte im Jahre 1989. Zürich 1991

/TÜVBAYERN 1996/ TÜV Bayern Holding AG/Verlag (Hrsg.): Biodiesel für Fahrzeuge. München 1996

/TÜVRL 1989/ Weyrauther, G. et al. (TÜV Rheinland): Ermittlung der Abgasemissionen aus dem Flugverkehr über der Bundesrepublik Deutschland. Berichte des Umweltbundesamtes 6/89, Erich Schmidt Verlag, Berlin 1989

/TÜVRL 1995/ Hassel, D., Jost, P., Weber, F.-J., Dursbeck, F., Plettau, D. (TÜV Rheinland): Abgas-Emissionsverhalten von Nutzfahrzeugen in der BRD für das Bezugsjahr 1990. Im Auftrag des Umweltbundesamtes, Berlin 1995

/UBA 1989/ Umweltbundesamt (Hrsg.): Luftreinhaltung '88: Tendenzen, Probleme, Lösungen. Erich Schmidt Verlag, Berlin 1989

/UBA 1992/ Umweltbundesamt (Hrsg.): Ökobilanzen für Produkte: Bedeutung, Sachstand, Perspektiven. UBA-Texte 38/92, Berlin 1992

/UBA 1994/ Umweltbundesamt: Persönliche Mitteilung, 1994

/UBA 1995a/ Umweltbundesamt (Hrsg.): Ökobilanz für Getränkeverpackungen. UBA-Texte 52/95, Berlin 1995

/UBA 1995b/ Umweltbundesamt (Hrsg.): Methodik der produktbezogenen Ökobilanzen – Wirkungsbilanz und Bewertung. UBA-Texte 23/95, Berlin 1995

/UBA 1995c/ Umweltbundesamt (Hrsg.): Jahresbericht 1994, Berlin 1995

/UBA 1998/ Nöcker, H., Umweltbundesamt: Persönliche Mitteilungen, 1998

/UN 1995/ United Nations Department for Economic and Social Information and Policy Analysis: Energy statistics yearbook. New York 1995

/VDEW 1998/ Vereinigung deutscher Elektrizitätswerke (Hrsg.): Die öffentliche Elektrizitätsversorgung 1997. VDEW, Frankfurt a. M. 1998

/VDI 1992/ Verein Deutscher Ingenieure (Hrsg.): Technikfolgenabschätzung. VDI-Verlag, Düsseldorf 1992

/VDI 1997/ Verein Deutscher Ingenieure (Hrsg.): VDI-Richtlinie 4600 „Kumulierter Energieaufwand“. Düsseldorf 1997

/VELLGUTH 1987/ Vellguth, G.: Emissionen bei Verwendung alternativer Kraftstoffe in Schlepper-Dieselmotoren. Grundl. Landtechnik 37 (1987) 207-213

/VERKEHR 1997/ Bundesministerium Verkehr (Hrsg.): Verkehr in Zahlen 1997, Bonn 1997

/WEC 1988/ Environmental Effects Arising from Electricity Supply and Utilisation and the Resulting Costs to the Utility. World Energy Conference Report, London 1988

/WEG 1994/ Wirtschaftsverband Erdöl- und Erdgasgewinnung: Persönliche Mitteilung, 1994

/WEG 1997/ Wirtschaftsverband Erdöl- und Erdgasgewinnung (Hrsg.): Jahresbericht ‘96, Hannover 1997

/WELSCHOF 1981/ Welschof, G.: Der Ackerschlepper – Mittelpunkt der Landtechnik. VDI-Berichte 407 (1981) 11-17

/WÖRGETTER et al. 1990/ Wörgetter, M., Wurst, F., Boos, R., Prey, T., Scheidl, K.: Emissionen beim Einsatz von Rapsölmethylester an einem Prüfstandsmotor. Forschungsberichte der Bundesanstalt für Landtechnik, Wieselburg/A 1990

/WÖRGETTER et al. 1993/ Wörgetter, M., Prankl, H., Schauflen, H.: Untersuchung der Emissionen eines Traktors mit Mischungen aus Dieselkraftstoff, Rapsölmethylester und n-Butanol. Forschungsberichte der Bundesanstalt für Landtechnik, Wieselburg/A 1993